THE OLD WEST

THE OLD WEST

THE OLD WEST

DAY BY DAY

Mike Flanagan

Facts On File®

AN INFOBASE HOLDINGS COMPANY

The Old West: Day by Day

Copyright © 1995 Mike Flanagan

Facts On File, Inc.
460 Park Avenue South
New York NY 10016

Library of Congress Cataloging-in-Publication Data
Flanagan, Mike.
   The old West: day by day / Mike Flanagan.
      p. cm.
   Updated and enl. ed. of: Days of the West. c 1987.
   Includes bibliographical references and index.
   ISBN 0-8160-2689-0
   1. West (U.S.)—History—Chronology. 2. West (U.S.)—History—
Miscellanea. I. Flanagan, Mike. Days of the West. II. Title.
F591.F53 1995
978′.02′0202—dc20   94-4663

Text and jacket design by Catherine Rincon Hyman
Printed in the United States of America

VB VC 10 9 8 7 6 5 4 3 2 1

This book is printed on acid-free paper.

CONTENTS

ACKNOWLEDGMENTS

M any people helped with this project along the way. My first debt of gratitude must go to the hundreds of unnamed journalists and historians whose knowledge of long-past current events now reside in microfilm files from another century. Their eyewitness accounts proved invaluable.

Much of these works were found at the Western History Department of the Denver Public Library, whose staggering files are a priceless reminder that what you have here really is only the tip of the iceberg. A special thanks to department manager Eleanor Gehres and the master of western photographic images Augie Mastrogiuseppe, as well as the excellent staff.

My wife, Nancy Flanagan, gets special credit for helping in the preparation of this package, the tightening of the prose, and all the other detail work that is always handled by my first and best editor.

Other historical societies and organizations who provided material for this book include the Colorado State Historical Society of Denver, Colorado, the Arizona Historical Foundation, Hayden Library of Tempe, Arizona, the Arizona Historical Society, Manuscripts Division of Tucson, Arizona, the Idaho State Historical Society, of Boise, Idaho, the University of Kansas Kenneth Spencer Research Library Kansas Collection of Lawrence, Kansas, the University of Minnesota Libraries-Manuscript Division of St. Paul, Minnesota, the Missouri Historical Society Archives of St. Louis, Missouri, the Montana State University Library Special Collections of Bozeman, Montana, the Montana Historical Society Division of Archives and Manuscripts of Helena Montana, the California Historical Society Archives of San Francisco, California, the Nevada Historical Society Archives of Reno, Nevada, the Utah State Historical Society Archives of Salt Lake City, Utah, the Oklahoma Historical Society Archives of Oklahoma City, Oklahoma, the Kansas State Historical Society Museum Archives of Topeka, Kansas, the Nebraska State Historical Society Archives of Lincoln, Nebraska, the Washington State Historical Society Archives of Tacoma, Washington, and the Oregon Historical Society Archives of Portland, Oregon. These invaluable sources keep records of the western expansion that have eluded many history books, and provided unique and rare perspectives.

Other thanks go to Roger Rountree for help in the photographic department and Harry Chrisman for his authentic voice of the West and his encouragement. I also would like to thank Colorado Public Radio for their endless patience with the directions I take.

INTRODUCTION

"The West is dead!
You may lose a sweetheart.
But you won't forget her."
—Charles M. Russell
Good Medicine: The Illustrated Letters of Charles M. Russell

The Old West brought forth guidebooks. There were books for the Oregon Trail, books on the best way to the goldfields, books that told you the watering holes along the way and how to set up a sluice once you got there. With the idea to transport Texas longhorns from the Kansas railheads to the beef-hungry East, there were books about how to get rich in the cattle business. And for those who never accepted the challenge of Manifest Destiny but nevertheless longed for the adventure, there were books that told of what life was like in the Wild West.

Some of these communiqués from the last century are still quite helpful, but others have become comical with the passage of time. The selling of the West began as any other enterprise, with the germ to assist and profit. It behooved rail companies to have towns spring up alongside their otherwise desolate tracks. Town builders welcomed anyone who might enhance their community, and they often took strong measures against detractors.

The survival of transplanted Europeans in an often hostile region depended on community. For community, one had to have people. For the individuals, enticed by the promise of a new beginning and a first-time belonging, there was an urgency to settle. What

came next was a push unlike any other across a continent. A scant 42 years separated the discovery of gold in California from the last blood spilled in the "Indian Wars." A quarter century—from the end of the Civil War until 1890—was all it took either to relocate or eliminate the native population of a continent. The westward expansion swept over the previous tenants like a great wave: Like wildfire, a new people, armed to the teeth, engulfed and then devoured the land, as well as the people.

The West that captured the American imagination changed almost yearly. Daniel Boone's West was already won by the time Davy Crockett sought his. John Charles Frémont explored another West, just ahead of the masses who filled it. George A. Custer's frontier was an extension of the Civil War, but with brand new enemies of his Union. By the time of Billy the Kid and Jesse James, conquest had given way to existence in a hard-scrabble society of law and rough justice. No sooner did these hombres bite the dust than William F. Cody saw yet another horizon, a regional marriage of reality and mythology, all in the name of show business.

This is a guidebook to the Old West, arranged by the rules of time. Its main focus is on the boom-to-bust years, 1848 to 1890. The history of the region is told in some 15,000 incidents—events ranging from happenings that shaped and changed the trans-Mississippi West to the lesser-known episodes that made up daily life in a changing region. Here, in linear juxtaposition, is a series of events connected by geography. Looking back a century after the dust settled, we are afforded a perspective unavailable at the time.

In preparing this chronicle, there were many factors to consider. Westward expansion occurred simultaneously in mining camps, in metropolitan areas, on the Great Plains, in the mountains, in the deserts, and, yes, in the imagination. The continental metamorphosis was too much to fathom, even for those who witnessed it. And romance, riding in on a golden palomino and resplendent in white hat and spurs, glossed over the blemishes with tales of honor. Western history is therefore loaded with credibility gaps.

This book is presented in three sections, starting with a brief prologue of major events from the years 50,000 B.C. to A.D. 1847. Beginning with 1848 and concluding with 1890, there is a day-by-day chronology of happenings both great and small. An epilogue highlights western occurrences of the last century. Descriptions of events are purposely brief, and the reader is encouraged to use them as a springboard to further investigation.

In the 1848–1890 section, bulleted lists denote events that occurred on the same day. When their exact dates are uncertain save for the month, events are included at the end of that month's listings. Some incidents, traceable only to their years, appear at the end of a given year in the "Also" section. National headlines are included to add a sense of events that occurred outside the West.

Scattered throughout the text are boxes highlighting dozens of biographical chronologies and historical events that are of particular interest to the reader. In these boxes one will find complete chronological summaries of the lives of figures such as Wyatt Earp and Butch Cassidy; these are typically located near the person's birth date or where the individual is first mentioned. Events such as the construction of the transcontinental telegraph and the massacre at Sand Creek are described in detail at the date on which the central event occurred.

In many instances, we have been left with clear recaps of what happened when and where. In others, we have had to piece together information from available sources—books, newspapers, magazines, diaries, and so forth. Trying to find agreement among sources has been just one of the challenges of preparing this work.

For instance, the U.S. government recorded 1,065 battles between the United States Army and the American Indians from 1866 to 1891. Many are listed here. The Adjutant General's office almost uniformly identified the adversaries as "Indians" rather than giving tribal names. Sometimes, in the fury of a surprise encounter, soldiers did not know whom they were fighting. Other times, they clearly did not care. In many instances when our sources are the official government reports, we have used their language. Some of these accounts and their battle estimates have been questioned over the years; hence entries with such information are listed as "reported." To omit them would dilute the daily sense of an undeclared war that took place over four decades.

For whatever reasons—rumors to encourage migration, a sense of regional pride, or the need to have a good story by deadline—the history of the Old West is loaded with exaggeration. Like any other historical period, there were slow news days. But to assume that the settling of half the country entailed some logical, orderly progression of events, ideas, and philosophies is to miss the point. For this reason, the action in the following pages tends to follow the "hot spots." When historical disagreement abounds, sources that have proven reliable in similar instances were selected.

This is the story of the Old West, told with facts and minimum editorializing. It is a tool for readers who like an orderly progression in their history, for writers who like to focus on all aspects of life in a certain time, for historians who crave perspective, and for anyone who may be curious about America's mercurial frontier. It can be read from first to last, in segments, or however you wish to follow the trail.

—Mike Flanagan
Denver, Colorado

PROLOGUE

50,000 B.C.—A.D. 1847

50,000 B.C.—5000 B.C.

Paleo-Siberians migrate to North America from Asia via the Bering Strait Land Bridge.

The Projectile Point cultures develop, using flint and obsidian to craft spears, knives, and other tools.

Big-game hunters follow herds of mastodons and woolly mammoths.

The Sandia Spear-Point culture develops in the Sandia Mountains of present New Mexico, fashioning spear points with round bases and bulges on one side.

The Ice Age ends.

Woolly mammoths, mastodons, saber-toothed tigers, and bighorn bisons become extinct.

The Desert culture thrives in the Great Basin region of present Nevada, Arizona, and Utah.

The Clovis or Llano Spear-Point culture evolves in eastern New Mexico, using slim-styled spear points.

The Folsom Spear-Point culture thrives in northeastern New Mexico and throughout the Great Plains, using shorter spear points with fluting on both sides.

7500 B.C.—1500 B.C.

The Plano Spear-Point culture develops in present Texas, stampeding bighorn bison over cliffs or into special corrals.

Throughout the Southwest, squash, pumpkins, maize, beans, gourds, and peppers are cultivated.

The Cochise culture, an offshoot of the Desert culture, emerges in present New Mexico and Arizona.

The Old Cordilleran or Cascade culture originates in the Columbia River valley.

The Bitterroot peoples inhabit the Alpha Rockshelter near the Salmon River in present Idaho.

3600 B.C.—1500 B.C.

The beaver-tooth gouge, a woodworking tool, is used in the Canadian subarctic area.

Cave dwellers in present Montana draw men and animals on walls.

Irrigation is attempted for the first time.

The earliest pottery to be discovered in North America is made near present Guerrero, Mexico.

The weaving of cloth begins.

1500 B.C.—A.D. 1000

Villages appear, and agriculture, stone carving, pottery, and weaving are practiced by tribes.

The Olmec people develop an agricultural culture in Mexico.

Teotihuacán becomes the largest city in the Americas. The 200-foot-high Pyramid of the Sun is constructed in the Valley of Mexico.

Dogs are domesticated in North America.

Hunters use canoes in eastern North America.

The Poverty Point people begin to inhabit the Arkansas River regions of northern Louisiana.

The Olmec culture is at its height in Mexico.

The Mound Building cultures of Adena and Hopewell emerge and spread through the Ohio Valley.

The Pinto Basin inhabitants in southeastern California pulverize hard-shell seeds, mainly acorns, for dietary purposes.

The Poverty Point civilization reaches its peak in Louisiana.

The Anasazi culture thrives in the Southwest.

300—1000

The Basket Maker II culture thrives in New Mexico; the people are mostly farmers and basket weavers.

The Basket Maker III culture in New Mexico builds slab houses, raises beans, corn, squash, and tobacco, and introduces southwestern pottery.

The Mayan civilization flourishes in Central America.

The Anasazi Indians occupy Arizona's Canyon de Chelly and farm near present Mesa Verde, Colorado.

The Pueblo I people, possibly from northwestern New Mexico, conquer and absorb the Basket Makers in southwestern New Mexico. In addition to pottery, they introduce the bow and arrow, and they begin living in above-ground communal centers.

The Ancestral Apaches break from the Athapascan people in the north and migrate to the southwest.

The Cochise people, prehistoric Indians, live near present Bisbee, Arizona.

Teotihuacán, with a population larger than Rome's, thrives in Central America until the year 700.

The Mississippian culture flourishes in the lower Mississippi River valleys.

987

Quetzalcóatl, the priest-ruler of the Toltecs of central Mexico, abdicates.

1000

The Norseman Leif Ericsson explores parts of North America.

1025

Ancestral Navajo break from the Athapascans and migrate to the southwest.

1050

Irrigation brings water to the city of Casas Grandes in the present state of Chihuahua, Mexico.

1100

The Hohokam Indians build more than 200 miles of canals in present Arizona.

The Pueblo II people in New Mexico develop unit-type houses and group dwellings on the order of villages.

1200

Anasazi Indians, the "apartment builders," live in Arizona and Colorado. One of their largest ruins is a pueblo at Kinishba, Arizona.

People live in Oraibi, Arizona, the oldest continually inhabited settlement in the present United States.

1200–1500

The Aztec culture flourishes in Mexico.

1250

The Mogollon Indians, residents of present Arizona since 500 B.C., disappear.

1276

A 23-year drought begins in the Southwest around Mesa Verde.

1300

The Pueblo III culture flourishes in New Mexico.

1325

The Aztecs build Tenochtitlán on Lake Texcoco, on the site of present Mexico City. The culture, which practices agriculture as well as human sacrifice, flourishes.

1350

The Pueblo IV culture begins; it will become the most widespread Pueblo culture expansion in New Mexico.

1400

Hohokam Indians depart the Salt and Gila River valleys.

The Southern Death cult emerges from the Mississippian culture and practices human sacrifice.

1444

Moctezuma I rules the Aztecs.

1480

The 20-ton Aztec Calendar Stone is completed, with an image of the Sun God.

1492

October 12: Christopher Columbus lands at San Salvador.

1497

John Cabot explores the east coast of North America; he kidnaps three Micmac Indians.

1497–1503

Amerigo Vespucci explores South America and the West Indies.

1500

The first European diseases appear among North American Indians.

1507

The Western Hemisphere is first referred to as America.

1510

The Spanish conquistador Francisco Vásquez de Coronado is born.

Garcí Rodríguez Ordóñez de Montalvo provides a written description of California in *Las Sergas de Esplandían:* "At the right hand of the Indies there is an island called California . . . inhabited by black women without a single man among them . . . in the manner of Amazons."

1512

The Spanish "Law of Burgos" sanctions making Indians into slaves.

Pope Julius II issues a papal decree saying Indians are descendants of Adam and Eve.

1513

The explorer Vasco Núñez de Balboa crosses the Isthmus of Panama and discovers the Pacific Ocean.

1513–1521

The Spanish explorer Juan Ponce de León explores Florida.

1517–1521

Hernán Cortés conquers the Aztecs, ending their empire. The Aztec ruler Moctezuma II (1502–1520) is killed in the fighting.

1519

Hernán Cortés brings the first horses to Mexico.

1521

Gregorio de Villalobos brings seven Andalusian calves by boat from Santo Domingo to Vera Cruz; these are the first cattle to appear on the mainland.

1526

The explorer Don Jose de Basconales crosses Arizona on a trip to Zuni country.

1528

The explorer Alvar Núñez Cabeza de Vaca is washed ashore at Galveston Island and accidentally discovers Texas.

1533

"California" is the name Hernán Cortés gives to the southern tip of the present state of California.

1534–1541

The French explorer Jacques Cartier travels the St. Lawrence River.

1535

Francisco Vásquez de Coronado arrives in Mexico with the first Spanish government officials.

1536

Cabeza de Vaca begins the legend of the Seven Cities of Cibola after a trip through present Texas and Arizona. Indians in the south tell him of northern pueblos.

1538

Francisco Vásquez de Coronado becomes the governor of Nueva Galicia.

1539

The Franciscan friar Marcos de Niza, in present Arizona, searches for the legendary Seven Cities of Cibola with the black Morrocan slave Estevan.

1540

Francisco Vásquez de Coronado begins his search for Cibola throughout the southwest. One of his 300 men, Cárdenas, discovers the Grand Canyon. Another member of the expedition, Díaz, explores the lower Colorado River area.

Hernando de Alarcón leaves Acapulco to explore the Sea of Cortés, the present Gulf of California. He also navigates a boat on the lower Colorado River to the mouth of the Gila.

1541

Diáz dies in the desert near Ojo, Arizona.

Francisco Vásquez de Coronado's party crosses the Arkansas River in present Kansas as far north as the present Kansas-Nebraska border.

The explorer Hernando de Soto claims Florida for Spain and explores Arkansas and Oklahoma.

Present Texas is called "Tejas," a Spanish version of a Caddo word meaning "allies."

1542

Francisco Vásquez de Coronado returns to Mexico to report failure in his attempt to find the cities of gold.

The explorer Juan Rodríguez Cabrillo sails into San Diego Bay. His pilot, Bartolome Ferrelo, will continue as far north as present Oregon.

1543

The Franciscans Juan de Padilla and Luis de Escalona become the first missionaries in New Mexico.

1550

The Indian population of Spanish America is approximately 7 million.

1554

Francisco Vásquez de Coronado, 44, dies in Mexico City.

1560–1570

Mohawk, Oneida, Onondaga, Cayuga, and Seneca Indians form the Iroquois League of Five Nations.

1565

St. Augustine is founded in Florida.

1569

A Mercator map indicates Hispania Noua, New Spain.

1579

The British explorer Sir Francis Drake sails into a northern California bay and names it Nova Albion for Queen Elizabeth. His trip will take him as far north as present Oregon.

1581

Antonio de Espejo and the Faran expedition journey up the Rio Grande through present Arizona.

Many Franciscans are reported killed by Indians in New Mexico.

1582

The expedition of Antonio de Espejo sets out to learn what happened to the Franciscans in New Mexico; it locates silver deposits near present Prescott, Arizona.

1583

Luxán's journal of Antonio de Espejo's expedition is the first written account to use the term "New Mexico."

1585

The first British settlement in North America is established on Roanoke Island, North Carolina.

1587

Virginia Dare is the first British child born in America, on Roanoke Island.

1590

The first unauthorized colonization in New Mexico is attempted by Captain Gaspar Castaño de Sosa and 170 followers. He will be arrested after one year.

1591

The colonists of Roanoke Island disappear.

1593

More unauthorized exploration occurs in New Mexico, this time by two groups led by Captains Humaña and Bonilla.

1595

The Spanish official Don Juan de Oñate receives a contract for colonization in New Mexico.

1598

Spain's sovereignty over "lands, pueblos, cities, villas, of whatsoever nature now founded in the kingdom and province of New Mexico" is proclaimed by Juan de Oñate. The territory stretches from present Texas to Calfornia. The settlement of San Juan is begun.

1599

Juan de Oñate enters Arizona from the Rio Grande.
Spanish forces under Juan de Oñate kill 800 Indians and win the Battle of Acoma.

1600

The Indian population of Spanish America has dropped from 7 million to 1 million in the last 50 years, the primary cause being European diseases.
The Spanish introduce sheep to the Southwest.

1600–1770

Horses spread from Mexico throughout the Southwest and the Great Plains.

1601

Don Juan de Oñate, governor of New Mexico, explores the northeast, probably as far as present Wichita, Kansas.

1602

The explorer Sebastian Vizcaino sails into San Miguel Bay and renames it San Diego de Alcala.

1603

The explorer Martin d'Aguilar sails past present Oregon.

1605

Don Juan de Oñate, returning from the Gulf of California, carves his name on Inscription Rock at present El Morro National Monument.

1607

Jamestown, the first permanent British settlement in America, is established.

1609

Santa Fe becomes the first permanent Spanish settlement in the Southwest.

1610

The formal founding of Santa Fe, La Villa Real de la Santa Fé de San Francisco de Assisi (the Royal City of the Holy Faith of St. Francis of a Assisi), is proclaimed by Governor Don Pedro de Peralta.
Gaspar Pérez de Villagrá pens his narrative in verse, "Historia de la Nueva México," which is published in Spain. He is the first American poet.

1613

Governor Don Pedro de Peralta is held prisoner for a year by Fray Isidro Orodóñez, agent of the Inquisition.
Pocahontas, an Algonquin Indian, is captured by British colonists in Virginia; she converts to Christianity and weds John Rolfe.

1615

The Wampanoag Squanto, who will figure in the Pilgrim saga, is kidnapped by settlers and taken to England.

1616–1620

Smallpox ravages the New England Indians.

1617

Eleven mission churches operate in New Mexico.
Pocahontas, the wife of John Rolfe, contracts a European malady and dies in England.

1619

Squanto returns to North America.

1620

Pilgrims land at Plymouth Rock in present Massachusetts. Squanto shows them how to plant corn and use fish as fertilizer.

1624

Virginia becomes a royal colony.

1625

The Spaniard Fray Alonzo de Benavides arrives in Santa Fe to assume his duties as custodian of the Franciscan mission province and agent of the Inquisition.

1626

The Dutch administrator Peter Minuit buys Manhattan Island from the Canarsee Indians.

1629–1633

Missions are founded among the Hopi, Zuni, and Acoma tribes.

1630

The Puritans settle Boston.
Fray Alonso de Benavides writes *Memorial*.

1632

In separate incidents, New Mexico Indians kill Francisco de Letrado and Fray Pedro de Miranda.

1633

The use of peyote and the practices of bigamy and witchcraft are just a few of the abuses investigated by Fray Estevan de Perea in New Mexico.

1642

The English clergyman Roger Williams, founder of Rhode Island, pens the *Indian-English Dictionary,* which is published in England.

1644

Religous persecution of the Indians occurs in New Mexico: 40 are hanged for refusing to relinquish their native religion and convert to Catholicism.

1650

A plot by members of the Apache tribe and residents of the pueblos of Alameda, Cochití, Isleta, Jémez, and San Felipe to drive away the Spaniards is discovered by the authorities; nine are hanged, the others are sold into slavery.

1659

Franciscans from New Mexico establish a mission at present Juárez, Mexico.

1661

Sacred kivas of the Pueblo Indians are ransacked and destroyed by Spanish soldiers in an effort to suppress the religion of the natives.

1673

The French explorers Father Jacques Marquette and Louis Joliet explore the North American interior from Lake Michigan down the Mississippi to the Arkansas River.

1674

Father Marquette establishes a mission at present Chicago.

1675

Four Indians are hanged in New Mexico and another 43 are whipped and sold into slavery after a Spanish tribunal convicts them of bewitching the superior of the Franciscan Monastery at San Ildefonso.
In King Philip's War, Wampanoag Indians under the sachem King Philip raid a number of frontier settlements in New England.

1676

Apaches destroy pueblos and churches in New Mexico, killing Spaniards as well as Indians who were converting. Those apprehended are hanged or sold into slavery.
King Philip's War ends after Connecticut troops and Mohegan Indians drive the Wampanoags back into New Hampshire. King Philip is slain and resistance is extinguished.

1679

Sioux and Ojibway Indians are urged to talk peace by French explorer Daniel Duluth.

1680

In the Pueblo Revolt, Hopis led by Po-pé turn against missionaries in the Southwest; hundreds of Spaniards are driven from New Mexico and many are killed.
The Coronielli map is the first to note that the Rio Grande empties into the Gulf of Mexico instead of the Gulf of California.

1682

Father Zenobe Membre, chaplain of a minor French expedition, reaches the mouth of the Missouri River after descending the Mississippi.
The Sovereignty and Goodness of God, or The Narrative of Mrs. Mary Rowlandson is the first narrative written by a person held captive by Indians to be published in English.

1685

The Nuestra Señora del Pilar de Zaragosa mine is registered in the Fray Cristóbal Mountains, New Mexico.

1689

King William's War begins as the British battle the French for Canada.

1690

The horse is used by the tribes of the Southern Plains.

1692

Father Kino begins missionary work in the Santa Cruz and San Pedro Valleys.

Governor Don Diego de Vargas begins the reconquest of New Mexico. The Indians at Santa Fe yield peaceably on September 13.

1693

The recolonization of New Mexico is begun by Governor De Vargas and 70 families, 100 soldiers, and 17 Franciscans.

1695

The Pima uprising against the Spanish in the Southwest takes place.

1696

The final defeat of the Pueblos occurs; many Pueblo governors are executed.

1697

The end of King William's War also marks the end of the first phase of the 75-year French and Indian Wars.

1700

Father Kino founds the San Xavier del Bac Mission near Tucson.

The Pueblo V culture flourishes in New Mexico, near the present Pueblo.

Father Gabriel Marest of the Kaskaskia mission writes of the Missouri River: "Its real name is the Pekitanou and the French call it the Missouri because this people is the first you meet there."

1706

The Spanish official Juan de Ulibarri of Santa Fe establishes relations with friendly Apaches. He claims for Spain the upper Arkansas River area, including present Colorado, and names it Santo Domingo.

Albuquerque is established by Governor Don Francisco Cuervo y Valdés.

1711

Father Kino dies.

The Tuscarora War begins with a massacre of settlers in North Carolina.

1712

Entrepreneur Sieur Antoine Crozat secures a monopoly on the western fur trade in an area stretching from the Carolinas to New Mexico. The governor of the new territory is the founder of Detroit, Sieur Antoine de la Mothe Cadillac.

The first fiesta season is proclaimed in Santa Fe.

1715

The Yamasee War begins in South Carolina. The Yamasee Indians, unhappy with corrupt English traders, wage war on the colonists and kill the traders among them, as well as some 300 settlers.

1716

Governor Felix Martínez fails to conquer the Hopi pueblo Indians.

Members of the Ramon Expedition hold the first horse race in Texas.

1718

The mission San Antonio de Valero, the Alamo, is founded by Spanish governor Martin de Alarcon.

1720

Pawnee Indians and French forces combine to destroy the expedition of Captain Pedro de Villasur, who sought to investigate French activity on the northeastern frontier of New Mexico.

Pontiac, the future chief of the Ottawa Indians, is born.

1721

The first public schools appear in New Mexico.

The first smallpox inoculations are given in the Southwest.

1725

The first known scalping of Indians by white men occurs in New Hampshire. The Boston treasury offers £100 per scalp.

The Spanish government forbids trading with the French.

1729

The French governor in Louisiana orders the Natchez tribe to vacate its lands so he can use them as his plantation. The Natchez Indians kill 200 French at

Fort Rosalie. French troops are sent in to defeat the Natchez.

1730
Cherokee Indian representatives confer with King George II in England.

1734
November 2: Daniel Boone is born in Berks County, Pennsylvania.

1738
A smallpox epidemic reduces the Cherokee population from 20,000 to about 10,000.

1739
What is known today as the Platte River is named by the exploring brothers Paul and Peter Mallet, who call it the "Plate." From there, they proceed southward until they reach Santa Fe.

1740
The Mallet brothers abandon their horses and build a canoe to travel on a river that will be named the Canadian, in honor of their nationality.

1743
Pierre de la Verendrye makes his western explorations and writes the first account of present Montana.
A map by Bellin shows Nouveau Mexique and Santa Fe.

1744–1748
King George's War, the third intercolonial war, sees the French, with Indian allies, conducting a border conflict against the British from New York to Maine.

1749
Great Britain grants 200,000 acres of upper Ohio to a group of colonists from Virginia.

1751
A presidio is established at Tubac, Arizona.
Pima Indians revolt, killing many Jesuit priests in present Arizona.
In Illinois a war between Pawnees and Osage is fought.

1752
Spanish soldiers build a fort at Tubac, thereby establishing the first white settlement in Arizona.

1753
The surveyor George Washington, 21, works in Ohio.
Daniel Boone moves to North Carolina.

1754
The French and Indian War opens with a French attack on George Washington's troops near Fort Duquesne (present Pittsburgh).

1755
March 11: The Scottish explorer and fur trader Sir Alexander MacKenzie is born.

Also in 1755:
The British bounty on enemy tribes is £40 per scalp.
Daniel Boone participates in General Braddock's campaign against the French.

1760
Cherokees and colonists war in the Carolinas.

1762
In the secret Treaty of Fontainebleau, France cedes Louisiana west of the Mississippi and the Isle d'Orleans to Spain.

1763
July 17: John Jacob Astor is born near Heidelberg, Germany.

Also in 1763:
The French and Indian War ends with the Treaty of Paris.
Canada passes from France to Britain, and Florida passes from Spain to Britain. Britain also acquires the half of Louisiana east of the Mississippi.

1764
In Pontiac's Rebellion, the Ottawas fight against the British in the Great Lakes areas.
The Sugar Act is passed by the British parliament.

1765
Major Robert Rogers is the first person known to call the northwestern region of the present United States "Ouragon."
The Stamp Act is passed by the British parliament.

1766
Antonio de Ulloa becomes the first Spanish governor of Louisiana.
Chief Pontiac surrenders to the British at Oswego.

1767
March 15: Andrew Jackson is born in Waxhaw, South Carolina.

Also in 1767:

A royal Spanish decree orders all Jesuits out of Spanish dominions in the Old World and the New.

A major flood occurs in Santa Fe.

1769

Daniel Boone leaves North Carolina to explore in Kentucky via the Cumberland Gap; he is captured by Shawnees in December.

Missions are established in California from San Diego to San Francisco.

Chief Pontiac is assassinated by an Illinois Indian at Cahokia.

1770

March 5: The "Boston Massacre" occurs when British troops fire on civilians, killing five.

Also in 1770:

August 1: The explorer William Clark is born in Caroline County, Virginia.

The explorer Garces treks through southwestern Arizona.

The Cherokee scholar Sequoyah is born in present Tennessee.

The 10,000 Mandan Indians are reduced to about 1,600 following a smallpox epidemic spread by French and Spanish traders.

1773

Mexican Indians discover Mayan ruins at Palenque.

In the Boston Tea Party, colonists dressed as Indians toss shipments of tea into Boston Harbor to protest the Tea Act.

1774

August 18: The explorer Meriwether Lewis is born in Albemarle County, Virginia.

Also in 1774:

Garces and Anza explore the Gila River region.

Shawnees and settlers fight in Virginia's Lord Dunmore's War.

The explorer Juan Pérez sails his ship along the Oregon coast.

The Continental Congress is called for by the Virginia House of Burgesses.

1775

Daniel Boone opens the Wilderness Road through the Cumberland Gap; he founds Boonesborough in Kentucky.

Daniel Boone (1734–1820), America's first celebrity pioneer. (New York Public Library)

Standing Bull and the Teton Sioux reach the Black Hills of present South Dakota.

Cherokees sell parts of present Kentucky to the Transylvania Company.

The explorers Bruno Heceta and Juan Francisco de Bodega y Quadra are the first Europeans known to set foot on the soil of what will be the northwest United States when they land at present Washington.

The American Revolution begins: Paul Revere rides from Charleston to Lexington, Massachusetts; the British are defeated at Lexington; the Second Continental Congress assembles in Philadelphia; the British are victorious at Bunker Hill; George Washington is named commander in chief of the revolutionary army.

1776

The presidio of San Francisco is founded by Juan Bautista de Anza and 247 colonists.

A Spanish fort is established at Tucson.

Father Garces is the first Spaniard recorded as visiting a Mohave settlement near present Needles, California.

Fort Boonesboro in 1775. (New York Public Library)

The Sioux, moving from Minnesota, cross the Missouri River for the first time and acquire large numbers of horses.

Father Silvestre Velez de Escalante, Athanasio Dominguez, and eight companions tour present Arizona, Utah, Colorado, and New Mexico and see, among other things, the Grand Canyon and the Great Salt Lake.

In the American Revolution, Washington drives the British from Boston; the Declaration of Independence is signed on July 4; Washington defeats the Hessians in Trenton, New Jersey.

1777

The Escalante Expedition ends in Santa Fe.

Captain James Cook, on his third voyage, explores the Pacific Northwest.

The mission Santa Clara de Asis is founded in California.

The first pueblo in California is established—San Jose de Guadalupe.

In the American Revolution, the British are defeated at Princeton, New Jersey; the colonists are defeated at Germantown and Brandywine, Pennsylvania; the

British under General John Burgoyne are defeated at Bemis Heights and Saratoga, New York.

1778

Captain James Cook sails past Washington and Oregon.

Daniel Boone is captured by the Shawnee Indians. He lives with them for three months, but escapes after hearing that Chief Blackfish is plotting to attack Boonesborough. He returns in time to help successfully defend against an attack by the British and the Indians from March 7 to September 20.

Jonathan Carver writes *Travels through the Interior Parts of North America in the Years 1766, 1767, 1768,* in which the word "Oregon" appears in print for the first time.

The Canadian plains and Rockies are explored by Peter Pond.

Indian massacres are reported at Cherry Valley, New York, and Wyoming, Pennsylvania.

The first U.S. treaty with Indians is with the Delaware tribe.

In the American Revolution, the colonies align with Holland and France; Washington defeats the British at Monmouth, New Jersey.

1779

January 5: The explorer Zebulon Pike is born in Lamberton, New Jersey.

Also in 1779:

Daniel Boone's political career begins as he serves in the Virginia General Assembly.

Congress sends troops to protect settlers from Indians in Pennsylvania's Wyoming Valley.

In the Southwest, Governor De Anza's campaign against the Comanches results in 38 warriors killed northeast of Santa Fe. De Anza also passes well within view of what will later be "discovered" by Zebulon Pike—Pike's Peak.

In the American Revolution, British troops surrender at Vincennes on the Wabash River, in present Indiana.

1780

After three years of drought in New Mexico, smallpox spreads among the Pueblo and the Moquis Indians and the Spanish.

A 20-year cycle of smallpox in New Mexico and Texas begins.

In the American Revolution, Charleston, South Carolina, surrenders to the British, who also win at Camden, New Jersey. The colonists are victorious at King's Mountain, North Carolina.

1781

A massacre at Yuma nearly wipes out a white colony; the Indians slay Father Garces.

Los Angeles is founded.

In the American Revolution, colonists defeat the British at Cowpens and Eutaw, North Carolina. The British surrender at Yorktown, Virginia, and depart Charleston, South Carolina, and Savannah, Georgia. The Articles of Confederation are ratified.

1782

The Mexican military conquest of the Yumas takes place.

Ninety-six Christian Delaware Indians are massacred by soldiers at Gnadenhutten, Ohio, in retaliation for raids conducted by other tribes.

Indians and Loyalists kill Colonel William Crawford, who gave the order for the massacre at Gnadenhutten.

Letters from an American Farmer, by Hector St. John Crèvecoeur, is the first book on the philosophy of frontier living.

Peace talks between the Americans and the British take place in Paris.

1783

The American Revolution ends, under the Treaty of Paris, the United States borders extend to the Mississippi River. Florida is ceded to Spain by Great Britain.

The Continental Congress warns squatters to stay off Indian land.

John Jacob Astor, 20 and penniless, arrives in New York.

John Ledyard writes *A Journal of Captain Cook's Last Voyage to the Pacific Ocean.*

1784

The first Russian settlement in Alaska is established at Three Saints Bay on Kodiak Island.

Thomas Jefferson's congressional committee proposes a temporary government in the western territories.

1785

With the signing of the Treaty of Fort McIntosh, the Chippewa, Delaware, Ottawa, and Wyandot Indians cede nearly all of present Ohio to the United States.

The Land Ordinance of 1785, passed by Congress, provides for six-mile-square townships in the northwest territories.

A Voyage to the Pacific Ocean, by Captain James Cook, is published.

1786

August 17: The frontiersman and politician David Crockett is born in Greene County, Tennessee.

Also in 1786:

Indian affairs come under the jurisdiction of the secretary of war.

Daniel Boone is elected to the Kentucky legislature.

Bernando de Galvez becomes the viceroy of "New Spain."

1787

The Northwest Ordinance, passed by Congress, states in part that "[Indian] land and property shall never be taken from them without their consent."

The Santa Fe Trail, a route from San Antonio north to the Red and Canadian Rivers and then on to Santa Fe, is traced by Pedro Vial.

1788

The first American to land in Oregon is Captain Robert Gray. The first black on Oregon soil is Markus Lopius, a member of the party on board Gray's sloops.

1789

The Treaty of Fort Hamar establishes principles of payment for land with the Ohio Indians.

George Washington is inaugurated the first U.S. president.

The French Revolution begins.

The author James Fenimore Cooper is born.

1790

Mexico and the Apaches make a peace that will last 32 years.

The population of New Mexico, including Indians, is 30,953.

Spain cedes the Pacific Northwest to the United States and Great Britain in the Treaty of Nootka.

John Meares publishes a travel journal, *Voyages Made in the Years 1788 and 1789.*

The Little Turtle's War or the Miami War occurs in the Old Northwest. Little Turtle, a Miami chief, leads an allied force of Shawnees, Delawares, and Wyandots in short attacks throughout the Old Northwest. They are eventually brought to peace talks by a 3,000-man force led by General "Mad" Anthony Wayne.

The Apache chief Mangas Coloradas is born.

1791

Most Cherokee lands are ceded to the United States in the Treaty of Holston River, in return for a promise that the Indians will be able to stay on their remaining lands for all time.

The British navigator George Vancouver explores the Pacific Northwest.

The Bill of Rights is ratified.

1792

Captain Robert Gray discovers and names the Columbia River and Mount Hood.

Trailblazer Pedro Vial journeys from Santa Fe to St. Louis and completes the first trek over what will later become the Santa Fe Trail.

Kentucky becomes a state.

1793

Sam Houston, the future president of Texas, is born in Rockbridge County, Virginia.

Alexander MacKenzie, a Scottish fur trader and explorer, and his party reaches the Pacific, completing the first continental crossing north of Mexico, from Saskatchewan to Dean Channel.

The Texas revolutionary Stephen Austin is born in Virginia.

1794

The future Mexican president Antonio López de Santa Anna is born in Jalapa, Vera Cruz, Mexico.

The Missouri Company is formed in St. Louis to explore and trade on the upper Missouri River.

General "Mad" Anthony Wayne defeats 2,000 Ohio Indians at the Battle of Fallen Timbers.

1796

July 16: The artist George Catlin is born in Wilkes-Barre, Pennsylvania.

Also in 1796:

The first American ship to explore California's coastline is Ebenezer Door's *Otter.*

James Bowie, the Texas revolutionary and inventor of the Bowie knife, is born in Logan County, Kentucky.

1797

The trader Francisco Derouin reports in St. Louis about raging battles between Kansa and Otoe Indians.

Smallpox ravages Mexican Indians.

After 14 years, construction is completed on the San Xavier Mission in present Arizona.

1799

January 6: Explorer and fur trader Jedediah Strong Smith is born in Bainbridge, New York.

September 21: Mountain man Bill Sublette is born in Lincoln County, Kentucky.

Also in 1799:

The Russian explorer A. A. Baranov's "Song" is the first poem composed in the West.

1800

The Harrison Land Act of 1800 provides liberal credit terms for western land purchases.

The Sioux control the region bordered by the Black Hills in the west, the Missouri River in the east, and the Platte River to the south.

Under a secret treaty, Napoleon reacquires Louisiana from Spain.

The Santa Rita copper deposit is discovered near present Silver City, New Mexico, by Lieutenant Colonel Carrisco.

Approximately 40,000,000 bison roam the North American continent.

1801

March 4: Thomas Jefferson is inaugurated president.

June 1: The religious leader Brigham Young is born in Whittingham, Vermont.

Also in 1801:

George Vancouver publishes his travel journal *A Voyage of Discovery to the North Pacific Ocean and Round the World.*

1802

January 9: Western University, the future Ohio University, is chartered at Athens.

April 30: The first Enabling Act instructs the organizers of territories on how to prepare for statehood.

September 4: The missionary Marcus Whitman is born in Rushville, New York.

November 29: An Ohio convention approves a constitution.

Also in 1802:

The first non-Indian child, an African American, is born in present North Dakota.

The Le Raye expedition from North Dakota travels to the Yellowstone, Big Horn, and Stillwaters Rivers.

John Chapman, "Johnny Appleseed," arrives in Ohio with apple seeds from New York and Pennsylvania.

Federal law prohibits the sale of liquor to Indians.

1803

January 18: President Jefferson asks Congress for $2,500 to fund a mission to the Indians "even to the Western ocean."

March 1: Ohio becomes a state.

April 11: Negotiations begin between France and the United States over the entire Louisiana Territory.

May 2: France cedes Louisiana, a territory of 828,000 square miles, to the United States for 80 million francs, or $15 million.

June 7: Indiana Governor William Henry Harrison signs treaties with Indians to obtain land along the Wabash River.

August 13: Meriwether Lewis and William Clark descend the Ohio River on the first leg of their western journey.

1804

March 9: Upper Louisiana is officially transferred from France to the United States.

Captain Meriwether Lewis arrives in St. Louis.

March 17: Mountain man Felix James Bridger is born in Richmond, Virginia.

March 26: The Land Act offers a minimum of 160 western acres at $1.64 per acre.

Congress divides Louisiana into the Territory of Orleans and the District of Louisiana.

May 14: The Lewis and Clark expedition starts up the Missouri River from St. Louis.

October 1: William Henry Harrison, governor of Indiana Territory, arrives in Missouri to establish a territorial government.

October 27: Lewis and Clark camp for the winter near present Bismarck, North Dakota, having covered 1,600 miles in less than six months. Touissant Charbonneau is hired as an interpreter at a Mandan village on the upper Missouri. His bride is the teenager Sacagawea.

Also in 1804:

President Jefferson appoints Pierre Chouteau the Louisiana agent for Indian affairs.

The Spanish defeat the Navajo Indians at Canyon de Chelly.

William C. Claiborne becomes the governor of the Territory of Orleans.

Sac and Fox Indians cede 5 million acres of present Wisconsin to the United States.

1805

January 11: The Michigan Territory is established; Congress changes the District of Louisiana to the Territory of Louisiana.

February 11: Sacagawea gives birth at a Mandan village near present Bismarck.

March 4: Thomas Jefferson is inaugurated for his second term as president.

April 7: The Lewis and Clark expedition resumes its trek up the Missouri River.

April 26: The Lewis and Clark expedition reaches the mouth of the Yellowstone River.

Captain Meriwether Lewis (1774–1809), Jefferson's private secretary and member of the 1st U.S. Infantry Regiment. (New York Public Library)

August 15: The Lewis and Clark expedition reaches the Continental Divide.

October 10: Lewis and Clark discover the Snake River, which flows to the west.

November 2: Lewis and Clark reach the Cascade Mountains.

November 7: Lewis and Clark's Corps of Discovery arrives at the headwaters of the Columbia River.

December 7: Lewis and Clark pitch their winter camp at Fort Clatsop in Oregon.

Also in 1805:
The first vaccinations are administered in New Mexico.
The Kentuckian James Purcell reaches Santa Fe after three years of wandering, having left St. Louis in 1802.
Zebulon Pike sets out on his northern voyage, presumably to locate the source of the Mississippi River.
General James Wilkinson is appointed governor of the Louisiana Territory. He will soon plot with Aaron Burr to establish a new country in the western territories.

1806

February 19: President Jefferson issues his first report on the success of Lewis and Clark.

April 30: Upon returning to St. Louis, Zebulon Pike incorrectly identifies Lake Cass as the source of the Mississippi. Geographers will accept his erroneous information until 1832.

June 15: Lewis and Clark begin their ascent of the western slope of the Rocky Mountains on their return trip from the Pacific. John Colter will leave the expedition shortly to trap beaver with two mountain men in the Yellowstone country.

July 15: Zebulon Pike begins his western expedition from Fort Belle Fountain, near St. Louis.

September 23: Lewis and Clark return to St. Louis, having logged 7,689 miles in 2 years, 4 months, and 10 days.

October 11: Wilkinson receives from Burr a dispatch suggesting that a war between Spain and the United States might help their scheme to set up a new country in the western territories.

November 15: In regard to Pikes Peak, which he discovers, Zebulon Pike writes, "I believe no human being could have ascended to its pinical."

Also in 1806:
The War Department establishes the Office of Superintendent of Indian Trade under the secretary of war.
Davy Crockett marries Polly Finley in Tennessee.

1807

January 22: President Jefferson informs Congress of Aaron Burr's alleged plot to form a separate country in the Southwest.

February 26: After Zebulon Pike reaches the Rio Grande near present Alamosa, Colorado, and builds a stockade, he and his party are met by 100 Spanish dragoons and militia. Pike is arrested on suspicion of spying.

March 3: Zebulon Pike and his men, prisoners of Mex-

Zebulon Montgomery Pike (1779–1813). Is he really off course, or on a spy mission? (Independence National Historical Park Collection)

ico, arrive in Santa Fe. The next morning, they are marched toward Chihuahua.

April 1: Zebulon Pike is interrogated at Chihuahua by General Nemesio Salcedo.

July 1: The Pike expedition is released by Spanish troops at Natchitoches, Louisiana.

September 1: Burr's treason trial ends in an acquittal.

November 21: Manuel Lisa establishes a trading post at the mouth of the Big Horn River.

Also in 1807:
Jefferson receives the first report from Lewis and Clark.
Meriwether Lewis succeeds General Wilkinson as governor of the Louisiana Territory.
Governor Alencaster inaugurates measures to prevent American influences from entering New Mexico.
John Colter, the first white man in Wyoming, discovers the Yellowstone country.

1808

April: John Jacob Astor establishes the American Fur Company.

July 12: The *Missouri Gazette* is the first newspaper published west of the Mississippi River.

July 16: Manuel Lisa, William Clark, and Pierre Chouteau establish the Missouri Fur Company.

October 16: Kansa Indians are banned from Fort Clark because of "insolent and violent conduct."

November 10: Osage Indians cede parts of present Missouri and Arkansas to the United States in return for a reservation in Oklahoma.

Also in 1808:

David Thompson of the North-West Company explores present Montana via the Kootenay River.

The United States prohibits the importation of slaves from Africa.

1809

March 1: The Illinois Territory is established.

July 2: The Shawnee chief Tecumseh urges the defense of western lands against whites.

August 9: William Barret Travis, the future hero of the Alamo, is born in Saluda County, South Carolina.

September 30: The Treaty of Fort Wayne, which grants the United States 2.5 million acres of Indian lands in Ohio and Indiana, is negotiated by General William Henry Harrison.

October 11: Meriwether Lewis dies at the age of 35; whether his death was a murder or a suicide is never proven.

December 24: Christopher Houston "Kit" Carson is born in Madison County, Kentucky.

Also in 1809:

A famous poem, "Gertrude of Wyoming," is published by Thomas Campbell; it concerns a 1778 massacre in Pennsylvania's Wyoming Valley. The title will be popular enough to become a territorial moniker in 1868.

Manuel Lisa and his party are arrested by Mexican authorities and taken to Chihuahua, where they will remain in jail for two years.

1810

June 23: The Pacific Fur Company is organized by John Jacob Astor.

September 8: The *Tonquin,* carrying 33 members of Astor's Pacific Fur Company, sails from New York for Oregon.

Also in 1810:

Father Hidalgo leads the Mexican Revolution for independence against Spain.

Zebulon Pike publishes *An Account of Expeditions to the Sources of the Mississippi and through the Western Parts.*

1811

February 2: Russian settlers establish Fort Foss on Bodega Bay, just north of San Francisco.

February 3: The journalist and politician Horace Greeley is born in Amherst, New Jersey.

September: The *New Orleans* is the first steamboat on the Mississippi.

November: Harrison defeats Tecumseh's brother, Tenskwatawa, on the Tippecanoe Creek in Indiana, effectively ending the Tecumseh Rebellion.

December 16: The largest recorded earthquake in U.S. history is centered at New Madrid, Missouri; the Mississippi River will flow north for a time.

Also in 1811:

Madame Dorion is the first woman to cross the Great Plains to settle in Oregon.

Representatives of J. J. Astor's company found Astoria, the first permanent settlement in the Pacific Northwest.

1812

January 12: The steamboat *New Orleans* becomes the first to make the Pittsburgh–New Orleans run.

April 30: Louisiana enters the Union as the 18th state.

June 4: The Territory of Missouri is created from the land not used in the creation of the state of Louisiana.

October 22: Frontiersman John "Grizzly" Adams is born in Medway, Massachusetts.

Also in 1812:

South Pass, a passage through the Rockies that will become a favorite of emigrants, discovered by Robert Stuart of the Pacific Fur Company.

The War of 1812 drives the British from most of the Northwest frontier.

1813

January 21: The military leader and explorer John Charles Frémont is born in Savannah, Georgia.

March 4: James Madison is inaugurated president for the second time.

April 27: Zebulon Pike, 34, is killed while leading his troops in the War of 1812's Battle of York.

May 9: Fort Meigs in present Ohio is defended by General William Henry Harrison against Tecumseh and British troops.

September 9: Captain Oliver Perry defeats the British on Lake Erie.

October 5: Chief Tecumseh is killed in battle at Ontario, Canada, where he was serving as a brigadier general for the British.

Also in 1813:

Astoria is sold to the British North-West Company and renamed Fort George.

Davy Crockett participates in Andrew Jackson's campaign against the Creek Indians in Alabama. In the Treaty of Fort Jackson, which will end the Creek War in 1814 the United States takes most of the Creek lands.

1814

August 8: Wyoming political figure Esther Hobart McQuigg (Ester Morris) is born in Tioga County, New York.

August 24: Washington, D.C., is burned by the British during the War of 1812.

September 28: Davy Crockett reenlists to fight the Creek Indians.

Also in 1814:

The first livestock introduced to the Pacific Northwest arrives by ship from California.

Shawnee leader Tecumseh (c. 1768–1813) is slain at the Battle of the Thames on October 5, 1813. (Library of Congress)

History of the Expedition, the first published account of the Lewis and Clark expedition, appears; it is edited by Nicholas Biddle and Paul Allen.

1815

January 8: In the Battle of New Orleans, General Andrew Jackson's 4,500 troops inflict 2,000 casualties on the British.

Also in 1815:

General William Clark negotiates the Portage des Sioux Treaty in Missouri.

James Bowie arrives in New Orleans, where he works in the slave trade and rides alligators.

1816

September 14: The novelist Hamlin Garland is born in West Salem, Wisconsin.

December 11: Indiana becomes the 19th state.

1817

March 3: A commercial steamboat route between Louisville and New Orleans is opened.

July 4: Construction of the Erie Canal begins at Rome, New York.

November 17: Davy Crockett becomes justice of the peace of Lawrence County, Tennessee.

December 10: Mississippi becomes the 20th state.

Also in 1817:

In the First Seminole War, Andrew Jackson invades Florida.

The name "Oregon" appears in William Cullen Bryant's poem "Thanatopsis."

The Senate Committee on Public Lands urges that Indians be removed from eastern lands and compensated with land in the west.

1818

January 8: The first petition for Missouri statehood is received by Congress.

April 1: Davy Crockett becomes the town commissioner of Lawrenceburg, Tennessee.

May 20: William G. Fargo, the cofounder of Wells, Fargo and Company, is born in Pompey, New York.

October 20: The Convention of 1818 with England fixes the Canadian boundary at the 49th parallel from Lake of the Woods to the summit of the Rockies. Fort George in Oregon Country returns to American ownership.

December 3: Illinois becomes the 23rd state.

Also in 1818:
Madeiro Gonzales establishes an American Fur Company trading post on the South Platte River.

Quapah Indians cede lands between the Red and Arkansas Rivers to the United States.

1819

February 13: The Missouri Bill is introduced in Congress in preparation for statehood.

March 2: Congress establishes Arkansas Territory.

June 6: Stephen H. Long's exploration of the Southwest begins; his mission from Secretary of War John C. Calhoun is to find the source of the Red River. Long will sight and name Long's Peak in present Colorado.

December 14: Alabama becomes the 22nd state.

Also in 1819:
Boundaries are established for Texas, Nevada, and California.

The Kickapoo Indians begin a five-year-long resistance to their removal from Illinois.

Navajos in Arizona go to war with Mexico.

Spain cedes Florida to the United States.

The *Independence* is the first steamboat on the Missouri River.

1820

February 17: The Missouri Compromise allows for the entry into the Union of Maine as a free state and of Missouri a slave state.

March 6: Congress passes the Missouri statehood bill, which will allow the state's electorate to decide on the issue of slavery within the state's boundaries.

April 24: The Land Act of 1820 sets 80 acres as the minimum amount of land one can purchase at $1.25 per acre.

July 15: Members of the Long expedition become the first to climb Pike's Peak. Earlier on the trek, Major Stephen Long wrote that what will one day become Nebraska is "wholly unfit for farming."

August 12: Manuel Lisa, 49, dies in Missouri.

September 26: Daniel Boone, 86, dies in Missouri.

Also in 1820:
Ohio has 600,000 residents and is thus the most populous state in the West.

1821

January 17: Mexico permits Moses Austin and 300 colonizers to enter Texas. Although Austin will soon die, his son, Stephen will go to Texas to claim the lands obtained by his father.

February 24: Mexico declares its independence from Spain.

March 2: The Relief Act allows price adjustments on western lands.

March 5: President James Monroe is inaugurated president for a second term.

August 10: Missouri is admitted to the Union as the 24th state, with a population of 65,000.

November 16: William Becknell arrives in Santa Fe, having traveled over what will become the Santa Fe Trail.

Also in 1821:
Arizona and New Mexico become provinces of Mexico.

Davy Crockett runs for the Tennessee legislature; the same year, he explores the Ohio River country.

The Hudson's Bay Company merges with and absorbs the North-West Company.

Sequoyah completes his 86-character Cherokee syllabary.

1822

February 9: The American Indian Society is organized.

February 13: Missouri lieutenant governor William Ashley places an ad in the *Missouri Gazette and Public Advisor* seeking 100 "enterprising young men" to trap along the Missouri River. Jedediah Smith and Jim Bridger are among the applicants.

May 22: William Becknell sets off on his second trip from Missouri to Santa Fe.

December 12: The United States recognizes independent Mexico.

Also in 1822:
Henry Rowe Schoolcraft begins his ethnological study of Indians.

The Office of Indian Trade is abolished by Congress.

The Stephen Long expedition is described in Edwin James's *Account of an Expedition from Pittsburgh to the Rocky Mountains.*

1823

March 20: The dime novelist E. Z. C. Judson, who will earn fame under the pen name Ned Buntline, is born in Stamford, New York.

April 23: Stephen Austin goes to Mexico to confirm the settlement of Texas.

September 26: The author Francis Parkman (*The Oregon Trail*) is born in Boston.

December 2: President Monroe introduces his "Monroe Doctrine" to Congress.

Also in 1823:

General William Ashley's trading party is attacked by Arikara Indians on the Yellowstone River.

Jedediah Smith leads an overland party to the Black Hills.

The Navajos make peace with Mexico.

Sam Houston is elected to Congress from Tennessee.

Secretary of War Calhoun recommends to Congress the removal of Indians from the East.

Seminoles in Florida agree to live on a 4-million-acre reservation in their native state.

The Texas Rangers, a state law enforcement organization, are formed.

The fictional western hero springs to life in James Fenimore Cooper's *The Pioneers,* the first of his five "Leatherstocking Tales."

The Jones-Immel party is massacred on the Yellowstone River.

1824

February: Jedediah Smith leads trappers through the South Pass of the Rockies in Wyoming.

April 17: An agreement with Russia sets 54°40′ as the boundary between the American and the Russian territories in the Pacific Northwest.

May 7: New Mexico becomes a territory of the Republic of Mexico under political chief Bartolomé Baca. Texas and Coahuila are organized as Mexican states.

June 17: The Bureau of Indian Affairs is created as part of the War Department.

August 15: The Lincoln County War figure John Chisum is born in Madison County Tennessee.

October 8: Brigham Young, 23, marries Miriam Works of New York, his first wife.

October 22: Davy Crockett's state political career ends when the Tennessee legislature adjourns.

Also in 1824:

The pioneer Dr. John McLoughlin arrives in Oregon.

The Hudson's Bay Company transfers its headquarters from Fort George to Fort Vancouver.

1825

January 27: Congress approves the Indian Territory, an area in present Kansas and Oklahoma to which eastern tribes are to be relocated.

February 12: Creek Indians cede all of their lands in Georgia to the United States and agree to leave in 17 months.

March 24: The Mexican state of Texas-Coahuila declares itself open for American settlers.

James Bridger (1804–1881). When he tastes the waters of the Great Salt Lake, he declares he has found a route to the Pacific. (Kansas State Historical Society, Topeka)

May 12: Jim Bridger explores the Great Salt Lake, sure that he has reached the Pacific Ocean.

August 10: Osage Indians cede their lands to the United States with a treaty at Council Grove, Kansas.

August 19: Sioux, Iowa, Chippewa, Sauk, and Fox Indians agree to boundary limitations.

October 26: The Erie Canal opens; it connects New York City (via the Hudson River) and Lake Erie.

Also in 1825:

Dr. John McLoughlin brings wheat to Oregon.

The first rendezvous, the mountain man's raucous swap meet, occurs on Henry's Fork on the Green River in present Utah. Jed Smith becomes partners with William Ashley. The rendezvous will become an annual event in which thousands will gather for fur trading, dining, drinking, horse racing, and so forth.

Kit Carson traps with Sylvester and James Ohio Pattie in the Gila Valley.

Roy Bean, the self-proclaimed "Law West of the Pecos," is born in Kentucky.

The trapper Bill Williams works the far Northwest down to Sonora.

U.S. surveyors map the route of the Santa Fe Trail.

1826

November 27: Following the second mountain man rendezvous, Jedediah Smith and his party arrive in San Diego, having completed the first overland expedition from Utah to California.

December 16: Benjamin Edwards declares himself the supreme potentate of the Republic of Fredonia at Nacogdoches, Texas. Stephen Austin ends the revolt.

Also in 1826:

A survey of Cherokees reports 22,000 cattle, 7,600 horses, 46,000 swine, 2,500 sheep, 762 looms, 2,488 spinning wheels, 172 wagons, 2,942 plows, 10 sawmills, 31 grist mills, 62 blacksmith shops, 18 schools, and 18 ferries.

Dr. John McLoughlin plants barley, oats, corn, and timothy grass in Oregon.

The first English novel set in the Southwest is Timothy Flint's *Francis Berrian.*

Kansas becomes Indian Territory for tribes that have ceded eastern lands, including the Kickapoo, Iowa, Sauk, Fox, Delaware, Potawatomi, and Shawnee.

1827

May 8: The Fort Leavenworth site is chosen as an outpost in Kansas for Santa Fe Trail travelers.

July 3: Jedediah Smith returns with three of his original party to the Great Salt Lake, then plans a return trip to California.

July 26: The Cherokees declare themselves a sovereign nation (their constitution is partially based on the U.S. Constitution); the Georgia legislature nullifies the act.

September 19: Jim Bowie slays banker Morris Wright with his famous invention, the Bowie knife, not long after Wright turns down his loan request.

Also in 1827:

The Winnebago Indians stage an uprising in Wisconsin.

Davy Crockett is elected to the U.S. House of Representatives.

Dr. McLoughlin erects the first sawmill in the Pacific Northwest.

Franciscans are expelled from the New Republic of Mexico.

Sam Houston is elected governor of Tennessee.

The first magazine to be published west of the Allegheny Mountains is Timothy Flint's *Western Monthly Review.*

1828

February 21: The *Cherokee Phoenix* begins publication; founded by Sequoyah and Elias Boudinot, it is the first American newspaper published in an Indian language.

July 8: Jedediah Smith's party reaches the Pacific Northwest; 15 of the 18 people in the original party

are killed by Kelawatset Indians on the Umpqua River.

August 22: Napoleon Boone, grandson of Daniel, is the second white child and first white boy born in present Kansas.

Also in 1828:

Fort Union is established by the American Fur Company in present Montana.

Placer gold mines, deposits of gravel, sand, and gold, are discovered south of Santa Fe.

Recent gold discoveries prompt Georgia to annex Indian lands.

1829

March 4: President Andrew Jackson, in his inaugural address, asks for just treatment of, and a liberal policy toward, the Indians.

July 26: The Ottawa, Chippewa, and Potawatomi Indians cede much of Michigan Territory to the United States.

August 25: Mexico turns down a request of President Jackson to buy Texas.

Also in 1829:

Bent's Fort is built by the brothers Charles, George, Robert, and William Bent near present La Junta, Colorado.

Jedediah Smith appears at his first rendezvous in two years.

Dr. John McLoughlin claims the site of Oregon City for the Hudson's Bay Company.

Geronimo, the future Apache leader, is born near the headwaters of the Gila River in Arizona.

Kit Carson travels west with an expedition to California.

Sam Houston resigns as Tennessee governor. He lives for a time among the Cherokee Indians.

The first U.S. military escort for a shipment on the Santa Fe Trail includes 170 troops from Fort Leavenworth led by Captain Bennett Riley.

1830

April 6: The Church of Jesus Christ of Latter-day Saints (Mormons) is formed at Fayette, New York, by Joseph Smith and six others.

Mexico prohibits Americans from settling in Texas.

April 10: William L. Sublette and 81 men leave St. Louis for this year's mountain man rendezvous. His are the first wagons to travel as far as the Rocky Mountains.

May 28: President Jackson signs the Indian Removal

Act, which will relocate several southeastern tribes to Indian Territory.

May 29: The Preemption Act sets a price of $1.25 an acre for settlers who wish to purchase lands they cultivated in the past year.

July 15: Sioux, Sac, Fox, and other tribes sign a treaty giving the United States most of Iowa, Missouri, and Minnesota.

September 30: Choctaws give the United States 8 million acres east of the Mississippi in exchange for land in present Oklahoma.

Also in 1830:

The Hudson's Bay Company plants potatoes at Oregon City.

Jedediah Smith enters the Santa Fe trade.

Jim Bridger camps in the Powder River valley.

Donald Mackenzie negotiates a truce between the Blackfeet and Assiniboine Indians.

The first oxen are used on the Santa Fe Trail.

Victorio, the Apache leader, is born.

1831

April 25: *The Lion of the West,* a play loosely based on the Davy Crockett legend, opens in New York with James Hackett as Nimrod Wildfire.

May 27: Jedediah Strong Smith is slain by Comanches on the Cimarron River on the Santa Fe Trail.

June 27: Chief Black Hawk agrees to move his Sac Indians west of the Mississippi River.

October 29: A smallpox epidemic occurs among Pawnees; agent John Dougherty reports "no one under 33 years of age escaped the monstrous disease."

Also in 1831:

A description of California and the Southwest appears in James Ohio Pattie's *The Personal Narrative of James O. Pattie.*

A revolt in California leads to the resignation of Governor Manuel Victoria.

The removal of the Choctaw from western Alabama and Mississippi to present Oklahoma begins.

Cyrus McCormick invents the reaper for cutting grain.

A delegation of Flathead and Nez Percé Indians visits St. Louis and asks missionaries to come to Oregon.

James Bowie further develops the Bowie knife. It measures 15 inches and weighs two pounds.

Kit Carson begins a decade of trapping in the Rockies.

Tatanka Iyotake, the future Sioux leader Sitting Bull, is born near Bullhead in present South Dakota.

The Supreme Court declares the Cherokees a "domestic dependent" in *Cherokee Nation v. Georgia.*

1832

February 6: *The Emigrant,* a book published in Ann Arbor, Michigan, includes the first suggestion for a transcontinental railroad to appear in print.

March 26: The American Fur Company's steamship *Yellowstone* leaves on her second expedition up the Missouri. Among the passengers boarding at St. Louis is the artist George Catlin.

April–August: The Black Hawk War occurs in the Illinois and Michigan territories. Sac and Fox Indians try to regain lands ceded to the United States. The Indians are defeated at Bad Axe River, Wisconsin. Sauk chief Black Hawk surrenders and is incarcerated for one year.

May 5: The historian Hubert Howe Bancroft is born in Granville, Ohio.

July 24: Captain Benjamin L. E. Bonneville leads 110 men and 20 wagons across the Continental Divide at South Pass. Bonneville notes the presence of buffalo on the Great Plains: "As far as the eye could reach, the country seemed blackened by innumerable herds." His wagons are the first through South Pass and the first to cross the Continental Divide.

October: George Catlin paints portraits of the Mandan chief Four Bears and of Shawnees and Delawares near St. Louis.

October: Asiatic cholera claims the lives of 6,000 people in New Orleans, including the wife and two children of James Bowie.

October 14: The Chickasaw Indians agree to give up all their lands east of the Mississippi River.

October–November: The author Washington Irving embarks on a 400-mile tour of present Oklahoma with a company of mounted rangers. Irving will write of his travels through a "part of the Pawnee hunting grounds where no party of white men had yet penetrated."

December 28: St. Louis University is chartered.

Also in 1832:

After continuous raids and debauchery by white settlers in Georgia, the Creeks accept a treaty calling for their removal from the state.

Stephen Austin and 8,000 settlers live in the Texas colonies.

The Seminole removal policy is approved, despite strong opposition from a majority of the tribe.

Indians and fur trappers battle at Pierre's Hole, Idaho.

The first poem composed in English by a white in the West is Albert Pike's "The Fall of Poland," in *Prose Sketches and Poems Written in the Western Country.*

The first fictional tales about Davy Crockett appear.

The first steamboat reaches Fort Union, Montana.

Brigham Young leads a group of Mormons to Ohio.

Sam Houston, commissioned by President Jackson to meet with the Indians, arrives in Texas.

Congress prohibits the sale of liquor in "Indian country."

1833

January: *The Life and Adventures of Colonel David Crockett of West Tennessee,* by Mathew St. Clair Clarke, receives copyright protection.

January 1: Antonio López de Santa Anna begins his term as president of Mexico.

March 4: Andrew Jackson is inaugurated president for a second term.

April: Prince Maximilian of Wied Neuwied and the Swiss artist Karl Bodmer travel aboard the *Yellowstone* on her third voyage up the Missouri River. Bodmer paints Teton Sioux and Assiniboines of the Upper Missouri. Maximilian collects specimens of plants and animals, and he will later publish his findings in *Travels in the Interior of North America.* On the trip, Maximilian counts 2,100 Hidatsa Indians.

April: Texans at San Felipe vote to become independent of Mexico.

May: The Mormons adopt the name "Latter-day Saints."

July: Stephen Austin arrives in Mexico City with his proposal to separate Texas from Coahuila.

November: The Joe Walker expedition to California is the first party of whites to camp in Yellowstone Valley; the journey marks the discovery of Walker Pass in the Sierra Nevada.

Also in 1833:

The removal of Choctaws to present Oklahoma ends.

The removal of Creeks to Oklahoma begins; a protest by 1,500 is answered by General T. S. Jesup and 11,000 troops.

The first Oregon timber is shipped to China.

Fort Mackenzie is erected on the Missouri River, Fort Cass on the Yellowstone River.

The first gold lode west of the Mississippi is discovered at Sierra de Oro (Mountain of Gold), New Mexico, later known as the Ortiz Mine.

Samuel Colt invents and begins producing the revolver.

1834

January 3: Stephen Austin is arrested by the government in Mexico for inciting Texans to rebel.

June 30: The Department of Indian Affairs is established.

July: The annual mountain man rendezvous takes place at Beaver River; Tennessee fur trader Joe Walker attends.

October 28: The United States demands that the Seminole tribe vacate Florida.

Also in 1834:

Brigham Young, recently designated an apostle, is a traveling missionary in the United States and Great Britain.

Chickasaws sign a treaty agreeing to their removal from northern Mississippi and western Tennessee to Indian Territory in present Oklahoma.

John Sutter, 32, flees Germany to avoid bad debts. He sails across the Atlantic. The land he settles in California will be the place where gold is discovered.

Davy Crockett appears at a series of speaking engagements in the East.

Dr. John McLoughlin sends to London the remains of a mastodon found in Oregon.

J. J. Astor leaves the fur business for real estate ventures.

New Mexico's first newspaper is called (in English) *The Dawn of Liberty.* It is produced on the first printing press in Santa Fe, owned by Don Ramón Abreu.

1835

February 24: The *Shawnee Sun* becomes the first Kansas newspaper; it is printed by Jotham Meeker.

June 30: Colonel William B. Travis captures Fort Anahuac from a Mexican garrison as a prelude to the Texas Revolution.

October 10: Gail Borden begins publishing a newspaper, the *Telegraph and Texas Register.*

November: After failing reelection to Congress, Davy Crockett tells voters: "You can all go to hell. I'm going to Texas!"

November 30: Samuel Clemens, whose pen name will be Mark Twain, is born in Florida, Missouri.

December 4: Texans win the first battle of the Alamo as Texas leader Ben Milam's troops drive General Cos and his Mexicans from the mission-fortress in San Antonio. Ben Milam dies during the battle.

December 15: The Mexican dictator Santa Anna issues his constitution for Mexican territories.

December 29: With the Treaty of New Echota—signed by 20 Cherokees, none a chief—binding to the Cherokee nation, the United States forces the Cherokees to surrender their eastern lands. The payoff is $5 million and some land in Oklahoma. The Indians' removal, which will kill 10 percent of the tribe, begins.

A romantic portrait of Davy Crockett falling at the Alamo. Some maintain he was found after the battle and executed by Santa Anna. (Library of Congress)

Also in 1835:

Fort Van Buren is built on the Yellowstone River.

Padre Antonio José Martinzea prints pamphlets and school manuals at Taos in present New Mexico.

Sam Houston becomes commander of the Texas Army.

Texas Rangers reorganize with a force of 150 men.

The Second Seminole War begins in Florida.

Washington Irving publishes *A Tour of the Prairies.*

1836

February 8: Davy Crockett arrives at the Alamo.

February 11: William B. Travis assumes command at the Alamo.

February 23–March 6: In the Battle of the Alamo, fewer than 200 Texans initially hold out against an assault force of 1,800 Mexican troops. On the day of the final onslaught, William Travis is one of the first to die, followed by James Bowie and then Davy Crockett (who may have been put to death by a firing squad after the battle). Santa Anna orders the 187 bodies tossed on a funeral pyre.

February 25: Samuel Colt receives Patent No. 138 for "an improvement on revolving fire-arms."

March 2: Texas declares its independence from Mexico in the village of Washington-on-the-Brazos, on Sam Houston's 43rd birthday.

March 5: Cattleman Charles Goodnight is born in Madison County, Illinois.

March 27: In the Goliad Massacre, troops under General Urrea put to the sword 417 Texas revolutionary prisoners from the Battle of Coleto Creek.

April 21: Sam Houston's force of 783 men surprises Santa Anna's troops in the Battle of San Jacinto. Seven Texans are killed, while 630 Mexicans die and 730 are taken prisoner, including Santa Anna, who is forced to sign surrender papers and recognize Texas's independence.

May 19: Cynthia Parker, 9, is kidnapped from Parker's Fort, Texas, by a Comanche, Kiowa, and Caddo raiding party. She will remain a captive for years, during which time she will become the mother of Quanah Parker, the last chief the Comanches.

August 25: The author Bret Harte is born in Albany, New York.

September 1: Dr. Marcus Whitman and H. H. Spalding, Protestant missionaries, lead a party to Oregon; Narcissa Whitman and Eliza Spalding are the first white women to travel the Oregon Trail.

October 22: Sam Houston becomes the first president of Texas.

December 27: Stephen Austin dies at 43.

Also in 1836:

Arkansas becomes a state.

John Charles Frémont works on railroad survey crews for the Charleston and Cincinnati Railroad.

1 8 3 6

Seminole Indians, led by Osceola, go on the warpath in Florida to protest against the removal of Indians.

The first steamboat on the Pacific, the *Beaver,* arrives at Fort Vancouver.

Washington Irving publishes *Astoria.*

1837

January 26: Michigan becomes the 26th state.

March 3: President Jackson recognizes the Republic of Texas.

March 4: Martin Van Buren is inaugurated the 8th president.

May 27: The future lawman James Butler "Wild Bill" Hickok is born in Homer, Illinois.

June: The steamship *St. Peter's* journeys up the Missouri carrying smallpox. The Mandan Indian population, estimated at 15,000 in 1738, will decline from 2,000 in June to 138 in October following a smallpox pandemic. Also heavily affected are the Hidatsa and Arikara tribes.

July 31: Guerrilla leader William Clarke Quantrill is born at Canal Dover, Ohio.

Also in 1837:

An uprising occurs in New Mexico over the revised Mexican constitution; Governor Albino Pérez is assassinated.

Ten thousand people live in St. Louis, 60,000 in New Orleans.

The artist Alfred Jacob Miller, on a Rocky Mountain expedition, paints Fort William, which later becomes Fort Laramie.

The removal of Chickasaws from western Alabama and Tennessee to Oklahoma begins; the tribe is ravaged by cholera and badgered by whiskey salesmen.

Ewing Young becomes the first person to drive sheep from California to Oregon City.

The Mexican state of Chihuahua offers a bounty on Apache scalps: 100 pesos for those of men, 50 for those of women, 25 for those of children.

Washington Irving publishes *The Adventures of Captain Bonneville.*

1838

January 31: The Seminole leader Osceola dies in prison at Charleston, South Carolina.

April 21: The naturalist John Muir is born in Dunbar, Scotland.

July 4: Iowa becomes a territory formed from the old Wisconsin Territory.

September 1: The explorer William Clark dies at 68.

October 8: At Battle Creek, Texas, only seven out of 25 surveyors survive an attack by 300 Kickapoo Indians.

October 30: In the Haun's Hill Massacre, Nehemiah Comstock and 200 men attack a Mormon camp in Missouri, slaughtering 20 men, women, and children.

Also in 1838:

Black Hawk dies.

Brigham Young moves the Latter-day Saints to Nauvoo, Illinois.

John Charles Frémont explores Minnesota.

New Mexico rebel leaders are rounded up and shot. General Manuel Armijo is in power.

Smallpox spreads across the plains; the Assiniboins infect the Cree, of which some 7,000 die. The death toll among the Blackfeet reaches 6,000. As tribes flee, smallpox spreads among the Crow, Dakota, Pawnee, Osage, Winnebago, Sioux, and Choctaw.

The first moonshine is made in Oregon.

The first temperance society is organized in Oregon.

The first western cattle drive arrives in California.

The "Trail of Tears" begins as General Winfield Scott and 7,000 soldiers arrive in Georgia to enforce the removal of the Cherokee. The winter departure kills 25 percent of the 16,000 Cherokees.

Tubac, Arizona, becomes a pueblo.

1839

February 11: The University of Missouri is chartered at Columbus.

August: John August Sutter arrives in California from Germany, via Hawaii.

December 5: The future military leader George Armstrong Custer is born in New Rumley, Ohio.

Also in 1839:

John K. Townsend writes *Narrative of a Journey Across the Roc¹ ; Mountains and the Colorado River to the Sandwich Islands.*

The Kiowa Indians call the winter of 1839–1840 "smallpox winter." Cases are reported as far north as the Hudson's Bay Company's posts in Canada, and as far south as Apache and Comanche country.

John Lloyd Stephens and Frederick Catherwood discover Mayan ruins in Central America.

The first printing press in the Northwest arrives at Lapwai (in present Idaho) from Honolulu; it prints the first book ever published in the region, a Nez Percé schoolbook.

1840

March 19: San Antonio whites invite the Comanches to talk peace. A fight breaks out when settlers lock the doors of the Council House; 35 Indians are killed in the melee.

March 29: Antonio Zapata, found guilty of treason in Mexico, is beheaded.

August 12: Texas troops kill 80 Comanches in the Battle of Plum Creek.

Also in 1840:

Father De Smet explores in Montana.

Richard Henry Dana's *Two Years Before the Mast* is published.

The total number of Indian lives lost to smallpox from 1837 to 1840 is elusive. Experts believe there were no fewer than 100,000 deaths, perhaps as many as 300,000.

1841

February 11: The only mutiny in Texas history is staged by the crew of the *San Antonio*.

March 4: William Henry Harrison becomes the 9th president of the United States.

April 4: Upon the death of Harrison, John Tyler becomes the 10th president.

September 18: Mexican and Texas forces clash east of San Antonio in the Battle of Salado Creek.

October 2: The lawman John Slaughter is born in Sabine Parish, Louisiana.

December 16: Missouri senator Lewis Linn introduces legislation in Congress to encourage migration to Oregon; the bill will eventually fail.

Also in 1841:

Brigham Young becomes president of the Mormon's Quorum of the Twelve Apostles.

The future Sioux chief Crazy Horse is born.

Father De Smet founds St. Mary's Mission in present Montana.

France severs diplomatic relations with the Republic of Texas after an Austin hotel keeper slaughters the French minister's pigs.

The artist George Catlin's works appear in *North American Indians*.

Red Cloud kills a rival chief, thereby splitting Sioux alliances for 40 years.

Texas Rangers engage Comanche forces in the Battle of Bandera Pass.

The first covered wagons to travel the Oregon Trail arrive in Sacramento.

The Port of Houston opens.

The *Star of Oregon,* the first ship built by Americans in Oregon, is launched.

1842

May: John C. Frémont's first exploration of the Rocky Mountains is with the guide Kit Carson.

Christopher Houston "Kit" Carson (1809–1868) and John Charles Frémont (1813–1890) meet in 1842. Carson guides the first Frémont expedition as well as two subsequent ones. Their fame spreads from the Rockies to Oregon. (New York Public Library)

The first wagons depart St. Louis to follow the Oregon Trail.

September: More fighting occurs between Mexicans and Texans. Mexican troops recapture the Alamo for a brief period. The "Dawson Massacre" occurs when Nicholas Dawson and 35 reinforcements are killed by the Mexican army.

Also in 1842:

The last battle of the Second Seminole War is fought. General Zachary Taylor estimates that about 3,000 Indians have been removed from Florida at a cost of $20 million and the lives of 1,500 soldiers.

Charles Dickens tours the Great Plains.

Oregon's Willamette University is the first college west of the Mississippi.

1843

January 10: The outlaw Frank James is born in Clay County, Missouri.

February 3: The Oregon Bill, intended to encourage migration, passes in the Senate but dies in the House.

March 25: In the "Black Bean Affair," 170 Texans from the Mier Expedition, which had forced a battle and had slain 500 Mexicans, are captured inside Mexico. Governor Francisco Mexía orders every tenth man shot. The condemned are chosen by lottery, each Texan reaching into a jar filled with white beans and 17 black ones. Those who draw the black beans are executed, the others released.

April 4: The photographer William Henry Jackson is born in Keesville, New York.

May: Early Oregon Trail travelers head for the Pacific Northwest; 900 will arrive at Willamette Valley.

May 29: John Charles Frémont's second expedition, guided by Kit Carson, will go through the Snake River valley and on to California's San Joaquin valley.

June 15: Texas and Mexico declare a truce.

November 20: The Blacksnake Hills trading post is renamed St. Joseph, Missouri.

Also in 1843:

Oregon adopts the Organic Laws, putting a provisional government in place.

Jim Bridger and Louis Vasquez establish Fort Bridger, Wyoming.

Fort Chadron opens on the Missouri River in present Montana.

Fort Sarpy and Fort Alexander are built on the Yellowstone.

John J. Audubon paints the birds of the upper Missouri River.

President Santa Anna orders the Taos customs house closed.

Frederick Marryat writes *The Travels and Adventures of Monsieur R. Violet in California, Sonora, and West Texas.*

Thomas J. Farnham writes *Travels in the Great Western Prairies.*

Father De Smet writes *Letters and Sketches.*

Sequoyah, inventor of the Cherokee alphabet, dies.

1844

January 15: The outlaw Coleman Younger is born near Lee's Summit, Missouri.

March 6: The second Frémont Expedition reaches Sutter's Fort on the Sacramento River.

May 22: Samuel F. B. Morse displays the telegraph.

June 27: The Mormon founder Joseph Smith is executed by a mob in Carthage, Illinois. He and his brother Hyrum were arrested and jailed for allegedly wrecking the printing press of the *Nauvoo Expositor.*

Rumors of polygamy fuel an angry mob that pulls the men from their cells and lynches them in the streets.

August 7: John Charles Frémont returns to St. Louis.

August 8: Brigham Young is chosen to succeed Joseph Smith as leader of the Mormons.

November 1: Iowa voters adopt a new constitution.

December 3: President Tyler asks Congress to approve the annexation of Texas.

December 12: Anson Jones becomes the second president of Texas.

Also in 1844:

Amos Lovejoy lays out the first plots of land in the future Portland, Oregon

The first wagon train reaches Sutter's Fort in California.

George Wilkins Kendall writes *Narrative of the Texas–Santa Fe Expedition.*

Josiah Gregg writes *Commerce of the Prairies.*

The *Cherokee Advocate* is published in present Oklahoma. U.S. troops confiscate the printing press.

The first printing press in New Mexico is moved from Taos to Santa Fe in order to print the official newspaper *La Verdad (Truth).*

1845

February 1: The University of Waco (the future Baylor University) is chartered.

March 1: The United States annexes Texas.

March 4: James K. Polk is inaugurated president.

March 28: Mexico breaks diplomatic relations with the United States.

May: John Charles Frémont's third expedition sets out from Missouri.

May 28: President Polk sends troops to guard the Texas border.

December 29, 1845: Texas enters the Union. (Library of Congress)

July 4: Texas accepts annexation at a convention chaired by President Anson Jones

July 23: The mountain man William Sublette, 45, dies of tuberculosis at Cape May, New Jersey.

July 31: General Zachary Taylor has 1,500 troops encamped on the Nueces River in Texas.

September 16: President Polk attempts to purchase from Mexico disputed territories in New Mexico, California, and in Texas south of the Nueces River for $40 million.

October 13: Texas voters approve annexation as well as a new constitution.

December 27: The United States refuses to renew its offer of the 49th parallel as a boundary with Great Britain's territory in the Northwest, making good on Polk's promise of "54°40′ or Fight."

December 29: Texas becomes the 28th state. Sam Houston is elected to the U.S. Senate.

Also in 1845:

The first grist mill in Montana is constructed by Father Ravalli at St. Mary's.

The editor John L. O'Sullivan coins the term "Manifest Destiny" in an editorial.

Colonel Stephen W. Kearny displays a show of force by marching dragoons up the Platte River and warning Oglalas against trifling with emigrants.

Five thousand people travel on the Oregon Trail.

1846

February 26: The scout, hunter, and showman William F. Cody, Buffalo Bill, is born in Le Claire, Iowa.

May: Francis Parkman travels the Oregon Trail.

May 9: General Zachary Taylor's troops defeat Mexicans at Palo Alto, where he reports 400 Mexicans dead.

May 11: President Polk declares war on Mexico.

June 3: General Stephen Watts Kearny and his Army of the West receive orders to take possession of California, with help from the sea provided by Commodore John Sloat.

June 14: In California's Bear Flag Revolt, William B. Ide and homesteaders take over Sonoma and declare California independent. Captain John C. Frémont joins them in raising a flag with a bear as its emblem.

June 15: The Oregon Treaty between Great Britain and the United States is signed, setting the dividing line between their territories in the Pacific Northwest at the 49th parallel.

July 5: Captain John C. Frémont is chosen to lead the Republic of California.

July 7: Declaring that California belongs to the United

James and Margaret Reed, survivors of the Donner tragedy. (California Department of Parks and Recreation)

States, Commodore John Sloat occupies Monterey, California,

July 9: Commander John Montgomery's forces take San Francisco.

July 24: John Charles Frémont organizes the California Battalion.

August 2: General Stephen Watts Kearny's army marches from Bent's Fort in Colorado toward New Mexico.

August 15: The first newspaper published in California is the *Californian*.

August 17: The annexation of California is announced by Commodore David Stockton, who seizes Los Angeles and proclaims himself governor.

August 18: Colonel Stephen Kearny takes Santa Fe without firing a shot and declares New Mexico to be under American rule. Charles Bent is named governor of New Mexico.

September 25: General Zachary Taylor's forces capture Monterrey, Mexico. Colonel Stephen Kearny departs Santa Fe for California.

October: The Mormon Battalion takes possession of Tucson and raises the American flag to designate Cooke's Wagon Road from Santa Fe to the Pacific.

November: The Donner party, enroute to California from Illinois, circle their wagons to face winter at Truckee Meadows in the Sierra Nevada.

November 16: General Zachary Taylor captures Saltillo during the Mexican War.

November 25: Carry Amelia Moore, the future prohibitionist Carry Nation, is born in Kentucky.

December: Alexander Doniphan defeats the Mexicans at El Brazito in the only Mexican War battle fought in New Mexico; two days later he occupies El Paso.

December 28: Iowa becomes the 29th state.

September 14, 1847. General Winfield Scott marches his troops into the Grand Plaza of Mexico City and raises the American flag. (Library of Congress)

Also in 1846:

Alexander Doniphan makes the first U.S. treaty with the Navajo.

The first newspaper published west of the Mississippi is the *Oregon Spectator*.

Fort Lewis is built on the Missouri River near the mouth of the Maria River.

John C. Frémont writes *Narrative of the Exploring Expedition to the Rocky Mountains in the Year 1842*.

Massachusetts representative Robert Winthrop is the first politician to use the term "Manifest Destiny" (John O'Sullivan coined it in 1845).

"Texas Jack" Omohundro and Nate Salsbury are born.

Led by Brigham Young, the Mormons leave Nauvoo, Illinois, and head west.

The U.S. government reports that the Kansa tribe is "very ill with autumnal diseases."

1847

January 10: Commodore Robert F. Stockton and General Stephen Kearny recapture Los Angeles from Mexican rebels. The fighting ends in California.

January 16: John Charles Frémont is appointed governor of California.

January 20: In the Taos Revolt, Taos Indians and revolutionists assassinate many officials, including Governor Bent. Colonel Price puts down the revolt.

February 19: Rescuers reach the ill-fated Donner party at Donner Lake near Truckee Pass in the Sierra Nevada. Of the 86 who started out, 36 have perished since November. Survivors are found eating stew containing human flesh.

February 22–24: In the Battle of Buena Vista, 15,000 troops under Santa Anna are defeated by Zachary Taylor's 5,000 men.

February 28: Colonel Alexander Doniphan defeats Mexican forces in the Battle of Sacramento.

March 16: Mormons under Brigham Young depart Council Bluffs, Iowa, for the Great Salt Lake region.

March 29: General Winfield Scott captures Vera Cruz.

May 31: Stephen Kearny appoints Colonel Richard Mason governor of California.

June 6: Nicholas Trist is sent to negotiate peace with Santa Anna.

July 23–24: Mormons arrive at the Great Salt Lake; Brigham Young declares, "This is the place."

September 5: The future outlaw Jesse Woodson James is born in Missouri.

September 7: The Mexican government rejects the U.S. terms for peace.

September 13–14: Major General Winfield Scott's army takes the Chapultepec Palace outside Mexico City. The next day, his army enters Mexico City and raises the American flag over the National Palace.

November 29: The "Whitman Massacre" occurs in Oregon. Cayuse Indians, convinced that missionary Marcus Whitman and his settlers have brought a plague of measles, raid the mission at Waiilatpu, near Walla Walla. Whitman, his wife Narcissa, and a dozen other whites are slain. The Cayuse War begins.

Also in 1847:

David H. Coyner writes *The Lost Trappers*.

The first English-language newspaper in New Mexico, the *Santa Fe Republican* is published.

Yerba Buena is renamed San Francisco; the first newspaper in San Francisco, the *California Star,* is published.

THE WEST

1848—1890

1848

"Full flowing streams, mighty timber, large crops, luxuriant clover, fragrant flowers, gold and silver. Great country, this."

—Sam Brannan, *California Star*

JANUARY

2. The mountain man James Beckwourth departs Fort Leavenworth, heading for Bent's Fort.

▪ James B. Grant, Colorado governor from 1883–1885, is born in Russell County, Alabama.

5. *Commerce of the Lakes and Western Rivers,* published on this date by Colonel J. J. Albert, includes Lieutenant Colonel Stephen H. Long's report on the extent of steam navigation on western waters, including estimates for the Missouri (1,800 miles), Yellowstone (300 miles), Platte (40 miles), Kansas (150 miles), Osage (275 miles), and Grand (90 miles) Rivers.

▪ Francis X. Aubry, traveling alone, arrives in Independence, Missouri, after a 14-day horse ride from Santa Fe.

▪ Henry Jacquis, chief of the Wyandot Nation, dies in Kansas City.

9. The first commercial bank in San Francisco is established.

15. The *California Star* announces that the California Star Express, a stagecoach, will leave San Francisco on April 1, bound for Salt Lake and Independence, Missouri, and will carry letters for 50 cents. The coach is expected to reach Missouri in 60 days.

▪ Jim Younger, the future outlaw, is born near Lee's Summit, Missouri.

24. James Marshall discovers gold in California.

28. James Marshall tells John Sutter of his discovery.

30. From Henry Bigler's journal, describing events at Sutter's Mill: "Sunday 30 clear & has been all the last week our metal has been tride and prooves to be goald it is thought to be rich We have pict up more than a hundred dollars woth last week."

31. John Charles Frémont is found guilty of mutiny, disobedience, and prejudicial conduct for having taken the reins of government in California. The charges were placed by General Stephen Kearny.

GOLD IN CALIFORNIA
JANUARY 24, 1848

While building a sawmill for John Augustus Sutter on the south fork of the American River, some 50 miles northeast of Sutter's Fort, the New Jersey mechanic James Wilson Marshall discovered gold. Said Marshall, when recalling the event, "I went down as usual and after shutting off the water from the race I stepped into it, near the lower end, and there upon the rock about six inches beneath the water I discovered the gold. I picked up one or two pieces and examined them attentively. I then tried it between two rocks and found that it could be beaten into a different shape but not broken."

Despite his monumental find, Marshall made no money in the ensuing rush to riches.

Sutters Fort in 1848, the site of the first California gold discovery. (Library of Congress)

Following the court-martial, Frémont is dismissed from the army.

Also in January 1848:
San Francisco's population is estimated at 900.

FEBRUARY

1. The missionaries S. M. Irvin and William Hamilton publish a brief history of the Iowa and Sac tribes in Kansas.
2. The Treaty of Guadalupe Hidalgo is signed.
- The first Chinese arrive in San Francisco aboard the brigantine *Eagle*.
5. Myra Maybelle Shirley, the future "Bandit Queen" Belle Starr, is born near Medoc, Missouri.
7. A contract to deliver 30,000 pounds of flour to Sac and Fox Indians of the Mississippi River region is obtained by Hugh Hamilton.
9. The Oregon Bill, which will provide for statehood without slavery, is reintroduced in the House.
12. The *Santa Fe Republican* reports that James Beckwourth and his traveling companions are safe at

BELLE STARR
FEBRUARY 5, 1848—FEBRUARY 2, 1889

1848: Myra Belle Shirley is born on a farm near Carthage, Missouri.

1866: Unwed, Starr bears Cole Younger a daughter, Pearl, in Texas. While working as a dealer in Dallas gaming house, she become Mrs. James Reed.

1871: The Reeds move to California, where Belle has another baby. Following this, the family relocates to Texas where the new parents earn a living stealing horses.

1874: Belle is widowed when James Reed is slain by bounty hunters. For spite, Belle refuses to identify the body, which means the bounty cannot be paid.

1880: Following six common-law marriages, Belle weds Sam Starr. They make their home at Eufala, Oklahoma.

1882: Belle Starr is arrested on a horse-thieving charge.

1885: Belle allegedly has a love affair with John Middleton, a known murderer.

1886: Sam Starr gets into a gunfight with the lawman Frank West, in which both are mortally wounded. Following a period of mourning, the widow enters into a common-law marriage with Bill Julyi, who becomes Bill July Starr.

1889: Belle Starr is murdered, shot in the back by an unknown assailant as she rides home.

THE TREATY OF GUADALUPE HIDALGO
FEBRUARY 2, 1848

The treaty ended the Mexican War that officially began on May 13, 1846. The United States obtained from Mexico upper California, New Mexico, Utah, Nevada, most of Arizona, and a portion of Colorado, for a lump payment of $15 million. The land itself covered an area extending from Texas to the Pacific and up to Oregon, some 1,193,061 square miles. The United States also agreed to pay the $3.25 million in American claims against Mexico.

Fort Bent. They tell of an attack by Pawnees on the plains of Kansas and claim they killed two and wounded three.

23. The first steamboat of the season, the *Tamerlane*, reaches Weston, Missouri. Another 192 will follow this year.
23. The Treaty of Guadalupe Hidalgo is presented to the Senate by President James Polk.
25. Edward H. Harriman, the future head of the Union Pacific Railroad and founder of the Boys Club, is born in Hempstead, New York.
- The poet Walt Whitman arrives in New Orleans to work for the *New Orleans Crescent;* the job will last only a few months.
29. A military armistice suspending hostilities in the Mexican War takes effect.

James Beckwourth (c. 1800–1866), the explorer referred to in the February 12, 1848, Santa Fe Republican. An African-American mountain man, his career is launched on General William Ashley's 1824 fur-trapping expedition. (Denver Public Library, Western History Department)

Also in February 1848:
The U.S. government reports that the Kansa tribe is "terribly destitute."

National Headlines/February 1848:
23. REP. JOHN QUINCY ADAMS, FORMER PRESIDENT, DIES AT 80 IN HOUSE OF REPRESENTATIVES

MARCH

1. In response to the January 15 offer of the *California Star*, the rival *Californian* announces its own mail route to Salt Lake City and Wyoming. Letters will be carried for 12.5 cents, and departure is set for April 15.
■ Nah-ko-min, the main chief of the Delawares since 1835, dies on a reserve north of the Kansas River in present Wyandotte county.

5. The wagon train known as "Fisher's Express" is reported to be "suffering much" on the road from Fort Leavenworth to Santa Fe; frostbite is said to be the main difficulty.

8. A wagon train from Santa Fe arrives in St. Louis after a journey of 22 or 32 days; members of the train disagree on exactly how long it took.

10. The Treaty of Guadalupe Hidalgo is ratified by the Senate by a vote of 38 to 14.

15. The first published account of the discovery of gold in California receives little notice when it appears in the *San Francisco Californian*.

17. Nicholas P. Trist, who represented the United States in the negotiation of the Treaty of Guadalupe Hidalgo, is arrested because he negotiated the treaty after being ordered home.

18. The second published account of the discovery of gold in California appears in the *California Star*. The *Star* also reports San Francisco's white population as being 575 adult males, 177 adult females, and 60 children.

19. Wyatt Berry Stapp Earp, lawman, is born to farmers Nicholas P. and Virginia Ann Earp in Monmouth, Illinois. He is named for his father's Mexican War commander.

20. An express from Santa Fe arrives at Fort Leavenworth, where everyone catches up on the latest newspapers, those dated as recently as February 24.
■ The Pottawatomie Baptist Mission reopens in Shawnee County, Kansas; 17 children will attend school until August 20.

24. Black Dog, chief of the Osage, dies at his home near present Claremore, Oklahoma. George Catlin had painted the seven-foot, 270-pound chief in 1834, calling him "in height and in girth, above all of his tribe."

29. John Jacob Astor, fur magnate and richest man in America, dies in New York City. He leaves an estate worth $20,000,000.

30. The last military action of the Mexican War occurs at Todos Santos in Lower California.

Also in March 1848:
F. X. Aubry arrives in Santa Fe with a wagon train. His announcement that he will make the return trip to Independence in ten days shocks the city. Says the *Santa Fe Republican,* "If energy and perseverance can accomplish a feat of that kind, Aubry is the man." To accomplish his goal, Aubry arranges for relay horses to be waiting at strategic points along the way.

WYATT EARP
MARCH 19, 1848—JANUARY 13, 1929

1848: Wyatt Earp is born at Monmouth, Illinois.

1864: Migrates with his family to San Bernardino, California.

1868: Working as a stagecoach driver, he returns to Monmouth, then leaves to work on the Union Pacific Railroad in Wyoming.

1870: Earp weds Willa Sutherland at Lamar, Missouri. She dies four months later.

1871: Earp jumps a $500 bail after being arrested as a horse thief near present Muskogee, Oklahoma

1872: He works as a buffalo hunter on the Salt Fork of the Arkansas River.

1875: He begins serving an eight-month stint as a policeman in Wichita, Kansas

1876: Earp is dismissed from the Wichita police force following fisticuffs with town-marshal candidate Bill Smith. He drifts to Dodge City, where he deals faro (a gambling game) and joins the police force.

1877: He resigns his Dodge City position to hunt for gold in the Black Hills.

1878: Back in Dodge City, Earp becomes assistant marshal. During a disturbance, he shoots his first man, gunman George Hoyt, who dies four weeks later from infection.

1879: Following brief stays at Mobeetie, Texas, and Las Vegas, New Mexico, Earp and his common law wife, Mattie Blaylock, arrive in Tombstone, Arizona, with his brothers. There, his first job is as a shotgun messenger for Wells Fargo.

1880: He becomes a part-owner of the Oriental Saloon. When brother Virgil is advanced to town marshal, Earp becomes his deputy.

1881: The feud between the Earp brothers and the "cowboy element" around Tombstone festers and culminates in the "Gunfight at the O.K. Corral."

1882: After taking out his revenge on the alleged attackers of brothers Virgil and Morgan, Wyatt leaves for Colorado.

1883: He assists lawman Luke Short at Dodge City.

1884: While operating two saloons in Idaho, Earp is involved in a mining claim that results in legal problems. Also that year, he is wounded during a poker game in Lake City, Colorado.

1888: Mattie Earp, 30, who became a prostitute after Wyatt left her, commits suicide. Earp has remarried since the desertion, to vaudevillian Josephine Sarah Marcus.

1889: He completes three years of managing a San Francisco bar, then relocates to San Diego to run a gambling hall.

1896: He referees the Bob Fitzsimmons–Tom Sharkey boxing match and is accused of throwing the decision for Sharkey.

1897: Lured by the Alaska gold rush, Wyatt runs a saloon in Nome from 1897–1901.

1901–1906: He prospects with his wife in Nevada and runs a bar at Tonopah.

1906: Earp moves to Los Angeles, where he finds employment as a bank guard.

1911: Earp is charged with vagrancy and running a bunco operation.

1920s: He serves as an unpaid consultant for some Hollywood silent westerns.

1928: After dictating his story to author Stuart Lake, Earp makes a nostalgic last trip to Tombstone, where he is a forgotten man.

1929: Earp, 80, dies in his sleep January 13 at his home at 4004 West 17th in Los Angeles.

1931: Stuart Lake's biography, *Wyatt Earp, Frontier Marshal,* is published and makes Earp famous.

The Texas state legislature creates the County of Santa Fe, extending about 100,000 square miles outside its present boundary. The land covers everything between the Pecos River and the Rio Grande, and north to the 42nd parallel, just north of present Rawlins, Wyoming.

APRIL

1. Crawford Seminary, a Methodist church and trade school for Quapaws, opens on the military road between Fort Leavenworth and Fort Smith.

2. The overland mail service started by the *California Star* departs San Francisco for Independence.

ASTORIA

The first attempt to establish organized trade in the great West was a major disaster. In his zeal for undiluted mercantile power, John Jacob Astor, America's first recorded millionaire, cast his fate to the winds of the Pacific.

The son of a butcher, Johan Jakob Astor was born in Germany on July 17, 1763. At age 20, with $25 and five flutes to sell, he booked passage for America. By 1790, he had married a rich widow's daughter and had established his own fur outlet. In ten years he amassed $250,000, trading regularly with London and China.

He organized the American Fur Company in 1808 with $1 million in capital. To that company, in 1810, he attached the Pacific Fur Company, which would operate from the soon-to-be-established west coast office known as Astoria, at the

John Jacob Astor (1763–1848). The wealthiest man in America makes his fortune in the western fur trade. (Library of Congress)

mouth of Oregon's Columbia River. Astor sent two expeditions to the promised land. One was to sail around Cape Horn, then north to the mouth of the Columbia. An overland group of sixty men was to trek up the Missouri, then down the Columbia to the Pacific.

On September 8, 1810, the *Tonquin* with a crew of 33 sailed out of New York Harbor, escorted by none other than the dark frigate *Constitution,* "Old Ironsides." Almost immediately, the expedition encountered trouble. The ship's commander Lieutenant Jonathan Thorn, was unpopular with the crew; in his journal, partner Alexander McKay noted, "I fear we are in the hands of a maniac." At the Falkland Islands, five crew members sent for fresh water were tardy in returning. Thorn pulled up anchor, and the men were forced to row frantically for three hours in order to reach the ship.

By late March 1811, the *Tonquin* had reached the choppy mouth of the Columbia. Thorn ordered first mate Ebenezer Fox into a small boat with inexperienced seamen and told him to find a passage. Fox pleaded his case for not going, but to no avail. The waters were ferocious, and those aboard the *Tonquin* watched as the sea swallowed the boat and its crew of five. Before the *Tonquin* was finally able to dock in the bay, eight additional crew members were lost at what is now called Cape Disappointment.

Then came the problems of building Astoria. The overland team had not arrived, and the tools on the *Tonquin* were minimal. Thorn fumed for two months as he waited for ground to be cleared. Finally, on June 1, he could take no more. With many of the supplies still on board, he took the vessel north to trade with Indians. Duncan McDougal was left in charge on land, while McKay would accompany Thorn. McKay confided to his cohorts that if they ever saw him again, it would be a miracle.

At Nootka Bay, Thorn's attitude proved fatal. During an onboard swapping session, he struck a Salish chief in the face with a pelt. A free-for-all broke out, and McKay was tossed overboard into a canoe, where he was hacked to death by Indian women wielding cooking tools. Thorn fought gallantly but fell under a dozen attackers. The war-

(continued)

(continued)

riors departed at sunset with plans to return the next day for the great unloading.

At dawn they were greeted by a strange sight. A wounded crewman, possibly clerk James Lewis, was on deck, gesturing for them to come aboard. In an hour, a hundred Indians were on the deck, some looking for the seaman, others looting. At the most opportune moment, the 290-ton *Tonquin* and everyone on board was blown to smithereens. Horrified squaws and children saw body parts wash ashore for days.

The overland Astorians had not fared much better. Delayed in St. Louis until October 21, 1810, they set off under the leadership of New Jersey businessman Wilson P. Hunt, whose wilderness savvy was on a par with Thorn's interpersonal skills. The expedition covered only 500 miles before it was forced to stop for the winter. Resuming its trek the following May, it crossed the Rockies at South Pass, then made a deadly error. Canoes were chosen to shoot the rapids of the Snake River, which is surrounded by the mile-high walls of Hell's Canyon. Four members drowned and another went insane.

Forty-five haggard survivors arrived at Fort Asttoria on February 15, 1812, having traveled 3,500 miles to cover the 1,800 miles separating two points on the map. A small ship was constructed and used for trading along the Columbia. The supply boat *Beaver* arrived in May, 1813.

When the United States and Great Britain locked into the War of 1812, Astoria's future became clouded. To reinforce his outpost, Astor sent the speedy *Lark* to break a British blockade, which it did, only to sink in a hurricane near Hawaii.

Faced with certain British occupation, the Astorians cut their losses: they sold $200,000 in furs for less than $80,000 to the North West Company and got out. Captain William Black of the HMS *Raccoon* claimed the post for the crown and renamed it Fort George on December 13, 1813. Astoria's books closed showing no profit and 65 lives lost.

The treaty of Ghent returned Astoria to America, but Astor was no longer interested in pursuing his dream. Such a setback would have been cataclysmic for some investors, but not for John Jacob Astor. When asked about the disappointment of Astoria, Astor waxed philosophical: "But for the war, I would have been the richest man that ever lived."

---

3. The first American public school opens in San Francisco.

5–18. The Swiss artist Rudolph Friedrich Kurz is on board the *Tamerlane* for her overly long voyage from St. Louis to St. Joseph. He will work in a St. Joseph studio until May 1850.

18. Sarah Malin becomes Brigham Young's 44th wife.

21. Francis X. Aubry, on the road from Independence since March, arrives in Santa Fe with 15 wagons.

26. A party of 30 traders reaches St. Louis from Santa Fe after a 27-day trip.

29. The *Independence Expositor* reports that wagon trains are being delayed by dry conditions and a scarcity of grass on the Santa Fe Trail.

Also in April 1848:
The Pacific Steamship Company announces it will deliver mail via the Isthmus of Panama.

MAY

3. Although the presence of gold is still just a rumor in California, the *Californian* states that "seven men with picks and spades could gather $1,600 worth of gold in fifteen days."

5. Kit Carson and a party of 27 set out from Los Angeles for Santa Fe.

6. Editor Samuel Brannan of the *California Star*, a bottle of gold dust in hand returns from the diggings with this report: "Full flowing streams, mighty timber, large crops, luxuriant clover, fragrant flowers, gold and silver. Great country, this."

12. Samuel Brannan spreads news that gold has been found on the American River, starting a California business boom.

17. The *California Star* announces that another express stagecoach will leave its offices this morning for Independence via Salt Lake.

19. F. X. Aubry thunders into the night, intent on making the Santa Fe–Independence run in 10 days. On the way he is captured by Comanches, who steal the mail he is carrying and most of his provisions. After a night escape, he manages to run to his next horse and ride on. When that horse dies of exhaustion in Kansas, Aubry has to make 40 miles to Fort Mann, near present Dodge City, on foot.

20. Two of three trading boats belonging to Joseph Picotte and carrying "upwards of 800 bales of buf-

falo robes" down the Missouri arrive at St. Louis. The third was snagged above Council Bluffs and sank.

21. William Bent and a party including New Mexico's attorney general arrive in St. Louis aboard the *Whirlwind,* having covered the Santa Fe Trail from Bent's Fort since April 22. They report "cold weather, no Indians."

22. James J. Dolan, a Lincoln County War figure, is born in Loughrea, County Galway, Ireland.

25. White Cloud and a raiding party of Iowas return to their home in present Doniphan County, Kansas, with scalps following a successful attack on a Pawnee village that killed six men, three women, and two children.

- The Mexican Congress ratifies the Treaty of Guadalupe Hidalgo.

26. The *Californian* reports: "The whole country, from San Francisco to Los Angeles, and from the seashore to the base of Sierra Nevada, resounds with the sordid cry of gold! Gold!! GOLD!!! while the field is left unplanted, the house half builded, and everything neglected but the manufacturers of shovels and picks."

28. Francis X. Aubry rides into Independence, Missouri, an hour after sunrise, having completed 780 miles of the Santa Fe Trail in eight days and 10 hours, shaving 5.5 days off his time of January 5. Newspapers call him "the Telegraph."

- Captain L. C. Easton receives a contract to bring 400 head of cattle from Fort Leavenworth to Santa Fe.

29. The *Californian* closes it doors; editor Benjamin R. Buckelew and employees have left to seek gold. The *Star* humorously wrote, "Gone to ———. The *Californian* ceased issue with the annunciatory slip of Tuesday last. Verdict of inquest———fever."

30. Lieutenant Colonel William Gilpin and his volunteers arrive at Fort Mann after an excursion against hostiles in the area, and are greeted by chiefs of the Cheyenne, Arapaho, and Kiowa who wish to talk peace.

- A "Mr. Fink" arrives in St. Louis aboard the *Reveille,* fresh from the Santa Fe Trail. He reports his party was attacked 30 miles from Fort Mann by mounted Comanches, but only one of his traders was wounded.

- The instruments of ratification for the Treaty of Guadalupe Hidalgo are formally exchanged by the United States and Mexico.

31. At Mormon Winter Quarters, Brigham Young organizes followers into companies, 1,891 people in 623 wagons, for the upcoming migration.

Also in May 1848:

A flock of seagulls saves Mormon farmers in Utah when the birds swoop down to feast on crickets that have been devouring crops on Salt Lake farms.

Auguste A. L. Trécul visits Kansas to gather animal and plant samples for the National Museum of Natural History in Paris.

Traffic on the Oregon Trail appears to be down from 1847. Since April, agent Thomas Fitzpatrick has counted 364 wagons carrying about 1,700 people departing Missouri.

National Headlines/May 1848:

26. DEMOCRATS NOMINATE CASS

29. WISCONSIN BECOMES 30th STATE

JUNE

1. It is reported that a paymaster, Major William Singer, having left Santa Fe on May 3, abandoned "his entire baggage, including his pay rolls, horses, four mules, and his wagon" when set upon by mounted Indians on May 15. His group of seven successfully completed its run to Fort Mann.

6. Superintendent T. H. Harvey of St. Louis learns of the death in April or May of Keokuk, the approximately 60-year-old Sac chief.

12. Following the end of the Mexican War, U.S. military forces leave Mexico City.

14. The *Daily Reveille* reports that the *Mandan* arrived at St. Louis with 1,833 packs of buffalo robes.

18. The American Fur Company's boat on the Missouri strikes a snag and sinks near St. Joseph; one person drowns and the fur shipment is completely lost.

20. The offices of the *California Star* close. The newspaper folds as editor Edward Kemble heads for the goldfields.

24. Brigham Young's Mormons celebrate their first year in Utah.

29. James S. Rains succeeds Solomon P. Sublette as agent of the Osage River Agency.

Also in June 1848:

Hardly any males remain in the California towns of Monterey, San Francisco, San Jose, and Santa Cruz—they have all left for mining country.

The future historian Hubert Howe Bancroft, 16, is hired by brother-in-law George Derby to work in a Buffalo, New York, bookstore.

Lieutenant Daniel P. Woodbury and 175 men arrive at the Platte in present Nebraska, where they begin construction of Fort Kearny, which is intended to help protect Oregon Trail settlers from Indians.

9. WHIGS NOMINATE A TAYLOR-FILLMORE TICKET

JULY

1. The Missouri Hotel opens in Kansas City, Missouri.
4. President Polk declares the Treaty of Guadalupe Hidalgo in effect.
7. One hundred Missouri volunteers under Captain John C. Griffin leave Fort Mann on a mission against the Comanches.
9. Captain John C. Griffin comes upon a large deserted campsite and sets off after the Comanches. Three hours later, the enemy is engaged. Griffin claims 30 enemy are killed, as opposed to one of his soldiers wounded. Other reports say Griffin's men killed only a few Indians.
13. Lieutenant Colonel Clifton Wharton, 46, the commander of Fort Leavenworth since 1844, dies.
13. Mountain man Jim Beckwourth arrives at Fort Leavenworth from Santa Fe in 17 days.
15. Captain Thomas Jones and 101 Missouri mounted volunteers, packing a "brass six-pounder," depart Fort Mann on a mission against the Comanches.
18. The *Santa Fe Republican* observes, "Not a day passes now without the arrival of large trains from the United States, laden with all kinds of merchandise."
20. Captain Thomas Jones and his volunteers engage the Comanches in woods near the Cimarron River (present Woods County, Oklahoma), killing 21 of 41.
25. California military governor Colonel Richard Mason issues a proclamation asking for public cooperation in apprehending deserters who have left for the goldfields.
26. Fighting erupts between Pawnees and Pottawatomies in the buffalo country of the Kansas River. Although there are conflicting versions of the battle, the Pottawatomies return with five scalps.
29. The *New York Weekly Tribune* reports that the only white man killed in Kansas by Indians in 1848 was a member of "Brown's train"—he was killed by Comanches at Walnut Creek.

Also in July 1848:
Colorado mining magnate Winfield Scott Stratton is born in Jeffersonville, Indiana.

National Headlines/July 1848:
19. FIRST WOMEN'S RIGHTS CONVENTION AT SENECA FALLS, NY

AUGUST

2. The House passes the Oregon Bill.
■ The last U.S. forces leave Vera Cruz following the end of the Mexican War.
5. Francis X. Aubry arrives in Santa Fe a few hours ahead of the second wagon train he has brought this year. While in Santa Fe, he bets a group of men, which may have included Kit Carson, $1,000 that he can make the return trip to Independence in six days.
6. The Pawnees give up their rights to Grand Island, Nebraska, and surrounding lands. The signing at Fort Childs is delayed, awaiting the arrival of $2,000 in merchandise for the Pawnees.
7. California military governor Colonel Richard B. Mason issues the Laws for the Better Government of California.
9. The Mormon fort at Great Salt Lake City has 450 buildings, including three sawmills and a flour mill.
10. A major Mormon feast at Great Salt Lake City celebrates the first harvest.
13. The Senate passes the Oregon Bill.
14. President Polk signs the Oregon Bill creating the territorial government of Oregon, which will not allow slavery. Abraham Lincoln is asked to be the first governor, but he declines. The Mexican War hero Joseph Lane accepts the position.
15. Jacob Thierer wins a government contract to supply beef for Fort Leavenworth for a year.
17. Navy Lieutenant Edward F. Beale arrives in Mexico City and spreads word of the discovery of gold in California.
19. The *New York Herald* reports news of the California gold discovery.
28. The first English school in Santa Fe is founded.

SEPTEMBER

2. The *Californian* publishes its third issue since suspending continuous operations in May so that employees could hunt for gold.
9. St. Mary's, a Potawatomi Catholic mission, is established in Kansas by Father Felix L. Verreydt.
12. Francis X. Aubry departs Santa Fe alone on another of his famous whirlwind tours of the Santa Fe Trail. His drinking buddies meet him in the streets for a hearty dawn send-off, complete with cheers and pistol shots. Then, with a holler and a whack to his horse's rump, he is off in a cloud of dust.
18. Marching home, volunteers from Missouri and Illinois who fought in the Mexican War begin arriving at Fort Leavenworth and Independence.

AUBRY'S WILD RIDE
SEPTEMBER 12–17, 1848

A hundred miles out of Santa Fe, a wagon train led by Alexander Majors saw Francis X. Aubry gallop past on a yellow mare named Dolly. Rain began to fall soon thereafter, as Aubry drew closer to Point of Rock, southeast of Raton. At Aubry's first relay point, Indians had scalped his aide and stolen the horses.

Aubry rode Dolly 200 miles during the next 26 hours, until he saw another wagon train. Aubry purchased a fresh mount from the train and left instructions to return Dolly to a Santa Fe stable. Tying himself in the saddle to catch brief naps, Aubry continued his prairie marathon.

To his relief, the three horses that had been secluded near the Cimarron River were waiting peacefully. With newfound energy, Aubry ran the horses to death but covered only 30 miles in the process. He covered the last 20 miles to Fort Mann on foot and then collapsed.

After a two-hour nap, Aubry bought another horse and rode east. At Council Grove, he gulped down a pot of coffee and lined up new horses for the last leg of his journey—150 miles in rain and mud. On the 17th, he staggered into the lobby of the Merchants Hotel in Independence and dropped to the carpet, having broken his own record for the 780-mile Santa Fe Trail for the second time this year. He made the ride in five days, 16 hours. At 23, the "skimmer of the plains" had a record that would never be broken.

20. Brigham Young arrives with a wave of immigrants at Salt Lake City.
25. The Western Academy, in Johnson County, becomes the first high school in Kansas.

OCTOBER

2. Kit Carson departs the town of Kansas (Kansas City) for the "Far West."
6. The *Liberty Tribune* reprints a story from the *New Orleans Picayune* about discoveries of gold in "Upper California."
8. Francis X. Aubry departs Independence for Santa Fe, leading his third wagon train on the Santa Fe Trail this year.
10–17. A major council of neighboring tribes is held on the Delaware Indians' reserve near Fort Leavenworth: representatives of that tribe and of the Wyandots, Peorias, Shawnees, Ottawas, Potawatomis, Kickapoos, Kansa, Chippewas, Weas, and Miamis are in attendance. Representatives of the Sac and Fox also attend, but depart following a speech about an early war they fought with the Wyandots.
13. Apache raiders scatter 240 head of government livestock and kill a stockman near Las Vegas, New Mexico.
14. Sacramento, California, is founded by John Sutter's son.
■ The *Liberty Tribune* reports that B. F. Choteau arrived in Santa Fe on the 4th of July with news of California gold.
■ New Mexicans hold a convention in Santa Fe to petition Congress for a territorial government. The convention also opposes the dismemberment of New Mexico in favor of Texas and requests protection against the introduction of slavery.
19. John Charles Frémont's fourth western expedition sets out from a camp near Westport, Missouri.
20. The *St. Joseph Gazette* reprints a story about the discovery of gold that appeared in the *New York Sun*.
22. At Rialto, Missouri, a ferryboat strikes a snag and sinks in the Missouri; nine men and six horses are rescued.
24. Kit Carson arrives in Taos on a trading mission.
25. En route to California, the U.S. First Dragoons reach Tucson.
26. Fort Ringgold is established at Rio Grande City, Texas, by Captain J. H. LaMotte.
27. The *St. Joseph Gazette* quotes the *Washington Union*: "An immense bed of gold, 100 miles in extent . . . in California."
29. John Charles Frémont's party passes present Salina, Kansas, where it sights a herd of buffalo.
■ From Kansas City, the missionary Allen Ward writes: "The town of Kansas . . . now contains I think upwards of 300 houses & is rapidly improving."
31. General Stephen Watts Kearny, 54, commander of the Army of the West in the Mexican War, dies in St. Louis.
■ Boston Custer, George Armstrong's brother, is born.

Also in October 1848:
The steamer *California* departs New York for San Francisco.

THE WHITMAN MASSACRE

Marcus and Narcissa Whitman were missionaries who worked to Christianize the western Indians. Filled with faith, hope, and charity, they became entangled in the inevitable struggle between cultures. Their names came to symbolize the worst that could happen in the Old West.

Marcus Whitman at first wanted to be a minister for his Congregational church, but he simply could not afford the seven-year education required for that vocation. Choosing a less expensive curriculum, he graduated in 1832 from a Fairfield, New York, medical school at age 30 and began practicing in the village of Wheeler. Caught up by the wave of enthusiasm for bringing Christ to the savages, he applied to the American Board of Foreign Missions in Boston in 1834.

Narcissa Prentiss of Amity also had requested a western assignment, but officials balked at the idea of sending a woman. Perhaps if she were married to someone who was similarly bent on saving the region, something might be arranged. After an introduction by the Reverend Samuel Parker, Marcus and Narcissa fell in love, their flame kindled by a common goal.

So it was decided. Whitman would join Parker on a fact-finding expedition. In the spring of 1835, the two set out from St. Louis with a group of trappers to inspect the Oregon Trail. Making their way toward Fort Laramie, Whitman observed that if covered wagons could make the journey, so could women and children. Now his dreams included colonization. The pair parted at Green River—Parker to go on to the Oregon country while Whitman returned for Narcissa.

Marcus and Narcissa were wed on February 16, 1836, in Angelica, New York, and planned to spend their honeymoon in the Wild West. Joined by Henry and Eliza Spalding and carpenter William Gray, they journeyed by river to St. Louis. From Independence, their two wagons left with a party of fur traders.

On September 1, 1836, six months and 4,000 difficult miles later, they reached Fort Walla Walla in the future state of Washington. Narcissa and Eliza had become the first white women to cross the Rocky Mountains. Mrs. Whitman had kept a detailed journal, a priceless, honest document of life on the Oregon Trail.

The couples wisely chose to live 120 miles apart. Following a trip to Fort Vancouver for supplies, Spalding chose to minister to the Nez Perce on the Clearwater River. Whitman would build his cabin 25 miles from Walla Walla at Waiilatpu, the "place of the rye grass" in Cayuse country in present Oregon. The Nez Percé told him to reconsider: The Cayuse had a "difficulty" with the white man.

The Whitmans' mission weathered triumph and tragedy. A lean-to expanded into a small cabin, then into a two-bedroom home with a kitchen. On Narcissa's 29th birthday, March 14, 1837, she gave birth to a healthy Alice Clarissa. As more missionaries arrived, the grounds were expanded. Other homes were built, along with a missionary house, a small school, a blacksmith shop, and a gristmill. Everything was progressing well.

In 1839, however, the Whitmans' daughter drowned in the Walla Walla River, a tragedy from which Narcissa never really recovered. Then in 1842, the Board of Missions in Boston ordered the closing of their mission. Determined to reverse this order, Marcus Whitman ventured a bold ride to the East in the dead of winter. Board officials were impressed by his sincerity and rescinded their order. Marcus returned to the West with a party of settlers in 1843.

Relations with the Indians deteriorated. The Cayuses' attitude toward Dr. Whitman degenerated from curiosity to distrust to outright hatred. Gradually, Whitman's focus had switched from converting the Indians to aiding settlers. The pioneers were encroaching on the Indians and bringing disease.

A measles epidemic in the fall of 1847 claimed 197 Cayuses, half of the tribe. The Whitmans knew that if a medicine man's patient died, the relatives could kill the doctor. What they probably were not aware of were the vicious rumors—that the missionaries were receiving shipments of poison for the Indians. An Indian campfire council agreed that something would have to be done.

November 29, 1847, dawned cold and gloomy. Whitman had been up all night tending the 11 sick children out of the 42 that lived at the mission. Word came that the third child of Chief Tiloukaikt

(continued)

(continued)

had succumbed to measles. Whitman left for the burial. He returned that afternoon, exhausted.

It came as somewhat of a surprise that the grieving chief appeared soon thereafter at the Whitman home. With him were Tomahas and some other braves. More members of the tribe were sick and needed medicine.

Whitman met the Indians in the kitchen. While Tiloukaikt talked with the doctor, Tomahas stepped behind the doctor and, without warning, swung his tomahawk in a high, overhead arc, slamming the weapon full force into the top of Whitman's skull. Another brave fired a gun into the victim's neck. John Sayer was also present; he was slain when he went for his gun.

Eyewitness reports vary. Apparently, Whitman crawled outside as his assailants escaped. Narcissa and two other women carried him back into the house. Around the mission, a bloodbath was in progress. A frightened gardener banged on the door of the Whitman house, seeking shelter. Narcissa opened it and took a bullet under her left arm.

Warriors chopped away at the door. Just before the attackers broke into the house, Narcissa led a group of women and children to a second-floor bedroom. The Cayuse were held at bay by a rifle pointing from the bedroom. Finally, one of the Indians, Tamsucky, an old friend of the Whitmans', convinced Narcissa to surrender in return for safe passage to a nearby fort. "God has raised us up a friend!" one of the children heard her say.

Narcissa, weak from blood loss, was carried outside on a settee, where she was greeted by a hail of bullets. One Indian hoisted her body from the mud and whipped her face with a leather quirt. The carnage continued until 14 whites (11 men, one woman and two children) were dead. A family hiding beneath the floorboards of the home heard the doctor moaning long into the night.

Forty-seven hostages taken during the massacre were freed sometime later when officials from the Hudson's Bay Company paid their ransom. A force of 500 Willamette Valley settlers, outraged by the atrocity, went hunting for the offenders.

Mountain man Joseph Meek led the party that reburied the Whitmans and the other victims, including his own daughter, a task made even more grisly because the dead had been attacked by a pack of wolves. He urged his cousin, President James Polk, to provide protection for Oregon, a step that until then had been obstructed by British claims and the desire of the South for another slave state. On the day before he left office, Polk proclaimed Oregon a territory. By 1850, the population of the area had increased in 10 years from 200 to 13,000.

Five Cayuse braves, including Tomahas and Chief Tiloukaikt, surrendered after two years on the run and were sentenced to hang. Tiloukaikt, when asked why he had surrendered, said, "Did not your missionaries teach us that Christ died to save his people? So we die to save our people." By their martyrdom, the Whitmans had done the same.

NOVEMBER

1. Kit Carson, on a hunting/trading trek, arrives in Santa Fe.
7. John Charles Frémont's party reaches the Arkansas River in present Kansas.
9. The first U.S. post office in California opens in San Francisco at Pike and Clay Streets. The white population of the state is now estimated at 15,000.
10. Locals at Nauvoo, Illinois, outraged by reports of the Mormons' polygamy, set the Mormon temple on fire.
12. John Charles Frémont's party reaches Big Timbers, where a conference of some 6,000 Arapahos, Kiowas, Comanches, and Apaches with agent Thomas Fitzpatrick is in progress.
16. John Charles Frémont's party reaches Bent's Fort.

From here, they will travel on to Pueblo, then into the Rockies in winter.
17. John Charles Frémont, in a dispatch from Bent's Fort, notes that agent Thomas Fitzpatrick has convinced the Kiowas to break relations with the Comanches and come live in peace with the Arapahos and Cheyennes.
18. Father Pierre-Jean De Smet arrives via steamboat in St. Louis after a tour of the western tribes, including much time spent among the Sioux.
27. The U.S. 1st Dragoons cross the Colorado River at Yuma, Arizona.
29. This date marks the first anniversary of the "Whitman Massacre" in Oregon—the murder of missionary Marcus Whitman, his wife Narcissa, and 12 others by Cayuse Indians at Waiilatpu.

7. TAYLOR DEFEATS CASS FOR PRESIDENCY

DECEMBER

5. President Polk informs Congress of the discovery of gold in California; the Gold Rush begins in earnest. Some 40,000 settlers will arrive in California in the next year. The state's population will reach 100,000 in 1850.
24. A fire results in $1 million in damages to San Francisco's entertainment and gambling districts.
30. Fort Childs, in present Nebraska, is officially renamed Fort Kearny.

Also in December 1848:

Senator A. H. Sevier dies. He had been recently appointed by President Polk as the U.S. boundary commissioner under terms of the Treaty of Guadalupe Hidalgo.

Also in 1848:

Final tally for the Mexican War—U.S. killed: 1,721 of wounds, 11,155 of disease; U.S. wounded: 4,102; military expenditure: $97,500,000.

Nationwide, native Americans are currently operating 87 boarding schools and 16 manual arts training schools.

In Indian Territory, the Chickasaw Nation establishes two boarding schools, the Chickasaw Academy for boys and the Wapanucka Institute for girls.

Samuel Clemens, 13, is an apprentice to printer Joseph P. Ament, the publisher of the *Missouri Courier* at Hannibal.

Friedrich Gerstäcker writes *Die Flusspiraten des Mississippi* (River Pirates of the Mississippi).

Roy Bean, 23, organizes a trading expedition to Chihuahua with his brother, but an unspecified difficulty finds them leaving Mexico in haste for California.

Theodore Gentilz paints a portrait of the Alamo 12 years after the famous battle. The mission is covered in weeds and nearly in ruins.

John Charles Frémont writes of his first expedition to California in *Geographical Memoir upon Upper California*.

The *Choctaw Telegraph* is founded at Doaksville, Indian Territory.

Public-domain land in Texas is listed at 181,965,332 acres.

Rutherford B. Hayes notes in his diary that the social life in Texas is the same as that found anywhere else.

Walt Whitman catches his first glimpse of the Great Plains from a Mississippi steamboat.

Texas in 1848, a book of general description, is written by Viktor Bracht.

There are about 350,000 head of cattle in Texas.

California produces $250,000 in gold.

1849

"The untransacted destiny of the American people is to subdue the continent—to rush over this vast field to the Pacific Ocean—to animate the many hundred millions of its people and to cheer them upward—to set the principle of self-government at work—to agitate these Herculean masses—to establish a new order in human affairs—to set free the enslaved—to regenerate superannuated nations—to change darkness into light—to stir up the sleep of a hundred centuries—to teach old nations a new civilization—to confirm the destiny of the human race—to carry the career of mankind to its culminating point—to cause stagnant people to be reborn—to perfect science—to emblazon history with the conquest of peace—to shed a new and resplendent glory upon mankind—to unite the world in one social family—to dissolve the spell of tyranny and exalt charity—to absolve the curse that weighs down humanity, and to shed blessing round the world!"

—William Gilpin

JANUARY

21. John Charles Frémont appears at Beaubien's store in Taos, where Kit Carson, Dick Owens, and Lucien Maxwell are passing the evening. Frémont discusses his disastrous fourth western expedition, including the 18-foot snows he encountered in the San Juans. A rescue party is organized to retrieve the remainder of his command, which includes 34 of the original 44. Carson and his wife, Josefa, care for Frémont.

Also in January 1849:

San Francisco organizes a volunteer fire department of three engine companies.

The Swiss artist Rudolph Friedrich Kurz, living in St. Joseph, reports the appearance in that town of the first gold seekers ("two rich merchants from New York . . . traveled in a sleigh direct from their home to this place") heading for California.

FEBRUARY

5. The temperature in Salt Lake City hits −33 degrees.

7. The *St. Louis Daily Union* carries a Turner & Allen advertisement that reads:

PIONEER PASSENGER TRAIN FOR
CALIFORNIA!
OVERLAND BY SOUTH PASS

A $200 fare will guarantee passage with 100 pounds of baggage in a six-seater stagecoach.

12. The C.B.&Q. Railroad is incorporated.

■ A public meeting sets up a temporary government for San Francisco.

18. California's first regular steamboat service begins with the arrival of the Pacific Mail's *California.*

23. The mountain man Miles Goodyear writes a letter to the *Missouri Republican,* recommending a spot upriver from Fort Kearny in present Nebraska as a good starting point for settlers headed west.

27. William Jewell College is chartered at Liberty, Missouri.

28. The steamer *Californian* sails into San Francisco Bay with 265 passengers, the first gold seekers to arrive by ship.

■ General Persifer F. Smith becomes military governor of California.

Also in February 1849:

St. Joseph, Missouri, reports "thousands" of immigrants passing through town on their way to California. The city itself claims 1,800 residents.

Some 100,000 Indians of various tribes live in California at the beginning of the Gold Rush.

MARCH

2. Newly appointed Oregon governor Joseph Lane arrives in Oregon Territory.

3. President Polk signs the act creating Minnesota Territory; Alexander Ramsey, a Philadelphia Whig, becomes the first governor. The territory's population of 5,000 is concentrated primarily around St. Paul, near Fort Snelling.

BRIGHAM YOUNG
JUNE 1, 1801—AUGUST 23, 1877

1801: Young is born in Whittingham, Vermont, the 9th of 11 children.

1817: He is self-employed as a carpenter and painter.

1824: Young weds Miriam Works and moves to New York.

1831: He sees a copy of *The Book of Mormon.*

1832: Baptized into the Mormon Church, he meets Joseph Smith.

1833: Young moves to Kirtland, Ohio.

1834: A widower, he marries his second wife, Mary Ann Angell. With the Zion's Camp movement, he becomes involved in a struggle for control of Jackson County, Missouri.

1835: Young becomes an apostle and travels in the United States and England as a missionary.

1837: He supports Joseph Smith during a church financial crisis.

1838: Young helps to move his people to Far West, Missouri, then to Nauvoo, Illinois.

1840: He goes on a missionary trip to England.

1841: He becomes president of the Quorum of the Twelve Apostles.

1842: Young takes his first plural wife, Lucy Decker, 20.

1843: He weds Harriet Elizabeth Cook ("Harriet the Neglected") and Augusta Adams Cobb on the same day, November 2.

1844: Young assumes church leadership following Joseph Smith's murder at Carthage, Illinois. He enters into three marriages: with Clara Decker, 14; Susan Snively, 29; and Clara Ross, 30.

1845: Brigham Heber, "the first child of Mormon polygamy," is born, the first of six children Young will have with Lucy Decker. Young takes his 12th wife, Emmeline Free, who will bear him 10 children.

1846: On February 3, he weds five women ranging in age from 18 to 55. Three days later, he takes wives number 38, 39, 40, and 41. The Mormons exodus from Nauvoo begins.

1847: The exodus resumes in the spring from Council Bluffs, Iowa. The Mormons reach Utah on July 24.

1850: Young is elected first governor of the Territory of Utah and the superintendent of Indian affairs.

1852: He publicly acknowledges polygamy for the first time.

1855: He originates the handcart migration.

1856: The Republican Party platform condemns polygamy.

1857: Young obtains a mail and freight contract from the United States. Federal troops are sent to the Mormon state. Salt Lake City is evacuated. President James Buchanan names Alfred Cumming to replace Young as the Utah territorial governor.

1861: Young becomes involved in the construction of the transcontinental telegraph line.

1865: He takes his 50th bride.

1868: He aids in the construction of the transcontinental railroad.

1870: He takes his last bride, Lydia Farnsworth, 62.

1871: Accused of bigamy, Young's trial ends when charges are dropped on a technicality.

1872: He is sued for divorce by Ann Eliza Webb, who claims "neglect, unkindness, cruel and inhuman treatment, absolute desertion."

1875: Ann Eliza Webb publishes her memoirs, *Wife No. 19, or The Story of a Life in Bondage.*

1877: Brigham Young dies of peritonitis at 76. At the time of his death, his Mormon stronghold numbers 140,000.

- The Home Department, the future Department of the Interior, is established by Congress to deal with many western settlement issues, including public lands. It will also oversee the Bureau of Indian Affairs, previously a concern of the War Department.
- Camp Crawford is established at Laredo, Texas.
5. The constitution of the Mormon State of Deseret is drafted by a convention at Salt Lake City that also elects a legislature.
7. The botanist and horticulturist Luther Burbank is born in Lancaster, Massachusetts.
8. The steamboat *St. Joseph* is unable to travel beyond Kansas City, Missouri, because of extensive ice on the Missouri River.
9. The *St. Louis Daily Union* again advertises passenger service to California: the first coach is set to leave on April 25, the second on May 20.
- Utah elects Brigham Young governor.
10. The Missouri legislature votes for "popular sovereignty": hopes to keep Congress out of the slavery issue by resolving that "the right to prohibit slavery in any territory belongs exclusively to the people thereof."
- The Mormons vote to form the State of Deseret in present Utah and to uphold the United States Constitution.
13. The 1st Dragoons under First Lieutenant J. Whittesley engage Indians at El Cetro del Oya, New Mexico. Two soldiers are reported killed.
17. A fire in St. Louis consumes some 400 buildings and 27 steamships.
- A grand military ball in honor of St. Patrick's Day is held at Fort Leavenworth.
- Green Jones arrives in Independence with a February 2 issue of the *Santa Fe Republican* that gives an account of Frémont's recent disastrous exploration.
29. James C. Calhoun is appointed the Indian agent for New Mexico, the first such agent west of the Mississippi River.

Also in March 1849:

Some of the titles offered by St. Louis booksellers: *Emigrant's Guide to the Gold Mines of Upper California,* by E. Sandford Seymour; *Overland Journey from Fort Leavenworth to San Diego,* by Lieutenant William H. Emory; *The California and Oregon Trail,* by Francis Parkman; *The Emigrants' Guide to California,* by Joseph E. Ware; *The Gold Placers of California,* by Charles Foster; and *What I Saw in California,* by Edwin Bryant.

More than 17,000 people have sailed to California from eastern parts to join in the search for gold.

National Headlines/March 1849:
3. HOME DEPT (DEPT OF INTERIOR) CREATED
5. TAYLOR INAUGURATED 12TH PRESIDENT

APRIL

4. Captain Randolph B. March leads a company of 75 soldiers from Fort Smith to Santa Fe to guard settlers on their way to California.
6. Since March 31, 10 steamboats filled with gold seekers headed for California have arrived in St. Joseph. For example, the *Consignee* arrived from Pittsburgh with 240 men, 70 wagons, 90 mules, and some 100 tons of equipment
12. The first west coast mail to arrive in the East comes via Panama.
- The first San Francisco bankers to advertise are Roach & Woodworth in the *Alta California:* "To Gold Diggers, and others!! Remittances to the United States and Europe, can be made in sums from $10 to $10,000 in Bills of Exchange, Drafts, Letters of Credit, Gold Dust, or Coin, at the same rates as cost of transportation only."
13. General Bennett Riley becomes military governor of California.
14. Captain G. W. Paul leads the first party of 49ers, as gold rush participants are being called, on the Oregon–California Trail from Independence.
19. David D. Mitchell replaces Thomas H. Harvey as superintendent of Indian affairs in St. Louis.
- The first party of 49ers to travel the Oregon–California Trail from St. Joseph sets out, its members calling themselves the "St. Clair Mining Company."
25. Leonidas Chick, 9, dies of cholera in Kansas City, Missouri. This is the first death in what will become a major outbreak of the disease.
27. Fort Scott, Kansas, reports that 40 wagons headed for California in the past week.
28. John Fuller, 20, who accidentally shot himself on the way to California, is buried on the eastern bank of the Big Blue River.
30. Another 15 deaths from cholera are reported in Kansas City.

Also in April 1849:

Kit Carson farms in New Mexico, using the $2,000 he made in the past year as a guide and trapper.

MAY

1. William Bent, arriving in St. Louis with Upper Platte agent Thomas Fitzpatrick after a 46-day hike from Bent's Fort, reports 6 to 10 cholera deaths at

each encampment he passed on the California–Oregon Trail.

2. Independence reports 20 cholera deaths among emigrants in the past two weeks.

3. Although it may not be accurate, the *St. Joseph Gazette* estimates that 8,318 emigrants have passed through the city on their way to California.

4. Another San Francisco fire results in $3 million in damages to the banking and commercial district.

6. Fort Kearny, Nebraska, receives its first gold seeker heading for California.

7. Captain G. W. Paul's party of 49ers, having left Independence on April 14, passes Fort Kearny.

■ Since April 25, cholera deaths in Kansas City have averaged 10 per day.

8. The *Mary,* carrying 250 Mormons to Utah, reports 35 cholera deaths.

9. The St. Clair Mining Company arrives at Fort Kearny.

10. Jotham Meeker's journal records 5 to 11 cholera deaths in Independence during the past week.

11. The cholera outbreak is reported to be subsiding in Independence. St. Joseph reports that six cholera cases "terminated fatally" in the past five days. The *St. Joseph Gazette* says as many as 25 people died from the disease in one day at Fort Leavenworth.

12. The *Monroe,* carrying Mormons to Utah, docks at Jefferson City and reports 53 cholera deaths.

13. The first Turner and Allen stagecoach, billed as a "passenger train," from St. Louis to California, scheduled to depart on April 25, leaves about 10 miles west of Independence. It includes 20 passenger coaches, holding six people each, and 20 baggage wagons.

14. In St. Louis, the *Timour* docks with 680 bales of buffalo robes and 742 bales of hemp.

15. In the *Iowa Nation,* St. Louis physician B. B. Brown writes, "The Cholera is making fearful head on the road. . . ."

17. A fire in St. Louis destroys 15 city blocks and 25 steamboats, and does $4 million in damage.

21. Ruth McEnery, author of *A Golden Wedding and Other Tales* (1893), is born in Marksville, Louisiana.

27. Immigrants on their way to the California goldfields arrive in Salt Lake City.

31. The Wyandot Mining Company, consisting of 15 tribe members and some whites, sets out on the Oregon–California Trail.

Also in May 1849:

En route to Salt Lake City is future shipping magnate Ben Holladay, 29, his wagons filled with supplies and $70,000 in goods. Holladay, who supplied Ste-phen Kearny's Army of the West during the Mexican War, has mortgaged everything to buy government surplus wagons, oxen and mules. Brigham Young will remember Holladay as having been Colonel Alexander Doniphan's messenger in 1838, and he will give him his blessing to do business among the Mormons. In lieu of cash, Holladay will take payment in $6-a-head Mormon cattle, which he will then drive to California. The herd will be sold for about $180-a-head to the Pacific Mail Steamship Company.

A San Francisco town council passes ordinances requiring the building of additional wells and reservoirs to combat fires, and making it mandatory for property owners to keep six buckets of water on hand.

Charles Carson, the first child of Josefa and Kit Carson, dies in Taos.

The San Francisco Wharf Association is formed to construct new piers.

National Headlines/May 1849:
10. ASTOR PLACE RIOTS CLAIM 20 IN NYC

JUNE

3. Brigadier General Bennett Riley, California's military governor, issues a proclamation "recommending the formation of a State constitution, or a plan for a Territorial government."

5. Eleazar Adams, the father of Grizzly Adams, commits suicide.

6. Camp Worth is established in Texas by Brevet Major Ripley Arnold. It is named in honor of the Mexican War hero General William Jenkins Worth. Even though the camp is the site of the future Fort Worth, it will never be a fort.

15. No cholera deaths have been reported in the last 10 days in Independence.

18. The firm Whitney and Ely sends packages and letters from San Francisco to New York via Panama, New Orleans, and Havana.

■ The second Turner and Allen stagecoach from Missouri to California departs St. Louis.

18. William Russell's wagon train, en route from Fort Leavenworth to Santa Fe, reports nine dead from cholera and seven sick. The *Missouri Republican* reports that "the remainder of his teamsters, numbering some 35 or 40, left their teams . . . and cut for tall timber."

21. Three more banks advertise their services in the pages of the *Alta California*: Simmons, Hutchinson and Company, Burgoyne and Company, and Moffat and Company.

23. Fort Kearny reports that 5,516 wagons have passed

it on their way to California. "At moderate calculations, there are 20,000 persons and 60,000 animals now upon the road between this point and Fort Hall (Idaho)."

26. The U.S. Army purchases Fort Laramie for $4,000 from the American Fur Company.

Also in June 1849:

Cholera spreads to Texas, ravaging tribes, including the Comanche, Cheyenne, Apache, Kiowa, and Kiowa-Apache.

Since April, St. Joseph, Missouri, has recorded 1,500 covered wagons passing through town on the journey westward.

William Perkins's bill for a typical Sonora breakfast:

A small box of sardines	$ 5
Sea biscuits	1
A bottle of English ale	8
Eight lbs. of barley for horse	12
Total	$26

National Headlines/June 1849:

15. FORMER PRESIDENT JAMES K. POLK, 53, DIES IN NASHVILLE

JULY

2. Delegates from the proposed State of Deseret arrive in Washington to petition for admission to the Union as a free and independent state.

5. A woman known only as "Pretty Juanita" becomes the first person to be hanged in the gold camps of California. She stabbed a man to death when he insulted her.

6. In California, Commander Sloat proclaims that Mexican land grants will be honored by the United States.

12. A second cholera epidemic has already claimed 20 people in Kansas City.

14. The last Mormon wagon train for Utah this season departs eastern Nebraska for Salt Lake City.

15. A racially motivated gang of New Yorkers and Australians calling themselves the "Hounds" and vowing to keep San Francisco for "Americans" ransacks a small colony of Hispanic gold seekers; shacks are destroyed and many people are injured.

16. Some 230 San Franciscans, outraged at yesterday's attack by the "Hounds," organize under W. E. Spofford and arrest 20 members of the group who are then imprisoned aboard the USS *Warren.*

20. Pierre Melicourt Papin, 56, the American Fur Company's agent among the Osage, dies of cholera.

28. The first clipper ship to arrive in San Francisco is the *Memnon,* having made the journey from New York in 120 days.

Also in July 1849:

At Mormon Station, southeast of Reno, Nevada, flour sells for $2 a pound.

AUGUST

11. Reporting that 36 people have been murdered in Indian raids and that 1,300 head of livestock have disappeared, Governor George Wood sends three Texas Ranger companies to Corpus Christi to provide protection.

16. Captain Steen and the 1st Dragoons battle Apaches in New Mexico. Steen is wounded and an officer is killed.

17. Regular service between San Francisco and Sacramento is begun with the ship *George Washington.*

20–21. William Bent, disgusted by the U.S. government's refusal to meet his price for Bent's Fort, on the upper Arkansas, removes all of his property from the fort and blows it up.

28. Captain H. Stansbury arrives in Salt Lake City to begin a federal survey of the Great Salt Lake Valley.

29. Pawnees attack Thomas Fulton's wagon train, heading for Fort Kearny, on the Little Blue River. Fulton is robbed of everything, and the contents of the wagons are destroyed.

Also in August 1849:

San Francisco is broke and cannot afford to maintain police or jails, the chief administrator John W. Geary reports. To remedy the situation, licensing fees for gamblers are increased, a municipal court is created, a paid police force is organized, and the ship *Euphemia* is purchased for use as a jail.

In San Francisco, a carpenter can earn approximately $16 a day.

SEPTEMBER

1. At Colton Hall, Monterey, 48 delegates convene to draft the California state constitution, which will prohibit slavery.

3. The first Minnesota territorial legislature meets in St. Paul.

14. In Doniphan County, Kansas, a small party led by a Mr. Ritson is intercepted by Sac and Fox warriors led by the son of Chief Nesoquot. A 16-year-old Pawnee girl traveling with Ritson is kidnapped and decapitated.

16. Troops under Brevet Major James H. Carleton arrive at the Sac and Fox village and arrest those who killed the 16-year-old Pawnee girl two days earlier. White Cloud is also arrested for "bad conduct."

26. The fifth anniversary of the bilingual Indian Territory newspaper the *Cherokee Advocate* is celebrated.

Also in September 1849:

The first public school in Fort Des Moines, Iowa, is established.

Lieutenant A. W. Whipple, conducting a boundary survey near Yuma, Arizona, writes that the area is "populated only with Indians."

OCTOBER

1. In his report to the commissioner of Indian affairs, agent John Barrow notes more than 1,200 cholera deaths among the Pawnees during the spring and summer.

■ The thief William Sansom becomes the first prisoner in the Huntsville, Texas, prison.

6. The Perpetual Emigration Company is organized in Salt Lake City.

10. The California state constitution, which forbids slavery, is adopted.

12. The *St. Joseph Gazette* reports that the *Cumberland Valley* sank in early October after having struck a snag at the mouth of the Kansas River.

■ The first white birth recorded in Arizona is that of Gila Pancoast, who was born on the riverbank of the Gila River while his parents were journeying with an immigrant party. They completed their trip on this date.

13. The California state constitution is signed in Monterey; the convention adjourns after requesting statehood.

21. Three mail carriers on their way to Fort Leavenworth turn back to Fort Kearny when they run into 60 hostile Pawnees. Brevet Second Lieutenant Charles H. Ogle leads 20 members of the 1st Dragoons into an engagement with the Pawnees. Three members of the tribe are killed, and the dragoons report seven wounded, including Ogle, who takes an arrow in the mouth. More troops arrive to escort the mail carriers, but the Pawnees are nowhere to be found. The mail goes through.

25. California's Democratic Party is organized; Peter H. Burnett is nominated for governor.

29. Sioux and the 1st Dragoons under Captain R. H. Chilton do battle on the Platte River near Fort Kearny, Nebraska. One enlisted man is reported killed; there are no estimates of Sioux casualties.

31. Adams and Company becomes the first eastern express company to establish itself in California; its representative is Daniel H. Haskell.

Also in October 1849:

Jicarilla Apaches led by Lobo Blanco attack the wagon train of J. M. White at the Point of Rocks on the Santa Fe Trail, killing White and kidnapping his wife and daughter. One investigator believes the Indians were retaliating for having been fired upon by troops near Las Vegas, New Mexico.

The Wyandot Mining Company, having left Kansas in May, arrives in gold country and travels to the North Fork of the Feather River, where its enterprise enjoys success.

NOVEMBER

8. Adams and Company advertises San Francisco-to-New York express services in the *Alta California*.

KIT CARSON'S BELATED RESCUE ATTEMPT
NOVEMBER 28, 1849

In the wake of the October raid on J. M. White's wagon train, a rescue party was organized to search for the women of White's party. A company of the First Dragoons gathered at Taos, and Kit Carson was picked to guide them to the correct Apache camp. At site after site, Carson discovered articles of Mrs. White's clothing.

A week and a half later, the party came upon the camp. After a brief skirmish, the rescue party reached the campsite behind fleeing Apaches. Mrs. White's body, still warm and with an arrow through the heart, was found among the seven Indians killed. Carson later wrote: "In camp was found a book, the first of the kind I had ever seen, in which I was made a great hero, slaying Indians by the hundred, and I have often thought that as Mrs. White could read the same, she would pray for my appearance and that she might be saved."

On November 28, the Santa Fe *New Mexican* published its first issue, four pages, two in English and two in Spanish. The top story read: "We learn that the wife of the late Mr. J. M. White has, at last, been deprived of her suffering, having been shot by the Indians, who had her in possession. . . . The numerous murders and robberies committed since July last, by the Apaches, Navajos and Utahs, who encircle this Territory, admonish all concerned, that it is unsafe to attempt to come here, or to go hence, unless travelling parties are sufficiently strong to protect themselves."

---

10. George White Hair, the principal chief of the Osage, visits President Zachary Taylor in Washington.

13. The California state constitution is formally ratified. Also, the first state officials are elected, including Democratic governor Peter H. Burnett.

17. The 1st Dragoons skirmish with Apaches at Too Koon Kurre Butte on the Red River in New Mexico.

■ San Diego's first Masonic Lodge is organized.

17–19. Some 40 miles from the Arkansas River, a three-day blizzard kills all the oxen in the 20-wagon Santa Fe Trail party of Judge James Brown. Brown's nephew will return in January with a new team.

21. The 2nd Dragoons, under Brevet Captain J. Oakes, battle Indians near Fort Lincoln on the Rio Saco in Texas.

22. Austin College is chartered in Huntsville, Texas.

23. Joshua Abraham Norton, 31, a native Londoner who has lived in Cape Town, South Africa, since the age of 2, sails into San Francisco Bay aboard the German ship *Franzeska*. In the next four years, he will turn $40,000 into $250,000 through a series of investments. When the economic boom goes bust, Norton will reinvent himself as "Emperor Norton."

26. Susan James, the only sister of Frank and Jesse, is born in Kearney, Missouri.

Also in November 1849:

Congress appropriates a $1,500 ransom for J. M. White's daughter, but she is never recovered.

The French Bakery becomes the first commercial sourdough bakery in San Francisco.

There are some 500 ships abandoned in San Francisco Bay, their crews having joined in the search for gold.

DECEMBER

4. President Taylor asks Congress to admit California to the Union; Southern states balk because it would upset the balance between free and slave states.

9. The crew of the *Anna,* docking in St. Louis, pronounces the end of the river season. The Missouri is low and the weather is turning very cold.

10. The *Haydee* departs St. Louis, attempting to navigate the Missouri.

The Gold Rush. With more novices than millionaires, the rush still produces $10,000,000 in gold in 1849. (Library of Congress)

14. The *Haydee* returns to St. Louis, unable to get through the ice on the Missouri.

20. Following the first California elections that made Peter H. Burnett governor, military governor Bennett Riley respectfully resigns his post.

24. San Francisco's first big fire destroys 50 buildings.

Also in December 1849:

Great Salt Lake County is created, with Salt Lake City as its seat.

Since March, 549 vessels have dropped anchor in San Francisco.

W. H. Emory is named acting U.S. Boundary Commissioner under the terms of the Treaty of Guadalupe Hidalgo.

Also in 1849:

Dallas's first newspaper is published. Along with the city's first printing press, the city's first piano arrives by oxcart.

The Pacific Railroad is chartered in Missouri to link St. Louis with Kansas City.

Relations between the Apaches and Mexico remain poor. This year, the state of Chihuahua paid 17,896 pesos for the scalps of Apache men, women, and children.

John Muir, 11, migrates with his family from Scotland to a small farm in Wisconsin's Fox River region near Fort Winnebago.

George Horatio Derby, who will be known as John Phoenix, the first western humorist, arrives in California.

This year, 10,000 Australians made their way to the California goldfields.

A British perspective is offered in George Frederick Ruxton's *Life in the Far West*.

In Bonn, Germany, Dr. Ferdinand Roemer publishes his *Texas, with Particular Reference to German Immigration and the Physical Appearance of the Country, Described Through Personal Observation*.

Francis Parkman publishes *The California and Oregon Trail*.

California produces $10 million in gold.

Since 1820, a total of 43 Chinese have immigrated to the United States.

Brulé and Oglala Sioux, fleeing the cholera of the plains, return to their previous homes on South Dakota's White River. There, in a camp of standing tepees, they discover that every person in the village has died of the disease.

Nearly half of all Cheyennes die of cholera.

1850

"The West of which I speak is but another name for the Wild; and what I have been preparing to say is, that in Wildness is the preservation of the World."

—Henry David Thoreau

JANUARY

1. San Francisco's population is 35,000, of which 787 are Chinese.
■ The *St. Louis Intelligencer* publishes its first issue.
3. Camp Crawford, at Laredo, Texas, is renamed Fort McIntosh, after Brevet Colonel James S. McIntosh, who was killed in 1847 at Molino del Rey.
■ Beach and waterfront property is offered for sale in San Francisco.
5. The California Exchange opens in San Francisco.
16. The Eagle Theater opens in San Francisco.
19. The National Theater is dedicated in San Francisco.
21. The forced migrations of Florida Indians are completed.
■ *Le Californien,* a French newspaper, begins publication in San Francisco.
22. San Francisco's *Alta California,* until now a weekly, becomes the first daily newspaper in California.
23. San Francisco's second daily newspaper, the *Journal of Commerce,* begins publication.
28. Frederick D. Kohler becomes San Francisco's first fire chief.
29. The Compromise of 1850, a series of resolutions introduced by Senator Henry Clay, proposes that California be admitted to the Union as a free state and that territorial governments be organized in lands newly acquired from Mexico—specifically, New Mexico and Utah—with no mention of slavery. The boundaries of Texas would also be changed, and that state's public debt would be assumed by the United States.

Also in January 1850:

The first commercial ferry on the Colorado River is opened in Yuma by Dr. Able Lincoln. His timing is perfect: he will transport in the first year 60,000 passengers en route to the goldfields.

The Horton Hotel, with 96 rooms, opens in San Diego.

FEBRUARY

2. Apaches, perhaps Gileños or Membres, attack the village of Doña Ana on the Rio Grande, killing one person and wounding three.
■ The California state legislature creates San Diego County.
4. Immigrant Kansans reach the San Francisquito Ranch in California after a treacherous journey through Death Valley.
10. The Buffalo Bayou, Brazos, and Colorado, the first railroad in Texas and the second west of the Mississippi, is chartered.
18. A party of eight led by Preston Beck arrives in Independence, having left Santa Fe on January 27. The party reports 10 inches of snow on most of the prairie.
■ The California legislature creates 27 counties.
19. The National Theater opens in San Francisco.
20. Captain J. T. Sprague and the 8th Infantry battle Indians between Forts Inge and Duncan in Texas; one enlisted man is reported killed.
22. Earthquake shocks are reported in Salt Lake City.
27. The *St. Louis Reveille* publishes an ad for *A Journey to California,* by Major John Stemmons.

MARCH

3. In Texas, a guard on Chacon Creek is reported slain by Indians.
12. California asks Congress to grant it statehood.
23. The Phoenix Theater opens in San Francisco.
29. The *St. Joseph Gazette* reports: "Every boat that arrives at our wharf is crowded with Californians. . . . We suppose there are now in this place, and vicinity, upwards of 1,500."

Also in March 1850:

Gambling grows in San Francisco: in two years, 1,000 establishments have opened to a population of 25,000, mostly miners under 40 who bet with gold dust. Legendary gamblers include Jim Rynders, who won $89,000 in poker in three days and then lost it all the following week, and Ed Moses, who placed the largest single faro wager in American history—$60,000. Moses lost the bet and a total of $200,000 during an eight-hour session.

National Headlines/March 1850:

31. JOHN C. CALHOUN DIES IN WASHINGTON

APRIL

1. The county government of San Francisco is established.
4. The city of Los Angeles is incorporated and becomes the county seat. The first U.S. Census will list the population of the city as "8,329": "4,091 native white Mexicans, 4,193 domesticated Indians, and 295 Americans."
5. The Utah Territory begins the organization process.
6. Sergeant W. C. Holbrook and the 1st Dragoons engage Apaches near Rayado, New Mexico. Five Apache deaths are recorded.
7. Troops under Lieutenant W. W. Hudson engage Indians near Laredo Texas. Hudson is wounded.
9. At Fort Leavenworth, the government auctions off some 350 wagons and 200 ox yokes.
12. The *St. Joseph Gazette* reports "from 15 to 20" steamboats on the river between St. Joseph and St. Louis.
13. One observer reports 8,200 emigrants in St. Joseph are ready to make the trek to California. The season's first wagon train of gold seekers reaches Fort Kearny.
15. The city of San Francisco is incorporated; California's first public schools open there.
18. The U.S. Senate refers the resolutions for California statehood to a select committee.
19. Lieutenant W. W. Hudson dies of wounds he received on April 7.

Bavarian immigrant Levi Strauss (c. 1829–1902), the father of blue jeans. (Levi Strauss and Co.)

22. The California legislature passes a law protecting the rights of American Indians.
23. Yuma Indians attack the ferry at Yuma Crossing, killing 15. Three ferrymen escape.

Also in April 1850:

The Bavarian immigrant Levi Strauss arrives in San Francisco with rolls of canvas, intent on being a supplier of tents. A miner tells him there are plenty of tents to be had, but what are needed are durable trousers: "Pants don't wear worth a hoot up in the diggings."

National Headlines/April 1850:

27. STEAMSHIP SERVICE INAUGURATED BETWEEN NYC & LIVERPOOL

MAY

1. The San Francisco Chamber of Commerce is created.
3. The *St. Joseph Gazette* estimates there are 1,500 emigrants in Independence, 1,000 in Kansas City, 400 in Weston, and roughly 10,000 in Council Bluffs.
4. A fire destroys much of San Francisco.
5. Kit Carson and Tim Goodale set out with a train of 50 mules, packing goods from New Mexico to Fort Laramie. Upon Carson's arrival at the fort, one settler, expecting to meet the tall hero of dime novels, blurts, "You ain't the kind of Kit Carson I'm alookin' for."
6. The diarist John Warnock writes: "At Wolf creek is a log toll bridge built by the indians where they

CHRISTOPHER HOUSTON "KIT" CARSON
DECEMBER 24, 1809–MAY 23, 1868

1809: Carson is born in Madison County, Kentucky.

1812: He migrates with his family to Missouri.

1818: His father dies while felling a tree.

1824: Carson is apprenticed as a saddler to David Workman.

1826: He joins a wagon train bound for New Mexico.

1828: He goes west with a trapping expedition to California.

1831: Carson begins a decade of trapping in the Rockies. With Thomas Fitzpatrick, he goes as far north as the Salmon River.

1835: With 11 other trappers, he tracks a party of Blackfoot Indians 50 miles through the Idaho snow to recover 18 stolen horses. At the annual rendezvous, he has a famous fight with Shunar, a French trapper.

1841: Carson's first wife, an Arapaho named Waanibe, dies. He marries a Cheyenne, Making-Out-Road, who later divorces him by throwing all of his belongings out of the tepee.

1842: Carson is employed as a buffalo hunter for Bent's Fort. He converts to Catholicism in Taos and weds Josefa Jaramillo, 14. He guides John Charles Frémont's first expedition.

1843: Carson leads the second Frémont expedition through the Snake River valley and on to California's San Joaquin valley.

1845: He leads the third Frémont expedition through Colorado, Utah, and Nevada. In California, he participates in the Bear Flag Republic movement and guides General Stephen Kearny from New Mexico to California.

1847: Frémont's published memoirs make Carson a national hero.

1848: Carson carries news of the discovery of gold in California to Washington.

1849: He ranches near Taos and leads the unsuccessful attempt to rescue Mrs. White.

1850: He runs a major sheep-herding drive from Santa Fe to California.

1853: Carson leads a successful sheep drive from New Mexico to California. He is named the agent for the Ute Indians in Taos.

1854: Carson scouts for troops that fight Jicarilla Apaches in the Battle of Rio Caliente.

1861–1865: As a colonel in the New Mexico Volunteers, Carson is charged with protecting settlements from Indian attack during the Civil War.

1862: In the Civil War, he participates in the Battle of Valverde, then fights Mescalero Apaches in southeastern New Mexico under General James H. Carleton. Most Mescaleros surrender and are placed at Bosque Redondo.

1863–1864: Carson wages a scorched-earth campaign against the Navajos under Manuelito at Canyon de Chelly, burning crops and destroying livestock. By the summer of 1864, 8,000 Navajos have surrendered.

1864: Carson battles Kiowas and Comanches near Adobe Walls, Texas.

1865: Representing the army and the Little Arkansas Council, he parleys with Arapahos, Kiowas, Cheyennes, Comanches, and other tribes.

1867: Carson accompanies a Ute delegation to Washington.

1868: He is named superintendent of Indian affairs for Colorado Territory. Josefa dies 10 days after giving birth. Carson dies at age 59, on May 23 at Fort Lyon, Colorado.

---

charge 25¢ for each wagon that crosses. The Keeper of the bridge says 1,400 wagons had passed before us."

■ Ralph Ringwood, in one of his many letters from the Missouri frontier to Horace Greeley's *New York Herald,* reports: "On the first day of May ice to the thickness of an inch formed in the Missouri."

7. Foley's Olympic Amphitheater opens in San Francisco.

8. A Senate select committee recommends an Omnibus Bill for California, the territories, and the Texas–New Mexico boundary.

11. Construction begins on San Francisco's first brick building, the Naglee.

14. Alva Adams, who will serve as governor of Colorado in 1887–1889, 1897–1899, and 1905, is born in Iowa County, Wisconsin.

16. At Fort Kearny, Nebraska, Samuel Lane writes: "A

record kept at the fort showed that 1,952 wagons and 6,152 souls had preceded us."

- The *Saranak,* carrying 30 mountain men and some 600 bales of buffalo robes, arrives in St. Louis from Council Bluffs.

19. The 1st Dragoons engage Indians at Clear Lake and Pitt River, California; two enlisted men are reported wounded.

20. In St. Louis, the *Saluda* reports that all emigrants have left St. Joseph for California.

- Captain Merchant is wounded in a skirmish with Indians at Frio Pass, near Leona, Texas.

25. In New Mexico, a constitutional convention at Santa Fe frames a new constitution prohibiting slavery and establishing boundaries.

27. The walls of the Mormon temple at Nauvoo, the only remains left standing after the 1848 fire, are blown down by a hurricane.

30. In Kansas, Jotham Meeker writes that a "general war" is raging between Pawnees and a united front of Pottawatomie, Osage, Kickapoo, Shawnee, Sak and Fox, and Kansa Indians.

Also in May 1850:

Jicarilla Apaches and Utes attack an eastbound mail-carrying wagon train on the Santa Fe Trail, killing all 11 members. Lieutenant Ambrose Burnside's account of the incident will draw much attention to New Mexico's "Indian problem."

JUNE

1. The *San Francisco Daily Herald* begins publishing.

2. Several million dollars in property are believed lost in recent San Francisco fires.

3. Five Cayuse Indians found guilty in the "Whitman Massacre" are hanged in Oregon City in the territory's first application of capital punishment. (See November 29, 1848.)

- The *Robert Campbell* sets the fastest time ever for a steamboat traveling round-trip between St. Louis and Council Bluffs: seven days, six hours.

5. Patrick Floyd Garrett, the future lawman and killer of Billy the Kid, is born in Chambers County, Alabama.

12. Francis X. Aubry departs Santa Fe for Independence.

- The infantry engages the Indians near Laredo, Texas. Two enlisted men are reported wounded.

14. In San Francisco, a fire destroys some 300 buildings and 18 blocks of frame houses in 10 hours; the damage estimates top $5 million.

- The first Mormon missionaries to Scandinavia arrive in Copenhagen from Utah.

PAT GARRETT
JUNE 5, 1850—FEBRUARY 29, 1908

1850: Garrett is born in Chambers County, Alabama.

1853: He relocates with his family to an 1,800-acre Louisiana plantation.

1867: His mother dies, followed less than one year later by his father.

1869: Following a bitter fight with his brother-in-law over the estate, Garrett departs for the West to become a buffalo hunter.

1876: He kills his first man, the hunter Joe Briscoe, at a buffalo hunter's campfire in Texas.

1877: Comanche raids drive Garrett from the buffalo business. He drifts to Fort Sumner, New Mexico.

1879: He becomes a partner with Beaver Smith in a saloon and marries Juanita Gutierrez. She dies the same year of disease.

1880: Garrett weds his late wife's sister, Apolinaria Gutierrez. At his saloon, he makes friends with Billy the Kid—locals call them "Big Casino" and "Little Casino." He is elected Lincoln County sheriff and arrests the Kid on a murder charge at Stinking Springs in December.

1881: Billy the Kid escapes in April. On the night of July 31, Garrett catches up with his nemesis at Pete Maxwell's farm, where he waits in a darkened bedroom. The Kid enters, and Garrett fatally shoots him.

1882: Garrett writes *The Authentic Life of Billy, the Kid, the Noted Desperado of the Southwest, Whose Deeds of Daring Have Made His Name a Terror in New Mexico, Arizona, and Northern Mexico.* He returns to ranching.

1897: He serves as appointed sheriff of New Mexico's Doña Ana County.

1901: Garrett is appointed by President Theodore Roosevelt to be customs collector in El Paso.

1905: He buys a New Mexico horse ranch.

1908: On February 29, Pat Garrett is shot dead by Wayne Brazel, a disgruntled tenant.

---

15. The first issue of The *Deseret News* is published in Salt Lake City by Dr. Willard Richards.

16. The deaths of two enlisted men wounded in an Indian fight near Laredo, Texas, are reported.

20. A "state" constitution for New Mexico is ratified and sent to Congress. The state legislature also creates Socorro County.

22. Gold is discovered by Lewis Ralston and a group of Cherokee Indians near present Arvada, Colorado.

Also in June 1850:

J. R. Bartlett is named U.S. boundary commissioner under the terms of the Treaty of Guadalupe Hidalgo.

There are some 20 million bison on the North American continent, down from 40 million in 1800.

JULY

1. The first overland mail route west of the Missouri River is inaugurated with monthly service between Independence and Salt Lake City. Monthly U.S. postal service between Independence and Santa Fe begins with the departure of a Waldo, Hall and Company stagecoach.

■ There are 626 ships in San Francisco Bay and adjoining harbors.

■ A letter from Fort Laramie, by a person calling himself "Cheyenne," reports: "A man just from the frontier states he counted no less than 645 new graves along side the road."

■ The *California Courier* begins publication in San Francisco.

3. Francis X. Aubry arrives in Independence, having left Santa Fe on June 12. He reports making one 200-mile stretch on the same horse.

4. San Franciscans celebrate the 4th of July by dedicating a 111-foot flagpole.

■ The Dramatic Museum Theater opens in San Francisco.

11. Louis J. F. "Don Diego" Jaeger opens a new ferry at Yuma Crossing, despite the threat of attack from Yuma Indians.

25. Gold is discovered in Oregon's Rogue River country.

■ Troops and Indians clash at Pitt River, California; one enlisted man is reported wounded and another killed.

26. The 1st and 2nd Dragoons surprise a camp of 150 lodges at the headwaters of the Red River in New Mexico. One enlisted man is reported killed; no estimate of Indian casualties is reported.

27. An enlisted man wounded at Pitt River dies.

31. A territorial government is established in Utah, the former "State of Deseret." Brigham Young will become the first governor.

Also in July 1850:

Nine out of 10 people making the gold rush to California are males.

In Kansas City, 17 Belgian emigrants are reported dead of cholera, along with a Dr. Fulton, who attended them.

National Headlines/July 1850:

9. PRESIDENT TAYLOR DIES IN THE WHITE HOUSE

10. FILLMORE TAKES OATH OF OFFICE

AUGUST

3. The San Francisco *Evening Picayune* begins publication.

6. Fort Bridger, in present Wyoming, gets its first postmaster, Louis Vasquez.

9. The border between Texas and New Mexico is adjusted; Texas receives a $10 million federal appropriation to assume debts.

12. Brevet Captain J. Oakes is wounded leading Company G of the 2nd Dragoons against Indians between the Nueces River and the Rio Grande in Texas.

13. A bill admitting California to the Union as a free state passes the Senate, 34 to 18.

■ The Athenaeum I Theater opens in San Francisco.

14. In Sacramento, riots erupt as armed squatters protest the validity of Sutter's grant, the land where the gold was found.

■ Rowe's New Olympic Amphitheater opens in San Francisco.

15. The creation of the Territory of New Mexico is approved by the Senate by a vote of 27 to 10; slavery is not restricted in the territory.

25. A major force of dragoons departs Fort Leavenworth for New Mexico.

28. Mail that left Independence on August 1 arrives in Santa Fe.

■ Captain Stansbury completes his survey of Salt Lake City.

Also in August 1850:

The new U.S. boundary commissioner, J. R. Bartlett, reports to Texas.

SEPTEMBER

2. Eugene Field, the future journalist and poet ("Wynken, Blynken, and Nod") is born in St. Louis.

4. Brown, Russell and Company contract to move freight from Fort Leavenworth—some 600,000 pounds at $14.33 per hundred pounds.

6–9. The house adopts the five measures that will

become known as the Compromise of 1850. The combined Texas and New Mexico bills pass by a vote of 108 to 97, the Utah bill by a vote of 97 to 85.

7. A bill admitting California to the Union as the 31st state is adopted by the House, 150 to 56.

9. California becomes a state, while New Mexico and Utah become territories. California enters the Union as a free state in accordance with the act of Congress signed by President Millard Fillmore. The U.S. Census reports the 31st state has a population of 92,597. Fillmore also signs the Texas and New Mexico Act, providing for the organization of New Mexico Territory (including present Arizona), without restriction on slavery, as well as the adjustment of its boundary with Texas. The United States agrees to pay Texas $10 million to cover the debt Texas accrued before annexation, if that state abandons all claims on New Mexico. Fillmore then signs the Utah Act, which creates that territory and allows it to become free or slave depending on the constitution it adopts upon admittance to the Union. Brigham Young will be appointed governor and superintendent of Indian affairs for Utah Territory.

12. *La Gazette Républicaine* begins publication in San Francisco.

16. The year's first overland party from California arrives in St. Joseph.

17. Fire in San Francisco destroys 125 buildings and prompts looting.

27. Congress approves a monthly mail route running east from New Mexico, as well as the establishment of post offices.

28. President Fillmore formally appoints Brigham Young the first governor of Utah Territory.

30. Leland Stanford marries Jane Lathrop of Albany, New York.

■ Foley's Amphitheater opens in San Francisco.

Also in September 1850:

In San Francisco, the first city directory appears, containing 2,500 names.

In St. Louis, there are 32 wagonmakers employing 121 men and producing $146,585 worth of wagons annually.

James Denver, 30, arrives in Sacramento with a party of 26 gold seekers. From there, he travels north to Trinity County, where he begins trading between the mines and Humboldt Bay. A year later, he will be elected to the California state senate.

National Headlines/September 1850:
11. JENNY LIND WOWS NYC

OCTOBER

3. Brigham Young is sealed to Eliza Burgess, his 45th wife.

10. Samuel Clemens, 15, goes to work for his brother Orion, the publisher of the new Hannibal newspaper *Western Union*.

16. The Adelphi I Theater opens in San Francisco.

19. The steamer *Oregon* arrives in San Francisco with the news that California has been admitted to the Union.

30. The Jenny Lind Theater opens in San Francisco.

NOVEMBER

1. The missionary Jotham Meeker, a Kansas resident for 17 years, writes, "Think I have never known so dry a season as we have now had."

5. St. Mary's Mission in Montana is purchased from the Jesuits by John Owen for $250.

6. An executive order of President Fillmore reserves California's Angel Island, Yerba Buena Island, and Point San Jose for the military.

23. The date Bret Harte set for the beginning of his fictional narrative, *The Outcasts of Poker Flat*. In the celebrated work, gambler John Oakhurst notices "a change in the moral climate" of Harte's Poker Flat.

25. The state of Texas formally accepts the Compromise of 1850; it will receive $10 million from the U.S. government in settlement of the state's land claims, which reach to California.

27. Three companies of troops under Captain Samuel P. Heintzelman arrive at Yuma Crossing at the junction of the Gila and Colorado Rivers and name their fort Camp Independence.

Also in November 1850:

Since 1836, fewer than 15,000 Americans have migrated to Oregon on the Platte Valley–South Pass Oregon Trail. Since 1849, some 55,000 have survived the trek to California on the Overland and Ox-Bow Trails.

W. H. Emory is relieved of his duties as acting U.S. boundary commissioner, the position established by the terms of the Treaty of Guadalupe Hidalgo.

DECEMBER

7. John Oakhurst, Bret Harte's gambler hero in the short story "The Outcasts of Poker Flat," expires in the snow. On a deuce of clubs is his message: "Beneath this tree lies the body of John Oakhurst, who struck a streak of bad luck on the 23d of November, 1850, and handed in his checks on the 7th December, 1850."

- The Latter-day Saints organized their first church in Paris.
8. The Mormon Elder George Smith leads 30 families from Salt Lake City to settle the county of Iron, Utah.
- The *Public Balance,* a newspaper, is established in San Francisco.
13. The United States formally assumes control of Kansas south of the Arkansas River and west of the 100th meridian. The land had been claimed by Texas since 1835.
14. Foley's New Amphitheater opens in San Francisco.
24. The schooner *Invincible,* traveling from San Diego and loaded with supplies for Camp Independence, arrives at the mouth of the Colorado River but cannot sail on its shallow waters. Cocopah Indians take a message to the camp, and the supplies are retrieved by wagon.
26. The mail arrives in Independence from Salt Lake City and Santa Fe.
31. Since 1847, the population of California has increased from approximately 15,000 to 92,497.

Also in December 1850:

Fort Laramie reports that 55,000 settlers stopped there in 1850, most on their way to the California gold-fields; about 13,000 were Mormons en route to Utah. Three hundred and sixteen settlers died east of the fort, most from cholera.

The Sioux refer to this season as "the big smallpox winter."

Also in 1850:

Montana's Fort Lewis is renamed Fort Benton to honor Missouri Senator Thomas Hart Benton.

Forty-five ships carrying 500 passengers each sail from China to California.

Jim Bridger discovers Bridger's Pass while leading the Howard Stansbury expedition through the Wasatch and Rocky mountains.

William F. Cody, 3, moves with his family to Kansas.

Hector Lewis Garrad publishes *Wah-to-yah and the Taos Trail,* about his 1847 tour of the Santa Fe Trail.

The *Choctaw Intelligencer* begins publication in Indian Territory.

Bayard Taylor publishes *El Dorado.*

An estimated 500 ships are abandoned in San Francisco Bay, as crews desert to hunt for gold. Living in San

1850 CENSUS	
Arkansas	210,000
California	92,497 (roughly 86,000 males to 7,000 females)
Iowa	192,000
Kansas	107,000
Louisiana	518,000
Minnesota	6,000
Missouri	682,000
New Mexico (including present Arizona and a portion of Colorado)	61,547
Oregon	12,093
Texas	212,592 (20 percent of the white population is German)
Utah	11,380
Washington	1,000

Francisco during the Gold Rush requires a hefty investment: rooms rent for as much as $300 a month, an apple might cost $5, an egg $1.

California produces $41 million in gold.

The *Weekly Oregonian* begins publication in Portland.

The University of Utah begins operations at Salt Lake City as the state university of Deseret.

The Irish novelist Mayne Reid, who came to this country via New Orleans and found himself a lieutenant in the Mexican War, publishes his war romance *The Rifle Rangers.*

The African-American pioneer George Washington Bush files for 640 acres under the Donation Land Act; his request is denied because the act states that the land is "for white Americans." The Washington territorial legislature petitions Congress to grant a special privilege to Bush, who "by a constant and laborious cultivation . . . and by accommodating and charitable disposal of his produce to emigrants has contributed much towards the settlement of this Territory."

1851

"Go West, young man, go West."

—John Babson Lane Soule, *Terre Haute Express*

JANUARY

3. Brigham Young's provisional state of Deseret (Utah Territory) holds its first criminal jury trial.

9. Salt Lake City is incorporated, with Jedediah Grant as the first mayor.

▪ John McDougal is inaugurated governor of California following the resignation of Governor Peter Burnett.

▪ California's College of the Pacific is chartered.

17. Cheyennes and Arapahos sign a boundary treaty on the Platte River.

18. The California Circus Theater opens in San Francisco.

23. A toss of a coin determines the name of a new city incorporated in Oregon Territory: when the coin comes up heads, it means the town will be named for Portland, Maine, rather than for Boston, Massachusetts.

31. Protestants open the San Francisco Orphan Asylum, the first such institution in the state.

National Headlines/January 1851:
27. JOHN J. AUDUBON DIES

FEBRUARY

3. Brigham Young takes the oath of office as the governor of Utah Territory.

13. The University of Minnesota is established.

17. Alice Ivers, who will be known in the West as "Poker Alice," is born in Sudbury, England.

18. Westminster College is chartered in Fulton, Missouri.

19. An *Alta California* editorial pleads for an end to the lawlessness caused by the swarms of people rushing for gold.

25. Ben Holladay receives a two-year contract to haul army freight between Forts Kearny and Leavenworth.

Also in February 1851:
Construction is completed on the Kaw Methodist Mission in Council Grove, Kansas.

Discoveries of quartz in Amador County, California, cause a small boom in the area.

The Kansas River is reported "about run dry."

MARCH

1. Indians and the 6th Infantry clash near Fort Atkinson, Nebraska; Captain William Hoffman is wounded.

3. California appoints a land commission to settle Mexican and Spanish claims.

▪ James S. Calhoun becomes New Mexico's first governor under the Organic Act.

▪ Captain William Hoffman dies of wounds suffered in Nebraska on March 1.

10. The first wagon train to carry merchandise on the Santa Fe Trail this season, led by Francis X. Aubry, departs from Missouri.

22. A prairie fire destroys all the wagons in a train "near Chouteau's Island," according to co—wagon master George Cranmer, who blames Pawnees.

25. California's Yosemite Valley is discovered by Major

James D. Savage, who stumbles upon it while chasing a band of Indians.

28. A family of pioneers named Oatman arrive at the Pima villages from Tucson. Some days later, local Indians (sources name the Tonto Apaches or the Mohaves) kill the parents, leave the son for dead, and ride away with the two daughters.

Also in March 1851:

Kansas City has a population of 300.

APRIL

2. Mescalero Apaches sign a treaty with the United States.

5. The legislature of the provisional state of Deseret is dissolved because it was elected under the territorial bill.

8. Elizabeth Bacon, the future bride of George Custer, receives a journal on her 9th birthday; she lives in Monroe, Michigan.

17. The *Glasgow* (Missouri) *Weekly Times* welcomes the first newspaper to publish in Kansas, Missouri, the *Kansas Public Ledger*. Raves the *Times,* "It is a handsome sheet, neutral in politics. . . ."

■ Richens Wootton arrives in St. Louis after traveling 15 days on horseback from Santa Fe.

24. The future lawman Morgan Earp is born in Pella, Iowa.

25. A monthly mail service is established between Salt Lake City and Sacramento.

MAY

1. The first load of transcontinental mail departs the firm of Woodward and Chorpenning from Sacramento headed for Salt Lake City. Indians attack the wagon train almost immediately.

■ Kit Carson arrives in Kansas, Missouri, with 12 wagons, having been on the trail from New Mexico since March 17. He came by way of Bent's Fort.

2. Navigation on the Missouri is reported to be "difficult and hazardous."

3. San Francisco's fifth and largest fire since the onset of the Gold Rush wipes out 70 percent of the city, destroying 2,500 buildings, killing 30, and causing $7 million in damages. It is believed the fire was set by people looking to create a diversion while they looted.

4. Francis X. Aubry, en route to Missouri, passes a massive peace conference that Brevet Lieutenant Colonel William Hoffman is conducting with representatives of the Apaches, Kiowas, Arapahos, Cheyennes, and Comanches.

■ Lilly Coit, who will become a famous firefighter, arrives in San Francisco via the Golden Gate.

■ Much of St. Louis is destroyed by fire.

6. The San Francisco Chamber of Commerce is organized.

7. Under the direction of the Cherokee National Council, seminaries for male and female Indians are established at Park Hill near Tahlequah, Indian Territory. One observer notes that many whites in the territory cannot even sign their names, while the Indians are learning Greek and Latin.

8. The Independence *Occidental Messenger* reports that the first newspaper to publish in Kansas City, the *Kansas Public Ledger,* has gone out of business.

12. Francis X. Aubry arrives in Independence after a 19-day journey from Santa Fe.

13. A Dr. Long of St. Joseph departs for St. Lake City, driving a herd of 1,200 sheep.

15. A slave transaction occurs in the Potawatomi Nation when trader Thomas Stinson purchases "a certain Negro Man named Moses of the age of 26" from Alexander and Margret Boshman.

17. The first newspaper published in Los Angeles is *La Estrella de los Angeles,* or the *Los Angeles Star.* The paper appears with both Spanish and English text.

18. James Herbert Budd, the 19th governor of California (1895–1899), is born in Janesville, Wisconsin.

19. The Theater of Arts opens in San Francisco.

24. The *Morning Post* begins publication in San Francisco.

29. The *San Diego Herald* begins publication.

Also in May 1851:

Upon learning that about one-fifth of the Sac and Fox tribe in Missouri has perished from smallpox, agent W. P. Richardson orders vaccinations at the Great Nemaha Subagency. An epidemic is held in check: only 40 previously ill persons die out of 1,700 who are inoculated.

School begins at the Kaw Methodist Mission in Council Grove, Kansas; Thomas Sears Huffaker is the director.

National Headlines/May 1851:

29. 2ND WOMEN'S RIGHTS CONVENTION CONVENES

JUNE

6. Thus far this season, the following have passed Fort Kearny heading West: 837 wagons, 1,156 men, 928 women, 799 children, and 5,975 livestock.

■ San Francisco constructs a county jail, replacing the temporary one on board the *Euphemia.*

SMALLPOX

Early smallpox epidemics offered an unplanned germ warfare against the West's original inhabitants.

The first Indians affected were those of the village tribes of the upper Missouri River. Ten thousand Mandans had established an agrarian culture by the beginning of the 18th century, but a 1770 bout with the disease, spread by French and Spanish traders, reduced their ranks to around 1,600. The survivors relocated near a Hidatsa village on the Knife River in present North Dakota.

The Hidatsas and their neighbors, the Arikaras, had also suffered through the same early epidemics as well as attacks from the Sioux. Along with the Mandans, the Hidatsas and Arikaras survived on their crops, namely corn, squash, beans, and sunflowers. Lewis and Clark visited them in 1804. The artist George Catlin came in 1832 and painted his famous portrait of the Mandan chief Four Bears. Prince Maximilian of Wied-Neuwied appeared the next year and counted 2,100 Hidatsas. These early visitors reported a pleasant life in the villages. People lived in earthen lodges and traded produce among themselves and for necessities, including horses and guns. Some hunted buffalo. The three tribes welcomed the white traders and permitted convenient trading posts to be established.

In 1837, the American Fur Company steamship *St. Peter's* began another routine trade cruise up the Missouri. This time, in addition to the usual trinkets, furs, and foodstuffs, she carried death. As early as June 10 it was realized that smallpox was on board but, fearing monetary losses, officials did not turn back. At Fort Clark on June 19, a Mandan boarded the boat and stole a contaminated blanket from a dying watchman. Also on board were three Arikara women who had become infected and would soon be joining the Pawnees. The first sparks were thus ignited.

The ship continued to Fort Union, the nearest trading post for the Mandans, Hidatsas, and Arikaras. It also brought the new operator of the post, Jacob Halsey. Having realized he was carrying a deadly cargo, Halsey ordered the Indians away from the boat upon its arrival. The Indians, believing they were being duped into some sort of unfair trading scheme, refused. Halsey then ordered the ship's crew vaccinated, himself included. He recovered from his dose, but his wife and some crew members were not so lucky.

Smallpox was soon rampant at Fort Union. In the confusion, five Assiniboin warriors decided that no one would miss two fine army horses. A group of soldiers apprehended them, and the Indians agreed to return the horses with no questions asked. But one of the troopers had smallpox, and the five would-be thieves returned to their camp, sickened, and died. They were followed by 800 of their tribe whom they had infected.

Death by smallpox was one of nature's most horrible exits. An infected person would be unaware of exposure until about the ninth day, when he or she would be stricken with nausea, headaches, chills, fever, and convulsion. After four days of these symptoms and a scarlet skin coloration, a rash of flat red spots began covering first the face, then the rest of the body. Soon the victim swelled into a hideous mass of dark, oozing blisters. Many said it felt as if their leopard skin had been set ablaze. Those who survived this stage ultimately died when the infection spread internally.

Infected Indians often committed suicide. Some drowned themselves, others jumped into fires or impaled themselves on knives or arrows. Others ran off cliffs. After watching his wife and children die, Four Bears starved himself. Before he succumbed on July 30, 1837, he told his council, "I do not fear Death . . . but to die with my face rotten, that even the Wolves will shrink with horror at seeing me, and say to themselves, that is the 4 Bears the Friend of the Whites."

Of the 1,600 Mandans, 1,477 were dead before autumn. Catlin returned, only to write: "So have perished the friendly and hospitable Mandans. . . . Although it may be possible that some few individuals may yet be remaining, I think it is not probable. . . . As a nation, the Mandans are extinct, having no longer an existence. The Hidatsas and Arikaras suffered equally appalling losses.

The Assiniboins infected the Crees, of whom some 7,000 died. The death toll among the Blackfeet reached 6,000. As tribes tried to flee the scourge, smallpox spread among the Crows, Dakotas, Pawnees, Osages, Winnebagos, Sioux, and Choctaws. The Kiowas called the winter of 1839–1840 "Small-

(continued)

(continued)

pox Winter." Cases were reported as far north as the Hudson's Bay Company posts in Canada, and as far south as Apache and Comanche country.

Wrote one observer from New Orleans, "The destroying angel has visited the unfortunate sons of the wilderness with terrors never before known, and has converted the extensive hunting grounds, as well as the peaceful settlements of those tribes, into desolate and boundless cemeteries."

Perhaps what is most astounding in these events is the casual attitude with which the disaster was treated by the government, whose unstated policy was to let the disease "run its course." Congress had appropriated $12,000 toward Indian inoculation in 1832, but government action was focused more on President Andrew Jackson's program of forcibly removing the Indians of the southeast to locations in present Oklahoma than on combatting disease.

The total number of Indian lives lost to smallpox from 1837 to 1840 is unknown. Experts believe there were no fewer than 100,000 deaths, perhaps as many as 300,000. Almost every tribe suffered from the disease and some were wiped out. In truth, the winning of the West was well under way before the first shots were fired.

---

7. The steamship *St. Ange* departs St. Louis for a voyage up the Missouri. Cholera breaks out during the trip. On board is Father Pierre-Jean De Smet. Of the 80 passengers, 14 will die. De Smet will recover.

■ San Francisco's chief engineer reports that the city's fire equipment and the structure housing its fire department have been rendered useless by the latest fire. Also, the city treasury is out of funds.

9. Sam Brannan organizes San Francisco's first Committee of Vigilance, some 200 strong, following the robbery and abuse of merchant J. Jansen.

10. The San Francisco vigilance committee hangs an accused thief from the veranda of the city hotel. The man supposedly stole $1,500 from the safe of a Mr. Virgin and was caught while rowing across the bay.

13. William Bent arrives in St. Louis.

■ The Jenny Lind Theater reopens in San Francisco.

17. Luke Lea, 68(?), an agent of the Fort Leavenworth Agency, is killed when he falls from his horse.

19. A major peace council is convened by agent Thomas Fitzpatrick on the Arkansas River. William Bent estimates that 3,000 Arapahos, Cheyennes, Comanches, and Kiowas are in attendance.

21. San Luis, the first town in what will become Colorado, is founded by New Mexican colonists.

22. Another portion of San Francisco—most of what was spared in the May 1 blaze—is destroyed by fire.

25. "New Post on Arkansas," the site where the big peace conference convened by Thomas Fitzpatrick is being held, is renamed Fort Atkinson. Offended, the Cheyennes have already departed.

Also in June 1851:
A monument is erected 18 miles south of San Diego to mark the boundary with Mexico.

Reported cholera deaths this month include 45 in Independence and another 32 in Weston.

Fort Belknap, on the Brazos River near present Newcastle, Texas, is established by General William G. Belknap.

Francis X. Aubry departs Missouri with his second wagon train of the season, heading for New Mexico. En route, his train will suffer an outbreak of cholera.

Kit Carson is on the road to Bent's Fort with a party of 17, including his daughter and niece. En route, Carson becomes aware of a Cheyenne plot against him but manages to evade it.

JULY

2. Of the cholera epidemic, the Reverend John G. Pratt of the Delaware Baptist Mission writes in his journal, "The alarm is very general, but not so great as in the former visitation."

10. California Wesleyan College, the future University of the Pacific, is chartered in Santa Clara.

11. San Francisco's vigilance committee executes the accused murderer James Stuart on a wharf.

14. Santa Fe is made the territorial capital of New Mexico by the first legislative assembly elected under the Organic Act.

21. Sam Bass, the future Texas outlaw, is born near Mitchell in Lawrence County, Indiana.

23. In the Treaty of Traverse des Sioux, the tribe cedes Indian lands in northern Iowa and southern Minnesota to the United States.

28. In St. Joseph, cholera has claimed 13 lives in the past week.

AUGUST

1. The Adelphi II Theater opens in San Francisco.

6. A party of 23 men and one woman arrives in St. Joseph from Sacramento, having made the journey in 66 days.

8. Right Reverend Jean-Baptiste Lamy arrives in Santa Fe to become the bishop of the new Roman Catholic Diocese of Santa Fe.

18. San Francisco's first vigilance committee hangs its last two men, the suspected burglars Robert McKenzie and Samuel Whittaker. The men were being housed in the jail and were pulled out by the mob.

25. In his report to the commissioner of Indian affairs, agent Thomas Moseley, Jr., notes 40 cholera deaths among several tribes, including the Delaware and the Shawnee, in the past month.

26. The 1st Dragoons and Indians fight at the Gila and Pinto Rivers in New Mexico. One person is reported killed on each side.

29. Mail that left Salt Lake City on August 1 arrives in Independence, Missouri.

31. The Yankee clipper *Flying Cloud* arrives in San Francisco following an 81-day, 21-hour trip from New York. Captain Josiah Creesy says the vessel averaged 227 miles a day on the 5,912-mile voyage.

Also in August 1851:

In St. Louis, the artist Heinrich B. Möllhausen and Paul Wilhelm, Duke of Württemberg, begin a trip up the Missouri River that will put them on the Oregon–California Trail.

The Sac chief Hard Fish, 51(?), is buried at the Sac and Fox Agency in Kansas.

National Headlines/August 1851:

26. NATION'S FAVORITE TUNE IS FOSTER'S "OLD FOLKS AT HOME"

SEPTEMBER

3. The *London Morning Chronicle* criticizes California's "Committee of Vigilance."

4. Orion Clemens changes the name of his Hannibal newspaper from *Western Union* to the *Journal and Western Union*.

9. The San Francisco vigilance committee disbands.

11. Lieutenant Ambrose E. Burnside arrives at Fort Leavenworth, having traveled overland from New Mexico.

15. Fort Defiance is established in present Apache County, Arizona.

17. The first Treaty of Fort Laramie is signed.

22. The first meeting of the Utah territorial legislature convenes.

Also in September 1851:

Following a gold strike at Pinos Altos, 56-year-old Mangas Coloradas, an Apache chief, comes to peaceably discuss the future with community leaders. If it is gold they want, he offers to show them a place in Mexico where there is more. Thinking that he might be setting a trap, the prospectors bind Mangas to a tree and flog him. He is then released.

THE TREATY OF FORT LARAMIE
SEPTEMBER 17, 1851

The first Treaty of Fort Laramie was agreed to at the stockade that was founded in 1834 by William Sublette and Robert Campbell. Indian agent Thomas Fitzpatrick assembled at least 10,000 (some reports say 60,000) representatives of the Sioux, Cheyenne, Arapaho, Snake, and Crow tribes. Many Indian lands were surrendered to the government for a fee of $50,000 a year for 50 years (a typographical error in Washington changed the contract to 10 years). Boundaries for the different tribes were set, and whites were granted safe passage through the territory as well as the right to establish forts. About the month-long festivities at the Laramie Council, Father De Smet wrote of the nonstop eating: "No epoch in Indian annals probably shows a greater massacre of the canine race." Present at the Laramie Council was 10-year-old Curly, known to history as Crazy Horse.

A group of 640 Ottawas, Chippewas, and Potawatomis from Wisconsin arrive in Kansas to join relatives on the Pottawatomie reserve.

The town of Fort Des Moines, Iowa, is incorporated.

National Headlines/September, 1851:
14. JAMES FENIMORE COOPER DIES AT 62

OCTOBER
4. The Jenny Lind Theater re-reopens in San Francisco.
- Millard County is created in Utah; its county seat is Fillmore.
- The St. Louis and Missouri River Telegraph Company opens an office in Weston, Missouri.
11. Francis X. Aubry arrives in Independence ahead of his 30-wagon train.
16. The future gunfighter William Preston "Wild Bill" Longley is born in Austin County, Texas.
20. The American Theater opens in San Francisco.
29. Fillmore City is named the capital of Utah Territory.

NOVEMBER
1. Telegraph service westward is now available from St. Joseph, Missouri. A message telegraphed today announces: "The office of Morse's line of telegraph westward has been opened at this point for a few days."
11. Yuma Indians attack Yuma Crossing and Camp Independence in present Arizona, sinking the ferry. The garrison under Lieutenant T. J. Sweeny will be under siege into December, when it will run out of rations and withdraw.
- A post office opens at Fort Atkinson.
14. The party of Heinrich Möllhausen and Paul Wilhelm, Duke of Württemberg, is caught in a blizzard on the Little Blue in present Wyoming, on its return trip to the East. The next morning, they report a frozen mare and a temperature of −30°.
- Fort Phantom Hill is established in Jones County, Texas.
25. Heinrich Möllhausen and Paul Wilhelm are found by the mail stagecoach from Fort Laramie. There is room on board for only one person, so Möllhausen and Wilhelm flip a coin. Wilhelm wins and bids farewell to his traveling companion.
26. Independence receives word that 275 mules in a government wagon train have perished in a winter storm some 60 miles west of Council Grove, and that one man in the expedition has frozen to death.
27. San Diego is in a state of panic after a raid on the Warner ranch. The house is burned and the livestock stolen.

National Headlines/November 1851:
14. MOBY DICK PUBLISHED
30. POTATO FAMINE MEANS 250,000 IRISH IMMIGRANTS THIS YEAR

DECEMBER
1. The first wheeled wagon arrives at Fort Benton, Montana: it is driven by Alexander Culbertson.
10. The last steamboat on the "middle Missouri" this season, the *Kansas,* arrives in St. Louis.
- Maria Meeker, 17, daughter of the Baptist missionaries Jotham and Eleanor Meeker, weds Nathan L. Simpson in Westport, Missouri.
18. Juan Verdugo is hanged in San Diego for the raid on the Warner ranch.
29. Lola Montez makes her American debut in *Betley, the Tyrolean.* Soon she will be the rage in San Francisco.
31. Francis X. Aubry departs Santa Fe for Independence with a small party and 12 wagons.

Also in December 1851:
James's Traveler's Companion, Being a Complete Guide Through the Western States, by Stephen L. Massey, is published in Ohio.

Lola Montez (1818–1861), conqueror of Franz Liszt, Alexander Dumas, King Ludwig I of Bavaria, and gold-rush San Francisco. Says one reviewer, "She is the very comet of her sex." (Wells Fargo Bank History Room)

San Francisco undergoes massive rebuilding after the fires.

An outbreak of smallpox is reported among the Potawatomis near St. Mary's Mission in Kansas.

National Headlines/December 1851:
24. FIRE DESTROYS 2/3 OF THE BOOKS IN THE LIBRARY OF CONGRESS

Also in 1851:

John Babson Lane Soule, editor of the *Terre Haute Express,* is the first to print the slogan "Go West, young man, go West." It will soon be adopted by *New York Tribune* editor Horace Greeley, with whom it will forever be associated.

Santa Fe receives a city charter.

The Irish novelist Mayne Reid, a veteran of the Mexican War, publishes his second novel, *The Scalp Hunters.*

The future gunslinger Ben Thompson, 7, migrates with his family from his birthplace, Knottingley, Yorkshire, England, to Texas.

Construction begins on the first railroad in Texas.

California produces $60 million worth of gold.

Approximately 25,000 Chinese arrive in California.

1852

"All the past we leave behind,
We debouch upon a newer mightier world,
varied world,
Fresh and strong the world we seize, world
of labor and the march,
Pioneers! O pioneers!"

—Walt Whitman

JANUARY

5. Margaret Emma Custer, George Armstrong Custer's sister, is born.

8. Democrat John Bigler is inaugurated governor of California.

9. The following counties are established in New Mexico: Bernalillo, Dona Ana, Rio Arriba, San Miguel, Santa Fe, Socorro, Taos, and Valencia.

10. Antonia Garra is executed in San Diego after being convicted of leading an Indian revolution.

13. The 300-ton schooner *Captain Lincoln* runs aground 50 miles beyond its destination, Port Orford, Oregon. Much of the army wares she carries is rescued for an ongoing surplus sale.

15. Charles Pickett begins publishing The *Western American,* a weekly newspaper, in San Francisco.

16. The Tabernacle, with a seating capacity of almost 3,000, is completed in Salt Lake City.

23. The Osage chief George White Hair, 48 (?), dies of pneumonia in St. Paul, Kansas.

24–February 19. Three companies of the 2nd Dragoons battle Apaches near Laguna, on New Mexico's Jornado del Muerto in the Fra Cristobal Range. Five enlisted men are reported killed and no Apache deaths are recorded.

29. A telegraph dispatch to St. Louis from Parkville, Missouri, reports that a trading party of Delawares had arrived with "a quantity of gold dust." The Indians sold their dust but then refused an offer of $1,000 to tell where they had found it.

Also in January 1852:

A party of friendly Otoes discovers the artist Heinrich B. Möllhausen still surviving at what he calls "Sandy Hill Creek." The Indians will take him to the Missouri and the new settlement of Bethlehem.

FEBRUARY

3. The *Missouri Republican* reports that many Delaware Indians were slain in a trading meeting with Comanches.

5. Francis X. Aubry arrives in Independence.

6. The infantry under Captain I. B. Richardson battles the Apaches near Fort Webster, New Mexico. Three soldiers are killed and one is wounded. No Apache losses are recorded.

10. The *El Paso* becomes the first steamboat to reach Weston, Missouri, this year.

14. Missouri's *Savannah Sentinel* predicts 100,000 people will pass through the state this year en route to California and Oregon.

■ Utah's legislature requests that Congress provide the territory with telegraph and railroad service.

15. The first gold discovery in Montana is made by a Mr. Benetsee near Stevensville.
16. Word reaches St. Louis that 50 Potawatomis have died of smallpox. Today, Reverend S. M. Irvin writes: "The Ioway Nation has diminished over one half since this mission was first commenced. There are now not over 400 living souls of 830 the number of the Nation 15 years ago. Of six chiefs then living and acting, but one survives."
22. Four infantry companies and one dragoon company under Major S. P. Heintzelman arrive at Camp Independence at the Colorado River's Yuma Crossing to rebuild in the wake of the recent Indian attack (November 11, 1851). The new structure will become Fort Yuma, and Louis Jaeger will build another ferryboat.
26. A military reservation is created in San Diego.
29. John Calhoun writes of the Apache raid taking place in New Mexico: "the Indians have become bolder and bolder, and . . . we receive daily information of new outrages and murders committed by them. . . . An escort no longer affords any protection."

Also in February 1852:

Roy Bean is arrested in San Diego for participating in a duel.

Crawford School, an institution for Quapaw Indians in Kansas run by Methodist Episcopals, closes.

Kennekuk, a Kickapoo prophet, dies of smallpox in Leavenworth County.

Rain Walker, an Iowa chief, dies of smallpox in Doniphan County.

White Cloud, a former chief of the Iowas, dies of smallpox in Doniphan County.

MARCH

1. Three Michigan men arrive on foot in a blizzard at Fort Kearny.
■ Francis X. Aubry departs Independence for Santa Fe with his first wagon train of the year.
3. The following counties are created in Utah: Davis (named after the Mormon battalion captain Daniel C. Davis), Iron, Juab, Sanpete (named after the Indian chief San Pitch), Tooele (named after the Indian chief Tuilla), Utah (named after the Ute Indians), Washington, and Weber (named after John G. Weber, a trapper under General William Ashley).
5. Indians attack a herd guard on the east bank of the Colorado River near Camp Yuma, California. Five soldiers are killed in the ensuing battle with the First Dragoons.

DOC HOLLIDAY
1852–NOVEMBER 8, 1887

1852: Holliday is born in Georgia.

1862: He migrates with his family to a farm near Valdosta, Georgia.

1868: He is possibly involved in a plot to blow up a federal courthouse.

1872: Holliday practices dentistry in Atlanta upon graduation from the Pennsylvania College of Dental Surgery.

1873: He is diagnosed with tuberculosis.

1874: He opens a dental practice in Dallas, Texas. Holliday charges $3 per extraction and promises in a newspaper ad, "where satisfaction is not given, money will be refunded."

1875: He is jailed for wounding a saloon keeper. He kills another who had accused him of cheating at faro.

1877: He travels to Fort Griffin, Texas, and becomes involved with the prostitute "Big Nose" Katie Elder. He meets Wyatt Earp. Holliday disembowels Edward Bailey following another accusation of cheating. He relocates to Dodge City.

1880: Holliday arrives in Tombstone, Arizona, where he is reunited with Earp and Elder.

1881: Rumors fly that Holliday robbed the Benson-Tombstone stagecoach. He assists the Earps at the Gunfight at the O. K. Corral.

1882: He assists Wyatt Earp in avenging the attacks on Virgil and Morgan Earp.

1883: He gambles in Deadwood.

1884: Holliday shoots a Leadville bartender during an argument over a $5 loan.

1886: The *New York Sun* reports that he has killed 30 men. When asked about it, he replies: "I claim to have been a benefactor to the country."

1887: He checks into a sanatorium for the treatment of tuberculosis in Glenwood Springs, Colorado, and dies shortly thereafter at the age of 35.

10. The Perry brothers of Missouri advertise a passenger wagon train to California; the $150 fare includes 50 pounds of baggage.

17. John Randolph Benton, 22, the only son of Colonel Thomas Hart Benton, dies in St. Louis.

18. Contract mail carriers report their quickest trip yet from Santa Fe to Independence: 17 days.

■ Wells, Fargo and Company, is organized at New York's Astoria House as a joint stock association with an initial capital of $300,000. It will begin operations in the California gold country. Henry Wells and William G. Fargo had started American Express with John Butterfield in 1850. When the board of directors balked at the new project, Wells and Fargo gathered seven financial backers for to-day's meeting.

21. Although a birth record does not exist, John Henry Holliday, who will earn fame as the gunfighter-dentist Doc Holliday, is baptized in Griffin, Georgia. His parents are Major Henry B. and Alice Jane McKey Holliday.

APRIL

1. Hubert Howe Bancroft, 20, arrives in gold-crazy San Francisco by boat via Panama with a shipment of books to sell.

2. Abigail Scott, the 17-year-old future voting rights activist, departs Illinois with her family in a wagon train heading for Oregon.

8. Kansas City is the place for one to start a western sojourn, according to ads in the *Missouri Republican* that read:

KANSAS, MO.! CALIFORNIA! OREGON!
Aubry, Messervy, Huston, Kit Carson, and all the celebrated voyagers, invariably select Kansas as their starting point.

17. The author David W. Cartwright begins a western sojourn at St. Joseph with a party of 33 from Wisconsin. "A Tramp to California in 1852" will be the title of a chapter in his *Natural History of Western Wild Animals.*

19. A U.S. mail stagecoach arrives in Independence, having left Santa Fe on April 1.

■ The California Historical Society is founded.

21. According to the *St. Joseph Gazette:* "Every boat that arrives at our wharf, is crowded with California and Oregon emigrants. . . . Several hundred have landed at this place by water and overland, and still they come."

22. Captain Randolph B. Marcy and troops depart Fort Washita, northwest of present Durant, Oklahoma, to explore the Upper Red River.

23. Edwin Charles Markham, the future poet laureate of Oregon ("The Man with the Hoe"), is born in Oregon City.

24. The Missouri *Savannah Sentinel* observes, "The rush to California has now commenced in earnest."

29. The pioneer Lodisa Frizzell, in St. Joseph preparing for the California trek, notes that "200 Indians of the Pawtawattimees & Winnewbagoes came down the street" before moving on to Kansas.

30. The first emigrant wagon train of the season is seen at Fort Kearny.

Also in April 1852:

A measles epidemic spreads through the Osage Mission in Neosho County, Kansas, after a terminally ill Quapaw arrives. Some 45 students at the boarding school become ill in the first four days; 11 boys and one girl die.

The Reelfoot Williams gang stops the Nevada City coach and relieves the express box of $7,500. A posse kills three of the bandits, but Richard H. Barter, aka "Rattlesnake Dick," escapes.

Roy Bean, in a San Diego jail for duelling, escapes. He will resurface in San Gabriel and assist his brother Josh in running the Headquarters Saloon.

MAY

1. Martha "Calamity" Jane Canary is born in Princeton, Missouri, the daughter of Robert and Charlotte Canary.

7. In his *Autobiography,* the pioneer Theodore E. Potter describes what he saw on this day, six miles out of St. Joseph: "It was a grand sight to look over the prairie as far as the eye could discern and see the new white-covered wagons and tents clustered here and there. . . . At least 10,000 emigrants were camped within a distance of ten miles of this point."

8. Francis X. Aubry reaches Missouri with his second wagon train of the season from Santa Fe.

15. Jotham Meeker estimates that 800 wagons and 10,000 head of cattle have passed the Ottawa Baptist Mission, in present Kansas, this season. Today alone, some 30 wagons and 300 head of cattle were seen.

16. Fort Kearny reports the passing of 1,400 wagons so far this season.

19. The *St. Joseph Gazette* estimates that "35 or 40" immigrants are suffering from cholera near the city.

20. The formation of Wells Fargo and Company is announced in the pages of the *New York Times.* The company's board includes the following: Henry Wells, William G. Fargo, Johnston Livingston, Eli-

CALAMITY JANE
MAY 1, 1852–AUGUST 1, 1903

1852: Martha Jane Canary is born in Princeton, Missouri.

1865: She relocates with her family to Montana. Legend states that her parents relocated to Salt Lake City and died, at which time Jane was sent to live with various Utah families.

1869: She moves to Wyoming and works for a railroad.

1870: She befriends—possibly marries—Wild Bill Hickok.

1875: Dressed as a man, she joins Dr. Walter Jenney's geological expedition into the Black Hills.

1876: Jane scouts for General George Crook.

1885: She claims a marriage to a Clinton Burke, although no official record exists.

1893: She tours with Buffalo Bill's Wild West Show.

1896: Jane is seen in Minnesota in the show produced by Kohl and Middleton.

1901: She appears at the Pan-American Exposition in Buffalo, New York.

1903: Jane dies in Terry, near Deadwood, South Dakota. Her tombstone reads "Calamity Jane" and, in smaller letters, "Mrs. M. E. Burke."

jah Williams, Edwin B. Morgan, James McKay, Alpheus Reynolds, Alex M. C. Smith, and Henry D. Rice. Morgan is president and the company capitalized at $300,000 on March 18.

21. A scout arriving at Fort Kearny reports 30 cases of cholera and smallpox "on the St. Joseph and Independence roads."

25. An observer at Fort Kearny reports the passing of 2,870 wagons thus far this season.

▪ The *Evening Journal* is established in San Francisco.

26. Lodisa Frizzell's wagon train reaches Fort Kearny. She reports 2,657 wagons thus far and adds: "I do not think they can keep a correct account, & I do not think they try to get the number of those that pass on the north side of the river."

▪ Seth Doty, writing at Fort Kearny, observes that the trail of wagons is 700 miles long as of tonight, and is moving 15 or 20 miles a day.

Also in May 1852:

John Calhoun, New Mexico Indian agent, dies near Kansas, Missouri.

JUNE

1. In San Francisco, the newspaper *L'Echo du Pacifique* begins publishing only in French.

10. Andrew Goodyear reaches Fort Kearny and estimates that 7,000 wagons, with 30,000 people, have passed there so far this year.

11. Arriving in Independence, the trader Josiah Collins estimates that 5,325 wagons, 16,362 men, 3,242 women, and 4,266 children (total number of people, 23,870), as well as 59,392 head of cattle, 10,523 sheep, 4,606 mules, 6,538 horses, 150 turkeys, 4 ducks, 2 guinea fowls, and 1 hog, are making the trek to California this season. He counts 70 fresh graves.

16. The *St. Joseph Gazette* reports: "The emigrants are all gone, with the exception of a few straggling parties."

19. In a report to the *Sacramento Union,* Andrew Goodyear says that "much sickness existed among the emigration; we met some 400 wagons returning on account of sickness; one company of 72 men had lost 24 out of their company."

Also in June 1852:

The first Wells Fargo agent in California, Samuel P. Carter, arrives on the *Oregon.*

National Headlines/June 1852:

6. DEMOCRATS NOMINATE PIERCE ON 49TH BALLOT

JULY

3. An act of Congress authorizes the construction of a U.S. Mint in San Francisco.

▪ The first Wells Fargo advertisement appears in the *Alta California,* saying the company will "undertake a General Express Forwarding Agency and Commission." Offices are at 114 Montgomery Street.

4. The 2nd Infantry and Indians fight at the headwaters of the San Joaquin River in California. One trooper is wounded.

7. The trooper wounded on the San Joaquin River dies.

10. On board the *Tennessee* as it arrives in San Francisco is Reuben W. Washburn, who will handle banking for Wells Fargo. The ship suffered 11 cholera deaths in transit from New York.

22. Captain Randolph B. Marcy, having visited Wichita and Waco Indian villages in the region around present Rush Springs, Oklahoma, writes in his jour-

nal of the cultivation of "corn, pumpkins, beans, peas, and melons." He adds, "These people have no ploughs, or other agricultural implements, but a small hoe, with which they prepare the ground for the reception of the seed, and do all other necessary work in its cultivations; yet the prolific soil gives them bountiful returns."

27. The mercury hits 127 degrees in Salt Lake City.
29. Commodore Perry Owen, who will serve as a sheriff in the 1880s in Arizona, is born in Tennessee.
31. The *Oregon* sails from San Francisco, transporting the following amounts of gold: $600,000 for Adams and Company; $682,014 for Page, Bacon; and $21,710 for Wells Fargo.

Also in July 1852:
John Hawkins Clark writes in his journal, *Overland to the Gold Fields,* about his stay in Utah:

I called at a house where three women belonged to one man. These women were all young and had children. The father of this young brood is a yankee from the state of Maine. . . . Being a shrewd kind of a fellow he had located a farm in this neighborhood and, as he told me, was trying the experiment of building up a farm and raising a family. He has now a good farm well improved, and well stocked with cattle; three wives and nine children and not a soul on the place over twenty-seven years of age. If his 'experiment' is not a success, I do not think it is his fault.

In negotiations, Mangas Coloradas agrees to peace with the United States but not with Mexico. This situation will persist for eight years, during which time Mangas will align himself with his son-in-law, Cochise.

John R. Bartlett writes about Tubac, Arizona's oldest white settlement, founded as a Spanish frontier colony in 1752: "As for this God-forsaken place, when I have said that it contains a few dilapidated buildings and one old church, with a miserable population, I have said about all."

AUGUST

1. Agent Thomas Fitzpatrick receives $30,000 in goods to turn over to tribes that signed the Treaty of Fort Laramie in 1851.
■ The Zion M. E. Church is established in San Francisco.
2. California state senator James Denver slays *Alta California* editor Edward Gilbert in a duel that grew out of a political disagreement. The newspaper had printed a series of editorials criticizing California governor Bigler about a rescue mission to a wagon train of emigrants; as leader of the train, Denver felt duty-bound to answer.

The two meet in person for the first time at dawn at Oak Grove, near Sacramento. Gilbert fires quickly—the bullet plows into the dirt a few yards in front of his target. Denver smiles, then discharges his weapon in the air. Gilbert is given the option to apologize, but he refuses. Denver is heard to say, "I have no intention of standing here all day to be shot at." At the next call to fire, Denver's aim is true. "My God," he reportedly says, "I have killed the best man in California for that infernal Bigler." Two hours later, Denver takes his seat in the senate.

3. Another battle takes place at Yuma's Crossing as some 800 warriors attack Fort Yuma. Major S. P. Heintzelman reports victory.
6. At Fort Kearny, Captain Henry W. Wharton writes, "The great emigration of the present season is past and gone."
17. A contract is issued to John Duff and Company of Boston to build a 200-mile railroad between Hannibal and St. Joseph; completion time is scheduled for four years.
18. James Robinson is executed in San Diego for stealing a rowboat.
24. Captain William Steele and the 2nd Dragoons set out from Ft. Leavenworth on a march to New Mexico.
25. Francis X. Aubry arrives in Independence with his third wagon train of the year from Santa Fe.
■ Yuma Indians and the 2nd Infantry clash at the junction of the Colorado and Gila Rivers in California. Two troopers are wounded.
29. The Mormons admit to practicing polygamy when the revelation on the celestial law of marriage, dated 1843, is published by Brigham Young.

National Headlines/August 1852:
23. *UNCLE TOM'S CABIN* PUBLISHED

SEPTEMBER

3. A delegation of Sac and Fox Indians led by Keokuk visits the Indian Bureau in Washington, D. C.
■ In Arizona, the schooner *Capacity* arrives at the Colorado River with her cargo: a steam engine, a boiler, and enough lumber to build a steamboat.
4. Residents of Salt Lake City enter into a treaty with the chiefs of the Utes and Shoshones.
7. Thomas Jefferson Sutherland of the Iowa Mission, in Nebraska Territory, dies of typhus.
9. Orion Clemens changes the name of his newspaper to the *Daily Journal.*
28. The wagon train transporting Abigail Scott arrives in Salem, Oregon. On the trip, her mother died of cholera and her little brother of dysentery.

Also in September 1852:

Francis X. Aubry leaves Missouri on what will be his last trip on the Santa Fe Trail.

The future poet Joaquin Miller, 15, arrives in Oregon with his family, having traveled the Oregon Trail from Indiana.

OCTOBER

1. Of the measles epidemic, Indian agent W. J. J. Morrow writes: "The Osages were unusually sickly last winter and spring. It is estimated by many that not less than one thousand have died within the last twelve months."

14. The *New York Times* quotes an Oregon newspaper: "The emigration to Oregon this year is very large, 186 wagons having passed the 'Gate' on the other side of the mountains, and with them 750 persons, of whom 160 were females and 609 males. They had 1,000 head of cattle and 400 head of horses and mules."

21. Near St. Mary's Mission on the Potawatomi reservation in Nebraska Territory, citizens hold a meeting to set up a congressional election.

28. The San Franciscan William Walker attempts to conquer a part of Mexico.

Also in October 1852:

Wells Fargo announces semimonthly carriage service to Portland.

NOVEMBER

2. A catastrophic fire in Sacramento destroys 2,500 buildings—75 percent of the city—and does $5 million in damage. The headline of the *Alta California* reads: "SACRAMENTO IN ASHES!" Six Lives Known to Be Lost! Dreadful Destitution Among the Sufferers!"

3. Captain Lorenzo Sitgreaves and his survey party begins a journey on which they will travel the Little Colorado River, note Grand Falls, and then travel by way of the Colorado River to Fort Yuma. On the way, they will survey the Zuni, Little Colorado, and Rio Colorado Indians.

23. The water level of California's Lake Merced drops 30 feet after an earthquake-like shock.

24. Commodore Matthew Perry sails for Japan from San Francisco on the *Susquehanna.*

Also in November 1852:

French equipment for processing sugar beets arrives in Salt Lake City via wagon train.

National Headlines/November 1852:

2. PIERCE DEFEATS SCOTT FOR THE PRESIDENCY

DECEMBER

3. The first Colorado River steamboat, *Uncle Sam,* arrives at Fort Yuma.

6. Brigham Young, 60, is sealed to Mary Oldfield, his 46th bride.

19. The literary weekly *Golden Era* publishes its first issue in San Francisco.

■ On the Wyandot reservation in Kansas City, John Coon, Jr., is found guilty of murdering Curtis Punch.

23. The Chinese Theater opens in San Francisco.

24. The first locomotive to go into service in Texas is the *General Sherman.*

27. Wells Fargo announces additional service from San Francisco to New Orleans. In its first year of operation, the company has 12 California offices.

31. The richest year of the Gold Rush ends with California's gold production reaching an all-time high of $81.3 million. Production will level off to between $42 million and $47 million until 1862, and then drop to the $18-million-a-year range until well into the 1880s.

Also in 1852:

California's state census shows the population has risen to 264,000, only 22,000 of whom are women. San Francisco is the largest city, with 34,776 residents, up from 459 in 1847. The Indian population in California has dropped from 100,000 to 85,000 since 1849. This year, 18,000 Chinese immigrants arrived via San Francisco, 17 of them women.

One hundred thousand buffalo robes were received in St. Louis.

Tahlequah becomes the first incorporated town in what will become Oklahoma when it is incorporated under Cherokee tribal law.

The city of San Francisco purchases the Jenny Lind Theater for $200,000 and begins converting it into a courthouse and city hall.

The San Francisco customs house, which recorded 2,716 immigrants in 1851, records 18,400 in 1852.

The Bloomfield School opens in Indian Territory. It is the first missionary school for Chickasaw girls.

Flying Hawk, an Oglala Sioux, is born near present Rapid City, South Dakota. He will participate in his first wagon train attack at age 10. At age 20, he will lead a raiding party on the Crows that will capture 139 horses.

Jules Beril builds a shack at a site that will become Julesburg, Colorado.

While working with his brother William for the *Hannibal Journal,* Samuel Clemens, 16, sees his first work of fiction, "The Dandy Frightening the Squatter," appear in a Boston magazine.

Andrew S. Hallidie, the inventor of the cable car, arrives in San Francisco from London.

The recently widowed Elizabeth Ostrander Harte remarries and moves from Brooklyn to California. Her 16-year-old son, Francis Bret Harte, remains behind for the time being to work odd jobs, usually for lawyers or banks.

During the bitter winter, the black Washington pioneer George Washington Bush turns down a Seattle firm's lucrative offer for his surplus wheat and gives it to the hardest-hit settlers on Puget Sound.

Sixteen Czechoslovak families migrate to Austin County, Texas, to begin a town in what had previously been territory occupied by Germans.

The future general George Crook graduates near the bottom of his class at West Point.

1853

"You are now 640 miles from Independence,
and it is discouraging to tell you that you have not yet
travelled one-third of the long road to Oregon."

—*J. M. Shively, Route and distances to Oregon and California, with a description of watering places, crossings, dangerous Indians . . .*

JANUARY

2. The U.S. Land Commission opens hearings in San Francisco to examine land claims made under old "Spanish grants."

12. Willamette University is chartered in Salem, Oregon; it initially opened as the Oregon Institute in 1844, the first college on the Pacific coast.

16. The agricultural newspaper *California Farmer* begins publishing in San Francisco.

18. John Coon, Jr., a convicted murderer, is executed by a firing squad in Kansas City.

25. The Mormon missionaries O. Spencer and J. Houtz arrive in Berlin, Germany.

Also in January 1853:

U.S. Boundary Commissioner J. R. Bartlett departs Texas to return to the East. The boundary survey is suspended pending clarification and more negotiations between the United States and Mexico.

FEBRUARY

2. The Mormon missionaries O. Spencer and J. Houtz are banished from Berlin.

5. Henry Wells arrives in San Francisco on the *Oregon* to inspect his booming new business, Wells Fargo.

6. The *Tennessee,* with 1,600 passengers, runs onto rocks just north of the Golden Gate. The Adams Express messenger Thomas Gihon receives special accolades for helping women and children off the boat before asking whether he could remove his 14 trunks of packages and money.

7. Andrew Female College is chartered in Huntsville, Texas.

12. The *Alta California* reports on San Francisco's homeless: "There has never been so deplorable an exhibition of mendicancy in our streets as may be witnessed daily at this time . . . hundreds of destitute men and scores of women and children besieging the pockets of socity in publick and private, indoors and out."

14. John Hicks, 80, the "last hereditary chief of the Wyandot nation," dies on the tribe's reservation in present Kansas.

■ Ground is consecrated for the Temple in Salt Lake City.

15. The *Curiosity Shop,* a humorous weekly, is first published in San Francisco.

16. In one of the Pacific coast's worst shipwrecks, the *Independence* goes down off Santa Margarita Island, Baja California, drowning 300 passengers.

■ The biggest gold shipment to date leaves San Francisco—$4 million on three ships, the *Brother Jonathan,* the *Panama,* and the *California.*

21. The Coinage Act authorizes the minting of $3 gold pieces and reduces the silver that will be contained in coins of less than $1.

22. Washington University is chartered in St. Louis.

Also in February 1853:

The artist Albert Bierstadt, 23, spends the year studying in Düsseldorf.

The entrepreneur Levi Strauss, 23, who at first tried to earn a living in San Francisco by selling canvas tents, takes his unsold canvas to a tailor and has sturdy trousers fashioned. He begins producing "waist-high overalls," and in 1870 he will begin importing tough cotton cloth called *serge de Nimes* from Nimes, France.

MARCH

2. Congress divides Oregon Territory: the northern part, above the Columbia River and the 46th parallel, is designated Washington Territory, and Isaac Ingalls Stevens is its first governor.

3. Congress approves $150,000 for a railroad survey, to be conducted by the War Department, of all lands from the Mississippi River to the Pacific.

4. In his inaugural speech, President Franklin Pierce voices his support for the Compromise of 1850.

6. John Henry Tunstall, a Lincoln County War participant, is born in Middlesex County, England.

17. The *Wide West,* a literary newspaper, begins publishing in San Francisco.

24. First Lieutenant E. Russell of the 4th Infantry is killed in action in a skirmish with Indians near the Red Bluffs in California.

26. The *Occidental Messenger* reports: "Emigrants for California and Oregon are beginning to arrive by land and by river."

31. Louisiana State University is chartered in Alexandria.

APRIL

6. The cornerstone of the new Temple is laid in Salt Lake City.

8. Exploration for a rail route between the 47th and 49th parallels begins.

17. A U.S. Marine hospital is established at San Francisco's Presidio.

20. Four wagons and 25 horses take a company of 12 led by Isaac Evans from St. Joseph to Sacramento.

22. The steamboat *Kansas,* heading for Council Bluffs, strikes a snag and sinks near "Iowa Point." The cargo is a total loss, but all lives are spared. The boat had recently been purchased for $7,000.

■ Fort Scott is abandoned and its troops are directed to Fort Leavenworth.

28. The Chinese newspaper *Golden Hill News* begins publishing in San Francisco.

Also in April 1853:

An Adams Express agent is robbed of $7,000 by seven men at Mormon Island in gold country, prompting the company to post a $2,000 reward.

The *St. Joseph Gazette* reports that emigrants are "not as numerous" as they were last year.

William Tecumseh Sherman, having recently resigned his commission, arrives in San Francisco, where he will manage the Lucas, Turner and Company branch bank.

MAY

1. San Francisco's first Queen of May is Emma Jane Swasey

3. Wells Fargo's capital stock increases from $300,000 to $500,000.

6–7. Missouri senator Thomas Hart Benton speaks on the advantages of a central route for the transcontinental railroad in Kansas City, Independence, and Westport.

7. A major sheep drive leaves for California from Keokuk, Iowa. Benjamin and Thomas Flint and Llewellyn Bixby take 1,880 sheep, 11 yokes of oxen, 4 horses, 3 dogs, and 2 cows. Eight months later they will arrive and sell 900 wethers for $16 a head.

8. The head of the bandit Joaquin Murieta is displayed in a saloon in Stockton, California.

10. Contracts are let for the first 25 miles of the western end of the Hannibal–St. Joseph railroad.

12. The head of the bandit Joaquin Murieta is pickled in whisky and sent on a macabre national tour with the hand of Manuel "Three-Fingered Jack." The head will be lost in the San Francisco earthquake of 1906.

18. The *St. Joseph Gazette* estimates that 10,000 head of cattle have been driven across the river in that city, heading for California. It also predicts that 100,000 head will do the same during the spring season.

19. James Gadsden, representing the United States, begins talks with Mexico to settle the question of New

---

JOHN WESLEY HARDIN
MAY 26, 1853–AUGUST 19, 1895

1853: Hardin is born in Bonham, Texas.

1864: He knifes a classmate in an argument over a girl at Sumpter, Texas.

1868: He kills his first man, an ex-slave called
(continued)

Mage, for "shaking a stick" at him. Hardin shoots Mage with a Colt 44. He becomes a fugitive and reportedly slays three troopers who come after him.

1869: With his 19-year-old cousin Simp Dixon, he opens fire on a camp of "Yankee soldiers," killing two before he escapes. He kills James Bradley after a poker game in Towash, Texas.

1870: Texas governor Edmund Davis announces that Harding should be "killed, jailed, or hanged."

1871: On the Chisolm Trail, from Texas to Kansas, Hardin murders a Mexican trail boss. He leaves Abilene, Kansas, after shooting a man, who was keeping him awake with snoring, through a thin hotel wall. He travels to Gonzales County, Texas.

1872: Hardin weds Jane Bowen. He shoots a police officer dead and then is wounded in the leg by a posse in the ensuing chase. Jailed, he escapes by sawing through the prison's bars.

1873: In Texas, he participates in a family feud between the Taylors and the Suttons. He blasts Jack Helm, a Sutton supporter, with a shotgun.

1874: Following a horse race and while celebrating his 21st birthday, Hardin kills Deputy Sheriff Charles Webb in Comanche, Texas.

1875: He runs a saloon in Gainesville, Florida. He works briefly in Alabama in the cattle trade, then returns to Florida.

1877: He is arrested in Florida by Ranger John Armstrong and sentenced to 25 years in Rusk Prison in Texas. Since 1868, Hardin has killed more than 20 men.

1894: Hardin is released from prison. He studies law and sets up a practice in Gonzales.

1895: He weds Callie Lewis but then leaves her a few hours after the ceremony. He drifts to El Paso, where he is assassinated, shot in the back by John Selman while standing at the bar of the Acme Saloon.

Mexico's southern border, in preparation for the construction of a Texas-to-California railroad.

26. The future outlaw John Wesley Hardin is born in Bonham, Texas.

31. Fort Kearny's estimates of travelers to the West thus far this year: 4,937 men, 1,900 women, and 2,600 children in 2,084 wagons and driving 81,660 cattle.

Also in May 1853:

Abigail Scott weds Ben C. Duniway in Salem, Oregon Territory. At her request, the word "obey" is scratched from the traditional vows.

THE LOLA MONTEZ VISIT
MAY 1853

The news that Lola Montez, Europe's quintessential bad girl, was heading for San Francisco created an immediate sensation. Lonely gold miners fantasized over the world-class beauty. One newspaper compared the visit to "the application of fire to combustible matter."

Lola's reputation was well deserved. Born Maria Dolores Eliza Gilbert in Limerick, Ireland, in 1818, she adopted a new name to give credence to her Spanish dance act. By age 28, she had finished with two husbands and a host of lovers that included Franz Liszt and Alexander Dumas. As a danseuse, she had shocked Paris by lifting her leg and tossing a perfumed garter to the crowd. In 1846, she was in the royal bed of Bavaria's King Ludwig I as the Countess of Landsfelt.

In May 1853, "the most widely known and thoroughly discussed woman of the decade" sailed into San Francisco Bay. At 6:00 A.M. she was greeted by 5,000 miners. One newspaper observed, "she is the very comet of her sex."

At the Russ House Hotel, she received her 50 trunks of luggage. For five days she rested and delighted in the uproar. Said the *San Francisco Herald:* "She sways hearts and potentates and editors and public opinion . . . she is welcomed—so she permits herself to be seen, admired, sung, courted, and gone mad over here as elsewhere."

Her debut was at the American Theatre, playing Lady Teazle in Sheridan's *The School*
(continued)

(continued)

for Scandal. The second night, she danced *La Tarantula,* appearing in short skirts and flesh-colored tights. Lola writhed like a madwoman, jumping and jiggling, flinging fake arachnids to the floor and stamping on them. Her next performance was a confused *Lola Montez in Bavaria,* in which she played herself as a serious statesperson rather than as a king's whore.

Montez argued with her agent during a rehearsal, beat him soundly, and followed by firing him in public. In a calmer mood, she organized benefits for the Hebrew Benevolent Society and the Fireman's Fund. When it was announced she had raised $30,000 for the latter, the infatuated firefighters threw their helmets on stage in adoration. Before her departure, she threw a lavish party and married the Irish journalist Patrick Purdy Hull, whom she had met on her long sea voyage.

From San Francisco it was on to San Diego, another city conquered by her spider dance. When a local editor suggested she had paid her audience for its enthusiastic response, she replied: "You may choose between my dueling pistols or take your choice of a pill out of a pill box. Once shall be poisoned and the other not, and the chances are even." The editor declined.

Lola attempted to settle down in Grass Valley but soon tired of California as well as of her current husband. In 1855, she sailed for Australia and new horizons.

JUNE

3. Central College is chartered in Pella, Iowa.
16. The *Present and Future,* a daily newspaper, begins publishing in San Francisco.
27. Camp Centre, on the Republican Fork of the Kansas River, is renamed Fort Riley.

Also in June 1853:
Captain J. W. Gunnison explores in the Saguache Mountains of Colorado; his discoveries will prove invaluable to the railroads.
Percival Lowe will write of a Fort Leavenworth-to-Fort Atkinson excursion made this month by Company B, 1st dragoons, in his *Five Years a Dragoon* (1906).
Samuel Clemens, 17, leaves Hannibal for St. Louis,

where he goes to work as a compositor for the *Evening News.*

JULY

4. The *Sacramento Union* hails the party led by Isaac Evans as the "first of the great overland army of the present season."
7. Samuel P. Carter, California's first Wells Fargo agent, returns to the East Coast. He will be replaced by Colonel William Pardee.
24. A force of 800 Pawnees defeats some 1,000 Cheyennes and their allies approximately 60 miles southwest of Fort Kearny. The Pawnees report taking 25 scalps (and killing many more opponents) and 170 ponies.
25. Richard King, 29, and Juan Mendiola shake hands on the deal in which King acquires 15,500 acres of Texas for $300, or for slightly less than two cents an acre. King had researched the grasslands of present Nueces County on the Santa Gertrudis Creek, and found that the Mendiola family owned them under ancient Spanish grants.
26. The first issue of the *Industrial Luminary,* a weekly, is published in Parkville, Missouri.
▪ San Francisco's Music Hall opens.
27. U.S. Commissioner Thomas Fitzpatrick signs a peace treaty with members of the Comanche, Kiowa, and Plains Apache tribes at Fort Atkinson, Kansas; the treaty provides for the United States to make annual payments of $18,000 in goods for 10 years.

Also in July 1853:
San Francisco's Chinatown has a population of approximately 25,000.

National Headlines/July 1853:
14. PERRY IN JAPAN

AUGUST

4. The Ladies' Protection and Relief Society is organized in San Francisco.
12. The steamship *Polar Star* sets a record on the St. Louis-to-St. Joseph run—2 days, 20 hours.
14. Francis X. Aubry and a party of adventurers in Arizona are attacked by an estimated 200 Indians. Writes Aubry: "We shot them down so fast with our Colt's revolvers, that we soon produced confusion among them and put them to flight. We owe our lives to these fire-arms, the best that were ever invented, and now brought, by successive improvements, to a state of perfection."
15. Fort Kearny's final tally of settlers traveling west in

1853: 9,909 men, 2,252 women, and 3,058 children (total: 15,219) in 3,708 wagons. Also: 105,792 cattle, 5,477 horses, 2,190 mules, 48,495 sheep. Of the settlers, states the *Missouri Republican,* 1,661 males, 761 females, and 1,085 children are heading for Oregon.

24. Oregon's first governor, Joseph Lane, defeats a band of Indians at Table Rock, on the Rogue River near Jacksonville. Captain B. R. Alden is wounded.

29. Salt Lake City's council approves a protective "Spanish Wall" around the city; it will be as much as 12 feet tall in some places, 6 feet thick at the base, and some 9 miles in length.

31. Samuel Clemens leaves St. Louis for New York to work as a printer.

Also in August 1853:

John Charles Frémont's fifth expedition is organized. His route to the Rockies will approximate the future course of the Denver and Rio Grande Railroad's narrow-gauge track from Salida to Grand Junction, Colorado.

SEPTEMBER

1. The Stevens Expedition, exploring a northern transcontinental rail route, arrives at Fort Benton.

2. The Wells Fargo board learns its company has made a 40 percent or $30,000 profit in a little more than a year of operation.

11. San Francisco's first electric telegraph is opened, connecting San Francisco's Merchant Exchange with Point Lobos.

15. Russell, Waddell and Company, Alexander Majors, and J. B. Yager sign a contract at Fort Leavenworth to transport freight to Fort Union, New Mexico, at a rate of $16 per 100 pounds.

21. In Hannibal, Missouri, Orion Clemens edits his last issue of the *Daily Journal.*

22. John Charles Frémont's fifth and last exploration of the West starts from a camp near Westport, Missouri.

■ Fort Atkinson is abandoned and the remaining soldiers depart for Fort Riley.

28. The first temporary military post in Montana Territory is Cantonment Stevens in the Bitterroot Valley.

Also in September 1853:

Wells Fargo buys the express company of Alexander Todd.

OCTOBER

1. San Francisco's Olympic Theater opens.

8. William Walker of Yuba County, California, and a party of 45 prepare to sail on the *Carolina* to

Guaymas, in Mexico's Sonora state, supposedly to stop Apache raids into California.

17. Colonel William Walker and a party of 75 begin sailing from San Francisco to Lower California to establish a proslavery republic.

22. Minister James Gadsden is given the go-ahead to negotiate a purchase by the United States from Mexico of land south of the Gila River, including all of Lower California.

24. Indians and the 1st Dragoons clash near the Illinois River in Oregon; two soldiers are killed.

25. From John Charles Frémont's memoirs: "Went to Uniontown and nooned [had lunch]. This is a street of log-cabins. Nothing to be had here. . . . Lots of John Barleycorn which the men about were consuming."

26. At 6:00 A.M., the camp of Lieutenant J. W. Gunnison on Utah's Sevier River is attacked by Indians. Gunnison and a party of eight, including the botanist M. Creutzfeldt, are slain.

27. Samuel Clemens is in Philadelphia, "subbing in the *Inquirer* office."

30. John Charles Frémont's fifth expedition sights prairie fires in present Saline County, Kansas.

NOVEMBER

3. At La Paz, on the southern tip of present Baja California, the Walker expedition declares the Republic of Lower California.

23. James Henderson becomes the governor of Texas, an office he will occupy for 28 days.

25. Henry Tifft Gage, who will become the 20th governor of California (1899–1903), is born near Geneva, New York.

26. William Barclay "Bat" Masterson is born in County Rouville, Quebec, Canada. He is the second of seven children of Thomas and Catherine Masterson.

■ Colonel Edwin B. Morgan resigns as Wells Fargo president and is replaced by Danford N. Barney.

Also in November 1853:

Fort Supply is established by Mormons in Wyoming's Black's Fork Valley. Wyoming's first experiment in irrigation will occur at the fort before it is abandoned in 1857.

John Charles Frémont's fifth expedition arrives at Bent's Fort.

Since 1851, Sonora has reported some 500 residents killed in Apache raids allegedly directed by Mangas Coloradas.

DECEMBER

8. The *Honduras* is the last steamboat of the season to arrive in St. Louis.

BAT MASTERSON
NOVEMBER 26, 1853–OCTOBER 25, 1921

1853: Masterson is born in Quebec, Canada.

1867: After living in Canada, New York, and Illinois, he migrates with his parents to Wichita, Kansas.

1872: He leaves home with his brother Ed and grades roadbeds for the Atchison, Topeka, and Santa Fe Railroad in Dodge City.

1874: As a buffalo hunter, Masterson participates in the Battle of Adobe Walls in the Texas panhandle. He scouts for General Nelson Miles.

1876: He kills Sergeant King in a gunfight in a Texas saloon. He returns to Dodge City and will become a peace officer.

1877: Operating a saloon in Dodge City, Masterson is appointed deputy sheriff of Ford County, Kansas. That fall, he is elected sheriff of the county.

1878: His brother Ed is killed in a Dodge City gunfight.

1879: Masterson is appointed deputy U.S. marshal. He is later defeated in the election for sheriff.

1880: He drifts through Nebraska, Colorado, and New Mexico and resides in Kansas City.

1881: He works for Wyatt Earp at the Oriental Saloon in Tombstone. He ventures to Dodge City to assist his brother Jim in a conflict that turns into a gunfight.

1882: Masterson serves as town marshal of Trinidad, Colorado, and then promotes sporting events.

1883: He returns to Dodge City to participate in the "Dodge City War."

1884: He lives in Fort Worth, then Denver. He gambles and writes sports articles.

1891: Masterson manages a large gambling hall in Denver and weds Emma Walters.

1902: He moves to New York City and works as a sports columnist for the *Morning Telegraph.*

1921: Masterson dies while working at his desk at the *Morning Telegraph.*

24. In a disaster on the high seas, the *San Francisco* sinks en route to California; 240 of the 700 passengers and crew drown.

- San Francisco's Guillot's Theater opens.

25. San Francisco's Metropolitan Theater, the first to be lit by gas, opens.

28. In a race to California between express companies, Adams's horses are faster than those of Wells Fargo in delivering President Franklin Pierce's December 5 message to Congress.

30. Negotiations for the acquisition from Mexico of the southernmost portions of present Arizona and New Mexico are completed. The treaty, known as the Gadsden Purchase, is signed in Mexico City. The new land, 29,142,400 acres, is bought by the United States for $10 million. Mexico, currently under the regime of Santa Anna, is very willing to make the deal. For the United States, the major benefit is believed to be a railroad pass through the Rockies. The Civil War will prevent that from ever being realized, but in 1856 gold and silver will be discovered in the new territory.

31. The first dance held in Nevada occurs on New Year's Eve in Dayton, 10 miles east of Carson City.

Also in December 1853:

Fort Gibson, northeast of present Muskogee, Oklahoma, reports that since its establishment in 1824, 9 officers and 561 privates have been buried there.

San Francisco has 12 daily newspapers, 6 weeklies, and 2 tri-weeklies (one in French, the other in German).

Also in 1853:

The city of Berkeley, California, is founded.

Kit Carson is appointed Indian agent in Taos.

San Antonio has four free public schools in what is believed to be the first free school system in Texas.

About 100 Sac and Fox Indians, recently transplanted to Kansas, battle 1,000 plains warriors over buffalo hunting rights.

Pen Knife Sketches, or Chips of the Old Block is written by Alonzo Delano.

San Francisco's Kong Chow Temple is completed; it is the first Buddhist temple in the nation.

Lieutenant A. W. Whipple conducts a railroad survey along the 35th parallel. The artist Heinrich B. Möllhausen, who accompanies the crew, paints a view of Fort Smith, Arkansas.

Captain John W. Gunnison leads a U.S. survey for a possible transcontinental railroad route over Cochetopa Pass. After discovering and naming the Gunnison River, he moves on to Utah, where he is killed by Indians.

1854

"I love my wives . . . but to make a queen of one and peasants of the rest I have no such disposition. It is not the privilege of a woman to dictate the husband, and tell who or how many he shall take, or what he shall do with them when he gets them, but it is the duty of the woman to submit cheerfully."

—Brigham Young

JANUARY

1. The California Stage Company is organized, with a capital stock of $1 million and headquarters in Sacramento.

4. In Congress, Senator Stephen A. Douglas introduces a bill that would allow the question of slavery in the proposed Nebraska Territory to be put to a vote among the territory's population.

7. John C. Frémont and his party of 9 whites and 12 Delaware Indians arrive nearly starved at Parowan, in Utah.

11. Fort Bliss is established near El Paso, Texas.

13. Pacific University is chartered in Forest Grove, Oregon.

15. The first Protestant church in New Mexico Territory is dedicated in Santa Fe.

17. The Wells Fargo board of directors increases the company's working capital to $150,000. The San Francisco office moves to a new building at the corner of Montgomery and California streets.

■ Summit County is created in Utah.

18. William Walker establishes himself as president of the new "Republic of Sonora," which consists of the Mexican state of Sonora and Baja California.

■ The *St. Joseph Gazette* reports that Congress is considering splitting the large Nebraska Territory into three, to be named Nebraska, Kansas, and Cherokee.

■ Another Colorado River steamboat, the *General Jessup,* arrives at Yuma Crossing.

23. In Congress, Stephen Douglas introduces a bill that would divide Nebraska Territory into two, Kansas and Nebraska.

24. Lieutenants George Stoneman and John Park depart San Diego for Yuma Crossing, where they will survey a rail line to Doña Ana.

30. The ship *Golden Age* brings bad news to San Francisco—mercantile houses in the East are failing.

31. In Texas, an act establishing a uniform state school system is passed.

■ The Missouri River is frozen solid at St. Joseph; much foot traffic is reported on it.

FEBRUARY

11. The main streets of San Francisco are lit by coal gas.

15. Wells Fargo pays a dividend of 5 percent.

17. The *Alta California* reports that Wells Fargo has just shipped $30,000 on the steamer *California* via Panama, and $6,000 on the Nicaragua Steamship Company's *Brother Jonathan.*

22. The Rock Island line, of Illinois, becomes the first railroad to link the Atlantic Ocean with the Mississippi River.

23. Earl Fitzwilliam, a member of the British Parliament, arrives at Westport, Missouri, after wintering in Taos.

25. Sacramento becomes the capital of California.

MARCH

1. The first steamboat to arrive this year in St. Joseph from St. Louis is the *Polar Star,* having departed on February 21.

▪ The California Steam Navigation Company, a conglomerate of steamboat operators, is capitalized as a joint-stock company at $2 million.

▪ Well Fargo pays a dividend of 10 percent.

2. The *Alta California* reports that Wells Fargo has just shipped $60,800 on the *John L. Stephens,* as well as $63,100 on the *Sierra Nevada.*

5. Jicarilla Apaches and the 2nd Dragoons clash on New Mexico's Congillon River. Four soldiers are wounded and two are killed; no Apache casualties are recorded.

8. William Walker and 34 supporters surrender to military authorities in San Diego. Their new republic was rejected by the residents of Lower California and Sonora.

11. Dr. Willard Richards, editor of the *Deseret News,* dies in Salt Lake City.

12. Near Fort Arbuckle in Indian Territory, Lieutenant A. B. Tree and 20 enlisted men capture and kill a Kickapoo named Thunder, the alleged murderer of a Colonel Stein.

15. The Oto and Missouri tribes cede to the United States all their land west of the Missouri River, accepting in return a 10-mile-wide tract on the Big Blue River in Kansas.

17. The *Alta California* reports that Wells Fargo has just shipped $80,200 on the *Golden Gate,* and $69,550 on the *Cortes.*

25. William Walker, the half-bred chief of the Wyandots, writes: "Slavery exists here [in Kansas] among the Indians and whites in defiance of the Compromise of 1820."

30. A combined party of 250 Jicarilla Apaches and Utes attacks some 60 soldiers of the 1st Dragoons near Cianeguilla, New Mexico, and kills 22. The troops report killing 200 Indians.

▪ The mail arrives in Independence from Salt Lake City with the latest news, a February 2 issue of the *Deseret News.*

APRIL

3. With the opening of a branch mint in San Francisco, the United States ends the private coinage of gold.

8. Companies of the 1st and 2nd Dragoons report one dead following a clash with Apaches at Ojo Caliente, New Mexico.

Emigrants on the plains. Manifest Destiny is nearly a reality.   (Library of Congress)

11. Representatives of the Shawnee and Delaware tribes board the *Polar Star* in Kansas City on a trip to Washington for treaty signings.

21. Kickapoo, Iowa, and Sac and Fox delegates board the *Honduras* in St. Joseph, on their way to land cession meetings in Washington.

■ Alexander Majors contracts with the United States to transport army freight from Fort Leavenworth to Fort Laramie for $7.90 per 100 pounds.

25. President Pierce signs the Gadsden Purchase.

26. Eli Thayer and concerned Bostonians organize the Massachusetts Emigrant Aid Society to promote the settlement of antislavery groups in Kansas.

■ The *St. Joseph Gazette* reports crowded conditions in the city because of the influx of emigrants in the new season: "Our Hotels are full, and still they come."

28. Alexander Majors and William H. Russell contract with the United States to carry army freight from Fort Leavenworth to Albuquerque for $10.83 per 100 pounds.

Also in April 1854:

John W. Whitfield, the former Potawatomi agent, is named Indian agent at the Upper Platte Agency following the death of Thomas Fitzpatrick. Richard C. Brown is appointed agent of the Pottawatomies.

San Francisco's first economic depression is underway, caused by declining gold production.

MAY

1. Majors and Russell's first wagon train from Fort Leavenworth to Albuquerque gets underway. In the train is James A. Little, who will write of his experiences in *What I Saw on the Old Santa Fe Trail* (1904).

6. The Delaware Indians cede most of their lands in present Kansas to the United States.

■ San Francisco's Catholic Church begins publishing the *Weekly Catholic Standard.*

9. At Lake Trinidad in Texas, a company of 11 mounted riflemen under Lieutenant G. B. Cosby is attacked by "about 40 Indians." Two soldiers are killed and Cosby is wounded.

10. The Shawnees cede 1.6 million acres of present Kansas to the United States, which in turn re-cedes to the Shawnees a 200,000-acre tract in Indian Territory.

17. The Iowa tribe cedes 400 sections of present northeastern Kansas to the United States.

18. The Sac and Fox Indians cede to the United States all but 32,000 acres of their land in northeastern Kansas, while the Kickapoos cede 150,000 acres in the same area.

19. The weekly newspaper the *Daily Sun* begins publishing in San Francisco.

22. The Kansas-Nebraska Bill passes in the House by a vote of 113 to 100.

25. The new Potawatomi agent Richard C. Brown arrives at his headquarters in Westport, Missouri.

26. After an evening-long session, the Senate passes the Kansas-Nebraska Act at 1:15 A.M. by a vote of 37–14. Stephen A. Douglas had introduced the bill earlier in the year (Jan. 4) to organize two territories that would allow settlers to decide for themselves the issue of slavery, which was excluded up until this point under the Missouri Compromise. The new bill says that states may now form "with or without slavery, as their constitution may prescribe at the time of admission." Douglas's motives are the subject of much debate—they have been described as a reason to remove Indians from the Platte area, and to see the transcontinental railroad take a central route that would favor his home state of Illinois. Whatever the intent, the result becomes a source of antagonism and controversy, one that will further divide North and South.

■ Writes one observer to the evening on Capitol Hill, "Intoxication and anger made memorable the night scenes in the Senate and House."

27. The telegraph line from Fort Point to San Francisco is completed.

30. The signing of the Kansas-Nebraska Act by President Pierce creates the twin territories of Kansas and Nebraska out of what had formerly been called Unorganized Territory. Of the original lands of the Louisiana Purchase of 1803, only Indian Territory, south of 37° north latitude, remains unorganized.

■ The Peorias, Kaskaskias, Piankeshaws, and Weas cede most of their small reserves in Kansas to the United States.

Also in May 1854:

Senator John B. Weller of California submits to Congress a petition, signed by 75,000 residents, demanding an overland mail service.

Samuel Clemens is in Philadelphia, working for the *Ledger* and the *North American.*

JUNE

6. Sir George Gore's buffalo-slaughtering expedition is camped west of Westport, Missouri, ready to leave for Fort Laramie. From there the party will number 41, with as many dogs; Gore himself has brought along 75 rifles and a collapsible brass bed.

8. Fort Towson, established in 1824 east of present Hugo, Oklahoma, is abandoned.

10. William F. Cody, 8, moves with his family to the Salt Creek Valley near Fort Leavenworth in Kansas Territory.

13. The town company of Leavenworth is established by Missourians at Weston, Missouri.

18. Thirty cases of cholera are reported in Independence.

22. The first steamboat to travel the Colorado River, the *Uncle Sam*, sinks near Pilot Knob.

■ The Accumulating Fund Association is incorporated in San Francisco.

■ Richard C. Brown, the agent of the Potawatomi, dies of cholera.

25. The *New York Tribune* reports that Wells Fargo has shipped $138,000 on the *Pacific* via San Juan.

29. Andrew Reeder is appointed the first territorial governor of Kansas. New international borders between Mexico and what will become parts of Arizona and New Mexico are approved as the Gadsden Purchase is signed by President Pierce.

■ A Lieutenant Maxwell is reported killed in a skirmish with Apaches south of Fort Union, New Mexico.

Also in June 1854:

Nat Love, who will earn fame as the cowboy Deadwood Dick, is born to slave parents on the Robert Love plantation in Davidson County, Tennessee.

JULY

4. The United States officially takes possession of the land bought from Mexico in the Gadsden Purchase.

■ William Matthew "Bill" Tilghman, the future lawman, senator, and businessman, is born in Fort Dodge, Iowa. Little Billy will still be in diapers the first time someone shoots at him when the family, having relocated to Fort Ridgely, Minnesota, is attacked by Sioux; a flying arrow will hit his mother in the arm as she is holding him.

11. A Captain Van Buren is reported wounded when

he and his 16 soldiers are attacked by Comanches near San Diego, Texas.

17. The first party of pioneers from Boston departs for Kansas.

22. An act of Congress extends U.S. land laws to New Mexico and creates the office of U.S. surveyor general for the territory.

25. David Belasco, the future playwright, director, and producer, is born in San Francisco.

27. The Atchison town company is founded in Missouri.

Also in July 1854:

A federal land office opens in Kansas Territory.

Wells Fargo buys out Hunter and Company, a competitor.

The first publicly maintained school in San Diego is established by Fanny Stevens.

AUGUST

4. Congress officially awards lands acquired in the Gadsden Purchase to New Mexico.

5. San Francisco's People's Theater opens.

10. Fort Tejón, the future home of the U.S. Camel Corps, is established northwest of Los Angeles to guard the pass through the Tehachapi Mountains.

17. A tense situation develops on the Oregon Trail near Fort Laramie when High Forehead, a Miniconjou Sioux, kills an old cow that belonged to a Mormon wagon train. Chief Conquering Bear goes to Fort Laramie with an offer of restitution, but Lieutenant Hugh Fleming insists on the arrest of High Forehead.

18. Francis X. Aubry, "the skimmer of the plains," argues with Colonel Richard H. Weightman, a local editor, in a Santa Fe bar. On hearing that Weightman's newspaper had folded, Aubry remarks that the "lying paper deserved to die." Weightman stabs Aubry with a bowie knife, and Aubry dies about 10 minutes later. The assailant claims self-defense and will be acquitted.

19. The "Grattan Fight" occurs near Fort Laramie. The trouble begins when Lieutenant John Grattan, an interpreter, and 29 infantrymen from Company G of the 6th Infantry arrive at the camp of the Brulé Sioux near the fort. Chief Conquering Bear again attempts to make peace, but Grattan answers with howitzer fire. Conquering Bear is slain in the first volley. Oglalas and Brulés under Little Thunder attack the troops, killing Grattan and all but one of his men, who makes it back to the fort. This is the first armed confrontation between the U.S. Army and the Sioux. One of the witnesses to the Grattan Fight is 13-year-old Crazy Horse.

SEPTEMBER

5. One trooper is reported wounded in a small skirmish with Indians near Rio Grande, Texas.

9. Brigham Young is reappointed governor of Utah.

15. The first newspaper in Kansas, the *Kansas Weekly Herald,* begins publication in Leavenworth. It estimates the city's population at "99 men, 1 woman, 0 babies, Total 100."

21. The first sale of city lots in Atchison, Kansas, takes place.

25. The *Prometheus* arrives in New York carrying the following amounts of gold from California: $417,000 for Duncan, Sherman and Company; $224,236 for Adams; and $110,500 for Wells Fargo.

▪ A German newspaper, the *Abend Zeitung,* begins publication in San Francisco.

26. A report on San Francisco in the *New York Tribune* notes: "The city is improving at a wonderful rate. The streets in the business portion of the city are being rapidly filled up three, four, five and six feet, to the new grade; and the old houses are raising and new ones building on all sides."

Also in September 1854:

Wells Fargo pays a dividend of 5 percent, making a total of 15 percent for the year.

OCTOBER

4. Andrew H. Reeder, the first territorial governor of Kansas, arrives at Fort Leavenworth, where he will maintain an office for approximately 50 days.

6. In San Francisco, the North Beach and Fisherman's Wharf districts are being developed by "Honest" Harry Meiggs, who, using fraudulent warrants, is also building a road around the base of the Hill. When his scheme becomes public, Meiggs departs for Chile, leaving behind some $800,000 in liabilities.

▪ The Boston pioneers name their proposed Kansas settlement Lawrence, after Amos A. Lawrence.

7. Fort Davis is established southeast of El Paso, Texas, by Lieutenant Colonel Washington Seawell.

11. Captain B. H. Arthur and his 1st Infantry troops kill two Lipan Indians at Live Oak Creek, Texas.

26. Lawrence Carter becomes the first child born in Lawrence, Kansas.

31. The *Nebraska Palladium* reports that "the number of females at present holding office of Post Master is 128." The paper also says the women in the position are paid the same as men, and that no other occupation can make a similar claim.

NOVEMBER

1. Three members of the 8th Infantry are killed in a battle with Indians near Fort Davis, Texas.
4. Construction of the lighthouse on Alcatraz Island, in San Francisco Bay, is completed.
17. It is reported that the following express companies have shipped these amounts of gold from California via Panama: Page and Bacon, $417,000; Adams, $350,000; Wells Fargo, $177,000.
19. Sam Houston is baptized. When told that his sins have been washed away, he replies, "Lord, help the fish down below."
24. Kansas Territory's governor Andrew H. Reeder moves his office from Fort Leavenworth to the Shawnee Methodist Mission, where he will remain until June 1855.
29. J. W. Whitfield is elected to Congress as a Kansas representative. His cause was helped by 1,600 armed ruffians who crossed the border from Missouri to vote for him.

Also in November 1854:
The San Diego and Gila Southern Pacific and Atlantic Railroad is organized by citizens of San Diego.

DECEMBER

3. The migration of Poles to Texas begins with the arrival of 100 in Galveston.
4. The American II Theater opens in San Francisco.
5. Topeka, Kansas, is founded.
6. Cora Leavenworth Kyle becomes the first baby born in Leavenworth, Kansas.
10. The future cattle baron Richard King weds Henrietta Chamberlain. In addition to the 15,500 acres he acquired in 1853, this year he purchased an adjacent 53,000 acres west of the Santa Gertrudis in Texas for $1,800. Before he is through, King's holdings will total 1.25 million acres in four counties.
25. The settlement of Fort Pueblo, Colorado, is wiped out by Ute Indians as revenge for a recent outbreak of smallpox. Prospectors from St. Louis will come upon the site in 1858 and begin establishing the present town of Pueblo.
28. The shipping firm of William Russell, W. B. Waddell, and Alexander Majors obtains a government subsidy to provide freight service from Fort Leavenworth to California.
31. Since April, the U.S. Mint in San Francisco has coined $4,084,207 in gold pieces.

Also in 1854:
Indian commissioner George Manypenny calls for an end to the removal of Indians from their lands: "By alternate persuasion and force, some of these tribes have been removed, step by step, from mountains to valley, and from river to plain, until they have been pushed half-way across the continent. They can go no further. On the ground they now occupy, the crises must be met, and their future determined."

The *Nebraska Palladium* becomes the first newspaper published in Nebraska Territory.

A French colony headed by Victor Considerant settles near Dallas, Texas.

The Texas legislature appropriates $2 million for public education.

Father Leopole Moczygemba and Johann Twohig bring a group of Polish settlers to the San Antonio River region of Texas.

The clipper *Flying Cloud* sets a record on the Boston–San Francisco voyage around Cape Horn—89 days, 8 hours.

The Knights of the Golden Circle is organized in Texas, with the goal of preserving slavery.

The construction of San Francisco's first railroad is engineered by Theodore Dehone Judah of Erie Canal fame.

Smallpox breaks out among the Utes of Colorado.

Samuel Clemens leaves Philadelphia for St. Louis, where again he will be employed briefly by the *Evening Post*.

Bret Harte, 18, and his sister journey from Brooklyn to San Francisco, by ship via Nicaragua, to join their mother, who relocated there in 1852.

Prospectors find a copper vein 100 miles southeast of Fort Yuma. Ajo, the town they established, becomes the site of the first copper mine in Arizona.

Alonzo Delano writes *Across the Plains and Among the Diggings.*

The Life and Adventures of Joaquin Murieta, the Celebrated California Bandit, by John Rollin Ridge, becomes the first novel published by a Native American. The grandson of Cherokee leader Major Ridge and the son of John Rollin, Ridge survived the Trail of Tears during the Cherokee Removal from Georgia in 1837, only to witness the murder of his father at age 12. His book is a groundbreaker for the western genre and firmly establishes Murieta's status as a folk hero.

The anthropologist John Russell Bartlett, whose surveys were crucial to the Gadsden Purchase, publishes his illustrated journal *Personal Narrative of Explorations and Incidents Connected with the United States and Mexican Boundary Commission.*

The first novel about the Northwest is Margaret Jewett Bailey's *The Grains, or Passages in the Life of Ruth Rover.*

Smith and Wesson invent their revolver.

1855

"If I owned Texas and Hell, I would rent out Texas and live in hell."
—General Philip H. Sheridan

JANUARY

1. Nebraska's first territorial legislature convenes in Omaha.

■ The Deseret Iron Company produces its first iron.

4. The Chinese newspaper *Oriental* begins publishing in San Francisco.

7. Captain W. L. Elliott reports "several Comanches killed" in a fight on the Pecos River in Texas.

15. Captain J. H. Whittlesey of Company H of the 1st Dragoons is wounded in a skirmish with Apaches in New Mexico's White Mountains southeast of Los Lunas.

16. Nebraska's first territorial legislature meets in Omaha City.

18. The future "Silver King" Horace Tabor weds Augusta L. Pierce in Maine. They will relocate to Riley County, Kansas, where they will farm 160 acres and where Tabor will be elected to the Topeka territorial legislature.

19. Captain Henry W. Stanton and two of his soldiers are killed in a skirmish with Apaches on the Rio Penasco in New Mexico.

21. John Moses Browning, the future gun designer, is born in Ogden, Utah. He will obtain a patent on the breech-loading single shot rifle in 1879, and will invent the Browning automatic pistol in 1911, the Browning machine gun in 1917, and the Browning automatic rifle in 1918.

25. Iowa Wesleyan College is chartered in Mount Pleasant, Iowa.

28. Today's completion of W. H. Aspinwall's Panama Railroad cuts the trip from New York to California to five weeks, as compared with the six-month, 19,000-mile journey around Cape Horn.

29. Walchor (Wakara, Walker), a Ute chief, is secretly killed at Meadow Creek, Utah, by two men identified only as Jordan and Mr. Chandless.

■ Captain J. H. Whittlesey dies of wounds he suffered on January 15.

30. Congress grants the black Washington pioneer George Washington Bush his 640 acres under the Donation Land Act, officially giving him the right to stay on the land he improved during the past 10 years. Bush had requested the tract in 1850.

31. The boundary commissioner William H. Emory arrives at the Rio Grande to begin a border survey of the Gadsden Purchase.

Also in January 1855:

Captain Richard Ewell leads a campaign against wintering Mescaleros in New Mexico, destroying many villages.

One-third of San Francisco's 1,000 stores are vacant due to an economic depression.

FEBRUARY

15. Wells Fargo's directors vote a 5 percent dividend.

17. Charles Angelo Siringo, author of *A Texas Cowboy, or Fifteen Years on the Hurricane Deck of a Spanish Pony* (1885), is born on the Matagorda Peninsula of Texas.

■ The mail steamer *Oregon* arrives in San Francisco with the news that the St. Louis, Missouri firm of

THE FIRST GEORGE BUSH

History's first George Bush was not the 41st president of the United States. George Washington Bush was born in Philadelphia on September 4, 1781. His parents were slaves owned by Mr. Stevenson, a shipping magnate. George received his elementary education at a Quaker school.

When Stevenson relocated to Cumberland County, Tennessee, the Bush family went along. As the Stevensons grew older, they were cared for by their devoted servants. When Mr. Stevenson died, the Bushes received their freedom and a portion of the estate.

At 18 years of age, George Bush was raising livestock in Illinois. During the War of 1812, Bush fought under General Andrew Jackson at the Battle of New Orleans. In 1816, he farmed in Platte County, Missouri. During the 1820s, he worked for two St. Louis fur traders. His travels took him across the West and up the Pacific coast. When he was 50, he married the German-American Isabella James, and they farmed in Missouri. During the years 1831–1843, Bush became one of the wealthier men on the frontier. Isabella bore him five sons.

An African-American in a slave state did not need much imagination to see what kind of future lay ahead for his sons and their families. At age 63, Bush prepared for one last adventure. His enthusiasm for a migration to Oregon caught on with at least five neighboring families. In the spring of 1844, a group led by Bush and Michael T. Simmons joined a wagon train that had begun in Kentucky. Eighty Conestogas set out to cut another groove in the Oregon Trail. Bush felt secure; he had $3,000 in silver nailed under a false bottom in his wagon.

All went well until the party reached The Dalles on the Columbia River between present Washington and Oregon. Here, Bush found he had stepped into a political hornet's nest. For starters, the racism that George Bush had tried to plow under in Missouri had sprung full bloom in Oregon Territory. That summer, the provisional government had voted to adopt the laws of Iowa Territory. Slavery was banned, but a new exclusion prevented blacks not currently living in the territory from becoming property owners. The penalty for disobedience was 20 to 39 lashes.

The new settlers were stunned. Bush was an important member of the expedition; he had financed two of the families. Wrote member John Minton, "they were all Americans, they would take no part in ill treating G. W. Bush on account of his color." If Bush could not enter Oregon, neither would they. Twenty miles east of Fort Vancouver, the party camped for a year on the Washougal River, planning its move.

The exclusion applied to the land south of the Columbia. Above that line was land involved in a stalemated dispute with Great Britain. Three forts had been built there in the name of the crown: Fort Langley on the Fraser River, Fort Nisqually on Puget Sound, and Fort Vancouver. At the last, factor John McLoughlin's instructions from the Hudson's Bay Company were to direct American settlers into the Willamette Valley, out of the "British zone."

The pioneers decided to take their chances north of the border. Without ceremony, the 32 men, women, and children rolled into the forbidden area in October 1845. Michael Simmons claimed a site by the Deschutes River near present Olympia. Bush took a nearby field that would later be called Bush Prairie. The others staked claims within a six-mile radius. The settlers were allowed to stay and to trade at Fort Nisqually because of Bush's previous employment with the Hudson's Bay Company.

On June 15, 1846, the matter between the two countries was resolved. Great Britain agreed to the 49th parallel as the boundary line and retained Vancouver Island. No doubt, the new settlers influenced the treaty, and the British realized a flood of humanity was on its way; better to negotiate than to forfeit the entire area.

Still, Bush faced problems. The law he had avoided was now in effect up to the 49th parallel. Simmons, who had become a justice of the peace, protested loudly. Under a special act from the provisional territorial government, Bush was allowed to stay and raise his wheat. In 1847, he helped fund the first sawmill on Puget Sound. He also imported the area's first mower and reaper.

In 1850, Bush filed for 640 acres under the Donation Land Act, but was denied because of the wording "for white Americans." The Washington territorial legislature petitioned Congress to grant special privilege to Bush, who "by a constant and

(continued)

(continued)

laborious cultivation . . . and by accommodating and charitable disposal of his produce to emigrants has contributed much towards the settlement of this Territory." The historian Ezra Meeker explained the dilemma: "He was a true American and yet without a country; he owed allegiance to the flag and yet the flag would not own him; he was firmly held to obey the law and yet the law would not protect him."

While Bush anxiously awaited the ruling, the bitter winter of 1852 struck. A Seattle firm offered him top dollar for his surplus wheat, but Bush turned it down. Instead, he gave the wheat to the settlers on Puget Sound. Finally, on January 30, 1855, Congress granted him the right to stay on the land he had improved during the past 10 years. Bush farmed another eight years and died at age 82 in 1863; Isabella followed in 1867. His first son, William, went on to raise prize-winning wheat and was elected to the first Washington state legislature.

Page, Bacon has failed. The firm was the parent company of the express company of the same name.

18. A bank panic in San Francisco begins as the Page, Bacon bank sees the first of a four-day run.

21. The Massachusetts Emigrant Aid Society is reincorporated as the New England Emigrant Aid Company. It will found Lawrence and other Kansas Free State communities from its base in Worcester, Massachusetts.

22. Financial panic continues to sweep California. A run on the Page, Bacon bank ends today when the bank closes after paying out $600,000 in four days. Other banks will close in the next few days after paying out all their funds to depositors.

23. The French-Canadian Louis Remme sells his cattle for $12,500 in Sacramento and deposits his money in the Adams bank.

24. The Adams Express Company goes into receivership. In Sacramento, Louis Remme learns that the Adams Company has failed. Seeing a long line at the bank, he realizes he will never get his $12,500, which he deposited the day before. Knowing that the news will not have reached his hometown of Portland, he travels 42 miles by boat to Knight's Landing. From there, he buys horses along the way to finish his 700-mile race against the steamer *Columbia,* which is carrying the financial news.

■ Troops destroy a Mescalero Apache village in New Mexico.

■ Two members of the 1st Dragoons are fatally wounded in a fight with Apaches in the White Mountains of New Mexico.

25. In the *Alta California,* Wells Fargo's managers announce they have "completed a balance of their accounts this day, and find to the credit of their house, above every liability, $389,105.23; and only

CHARLES SIRINGO
FEBRUARY 7, 1855—OCTOBER 19, 1928

1855: Siringo is born in Matagorda County, Texas.

1856: His father dies.

1860: He ropes cows and holds them for milking.

1869: Siringo attends school in St. Louis and works on Mississippi steamboats.

1871: He works as a cowboy on the frontier.

1875: He is wounded by Sam Grant in an argument over misappropriated livestock.

1877: In a barroom brawl in Dodge City, Siringo gets a beer mug bounced off his forehead by bartender Bat Masterson.

1878: He meets Billy the Kid in west Texas.

1882: Following a cattle drive to Caldwell, Kansas, Siringo weds a 15-year-old. He supports her by running a cigar store that sells ice cream, oysters, and a "genuine cowpuncher coffee that will almost stand alone."

1883: He pens a reminiscence of Billy the Kid for a local newspaper.

1885: His *A Texas Cowboy, or Fifteen Years on the Hurricane Deck of a Spanish Pony* is published by M. Umbdenstock and Company of Chicago.

1886: He reprints his 1885 book with a 30-page addendum on "how to get rich and go broke in the cattle business."

(continued)

(continued)

1887: He becomes an operative for the Pinkerton Detective Agency, stationed in the Denver office.

1899: Siringo begins a four-year, fruitless search for Butch Cassidy, the Sundance Kid, and the other members of the Wild Bunch.

1907: He retires from the Pinkerton Agency with 22 years' service.

1912: Following a two-year legal battle with the Pinkerton Agency, Siringo publishes his detective memoirs, *A Cowboy Detective.*

1915: Still angry over his former employer's litigation over his previous book, he publishes "Two Evil Isms: Pinkertonism and Anarchism."

1919: He publishes *A Lone Star Cowboy.*

1920: He publishes *History of Billy the Kid.*

1927: Siringo publishes *Riata and Spurs.*

1928: He dies at age 73 in Venice, California. Siringo is eulogized by author J. Frank Dobie: "Charlie Siringo had almost nothing to say on life; he reported actions. He put down something valid on a class of livers, as remote now from the Atomic Age as Rameses II. His cowboys and gunmen were not of Hollywood and folklore. He was an honest reporter."

ask of their friends a few days to convert some of their assets, to resume payment."

MARCH

1. Six days and 700 miles after departing Sacramento, the French-Canadian cattleman Louis Remme arrives in Portland ahead of the steamer carrying the news of the failure of the Adams banks. He goes to the Adams branch office and retrieves his $12,500 in gold, one hour before the arrival of the *Columbia.*

3. President Franklin Pierce's secretary of war, Jefferson Davis, persuades Congress to appropriate $30,000 for "the purchase and importation of camels and dromedaries to be employed for military purposes." Major Henry Wayne will be sent to London to study zoo camels, while David Porter will sail for Pisa, Italy. Comments one observer who will see them purchase three camels for $20 apiece

in Tunis, "every sore-backed and superannuated camel in Asia Minor was doctored up and hurried to the coast to be offered . . . at a grievous sacrifice of ten times its value."

9. Warren Earp, the lawman and stagecoach driver, is born in Pella, Iowa.

19. One hundred Apache and Utah Indians converge on troops under Captain H. Brooks at Cochotope Pass, New Mexico.

21. The same Apache and Utah Indians meet Captain Brooks's troops again and fight a two-day battle at Puncha Pass on the Arkansas River. One trooper is killed and 50 Indians are reported dead.

23. According to the *Cincinnati Gazette,* "Many persons have left here for Kansas and 600 are now ready to go." One party is reported taking along a frame schoolhouse.

30. Voters in Kansas elect a proslavery territorial legislature, in an election filled with fraud and confusion. Some 5,000 Missouri pro-slavers cross the border to vote. Governor Andrew H. Reeder refuses to invalidate the election, which shows 6,300 ballots cast where there were 3,000 registered voters.

APRIL

7. The *Fireman's Journal* begins publication in San Francisco.

16. Today marks the 250th anniversary of the oldest inscription on the great stone at El Morro, New Mexico. The area itself is a rock just over four miles in circumference. Travelers signed it from the time of the explorer Don Juan de Oñate, who autographed it on April 16, 1605, until 1906, when the area was designated El Morro National Monument.

28. Santa Clara University is chartered in California.

29. Utah and Apache Indians again engage Captain H. Brooks's dragoons and artillery, this time near the headwaters of the Arkansas River.

30. The College of California is chartered in Oakland.

Also in April 1855:

Kansas City's population is just under 1,000.

The American Fur Company sells Fort Pierre in present South Dakota for $45,000.

MAY

5. Fort Stanton is founded in New Mexico.

11. The Mormons sign a peace treaty with the Utes.

14. The capital stock of Wells Fargo increases to $600,000.

30. William Bringhurst and a party of 30 are ordered to present Nevada "to go to Las Vegas, build a fort there to protect immigrants and the United States

mail from the Indians, and to teach the latter how to raise corn, wheat, potatoes, squash, and melons."

JUNE

13. Captain C. L. Stevenson loses four soldiers of the 5th Infantry in a fight with Indians near the junction of the Pecos River and Delaware Creek, in New Mexico.

14. William Bringhurst's party arrives in Nevada to build Las Vegas Fort.

16. The first of approximately 550 French, Belgian, and Swiss settlers arrive at La Reunion, about four miles west of Dallas, Texas, via oxcart from Houston. The French leader is Victor Considerant; the Swiss are guided by Carl Burkli. Among the group are scientists, artists, authors, naturalists, and musicians. The community will struggle for three years, after which many of the settlers will move to Dallas or return home.

18. The establishment of Fort Lemhi, a stockade built around 25 cabins by 27 Mormon pioneers sent by Brigham Young, represents the first attempt at a permanent settlement in Idaho.

19. Brigham Young is sealed to Catherine Reeves, 51, his 47th bride.

Also in June 1855:

Kansas territorial governor Andrew H. Reeder moves his headquarters again, this time from the Shawnee Methodist Mission to Pawnee, a town near Fort Riley.

JULY

2. Kansas territorial governor Andrew H. Reeder convenes the first territorial legislature in Pawnee.

6. The Kansas territorial legislature adjourns to Shawnee Mission, over the protests of Governor Reeder.

16. The Kansas legislature, meeting at Shawnee Mission, approves tough proslavery measures, and expels antislavery legislators.

- Under the terms of the Council Grove Treaty, Flathead Indians agree to move from the Bitterroot range to the Jocko Valley near Missoula, Montana.

22. Mounted riflemen under Captain C. F. Ruff kill 13 Mescalero Apaches in a fight near Eagle Springs, Texas.

27. Waterloo becomes the county seat of Black Hawk County, Iowa.

31. President Pierce removes Andrew Reeder as Kansas territorial governor, charging that he speculated on land in Kansas. Wilson Shannon, who is proslavery, is installed as governor.

Also in July 1855:

Trade along the Sante Fe Trail is valued at approximately $5 million annually.

Molasses is produced from sugar beets in Utah.

AUGUST

3. Brevet Major Edmund A. Ogden, 44(?), dies of cholera during an outbreak at Fort Riley.

4. Kansas free-state supporters in Lawrence call for their own constitutional convention.

7. The United States signs a treaty of friendship with the western Shoshone Indians of northeastern Nevada at Haws' ranch in Elko County, Nevada. Congress will refuse to recognize the document negotiated by Indian Agent Garland Hurt and, hence, will never deliver the promised food and goods to the Indians. Bitter Shoshone raiding parties will attack settlers along the Humboldt River for the next six years.

- The "Know Nothing" Party holds its state convention in Sacramento.

18. The Kansas territorial legislature names Lecompton as the new capital.

23. John Brown leaves Chicago for Kansas.

Also in August 1855:

The U.S. government reports that members of the Kansa tribe have "lost all confidence in each other due to destitution."

SEPTEMBER

3. The Battle of the Blue Water takes place in Nebraska.

- In civil-war-torn Nicaragua, California adventurer William Walker declares himself a dictator. He will rule for a few years.

5. Opponents of slavery in Kansas convene at Big Springs and vote not to recognize the proslavery territorial legislature. The Free-State Party is formed, and it is urged that Kansas be admitted to the Union as such.

11. Las Vegas Fort, Nevada, established in June, reports ripe melons.

12. Wells Fargo's directors vote a dividend of 5 percent, making a total of 10 percent for the year.

28. The Puget Sound Anti-Chinese Congress meets to discuss new ways to frighten Chinese immigrants from Washington.

30. Governor Brigham Young devises a "handcart solution" to bring his followers to Utah: They will push and pull carts along the trail instead of riding in the traditional covered wagons. Between 1856 and

THE BATTLE OF BLUE WATER
SEPTEMBER 3, 1855

In the wake of the Grattan Fight (August 19, 1854), as well as the murder of a mail coach driver and his assistant a few months earlier, the United States sent troops against the Northern Plains tribes with the intent of gaining revenge.

Brigadier General W. S. Harney cut short his European vacation to lead 600 infantry, cavalry, and artillery troops (from the 2nd Dragoons, the 4th Artillery, and the 6th and 10th Infantries) from Fort Kearny, Nebraska. They encountered Little Thunder's Brulé Sioux encampment on Blue Water Creek, north of the North Platte River near present Lewellan, Nebraska. Following a sham peace conference, Harney's forces surrounded the camp and opened fire. Of the 250 Indians in the camp, 85 died and 70 women and children were captured. The attack was witnessed by a teenaged Crazy Horse, who was returning to Little Thunder's camp from a hunt. U.S. Army reports cite 22 troops killed and 35 wounded. In the days following the confrontation, Harney marched his men and their captives through Sioux country in a show of strength, and reported no further conflicts.

1860, 2,962 immigrants will arrive in Utah using 655 handcarts.

Also in September 1855:

A fire in Grass Valley, California, provides Wells Fargo agent Alonzo Delano a chance to advertise: "A fire broke out in the United States Hotel and rapidly spread to the adjoining buildings. The vault of Wells Fargo & Company withstood the hottest of the fire and preserved its valuable contents."

The Deseret Horticultural Society is organized.

OCTOBER

1. John W. Whitfield is re-elected a Kansas delegate to Congress, thanks to the votes of "Border Ruffians."
6–9. Two companies of the 4th Infantry under Captain G. O. Halton battle an estimated 1,500 Yakima warriors in the Toponish Simcoe Valley of Oregon.

8. The *Daily Evening Bulletin* begins publishing in San Francisco.
9. Kansas free-soilers elect former Governor Reeder a territorial delegate to Congress.
15. St. Ignatius Academy, the future University of San Francisco, opens.
17. The region between Missouri and the Yellowstone River becomes a "common" hunting ground in accordance with the Blackfoot Treaty.
19. At Fort Benton, Montana, Crows report 400 small-pox deaths.
23. Kansas free-soilers convene in Topeka and will meet until November 12. They will adopt a constitution that forbids slavery, as well as another ordinance targeted at preventing blacks from living in Kansas.
25. Rogue River Indians attack a detachment of 12 soldiers and kill two between Cow and Grave Creeks in Oregon.
30. Paul Bauer, the future saddle maker, is born in Yorktown, Texas.
31. Troops from dragoon, artillery, and infantry units engage Rogue River Indians in a two-day battle at Hungry Hill, between Cow and Grave Creeks in Oregon. Two soldiers are killed; no estimate of Indian casualties is available.

Also in October 1855:

Construction of a stockade begins at Fort Stanton, New Mexico.

Mormons report a third of their crops are destroyed by grasshoppers.

NOVEMBER

1. Disaster strikes a VIP test of the Pacific Railroad's new 750-foot bridge at Gasconode, Missouri. A makeshift wooden trestle sends many cars into the shallow Gasconode River. The passengers, mostly dignitaries from the railroad and military, suffer 22 fatalities and numerous injuries.
3. The mayor of Tacoma, Washington, his sheriff, and deputies lead a mob through the Chinese sector of the town, looting and evicting the Chinese.
4–5. Troops under First Lieutenant W. H. Slaughter and settlers on Washington's White River battle Rogue River Indians. One soldier and 19 settlers are killed; there is no estimate of Indian casualties.
6–7. First Lieutenant Slaughter continues the fight with Rogue River Indians at the Puyallup River; two more soldiers are killed.
10. Henry Wadsworth Longfellow publishes "The Song of Hiawatha."
14. Kansas governor Shannon organizes the "Law and

Order Party" at a proslavery meeting in Leavenworth.

26. The two-week-long Wakarusa War begins near Lawrence, Kansas: Free-staters battle 1,500 proslavery Missourians.

DECEMBER

4. First Lieutenant W. H. Slaughter is killed in action in a fight with Rogue River Indians at Bennans Prairie, Washington.

8. President Pierce issues a proclamation condemning William Walker's Nicaraguan dictatorship.

11. The last official acts of the Kansas territorial legislature take place.

15. Kansas now has two constitutions, pro- and antislave. Today, the free-soilers approve the Topeka constitution, which includes the clause banning blacks from entering the territory.

■ The first issue of *Frank Leslie's Illustrated Newspaper* appears in New York. Some of the earliest illustrations of the Wild West will grace its pages in the coming years.

24. The *Weekly Sunday Times* is established by James P. Casey in San Francisco.

31. Wells Fargo now has branches in 55 towns in California, Arizona Territory, Idaho Territory, and Oregon.

Also in 1855:

In San Francisco, the banking panic results in 197 business failures.

Nebraska Territory is explored by Dr. Ferdinand V. Hayden and Lieutenant G. K. Warren.

Using information he received from a prostitute, Rattlesnake Dick robs a Wells Fargo mule train of $80,000.

More than 5,000 New Orleans residents have died of yellow fever in the past two years.

The first Pacific Coast lighthouse goes into service off San Diego.

Brigham Young claims that a "single drop of Negro blood" makes a man unfit for the Mormon priesthood.

Mrs. Maria Ward publishes *Female Life Among the Mormons.*

Sir George Gore begins a two-year hunting trip from the Platte to the Columbia. Colorado's Gore mountain range will be named for him.

General William Larimer founds Larimer City, Nebraska.

Montana governor Stevens signs treaties with the Salish and Blackfeet Indians at Council Grove and at the mouth of the Judith River.

Since 1848, the cattle population of Texas has increased from 350,000 to 1 million.

1856

"The West begins where the average annual rainfall drops below twenty inches. When you reach the line which marks that drop—for convenience, the one hundredth meridian—you have reached the West."

—Bernard De Voto

JANUARY

5. Beaver and Cache Counties are created in Utah.

8. Borax is first discovered in the United States by John Veatch at a spring in California.

9. California's "Know Nothing" Party elects its candidate, J. Neely Johnson, governor.

15. Kansas free-soilers elect Charles Robinson governor, along with the members of a new legislature.

22. *Eco del Pacifico,* a Spanish daily, begins publishing in San Francisco.

24. President Franklin Pierce declares the January 15 election in Kansas an "act of rebellion." Pierce appoints Wilson Shannon as governor.

FEBRUARY

11. As tensions mount in "bleeding Kansas," President Pierce commits his administration to a proslavery stance when he orders "all persons engaged in unlawful combinations against the constituted authority of the Territory of Kansas or of the United States to disperse and retire peaceably to their respective abodes."

22. In Oregon, the "Geisel Family Massacre" occurs when the males in the pioneer family are put to death by Indians and the females are captured.

■ The first railroad trip west of Missouri is taken by "a trainload of merrymakers" on the Sacramento Valley Railroad, 22.5 miles of track constructed since 1853 and connecting Sacramento to Folsom in the Comstock Lode country.

■ Two soldiers are wounded in a scrape between the 2nd Cavalry and Indians at the headwaters of the Nueces River, in Texas.

28. Solomon Warner arrives in Tucson from Yuma with a pack train of 13 mules loaded with goods for a new general store.

National Headlines/February 1856
22. KNOW NOTHINGS NOMINATE FILLMORE

MARCH

1. Colonel Casey and Captain Keys lead 26 men in the relief of Lieutenant Kantz's soldiers, who were battling Indians on the White River in Washington Territory.

4. In Kansas Territory, the antislavery Topeka legislature petitions the United States for statehood and elects Andrew Reeder and James Lane as senators.

13. The *Daily Globe* begins publishing in San Francisco.

14. Brigham Young takes 25-year-old Emeline Barney as his 48th bride.

17. Senator Stephen Douglas, a Democrat from Illinois, introduces in Congress a bill that would admit Kansas as a state after a new territorial constitutional convention is held. He calls the Topeka antislavery legislature "lawless." Republicans favor the "Topeka Constitution," which bans slavery and black residency.

■ A state constitution for Utah is adopted in Salt Lake City.

19. A federal investigation of voter fraud in Kansas reveals that 6,000 votes were cast by 2,905 registered voters.

20. Company B of the 3rd Artillery reports eight Rogue River Indians killed and eight wounded in a fight at the mouth of Oregon's Rogue River.

■ Troops battle Apaches near Fort Thron in New Mexico's Almagre Mountains; one soldier is reported wounded.

21. First Lieutenant J. E. Slaughter leads a detachment of the 1st Artillery against Indians near Fort McIntosh, Texas. Two Indians are reported wounded.

23. According to the New York *Evening Post,* at a New Haven, Connecticut, meeting called to assist the Kansas Emigrant Aid Society, Henry Ward Beecher said that "the Sharp rifle was truly moral agency and that there was more moral power in one of those instruments so far as the slaveholders of Kansas were concerned than a hundred Bibles. You might just as well read the Bible to buffalos as to those fellows who follow Atchison and Stringfellow." The term "Beecher's Bibles" will become a popular slang for Sharp's rifles.

24. The Sonora Exploring and Mining Company is organized by Charles D. Poston in Arizona. Fort Yuma's Major Heintzelman is named president of the company, whose first order of business is to purchase the Arivaca Ranch and work its mines.

■ Two soldiers die in an attack by Rogue River Indians on Oregon's Illinois River.

26. One soldier is reported killed in an Indian attack against a blockhouse at the Cascades of the Columbia River in Washington.

■ In Oregon, Captain E. O. C. Ord leads two companies of troops against a Mackanootney Indian village.

27. A new state constitution is adopted in Utah.

27–28. Dragoons, infantry, and artillery are involved in a battle against Indians at the Casacades of the Columbia River in Washington.

APRIL

1. The Western Union Telegraph Company is established in Rochester, New York, to provide communications west of the Mississippi River.

9. Lieutenant Colonel Robert E. Lee is assigned to Camp Cooper, Texas.

13. Captain T. Claiborne and his troops capture four Indians, kill one, and wound another in a scrape on the Turkey Branch at the headwaters of the Nueces River in Texas.

16. Publishers Whitman and Searl of Lawrence issue a map of Kansas.

20. The proslavery government of Kansas Territory is formally established in Lecompton.

21. The first bridge across the Mississippi River connects Davenport, Iowa, with Rock Island, Illinois, and supports rail traffic.

22. The Fort Des Moines becomes the first train to cross the bridge spanning the Mississippi River at Davenport, Iowa, and Rock Island, Illinois.

25. The 9th Infantry battles Indians on Cedar Creek in Washington.

29. Captain E. O. C. Ord leads the 3rd Artillery against Chetco Indians in Oregon; two Indians are killed, three are wounded, and "several" are captured.

MAY

1. Captain James Oakes and the 2nd Cavalry battle Indians at the headwaters of the Concho River in Texas; they report one Indian killed.

1–9. The 9th Infantry under Second Lieutenant D. B. McKibbin engages Indians at the headwaters of the Nasqually River in Washington. The official report lists three Indians killed, 16 captured.

6. The only railroad bridge across the Mississippi, linking Rock Island, Illinois, with Davenport, Iowa, is rammed and wrecked by the steamboat *Effie Alton,* whose captain had called the bridge "a nuisance and an obstruction." A bitter fight between the rivermen and the railroads begins, with attorney Abraham Lincoln representing the latter.

14. James King of William, editor of the San Francisco *Bulletin,* is shot by *Sunday Times* publisher James P. Casey. In a political feud, King had revealed that Casey had done time in Sing Sing, a prison in Ossining, New York. As King of William is leaving his office and crossing a street in front of a Pacific Express Company building, Casey puts a bullet

May 14, 1856. On the streets of San Francisco, James P. Casey levels his pistol at James King of William.
(Library of Congress)

in him. Casey then turns himself in to the police.

- The ship carrying camels for the U.S. Army's experiment in the southwest docks at Indianola, Texas, about 120 miles southwest of Galveston. The camels, grouchy after a three-month ocean voyage and inconvenienced by a doctor whose remedy for swollen knee was tea and gunpowder, initially refuse to disembark. When the herders tickle the camels' noses with a chameleon's tail, they finally budge. The new "Camel Corps" is said to be "exhilarated" to be on land, and after sufficient rest, the animals are driven 60 miles to Camp Verde, near San Antonio, which will become known as "Little Egypt."

15. San Francisco's second Vigilance Committee is organized when some 3,000 men meet in a Sacramento Street building that will become known as "Fort Gunnybags" because of all the sandbags on hand for fortification.

- A former resident of New Hampshire now living in San Francisco comments on the Sunday mood of the group: "When you see these damned psalm-singing Yankees turn out of their churches, shoulder their guns, and march away like that, you may know that hell is going to crack shortly."

16. California governor Neely Johnson's in-person plea to the vigilantes to disband goes unheeded.

18. The Vigilance Committee orders *Sunday Times* editor James P. Casey and the prisoner Charles Cora to be brought from jail to stand trial.

19. In the Senate, Massachusetts Republican senator Charles Sumner delivers a speech entitled "The Crime Against Kansas," in which he denounces the territory's proslavery factions. South Carolina Senator Andrew P. Butler is a target of the speech. Three days later, Sumner will be beaten with a cane by Butler's cousin, Representative Preston S. Brooks.

21. James King of William dies of gunshot wounds he received on May 14.

- The Free State Hotel in Lawrence, Kansas, is burned by a proslavery posse. One man is killed.

22. The editor James P. Casey and Charles Cora are executed by the San Francisco Vigilance Committee. Some 8,000 vigilantes march on the city's prison and bodily remove Casey, jailed for the murder of James King of William, and Cora, convicted of killing a U.S. marshal. Hasty trials, convictions, and twin death sentences follow. Casey, 29, is publicly lynched following King's funeral; his last words are, "Oh, God! My poor mother! Oh, God!" Both Casey and Cora are hanged from gallows at Fort Gunnybags.

24–25. In retaliation for the raid on Lawrence, Kansas, on May 21, the abolitionist John Brown leads a small band against Kansans who favor slavery at Dutch Henry's Crossing on Pottawatomie Creek; Brown's men kill five of their opponents.

27. George Armstrong Custer, a student at Ohio's Hopedale Normal School, writes to Representative John Bingham, inquiring about the qualifications for entering West Point.

- Captain A. J. Lindsay and Company H of the Mounted Riflemen battle Indians on Devil's River, near Fort Clark, Texas.

27–28. Colonel Buchennan leads the 1st Dragoons and infantry troops against Rogue River Indians at the Big Bend of the Rogue River in Oregon.

29. Arizona's Camp Moore is renamed Fort Buchanan.

GEORGE ARMSTRONG CUSTER
DECEMBER 5, 1839–JUNE 25, 1876

1839: Custer is born in New Rumley, Ohio.

1856: Sponsored by Representative John Bingham, he enters West Point.

1861: Custer graduates last in his class at West Point; he is assigned to the 5th Cavalry in the Army of the Potomac. Custer fights in the First Battle of Bull Run during the Civil War.

1863: He is promoted to the rank of brigadier general, then to major general in the regular army. He leads a cavalry engagement agains Jeb Stuart at Gettysburg, Pennsylvania.

1864: He marries Elizabeth Bacon in Monroe, Michigan.

1865: At the end of the Civil War, Custer returns to the rank of captain; he is then promoted to lieutenant colonel in the newly created 7th Cavalry. He is later assigned to Fort Riley, Kansas.

1867: Custer becomes the chief commanding officer in the Hancock Campaign against the Southern Cheyennes. Court-martialed for deserting his command without permission in order to visit his wife—and for reported abuses during the campaign—he is suspended from service.

1868: Custer is restored to his command. He
(continued)

(continued)

participates in the winter campaign to encourage Cheyennes and Arapahos to return to their Indian Territory reservations. In the Battle on the Washita, his 7th Cavalry destroys a Cheyenne village in Indian Territory.

1869: He camps near Fort Hays.

1872: He serves as a guide for the Grand Duke Alexis's buffalo hunt.

1873: Custer explores the Yellowstone region.

1874: He leads an expedition into the Black Hills of Dakota Territory that discovers gold. He publishes *My Life on the Plains*.

1876: Custer is assigned to assist in moving the Sioux and Cheyennes onto their reservations. He is removed from command after implicating President Ulysses S. Grant's brother in a military scandal; later, he is restored by public demand. He leads the 7th Cavalry in the Battle of the Little Bighorn and is killed in action.

JUNE

2–6. The Democratic Party's national convention in Cincinnati reaffirms the Compromise of 1850 and calls the Kansas-Nebraska Act the safest solution to the issue of slavery in the territories.

3. California governor Neely Johnson declares San Francisco in a state of insurrection.

4. Governor Wilson Shannon of Kansas orders irregular armed units to disperse.

5. The arms magnate Samuel Colt weds Elizabeth Jarvis. After a European honeymoon, they will settle into Armsmear, his $2 million in Connecticut.

9. San Francisco's Vigilance Committee has its own cavalry battalion, a French legion, three regiments of infantry, and six brass cannons. In its headquarters, "Fort Gunnybags," members are busy compiling lists of known felons.

■ A hundred handcarts pushed by 497 Mormons depart Iowa City for Salt Lake City.

14. James Burch wins a $149,800-a-year contract to establish a mail route between San Diego and San Antonio.

17. The Republican Party's national convention, meeting in Philadelphia, nominates Colonel John C. Frémont of California as its candidate for president.

Populating the promised land—Mormon handcarts en route to the land of Brigham Young. (Library of Congress)

The party's platform calls on Congress to "prohibit in the Territories those twin relics of barbarism—Polygamy and Slavery." The platform also urges the admission of Kansas as a free state.

Also in June 1856:

General William S. Harney establishes Fort Randall in present South Dakota.

National Headlines/June 1856:

6. DEMOCRATS NOMINATE BUCHANAN

JULY

1. Captain E. VanDorn reports "2 Indians killed, 1 wounded" after leading 2nd Cavalry troops in a battle at the source of the Colorado and Brazos Rivers in Texas.

3. Statehood for Kansas under the terms of the antislavery Topeka Constitution is approved by the House of Representatives. The Senate rejects these terms.

7. The Great Overland Contract is awarded to the Butterfield Stage Company by President Pierce; San Francisco is the western terminus of the route.

18. After staging a major parade and show of support, San Francisco's Vigilance Committee disbands, taking credit for the executions of 25 "dangerous" criminals and the departure from the city of another 800. Although these numbers cannot be verified, it is known that the committee executed four criminals before it disbanded.

20. The Handcart Migration—the Mormons' journey from Florence, Nebraska, to the Great Salt Lake—begins. Nearly three thousand Latter-day Saints will cross the prairies over the next four years pushing and pulling their belongings in wheelbarrow-like vehicles.

22. "Lane's army," 300 free-state settlers who have traveled through Iowa with James Lane, cross the Missouri River at Nebraska City enroute to Kansas.

29. The murderers Joseph Hetherington and Philander Brace are lynched by San Francisco vigilantes.

31. Fort Lookout is established on the Missouri River in Nebraska Territory.

AUGUST

1. The proslavery delegates from Kansas are refused seats in the House of Representatives.

4. Fort Randall is established on the Missouri River in Nebraska Territory.

8. Fort Simcoe is established in Washington Territory to protect settlers from Yakima Indians.

9. Mail service is established between San Diego and San Antonio.

10. Disaster strikes the gulf resort of Last Island, Louisiana, when huge waves submerge the island; an estimated 400 people drown.

11. One of the first attempts to rob a stagecoach in the California mining regions occurs on the Langton Express route between Comptonville and Marysville. Six bandits make the attempt; three are wounded and one is killed. Three passengers are also wounded, and the wife of a Marysville banker is killed. The stagecoach gets away with its cargo, $100,000 in raw gold.

13. The Kansas Free State Militia captures the proslavery town of Franklin.

■ The first ship built in San Diego, the *Loma,* is launched.

16. Gail Borden, of Texas, patents a milk-concentrating process in his search for perfect condensed milk. He got the idea after a trip to England, where he was honored by Queen Victoria for inventing the meat biscuit. On the journey home, diseased cows aboard ship were unable to give milk, and Borden and other passengers were forced to listen to the wails of starving babies. Upon being issued Patent No. 15,553, Borden quips: "I shall . . . within one year either be a citizen of the world, known in every civilized country, or, I shall be a retired, humble individual in the back woods of Texas."

18. Kansas territorial governor Shannon resigns. Daniel Woodson, who favors slavery, is chosen as the interim governor.

23. The first wagon road across the Sierra Nevada is opened.

25. Proclaiming his territory to be in a state of insurrection, Kansas governor Woodson calls out the proslavery militia.

26. At a convention in Tucson, 260 Arizonans petition Congress for territorial status. Their motion will not be granted.

29. Joshua Norton files a petition of insolvency in San Francisco.

30. John Brown and 40 supporters are driven from Osawatomie, Kansas, by some 300 members of the proslavery Kansas militia.

EMPEROR NORTON

For nearly a quarter of a century, the United States was ruled by a kind and benevolent emperor. A favorite of reporters and tourists, Norton I was a dignified potentate who reigned from San Francisco.

Joshua Abraham Norton was born in London in 1818. When he was 2 years old, his parents, John and Sarah, took him and two siblings to Cape Town, South Africa. Raised in a colony of Jewish pioneers, he learned the shipping business. News of the California Gold Rush coincided with the death of his father, a widower; it seemed like a good time for Norton to strike out on his own.

Norton was 31 on November 23, 1849, the day he sailed into San Francisco Bay aboard the German ship *Franzeska.* There, he engaged in an assortment of speculative businesses in a town whose population would boom from 500 to 30,000 in a year. In four years, he turned the $40,000 he had brought with him into $250,000.

Famine in China drove the price of rice there from 4 cents to 36 cents a pound. Hoping to corner the San Francisco market, Norton bought a 200,000-pound shipment of rice for $25,000. The deal done, unexpected rice-laden ships from afar began arriving in California and the price of rice fell to 3 cents a pound. This, along with lawsuits and other reversals, left Norton bankrupt. His insolvency petition, filed on August 29, 1856, listed debts of $55,811, losses of $45,000, and assets of $15,000. The burden was obviously too much. In September 1859, he strolled into the offices of the *Bulletin* with an announcement for publication:

(continued)

(continued)

At the peremptory request and desire of a large majority of the citizens of the United States, I, Joshua Norton . . . declare and proclaim myself Emperor of the U.S., and . . . do hereby order and direct the representatives of the different States of the Union to assemble in the Musical Hall of this city on the 1st day of February next, then and there to make such alterations in the existing laws of the Union as may ameliorate the evils under which the country is laboring, and thereby cause confidence to exist, both at home and abroad in our stability and integrity.

—Norton I, Emperor of the United States

The reign had begun. San Francisco took his misguided majesty to its collective heart, encouraged his diplomacy, and defended his causes. In his next releases, he abolished Congress, fired the governor of Virginia for the hanging of John Brown, and then ordered General Winfield Scott to "clear the halls of Congress" when that body ignored his edict. Another early decree, scoffed at along with the rest, presented Norton's idea to construct a bridge on the exact location of today's Golden Gate Bridge.

In 1860, Norton ordered that the Republic of the United States be dissolved, to "establish in its stead" an Absolute Monarchy. Soon, he added "Protector of Mexico" to his title. Next, he abolished the Supreme Court. At the outset of the Civil War, he fired both Abraham Lincoln and Jefferson Davis. After the conflict, he found fault with Andrew Johnson: "If found guilty, behead him or send him here to black the Emperor's boots."

Once, Norton broke the window of a restaurant for displaying a "disrespectful" portrait of His Majesty dining with the city's mongrel celebrities, Bummer and Lazarus. Arrested for vagrancy in 1867 by a rookie officer, he was released with an apology from the chief of police, who said Norton "had shed no blood, robbed no one, and despoiled no country; which is more than can be said of his fellows in that line."

For 21 years the charade continued. On the night of January 8, 1880, Emperor Norton was found slumped at the corner of California and Grant. Those on the scene tried to revive him, but he was gone. The cause of death was listed as "sanguineous apoplexy."

Ten thousand people attended the royal funeral. His remains were first interred in the Masonic Cemetery, then moved in 1934 to Woodlawn, where he now rests under a monument that reads: NORTON I, EMPEROR OF THE UNITED STATES AND PROTECTOR OF MEXICO.

The debate over Norton's sincerity has ceased. Instead, he is remembered as a leader who never meddled in international affairs, never levied an unfair tax, and never sent a boy to war.

- Congress adjourns without taking any further action on Kansas statehood.
31. The first transcontinental mail arrives in San Diego 53 days after leaving San Antonio.

Also in August 1856:
Stagecoach robberies in the Comstock country continue at an alarming rate; many are blamed on the gangs of Tom Bell and Rattlesnake Dick.

SEPTEMBER
9. John W. Geary, the former mayor of San Francisco appointed by the president to succeed acting Kansas governor Woodson, arrives in Kansas.
11. Colonel Harvey surprises and captures a proslavery camp on Slough Creek, Kansas.
13. Mormons in Utah revive the Doctrine of Blood Atonement, the belief that some sins can be washed away only by the letting of blood.
15. At the request of Kansas governor Geary, federal troops are used to divert a band of 2,500 Missouri border thugs intent on raiding Lawrence, Kansas.
16. The free-stater David Buffum is murdered by Charles Hays near Lecompton.
26. The first two of the Mormon handcart brigades that left Iowa City on June 9 arrive in Salt Lake City. They are met by a huge celebration, complete with brass band.
28. Robert E. Lee arrives at Fort Ringgold, Texas, to conduct his court-martial duties.

Also in September 1856:
Samuel Clemens leaves Keokuk, Iowa, for Cincinnati, where he will work as a printer.

OCTOBER

18. A. T. Noel Byron, the widow of Lord Byron, sends to Harriet Beecher Stowe 65 pounds sterling "toward the relief of the sufferers in Kansas."

30. The court-martial at which Robert E. Lee is presiding adjourns at Fort Ringgold, Texas, to reconvene at Fort Brown, Texas.

Also in October 1856:

Another Mormon handcart brigade that left Iowa City in June arrives in Salt Lake City.

NOVEMBER

2. Grizzly Adams makes his theatrical debut in San Francisco's Union Theatre.

4. James F. Curtis becomes San Francisco's first police chief.

▪ James Buchanan Gillett, the future Texas Ranger, is born in Austin, Texas.

17. Fort Buchanan becomes the first army post constructed in the Gadsden Purchase lands.

18. Lieutenant W. A. Bradfute leads a detachment of the 2nd Cavalry against Comanches on the Concho River in Texas.

▪ Representative John Bingham of Ohio sends a letter to Secretary of War Jefferson Davis, nominating George Armstrong Custer to West Point.

22. The *Alta California* reports the following shipments of gold: Wells Fargo—$426,531; Drexel, Sather and Church—$325,000.

26. Lieutenant W. A. Bradfute again leads a detachment of the 2nd Cavalry against Comanches on the Concho River in Texas; four Indians are killed and one is captured.

29. Maguire's Opera House opens in San Francisco.

Also in November 1856:

Horace Tabor is elected to the Topeka legislature on the Free-Soil ticket.

National Headlines/November 1856:
4. BUCHANAN DEFEATS FREMONT

DECEMBER

1. The *Daily Morning Call* begins publishing in San Francisco. The newspaper is named after a popular play.

2. In his farewell address to Congress, President Pierce voices regret that Kansas "was made the battlefield, not so much of opposing factions or interests within itself as of the conflicting passions of the whole people of the United States."

3. Kansas and Iowa are devastated by a three-day blizzard.

4. Fort Buchanan becomes the first post office in southern Arizona.

8. The Utah legislature meets in Fillmore and adjourns to Salt Lake City.

13. William Walker, the wandering dictator from California, is forced from Granada, Nicaragua, by loyalist troops.

18. Lieutenant J. B. Witherell leads a detachment of the 2nd Cavalry against Indians near Fort Clark, on the Rio Grande in Texas.

▪ The Utah legislature meets in Salt Lake City.

22. Comanches and the 2nd Cavalry clash at the headwaters of the Concho River in Texas. Two soldiers and three Indians are killed.

31. For 1856, Wells Fargo reports a gross income of $251,400 from transportation (people) and a net income of $44,349 from express (freight) services.

Also in December 1856:

Since November 1855, the battle over slavery that has raged in "Bleeding Kansas" has claimed 200 lives and caused $2 million in property damage.

Also in 1856:

The Indian population in California stands at 50,000, compared to 100,000 in 1849.

The banking panic continues to affect San Francisco, where 140 failures occurred during the year.

During 1855 and 1856, Mark Twain lives in Keokuk, Iowa, assisting his brother Orion, a printer, at the Ben Franklin Book and Job Printing Office. Twain makes his first literary money here, selling letters written under the name Thomas Jefferson Snodgrass for $5 each to the Keokuk *Evening Post*.

Cattle are driven from Texas to Montana by Captain Richard Grant.

Harpers Weekly begins publishing in New York.

The city of Dallas, Texas, is incorporated.

Rattlesnake Dick robs a Rhodes and Lusk Express coach of $26,000.

Following an investigation of Pueblo Indian land claims in New Mexico, the U.S. surveyor general recommends the confirmation of land grants to 18 pueblos.

Hubert Howe Bancroft opens a San Francisco bookstore. Soon the operation will expand to 300 employees in printing and publishing. The first books published by H. H. Bancroft and Company are law books.

James Beckwourth, the black mountain man and one-time chief of the Crows, dictates his memoirs to T. D. Bonner: *The Life and Adventures of James P. Beckwourth*.

George Horatio Derby, aka "Squibob" or "John Phoenix," publishes *Phoenixiana*, a collection of parodies.

John Thomas O'Keefe, who will earn fame as the "Pike's Peak Prevaricator," is born in New York City.

1857

"If you have no family or friends to aid you,
and no prospect opened to you . . .
turn your face to the great West, and there build up a home and fortune."

—Horace Greeley

JANUARY

1. Montana's Fort Owen reports a temperature of −30°
   and 15 inches of snow on the ground.
12–**February 14.** At Lecompton, Kansas, the proslavery territorial legislature calls for the convening of
   a constitutional convention; the public will not be
   required to approve a new constitution.
16. The Concert Hall opens in San Francisco.

Also in January 1857:
Henry Newton Brown, the future lawman and bandit,
   is born in Cold Spring Township, Missouri.

FEBRUARY

16. Fort Des Moines, Iowa, officially becomes the city
   of Des Moines.

MARCH

1. Using Jaeger's ferry, one Henry A. Crabb and a
   group of followers invade Mexico with the objective
   of taking over the state of Sonora.
3. The Butterfield Overland Mail's stage service is inaugurated between Memphis, Tennessee, and Tipton, Missouri.
▪ Congress authorizes the postmaster general to seek
   bids for an overland stagecoach service to carry
   mail and passengers between the Missouri River
   and San Francisco.
▪ Fort Abercrombie is established on the west bank
   of the Red River south of present Fargo, North

Dakota. It is named for the commander of the
founding party, Lieutenant Colonel John J. Abercrombie.
4. Kansas governor Geary resigns, citing frustration
   with the struggle to bring self-government to his territory.
9. First Lieutenant A. Gibbs is wounded in an encounter with Indians on the northern slope of the Sierra
   de los Mimbres in New Mexico. Six Indians are
   reported killed.
10. Isaac Cody dies after coming down with a chill
   during a rainstorm. His 11-year-old son, William F.
   Cody, will soon go to work as a messenger boy for
   the wagon trains of Majors and Russell that run
   from Fort Leavenworth to Fort Kearny.
11. Lieutenant L. L. Baker and a detachment of
   mounted riflemen engage Apaches at Ojo del
   Muerto, New Mexico. Two soldiers are killed and
   two are wounded; seven Indians are killed and four
   are wounded.
26. Former treasury secretary Robert J. Walker is appointed Kansas territorial governor.
▪ At Rivas, Nicaragua, Central American troops lay
   siege to the dictatorship of William Walker.
29. Captain Alexander Fancher's wagon train, which
   includes nearly 150 men, women, and children,
   departs Arkansas en route to California.

National Headlines/March 1857
6. DRED SCOTT VS. SANDFORD DECIDED

APRIL

6. Henry A. Crabb's invaders are annihilated when they encounter Mexican military forces at Caborca.

7. Snow falls in every state of the Union during a freak late-season freeze. Temperatures in Houston dip to 21°.

29. The army's Division of the Pacific establishes its headquarters in San Francisco.

MAY

13. The California and New York Steamship Company is incorporated in San Francisco, with Leland Stanford as director.

20. President James Buchanan declares Utah in a "state of rebellion" for a variety of reasons, including the practice of polygamy, and orders federal troops to the territory.

■ The *Sonora* leaves San Francisco with $2.3 million in gold.

21. The rule of William Walker officially ends in Nicaragua, thanks to the forces provided by other countries and an army hired by Cornelius Vanderbilt.

24. Lieutenant Colonel Crittenden leads the Gila Expedition against the Apaches in the Mogollon Mountains of New Mexico. Seven Indians are reported killed and nine captured.

26. In his inaugural address, Robert Walker, Kansas Territory's new governor, calls for cooperation and promises a fair vote on any new constitution.

Also in May 1857:
The artist, architect, and author Frederick Law Olmstead writes *Trip on the Southwestern Frontier.*

JUNE

10. Brigham Young obtains a contract for his XY Company to haul mail and freight for the U.S. government.

■ First Lieutenant George Crook, leading the 4th Infantry against Indians at Pitt River Canyon, California, is wounded by an arrow.

15. The proslavery Kansas legislature meets in Lecompton.

■ San Francisco Water Works is established.

22. James E. Birch wins a contract from the U.S. government to carry mail and passengers on a semimonthly basis between San Antonio and San Diego, via Tucson. Because his passengers will be asked sometimes to ride mules from Fort Yuma to California, the service will become known as the "Jackass Mail."

25. In the initial expedition of the 1st Army Camel Corps, the beasts of burden of the 2nd Cavalry, led by Edward Beale, begin blazing a new supply trail to California. A convoy of troops, mules, horses, civilians, and 75 camels and their drivers leave San Antonio on the first leg of a journey that will take them to El Paso and then Albuquerque. A few days out, they will meet 26 cowboys driving a large herd of cattle. Upon seeing, and smelling, the long-legged, shaggy strangers, the steers will initiate what old-timers call the "Big Stampede." During the two days the cowboys will spend rounding up what is left of their herd, the camels will make another 100 miles.

27. The Gila Expedition continues in New Mexico. On the Gila River, dragoons, riflemen, and infantry under Colonel Loving and Captain Clayborne launch a major attack against Apaches. Four soldiers are wounded and several Indians are killed, wounded, or captured.

■ Emerson Hough, author of *The Covered Wagon* (1922), is born in Newton, Iowa.

28. At Fort Leavenworth, Brigadier General W. S. Harney is ordered to take command of the army in Utah. He will be removed from that command after stating that he intends to "hang Brigham first and try him afterward." His successor will be Colonel Alexander.

29. Lieutenant J. E. B. Stuart is wounded during a campaign against Cheyennes at Soloman's Fork on the Kansas River in Kansas. Ten Indians are killed and 10 are wounded.

JULY

1. Henry Pittock's party of four reaches the top of Mount Hood.

9. The first stagecoach mail line between San Antonio and San Diego begins operating.

13. President Buchanan, hoping to quiet the "insurrection," names Alfred Cumming to replace Brigham Young as Utah's territorial governor. Young's response: "I am, and will be governor, and no power can hinder it until the Lord Almighty says, 'Brigham, you need not be governor any longer.'"

■ Delegates from districts in Minnesota meet in St. Paul to draft a constitution. The convention splits along party lines, with Democrats and Republicans each drafting their own constitutions. A committee is appointed to resolve the differences, but two slightly different constitutions will emerge from the convention.

15. Kansas governor Walker urges free-staters to participate in the territorial election scheduled for October.

18. Colonel Albert Sidney Johnston, under orders from President Buchanan, begins leading his troops from Fort Leavenworth to Utah. When the news of the march reaches the Mormon stronghold, Salt Lake City will be evacuated.

25. George Cooper Pardee, who will become the 21st governor of California (1903–1907), is born in San Francisco.

Also in July 1857:
George A. Custer, 21, enters West Point.

AUGUST

3. The wagon train of Captain Alexander Fancher arrives in Salt Lake City (see March 29). Oddly, word of the train's arrival does not appear in the *Deseret News,* a clue to historians that a conspiracy is under way. Merchants refuse to trade with the Arkansas travelers. Following this unusual reception, the train will leave on a southwesterly route.

5–12. Captain H. L. Scott commands dragoons and infantry against Pitt River Indians near Fort Crook in California.

7. A portion of the "Army of Utah," Colonel Albert S. Johnston's troops, arrives at Fort Kearny.

12. In Kansas, a company of dragoons passes through Lawrence with a wagon full of free-staters taken prisoner in Franklin.

15. San Francisco's Metropolitan Theater is destroyed by fire.

31. The first mail coach from San Antonio arrives in San Diego.

National Headlines/August 1857:
24. FINANCIAL PANIC OF '57 BEGINS

SEPTEMBER

1. Troops arrive at the Sweetwater River—some 1,400 men of the 5th and 10th Regiments. Another 1,000 troops will follow, bringing the total force to uphold federal law to 2,400. An invasion of Utah seems imminent.

3. Dr. John McLoughlin, the former factor of Fort Vancouver and the founder of Oregon City, Oregon, dies.

■ The Fancher wagon train arrives at Mountain Meadows, about 320 miles southwest of Salt Lake City.

7–11. The Mountain Meadows Massacre takes place.

11. Colonel Albert S. Johnston assumes command of the Utah Expedition from General Harney.

13. A written communication from Brigham Young, urging that the Fancher wagon train be allowed to pass unmolested, arrives in Cedar City.

THE MOUNTAIN MEADOWS MASSACRE
SEPTEMBER 7–11, 1857

The trouble for the Fancher wagon train began earlier, in Salt Lake City, where the settlers had arrived during a time of public hysteria. Fearing an imminent invasion by U.S. troops, Salt Lake merchants had refused to trade with the group. Disgruntled members of the party supposedly raised Mormon ire in settlements along the way by promising to return with a "small army." Fancher's party also named two bulls "Brigham" and "Heber," after Brigham Young and his right hand man, Heber Kimball. Rumor had it that another member of the party had boasted that he had "helped shoot the guts out of" church founder Joseph Smith, who was slain in 1844 by a mob in Carthage, Illinois. According to another rumor, the Fancher party had wronged several Indians along the way by selling them putrid meat and bad water.

Approximately 320 miles southwest of Salt Lake City, at the rim of the Great Basin, Fancher's wagons reached a ribbon of grassy land known as Mountain Meadows. That same day, Sunday, September 6, John D. Lee was leading a group of Saints and local Indian warriors to the pastoral site. Before arriving, Lee and his men donned Indian garb and war paint. The combined force of Mormon militia and Indian braves, some 300 strong, then surrounded the camp of Fancher's wagon train and opened fire at the first smell of breakfast. Perhaps seven men in Fancher's party died immediately, and another dozen were gravely wounded. Women and children caught in the cross fire scattered in panic. The surviving members of the party mounted a sturdy defense, returning fire from behind their wagons. What had been intended as a quick and ugly incident thus turned into a standoff.

By September 10, the Fancher party was running out of water. Three males who attempted to ride for help were captured and executed. Meanwhile, the attackers had determined that all witnesses who could talk must die. Under a white flag on September 11, *(continued)*

(continued)

John Lee told the Fancher party that it could appease the Indians. The men were separated from the women and children and shot dead on "Massacre Hill." The Indians then killed the women and older children while the Mormons finished off the sick. Seventeen very young children were spared and whisked away to homes in Salt Lake City.

Twenty years later, Lee became the only person brought to trial for the massacre; he was convicted and shot.

15. Brigham Young proclaims, "We are invaded by a hostile force, who are evidently assailing us to accomplish our overthrow and destruction." Young forbids any troops to enter Utah Territory and declares martial law.
16. John Butterfield and Waterman L. Ormsby obtain a government contract for their Butterfield Overland Mail to link St. Louis and San Francisco. The operation itself will join St. Louis and Memphis to Fort Smith, Arkansas, then follow a route from El Paso to Fort Yuma and on to Los Angeles and San Francisco. The $600,000-a-year contract will help the company grow to 1,000 employees and more than 100 Concord coaches.
29. Nathan D. Champion, the future cowboy and suspected rustler, is born in Williamson County, Texas.

Also in September 1857:

The *Central America,* carrying $1,595,497 in California gold, sinks off Cape Hatteras, North Carolina. Wells Fargo was perhaps the largest financial loser in the disaster, having shipped $260,000 in gold, although insurance with four London companies probably covered the loss. Not so lucky was the uninsured firm of Drexel, Sather and Church, which was forced to suspend operations for six months.

San Francisco's Mechanics Institute and the California Horticulture Society cosponsor the city's first fair. Among the fruit and flower displays are exhibits of vines and a demonstration of how a wine industry might be developed.

OCTOBER

4. Disgruntled Mormons led by Major Lot Smith burn two army provision trains, a total of 72 federal wagons, causing many problems for the invading army.

5. In an election, Kansas free-soilers win a majority of territorial legislative seats. The polls were strictly supervised by Governor Robert Walker, and fraudulent ballots were thrown out by Territorial Secretary Frederick P. Stanton.
6. The U.S. chess championship is won by Paul Murphy, 20, of New Orleans.
9. Nathaniel Maxcy Tabor, the first child of future silver king Horace Tabor and his wife, Augusta, is born on a farm in Topeka, Kansas.
10. James and Granville Stuart, destined for fame in Montana's mining industry, first enter the territory at Monida Pass.
13. Residents of Minnesota Territory vote to adopt a constitution and to apply for statehood. The territory's population has grown from 6,000 in 1850 to more than 150,000.
19. The Lecompton Convention meets in Kansas to draft a proslavery constitution.
30. Gertrude Atherton, author of *A Daughter of the Vine* (1899), is born in San Francisco.

Also in October 1857:

Governor James W. Grimes declares Des Moines the capital of Iowa.

National Headlines/October 1857:

23. BANKING PANIC IN THE EAST FORCES CLOSURES OF BANKING & MERCANTILE FIRMS

NOVEMBER

5. Bad weather, along with harassment from the Mormon Nauvoo Legion, prevents Colonel Johnston's Utah Expedition from entering the territory. Out of supplies, he chooses to winter his force at Fort Bridger.
8. The Lecompton Convention adjourns in Kansas after drafting a proslavery constitution and calling for a territorial election on the question of slavery.
10. In New Orleans, William Walker is arrested and charged with outfitting a steamship with guns and men for another attempted overthrow of the government of Nicaragua. Bail is set at $2,000.
14. Texas governor Elisha Pease calls out the Texas Rangers to help end the "Cart War," violent altercations between Texan and Mexican teamsters that have resulted in much bloodshed.
17. The *San Francisco Bulletin* prints a two-column list of national businesses that have failed during the past three weeks of financial panic.
19. Shawnee Indian lands in Kansas are declared open for purchase.

24. William Walker, having jumped bail in New Orleans, arrives in Greytown, Nicaragua, and resumes his presidency.

Also in November 1857:

William Levi "Buck" Taylor, America's first cowboy hero and star of Buffalo Bill's Wild West and of dime novels such as *Buck Taylor, King of the Cowboys* (1887), is born in Fredericksburg, Texas.

DECEMBER

7. Lieutenant W. W. Overell and a detachment of mounted riflemen, 12 soldiers in all, battle six Kiowa Indians in the Ladrone Mountains near Fort Craig, New Mexico. Five Indians are killed and one is captured.

■ The third territorial legislature of Kansas convenes in Lecompton.

■ Commodore Hiram Paulding lands his troops in Nicaragua in pursuit of William Walker.

8. Congress hears President Buchanan's call for funds to suppress the insurrection in Utah and his recommendation of territorial status for Arizona. Certain that the bill will be passed, Arizona authorities send Lieutenant Sylvester Mowry of Tucson to Washington. Congress will reject territorial status for Arizona, and Mowry will be sent home.

9. Senator Stephen A. Douglas speaks against the Lecompton constitution.

15. Johnson's Melodeon opens in San Francisco.

17. Governor Walker of Kansas resigns over the president's decision to accept the Lecompton constitution. Frederick P. Stanton is named acting governor.

21. The Lecompton constitution, which permits slavery, is approved by Kansas voters, 6,226 to 569. Free-staters are prohibited from voting, and fraud will later be discovered.

29. William Walker is brought by a federal marshal to Washington, D.C., where he learns he is not being charged by the U.S. government.

31. Antislavery factions in Kansas boycott a vote on a constitution that allows slavery.

Also in December 1857:

Horace Greeley estimates that 381,107 persons arrived in San Francisco by sea from 1849 to 1857. During that period, some $370,986,599 in gold was shipped east from California.

The state records of Iowa are transferred from Iowa City to Des Moines.

Also in 1857:

St. Louis and New York City are linked by rail.

Alonzo Delano pens the play *A Live Woman in the Mines.*

The first house of worship for Chinese in the United States, San Francisco's Kong Chow Temple on Pine Street, opens.

In St. Louis, the German immigrant Eberhard Anheuser adds a brewery to his successful soap business. Adolphus Busch, also from Germany, arrives in St. Louis and opens a brewer's supply shop.

John Deere of Moline, Illinois, produces 10,000 steel plows, many for use in the West.

Lieutenant Joseph Christmas Ives leads the first exploration of Grand Canyon; he is searching for a supply route for forces engaging the Mormons in Utah.

President Buchanan appoints James Denver commissioner of Indian affairs and sends him to Kansas Territory to negotiate treaties.

Mount St. Helens, a volcano in Washington, erupts.

Robert E. Lee visits Fort Brown in Brownsville, Texas, and comments on the tropical birds and plants.

Bret Harte works as a printer's devil for a newspaper in Union, California, a job that branches into editorializing. He earns extra income from tutoring, and his poems appear in San Francisco's *Golden Era* magazine.

Wells Fargo ships a total of $60 million in gold.

California's honey industry begins when Italian honeybees are introduced to San Diego.

Sylvester Mowry, the former commander of Fort Yuma, self-publishes *Memoir of the Proposed Territory of Arizona,* which promotes the idea of separation from New Mexico Territory.

James G. Swan publishes *The Northwest Coast.*

Since 1853, the United States has acquired 157 million acres from 52 treaties with Native American tribes.

1858

"We are satisfied with our prospects here and intend to stay until this country is fully explored. We have laid the foundation for a city, an outlet for this gold bonanza and for the Rocky Mountain region."

—Gen. William Larimer

JANUARY

1. The *Pacific Medical Journal* is established in San Francisco.
2. The Colorado River steamboat *General Jessup* becomes the first to navigate the river above Yuma, reaching a point some 20 miles above Hardyville.
4. Kansas voters reject the Lecompton constitution by a margin of 10,226 to 138 (24 voted to approve the constitution minus its slavery clause); citizens who favor slavery did not vote.
5. The third territorial legislature of Kansas adjourns to Lawrence.
7. President Buchanan informs the Senate of his displeasure with the William Walker affair in Nicaragua.
8. The third territorial legislature of Kansas begins holding sessions in Lawrence.
■ Democrat John B. Weller is sworn in as governor of California.
9. Texas politician Anson Jones commits suicide. It is believed he was despondent after failing to tally a single vote in the 1857 senatorial election.
25. William Walker goes to Mobile, Alabama, to drum up support for the "Americanization" of Central America.
28. Three members of Captain I. N. Palmer's cavalry are wounded in a scrape with Indians on the south branch of the Llano River in Texas.

Also in January 1858:

Having made it from San Antonio to Los Angeles with the Camel Corps, Edward Beale's expedition begins its return trip. Many camels are left behind; some are donated to the city to haul salt and borax, and others, including some shipped to San Francisco by a private operation, will be used in mining camps in California and Nevada. The rocky terrain, however, will make the use of camels in mining operations impractical. Reports one miner, "The sight of the camels stampeded more horses and mules in the camps than a first-class earthquake."

FEBRUARY

1. Wells Fargo pays a cash dividend of 5 percent.
2. President Buchanan asks Congress to admit Kansas, with its Lecompton constitution, to the Union, as a slave state.
13. The third territorial legislature of Kansas adjourns in Lawrence.
14. The first marriage in what will become Arizona Territory is officiated by Charles Poston in Tubac.
17. William Green Russell, who will be called "the greatest single cause of the Pike's Peak gold rush," and a party of nine depart Lumpkin County, Georgia. They will soon link with a band of Cherokees, and the party will expand to 21.
25. Relations between the Nez Percé and the Mormon settlers at Fort Lemhi, Idaho, turn sour shortly after

one George Hill becomes romantically involved with a chief's daughter. The Indians kill two settlers and wound five.

- Thomas Kane, who has appointed himself ambassador to the Mormons, journeys to Utah to urge Brigham Young to recognize Alfred Cumming as governor of the territory. Young says he will abide if the U.S. government's troops are withdrawn.

28. The first troops arrive at Fort Abercrombie in present North Dakota.

MARCH

6. The Catholic *Weekly Monitor* begins publishing in San Francisco.

11. Apaches clash with approximately 20 dragoons under First Lieutenant I. N. Moore in New Mexico's Huachuca Mountains. Moore reports one officer wounded and one Indian killed.

18. The Mormons decide to abandon Salt Lake City in the face of invasion by U.S. troops.

22. At age 20, James Butler Hickok, who will gain fame under the name "Wild Bill," is elected village constable of Monticello Township, Johnson County, Kansas.

23. The U.S. Senate approves Kansas statehood under the Lecompton constitution by a vote of 33 to 25.

- Over the governor's veto, the Kansas territorial legislature votes to move the capital to Minneola, where the third constitutional convention is meeting; the convention adjourns to Leavenworth.

National Headlines/March 1858:

4. MATTHEW PERRY DIES AT 64

APRIL

1. By a vote of 120 to 112, the U.S. House of Representatives amends the Kansas statehood bill to provide for another popular vote on the Lecompton constitution.

5. Brigham Young plans a mass evacuation of his followers from Salt Lake City to Provo.

6. President Buchanan accuses the Mormons of "levying war against the United States" and declares their government to be in a state of rebellion.

11. Gold seekers in what will become Colorado, certain that their numbers will increase with the arrival of more fortune hunters, call for a convention to petition the federal government for statehood.

12. Newly appointed governor Alfred Cumming arrives in Salt Lake City. When he tells the populace that federal troops are indeed on their way, 30,000 Mormons evacuate the city. They will hide in Provo until the confusion subsides.

21. Captain George Anderson reports one cavalryman killed in a fight with Indians near Fort Scott, Kansas.

26. The Chinese are prohibited from landing at any port in California under the terms of a bill passed today by Congress. The action will be the first of many attempts at restricting Chinese immigration.

30. Following the House's approval of a compromise proposed by Representative William H. English and aimed at appeasing the Senate, the latter adopts the amended Kansas statehood bill that was approved by the House on April 1.

Also in April 1858:
The Mormons abandon Fort Lemhi in Idaho.

MAY

4. President Buchanan signs the Kansas statehood bill authorizing a new popular vote in that territory on the Lecompton constitution. If the constitution is adopted, Kansas will become a slave state and receive land grants. If the constitution is not adopted, statehood will be postponed until a population of 93,420 is reached.

11. Minnesota is admitted to the Union as the 32nd state, the 17th free of slavery. The new state comprises the eastern portion of Minnesota Territory, which now covers only the area between the Missouri and Red Rivers.

12. A force of 200 Texas Rangers and Tonkawa Indians attack the Comanche camp of Chief Iron Shirt (about 65 lodges). Iron Shirt, so named for his suit of Spanish armor, is killed when a bullet passes through a gap in the garment.

- James Denver is appointed governor of Kansas Territory, which includes a third of the future state of Colorado.

17. A major battle takes place near Spokane Lake, Washington, as 25 members of the 1st Dragoons and 9th Infantry find themselves up against "800–1,000" Spokane Indians and members of other tribes. Five enlisted men and two officers perish.

19. The Marais des Cygnes Massacre occurs on the Kansas river of the same name: proslavery forces capture 11 free-soilers and kill five.

21. Utah governor Cumming meets with Colonel Albert Johnston and attests that no organized military force exists in the territory.

JUNE

2. The Adelphi Theater is destroyed by fire in San Francisco.

10. The U.S. Army takes charge of Fort Bridger in present Wyoming.

12. William Green Russell's party of 19 Georgians, accompanied by 46 Cherokees, arrives at Bent's Fort in present Colorado. The party will soon move on to the Cherry Creek diggings, near present Denver.

13. The steamship *Pennsylvania* explodes on the Mississippi River near Memphis, killing 160.

14. Governor Cumming of Utah proclaims, "peace is restored to our Territory." Mormons celebrate their presidential pardon "for all treasons and seditions."

24. Fort Garland is established in Colorado's San Luis Valley.

■ Two prospecting companies from Missouri join the Russell party from Georgia.

26. Federal troops from Camp Scott under Colonel Johnston march through Salt Lake City in a show of force but find that most of the Mormons have fled south to Provo. The troops bring a presidential pardon "to all who will submit themselves to the just authority of the federal government."

Also in June 1858:

The future Civil War guerrilla William Clarke Quantrill travels with an expedition hoping to strike it rich in the Pikes Peak gold rush.

National Headlines/June 1858:

17. LINCOLN OPENS ILLINOIS SENATE CAMPAIGN: "A HOUSE DIVIDED"

JULY

1. Mormon leaders tell their followers to return to Salt Lake City; the federal troops have departed.

4. Mormons who fled to Provo begin returning to Salt Lake City.

5. William Green Russell and his mixed party of whites and Cherokees from Lumpkin County, Georgia, discover Colorado gold. Their discovery is actually made in Kansas Territory, on the future site of Denver. They make camp on the South Platte River, eight miles above the mouth of Cherry Creek.

■ A new wagon road from Fort Yuma to El Paso that skirts the Gila Desert is finished.

24. The first weekly mail from back East arrives in Santa Fe.

Also in July 1858:

Frank Leslie's Illustrated Newspaper reports on the express business: "The business ten years ago was a novelty, but it is now one of the recognized institutions of the country."

Rattlesnake Dick is recognized in Auburn, Nevada. The man who spotted him is killed, as are two deputies, in the ensuing gun battle. Dick, twice wounded,

escapes to a point about a mile from town, where he shoots himself in the head rather than die slowly from his wounds.

National Headlines/July 1858:

24. LINCOLN CHALLENGES DOUGLAS TO DEBATE

AUGUST

2. Kansas voters again reject the Lecompton Constitution, 11,812 to 1,926.

■ Wells Fargo pays a cash dividend of 5 percent, making a total of 10 percent for the year.

5. Julia Holmes, 20, becomes the first white woman known to have climbed Pikes Peak.

15. Second Lieutenant J. K. Allen is slain in a battle with Indians on Washington's Yakima River.

24. Camp Floyd is established in Utah's Cedar Valley.

29. Twelve soldiers under Captain G. McLane, joined by 22 Mexicans, battle 300 Navajo warriors near Bear Springs, New Mexico. Ten Indians are reported killed, four are wounded and four are captured.

National Headlines/August 1858:

16. FIRST CABLE MESSAGE CROSSES THE ATLANTIC

21. LINCOLN–DOUGLAS BEGIN DEBATE SERIES

SEPTEMBER

1. Troops under Colonel Wright fight Spokane Indians at Four Lakes, Washington.

3. Arizona again petitions Congress for territorial status and names Sylvester Mowry as its congressional delegate. Congress will again turn down the request.

5–8. Troops under Colonel Wright again fight Spokane Indians, this time at Spokane Plain, Washington.

6–24. In Kansas Territory, Montana City is laid out on Cherry Creek, six miles from its confluence with the South Platte River. It is the first town to spring up as a result of the Pikes Peak gold rush.

9–15. A punitive mission against the Navajos is launched by Colonel Miles and Colonel Loving from Fort Defiance, New Mexico. They report two soldiers killed, against "many Navajo" deaths.

10. Infantry and Indians fight on Washington's O'Kanogan River.

15. A punitive mission against the Comanches is launched by Major Earl Van Dorn from Fort Belknap, Texas.

16. The first Butterfield Overland Mail coach leaves Tipton, Missouri (near St. Louis), for San Francisco. John Butterfield's creed is "Remember, boys, nothing on God's earth must stop the United States

Frank Leslie's Illustrated Newspaper, *October 23, 1858, depicts the Overland Mail going through.* (Library of Congress)

mail!" Butterfield is on board, along with reporter Waterman Ormsby.

19–24. Captain W. F. Brooks leads the 3rd Infantry against Navajos at Canyon de Chelly, near Fort Defiance, New Mexico Territory. Six Indians are reported killed.

20. Camp Walbach is established to protect immigrants traveling through Cheyenne Pass between Nebraska and Wyoming.

22. The first westbound stagecoach of Butterfield's Overland Mail stops for breakfast and fresh horses at Fort Belknap, Texas.

24. The town of St. Charles, the future city of Denver, is laid out on the east bank of the South Platte River.

28–29. Captain T. Duncand leads riflemen and infantry against Indians in New Mexico's Chusca Valley and Mountains, killing two.

Also in September 1858:

Texan Jacob Snively discovers gold along the Gila River near Yuma, Arizona. Gila City will sprout quickly but disappear by 1862.

National Headlines/September 1858:

2. TRANSATLANTIC CABLE BREAKS

OCTOBER

1. Comanches and the 2nd Cavalry fight near the Wichita Village of the Choctaw Nation in Indian Territory. Lieutenant C. Van Camp is among the four troops killed; Comanche losses are listed by the army as 56.

▪ The first Butterfield Overland stagecoach reaches Arizona through Stein's Pass.

▪ The *Daily Evening Telegram* is established in San Francisco.

▪ Jacob Hall receives a contract to provide monthly mail service between Kansas City and Stockton, California. His mule teams will cover the distance in about 60 days.

▪ After another fight at Bear Springs, New Mexico, Captain Andrew Lindsay reports two enlisted men killed, eight Indians dead, and "many Indians wounded."

2. Navajos kill one soldier in a fight at Laguna Chusca, near New Mexico's Fort Defiance.

■ The first Butterfield Overland stagecoach reaches Tucson.

3. The *Weekly California Home Journal* begins publication in San Francisco.

5. The first Butterfield Overland stagecoach crosses the Colorado River into California on Jaeger's ferry at 6:15 A.M.

7. The Butterfield Overland Mail's Concord stagecoach arrives in Los Angeles 20 days after leaving Tipton, Missouri. It ran day and night, nonstop, over 2,600 miles. The route was Tipton (St. Louis)–Fort Smith–Sherman, Texas–El Paso–Fort Yuma, New Mexico–Los Angeles. The last leg, to San Francisco, begins today.

■ A ticket on the Overland stagecoach from St. Louis to San Francisco, or in the other direction, is $150, or 10 cents a mile for destinations along the way. Coaches expect to make 120 miles a day.

9. The first Butterfield Overland stagecoach from the Pacific Coast reaches St. Louis and is transferred to a train for shipment east. The trip from San Francisco took 23 days and four hours.

■ "Many" Indians are reported killed in a battle with soldiers at Rio Pierce of the West, New Mexico.

10. The first Butterfield Overland stagecoach from Missouri reaches San Francisco, having covered 3,000 miles in 23 days and 23.5 hours. The *Alta California* declares the coach is faster than steamer mail by 10 days.

■ On board the first Overland stagecoach is *New York Herald Tribune* reporter Waterman Ormsby, who writes: "never did the night traveler approach a distant light, or the lonely mariner descry a sail, with more joy than did I the city of San Francisco."

■ Riflemen and infantry battle 150 Navajos at Ojo del Oso, New Mexico. Indian losses are reported to be heavy.

17. Captain George Lane and a company of mounted riflemen report a brush with 200 Navajos at Canyon Bonita, New Mexico. One soldier and three Indians are reported killed.

■ Boulder, Colorado, is founded by gold seekers from Nebraska. Within a year the city boasts hotels, a stamp mill, a sawmill, and Colorado's first public school.

18. Captain A. J. Lindsay reports "many Navajo killed and wounded" in a fight in New Mexico's Juan Chu Mountains.

19–November 18. The "Navajo Expedition" takes place in New Mexico. Two Zuni Indian scouts for the U.S. Army are reported wounded and one Navajo is killed in the month-long campaign.

27. Theodore Roosevelt, the future president and western enthusiast, is born in New York City.

29. The first grocery store in what will become Denver, Colorado, is opened by Charles Blake and Andre J. Williams of Iowa.

Also in October 1858:
Las Vegas Fort, Nevada, is abandoned.

NOVEMBER

1. On the west bank of the South Platte, opposite the new city of St. Charles, prospectors form the Auraria Town Company.

■ Jacob Hall's first eastbound mail run leaves Stockton, California, in a mule train. Mohave Indians will keep the mail from going through.

■ A small battle between soldiers and Indians occurs at Canon de Chelly, New Mexico Territory.

6. A constitution for the "Territory of Jefferson" (the future state of Colorado) is adopted; delegates are sent to Washington and Kansas to seek recognition of their territorial organization. The first governor of the short-lived territory will be R. W. Steele.

16. General William H. Larimer and a group from Kansas arrive and jump a land claim at St. Charles. A solitary guard, Charles Nichols, was left behind while other St. Charlesians returned to Kansas to file papers; he is no match for Larimer's group.

22. William Larimer's group votes to "assume" its claim and to rename St. Charles "Denver City," after the governor of Kansas, James Denver. Unknown to Larimer, Denver resigned the governorship three weeks earlier to return to an Indian affairs post.

23. The enterprising trader Jim Sanders becomes Denver's first "postal service" when he agrees to carry letters by wagon to Fort Laramie, Wyoming for 50 cents a piece. He will arrive back in Denver with the return mail—Christmas cards and so forth—on January 8.

26. *Frank Leslie's Illustrated Newspaper* prints a map of the Butterfield Overland Mail's route from St. Louis and Memphis to San Francisco. The stagecoach trip from San Francisco to southwest Missouri takes from 12 to 14 days.

Also in November 1858:
The first mail to reach San Francisco via Mexico's Isthmus of Tehuantepec arrives 18 days after leaving New Orleans.

DECEMBER

6. President Buchanan tells Congress that the territories are at peace with the federal government.

18. The first issue of *Territorial Enterprise* is published in Genoa, Nevada.

■ *Frank Leslie's Illustrated Newspaper* prints a map of the Panamanian and Nicaraguan routes to California.

20. Working from his base in Kansas, John Brown leads his only raid into Missouri, freeing 11 slaves and killing one supporter of slavery in the township of Henry.

23. The weekly newspaper *Telegraph Hill* begins publishing in San Francisco.

25. Denver celebrates its first Christmas.

Also in 1858:

Every army regiment in the West is on the march against Indians; each regiment, on average, marches 1,234 miles.

Council Grove, Kansas, is incorporated.

Wells Fargo ships $58 million in California gold.

Parts of southern Dakota are ceded to the United States by the Yankton Sioux.

DENVER'S FIRST CHRISTMAS
December 25, 1858

The small mining camp of Denver celebrated its first Christmas with a Taos Lightning blowout, courtesy of "Santa Claus," Richens Wootton, a merchant from Santa Fe.

At first, the camp had little to celebrate. Located 600 miles from a railroad and 200 miles from a post office, the community suffered instant holiday depression. Its 200 men, five women (four of them married), and perhaps a half-dozen children were certain they were not included on Santa's map. Unknown to them, Wootton and his wife and two children were slowly making their way to Denver from Fort Union, New Mexico, in two ox carts.

Christmas morning was described as "soft and genial as a May day, as beautiful as ever shone. Not a breeze whispered through the leafless cottonwoods." It was calm, and one could easily hear the sound of wagon wheels and the prancing and pawing of each ox. According to Henry Edward Warner, in a 1900 issue of the *Denver Times,* "the sun had just rubbed its sleepy eyes and peeped in on the little settlement . . . when Santa Claus made his appearance." Wootton unloaded his goods and set up his tent. That task completed, he rolled out a barrel from one of the wagons and cracked the top with an axe. Inside was Taos Lightning, a potent moonshine guaranteed to start an electrical storm in the head. It was the first whiskey in the diggings. Said Warner: "It went down like a swain on his knees to the object of his affections. It hit the stomach all in a lump and sent cheerful feeling up to the roots of a fellow's hair and back again to his toes, in one howling, rip-roaring succession of luxurious vibratory spasms of exquisite joy. It beat grand opera without even trying." "Uncle Dick gave the whole town a free blowout," said witness A. E. Pearce. "Everyone helped himself freely, using tin cups." William Larimer's son, 18-year-old William, Jr., said that "several did help themselves, and so often that they needed help to reach their cabins." According to General Larimer, the Methodist Reverend George W. Fisher's plans for a religious service were dashed: "Some were in favor, some were lukewarm and some opposed entirely to the program. This opposition grew when that arch opponent of religion, whisky, was introduced."

A bonfire and hoedown began in the streets. Men locked arms and danced to songs such as "The Star-Spangled Banner," "The Girl I Left Behind Me," and a new tune, "Root, Hog, or Die." "Active feet went into motion," one witness wrote, "and in the weird light we danced until midnight. Groups of Indians with their squaws and papooses filled the shadowy background. It was a picture that Rembrandt would have loved." Meanwhile, guests at the Murats' cabin, including Mrs. Wootton and her children, decorated the Christmas tree and sang "Silent Night."

As for the most popular man in town, Wootton was called "Uncle Dick" from that day on, and given a full share in the Auraria Town Company and land on which he would build his business. He made sure none of the celebrators drove home that night—many settled down for a long winter's nap on the banks of Cherry Creek.

The United States agrees to buy the Pipestone Quarry area, 11 million acres in what will become Dakota Territory, from the Yankton Sioux. The government appraises the value of the area as $13,750,000 but pays the Indians $1,650,000.

Gold is found in Deer Lodge Valley, Montana.

The Colorado gold rush attracts some 35,000 Easterners.

Juan Seguín publishes *Personal Memoirs,* which describes his participation in the battle at the Alamo and San Jacinto.

The *Chicasaw and Choctaw Herald* begins publishing at the Chickasaw capital of Tishomingo. From 1858 to 1899, a total of 205 newspapers will be launched in Nevada; all but 25 will fail.

In the Santa Cruz Valley near Tucson, William S. Oury's 100 heifers and four bulls become the first herd of fine cattle to pasture in Arizona.

Les Trappeurs de l'Arkansas (The Trappers of Arkansas) is written by Gustave Aimard.

Because of the expulsions of the Indians in the 1830s and the prolonged military campaigns against them in the East, approximately 100 Native Americans remain in Florida.

1859

"Next to outright gambling, the hardest way to obtain gold is to mine for it. . . . A good farmer or mechanic will usually make money faster . . . by sticking to his own business than by deserting it for gold-digging."

—Horace Greeley

JANUARY

1. The *Journal of Commerce* charts what Kansas City received from New Mexico in 1858 via the Santa Fe Trail:

	Amount	Value
Mexican wool (pounds)	1,051,000	$ 167,650
Goatskins	55,000	27,500
Dressed deerskins	60,000	175,000
Dry hides	61,857	170,107
Specie (in boxes)	—	1,527,789
Furs, other skins (estimate)	—	50,000

2. Religious services resume at Salt Lake City's Tabernacle.

3. In Kansas, the fourth territorial legislature assembles in Lecompton.

5. The fourth territorial legislature of Kansas adjourns to Lawrence.

7. The fourth territorial legislature of Kansas convenes in Lawrence.

▪ George Jackson discovers the first gold deposits in Colorado near present Idaho Springs.

9. Lieutenant Colonel Hoffman and 52 dragoons withstand an attack by 300 Mohaves in California. Hoffman reports 18 Mohaves killed.

13. California senator David C. Broderick is killed in a duel with Judge David S. Terry.

15. Gold is discovered at Gold Run in Boulder County, Colorado. Prospectors will wash out $100,000 worth of dust in hand rockers this season.

17. Benjamin Franklin, the favorite bear of Grizzly Adams, dies of a mysterious illness in San Francisco.

18. A post office is established in Auraria, Kansas Territory, and in St. Vrain, Nebraska Territory.

25. Sergeants J. Kelly and J. Berry, on leave in the Whetstone Springs area of New Mexico, are killed by Apaches.

Also in January 1859:

Denver's first trial is held in a grove of cottonwood trees on the banks of the Platte River. The defendant is convicted of stealing six cans of oysters valued at between $5 and $6 a can. With no jail for miles around, the judge orders 20 lashes, although the majority of witnesses want the culprit hanged. Finally, when it is discovered that the defendant was drunk on whiskey at the time, it is decided he shall simply be banned from the settlement and, if he returns, anyone may shoot him on sight.

FEBRUARY

1. John Brown takes the slaves he liberated in last December's invasion of Missouri from Kansas to Canada and freedom.

▪ The Eldorado, the first hotel in Denver, opens.

▪ Wells Fargo pays a cash dividend of 5 percent.

7. The Kansas legislature abolishes the western county of Arapahoe, causing a major headache for residents of the gold-mining areas, including Denver and Auraria.

8. Three soldiers are killed and eight are wounded in an attack by Mescalero Apaches at Dog Canyon in the Sacramento Mountains of New Mexico.

11. The fourth territorial legislature of Kansas adjourns in Lawrence.

13. A golden spike is driven in St. Joseph, Missouri, by "Uncle Joe" Robidoux to commemorate the completion of the last link in the Hannibal and St. Joseph Railroad. The valley of the upper Missouri River is now open to railroad service.

14. With a population of 50,000, Oregon enters the Union as the 33rd state, the 18th to be free. The first governor of the state is John Whiteaker.

17. Cadet George A. Custer receives three demerits at West Point for throwing snowballs.

23. In a proclamation issued today, Texas governor Hardin R. Runnels tells Texans to avoid hostilities against Indians.

24. Comanches battle the infantry and the cavalry at Caddo Creek near Fort Arbuckle in the Choctaw Nation. One soldier is killed; there are no estimates of Comanche casualties.

25. Fifty-eight Arizonians meet in Tubac and petition Congress to pay for a law enforcement organization known as the Arizona Rangers.

27–28. Seven Comanches are killed by Captain J. McIntosh's 1st Cavalry near Caddo Creek in the Choctaw Nation.

28. Congress establishes the Gila River Reservation in Arizona for Maricopa and Pima Indians.

Also in February 1859:

William N. Byers leaves Omaha, Nebraska, heading for the gold rush in Kansas Territory, where he will found the *Rocky Mountain News.*

MARCH

1. San Franciscans adopt an official city seal.

3. Editor Edward E. Cross begins publishing the *Weekly Arizonian* in Tubac. The territory's first newspaper reports that there were 19 acts of murder or robbery committed by Indians against whites from January 1 to February 21.

18. Cadet George A. Custer receives two demerits at West Point for throwing food in the mess hall.

23. The *Journal of Commerce* observes of Kansas City: "Fair skies, dry roads, Santa Fe trains, Pike's Peak emigrants, ox trains, mule wagons, horses, buggies, Mexicans, Indians, Mountain men, candidates and crinoline make up the panorama of life in Kansas City at the present writing."

National Headlines/March 1859:

7. FUGITIVE SLAVE ACT DECLARED CONSTITUTIONAL

APRIL

5. The "State of Jefferson" is formed by residents of what will become Colorado.

7. The first Protestant services in Arizona are led by Reverend Tuthill, a Methodist missionary in Tubac.

9. Samuel Clemens gets his Mississippi riverboat pilot's license.

10. Denver's first hanging takes place. A Hungarian immigrant had been found strangled in his bed, and suspicion centered on the brother-in-law, John Stoefel. A vigilance committee pulled the suspect out of the hills on April 9th; his outdoor trial is held at noon on this date. By 2:00 P.M., the terror-stricken defendant is out of his misery, swinging from a cottonwood tree on what will become the corner of 10th and Wazee. In the crowd of onlookers at the hanging is 17-year-old Dave Cook, the future lawman.

15. On the Colorado River, construction begins on Camp Colorado, which will assist emigrants en route to California; a week later, its name will be changed to Fort Mojave.

17. William N. Byers arrives at Cherry Creek from Omaha on horseback. In the young city of Denver, he will start the *Rocky Mountain News.*

18. A coach of the Leavenworth and Pikes Peak Express Company departs Fort Leavenworth to begin a trial run to the goldfields in the westernmost portion of Kansas Territory (in present Colorado).

19. Fort Mojave is established on the Colorado River in present Arizona.

20. William Byers's printing press arrives in Denver by wagon.

22. A post office is established in Boulder, Kansas Territory.

23. William Byers publishes the first issue of the *Rocky Mountain News,* beating his competition, John L. Merrick's *Cherry Creek Pioneer,* by 20 minutes. The *Pioneer* congratulates the winner and ceases publication with its first issue.

■ A copy of the *Rocky Mountain News* sells for 25 cents, payable in coin or gold dust.

Also in April 1859:

After attending a lecture on the West by the poet Bayard Taylor, the artist Albert Bierstadt, 29, joins General Frederick W. Lander's military expedition to survey a rail route through Wyoming's South Pass, from Fort Laramie to the Pacific. Bierstadt will spend the summer as an artist on horseback, sketching the Oregon Trail. From the Wind River Mountains, he writes: "The color of the mountains and of the plains . . . reminds one of the color of Italy; in fact, we have here the Italy of America in a primitive condition."

MAY

1. The first American Catholic priest in Arizona is Father Joseph P. Machebeuf, who relocates from Mesilla, New Mexico, to Tucson.
2. Captain A. G. Brackett's 2nd Cavalry kills two Comanches on the Great Comanche Trail in Texas.
3. Andy Adams, the future cowboy and author (*The Log of a Cowboy,* 1903), is born in Columbia City, Indiana.
6. John Gregory of Georgia finds lode gold at what will be called Gregory's Gulch, on the North Branch of Clear Creek near the new city of Denver. Horace Greeley, on his western venture, will call the area "the richest square mile on earth."
7. The first Leavenworth and Pikes Peak Express stagecoach arrives in Denver, having followed the Republican River from Fort Leavenworth.
9. In Utah, any gathering of armed men is declared illegal by Governor Cumming; this is his way of restraining both armed locals and U.S. Army troops.
10. The *New York Tribune* announces that editor Horace Greeley, 48, will follow his own advice and "Go West, Young Man": "Mr. Greeley left this city by the Erie Railroad last evening, on his way to the Pacific States."

Colorado's great newspaper race. Workers at the Rocky Mountain News *work on their first deadlines.* (Colorado State Historical Society)

Horace Greeley (1811–1872), in a sentimentalized portrait, gives his "Go West, Young Man" advice. (National Archives)

13. Six companies of the 2nd Cavalry under Captain E. K. Smith battle Comanches in the Nescutunga Valley of Texas. The army estimates that two soldiers are killed and 15 are wounded, while 49 Comanches are killed, five are wounded, and 36 are captured.
15. The first wagon road through the Rockies, from Walla Walla to Fort Benton, Montana, is begun by John Mullan.
■ Horace Greeley, on his western sojourn, pens his first letter to the *New York Tribune* from Atchison, Kansas.
23. Horace Greeley writes: "Leavenworth: room bells and baths make their final appearance."
24. Horace Greeley writes: "Topeka: beef steak and washbowls last visible."
26. Horace Greeley writes: "Manhattan [Kansas Territory]: potatoes and eggs last recognized . . . chairs ditto."
27. Horace Greeley writes: "Junction City: beds bid us goodbye."
30. At a Kansas creek crossing, Horace Greeley and his party lend a hand to an Ohio party whose wagon is stuck in the mud. When asked by one of the emigrants what he does, Greeley responds that he is with the *New York Tribune*. "That's old Greeley's paper, isn't?" asks the emigrant. "Yes sir," says Greeley.

12. SUSAN B. ANTHONY ADDRESSES NATIONAL WOMEN'S NYC CONVENTION

JUNE

1. Friendly Indians frighten the mules pulling Horace Greeley's Leavenworth and Pikes Peak Express stagecoach, causing it to overturn. Greeley makes light of the incident, but he will limp for a year from a leg injury. Also on board is *Boston Journal* correspondent Albert Deane Richardson.
5. Herman Lehman is born in Loyal Valley, Texas. The son of German settlers, he will be captured by Apaches and then live with Comanches.
6. Horace Greeley arrives in year-old Denver, where he notes that the inhabitants are "prone to deep drinking, soured in temper, always armed, bristling at a word, ready with the rifle, revolver, or bowie knife."
7. The Jefferson State Convention adjourns in Denver.
10. What will become known as the Comstock Lode is discovered. In Six Mile Canyon in present Nevada's Washoe Mountains (then Utah Territory), Patrick McLaughlin and Peter O'Riley discover silver nitrate ore. Their discovery will evolve into a $300 million silver and gold bonanza over the next two decades, and the Ophir Mine will become famous for its bluish quartz that assays at ¾ pure silver and ¼ gold. Henry Comstock will insist that he get some of the credit for the discovery because McLaughlin and O'Riley were using his water. Although the Comstock Lode will become one of the richest mining discoveries in American history, Comstock, McLaughlin, and O'Riley will each die broke.
17. The "Santa Ana Wind" in Santa Barbara, California, reportedly raises the temperature to 133°. Says one account: it "grew very hot after 2:00 pm; fine dust or pulverized clay filled air; fruit roasted on one side."
24. St. John's Day is celebrated in Tucson with cockfights, fistfights, and horse races.

Also in June 1859:
Golden, Colorado, is founded west of Denver, at the mouth of Clear Creek Canyon.

National Headlines/June 1859:
30. BLONDIN CROSSES NIAGARA FALLS ON A TIGHTROPE

JULY

2. The first newspaper bulletin on the discovery of the Comstock Lode appears in the *Nevada City Journal*.

- Salt Lake City obtains stagecoach and mail service.
3. In Arizona, citizens of Tucson and Mesilla meet and select Lieutenant Sylvester Mowry as their delegate to Congress. Congress will refuse to recognize Mowry's selection.
5. In Kansas Territory, a constitutional convention meets to debate the free state–slave state issue; it will frame a new constitution that will prohibit slavery.
8. Sylvester Mowry challenges the *Weekly Arizonian*'s editor Edward Cross to a duel after Cross suggests that Mowry inflated his figures on Arizona's population. In Tubac, the men duel with Burnside rifles at 40 paces—both shots miss and the men return to their homes.
13. Horace Greeley's interview with Brigham Young in Salt Lake City is published in the *New York Tribune*.
16. Arizona Apaches attack the Sonora Exploring and Mining Company, driving off a large number of livestock.
- U.S. Commissioner David Crawford signs a treaty with the Chippewa and Munsee tribes at the Sac and Fox agency in eastern Kansas.
29. Kansas's constitutional convention adjourns in Wyandotte.

AUGUST

1. Wells Fargo pays a cash dividend of 5 percent, making a total of 10 percent for the year.
3. Comanches are officially expelled from Texas; many

GREELEY'S WILD RIDE
AUGUST 1859

On his western travels, Horace Greeley boarded a stagecoach at Carson City, Nevada, bound for Placerville, California. His driver, Hank Monk, is reported by one observer to have "drank so much that he gave whiskey to his horses and watered himself, thus becoming sober enough to handle his drunken team." Greeley complained of the slowness of the team, saying he was "not going to a funeral." At the summit of a long grade, Monk cracked his whip and gave Greeley a ride to remember. Greeley was bounced like "corn in a popper," a Placerville innkeeper said. "The canvas roof of the coach was ripped in half a dozen places; Mr. Greeley's hat was all bashed in; the team was foamin' at the mouth."

---

are sent to a reservation in Indian Territory, present Oklahoma.

4. Having failed to kill the editor of the newspaper in a duel last month, Sylvester Mowry buys the *Weekly Arizonian* and begins publishing from Tucson.

5. Major L. A. Armistead of the 6th Infantry leads two officers and 50 enlisted men against 200 Mohave warriors near Fort Mojave, New Mexico Territory. The army reports three soldiers wounded and estimates 23 Mojaves killed, with "many" wounded and taken captive.

12. The play *Pike's Peak, or The Search for Riches,* by F. H. Conway, debuts in New York.

13. In a conversation on the front porch of the Pacific House in Council Bluffs, Iowa, the seed is planted for a transcontinental railroad. The lawyer Abraham Lincoln asks Grenville M. Dodge, "What's the best route for a Pacific railroad to the West?" Replies Dodge, "From this town out the Platte Valley." Over the next two hours, Dodge explains his dream route.

▪ The 2nd Dragoons under Lieutenant Ebenezer Gay fight Indians at Devils Gate Canyon near Box Elder, Utah.

SEPTEMBER

4. Concluding his western sojourn, Horace Greeley writes his last travel letter to the *New York Tribune* from San Francisco.

5. The U.S. Senate defeats the "State of Jefferson" proposition submitted by residents of the western part of Kansas Territory.

13. California Supreme Court judge David S. Terry kills Senator David C. Broderick, his political opponent, in a duel at Lake Merced.

▪ The *Leavenworth Times* notes that "the Denver people are rapidly providing themselves with the luxuries to which they were accustomed before leaving the East. We observe that the demand for champagne and other wines is increasing."

20. Theodore Judah and his wife, Anna, organize a California Convention on the Pacific Railway in San Francisco. Judah will be designated by the convention as an official lobbyist to assure passage of the Pacific Railway Act.

22. Clarina Nichols, the Kansas women's rights proponent, suggests that women use their power to get the vote: "If men didn't give them their rights, they would revolt—wouldn't marry. What a row that would make."

28. The Mexican outlaw Juan Nepumoceno Cortina raids Brownsville, Texas, with a force of about 100, killing many of his enemies in the process. The Mexican militia comes from Matamoros and is joined by a group of volunteers called the Brownsville Tigers. Cortina defeats them, destroying two pieces of artillery.

Also in September 1859:
In its first year of operation, the Butterfield Overland Mail shows $27,229.94 in postal receipts.
His business failure of 1856 behind him, Joshua Norton strolls into the news room of the *San Francisco Bulletin* with the announcement that his reign has begun. It is signed "Norton I, Emperor of the United States."

OCTOBER

1. U.S. Commissioner Alfred B. Greenwood signs a treaty with the Sak and Fox tribes at the Sak and Fox agency in eastern Kansas.

3. The first school in present Colorado opens in Auraria.

4. Kansas voters ratify the antislavery Wyandotte constitution, 10,421 to 5,530.

5. U.S. Commissioner Alfred B. Greenwood signs a treaty with the Kansa tribe at the Kansa agency in Council Grove, Kansas.

10. Jones and Cartwright, the largest freight firm operating out of Leavenworth, dispatches 21 wagon trains carrying 1,783 tons at 10 cents per pound. The firm will gross $356,500 on a $208,200 investment.

22. Construction begins on Fort Larned, northeast of Dodge City, in Kansas Territory.

24. Because of a lack of government from Kansas Territory, residents of the year-old cities of Denver and Auraria meet to plan their own government. The territory of Jefferson is proposed, extending from the 102nd to the 110th meridian, and from the 37th to the 43rd parallel. Congress will never recognize "Jefferson."

30. A detachment of 23 soldiers of the 1st Cavalry under First Lieutenant David Bell fights Kiowa Indians near Pawnee Fork, Kansas. Two Kiowas are reported killed.

Also in October 1859:
In Denver, construction is completed on a bridge over Cherry Creek at Larimer Street.

National Headlines/October 1859:
16. JOHN BROWN SEIZES HARPERS FERRY ARSENAL

NOVEMBER

1–14. Major O. L. Shepherd leads an expedition against Apaches near Tunicha, New Mexico. Two Indians are reported killed and six wounded.

7. Jefferson Territory's General Assembly convenes in Denver to set the territory's new government in operation.

12. Approximately 46,000 sheep are reported passing through Tucson en route to California.

12–17. New Mexico's "Pinal Apache Expedition" captures 22 Apaches.

17. The capital stock of Wells Fargo is increased from $600,000 to $1 million.

20 (or 28). Henry McCarty is believed to have been born at 70 Allen Street in East Side Manhattan's Irish Fourth Ward. The illegitimate son of Catherine McCarty will migrate with his mother from the New York slum to New Mexico Territory, where he will become known as Billy the Kid. The exact date and place of his birth remain a historical puzzle: he may have been born as early as 1855, perhaps in Marion County, Indiana.

Also in November 1859:

Albert Bierstadt returns to New York City. In his West 10th Street studio, he paints *The Wolf River, Kansas* and *Indian Encampment, Shoshone Village*.

National Headlines/November 1859:

28. WASHINGTON IRVING DIES

DECEMBER

3. A dozen soldiers engage Apaches in the Santa Teresa Mountains of New Mexico. Two Indians are reported killed, three wounded.

4. At Fort Union, New Mexico, Sergeant F. M. Cabe reports that two Kiowas were killed and "several wounded" by his mounted riflemen, who were escorting the mail.

5. Gilbert's Melodeon Theater opens in San Francisco.

14. Fort Brown, in Brownsville, Texas, is reinforced. Troops under Major S. P. Heintzelman engage and defeat the outlaw Juan Cortina at La Ebronal.

18. Fourteen soldiers fight 16 Apaches in the Santa Teresa Mountains of New Mexico. Two Apaches are killed and four are wounded.

24. Some 46 members of the 1st Dragoons battle Apaches in the Pinal Mountains of New Mexico. Six Indians are killed.

■ The entire population of Boulder, Colorado—200 men and 17 women—attends a Christmas dance at Bill Barney's dance hall.

BILLY THE KID
NOVEMBER 20, 1859–JULY 14, 1881

1859: Henry McCarty, the future Billy the Kid, is probably born in this year, perhaps in New York City.

1866: He lives with his mother, Catherine McCarty, and his brother Joseph in Marion County, Indiana.

1869: Catherine McCarty purchases a town lot in Wichita, Kansas.

1871: McCarty sells her Kansas land.

1873: Catherine McCarty weds William Antrim in Santa Fe.

1874: The Kid's mother, Catherine Antrim, dies in Silver City, New Mexico.

1875: The Kid is arrested for the first time, in Silver City, for stealing some laundry; he escapes from jail.

1877: He kills his first man, Frank P. Cahill, near Camp Grant, Arizona.

1878: The Kid becomes an active participant in New Mexico's Lincoln County War. He works for John Tunstall, who is slain later in the year. The Kid aligns himself with the McSween faction and is wounded in a gun battle. He is indicted for the murder of Sheriff Brady, becomes involved in the massive gunfight at the McSween ranch, and meets with Lew Wallace, territorial governor of New Mexico.

1879: The Kid is arrested by Sheriff Kimball. He escapes from jail in Lincoln.

1880: He avoids a trap set by Pat Garrett in Fort Sumner, New Mexico. He earns a living rustling cattle. Governor Wallace puts a $500 price on his head. The Kid is captured by a posse led by Pat Garrett at Stinking Springs. Jailed in Las Vegas, the Kid is subsequently moved to Santa Fe.

1881: Billy the Kid is convicted of murder and sentenced to hang. He kills two guards while escaping from jail in Lincoln. He is murdered by Pat Garrett in Pete Maxwell's bedroom in Fort Sumner.

- The first Christmas tree is lit in Wyoming, at Glenrock.

26. "Denver" is chosen over "Auraria" and "Highlands" as the official name of the city at the junction of the Platte River and Cherry Creek. The name honors James Denver, the governor of Kansas; unknown to the residents of the new city, Denver had recently resigned his office.
- A combined force of 173 Texas Rangers and 165 U.S. regulars attack the outlaw band of Juan Cortina in Rio Grande City, Texas. Hand-to-hand combat results in Cortina's retreat.
- The New Mexico Historical Society is organized.
- William Dennison Stephens, the 24th governor of California (1917–1922), is born in Eaton, Ohio.

27. One soldier is killed and another is wounded in a fight with Indians near Rio Grande City, Texas.
- George West's the *Western Mountaineer* becomes the first newspaper published in Golden, Colorado.

31. Wells Fargo currently operates 126 agencies.

Also in December 1859:
The San Francisco city directory notes that 1,570 firms failed in 1859, with 2,056 "remaining in business."

National Headlines/December 1859:
2. JOHN BROWN HANGED AT CHARLESTON FOR HARPERS FERRY INSURRECTION

Also in 1859:
The first medical school on the West Coast, the University of the Pacific, in Santa Clara, California, is founded by Dr. Elias Samuel Cooper. The school's name will be changed to Cooper Medical College.
The first newspaper in South Dakota, the *Democrat,* is published in Sioux Falls.
The first Jewish congregation in Houston is organized.
John Rowlands, 17, arrives in New Orleans penniless,

"Pikes Peak or Bust." For most, it's the latter.   (Library of Congress)

having worked his way across the Atlantic from Liverpool, England. A life of adventure awaits the young man, who will become famous as the journalist Henry Stanley.
Congress rejects a request of settlers in the Mesilla Valley and the Gadsden Purchase area south of the Gila River to separate Arizona from New Mexico.
Approximately 30,000 copies of the *Texas Almanac* are published.
Isaac Parker, 21, is admitted to the Ohio bar. He moves to St. Louis to establish a legal practice.
Richard Henry Dana returns to San Francisco after 24 years aboard the mail steamer *Golden Gate.* He calls the city "one of the capitals of the American Republic, and the sole emporious of a new world, the awakened Pacific."
Some 100,000 would-be prospectors travel to Colorado under the slogan "Pikes Peak or Bust."
During the 1850s, the United States fought 22 small wars with Indian tribes from Florida to Oregon.

1860

"Then enter, boys; cheerily, boys, enter and rest;
You know how we live, boys, and die in the west . . ."

—George Pope Morris

JANUARY

2. The fifth territorial legislature of Kansas convenes in Lecompton and then adjourns to Lawrence over the governor's veto.

7. The fifth territorial legislature of Kansas begins meeting in Lawrence.

■ Grizzly Adams and his menagerie set sail for New York from San Francisco.

16. Two Comanches are killed by the 2nd Cavalry near Camp Colorado in Texas.

17. Navajos attack 35 enlisted men guarding cattle near Fort Defiance, New Mexico; four soldiers are killed.

18. The fifth territorial legislature of Kansas adjourns in Lawrence.

18–22. A small group of soldiers battles Navajos near Fort Defiance, New Mexico.

25. Charles Curtis, the first Native American senator (1907–1913, 1915–1929) and the nation's 31st vice president under Herbert Hoover (1929–1933), is born on a farm near Topeka, Kansas.

26. Major Thomas and a detachment of the 2nd Cavalry kill four Comanches and wound "many" on Kickapoo Creek in Texas.

27. After meeting with a senator in Washington, William H. Russell wires his business associates at the Leavenworth and Pikes Peak Express Company: "Have determined to establish a Pony Express to Sacramento, California, commencing 3rd of April. Time 10 days." His partner, Alexander Majors, has the idea of posting relay stations across the West, one he got from witnessing one of F. X. Aubry's incredible Santa Fe–Independence runs in 1848.

31. Arizona County, including most of the western portion of the Gadsden Purchase, is established by the New Mexico legislature.

FEBRUARY

1. The French Savings and Loan Society is incorporated in San Francisco.

■ Mora County is created in New Mexico.

7. Mounted riflemen kill two Indians near Canyon Alamosa, New Mexico.

8. A large battle near Fort Defiance, New Mexico Territory, pits 44 soldiers against 500 Navajos. Sergeant Werner reports only one soldier wounded.

■ Meanwhile, at nearby Canyon del Muerto, 52 soldiers battle 40 Navajos, killing six and wounding five. Nearby, another group of 52 mounted riflemen under Captain George McLane battles 75 Navajo and reports killing 15.

13. Near Fort Mason, Texas, Captain R. W. Johnson and his company of the 2nd Cavalry report killing one Indian and wounding two.

14. Gordon William Lillie, the future showman "Pawnee Bill," is born in Bloomington, Illinois.

15. Wells Fargo pays a cash dividend of 5 percent.

23. Kansas legislators override Governor Samuel Medary's veto and approve the Wyandotte constitution, which would prohibit slavery.

MARCH

17. Members of the Japanese embassy arrive in San Francisco.

19. The politician and orator William Jennings Bryan is born in Salem, Illinois.

■ Cadet George A. Custer receives a total of seven demerits at West Point for "room grossly out of order" and "bread, butter, potatoes, plates, knives, and forks in quarters."

20. To resolve a threatened foreclosure by Wells Fargo over a $162,400 advance, the Overland Mail Company agrees to changes in their board of directors, as well as the removal of John Butterfield as president.

24. In San Francisco, the clipper *Andrew Jackson* arrives from New York after 89 days at sea.

APRIL

2. A territorial constitution is drawn up in Tucson by 31 citizens. Although the constitution is supposed to be binding until Congress can establish a legal government, none of its provisions will be enforced.

■ The first book printed in Arizona will be the 24-page pamphlet issued by today's constitutional convention, meeting in Tucson. J. Howard Wells is the printer.

3. The Pony Express begins operating out of St. Joseph, Missouri, owned and operated by the firm of Russell, Majors, and Waddell.

5. The towns of Denver and Auraria merge.

THE PONY EXPRESS
APRIL 3, 1860

The first Pony Express rider departed St. Joseph on this date at 7:15 P.M. The rider's name is still disputed by historians. Among the more frequently mentioned names are Henry Wallace, William "Buddy" Richardson, and John Frey. James Randal, John Roff, or Samuel Hamilton are among the names put forth for the rider of the first leg from San Francisco.

Whoever the "first" carrier was, in his mailbag were 49 letters, special editions of newspapers printed on tissue paper, private telegrams, and special dispatches for West Coast newspapers. The historic Pony Express route included St. Joseph, Fort Kearney, Fort Laramie, Fort Bridger, Salt Lake City, Camp Floyd, Carson City, Washoe Silver Mines, Placerville, Sacramento, and San Francisco. Future riders would leave St. Joseph at noon and Sacramento at 8:00 P.M. every day except Sunday.

■ The Arizona provisional government establishes a supreme court in Tucson.

7. The San Diego *Herald* ceases publication, citing the city being bypassed by the transcontinental mail route as the reason for its failure.

13. The first Pony Express rider to arrive in Sacramento is Tom Hamilton. Riders covered 1,966 miles in 11 days.

14. The first Pony Express rider arrives in San Francisco with dispatches, only 10 days after departing St. Joseph. The postage rate is $5 a half-ounce.

■ Four bodies, including that of Captain Knight, are recovered off the coast of Oregon after the *Friendship* breaks up in a storm.

■ The oldest town in Idaho, Franklin, is founded by Mormons just north of the Utah border.

18. Three dragoons are wounded and two Indians are killed in a scrape between soldiers and Paiutes near Camp Cady on Arizona's Mojave River.

26. On the future site of Leadville, Colorado, prospector Abe Lee lifts a glistening panful of gold from the icy Arkansas River and shouts, "By God, I've got California in this here pan!" California Gulch is born, along with the future boomtown of Oro City. The gold rush will produce about $10 million worth of the metal during the next three years.

30. Navajos attack New Mexico's Fort Defiance, killing one and wounding two.

■ The San Francisco *Bulletin* reports on the recent removal of John Butterfield as president of the Overland Mail.

MAY

1. San Francisco's first school for the deaf is founded.

■ Wells Fargo pays a cash dividend of 3 percent, making a total of 8 percent on the year, the first time since 1853 that the stock pays less than 10 percent in a year.

2. Lieutenant M. G. Carr's dragoons kill three Paiutes, wound one, and capture another near Arizona's Providence Mountains.

7. The last heard of the Mexican bandit Cortina is in the diary entry of Robert E. Lee: "He has left the frontier and withdrawn to the Ceritos with his property, horses, etc."

■ Julius Real is born in the hills of Texas. In 1913, he will stage the legislative "Whiskey Rebellion" to keep prohibition illegal in the Lone Star State.

9. In Oskaloosa, Kansas Territory, Samuel Peppard launches his "windwagon."

12. At Pyramid Lake, Nevada, Major William Ormsby and many members of his volunteer force are killed

THE VOYAGE OF THE WINDWAGON

The earliest explorers had likened the western plains to a vast sea of grass, complete with gale-force winds, a comparison that inspired the strangest vehicle ever to traverse the prairie. Samuel Peppard's cockeyed hybrid was a bizarre landship whose propulsion would come only from the wind sweeping down the plain.

Oskaloosa, Kansas Territory, about 40 miles northeast of Topeka, was a hotbed for humor in 1860. A long drought had made crop raising a memory and prompted the formation of the "Lazy Club." Members were forbidden to touch axes, shovels, or any other work implements. Abe Sinnard was declared the "laziest man in town" when he and Tom Noble stretched out in the path of an oncoming stagecoach. Noble rolled out of the way at the last minute, but the reclined Sinnard stopped the horses with a wave of his hand.

Peppard had no time for such nonsense. His foolishness was serious. Born in Ohio on September 30, 1833, he had lived in Iowa before coming to Kansas. On the banks of the Grasshopper River (later the Delaware), he had built a sawmill, but the economic slump, along with the Pikes Peak gold rush, now fired his imagination in a new direction. If he could ride like the wind, he might beat a few thousand gold seekers.

Construction of the windwagon began in the early months of 1860. As it took shape, a Topeka journalist described it as "made of rough lumber and shaped like a skiff . . . 8 feet long from prow to stern and 3 feet across amidships, and 2 feet deep. The bed was placed on a running gear with axles 6 feet apart, the wheels all the same size and about as large as the front wheels of a buggy."

A 10-foot mast was rigged to the front axle, to which Peppard attached two sails measuring 11 by 8 feet and 7 by 5 feet. If all went according to the blueprint, there would be room for four men and provisions. Upon completion, the West's weirdest wind surfer weighed 350 pounds.

On May 9, 1860, Peppard, Gid Coldon, Steve Randall, and J. T. Forbes hauled the wagon to the outskirts of town for a test run. A gust of wind caught the sails, blew the craft a few feet, picked it off the ground, then dropped it with a crashing thud.

Repairs began on what was being called "Peppard's Folly." Believing he could control his ship with the right balance of braking, rudder, and sail control, Peppard and company were ready to try again in a few days. This time, they loaded 400 pounds of supplies on board.

The breeze picked up and Peppard adjusted his sails. Another killer gust came along, but this time the sod sailor was ready to roll. The windwagon lunged forward, then out across the prairie, bumping along at a speedy clip toward the northwest. Observers could not believe it. Samuel Peppard was gone with the wind.

Cruising speeds varied with the wind. During one sprint, Peppard guessed, they made two miles in four minutes. When the wind died completely, sometimes for a whole day at a time, the four sat in their horseless carriage, smoking and swapping stories. Five days out, they realized they were not alone—they were being trailed by a small band of Indians. When the warriors got near enough to see the bizarre buggy, said Peppard, "we could plainly see each Indian rise in his saddle with a start of surprise." A race ensued—a rider on a gray mare managed to pull close before the wagon sped away toward the Oregon Trail.

Two weeks later, at Fort Kearny in present Nebraska, a reporter for *Frank Leslie's Illustrated Newspaper* wrote of the craft "running down in a westerly direction for the fort, under full sail, across the green prairie." The adventurers stayed at the fort a few days before the wheeled boat "again caught the breeze and went off at a dashing rate towards Pikes Peak."

At the fork of the Platte River, the windwagon turned with the South Platte, then entered present Colorado near Julesburg. Alas, the windwagon never completed her maiden voyage. In June, just south of Fort Morgan, she ran into a dust devil. The men were thrown out as winds whipped the wagon to a pile of rubble. Although the 500-mile voyage had ended in shipwreck, the venture was not completely "blown." Peppard, Forbes, Coldon, and Randall were picked up by a wagon train and taken to Denver.

Peppard never found gold. He was back in Oskaloosa for his 27th birthday that September. He went on to serve the Union with the 2nd Colorado Volunteers for three years of the Civil War, after which he married and became the father of 13 children. He died in 1916 at the age of 82, and was buried in Oskaloosa.

by Indians. The Pyramid Lake War began when white men at Williams Station, Nevada, kidnapped some Paiute girls. In retaliation, Indians torched the station and killed the whites on hand. In the wake of Ormsby's battle, a force of 500 Californians will be organized by Colonel John C. Hays.

23. At Fort Kearny, Nebraska, a correspondent for *Frank Leslie's Illustrated Newspaper* reports Samuel Peppard's windwagon heading toward Pike's Peak.

29. In his journal, windwagonmaster Samuel Peppard notes that he and his fellow sailors passed 625 teams of pioneers in one day.

30. U.S. Commissioner Thomas B. Sykes signs a treaty with Delaware Indians at Sarcoxie, on the Delaware reservation in Kansas.

Also in May 1860:

Perhaps as many as 8,000 Paiutes join forces in a concerted effort to drive the white man from Nevada and a portion of Utah. Across a 300-mile stretch, half of the Pony Express stations are attacked and 17 employees are killed.

The incredible journey of Pony Express rider Bob Haslam occurs during a Paiute uprising in Nevada: He rides 380 miles in 36 hours.

The Tabors—Horace, Augusta, and son Maxcy—arrive in California Gulch, the future Leadville, Colorado. Augusta is the first white woman in the gold diggings. Miners build her an 18-by-24-foot cabin in which she cooks several meals a day and sets up the first post office.

The future entrepreneur Barney Ford, a black man, is forced at gunpoint by angry whites to leave his Central City, Colorado, mining claims.

National Headlines/May 1860:
16. REPUBLICANS NOMINATE LINCOLN

JUNE

2. Colonel Hays and his men engage Paiutes near Pyramid Lake, Nevada, driving them north. Four soldiers are reported wounded. Fort Churchill will soon be erected on the nearby Carson River.

3. Killing more than 175 people, the "Great Comanche Tornado" levels much of the country between Cedar Rapids, Iowa, and Lake Michigan. The twister gets its name from a town it completely destroyed, Comanche, Iowa, on the Mississippi River.

9. The first dime novel is published by Irwin P. Beadle. *Malaeska, the Indian Wife of the White Hunter,* by Ann Sophia Stevens, is a potboiler on an interracial marriage gone bad; it will sell 65,000 copies.

23. Dragoons and Snake Indians battle near Harney Lake, Oregon. One Indian is killed and "many" are wounded.

30. Wells Fargo loses $11,811.25 in an Iowa Hill stagecoach robbery; $3,068.23 will be recovered.

Also in June 1860:

In Texas, roughly 3 million head of cattle run loose.

Paiutes in Nevada attack and burn many Pony Express stations. The owners calculate that the attacks cost the company $75,000, but only once do the Paiutes capture the mail bags; those letters will be the only ones lost during the 19-month life of the Express.

Settlers in Colorado begin irrigating land east of the Rockies.

The Yakima Agency Boarding School opens in Washington Territory with 25 pupils.

JULY

2. The American Fur Company steamboat *Chippewa* becomes the first to penetrate the upper Missouri when it lands at Fort Benton in Montana Territory. Also arriving today is the *Key West.*

4. The San Francisco Market Street Railroad begins operations, carrying commuters on the city's first street rails.

9. Kansas swelters; Lawrence and Fort Scott report temperatures of 115°.

▪ San Francisco's Olympic Theater closes.

11. Cavalry and dragoons report many Kiowa Indians "killed and wounded" in a fight at Blackwater Springs, near Bent's Fort.

13. Captain Joseph Stewart receives his orders to build Fort Churchill on the Carson River in Nevada. Special Order No. 67 is a result of trouble with the Indians during the past year. Whites had kidnapped young Paiute women, who were rescued by their own people at James Williams's trading post. The post was burned and five whites were killed in the action.

14. Owen Wister, the future author (*The Virginian,* 1902), is born in Philadelphia.

20. The first gold coins to be minted in Colorado are by Clark, Gruber and Company. The equipment was freighted by members of the company on railroads to the Missouri River, and beyond on ox carts. Meanwhile, other members of the firm constructed a two-story brick building on McGaa and G Street in Denver. Guests are invited for today's opening-day ceremonies. The first coin, a $10 Gold Eagle, is presented to *Rocky Mountain News* editor William Byers. During the next two years, the firm will coin $600,000 in gold.

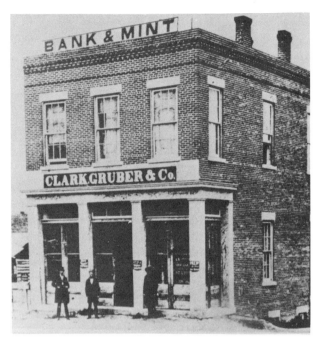

Denver's first mint is Clark, Gruber and Company. A private concern, it will be purchased by the U.S. government in 1863. (Colorado State Historical Society)

31. Wells Fargo posts a $2,839.30 loss in a stagecoach robbery at Trinity Hill.

AUGUST

2. Twenty mounted riflemen battle Navajos near Albuquerque, New Mexico. Two Indians are reported killed and two wounded.

6. Major John Sedgwick and six companies of the 1st Cavalry battle a combined force of Kiowas and Comanches on Cottonwood Creek in Kansas.

■ The Musical Hall opens in San Francisco.

11. Twenty-seven members of the 4th Artillery take on a force of 200 "Gashote and Parran" Indians at Fagan Canyon in Utah. One Indian is killed and "many" are wounded.

12. Temple Houston, the future attorney and adventurer and the son of Sam Houston, is the first person born in the Texas Governor's Mansion in Austin.

13. Phoebe Ann Moses, better known as Annie Oakley, is born in Darke County, Ohio, the fifth child of Susan and Jacob Moses.

26. The 1st Dragoons engages a force of 15 Apaches near Fort Buchanan, New Mexico, killing one.

26–27. Major G. H. Thomas is among those wounded in battle with Indians near the head of Clear Fork on the Brazos River.

27. Denver's *Rocky Mountain News* becomes a daily newspaper.

ANNIE OAKLEY
AUGUST 13, 1860–NOVEMBER 3, 1926

1860: Phoebe Ann Moses is born in Darke County, Ohio.

1866: Her father, Jacob Moses, dies of pneumonia. Annie will live in a series of foster homes, with varying degrees of success.

1870: As one of seven children at home, she works at the Darke County Infirmary.

1872: Annie rejoins her mother and provides for the family by hunting.

1875: At age 15, she defeats Frank Butler at a Cincinnati shooting match.

1876: She weds Frank Butler and stays at home for six years while Butler tours as a marksman.

1882: Annie steps in for Frank's partner, John Graham, at an exhibition in Springfield, Ohio. Soon after, they begin touring as "Butler and Oakley." On June 20, they repeat their marriage vows in Windsor, Canada.

1883: Annie tours with Butler in the play *Slocum's Oath*. She is met backstage in St. Paul by Sitting Bull.

1884: She tours with the Sells Brothers Circus.

1885: Annie joins Buffalo Bill's Wild West, in which she will star sporadically for 17 years.

1886: She performs two shooting shows a day at Erastina, a Staten Island resort.

1887: She meets Queen Victoria during a performance at the American Exhibition in London. She defeats Grand Duke Michael of Russia during a shooting match in England. Oakley leaves the Wild West for health reasons.

1888: Annie resumes her exhibition schedule, appearing with the Pawnee Bill Frontier Exhibition.

1889: She opens in Paris with Buffalo Bill's Wild West. She shoots a cigarette from the lips of Germany's Crown Prince Wilhelm.

1890: She appears with Buffalo Bill's Wild West in Berlin.

1901: Oakley is critically injured in a train wreck near Lexington, Kentucky.

(continued)

(continued)

> 1903: Annie is able to walk again after undergoing five operations. A short time thereafter, she resumes a limited schedule of public exhibitions.
>
> 1912: Oakley tours with Cody's farewell show.
>
> 1918: She demonstrates her shooting technique to soldiers in World War I.
>
> 1922: An auto accident leaves her in a wheelchair.
>
> 1926: Annie dies at the age of 66.

Also in August 1860:

Since the beginning of the Gold Rush in 1849, California's Indian population has decreased from 100,000 to 35,000.

William Russell expresses concern that the Pony Express is operating at a heavy loss and will not survive without federal aid.

SEPTEMBER

6. The 4th Artillery clashes with Indians on Deep Creek, in Utah.

12. Authorities in Nicaragua execute the adventurer William Walker, the former self-proclaimed ruler of that country who had recently tried to take over Honduras.

13. Five members of what was originally a party of 44 pioneers are separated in the wilderness following an Indian attack near Fort Hall, Idaho. Facing starvation, they resort to cannibalism.

18. Approximately 40 Indians attack troops guarding a herd near Fort Fauntleroy in New Mexico. The guards kill 10 Indians.

20. The first Western Stage Company mail coach leaves Denver for Omaha, inaugurating the first weekly U.S. mail service from Jefferson Territory.

■ James Norris Gillett, the 22nd governor of California (1907–1911), is born in Viroqua, Wisconsin.

23. Forty-seven soldiers and seven Indians battle in Navajo County, New Mexico.

24. Navajos and the 7th Infantry battle near Fort Fauntleroy, New Mexico.

25. Charles Edward Russell, the future publisher of the Hearst newspapers the *American* and the *Examiner,* is born in Davenport, Iowa.

26. Navajos and the 7th Infantry again battle near Fort Fauntleroy, New Mexico. Light casualties on both sides are reported.

30. Gold is discovered in Idaho, leading to the founding of Pierce.

Also in September 1860:

In Jefferson Territory, males outnumber females 20 to 1.

The population of California Gulch, Colorado, has increased from nine to 10,000 since spring. The area will soon be renamed Oro City.

John Muir, 22, enrolls at the University of Wisconsin.

National Headlines/September 1860:

7. SHIPS COLLIDE ON LAKE MICHIGAN; 400 KILLED

OCTOBER

3. Captain A. D. Nelson and a company of the 10th Infantry kill 10 Navajos in a fight in New Mexico's Tunicha Mountains.

■ Captain E. B. Hollaway's company of the 8th Infantry battles 50 Comanches at Chaparita, New Mexico, killing two and wounding "many."

4. The Hawaiian prince Kamehameha arrives in San Francisco for a visit.

8. The first telegraph line linking San Francisco and Los Angeles is completed.

10. Business is good in California, reports the *Alta:* "Perhaps at no previous period of our history has there been so widely diffused financial ease among the people of our state as at present."

13–18. Captain Thomas Clayborne leads a large force against Navajos near Cold Springs, New Mexico, killing seven, wounding one, and capturing six.

15. The first public school in what will become Colorado opens in Boulder with 40 students.

21. William F. "Billy the Kid" Claiborne (not to be confused with the true Kid) is born in Yazoo County, Mississippi.

24. Captain Thomas Clayborne and a small force kill three Navajos and capture another five in San Jose, New Mexico.

25. Grizzly Adams dies from an infected head wound he suffered while scuffling with Fremont, one of his bears, in New York.

26. Frank Eaton, the adventurer who will earn notoriety as Pistol Pete, is born in Hartford, Connecticut.

Also in October 1860:

James Butler Hickok is employed as a wagon driver for the freight company Russell, Majors and Waddell. En route from Independence to Santa Fe, Hickok encounters a cinnamon bear blocking Raton Pass. When she refuses to move, Bill attacks the bear with a bowie knife. The bears dies, but Hickok is badly mauled. After Hickok receives treatments in Kansas City, the firm transfers him to its Rock Creek station near present Fairbury, Nebraska.

NOVEMBER

7. The Jefferson Territory legislature meets today; it will remain in session for 40 days.

19. The opera star Adelina Patti debuts at New Orleans's French Opera House.

21. Tom Horn, the future hired gun and scout, is born in Memphis, Missouri.

27. A fire destroys San Francisco's Lyceum Theater.

Also in November 1860:

Albert Deane Richardson writes that Denver has a working mint, milk delivery, express and coach service to Missouri three times a week, a Catholic church, three newspapers, and two drugstores selling Chicago and New York newspapers that are only 10 days old. He also reports of the occupants of a crowded cemetery: "A large majority met violent deaths."

The population of Atchison, Kansas, has grown from 400 to 2,616 in the last two years.

National Headlines/November 1860:

6. LINCOLN ELECTED

DECEMBER

14. In Washington Territory, Missoula County is established, taking in all of present western Montana.

17. Texas Ranger captain Sul Ross raises 60 riders, Tonkawa Indian scouts, and citizen volunteers to go after Peta Nacona's Comanches on the Pease River. Ross finds a camp, but Peta Nacona and most of the men are away hunting. Ross will report that he killed Peta Nacona, although the victim was probably a Mexican slave named Joe who was trying to protect those in the village, mostly women and children. Charles Goodnight, riding with Ross, discovers in the village the former Cynthia Parker, who was kidnapped in 1836 and is now the wife of Peta Nacona, and her 18-month-old daughter Topsanah (Prairie Flower); both are returned to Camp Cooper. Shortly after this raid, Peta Nacona is believed to have died from an infected wound.

25. Newspapers accuse William Russell, the Pony Express partner, of using Indian Trust bonds to secure loans. Russell is arrested.

31. Wells Fargo shows a gross profit of $175,833.02 for 1860 and losses of $48,415.00 due to robberies and reward payments, for a net profit of $127,418.02. The company also shows a gross income of $430,293 from transportation and a net income of $151,128 from express services.

National Headlines/December 1860:

20. SOUTH CAROLINA SECEDES FROM UNION

Also in 1860:

The U.S. Signal Corps is established in New Mexico when Colonel E. R. S. Canby uses a heliograph, a system of mirrors, to communicate with his detachments during the campaign against the Navajos.

Thirty-one stagecoach lines operate in Texas.

The Pony Express delivers a presidential message to Sacramento in eight days.

Was 14-year-old William F. Cody a Pony Express rider? Cody claimed he was, and said he once carried the mail 322 miles without stopping. Company records do not list him as a rider, but they do not list many others who definitely rode. Express partner Alexander Majors verified Cody's claim.

The California Steam Navigation Company announces

1860 CENSUS	
Arkansas	435,450
California	379,994
San Francisco	56,802
Colorado	34,277
Denver	4,749
Dakota	4,837
Iowa	674,913
Kansas	107,206
Kansas City	7,000
Louisiana	708,002
Minnesota	172,000
Missouri	1,182,012
Nebraska	28,841
Nevada	6,857
New Mexico (including present Arizona and part of Colorado)	93,516
Oregon:	52,000
Texas:	604,215 (300 percent increase over 1850; 33 percent of population is black)
Utah:	40,273
Washington	11,594

it has paid "102 percent in dividends upon the par value of the stock, which, upon the average market value, is over 200 percent, leaving at the present time a handsome surplus of available assets on hand."

Drought forces the departure of 30,000 Kansas settlers.

"Norton I, Emperor of the United States" (the former Joshua Norton of San Francisco) orders that the Republic of the United States be dissolved in order to "establish in its stead" an absolute monarchy. He also adds "Protector of Mexico" to his title and abolishes the Supreme Court.

The seasoned frontier journalist Bret Harte resigns from the *Northern Californian* after criticizing a massacre of friendly Digger Indians by local thugs. He leaves Union to return to San Francisco.

The financially strapped freight firm Leavenworth and Pikes Peak Express turns to Russell, Majors and Waddell for help; the former is absorbed into the Central Overland California and Pike's Peak Express Company (C.O.C. & P.P.).

Gas street lights are installed in San Antonio.

The New Mexico legislature presses for a public-school law requiring at least one school per settlement.

Horace Greeley publishes *Overland Journey*.

The *Dial* becomes the first midwestern "little" magazine to be edited by Moncure Daniel Conway.

There are 735 steamboats working the Mississippi River and her tributaries, most with full gambling casinos on board.

The C.O.C. & P.P. cuts the rates on stagecoach passage from St. Joseph to Denver from $100 to $75.

Wells Fargo operated 147 offices this year, up from 55 in 1855.

After two years of operation, the Butterfield Overland Mail shows $119,766.76 in postal receipts.

While being tried by a miner's court in Central City, Colorado, the defendant known as "Pennsyltuck" brandishes a pistol and threatens the judge. Sheriff Keeler shoots and wounds Pennsyltuck, who is taken to a German doctor's house to recover. That same night, while he is asleep, a mob drags him from his bed and hangs him in his long-handled underwear.

The repeating rifle developed by shirt manufacturer Oliver F. Winchester, age 49, goes into production in New Haven, Connecticut. The Winchester Company also introduces an M1866 rifle with a .44 rimfire cartridge.

1861

"If we do not make common cause to save the good old ship of the Union on this voyage, nobody will have a chance to pilot her on another voyage."

—Abraham Lincoln

JANUARY

2. A force of 92 troopers battles Kiowa and Comanche warriors near Cold Spring, on the Cimarron River in New Mexico. Ten Indians are reported killed and "many" wounded.

3. A 5th Infantry soldier is killed by Navajos in New Mexico's Chusca Valley.

7. Four Indians are killed and 17 are captured during a scrape with infantry near Fort Fauntleroy, New Mexico.

8. The fifth territorial legislature of Kansas adjourns to Lawrence, where it will adjourn permanently when the territory acquires statehood.

10. The federal arsenal in Baton Rouge is seized by Louisiana state troops.

18. San Francisco's famed street mongrels, Bummer and Lazarus, appear in print for the first time in the *Daily Alta:*

> Three or four days ago, a poor, lean, mangy cur was attacked in the street by a larger dog, and was getting unmercifully walloped, when Bummer's ire being aroused at the unequal contest, he rushed in and gave the attacking canine such a rough handling that he was glad to quit the field yelping, and making the best dog time on record.

21. Sam Houston submits a resolution of secession to the Texas legislature.

26. Louisiana secedes from the Union.

29. Kansas, with a population of more than 100,000, enters the Union as the 34th state under the terms of the Wyandotte constitution, which prohibits slavery. The capital is Topeka.

National Headlines/January 1861:

9. MISSISSIPPI SECEDES
10. FLORIDA SECEDES
11. ALABAMA SECEDES
12. JEFFERSON DAVIS RESIGNS FROM SENATE
19. GEORGIA SECEDES

FEBRUARY

1. The Texas state convention votes 166 to 8 to secede from the Union. When Sam Houston refuses to take an oath of allegiance to the Confederacy, his office is declared vacant.

■ Congress halts the Butterfield Overland Mail's service in the wake of Texas's secession.

■ Wells Fargo pays a cash dividend of 3 percent.

3. Cadet George A. Custer receives two demerits at West Point for "long beard at inspection."

4. In New Mexico Territory, Chiricahua Apache leader Cochise meets with Second Lieutenant George H. Bascom under a white ceremonial flag at Apache Pass. During the meeting, Bascom attempts to detain Cochise, who reacts in a rage. Cochise slits his way through a tent, escapes into the night, and begins a 12-year war.

7. The Choctaw Nation pledges its allegiance to the Confederacy.

8. The federal arsenal in Little Rock is seized by Arkansas state troops.

13. The first medal of honor action occurs when Colonel Bernard John Dowling Irwin, an assistant surgeon, takes charge of the troops to defeat a party of hostile Chiricahua Indians at Apache Pass in New Mexico Territory. The medal itself will not be awarded until January 24, 1894.

15. Fort Pointis is completed near San Francisco.

16. The federal arsenal in San Antonio is seized by Texas state troops.

18. In Kansas, the Treaty of Fort Wise is signed. In a ceremony on the north bank of the Arkansas River, Cheyenne and Arapaho leaders give up their claim on much of present Colorado between the North Platte and Arkansas Rivers, even though their tribes are entitled to the land by the terms of an 1851 treaty. The tribes will relocate to a reservation situated between the Arkansas River and Sand Creek in the eastern portion of the state.

■ The remaining federal military posts in Texas are turned over to the Confederacy by General David E. Twiggs.

19. Lieutenant Bascom's troops withdraw from Apache Pass with nine captured Comanches.

23. Texas's ordinance of secession, passed on February 1, is formally ratified by a referendum. Texas becomes the seventh state to secede.

28. "Jefferson Territory" ceases to exist when President James Buchanan signs a bill creating the territory of Colorado. With an estimated population of 35,000, the new territory comprises parts of Nebraska and Utah Territories and what was formerly the western portion of Kansas Territory. Colorado Territory's border with New Mexico Territory is fixed at the 37th parallel, and its capital is Colorado City.

Also in February 1861:

The Pony Express is slowed by bad winter: letters take 30 to 40 days to reach their destination.

National Headlines/February 1861:

18. JEFFERSON DAVIS INAUGURATED AS PROVISIONAL CONFEDERATE PRESIDENT

MARCH

2. Congress creates the territories of Nevada and Dakota. The mining boom in Nevada has caused the population to swell to 20,000. Dakota Territory comprises land between the 43rd and 49th parallels formerly in Nebraska Territory.

■ The "independence" of Texas becomes official today.

The Overland stagecoach arrives in Denver. (Library of Congress)

■ Congress passes a law providing for a daily overland mail service on the Central Route and a Pony Express delivery semiweekly beginning July 1, to be subsidized by the government for $1 million. Russell, Majors, and Waddell, unable to undertake the added financial responsibilities, will see the contract go to John Butterfield's Overland Mail Company. The postmaster general will also order Butterfield to change from his southern route, where a number of attacks have recently occurred.

4. The Missouri state convention votes against secession.

6. Samuel Franklin Cody, the Wild West showman who will quit the business to pursue his aviation dreams, is born in Birdville, Texas.

10. Cadet George A. Custer receives two demerits at West Point for "long hair at inspection."

12. Congress annuls the government's contract with Butterfield Overland Mail for service on the southern route (the company's stations will be destroyed) to prevent use by hostile forces. Butterfield will obtain a government contract to provide six-times-a-week service between St. Louis and Placerville, California, for $1 million.

16. A beleaguered Sam Houston officially resigns the governorship of Texas because he refuses to accept the state's secession. Lieutenant governor William T. Clark takes his place.

■ Arkansas decides to put the question of secession to a vote of the people in a summer election.

■ The Overland Mail contracts with Wells Fargo to handle all express business coming from the East to points west of Salt Lake City, and all express originating in the West that is headed East.

31. The federal garrison at Fort Bliss, in El Paso, Texas, surrenders to state troops.

Also in March 1861:

The Cherokee Stand Watie becomes the Confederacy's only brigadier general; he will command two Cherokee regiments.

The Confederate government establishes a Bureau of Indian Affairs.

James Butler Hickok, still recuperating from last October's battle with a bear, arrives at Rock Creek station, Nebraska, where he is asked to tend stock. He immediately takes a dislike to acting superintendent David Colbert McCanles, who calls him "Duck Bill" and wrestles the limping Hickok into the dirt. Hickok gets a measure of revenge by sleeping with McCanles's mistress, the 26-year-old Sarah Shull.

National Headlines/March 1861:

4. LINCOLN INAUGURATED

APRIL

1. Some 1,400 grapevines arrive in California from Europe; the state's grape-growing industry begins.

3. Cadet George A. Custer receives three demerits at West Point for "throwing snowballs in vicinity of barracks."

11. The Metropolitan Theater opens in San Francisco.

14–15. Thirty members of the 6th Infantry battle Indians on California's Mad River. Twenty-five Indians are killed.

18. Arizona's Fort Defiance is abandoned.

21. General E. V. Sumner replaces Brigadier General Albert Sidney Johnston as commander of the Division of the Pacific in San Francisco. The War Department's decision reflects Sumner's strong attachment to the Union.

22. Troops from North Carolina commandeer the U.S. arsenal in Fayetteville, Arkansas, when that state's governor refuses to give it military protection.

23. Mormons organize a 200-wagon rescue party to travel to the Missouri River to retrieve some hard-luck immigrants.

24. In Denver, a town meeting debates whether to side with the Union or the Confederacy. Residents vote overwhelmingly to support the Union.

26. James Ryder Randall writes the song "Maryland, My Maryland" at New Roads, Louisiana, just northwest of Baton Rouge.

30. President Lincoln orders Union troops to leave Indian Territory.

National Headlines/April 1861:

12. WAR BEGINS; FORT SUMTER ATTACKED

17. VIRGINIA SECEDES

BOB HASLAM'S RIDE
MARCH 1861

One of the Pony Express riders to carry President Lincoln's inaugural address to California was Bob Haslam, who set his own personal endurance record in March 1861.

Between Smith's Creek and Cold Spring, Nevada, Haslam, riding "Old Buck," was attacked by Indians. He managed to shoot three from their horses during a running battle before an arrow struck his arm. Turning to look behind, he received another arrow in the mouth, breaking his jaw and dislodging five teeth. Haslam stuffed a bandanna into his mouth and made it to the next station, having covered 120 miles on 12 horses in eight hours. Lincoln's address arrived in California in seven days, 17 hours.

MAY

1. Soldiers at Fort Washita, in present Oklahoma, surrender their post to Confederates without any shots being fired.

■ Horace Wellman becomes supervisor at Rock Creek station, Nebraska, relieving David McCanles, who is selling the property to Russell, Majors and Waddell. This is a relief to employee James Butler Hickok, who has come to despise McCanles.

■ Construction of a San Francisco–Oakland railroad is authorized.

6. Arkansas becomes the 9th state to secede from the Union as the state legislature votes 69–1.

11. A pro-Union demonstration takes place in San Francisco as word of the Confederate victory at Fort Sumter arrives.

13. Lewiston, Idaho, is established as a service community for miners.

14. Sergeant Hartman's 4th Infantry detachment kills 14 Indians and captures 20 at Boulder Creek, California.

17. California's legislature unanimously adopts a resolution supporting the Union in the wake of the battle at Fort Sumter.

■ William Gilpin arrives in Denver to assume office as Colorado's first territorial governor. He notes that much of the population has returned to "the States" to participate in the Civil War.

22. In the "Cortina War" in Texas, Santos Benavides and a force of some 40 volunteers attack the Corti-

---

nistas near Laredo. Seven bandits are killed, 15 are wounded, and 11 are taken captive. The 11 prisoners are executed on the spot. Governor Edward Clark will reward Benavides with an engraved pistol.

29. Henry Robinson, one of the most feared Indian fighters in the state of Texas, and his daughter's fiancé are attacked by about 20 Indians while en route to Chalk Bluff. Both men are killed and scalped. Robinson is also deprived of the piece that gave him his nickname, Great Red Beard.

■ The USS *South Carolina* bombards Galveston, Texas.

■ Mounted riflemen clash with 70 Comanches in Chaparito, New Mexico. One Indian is reported killed.

■ San Francisco's Emperor Norton "fires" both Jefferson Davis and Abraham Lincoln, and is seen on the streets in Union and Confederate garb to show his impartiality.

National Headlines/May 1861:
20. NORTH CAROLINA SECEDES

JUNE

4. Members of the 4th Infantry kill eight Indians on California's Redwood Creek.

5. The Overland Mail Company agrees to put 600 horses, 25 stagecoaches, 25 drivers, 12 conductors, and other personnel totaling 150 on the road between Salt Lake City and Carson City.

6. His "territory" having become null and void with the formation of Colorado Territory, Provisional Governor Robert W. Steele resigns as chief executive of "Jefferson Territory." William Gilpin will assume the office of governor of Colorado Territory.

16. The Pacific Telegraph Act authorizes the construction of a telegraph line from San Francisco to Missouri.

17. General Nathaniel Lyon and his troops take Boonville, Missouri, for the Union, thereby securing control of the lower Missouri River.

18. Some 31 mounted riflemen report "many" Indians killed and wounded on New Mexico's Peanasco River.

20. Traveling by riverboat up the Minnesota River, Henry David Thoreau and Horace Mann, Jr., disembark at the Lower Sioux Indian Agency trading post of Redwood in Minnesota. Thoreau will meet Little Crow and write of his experiences during a ceremony: "the Indians, as usual, having the advantage in point of truth and earnestness, and therefore of eloquence."

23. Henry David Thoreau and Horace Mann, Jr., on their return to Massachusetts, stop at Red Wing, Minnesota, where they stay at the Metropolitan House and swim in the Mississippi River.

28. California's Central Pacific Railroad is organized by four Sacramento men, Charles Crocker, Mark Hopkins, Collis Huntington, and Leland Stanford.

Also in June 1861:
George A. Custer graduates last in his class of 34 at West Point. During his stay, he accumulated 726 demerits. His is commissioned a second lieutenant in the 2nd U.S. Cavalry.

National Headlines/June 1861:
3. STEPHEN A. DOUGLAS DEAD IN CHICAGO
8. TENNESSEE SECEDES

JULY

1. John Butterfield, under a contract with the Post Office Department, begins a daily coach service over the central route. His company, Butterfield Overland Mail, has subcontracted the C.O.C. & P.P. to provide service east of Salt Lake City, and the Pioneer Stage Line to run service between Carson and Placerville.

■ Lieutenant Colonel John R. Baylor's Confederate forces occupy Mesilla, New Mexico.

■ A new public school opens in San Francisco.

■ Wells Fargo begins pony express service from Placerville to San Francisco.

2. U.S. Commissioner William P. Dole signs a treaty with the Delaware tribe in Leavenworth, Kansas.

3. The Pony Express arrives in San Francisco with letters from New York.

4. Captain John Mullan and his party celebrate Independence Day on Idaho's Coeur d'Alene River, where he is supervising construction of the Mullan Road for immigrant travel. An American flag is raised atop a white pine.

■ Construction begins on a telegraph line from Omaha to Salt Lake City, via Julesburg.

5. In Carthage, Missouri, Union soldiers attack prosecessionist Missouri troops under Governor Claiborne Jackson. The Missourians outnumber Franz Sigel's federal troops by 3 to 1, and drive the invaders back. Approximately 40 Confederates are killed and 120 are wounded; 13 Union soldiers are killed and 31 are wounded.

■ Frank James and Cole Younger meet at the Battle of Carthage.

8. President Lincoln appoints William Gilpin governor of Colorado Territory.

- General Henry Hopkins Sibley is put in charge of Confederate troops in the New Mexico area.
10. Union troops demolish and then abandon Fort Breckenridge in present Arizona.
- Colorado Territory's Supreme Court convenes.
11. The steamboat *Chippewa,* loaded with a cargo of whiskey and gunpowder, explodes on Montana's Poplar Creek.
12. James Butler "Wild Bill" Hickok shoots it out with the McCanles Gang at Rock Creek station, Nebraska.

INCIDENT AT ROCK CREEK
JULY 12, 1861

The legend of James Butler "Wild Bill" Hickok began in earnest with his gunfight at Rock Creek station, Nebraska.

David Colbert McCanles, the original owner of the property, was involved in a long-standing feud with the firm of Russell, Majors and Waddell—he claimed the firm was using his property without full reimbursement. On this day, he arrived with a group of men to demand full payment. Company supervisor Horace Wellman was away, but his common-law wife, along with Sarah Shull, and Sarah Kelsey and Hickok were inside the small structure.

McCanles entered and threatened Hickok, demanding that he come out from behind a curtain or he would come after him. Wild Bill told him that if he tried that, there would be "one less son of a bitch." McCanles ripped back the curtain and Hickok put a bullet in his chest. McCanles staggered out, told his son to run, and fell dead. In the ensuing fight, Hickok wounded James Woods, who was finished off by Mrs. Wellman, who hacked him to death with a hoe. Hickok wounded another man, who was then killed by another employee.

Hickok was officially cleared of the murder of McCanles, and the incident went largely unnoticed until 1867, when the writer Colonel George W. Nichols penned a sensational "interview" with Hickok for *Harper's* magazine. Titled "Wild Bill," the article was a masterful blend of pulp journalism and applesauce, in which the dreaded McCanles "gang" grew to 10 members and tried to hang a local preacher before launching its ill-advised attack on Hickok.

---

14. Texas troops occupy Fort Bliss in El Paso.
21. Approximately 300 Indians under Cochise and Mangas Coloradas surround a mail coach en route to Tucson at Cook's Canyon. The seven guards hold out for three days before being killed. Cochise later admits he lost 175 men in the battle.
- In Virginia, Second Lieutenant George A. Custer is present at the Battle of Bull Run but does not participate in the fighting.
23. Confederate Captain John R. Baylor begins his invasion of New Mexico from El Paso. When it is learned that Baylor plans to attack Fort Fillmore, Major Isaac Lynde will order an evacuation. Baylor's troops will capture Lynde's entire force.
- Arizona's Fort Buchanan is torched and abandoned.
25. Confederate and Union troops skirmish in New Mexico after Major Isaac Lynde demands that the Southern forces surrender. The Union forces return to Fort Fillmore, which Lynde will abandon, and then move on to Fort Stanton 154 miles to the northeast.
26. The *California Daily Appeal,* having received a bulletin via Pony Express, prints an account of the Battle of Bull Run, which occurred on July 21.
- Confederate forces under Captain John Baylor gain control of New Mexico by driving Union troops from Fort Fillmore.

Also in July 1861:
The Pony Express reduces its postal rate from $5 per half-ounce to $1 per half-ounce.
During his brief hitch in the Confederate Army, Samuel Clemens (Mark Twain) returns to his birthplace, Florida, Missouri. The homecoming will be described in Twain's *The Private History of a Campaign that Failed* (1885). Twain's brother Orion has been appointed secretary of Nevada Territory; the two leave for Carson City.

National Headlines/July 1861:
21. CONFEDERACY HOLDS AT BULL RUN

AUGUST
1. After defeating Union troops at Fort Fillmore in New Mexico, Captain John Baylor claims all territory south of the 34th parallel as the Confederate Territory of Arizona. His government, based in Mesilla, will receive recognition from the Confederate Congress.
- The first territorial census in Colorado records a population of 25,329 (Denver's population is 2,603); males outnumber females 5 to 1. This number differs from earlier estimates because so many

Confederate soldiers bivouac at Las Moras, Texas.   (Library of Congress)

have left the gold fields to return home to fight in the Civil War.

2. Fort Stanton, in New Mexico, is evacuated by Union forces.

3. Sixty-eight residents meeting in Tucson declare their allegiance to the Confederacy, claiming that Arizona has been deserted by the Union. Granville Oury is chosen as a delegate to the Confederate Congress, which will refuse to seat him.

■ Residents of Tubac, Arizona, unprotected now that Union soldiers have been recalled for Civil War duty, will hold off a band of Indian and Mexican looters for three days before making a daring nighttime escape.

5. The Union general Nathaniel Lyon moves his troops out of Dug Springs, Missouri, upon hearing reports that a large detachment of Confederates is heading his way.

■ A company of the 1st Cavalry kills one Indian and wounds three others at Goose Lake, California.

10. Some 5,000 Union troops under Brigadier General Nathaniel Lyon are defeated by a force of 15,000 Confederates under Major General Sterling Price and Brigadier General Ben McCulloch at Wilson's Creek, Missouri. Lyon falls at Bloody Ridge. Confederate losses: 421 dead, 1,300 wounded. Union losses: 263 dead, 721 wounded.

12. Apaches attack a band of Confederates in Texas, killing 15.

14. Martial law is declared in St. Louis, Missouri, by the Union General John C. Frémont.

■ Orion and Samuel Clemens arrive by stagecoach in Carson City, Nevada. In addition to serving as his brother's secretary, Samuel will search for gold in the diggings and take extended breaks at Lake Tahoe.

15. General John Charles Frémont appeals to President Lincoln for federal aid in Missouri; he will be granted reinforcements by the War Department.

19. A group of proslavery Missourians proclaim their state a part of the Confederacy; they will soon be expelled by the state's free-soil majority.

20. The first criminal case filed in Denver is *United States v. Moses Adler*. Adler, a saloon keeper, is charged with murdering Thomas S. Rogers, a soldier in the Colorado Volunteers, "with a certain knife of the value of 50¢, inflicting a mortal wound near the heart."

■ Union and Confederate forces clash briefly in Jonesboro, Missouri.

27. The San Francisco *Daily Times* suspends operations.

30. Claiming that Missouri is subject to "helplessness of civil authority and total insecurity of life," General John Charles Frémont declares the state under martial law and orders the emancipation of the slaves of rebels. He also allows property to be confiscated from "those who would take up arms against the U.S."

Also in August 1861:

George A. Custer is transferred from the 2nd to the 5th Cavalry.

Another sign the boom times of the gold rush are over: the San Francisco carpenter who earned approximately $16 a day in 1849 now earns $4 a day.

Colorado's first territorial delegate to Congress is Hiram P. Bennett.

Richard King of Texas's King Ranch now owns some 20,000 head of cattle and 3,000 horses.

Kansas City's *Journal of Commerce* suspends publication.

SEPTEMBER

1. General Ulysses S. Grant assumes command of a Union army at Missouri's Cape Girardeau.

8. San Francisco's Stock Exchange Board is created to trade silver stocks.

9. The first Colorado territorial legislature meets in Denver to divide the territory into 18 counties. Colorado City is designated the capital. The new counties are Arapahoe, Boulder, Carbonate, Clear Creek, Costilla, Douglas, El Paso, Fremont, Gilpin, Guadalupe, Huerfano, Jefferson, Larimer, Park, Pueblo, San Miguel, Summit, and Weld.

■ New Mexico governor Connelly calls for volunteers to resist an invasion "by an armed force from the State of Texas."

■ The McClellan Guard is organized in San Francisco.

11. President Lincoln writes to General John Charles Frémont, questioning the legality of the latter's actions of August 30.

20. Union forces under Colonel Mulligan are defeated in Lexington, Missouri, largely because they could not obtain reinforcements from General John Charles Frémont. Frémont will receive additional criticism for his behavior.

23. When the editor of the *St. Louis Evening News* questions General Frémont's judgment regarding the battle in Lexington, the general orders the newspaper closed and the offending scribe arrested.

Also in September 1861:

A Wells Fargo shipment is robbed just outside of Placerville, California; three bandits make off with approximately $3,000 in gold coins.

OCTOBER

2. Union forces break up a Confederate camp at Charleston, Missouri.

4. Confederates sign treaties with the Seneca, Shawnee, and Cherokee tribes that will enable these Indians to join rebel forces in battle.

■ The artist Frederic Remington is born in Canton, New York.

5. Federal troops in California search for Confederate sympathizers at Temecula Ranch and Oak Grove.

7. General John Charles Frémont assembles a "too little, too late" expeditionary force to pursue General Sterling Price's Confederate force in Missouri.

12. Civil War–related clashes occur in Clintonville and Pomme de Terre, Missouri.

14. Former St. Louis mayor Jeff Thompson organizes the Missouri State Militia to rid the area of Union troops.

15. Jeff Thompson's militia attacks federal troops at Potosi, burns the Big River Bridge, and captures 50 Union soldiers.

16. Union forces recapture Lexington, Missouri.

18. Edward Creighton's crew, building the first transcontinental telegraph line west from Missouri, reaches Salt Lake City. Brigham Young sends a message to Abraham Lincoln over the new line.

■ Jeff Thompson's militia skirmishes with Union forces near Ironton, Missouri.

24. President Lincoln decides to terminate General John Charles Frémont's command in Missouri. General S. R. Curtis is dispatched to inform Frémont that he will be relieved of duty by General David Hunter.

■ The transcontinental telegraph line is completed.

25. General John Charles Frémont, aware that General Curtis is on the way with orders to relieve his command, pursues General Price's Confederate forces in Missouri.

26. The price to send a telegraphic message coast to coast is $6 for every 10 words.

27. General John Charles Frémont continues to pursue Price, whom he incorrectly believes to be in the vicinity of Springfield, Missouri.

A Pony Express rider hails telegraph construction workers. (National Archives)

THE TRANSCONTINENTAL TELEGRAPH
OCTOBER 24, 1861

James Gamble's crew constructing the telegraph line eastward from California reached Salt Lake City and linked lines with the crew from Missouri at Fort Bridger in present Wyoming. The first transcontinental telegraph message was sent from San Francisco by California's Supreme Court chief justice, Stephen Johnson Field, to President Lincoln in Washington, D.C. Field assured the president of California's allegiance to the Union from 3,595 miles away. Brigham Young had sent the first telegraph message from Salt Lake City to San Francisco.

With the telegraph a reality, the Pony Express suspended operations. In its 18 and one-half months of operation, the Pony Express lost an estimated $200,000 to $500,000. One calculation showed that each of the 34,753 pieces of mail it carried over a combined 650,000 miles cost $16 to deliver.

On the demise of the Pony Express, the *San Francisco Pacific* wrote:

> You came to us often with tidings that made your feet beautiful on . . . the mountains. . . . We have looked for you as those who wait for the morning, and how seldom did you fail us! When days were months and hours weeks, how you thrilled us out of our pain and suspense, to know the best or know the worst! You have served us well!

Also in October 1861:

Brigham Young instructs some 300 Mormon faithful to colonize a community called St. George, in southwestern Utah, and "to supply the territory with cotton, sugar, grapes, tobacco, figs, almonds, olive oil, and such other useful articles as the Lord has given us."

The U.S. government reports of the Kansa tribe: "Many are sick and without clothes."

NOVEMBER

2. President Lincoln's removal of General John Charles Frémont from the command of the Western Department becomes official.
5. Central City is chosen as the capital of Colorado Territory.
8. The city of Denver is incorporated.
■ The University of Colorado is incorporated in Boulder.
15. U.S. Commissioner William W. Ross signs a treaty with the Mission, Prairie, and Woods bands of the Potawatomi tribe at their Kansas agency.
16. In San Francisco, Wells Fargo receives 713 casks of butter shipped via Panama.
18. The last Pony Express ride is completed.
19. A Confederate attempt to seize Indian Territory is thwarted in a battle at Round Mountain.
20. Federal troops in California pursue a group of Confederate sympathizers known as the Showalter Party. Many days later, 18 members will be captured near Los Angeles, including rebel leader Daniel Showalter.
26. Albert Bacon Fall, the future politician and Teapot Dome scandal figure, is born in Frankfort, Kentucky.
28. The Provisional Congress at Richmond admits Mis-

Denver, Colorado. (Library of Congress)

souri to the Confederacy and admits her representatives. Missouri, however, never formally secedes.

Also in November 1861:

Smallpox affects many tribes in Texas, including the Comanche, Cheyenne, Arapaho, Kiowa, and Kiowa-Apache.

National Headlines/November 1861:

7. NORTH BLOCKADES SOUTHERN PORTS

DECEMBER

4. In Missouri, Union general Henry Halleck promises to arrest and execute anyone who aids the secessionist movement.
9. The Confederates are defeated in the Battle of Caving Banks in Indian Territory.
■ Near present Tulsa, Oklahoma, the pro-Southern forces of many tribes drive the pro-Union Creek Indians from the area around Bird Creek.
12. Isaac Parker, the future "Hanging Judge," weds Mary O'Toole in St. Louis.
24. Waco University is chartered in Texas; it will become part of Baylor University in 1886.
26. Confederate irregulars defeat pro-Union Indians at Chustenahlah in Indian Territory.
31. The California Powder Works incorporates with capital of $100,000.

Also in December 1861:

Two hundred wagons arrive at the site of St. George, the new Mormon colony in southwestern Utah.

Frederic Homer Balch, the poet and novelist (*The Bridge*

of the Gods, 1890), is born in Lebanon, Oregon.

General Henry H. Sibley reinforces Colonel John Baylor and takes over command of the Confederate column now known as the Army of New Mexico. He will establish his headquarters at Fort Bliss, in El Paso, Texas.

Also in 1861:

Informed that Union troops will not protect them on their reservations, 5,000 pro-Union Creeks under Chief Opothle begin a trek from Indian Territory to Kansas; they are joined by Chief Tustenuggee and 1,500 Seminoles. A white Confederate force attacks them but is driven back. Although Cherokees allied with the Confederates refuse to attack the Indians, other white Confederates continue a series of running battles. Only a handful of pro-Union Indians ultimately reach Kansas.

Balduin Möllhausen writes *Der Halbindianer* (The Half-Breed). This first novel will be followed by 178 novels, narratives, travel books, and other works on the Old West that will make Möllhausen Europe's most popular German author in the 1860s and 1870s.

Colorado furnished the Union Army with 4,903 soldiers.

The first California oil well is drilled at Eureka.

Fort Mojave is abandoned in Arizona.

There are 22 black slaves in New Mexico.

The Territorial University of Washington is established in Seattle.

Among other interesting feats it performed this year, Wells Fargo shipped a steam fire engine from Baltimore to Sacramento.

1862

> "The whites were always trying to make the Indians give up their life and live like white men—go to farming, work hard and do as they did—and the Indian did not know how to do that, and did not want to anyway. . . . If the Indians had tried to make the whites live like them, the whites would have resisted, and it was the same way with many Indians."
>
> —Big Eagle (Wamditanka), Santee Sioux

JANUARY

2. Floodwaters from the Colorado and Gila Rivers destroy Colorado City and submerge portions of Arizona between Fort Yuma and Pilot Knob.

10. Samuel Colt, 47, dies at his mansion, Armsmear. His estate is estimated at $15 million.

▪ Republican Leland Stanford is sworn in as California's governor.

11. Sarsfield Hall, a San Francisco boarding house, is destroyed by fire.

17. Morgan County is created in Utah with Grant as the county seat. Morgan Grant was a public official and the father of Herbert Grant, who will become president of the Latter-day Saints in 1940.

18. The Confederate Congress passes an act admitting the territories of Arizona and New Mexico into the Confederacy.

Also in January 1862:

Mountain man P. Weaver finds gold on the Colorado River in Arizona, and the town of La Paz is created; in four years, it will have 5,000 residents. After $8 million in gold is found, the river will change course and La Paz will become a ghost town.

The Treasury Department proposes to Congress that a branch mint be established in Denver. The department notes that Clark, Gruber and Company, a private mint, has coined $120,000 in gold in the past two years.

Clay Allison is discharged from the Tennessee Light Artillery after three months because of the effects of a childhood head injury. The official report reads: "Emotional or physical excitement produces paroxysmals of a mixed character, partly epileptic and partly maniacal."

A journey with no maps. Finding one's way in the Old West often depends on good relations with the natives. (Library of Congress)

National Headlines/January 1862:

31. LINCOLN ORDERS ARMY TO SEIZE MANASSAS JUNCTION RAILHEAD

FEBRUARY

12. St. Peter's Mission, near the Great Falls of the Missouri River, is taken over by Jesuits.

13. Jeff Pelkey becomes the first white person born in Montana Territory (at Hellgate).

14. Confederate president Jefferson Davis signs the act admitting Arizona and New Mexico to the Confederacy as territories.

21. At Valverde, New Mexico, General Henry H. Sibley's Confederate force of 2,600 men defeats the 3,800 Union soldiers under Colonel E. R. S. Canby and a New Mexico Volunteer Infantry that includes famed mountain man Kit Carson. After the battle, Sibley will take the cities of Albuquerque and Santa Fe. Canby lost 68 men, Sibley 31.

28. Captain Sherod Hunter and 200 Arizona Guards raise a Texas flag over Tucson and demand that the white residents swear an oath of allegiance to the Confederacy. A delegate is sent to Richmond.

Also in February 1862:

Samuel Clemens is in Aurora, Nevada, trying to strike it rich through mining. He is also writing letters to the Virginia City *Territorial Enterprise* under the name "Josh."

National Headlines/February 1862:

20. PRESIDENT'S SON DIES IN WHITE HOUSE

22. JEFFERSON DAVIS INAUGURATED FOLLOWING HIS ELECTION AS CONFEDERATE PRESIDENT

MARCH

1. General Samuel R. Curtis camps a force of some 10,500 Union soldiers on Sugar Creek in Arkansas. General Earl Van Dorn concentrates his Confederate forces in the area in an attempt to repel the Union drive.

■ Arizona's March H. McWillie is seated by the Confederate Congress as a delegate.

■ Lieutenant W. S. Pennock reports two enlisted men killed in a brush between Indians and the 1st Cavalry between Forts Craig and Union in New Mexico.

2. Edwin Milton Royle, author of *The Squaw Man* (1906), is born in Lexington, Missouri.

3. Acting Second Lieutenant R. Wall is wounded in a battle with Indians at Comanche Canyon, New Mexico.

6. The Salt Lake Theatre is dedicated.

6–8. The Battle of Pea Ridge takes place.

■ James Butler Hickok serves as a Union scout at the Battle of Pea Ridge.

10. Confederate troops occupy Santa Fe without oppo-

THE BATTLE OF PEA RIDGE
MARCH 6–8, 1862

The Battle of Pea Ridge, in Arkansas, was the most important Civil War battle fought west of the Mississippi.

On March 6, General Earl Van Dorn and about 17,000 Confederate soldiers were joined by Indian troops in an attack against one of General Samuel Curtis's divisions, commanded by General Franz Sigel, at Bentonville; Sigel's men were forced back into Curtis's camp. The next day, Curtis faced his army northwest. Van Dorn ordered General Benjamin McCulloch to attack Curtis's left. Union reinforcements arrived at 5:00 P.M.

On March 8, Confederate generals McCulloch and James McIntosh were both killed in heavy combat. Curtis moved against Van Dorn's concentrated strength. Low on ammunition, Van Dorn ordered a withdrawal to the Arkansas River to the north at about 10:00 P.M.

About 26,000 men saw action in the Union victory. Curtis reported 203 killed, 972 wounded, and 176 missing. Van Dorn cited 185 killed, 525 wounded, and 300 missing.

---

sition; the territorial government's seat is relocated to Las Vegas, New Mexico.

13. U.S. Commissioner H. W. Farnsworth signs a treaty with Kansa Indians at their agency near Council Grove, Kansas.

15. The 1st Colorado Cavalry defeats a detachment of Confederates.

18. Second Lieutenant Russell and 10 members of his 3rd Cavalry kill four Indians at Canyon Ladrone, New Mexico.

21. William Russell's Central Overland California and Pikes Peak Express Company is purchased by Benjamin Holladay. The Holladay Overland Mail and Express Company will operate between St. Louis and Salt Lake City, where it will connect with Wells Fargo to San Francisco.

26–28. The Battle of Glorietta Pass, sometimes referred to as the "Gettysburg of the West," occurs in New Mexico Territory. Pushing eastward in a forced march that included a snowstorm, Texas Confederates under General Henry H. Sibley are hoping to capture Fort Union. At La Glorietta Pass, about 20 miles southeast of Santa Fe, they are unexpectedly engaged by Union forces under Colonel John Slough. A detachment of First Colorado Volunteers is dispatched by Governor Gilpin and led by Major John Chivington. At a Santa Fe Trail stagecoach stop known as Pigeon's Ranch, Chivington finds the Confederate supply train and destroys all 73 wagons of the train. Confederates are pursued by General Canby's cavalry down the Rio Grande River into Texas. Of a force of 1,100 Confederates, 36 are listed as dead, 60 wounded. The Union force of 1,324 records 31 killed and 50 wounded. With this retreat, Confederate control of New Mexico becomes an impossibility.

26. Union troops capture 50 Confederates in a fight near Denver.
27. Kansas City's *Journal of Commerce* resumes publication.

Also in March 1862:
Clay Allison, 22, discovers a trooper of the 3rd Illinois Cavalry looting his mother's barn in Waynesboro, Tennessee, and shoots him dead.

Hiram S. Rumfield reports that the Butterfield Overland Mail fed $1,792 worth of beef to Indians along the company's routes in January, February, and March.

National Headlines/March 1862:
9. MONITOR, MERRIMAC CLASH

APRIL
6. The explorer John Wesley Powell loses his right arm during the Civil War battle of Shiloh in Tennessee.
8. Confederate troops abandon Sante Fe.
11. Union forces occupy Santa Fe.
15. The Battle of Peralta is the westernmost Civil War confrontation. At Picacho Pass in present Arizona, an advance unit of the California Column from Yuma, under General James H. Carleton, defeats a Confederate detachment of Captain Sherod Hunter's Texans. Upon learning of the battle, Confederate troops retreat from Tucson.
17. About 30 Indians attack a Holladay Overland Mail wagon train near Split Rock station in Utah. Six of the nine people in the train are wounded in the four-hour battle. The Indians get away with nine mules and partially destroy two wagons.
19. President Lincoln appoints Dr. John Evans the second territorial governor of Colorado.
21. In Washington, D.C., Congress approves a bill establishing a branch mint in Colorado.
25. Admiral David Farragut's Union forces seize control of New Orleans after Confederate forces leave it defenseless.

29. New Orleans is formally surrendered to Union forces.

Also in April 1862:
Captain Refugio Benavides organizes a Confederate company at Fort Ringgold, Texas; all but one of its members are Mexican-Texan.

Near Richmond, Virginia, George A. Custer ascends some 1,000 feet in a balloon to observe the movement of Confederate forces.

The U.S. government reports that the Kansa tribe is "completely destitute."

Wells Fargo carries the mail: In San Francisco, the company's green mailboxes can be seen standing next to Uncle Sam's red ones. The company's capital stock is increased to $2 million.

National Headlines/April 1862:
6–7. BATTLE OF SHILOH RAGES IN TENNESSEE
16. DAVIS APPROVES CONSCRIPTION

MAY
2. Granville Stuart and a Shoshone woman marry in Montana's Deer Lodge Valley.
5. Mexican forces under General Ignacio Zaragoza rout the French forces of Napolean III at the Battle of Puebla. The anniversary becomes a Mexican national holiday, Cinco de Mayo.
8. The first sluices for catching gold in Montana are erected at Gold Creek by James and Granville Stuart.
17. Colorado's second territorial governor, John Evans, arrives in Denver.
20. President Lincoln signs the Homestead Act, which will allow citizens or intended citizens over 21 years of age to claim 160 surveyed government acres after living on them for five years. Registration fees will not exceed $34. If a homesteader wanted to gain title earlier, the land could be bought for $1.25 an acre after 6 months.
■ Three divisions of the California Advance Guard under Colonel Joseph R. West enter Tucson to liberate the city, held by the Confederates since February. After much hollering and whooping in the center of town, amused residents inform the soldiers that the rebel detachment left a week earlier.
22. A party to rescue poor Mormons migrating to Utah is organized in Salt Lake City. The party includes 262 wagons, 293 teamsters, 2,880 oxen, and 143,315 pounds of flour.
25. Winnemucca, Numaga, and other chiefs of the Northern Paiutes in Nevada meet with Governor

James Nye on the Truckee River to exchange gifts and make peace with the whites in the region.

Also in May 1862:

The Confederacy's Thomas Legion, comprising 6,435 Cherokee soldiers, is organized.

JUNE

2. Slavery is officially banned in the Union's territories, by order of Congress.
5. George Armstong Custer is promoted to captain in the Union Army.
6. In Arizona, Lieutenant Sylvester Mowry is found guilty of treason by a military court convened by General James Carleton and is jailed in Tucson.
8. General James H. Carleton declares martial law in Tucson. He deems Arizona to be a territory "until such time as the President of the United States shall otherwise direct."
9. General John C. Frémont's forces are defeated by General Stonewall Jackson at Cross Keys, in the Shenandoah Valley campaign in Virginia.
16. The San Francisco Board of Supervisors approves a petition allowing Bummer and Lazarus to be excluded from the rules governing stray dogs. The petition calls for the "consecration of these two dogs as city property, to wander unmolested in pursuit of their daily food."
23. As if to show their appreciation for their new "preferred dog" status, Bummer and Lazarus stop a runaway team on Clay Street. The *Daily Alta* will print the following story on June 24:

> On reaching the corner of Kearny, "Bummer" rushed in front of the horses and held them at bay until a man came up and caught the team, "Lazarus" being on hand to check any further advances. These dogs may now be considered in the employ of the city, and of course are exempt from taxation.

24. John Bozeman, Thomas Stuart, and the rest of their party reach Gold Creek, Montana, having journeyed from Colorado.
28. U.S. Commissioner Charles B. Keith signs a treaty with the Kickapoo Indians at their agency in Kansas.

Also in June 1862:

Wells Fargo reports that nine sacks of mail and seven express sacks have been burned by Indians at Sweetwater, California. Another 21 mail sacks have been sliced open at Ice Springs, California.

The valedictorian of the graduating class at the Monroe (Michigan) Female Seminary is Elizabeth Bacon, the future bride of George A. Custer.

The U.S. government reports "many deaths for want of medicine" in the Kansa tribe.

JULY

1. President Lincoln signs the Pacific Railroad Act, authorizing the Central Pacific and the Union Pacific Railroads to build the country's first transcontinental railroad. The act adopts the "42nd Parallel route." Under the act's terms, the Central Pacific and the Union Pacific will be loaned capital at the rate of $16,000 per mile over prairie land, and $48,000 per mile over mountainous terrain. Also, it will grant the companies 10 sections of public land per mile for the track that will link the cities of Omaha and Sacramento. The goal is to complete the project in 1876, the nation's centennial.
■ Antipolygamy legislation aimed at Utah's Mormons is passed by Congress.
2. President Lincoln signs legislation awarding land for the construction of agricultural colleges to loyal states. Under the terms of the Morrill Land Grant Act, states will receive 30,000 acres for each member of Congress.
3. Union forces are victorious at Locust Grove in Indian Territory.
4. The first Masonic meeting in Wyoming is held on Independence Rock.
7. Colorado's second assembly meets at the current capital, Colorado City, and names Denver the territory's new capital.
11. San Francisco firemen salute the signing of the Pacific Railroad Act with a torchlight parade.
■ Colorado's second assembly adjourns to Denver.
14. Mangas Coloradas and Cochise lead an attack on a wagon train belonging to the California Column. Some 60 braves are killed in the incident, and the attackers are driven off.
15. The California Column's wagon train is attacked again by Mangas Coloradas and Cochise, this time at Apache Pass in present southern Arizona. Brigadier General James H. Carleton, on the trail of Confederates in Arizona, is leading a detachment to secure a spring because it looks as if the summer will be long. The attackers turn back after some 60

are killed by howitzer fire. Says one Apache after the fray, "We would have done well if you hadn't fired wagons at us."

- Wounded in the battle at Apache Pass, the aging Mangas Coloradas will be taken through the Chiricahua Mountains on a 100-mile trek to a doctor in Janos, Mexico. Upon arriving, Cochise will tell the physician: "If he [Coloradas] dies, everybody in Janos dies." Mangas will recover.

17. Piegan Indians and white settlers are attacked by Crow Indians on Montana's Marias River; one of the settlers is killed.

20. The fastest steamboat trip ever from Montana to St. Louis (12 days) begins as the *Emily* roars out of Fort Benton.

- Troops from the First and Second U.S. Cavalry establish temporary posts in Tubac, Arizona.

26. Fort Bowie is established southeast of Tucson, where General Carleton and his men secured a spring, to guard the eastern entrance to Apache Pass.

28. John White, William Eads, and a group of Colorado prospectors discover gold at Willard's or Grasshopper Creek, Montana. The boomtown of Bannack will spring up. Because of confusion about boundaries, the town will be in Oregon Territory, Idaho Territory and Montana Territory.

Also in July 1862:
General Henry Hopkins Sibley withdraws his forces from El Paso to San Antonio.

Impressed with his "Josh" letters, the Virginia City *Territorial Enterprise* hires Samuel L. Clemens at a salary of $25 a week.

George A. Custer is promoted to the rank of first lieutenant.

Precut houses are being shipped around Cape Horn to Nevada.

Trade along the Santa Fe Trail has increased in value from $5 million to $40 million a year since 1855.

National Headlines/July 1862:
12. CONGRESS AUTHORIZES MEDAL OF HONOR

AUGUST

2. Gold is discovered at Boise Basin, Idaho.
- The first Idaho newspaper, the *Golden Age,* is published in Lewiston.

10. Twenty miles from Fort Clark, on the Nueces River in Texas, a Confederate band called the Texas Rifles attacks a group of German-Texans and kills 32.

14. Colorado's second assembly names Golden as the new territorial capital

17. A Sioux "uprising" begins in Minnesota. Santee Sioux Indians under Chief Little Crow, facing starvation and angry because government supplies have not arrived at the Lower Sioux Agency near Fort Ridgely, launch a six-week campaign. Captain John S. Marsh leads 46 men from Fort Ridgely into an attack by warriors under White Dog at the Agency. Seeing his men dropping fast, Marsh orders a retreat. On the way back to the fort, to show his men it is possible to swim a treacherous stream, Marsh himself attempts to swim it and drowns.

18. Little Crow leads an attack on the Lower Sioux Agency near Fort Ridgely, Minnesota, killing 20 men and taking 12 women captive. Other raids on white settlements kill as many as 400.

- Federal troops reoccupy Fort Bliss in El Paso, Texas. Until the end of the Civil War, the troops will control the Rio Grande's Middle Valley.

20. Little Crow's warriors storm Fort Ridgely in southwestern Minnesota. Working with outdated cannon, a salty old artillery sergeant known as Jones repels the attack. After Little Crow is wounded, the final Indian charge is led by Mankato. The Sioux withdraw.

23. Little Crow's men, led by Mankato, battle 250 settlers on the outskirts of New Ulm, Minnesota. Captain William Dodd is killed and a portion of the town is burned.

24. A charge led by Judge Charles E. Flandrau of the Minnesota Supreme Court drives Little Crow's forces back from New Ulm.

28. Colonel Henry Hastings Sibley arrives at Fort Ridgely with 1,400 volunteers.

29. Colonel Henry Hastings Sibley arrives at the Lower Agency, where his troops bury 24 of Marsh's men and 20 citizens.

30. Sioux drive federal horses and cattle from Fort Abercrombie, near present Wahpeton, North Dakota.

National Headlines/August 1862:
30. SECOND BATTLE OF BULL RUN

SEPTEMBER

1. Major J. R. Brown and 200 men, closing in on Little Crow in Minnesota, camp at Birch Coulie.

2. Little Crow and his warriors attack Major J. R. Brown's encampment at dawn and immediately kill almost every horse. Colonel Henry H. Sibley, at the Lower Agency, hears gunfire in the distance and rushes to Brown's assistance; the Sioux retreat upon his arrival. Brown's casualties include 24 dead and 67 wounded. Little Crow will continue his war on Minnesota settlements.

5. A northern route from Minnesota to Montana is established by Jim Fisk's group.

9. James Wheelhouse is indicted in Pueblo, Colorado, on charges of selling a pint of whiskey for a quarter to an Indian.

11. William Sydney Porter is born in Greensboro, North Carolina. After spending time in a Texas prison on an embezzlement charge, Porter will become the short-story writer O. Henry, creator of the character "The Cisco Kid."

12. In San Francisco, Bummer and Lazarus make news when they team up on another Montgomery Street dog to steal his bone.

15. San Francisco begins raising a Union regiment to send to the Civil War.

18. In Minnesota, Colonel Henry Hastings Sibley takes 1,600 men on a march toward the Yellow Medicine River, where he has learned a village of hostages is located.

20. San Franciscans raise $100,000 for the war effort.

23. At Wood Lake, Minnesota, Little Crow attacks Colonel Sibley's advance party. Major Welsh's command rushes to the rescue. In thick woods, Little Crow attacks Welsh from the flank, and Welsh orders a retreat. Colonel Sibley orders five companies under Colonel Marshall to attack; the Sioux are beaten back; many, including Mankato, are killed.

26. With Little Crow's forces scattering, Colonel Sibley offers amnesty to three other chiefs. White captives numbering 269, mostly women and children, are returned to Sibley, and the conflict, which had claimed 644 citizens and 757 soldiers, essentially ends. Sibley will capture some 1,500 Sioux and imprison them at Fort Snelling.

■ Billy the Kid's stepfather, William H. Antrim, is honorably discharged from the Indiana Volunteer Infantry.

30. Bummer and Lazarus are accidentally locked overnight in the stationery and jewelry shop of Rosenfeldt and Collins. According to the *Alta California,* the dogs, "chaving at their confinement, had jumped through glass cases, and otherwise done considerable damage."

Also in September 1862:

Samuel Clemens moves to Virginia City in Nevada Territory to be near his $25-a-week job at the *Territorial Enterprise.*

National Headlines/September 1862:

15. STONEWALL JACKSON VICTORIOUS AT HARPERS FERRY

17. ANTIETAM BLOODIEST BATTLE OF CIVIL WAR

OCTOBER

9. Union forces under Commander William B. Renshaw capture Galveston, Texas. Having given the city fair warning, the harbor is secured without firing a shot. The U.S. flag is raised over the customs house, and the Galveston Fire Department appears in full parade uniform.

17. William Clarke Quantrill's raiders hit Johnson County, Kansas, killing three residents and burning 13 buildings. A few miles south of Shawnee, they kill two teamsters and steal their wagons.

22. The famous gold-rush hounds Bummer and Lazarus make their theatrical debut in a production of *Life in San Francisco,* at the city's Metropolitan Theatre.

31. Fort Sumner is established at Bosque Redondo, in the Pecos Valley of New Mexico.

■ Gold dust in Montana sells for $16 an ounce.

■ Hayden Carruth, who for 27 years will be a columnist for the *Woman's Home Companion,* is born in Lake City, Minnesota.

Also in October 1862:

In Gainesville, Texas, 19 men believed to be Union sympathizers are hanged in succession in the wake of the Peace Party Conspiracy. The Peace Party had originated in north Texas for the specific purpose of avoiding the draft. Confederate infiltrators arrested the men. Convictions were based on hearsay that the men had spoken against the confederacy.

NOVEMBER

5. In a massive court-martial, 392 Santee Sioux prisoners are tried on charges of extreme barbarity, that occurred during the recent violence in Minnesota. Of these, 307 will be sentenced to death and another 16 to prison. President Lincoln will commute all but 39 of the death sentences on December 6.

27. George Armstrong Custer meets his future bride, Elizabeth Bacon, at a Thanksgiving party.

29. General John Bankhead Magruder arrives in Texas to take charge of the Confederate forces there.

Also in November 1862:

Hiram S. Rumfield reports that the Butterfield Overland Mail spent $20,000 to feed the Indians along the company's routes with 400 head of cattle.

National Headlines/November 1862:

4. GATLING PATENTS GUN

5. LINCOLN RELIEVES McCLELLAN

DECEMBER

7. The Battle of Prairie Grove takes place near Fayetteville, Arkansas. Confederate General Thomas Hindman, with a force of 9,000 infantry, 2,000 cavalry, and 22 pieces of artillery, learns of an advancing Union force of 6,000 men under General Francis J. Herron. Herron is trying to link with forces under General James Blunt in Fayetteville, and Hindman decides to wedge himself between them. Hindman's cavalry drives Union horsemen back at 4:00 A.M. Herron mounts two assaults beginning at 1:00 P.M; both are repelled. By day's end, a fourth assault has failed. Hindman's force suffers 164 dead, 817 wounded, and 336 missing; Herron reports 175 of his men killed, 813 wounded, and 263 missing. Hindman claims victory but is forced to withdraw due to a lack of provisions and ammunition.

10. The British traveler Edward Shelly writes of meeting Buffalo Bill (William F. Cody) at Fort Benton on the Missouri, although he probably met Buffalo Bill Cramer.

26. Thirty-eight Santee Sioux are hanged from a large gallows built for the occasion at Mankato, Minnesota, for atrocities committed during the autumn uprising. Although 39 Indians were scheduled to be hanged, a last-minute reprieve saved one. As for Little Crow, who instigated the uprising, he is nowhere to be found.

29–31. Union forces are driven out of Galveston, Texas.

30. Company A, 5th Infantry, becomes the first troop to occupy Fort Sumner in New Mexico.

31. At the boom camp of Florence in Washington Territory, saloon keeper Henry J. "Cherokee Bob" Talbotte grants permission to William Willoughby to take his Cynthia to the local New Year's Eve dance. The ladies of Florence object to Cynthia's presence because Talbotte won her from William Mayfield in a poker game. Cynthia and Willoughby are ejected from the dance.

National Headlines/December 1862:
13. LEE VICTORIOUS AT FREDERICKSBURG

Also in 1862:
John Burwell Omohundro, Jr., 16, leaves his native Virginia for Texas and notoriety in the West as "Texas Jack."

Theodore Winthrop's novel *John Brent* is set in the Rocky Mountains and concerns the adventures of three men, a woman, and a wonder horse called Don Fulano. It would have been a promising start for one of the West's first novelists, but it was published posthumously: Winthrop died at the Civil War Battle of Great Bethel.

Jacob Waltz, 52, a naturalized American born in Prussia, migrates via Los Angeles to Arizona, where he registers a mining claim near Prescott. He will become the famed "Dutchman" of the "Lost Dutchman Mine."

Bret Harte weds Anna Griswold, who will bear him four children.

Stephen S. Harding becomes governor of Utah Territory; he will serve in that office until 1863.

The U.S. government buys the private mint of Clark, Gruber and Company in Denver for $25,000.

The humorist Charles Farrar Browne, writing under his pen name, publishes *Artemus Ward, His Book*.

To curb Indian attacks, Major General Grenville Dodge, commanding officer of the Army's Department of Missouri, orders a fort built near the site of the future cowboy capital, Dodge City, Kansas.

1863

"It is heart sickening to see what I have seen since I have been back here.
A desolated country and men and women and children, some of them almost naked.
Some on foot and some in old wagons. Oh God."

—Colonel Bazel Lazear, reacting to General Order No. 11

JANUARY

1. The Homestead Act takes effect today. The first claim, near present Beatrice in Gage County, Nebraska, is registered by Daniel Freeman.

■ Confederates under General John Bankhead Magruder retake the city of Galveston, Texas, which they will hold until the end of the Civil War.

■ Incensed about the events at the New Year's Eve dance in Florence, Washington Territory, Henry J. "Cherokee Bob" Talbotte and William Willoughby go gunning for dance-committee members Jacob Williams and Orlando Roberts. When the gun smoke clears, Willoughby lies dead and Talbotte is severely wounded.

5. "Cherokee Bob" Talbotte expires in the back room of his saloon in Florence.

8. The ground-breaking ceremonies for California's Central Pacific Railroad take place in Sacramento.

8–11. Union forces under General John McClernand and Admiral David Porter gain control of Fort Hindman, Arkansas. The Arkansas and White Rivers are now free for gunboats to pass, and Arkansas is now open to federal forces. Casualties—Union: 134 dead, 898 wounded, and 29 missing in action; Confederate: 28 dead, 81 wounded, and 4,720 prisoners.

10. Union gunboats pound Galveston, Texas.

17. Mangas Coloradas is murdered at a camp near Fort McLane on the Mimbres River.

24. Brigham Young weds Harriet Amelia Folsom, age 24, his 49th bride.

27. The Bear River Campaign culminates in a battle near Salt Lake City. General Patrick E. Connor had force-marched 700 volunteers of the 3rd California Infantry through Idaho in order to attack the Shoshone encampment of Bear Hunter, situated across the Bear River in Cache Valley near Salt Lake City. In today's four-hour battle, 224 Shoshones (some estimates say 350), including Bear Hunter, are killed and 164 women and children are taken prisoner. The army counts 21 troops dead and 46 wounded. Indian attacks along the California Trail will end, as will Indian control of southern Idaho and northern Utah.

28. The Society of California Pioneers is incorporated.

Also in January 1863:

George A. Custer serves with the temporary rank of captain under General George McClellan.

National Headlines/January 1863:

1. LINCOLN SIGNS EMANCIPATION PROCLAMATION

FEBRUARY

2. The great race to build the transcontinental railroad begins. Leland Stanford, president of the Central Pacific Railroad, strikes the ceremonial first spike in Sacramento. In 1869, at ceremonies completing the transcontinental railroad, he will strike the last one. Today, however, the Central Pacific faces seri-

MANGAS COLORADAS

arly accounts speak of Mangas Coloradas as if he were a giant—terrible in war, honorable in peace. Born around 1795 in southern New Mexico, his early years went unrecorded. He was a member of the Eastern Chiricahua (the "Red Paint People") or Mimbres Apache tribe. He grew up in a time of violence between his people and the Mexicans of Sonora and Chihuahua, who offered bounties for Apache scalps.

In 1835, a chief named Juan Jose and 35 Apaches were lured into a trap by the American businessman James Johnson. An afternoon of trading turned into a bloodbath, a scalps-for-profit scheme. To replace the fallen Juan Jose, a new chief was chosen, a six-foot, six-inch terror the Mexicans called Mangas Coloradas, or "Red Sleeves," so named for what became of his clothes in battle. Within weeks, Mangas had assembled a force of 400 warriors and began his raidings. The first to perish were 22 American trappers on the Gila River. From there, Mangas struck often, from Durango to the northern Navajo country, from the Davis Mountains of Texas to the Santa Ritas below Tucson.

On a foray into Sonora, Mangas kidnapped a Mexican girl to be his third wife. Outraged, the brothers of his Apache spouses challenged him. Mangas dueled Apache style, killing them both. After that, no one complained. His new bride bore him three daughters, one of whom became the wife of Apache leader Cochise.

Next, Mangas move to shut down the Santa Rita copper mines. He assaulted supply trains until the small settlement of 400 literally had to pack up and leave. Four days into the miners' sweltering march to Chihuahua, Mangas attacked. The half-dozen survivors made it to the presidio of Janos.

During the Mexican War in 1846, Mangas wished to make peace with the Americans. Colonel Stephen W. Kearny met with him but declined the offer of assistance. Mangas pledged friendship to the Americans and disappeared with his people into the hills around Santa Lucia Springs. But his raids into Mexico continued. Learning that Mangas had accepted a gesture of peace from the state of Chihuahua, Sonora's military governor, General Jose Carrasco, acted. While Apache men traded at Janos, Carrasco charged their camp, killing 130 (including the family of the young Geronimo) and capturing 90.

At the same time, the U.S. Army arrived at the abandoned Santa Rita mines along with hundreds of engineers and surveyors sent to evaluate the newly acquired land from Mexico. Mangas met with the U.S. Boundary Commission and agreed to coexist with the Americans. As a token of friendship, the army presented him a field officer's tunic.

Relations deteriorated when two kidnapped Mexican boys were taken from the Apaches by the army and returned home. Mangas complained to General John R. Bartlett, who resolved the matter with $250 in trinkets. Shortly thereafter, however, a Mexican laborer hired by the U.S. government killed an Apache man in an argument. When Bartlett refused to turn the accused over to the Indians for execution, Mangas felt betrayed. For retribution, he called upon Navajos to help him steal livestock from the Army. By the time the Boundary Commission departed, the Army had lost 300 head from their corrals. The Commission was replaced by more soldiers, who named the settlement Fort Webster.

New problems arose for Mangas. At Pinos Altos to the northwest in present New Mexico, a gold strike had lured 200 miners. In September 1851, the chief himself came to discuss the future with community leaders. If it was gold they wanted, he knew of a place in Mexico. Thinking he might be setting a trap, the prospectors bound Mangas to a tree and flogged him. Then they set him free, which was perhaps their biggest mistake.

Across the frontier, in Mexico, tales spread of terrible plunderings, murder, and torture, all directed by Mangas Coloradas. Wagon trains never reached their destinations. Sonora reported 500 residents killed in Apache attacks from 1851 to 1853.

In negotiations with the United States in July 1852, Mangas agreed to peace, but not with Mexico. The situation remained this way for eight years, during which time Mangas aligned himself with his son-in-law, the charismatic, young Cochise.

As power shifted from old to young, Cochise had his own difficulties with the U.S. Army. The aging Mangas fought at his side in 1862—ambushing troops at Apache Pass in the Chiricahua Mountains—and was severely wounded. Warriors escorted him on a 100-mile trek to a physician in Janos. Mangas recovered, then returned to his camp

(*continued*)

(continued)

near Pinos Altos for his last confrontation with the white man.

In January 1863, 40 prospectors under Joseph R. Walker were returning from a search for gold in California. In order to pass safely through this dangerous country, they hatched a scheme to kidnap a noted chief. John Swilling of the Walker party divulged his plan to 1st California Cavalry captain Edmond D. Shirland, who approved. A messenger ran to Mangas with word that the whites wished to talk peace. Mangas assembled a small entourage that included Geronimo and then rode out to investigate. Seeing the prospectors and their white flag, he proceeded.

When he reached the Walker party Mangas probably realized he had trusted one time too many. Rifles were leveled from all around. The old chief waved his followers away over their protests, then went quietly with his captors to the nearby, recently reoccupied Fort McLane. Here he was interrogated by General J. R. West, whose exact instructions have been clouded by history. Some sources indicate that West told the Guards to allow no escape, while another quotes him as saying: "Men, that old murderer has got away from every soldier command and has left a trail of blood 500 miles on the old stage line. I want him dead tomorrow morning."

On the night of January 17, 1863, two guards amused themselves by heating their bayonets in the fire and then putting them to their captive's bare feet. Mangas lifted himself on one elbow and told them he was not to be toyed with. The night air echoed with two rifle bursts, then four navy pistol shots.

Mangas's body lay by the fire until morning, when the soldiers dug a shallow grave. An army surgeon, hearing of the past evening's victory, rushed to the plot, exhumed the body, cut off the head and boiled it. He shipped the great skull to a New York phrenologist, who pronounced it bigger than Daniel Webster's.

The treachery surrounding the murder of Mangas Coloradas became an Apache rallying point in a doomed war. The martyred chief became a symbol for one people and a trophy for another.

ous financial problems: It has on hand only $156,000, yet the first 50 miles of track are estimated to cost $3 million.

■ Virginia City's *Territorial Enterprise* publishes the first letter with the byline "Mark Twain," Samuel Clemens's new pen name.

4. A party of prospectors led by Bill Fairweather departs Bannack in search of riches in the Yellowstone River.

20. Congress passes the Arizona Territorial Bill.

24. Arizona Territory is established, comprising the half of New Mexico Territory west of the 109th meridian. Prescott will become the new territory's capital.

National Headlines/February 1863:
10. BARNUM STAR GENERAL TOM THUMB WEDS

MARCH

2. Congress authorizes the Union Pacific Railroad to lay track with a gauge of four feet, eight and one-half inches, ignoring President Lincoln's suggestion of a five-foot gauge.

3. Congress creates Idaho Territory, where more than 20,000 miners have flocked to its goldfields. Idaho's initial borders make it larger than the state of Texas. Although the House of Representatives approved Ohio congressman James M. Ashley's suggestion that the new territory be called "Montana" (Latin for "mountainous"), the Senate preferred "Idaho."

3. Congress approves the establishment of a branch mint in Nevada and the removal of Indians from Kansas.

4. President Lincoln appoints John Gurley Arizona's territorial governor.

14. A Union flotilla commanded by Admiral David Farragut sails up the Mississippi River from New Orleans, past the Confederate base at Port Hudson, Louisiana.

15. Authorities seize the schooner. *J. M. Chapman* in San Francisco Bay and arrest five on charges of privateering.

22. An Overland Mail stagecoach is attacked by Indians near Eight Mile Station in Tooele County, Utah. The driver is killed and a passenger is wounded. Another passenger, Judge Mott, takes the reins and outruns his assailants.

Also in March 1863:
Some 500 Mescalero Apaches in southeastern New Mexico surrender to Colonel Kit Carson, who is spearheading a vigorous campaign by California and New Mexico volunteers. General James Carleton, commander of the Department of New Mexico,

establishes a reservation on the Pecos River's Bosque Redondo.

National Headlines/March 1863:
3. LINCOLN SIGNS CONSCRIPTION ACT

APRIL

5. In Utah, the Battle of Spanish Fork takes place. Colonel G. S. Evans leads 140 cavalrymen against 200 Indians, who are reportedly routed.
19. In Denver, a pile of garbage ignites behind the Cherokee House hotel on Blake Street near 15th. Winds whip the blaze into a citywide inferno that destroys most of the wooden structures in an area bordered by Market, Wazee, and 16th Streets, and Cherry Creek. The damages will be assessed at $350,000.
20. The Kountze Brothers Bank announces that it will finance the rebuilding of Denver at a healthy 25 percent-per-annum rate of interest. In a show of neutrality between Denver and Auraria factions, construction will take place in both Denver City, on Cherry Creek's northeast bank, and Auraria, on the southwest bank. New buildings will be constructed not only alongside Cherry Creek, but even in the creek's bed, despite warnings from local Indians that Cherry Creek tends to flood.
23. One of those to borrow money from the Kountze Brothers Bank is the black entrepreneur Barney Ford, who lost his barbershop in the fire. With a $9,000 loan, he opens the People's Restaurant on Blake Street and advertises fresh lemons, oysters, and Havana cigars. He will repay his loan, with the 25 percent interest, in 90 days.
29. William Randolph Hearst, the future publishing tycoon, is born in San Francisco. By his 50th year in journalism, he will own 25 daily newspapers, 17 Sunday papers, 13 magazines, 10 radio stations, and two wire services.

Also in April 1863:
Artist Albert Bierstadt and Fitz Hugh Ludlow, author of *The Hasheesh Eater,* arrive in Denver for what will be the painter's second western sojourn. They meet *Rocky Mountain News* editor William N. Byers, who takes them sight-seeing around Idaho Springs. Byers wrote about Bierstadt: "His enthusiasm was badly dampened, but the moment he caught the view, fatigue and hunger were forgotten. He said nothing, but his face was a picture of intense life and excitement."

Some 500 men leave Colorado to follow rumors of gold being present in Idaho and Montana.

MAY

5. A party led by James Stuart stakes out the site for a town at the mouth of the Bighorn River.
15. At Drum Creek in Kansas, Confederate officers are slain by Osage warriors.
18. Another mission is organized to rescue poor Mormons immigrating to Utah. A party from Salt Lake City sets out with 384 wagons, 488 teamsters, 3,604 oxen, and 225,969 pounds of flour.
19. Arizona's abandoned Fort Mojave is regarrisoned by troops of the California Column.
21–27. Union troops under General Nathaniel Banks attack Port Hudson on the Mississippi River, just above Baton Rouge. The siege ends after Confederates under General Franklin Garner inflict serious damage on their attackers.
24. Former road agent Henry Plummer assumes the office of sheriff of Bannack, Montana shortly after convincing the marshal to leave town.
26. Gold is discovered in Idaho Territory by a party of six led by Bill Fairweather: the party finds about $12 worth the first day, $180 worth the next. Fairweather and his colleagues name the site Alder Gulch and agree to keep it a secret. The site will become Virginia City.

National Headlines/May 1863:
10. STONEWALL JACKSON DIES; ACCIDENTALLY SHOT BY ONE OF HIS OWN MEN
14. GRANT TAKES JACKSON, MISSISSIPPI

JUNE

2. Bill Fairweather's group returns to Alder Gulch, although the road is already crowded with gold seekers. Fairweather's party are the first of some 15,000 fortune hunters who will begin Virginia City, Montana.
4. At the Farallone Egg Company on San Francisco Bay's Farallone Islands, a fight breaks out between company employees and a group of Italians. One person is killed and five are wounded.
6. Two desperados, James Melvine and William Cannon, are hanged by the citizens of Highland, Kansas.
12. The first Wyoming newspaper is published at Fort Bridger.
14. Union troops under General Nathaniel Banks again attack Port Hudson on the Mississippi River, only to be driven away again by Confederate defenders.
29. A gang of road agents known as the "Innocents" murder Deputy Dillingham in Alder Gulch.
30. George A. Custer, 23, is appointed a brigadier general of Union Army volunteers.

Also in June 1863:
Francis Fuller Victor's popular column "Florence Fane" appears regularly in the *Golden Era*.

Nelson Story, 25, arrives in Virginia City, Montana, having travelled with his wife from Denver. They bring two oxcarts filled with coffee, flour, cured pork, kettles, cloth, shovels, and various other supplies. They will start a small store.

National Headlines/June 1863:
3. LEE BEGINS 2ND INVASION OF THE NORTH
20. WEST VIRGINIA BECOMES 35TH STATE
28. LINCOLN NAMES MEADE TO COMMAND ARMY OF THE POTOMAC

JULY

1. Colonel James M. Williams and 800 members of the 1st Kansas Colored, together with 500 Indians, fight a force of Texas Confederates and Indians under Stand Watie at Cabin Creek, Kansas. The Union forces are victorious.

2. Chief Washakie of the Eastern Shoshone Tribe signs a treaty at Fort Bridger: He promises not to attack emigrants in return for $10,000 a year in goods for 20 years.

■ The Spring Valley Water Works begins supplying San Francisco with water from Lake Honda.

3. While deer hunting in Minnesota's north woods, Nathan Lampson and his son Chauncey come across two Indians stealing berries. Nathan fires, hitting one of them. As the wounded Sioux returns fire, he is killed by Chauncey. The body is scalped and taken to Hutchinson, where it is later identified as that of Little Crow, the leader of last fall's uprising. The body's identity is confirmed by Little Crow's son, Wo-wi-nap-sa.

■ Brigadier General George A. Custer leads a charge of the 7th Michigan Cavalry at the Battle of Gettysburg. In his report, he writes: "I challenge the annals of war to produce a more brilliant charge of cavalry."

4. General Theophilus Holmes, commander of the Confederacy's Trans-Mississippi Department, launches a futile assault on Union forces at Helena, Arkansas. In a five-hour battle, 173 of his troops are killed, 687 are wounded, and 776 are reported missing. Union casualties include 57 killed, 146 wounded, and 36 missing.

6. What will become Bozeman Trail is blazed as John M. Bozeman leaves Fort Laramie in present Wyoming for the Yellowstone Valley.

10. The territory of Idaho is organized in Lewiston by Governor William H. Wallace.

21. The San Francisco Normal School opens with an enrollment of six.

26. Sam Houston dies at the age of 70 in Huntsville, Texas. The man who played a crucial role in winning Texas's independence died convinced that his life was a failure because of his state's secession from the Union during the Civil War. His last words are "Texas, Texas! Margaret. . . ."

Also in July 1863:
A drought weighs heavily on the Great Plains. Writes rancher David Hodgson of Platteville, Colorado: "The dryest summer, the coldest winter, the worst flood, the biggest grasshoppers. . . .

National Headlines/July 1863:
3. BATTLE OF GETTYSBURG CLAIMS OVER 40,000 LIVES
4. CONFEDERATES SURRENDER VICKSBURG TO GRANT
11–18. ANTI-DRAFT RIOTS ROCK NEW YORK

AUGUST

3. Ira Aten, the future lawman, is born in Cairo, Illinois.

5. A tribe of Sioux kills 59 Pawnees at Massacre Canyon, Nebraska.

8. Several wagon trains are attacked in Nebraska Territory by Indians east of Fort Kearny; 14 men from the trains are killed and many women and children are taken captive.

21. William Quantrill's raiders devastate Lawrence, Kansas. Frank James and Cole Younger may have ridden with Quantrill in the raid.

■ The first private school in the area that will become Montana opens in Virginia City.

25. In the wake of the sacking of Lawrence, General Tom Ewing issues General Order No. 11. Under it, all residents of four Missouri border counties are ordered to vacate their homes within 15 days. Members of the 15th Kansas Cavalry will enforce the order, which will result in more burning and plundering. With only stone chimneys visible for hundreds of miles, the area became known as the Burnt District. Some 20,000 were left homeless.

29–30. Union forces capture Fort Esperanza on the Gulf Coast of Texas.

Also in August 1863:
The artist Albert Bierstadt and the author Fitz Hugh Ludlow tour the Yosemite Valley, then ride to Oregon and the Columbia River area. The Yosemite Valley will become one of Bierstadt's favorite subjects.

THE RAID ON LAWRENCE, KANSAS

The worst atrocity of the Civil War occurred when William Clarke Quantrill, 26, led his "raiders" in sacking Lawrence, Kansas, and slaughtering 150 male residents.

In early Civil War skirmishes, Quantrill fought alongside men who would later join his team. At the Battle of Dry Forks, on July 5, 1861, he discovered Cole Younger. A month later, at the Battle of Wilson's Creek, he met Frank James. A unique blend of charisma and evil, Quantrill was already a legend in a blood-red shirt, leading charges with a rebel yell, his .44 navy Colts blazing.

By November 1861, he was bored with the organized military and had begun piecing together "Quantrill's raiders." In February of 1862, his bushwhackers attacked a group of anti-slavery Kansas Jayhawkers. Throughout that summer, his band of border thugs grew larger. At times, he and his followers joined Confederate regulars for battle, but more often than not, they carried out their guerrilla fantasies sporadically, hitting and running at any hour, whenever they encountered the enemy. Following the August 1862 capture of Independence, Missouri, he was promoted to captain in the regular army, though most of his activity remained highly irregular.

Before a flickering fire on a humid summer night in the Missouri woods in 1863, Quantrill poured out his heart to the 448 men around him. Lawrence, the most beautiful town in Kansas, would be a perfect target. There it lay, 40 miles inside the border, an "abolitionist stronghold" of 1,200.

A special hit list was furnished so that no one would be overlooked. At the top of the list was the Union activist Senator Jim Lane, whom Quantrill wanted to take back to Missouri for a public lynching (Lane would survive, witnessing the attack from a cornfield). "Let's go to Lawrence," cried Quantrill. "We can get more revenge and more money there than anywhere else."

The men covered the distance in two days and two moonless nights, strapping themselves in their saddles to sleep. At dawn on August 21, decked in a guerrilla tunic and with four pistols jammed into his belt, Quantrill led his charge upon the sleeping town.

The first to be killed was Reverend S. S. Snyder, gunned down while milking his cow as the gang roared in from the southeast. The remnants of a 14th Cavalry camp were discovered, and 17 Union recruits died in their tents. Quantrill took a squadron to the Eldridge Hotel and demanded its surrender. When a sheet-waving Captain A. R. Banks asked his purpose, Quantrill replied, "Plunder!" He robbed the guests, threw them in the street, then set up his headquarters in the lobby. Before disappearing inside, he waved his hands wildly and screamed, "Kill, kill, kill!"

Every man on the street was cut down, as were many boys. Quantrill's "cleansing" of Lawrence quickly turned into a drunken orgy of slaughter. Men were dragged from their houses and killed in front of their families. As one wife watched in horror from a window, a raider turned to her and laughed, "We are friends from Hell!"

At 9:00 A.M. a lookout on Mount Oread reported an advancing column of Union soldiers. In three hours, 150 males had been killed. The entire business district and many homes—185 buildings in all—were burned to the ground. On orders from their chieftain, there had been no rape.

Losses in property and theft would total $2 million, but the true tragedy would be felt long after the raiders disappeared over the Kansas horizon. Left behind in a pile of smoking rubble were 80 widows and 250 fatherless children. Only one of the raiders had died—Larkin Skaggs, who passed out drunk and was scalped by a local Indian. The survivors of Lawrence tore his body to shreds.

Quantrill was not finished. On his way to hide out in Texas that October, he and his men ambushed and killed 100 Union soldiers at Baxter Springs, Kansas. Infighting in the Lone Star State eventually broke up the old gang. Some followed Bloody Bill, others George Todd. Quantrill went back to Missouri and lived for a time with Kate Clarke. One of the most wanted men in the Confederacy, he led a band of 11 faithful into Kentucky in 1865, where he was cornered in a Louisville barn on May 10. He was shot in the back while running for the woods. Paralyzed below the shoulders, he lingered in a military hospital until he died on June 6. He was 28

(continued)

(continued)

The town of Lawrence was rebuilt. The years managed to obscure but not remove the stigma of what happened there. The legacy of the psychotic guerrilla leader who could inspire men to do their worst influenced many in the Old West; indeed, his tactics were used by the James boys, the Youngers, and other, less stellar figures who "rode with Quantrill." In one of history's most tragic chapters, Quantrill remains a footnote engraved in blood.

General Frederick Steele, the Union commander in Helena, Arkansas, begins the attack on Little Rock.

Indian raids are the reason for a directive issued to Denver's postmaster to forward all eastbound mail to San Francisco for water passage.

Los Angeles continues to suffer through a two-year drought (1862–1864) that will kill thousands of head of cattle. Armed guards are posted at vineyards to keep out starving animals.

SEPTEMBER

1. Fort Smith, Arkansas, is taken by Union troops under General James G. Blunt.

- Oakland and San Francisco are connected by the Oakland Ferry–Railroad Line, the first system of its kind in the nation.

3. The Battle of Whitestone Hill occurs west of the James River in present North Dakota. Troopers under General Alfred Sully attack a Santee Sioux camp that is being abandoned. Sully loses 20 men,

Bulls circle to protect the herd from a wolf attack on the plains. (Library of Congress)

and 50 are reported wounded. Indian losses are reported as 150 killed and 156 taken prisoner. All Indian ponies are slain and their bodies burned along with 200 tons of dried buffalo meat and 300 tepees.

8. At Sabine Pass on the Texas coast northeast of Galveston, Confederates under Lieutenant Dick Dowling repel a Union naval landing, sinking two of four ships. Some 60 Union soldiers are taken captive.

10. Little Rock, Arkansas, is taken by Union forces under General Frederick Steele. Confederate forces under General Sterling Price withdraw to the southwestern portion of the state. Confederate governor Harris Flanigan will now govern the state from Washington, Arkansas.

13. The War Department turns down General James Carleton's request for cavalry to protect the goldfields in Arizona.

17. A Pueblo, Colorado, grand jury indicts Jose Felipe Enosio Espinosa for the murder of William Smith last June 30. It is believed that Espinosa, his brother Vivian, and their nephew, Julian, are responsible for between 22 and 30 murders, the result of a pact they signed to kill 600 whites.

Also in September 1863:

Sidney Edgerton of Ohio, the recently appointed chief justice of Idaho Territory, arrives with his family in Bannack. Because of the weather, they decide to winter there. Edgerton will urge Congress to form a new territory in the area, leading to the creation of Montana Territory the following year.

Cass County, Missouri, whose population until recently was 10,000, registers only 600 as of mid-September as a result of the infamous General Order No. 11.

The federal mint in Denver begins operations as an Assay Office, melting and stamping bullion. Bars are stamped "U.S. Branch Mint, Denver."

National Headlines/September 1863:
20. REBEL VICTORY AT CHICKAMAUGA

OCTOBER

1. Twelve chiefs of the Western Shoshone Tribe in Nevada sign a peace treaty with the United States at Ruby Valley in Elko County.

3. Lazarus, one of the "original dogs" of gold-rush San Francisco, is found dead, allegedly poisoned by a man who had accused the old dog of biting his son. An Edward Jump cartoon titled "Funeral of Lazarus," portraying a fictitious ceremony, will lead one source to incorrectly assert that 10,000 people

attended to pay their respects, the most ever for a dog's funeral.

6. Quantrill's raiders defeat Union cavalrymen at Baxter Springs, Kansas.

10. The first telegraph line to Denver, strung from Julesburg, is completed.

14. E. P. Williams resigns as director of Wells Fargo. Elected to succeed him is the company's longtime treasurer, Charles F. Latham.

15. Ceremonies are held at the opening of the San Francisco and San Jose Railroad.

20. San Francisco's *Democratic Press* begins publishing.

23. Another San Francisco fire claims portions of the financial district. Members of the Russian Navy whose ship is docked in San Francisco help fight the fire.

28. Following up on the death of the gold-rush dog Lazarus on October 3, the *Bulletin* reports: "Lazarus has risen and is stuffed. A skillful taxidermist has taken away from him all that was fleshy, and left on him only what is imperishable. Bright dogs can never die!"

■ A telegraph cable from Fort Point to Lime Point in San Francisco is completed.

31. Tom "Black Jack" Ketchum, the future outlaw, is born in San Saba County, Texas.

Also in October 1863:
John Muir, 25, drops out of the University of Wisconsin.

National Headlines/October 1863:
16. GRANT TO COMMAND MILITARY DIVISION OF THE MISSISSIPPI

NOVEMBER

1. Construction begins on a fort on Angel Island, off San Francisco.

2. Union forces directed by General Nathaniel Banks take Brazos Island in southern Texas.

7. The Santa Fe *New Mexican* states: "Now is a good time to enlist as a volunteer. . . . The laboring man can find no mode so easy, redoubtable and profitable, to discharge himself from poverty and servitude, as enlisting as a volunteer. The duties of the service promote patriotism, punctuality, courage and manliness."

13. Chipita Rodriguez becomes the first woman to be legally hanged in Texas. She was convicted of murdering John Savage.

14. Henry Plummer and three accomplices rob Henry Tilden at Horse Prairie, Montana.

17. President Lincoln designates Council Bluffs, Iowa, the eastern terminus of the Union Pacific Railroad.

Also in November 1863:
Union forces capture Brownsville, Texas.
San Francisco makes an outright gift of $450,000 to the Central Pacific Railroad after a bond issue approved by voters is rejected by the Board of Supervisors.

National Headlines/November 1863:
20. LINCOLN DELIVERS GETTYSBURG ADDRESS
25. GRANT VICTORIOUS AT CHATTANOOGA

DECEMBER

2. In ceremonies officiated by Nebraska governor Saunders, ground is broken in Omaha to begin construction on the Union Pacific Railroad.

■ Mohave chief Irataba arrives in San Francisco for a visit.

7. George Ives, a member of the "Innocents," robs and then kills Nick Thiebalt in Montana's Ruby Valley.

10. Californians elect their first four-year-term governor, Frederick F. Low of the Union Party.

12. The governor of New Mexico reports to the House of Representatives that progress is being made to improve relations with local Indians. He adds: "It is my disagreeable duty to again repeat that our Territory still suffers from the hostility of the Indian tribes which surround us."

18. George Ives, suspected murderer of Nicholas Thiebalt, becomes the first member of the Innocents gang to be captured by vigilantes in Montana's Ruby Valley.

19. After a quick trial, George Ives is hanged at Bannack, Montana, for the murder of Nicholas Thiebalt.

23. Montana vigilantes, men from Bannack, Virginia City, and Neveda City, complete their organization at John Lott's store in Bannack. Their stated purpose

Vigilante justice. In Montana, vigilantes include Nathaniel P. Langford, the father of Yellowstone National Park, and Wilbur Fisk Sanders, who will become one of Montana's first U.S. senators. (Library of Congress)

is to rid the territory of the Innocents gang of road agents. Some 2,000 men join the group. The original document of the vigilantes reads in part:

> We the undersigned uniting ourselves in a party for the laudible purpos of arresting thievs & murderers & recovering stollen propperty do pledge ourselvs & our sacred honor each to all others & solemnly swear that we will reveal no secrets, violate no laws of right & not desert each other or our standerd of justice so help us God.

25. Indians holed up in log buildings near Fort Gaston, California, open fire on troops. Under cover of darkness, every Indian escapes, but the dwellings are destroyed by the troops' howitzers.

29. In Navajo Springs, John Goodwin is sworn in as the territorial governor of Arizona.

National Headlines/December 1863:
8. LINCOLN ISSUES PROCLAMATION OF AMNESTY & RECONSTRUCTION

Also in 1863:
Jose and Vivian Espinosa hold up a wagon north of Santa Fe, tie the Mexican teamster to the wagon, and drag him to his death.

The sensation of the Virginia City, Nevada Territory, theatrical season is actress Adah Isaacs Menken, who appears in "Mazeppa, or The Wild Horse," at the climax of which she rides up a mountain trail on horseback, clad only in thin gauze. Miners name a mining district "Menken" and start the Menken Shaft and Tunnel Company. Fans lavish her with gold and silver when it is time for her to leave.

Theodore Winthrop's *The Canoe and the Saddle,* an excellent account of travel in the far west, is published.

Frank Butler, 13, the future husband of Annie Oakley, works his passage from Ireland to New York, where he holds a series of odd jobs.

The Oglala Sioux artist Amos Bad Heart, who at age 14 will witness the Battle of the Little Bighorn, is born.

John Kuner begins his canning business in Denver.

Jim Younger, 15, and John Younger, 10, surprise and kill four Union soldiers camped in Missouri.

Young "Texas Jack" Omohundro, 17, enlists in the Confederate Army, in which he will serve for the duration of the war.

Bret Harte begins working at the U.S. Mint in San Francisco.

1864

"Nothing lives long, except the earth and the mountains."
—White Antelope

JANUARY

1. Snow and gale-force winds are reported across the Midwest; the high in Minneapolis is −25°.

4. Two members of the Innocents gang, Erastus "Red" Yager and G. Brown, are hanged by vigilantes from a cottonwood in Stinkingwater Valley near Laurin, Montana. Before he meets his maker, Yager divulges the names of 25 of Henry Plummer's criminal associates and reveals the gang's code word, "Innocents."

6. Colonel Kit Carson leads a 300-man force from Fort Canby to carry out punitive raids on Navajos in Canyon de Chelly in present Arizona. Some 12,000 Navajos will surrender in the coming months. From January to March, about 8,000 prisoners will be marched 300 miles on the "Long March" or the "March of Tears" to the Bosque Redondo Reservation, resulting in the deaths of hundreds along the way. The Navajos will be held in a prison camp until 1868.

10. Vigilantes hang Sheriff Henry Plummer in Bannack, Montana. The leader of the "Innocents" begged for his life, to no avail. He was executed on crude gallows that he had constructed.

11. An estimated 24 Innocents have been hanged since December 21, 1863, by Montana vigilantes.

■ In San Francisco, stable grooms go on strike for higher wages.

14. Vigilantes lynch five Innocents on the corner of Wallace and Van Buren Streets in Virginia City, Montana. One of those to swing is highwayman Jack Gallagher, one of Henry Plummer's deputies, who is suspected of robbing and murdering a Mormon who flashed a large bankroll.

15. Stephen Marshland, a member of Henry Plummer's Innocents gang, is lynched by vigilantes at Big Hole, Wyoming.

16. The completion of the San Francisco and San Jose Railroad is commemorated with a lavish dinner in San Francisco.

■ The counties of Kane (named for the Mormon colonel Thomas L. Kaine) and Richland (named for the Mormon apostle Charles C. Rich) are created

Henry Plummer (1837–1864) is executed on January 10, 1864, in a scene like this one. Plummer's gang reportedly robbed or killed at least a hundred people. (Library of Congress)

in Utah. Richland will be renamed Rich County in 1868.

17. An overnight low of -40^0 is registered in Bannack, Montana. Says Governor Edgerton's wife, "I was afraid the children would freeze their noses and ears."

19. Bill Barton is hanged by vigilantes in Deer Lodge, Montana.

22. Arkansas inaugurates a free-state governor, Isaac Murphy, the only member of the 1861 convention to vote against secession.

23. Item from the Santa Fe *New Mexican:* "At a fandango a few evenings since, two of the females became insulted and enraged at each other, and . . . American men present endeavored to inflame the ill will and violence. . . . A ring was formed and knives placed in the hands of each, for a desperate fight. We hope no American will so far forget the dignity of human nature—his name and race—as to be found encouraging, again, such an exhibition of passion and violence."

24. Ely S. Parker, also known by his Seneca name "Donehogawa," a captain of engineers in the 7th Corps and with General Grant in the Vicksburg campaign, submits a four-point peace plan to Grant outlining a conclusion to the Civil War. (In 1873, Parker will become the first Indian to serve as commissioner of Indian affairs.)

26. "Whiskey" Bill Graves is hanged by vigilantes at Fort Owen, Montana.

Also in January 1864:
Virginia City in present Montana is incorporated.

National Headlines/January 1864:
13. STEPHEN FOSTER DIES IN POVERTY

FEBRUARY

1. In Nevada, William Johnson is slain by a gang of horse thieves led by John Daly for killing horse thief Jim Sears.

■ Colorado's third assembly convenes in Golden and then adjourns to Denver.

3. Montana vigilantes hang Bill Hunter, the last of the Innocents, in Gallatin Valley.

5. Since December 20, 1863, Montana vigilantes have lynched 24.

8. Jim Daly and three members of his gang are hanged in Aurora, Nevada, for the murder of William Johnson.

9. George Armstrong Custer marries Elizabeth Bacon in the Presbyterian Church in Monroe, Michigan.

15. "Texas Jack" Omohundro, 18, enlists as a private in Company G of the 5th Virginia Cavalry.

19. William F. Cody, 18, enlists in Company H of the 7th Kansas Volunteer Cavalry.

20. Kate Virginia Caven becomes the first white child born in Virginia City in present Montana.

22. Louisiana's Union government in New Orleans chooses Georg Michael Hahn as governor.

23. At Bloody Tanks, Arizona, local Tonto Apaches are lured to an Arizona peace conference by pioneer King S. Woolsey, who claims to be the personal representative of President Lincoln. The reason? Gold has been discovered at nearby Prescott. After the warriors are fed pinole loaded with strychnine, Woolsey signals his men to open fire; Woolsey personally kills the chief sitting next to him. Estimates of the Indians killed differ: some accounts say 20, but others put the number closer to 200.

28. George Armstrong Custer leaves his new bride to continue fighting in the Civil War.

MARCH

4. Reverend Thomas Starr King dies in San Francisco.

5. Denver University is incorporated.

9. The first issue of the *Arizona Miner* is published at Fort Whipple by the territory's secretary of state, Robert C. McCormick.

10. Vigilantes hang Joseph A. Slade in Virginia City in present Montana.

11. Tonto Apaches, angered by the treachery against their fellow tribesmen at the recent "peace conference" at Bloody Tanks, Arizona, kill three Hassayampa Canyon miners and five Mexicans. They then attack a wagon train and kill another two people.

18. In Arkansas, a convention votes to abolish slavery and swears allegiance to the Union.

19. Confederates under Santos Benavides, some 42 regulars and 30 militiamen, repulse a Union charge of 200 men at Fort McIntosh in Laredo, Texas.

■ The artist Charles Marion Russell is born in Oak Hill, Missouri.

21. President Lincoln signs an act enabling Colorado to hold a territorial convention to draft a petition for statehood.

National Headlines/March 1864:
12. GRANT NAMED GENERAL IN CHIEF OF UNION ARMIES

APRIL

6. The constitutional convention in New Orleans votes to abolish slavery in Louisiana and adopts a new constitution.

8. At Sabine Crossroads near Mansfield, Louisiana, a confederate force of 9,000 men halts 12,000 Union soldiers under General Banks, who are advancing through the Red River Valley toward Shreveport. General Frederick Steele, who had planned to link with Banks, remains in Camden, Arkansas, as Confederates marshal their forces. Losses—Union: 113 killed, 581 wounded, and 1,541 missing in action; Confederates: 1,000 killed and wounded.

9. Arizona Territory is divided into three judicial districts.

15. In San Francisco, General Wright issues an order forbidding ships entering the harbor to pass north of Alcatraz Island.

16. Tom Harris, who begins planting near Fort Owen, becomes Montana's first full-time farmer.

18. In Arkansas, Confederate troops cut General Frederick Steele's supply lines at Poison Spring.

25. General Frederick Steele's supply lines are damaged further by Confederate action at Marks' Mills. Steele retreats.

28. Fire destroys the officers' quarters of the Black Point Battery in San Francisco.

30. In the last major Civil War engagement in Arkansas, Confederate forces attack General Frederick Steele's retreating army at Jenkins' Ferry, but are unable to prevent Steele from reaching Little Rock.

Also in April 1864:
A sawmill is built at Alder Gulch in present Montana.

National Headlines/April 1864:
8. SENATE PASSES 13TH AMENDMENT
22. U.S. COINS TO SAY "IN GOD WE TRUST"
30. JOE DAVIS, SON OF JEFFERSON, DIES IN FALL

MAY

1. In the 13 months since Denver's big fire, development has proceeded. The new City Hall and the Trinity Methodist Church have been constructed in the bed of Cherry Creek, as has William N. Byers's five-year-old newspaper, the *Rocky Mountain News,* which is perched on stilts like a beach house. Denver now has a population of 3,000 and some 30 major buildings.

4. Boundary supervisors in Arizona name one of their new precincts Phoenix.

8. Tucson is declared an incorporated city; its officials are named by Governor Goodwin.

12. "Captain Jack" Crawford is wounded in the battle of Spotsylvania Court House. He will begin his literary career by writing poetry while recuperating at Philadelphia's Saterlee Hospital.

14. In Virginia City, Montana, five persons are hanged; the town's Boothill is opened.

17. Samuel Bancroft sells his land on the South Platte River near Julesburg in present Colorado to the military, which in turn will establish on it Camp Rankin and then Fort Sedgwick.

18. Maguire's Academy of Music opens in San Francisco.

19. Cherry Creek floods Denver at midnight. Rescue efforts will be organized by the 1st Colorado Volunteers under Colonel John M. Chivington.

21. The city of Denver purchases two ferryboats for transportation on the Platte River.

24. The first official census of Arizona is completed by U.S. Marshal Milton Duffield. The total population

---

THE DENVER FLOOD
MAY 19, 1864

That anyone would want to build a home near Cherry Creek in the first place had mystified local Indians. When the first prospectors arrived on the site of present Denver in 1858, the original inhabitants had warned them about potential flooding. To be sure, the unobtrusive creek appeared to be a mere trickle, but looks could be deceiving, especially when heavy rains fell in the mountains.

Cherry Creek's limited written history may have contributed to the early settlers' lack of respect. Colonel Henry Dodge had recorded that the creek bed was dry in 1835. Author Francis Parkman (*The Oregon Trail*) noted in 1846 that he had to dig a hole in the sand in order to find drinking water.

It had rained steadily for several days before May 19, 1864. That afternoon, tremendous dark clouds appeared in the east. As upstanding citizens turned in for the evening and revelers crowded into the gambling halls and brothels, the consensus was that Denver was in for just another rainy night.

At about midnight, Cherry Creek began spilling into the dirt streets. The alarm went out. Sleepers awoke to water seeping into their homes. Many were saved by clinging to their rooftops until the calamity passed. Less than two hours after the flooding began, one survivor would write that there was "a strange sound in the south like the noise of

(continued)

(continued)

the wind, which increased to a mighty roar as a great wall of water, bearing on its crest trees and other drift, rushed toward the settlement."

Like a tidal wave, the water slammed through the city. Pioneer journalist O. J. Goldrick would write in his eyewitness account:

> Hark! What and where was this? A torrent or tornado? Where can it be coming from and whither going? Presently the great noise of mighty waters, like the roaring of Niagara, or the rumbling of an enraged Etna, burst upon us, distinctly and regularly in its sounding steps as the approach of a tremendous train of locomotives. . . . The tempestuous torrent swept along, now 20 feet in the channel's bed, and bridging bank to bank with billows high as hills piled upon hills—with broken buildings, tables, bedsteads, baggage, boulders, mammoth trees, leviathan logs and human beings buffeted with the billowcrests, and beckoning us to save them.

In one great swoop, the trappings of civilization were washed away. Four men working on the second floor of the *Rocky Mountain News* were throwninto the swirling waters as the building itself collapsed. They were rescued by men with ropes who had ridden the Trinity Church to its landing place, the new shore of Market Street. William Byers, his wife, and two children were at home at the time, in a house that floated 30 feet before anchoring in a grove of cottonwood trees.

Bridges at Larimer and Market Street crumbled. The law offices of Charles and Hunt were never seen again. The city jail and its one inmate went careening down Cherry Creek. The prisoner managed to latch onto a floating tree for safety. Another resident, Martin Wall, surfed for three miles on top of the jailhouse roof. The City Hall, including its iron safe with hundreds of land titles, town company records, and municipal documents, disappeared completely.

Dawn lit the scene of the disaster, revealing water depths of five feet in some areas of the city. Waters began to recede at about 7:00 A.M. and the cleanup began. Horrible stories emerged from Denver's night of terror, tales of children splashing helplessly in the black waters. An official body count was impossible to compile, but at least 15 persons were known dead. Byers listed his *Rocky Mountain News* as a total loss, valued at $19,200. Estimates of the total damage ranged from $250,000 to $1 million.

---

is 4,573, including soldiers stationed there. To obtain territorial status, Arizona had reported to Congress that the population was 6,500.

26. Montana Territory is created from a portion of Idaho Territory. The first capital is Bannack. Ohio congressman James M. Ashley, a Republican, had lobbied heavily against naming the territory in honor of the Democrat Thomas Jefferson; his preference for "Montana" was finally chosen. For governor, President Lincoln chooses Sidney Edgerton, the Ohio lawyer who first suggested the area as a separate territory.

30. Arizona's territorial government is moved from Fort Whipple to Granite Creek, which is renamed Prescott. City lots go on sale.

Also in May 1864:

In the first year of mining at Alder Gulch in present Montana, $10 million in gold dust has been found by 10,000 miners.

Mark Twain leaves the *Territorial Enterprise* in Virginia City to go to work for San Francisco's *Morning Call*.

He was invited to leave Nevada after he broke the law by challenging a rival reporter to a duel. Soon he will begin his friendship with Bret Harte.

National Headlines/May 1864:

6. GRANT, LEE DO BATTLE IN WILDERNESS

18. NATHANIEL HAWTHORNE DIES

JUNE

11. Gale-driven waters wash away some 300 feet of Meigg's Wharf in San Francisco.

18. Indians of various tribes, including Cheyennes and Arapahos, are believed to be responsible for the massacre of an entire family some 25 miles east of Denver.

22. Sidney Edgerton becomes the first territorial governor of Montana.

24. All "friendly Indians" in Colorado are ordered to report to the reservation at Sand Creek because of recent tensions. Governor John Evans issues a circular that refers to recent attacks on whites by Cheyennes: "For this the Great Father is angry and will

Samuel Clemens (Mark Twain), San Francisco journalist. (National Archives)

certainly hunt them out and punish them, but he does not want to injure those who remain friendly to the whites; he desires to protect and take care of them."

30. Yosemite Valley Park, on the western slope of the Sierra Nevadas in California, becomes the first state park in the United States. The park is named for the Yosemite Indians, who called the valley "Ahwahnee," or "place of deep grass."

Also in June 1864:
Fort Ellsworth is established in Kansas; it is named for Lieutenant Allen Ellsworth of the 7th Iowa.

National Headlines/June 1864:
7. LINCOLN NOMINATED AT BALTIMORE
10. MAXIMILIAN EMPEROR OF MEXICO
21. CONFEDERATES HOLD PETERSBURG

JULY
2. The Northern Pacific Railroad is chartered by Congress to build a railway from Lake Superior to Portland, Oregon.

4. With the nation facing labor shortages caused by the Civil War, Congress passes the Immigration Act, which will allow companies such as the Central Pacific Railroad to import Chinese laborers.
■   Colorado's constitutional convention opens in Golden.
■   The Bank of California opens in San Francisco.
■   The *Daily Telegraph* begins publishing in Salt Lake City.
5. At his office in New York, Horace Greeley receives a letter containing a Confederate peace proposal and calling for meetings to be held in Canada. Greeley forwards the letter to President Lincoln.
8. In Montana, Jim Bridger leads his first wagon train, which departs Bozeman for Virginia City.
14. Rich deposits of gold are discovered by John Cowan at Last Chance Gulch, the site of present Helena, Montana.
18. Horace Greeley is sent by President Lincoln to what will be fruitless peace talks with Confederate representatives.
■   Territorial elections are held in Arizona; Charles Poston is elected delegate to Congress.
26. Texas guerrillas arrive in southern Colorado from New Mexico; depredations in the area begin.
■   Agent Samuel Colley writes to Governor Evans of Colorado that the Indians on the plains are not complying with his order of June 24: "I now think a little powder and lead is the best food for them."
27. The first application for land in Arizona under the Homestead Act is made by John B. Allen.
28. The Battle of Killdeer Mountain, or Tah-kah-o-kuty (Place where they kill deer), occurs on the Little Missouri River in the western portion of present North Dakota. General Alfred Sully's troops attack Sitting Bull's camp. Sully calls the badlands "Hell with the fires out." Sitting Bull witnesses a new kind of war, one made on women and children.
30. Silver is discovered north of Bannack, Montana.

Also in July 1864:
In Texas, smallpox plagues the Wichita and othe tribes.
General George A. Custer is ordered to lead 4,000 troops to Houston, Texas, as a show of force to Confederate sympathizers. He is accompanied by his new bride, Elizabeth, whom the soldiers dub "Lady Custer." In her memoirs, she will write about her husband's kindness to a newborn pup, but will neglect to write about the lashes he orders for his men for the smallest infractions.

A peaceful morning at a Dakota village, much like Sitting Bull's camp, which was attacked by General Sully on July 28, 1864. (Library of Congress)

AUGUST

4. Merchants in Boise, Idaho, begin closing shops on Sundays.

12. General Alfred Sully's party reaches the Yellowstone River some 30 miles from its mouth. His campaign against the Plains Indians is one of the largest so far.

14. Fort Collins is established in Colorado to guard the Overland Trail. It will be abandoned in 1867.

19–20. Crow Creek rancher Elbridge Gerry rides to Denver to warn of an impending Cheyenne attack on settlements on the South Platte River. A show of force by troops will alter the plan considerably. Cheyennes will scatter Gerry's livestock in retaliation.

27. The *Montana Post,* the first newspaper in the new territory, begins publishing in Virginia City.

30. Gold is discovered at Emigrant Gulch near Livingston, Montana.

31. The Cosmopolitan Hotel opens in San Francisco.

Also in August 1864:

Colorado governor John Evans instructs "all citizens of Colorado . . . to go in pursuit of all hostile Indians on the plains, scrupulously avoiding those who have responded to my call to rendezvous at the points indicated; also to kill and destroy as enemies of the country wherever they may be found, all such hostile Indians."

National Headlines/August 1864:

29. DEMOCRATS NOMINATE McCLELLAN AT CHICAGO

SEPTEMBER

1. Hunkpapa Sioux attack an immigrant train of 80 wagons under the escort of Captain James Fisk near present Rhame, North Dakota. Twelve members of the train are killed outright; the remainder continue a running fight for 10 miles until they can make camp. Overnight, the immigrants leave out poisoned hardtack for the Indians.

4. The Bank of California opens a branch office in Gold Hill.

5. Louisiana voters ratify a constitution that abolishes slavery.

11. California's Fort Tejon is abandoned as a military outpost.

12. A government supply train of 205 wagons departs Fort Scott, Kansas, for Fort Gibson to the south in Indian Territory.

14. Gold is discovered at German Gulch, Montana.

17. Near present Rhame, North Dakota, additional troops arrive to assist Captain Fisk. Many of the Sioux who had besieged Fisk's wagon train have died from eating poisoned hardtack; the remainder have packed up and left.
- John Dolan is hanged in Virginia City, Montana Territory, for allegedly stealing $700 from a friend.
- John C. Frémont, who won the Radical Republican Party's nomination for president in May, withdraws his candidacy in favor of Lincoln.
- The first bank in Montana opens in Virginia City.
19. On Cabin Creek, Brigadier General Stand Watie and 1,500 Indians and Texans capture most of the Union supply train that departed Fort Scott on September 12. The captured wagons and their contents are valued at $1.5 million.
22. Governor Sidney Edgerton orders Montana's first territorial election.
26. In Prescott, Arizona's first territorial legislature convenes. A university and a board of regents is established, $1,500 is set aside for education, and the counties of Pima, Yuma, Mojave, and Yavapai are created.
27. Bloody Bill Anderson's Confederate guerrillas, including 17-year-old Jesse James, plunder Centralia, Missouri, killing up to 24 residents. Next, they hold up a wagon train as it enters the town and execute 20 unarmed Union soldiers.

Teenager Jesse Woodson James (1847–1882), one of Bloody Bill Anderson's youngest guerrillas. Around the time this photo was taken, he blew off his left middle finger while cleaning a pistol. (Missouri State Historical Society)

- Union forces at Pilot Knob, Missouri, ward off an attack by a force of Confederate cavalry.
- The Union Lode is discovered by James Whitlatch at Orofino Gulch near Helena, Montana. Whitlatch will become the territory's first millionaire.
28. At Camp Weld, Colorado, seven chiefs, including Black Kettle and White Antelope, are accused by Governor Evans, Colonel John Chivington, and Major Edward Wynkoop of leading numerous attacks by Cheyennes and Arapahos. The Indians proclaim their innocence and blame the Sioux. Says Chivington, "My rule for fighting white men or Indians is to fight them until they lay down their arms and submit to military authority." The chiefs are ordered to move to Sand Creek, where they are promised safety.

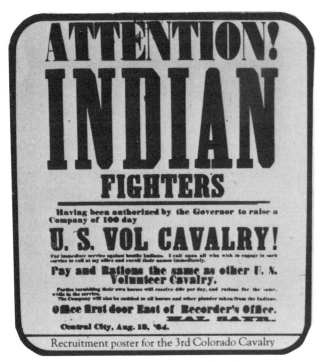

Another employment opportunity in the Old West. (Colorado State Historical Society)

Participants at the Camp Weld, Colorado, talks pause for a photograph on September 28, 1864. Major Edward Wynkoop kneels at the left. Black Kettle is seated behind him, third from left. (Colorado Historical Society)

Also in September 1864:

In New Mexico Territory, troops under Colonel Kit Carson defeat Navajo forces and capture war leader Barboncita at Canyon de Chelly. Some 7,000 captured Navajo are transferred to Bosque Redondo, a grove of woods near Fort Sumner on the Pecos River; disarmed, they will be taught to farm.

The Belmont Lode silver deposit is discovered near Georgetown, Colorado.

OCTOBER

2. General Pierre G. T. Beauregard is put in command of the Confederacy's Division of the West by President Jefferson Davis.

5. Clarence King writes: "Late in the afternoon of October 5, 1864, a party of us reached the edge of Yosemite, and looking down into the valley, saw that the summer haze had been banished from the regions by autumnal frosts and wind. We looked in the gulf through air as clear as a vacuum, discerning small objects upon valley-floor and cliff-front."

8. Superintendent of Indian Affairs W. G. Coffin signs a treaty with the Sauk and Fox and representatives of 13 other tribes at the Sauk and Fox agency near Quenemo, Kansas.

■ The first Catholic services in Helena, Montana Territory, are conducted at Silver Creek.

11. Colorado voters reject the proposed state constitution.

17. An Indian boarding school at St. Ignatius Mission, Montana, is founded by four Sisters of Providence from Montreal, Canada.

22. Serving with the Army of the Potomac, Brigadier General George A. Custer sees action in the Shenandoah Valley of Virginia.

23. The Confederacy is expelled from Missouri in the Battle of Westport: 20,000 Union troops attack Generals Price and Shelby's 8,000 Confederates.

24. Voters in Montana Territory elect their first public officials.

25. Robert Zachary, a member of Henry Plummer's Innocents gang, is hanged by vigilantes in Montana.

Zachary was apprehended this morning, allowed to write a letter to his mother, and then executed before lunch.

- ■ Confederates retreat at the Battle of Mine Creek in Kansas.
- **26.** Guerrilla leader "Bloody" Bill Anderson, 24, is shot dead by Union troops near Richmond, Missouri.
- **30.** Last Chance Gulch is renamed Helena, Montana Territory.
- **31.** Nevada becomes the 36th state of the Union. Although Nevada's population of 40,000 is too small to satisfy the legal requirement for statehood, President Lincoln approves its admittance in order to help with passage of the 13th Amendment, which prohibits slavery. The text of the new state's constitution was telegraphed to Washington at a cost of of $3,416.

National Headlines/October 1864:
22. REBELS ROUTED AT SHENANDOAH

NOVEMBER

- **6.** In Virginia City, the first permanent church in Montana Territory offers Methodist services.
- **8.** San Francisco casts more votes for Lincoln than does Boston—a total of 21,024—even though the latter has twice San Francisco's population.
- **14.** The Union ironclad ship *Comanche* is launched in San Francisco.
- **24.** In Colorado, Colonel John Chivington assumes command of an expedition against the Indians living at Sand Creek. On one occasion he is heard to say, "Damn any man who is in sympathy with an Indian."
- **26.** The First Battle of Adobe Walls takes place in Texas.
- **28.** In Colorado, James Beckwourth, a 69-year-old mulatto who at one time lived with the Crow Indians, is threatened with hanging if he refuses to guide Colonel John Chivington's cavalrymen to Black Kettle's camp at Sand Creek. Beckwourth reluctantly complies. Half way to the camp, the party comes upon the farmhouse of Robert Bent (the eldest son of William Bent), with whom Chivington replaces Beckwourth.
- **29.** The Sand Creek Massacre occurs in Colorado.

National Headlines/November 1864:
8. LINCOLN DEFEATS McCLELLAN FOR 2ND TERM
16. SHERMAN BURNS ATLANTA
25. CONFEDERATE PLOT TO BURN NYC FAILS

THE BATTLE OF ADOBE WALLS
NOVEMBER 26, 1864

In present Hutchinson County, Texas, Colonel Kit Carson led 14 officers and 321 enlisted men of the 1st Cavalry, New Mexico Volunteers, in an assault on Kiowas and Comanches at their winter quarters. Carson's soldiers routed a camp of 150 Kiowas at 8:30 A.M. and then pushed on to Adobe Walls, the ruins of a trading post constructed by William Bent around 1843. A camp of Comanches was within a mile; Carson's men faced a force of "many thousand" Comanche and Kiowa during the charges on Adobe Walls. Because they were using two mountain howitzers, Carson's men suffered only 25 dead. When Indian forces pulled away at dusk, Carson ordered the Kiowa camp that was attacked that morning burned. On November 27, Carson ordered his men out of the area.

MASSACRE AT SAND CREEK
NOVEMBER 29, 1864

Colonel John M. Chivington and 1,000 members of the Third Colorado Volunteers attacked Black Kettle's camp of about 600 Cheyennes and Arapahos in Colorado Territory, north of Fort Bent. The Indian encampment poignantly flew the American flag. Although Chivington claimed 400 to 500 Indians were killed, it is believed that 105 women and children died along with 28 men.

Atrocities were numerous. Two soldiers found a frightened 5-year-old girl and gunned her down. Another group of soldiers killed a pregnant woman, sliced open her womb, removed the fetus and dashed it against the ground. Many dead were scalped. Trophies, including pubic scalps from Indian women, were displayed a few days later during intermission at a Denver theater.

Chivington claimed that only nine of his soldiers died and 38 were wounded. His report
(continued)

(continued)

read in part: "It may, perhaps, be unnecessary for me to state that I captured no prisoners." Before Chief White Antelope died in the attack, he sang: "Nothing lives long, except the earth and the mountains." Black Kettle and his wife managed to escape.

In his testimony before a congressional investigating committee, Lieutenant James Connor described the scene at Sand Creek:

> I did not see a body of man, woman, or child but was scalped, and in many instances their bodies were mutilated in the most horrible manner—men, women, and children's privates cut out. . . . I heard of one instance of a child a few months old being thrown in the feed-box of a wagon, and after being carried some distance left on the ground to perish; I also heard of numerous instances in which men had cut out the private parts of females and stretched them over the saddlebows, and wore them over their hats while riding in the ranks. All these matters were a subject of general conversation, and could not help being known by Col. J. M. Chivington.

DECEMBER

2. Beaver Dams, the present Littlefield, is the first agricultural settlement in northern Arizona established by the Mormons.

3. Gold is discovered at Confederate Gulch near Townsend, Montana.

7. Arizona's territorial legislature appropriates $250 for the first public school at San Xavier.

12. Montana Territory's first legislative assembly meets in Bannack.

15. Wells Fargo purchases the Pioneer Stage Line from Louis McLane for $175,000 in gold.

19. The family of Nicholas P. Earp, which includes son Wyatt and six other children, completes a wagon-train trip from Iowa to San Bernardino, California.

22. The railroad linking Kansas City and Lawrence, Kansas, is completed.

23. The Santa Fe *New Mexican* reports: "Near the Pecos Church, the bodies of some fifteen Navajo Indians were observed a week or two since, exposed to the view of the traveller and the instincts of the wolf. The Superintendent of Indian Affairs . . . has made arrangements for their burial. These poor creatures were prisoners of war on their way to Fort Sumner, and perished with starvation during the severe weather . . . and were permitted to go without burial for five or six weeks."

24. Boise is designated the capital of Idaho Territory.

26. The first session of Arizona's Supreme Court is held in Prescott.

30. Virginia City becomes Montana Territory's first incorporated town.

31. Wells Fargo shows a profit of $184,699.43 for 1864.

Also in December 1864:

Author Artemus Ward visits Virginia City, Montana Territory, using an office at the *Territorial Enterprise* as headquarters.

Mark Twain spends the winter at Dick Stoker's cabin in the goldfields west of Sonora, California.

Hard times continue in Los Angeles as a result of the great drought of 1862–1864. No county taxes will be collected this year. Four downtown business lots are offered for sale at 63 cents apiece to pay back taxes; no one buys them.

National Headlines/December 1864:

24. SHERMAN'S PRESENT TO LINCOLN: SAVANNAH

Also in 1864:

Bret Harte becomes secretary of the U.S. branch mint in San Francisco.

The 37th Iowa Volunteer Infantry is made up of seniors whose average age is 57; one man in the regiment is over 80, while more than 100 members are in their 60s.

In Sumpter, Texas, John Wesley Hardin, 11, stabs a classmate in an argument over a girl.

Captain Jacob Downing and his cavalrymen engage Cheyennes at Cedar Canyon near present Sterling, Colorado.

The University of Kansas is established in Lawrence.

The *Frontier Scout* becomes the first newspaper to be published in North Dakota, at Fort Union.

Albert Bierstadt's painting *The Rocky Mountains* is exhibited at New York City's Metropolitan Fair. Measuring some 6 feet by 10 feet, it depicts a supreme Western fantasy—an Indian camp on the banks of sunlit waters, dwarfed by magnificent, clouded peaks.

The first salmon cannery in the United States is built by John William and George Hume on the Sacramento River in California. Although this cannery fails, their second one, at Eagle Fish, Washington, will succeed. Salmon canneries will soon become a fixture of the Pacific Northwest.

John M. Bozeman leads the first wagon train on the Bozeman Trail from Fort Laramie, in present Wyoming, to Bozeman, Montana.

The Colorado gold rush has run its course.

The journalist J. Ross Browne publishes *Crusoe's Island.*

The first military steamboat is reported on the Yellowstone River.

A congressional investigation calls the events of November 29 at Sand Creek, Colorado Territory, "a foul and dastardly massacre."

The United States auctions off the remaining animals of its "Camel Corps," with which the army experimented in California and Arizona; most are sold to circuses and curious ranchers. Many private owners will eventually give the animals their freedom, and this will lead to a rash of camel sightings in the southwest. An irate rancher will fell a campfire-attacking beast known as "La Phantasmia" in southwest Arizona in 1900; other sightings will be reported in Nevada in 1907 and California in 1929.

1865

"Finally, swift and terrible retribution is the only preventive of crime, while society is organizing in the far West. The long delay of justice, the wearisome proceedings, the remembrance of old friendships, etc., create a sympathy for the offender, so strong as to cause a hatred of the avenging law, instead of inspiring a horror of the crime."

—Thomas J. Dimsdale, *The Vigilantes of Montana*

JANUARY

1. Captain Simon Snyder and a detachment of the 5th Infantry kill four Apaches at Sycamore Springs, Arizona.

5. Near Julesburg, Colorado, Indians attack a Holladay Overland Mail and Express stagecoach and steal $1,802 being shipped by Denver merchants Norman Campbell and Samuel Jones.

▪ More's Wharf in San Francisco collapses.

7. More than 1,000 Sioux and Cheyenne warriors attack the trading post in Julesburg, Colorado in retaliation for the massacre at Sand Creek. Decoys lure soldiers from the stockade and kill 14 of them.

8. Three hundred and seventy members of the Texas militia attack, and are defeated by, a band of 1,400 Kickapoos under Chief No-Ko-Wat at Dove Creek near San Angelo, Texas.

▪ Brigham Young marries the 20-year-old Mary Van Cott, who is believed to be his 50th bride.

11. At Yellowstone City, Montana, a plug of tobacco costs $5 a pound.

12. Canada McOllough writes his account of recent events from Clear Water Ranch, Colorado: "There were 1,500 Indians at Julesburg last Saturday, January 7th. They killed nineteen white men, took the station, destroyed the mail, and took $30,000 in money. Two soldiers were killed."

16. The *San Francisco Dramatic Chronicle* begins publication; it will become the *Morning Chronicle*.

▪ The counties of Piute (named for the Indian tribe) and Sevier (named for Tennessee governor John Sevier) are created in Utah.

24. Captain Simon Snyder and a detachment of the 5th Infantry kill 20 Apaches at Little Cienega, Arizona.

Also in January 1865:

Mark Twain visits the diggings around Angels Camp, California, where he supposedly hears a tall tale about a frog-jumping contest from Ben Coon, a bartender at the Angels Hotel. Twain returns to San Francisco and begins work on his version of the story, "Jim Smiley and His Jumping Frog."

As a result of Colonel John Chivington's massacre of Indians at Sand Creek the previous November, a series of attacks occur on settlers in the valley of the South Platte in Colorado Territory. Wagon trains are a major target of the enraged Cheyennes, Arapahos, and Sioux. The American Ranch is burned. Wagons, ranch buildings, and telegraph lines are destroyed along a 75-mile stretch of the South Platte.

Six tons of mail that have accumulated in Denver are escorted east by 40 soldiers and some 20 travelers.

FEBRUARY

2. Another Indian raid on Julesburg occurs when George and Charles Bent lead Cheyenne Dog Soldiers against the trading post in northeastern Colorado. Many settlers are scalped in retaliation for the Sand Creek Massacre. A Mr. Foster of Denver reports that wagons containing 600 pounds of flour are burned.

- The Montana Historical Society is the first such organization to be established in the region.
- The first school laws requiring education for children are enacted in Montana.

5. The territorial legislature establishes the nine original counties of Montana; the territorial seal is also adopted by the legislature.

6. In Montana, Virginia City holds its first municipal elections.

- W. D. deLacey earns a commission from Montana's first legislature to draw an official map of the territory.

7. Virginia City is named the territorial capital of Montana.

27. The gunfighter and lawyer Elfego Baca is born in Socorro, New Mexico, shortly after his mother competed in a ball game.

MARCH

1. The bell atop San Francisco's City Hall is removed to the Old Union Hotel.

17. The *Montana Post* reports: "Only 22 sacks of flour in Silver Bow City, roads near impassable; two to twelve feet of snow in Deer Lodge."

24. Captain Simon Snyder and a detachment of the 5th Infantry battle Apaches near Fort Whipple, Arizona.

28. The Military District of the Plains is created.

Also in March 1865:

Ben Holladay buys the Butterfield Overland Mail, which gives him control over some 5,000 miles of stagecoach lines. Holladay's company employs 700 and has 1,500 horses, 700 mules, and 80 coaches and wagons.

National Headlines/March 1865:

2. LINCOLN REJECTS LEE PEACE PLAN; CALLS FOR UNCONDITIONAL SURRENDER

APRIL

1. The 161-foot stern-wheeler *Bertrand* strikes a snag in the Missouri River and sinks in 10 minutes. Some 150 tons of cargo will be salvaged in 1969 at the DeSoto National Wildlife Refuge in Iowa.

9. Ely S. Parker, also known as Donehogawa, a member of General Grant's army, is asked to write out General Lee's terms of surrender at Appomatox, because of his excellent penmanship.

10. After the Confederate general Robert E. Lee surrenders to General Ulysses S. Grant's Union army in Appomatox Courthouse, Virginia, General Phil Sheridan buys the table used by Grant and Lee. He then presents it to Major General George Armstrong Custer to give to his wife, Elizabeth. Custer will march home in style, the peace table strapped across the back of his saddle.

- A proposition to build a telegraph line is introduced in Utah.

15. In the wake of President Lincoln's assassination on the 14th, anti-southern riots occur in San Francisco. One innocent victim is French editor Etienne Derbec's newspaper *L'Echo du Pacifique,* which is destroyed because he is a "foreigner."

- Kansas governor Crawford designates April 23 as a date of fasting and prayer for the late President Lincoln.

17. In Montana Territory, flour shortages ignite "bread riots" in Virginia City.

21. The luxury steamship *Sultana* departs New Orleans for Cincinnati with one boiler in serious need of repair. Engineers work frantically. On board are 100 passengers, a crew of 80, and 100 horses and various other livestock, including a 10-foot alligator.

THE SULTANA EXPLODES
APRIL 27, 1865

The 1,720-ton *Sultana* was built in 1863 at a cost of $80,000. The luxury steamship had a capacity of 376 passengers and crew and was already carrying at least 180 when, on April 25, she stopped in Vicksburg, Mississippi, to take on some 2,400 Union soldiers who had just been released from Confederate prisons.

After docking in Memphis, the *Sultana* was navigating through a series of islands known as the Hens and Chickens when a weak boiler exploded with such force that literally hundreds of sleeping soldiers were either killed instantly or blown into the river. Those left on board faced a raging fire that quickly engulfed the ship. The *Bostona* appeared on the scene and was able to rescue some. At least 200 passengers pulled from the waters died in Memphis. The U.S. Customs Service in Memphis estimated that 1,547 died in the worst ship disaster in American history; 1,450 were Union soldiers.

24. San Francisco inaugurates a police telegraph and a fire alarm system.

25. The steamship *Sultana* stops in Vicksburg to pick up at least 2,400 Union soldiers. She pulls from the wharf low in the water. A clerk speculates it is possible the ship will make Mississippi River history, but he privately doubts the ship will make it to Cairo, Illinois.

26. The steamship *Sultana* pulls into Memphis at approximately 7:00 P.M. Many soldiers disembark and return to the ship intoxicated. At about midnight, the *Sultana* starts out again.

27. The steamship *Sultana* explodes on the Mississippi River.

Also in April 1865:

In Utah, war breaks out between Blackhawk Indians and settlers; the on-and-off affair will last until late 1867.

National Headlines/April 1865:

5. RICHMOND OCCUPIED

9. LEE SURRENDERS TO GRANT

14. LINCOLN SHOT AT FORD'S THEATER

15. LINCOLN DEAD; ANDREW JOHNSON INAUGURATED

26. BOOTH TRACKED DOWN; KILLED IN VIRGINIA

MAY

1. William F. Cody meets his future bride, Louisa Frederici, in St. Louis.

■ The Olympic Melodeon opens in San Francisco.

10. David Moffat, 25, begins working as a clerk in the First National Bank of Denver. Born in New York, he has worked in the banking industry in Iowa and Nebraska. He will ascend to the presidency of the First National Bank of Denver in 1880 and be instrumental in bringing railroads to Colorado.

12–13. In the Battle of Palmito Hill, the last battle of the Civil War, Union colonel Theodore H. Barrett attacks Confederates near Brownsville, Texas, and loses two-thirds of his command.

13. At White's Ranch, Texas, Sergeant Crocker of an all-black Union unit dies; his is the last recorded death of the Civil War.

■ Artemus Ward (Charles F. Browne), thanking the Leavenworth Typographical Union for electing him an honorary member, observes that he has "never been elected anything."

20. The last Confederate surrender takes place when General E. Kirby Smith surrenders the forces west of the Mississippi River.

25. Braves from a Blood tribe slay 10 woodcutters from the steamboat *Cutter* on Montana's Marias River.

27. Speaker of the U.S. House of Representatives Schuyler Colfax, en route to Virginia City, Nevada, by Overland stagecoach, arrives in Denver. He is greeted at a $16-a-head ball and has a major street named for him.

Also in May 1865:

The occupation of Texas by what will become a force of 50,000 federal troops begins.

Cattle in Texas, most running loose since the beginning of the Civil War, now number 5 million head, up from 1 million in 1855.

Since October 1864, 81 men have died at Fort Rice, just southeast of present Bismarck, North Dakota. Eight were killed by Indians and 37 died of scurvy.

In Denver, the entrepreneur Barney Ford sells his People's Restaurant for $23,400; he began it in the wake of the 1863 fire with a $9,000 loan.

National Headlines/May 1865:

4. LINCOLN BURIED AT SPRINGFIELD

10. JEFFERSON DAVIS CAPTURED IN GEORGIA

JUNE

3. Speaker of the House of Representatives Schuyler Colfax departs Denver on his mission to carry out Lincoln's last wish—to deliver a message of encouragement to the miners in Nevada.

5. A treaty with Indians in Utah is negotiated by Colonel O. H. Irish.

6. The guerrilla leader William Clarke Quantrill, 25, dies of gunshot wounds suffered at the hands of Union forces in Louisville, Kentucky.

■ A constitution prohibiting slavery is approved by Missouri voters.

8. Schuyler Colfax arrives in Salt Lake City, en route to Virginia City, Nevada.

10. John Keene becomes the first person to swing from Helena's "Hanging Tree."

11. Some 2,000 Sioux Indians, living under United States protection near Fort Laramie in Idaho Territory, begin a forced move to Fort Kearney, Nebraska, under the direction of Major General G. M. Dodge. Many atrocities will be reported along the way: young men will be beaten and maidens raped.

■ Bandits are foiled in their attempt to rob the Texas state treasury in Austin.

13. Crazy Horse sneaks into the camp of the Sioux being relocated to Fort Kearney. With other leaders, he plots an escape.

14. Crazy Horse leads an excape of Indians, mostly Sioux, from the U.S. cavalry.

19. General Robert S. Granger, commander of the Texas militia, retakes Galveston and issues a proclamation notifying blacks that they are free under the Emancipation Proclamation, which officially took effect six months earlier, on January 1, 1863. The regional annual holiday of Juneteenth is established, recognizing Emancipation Day in Texas.

23. The last Confederate general to surrender is the Cherokee chief Stand Watie; he turns his sword over to Union commissioners at Doaksville in the Choctaw Nation in present Oklahoma, at the abandoned Fort Towson.

24. Speaker of the House Schuyler Colfax arrives in Virginia City, Nevada. He brings a message of encouragement to the miners from the late President Lincoln, as well as a box containing a headstone and footstone for the neglected grave of Hosea B. Grosch, the discoverer of the Comstock Lode.

28. Indians slay Captain Burns and his troops at Avon, Montana.

29. The Olympic Melodeon theater closes in San Francisco.

30. The quartermaster general of the army reports that for the fiscal year ending today, the service paid $6,187,525 to civilian fright services to transport its supplies from Missouri to New Mexico and Utah.

Also in June 1865:
Navajo war chief Barboncita and about 500 of his people escape Bosque Redondo in eastern New Mexico. They will join forces with Manuelito.

Utah signs treaties with most of the territory's tribes.

JULY

1. Camp Tyler is established on the South Platte River Road in present Colorado. It will later be called Fort Morgan.

3. General Patrick E. Connor arrives at Fort Laramie in present Wyoming with orders to protect the Overland Mail Company's stagecoaches from Arapaho Indians.

10. The Union Pacific Railroad, building westward from Omaha, Nebraska, lays the first rails of its stretch of the transcontinental railroad, which will become the "greatest public work of this century." All materials and rolling stock needed for the construction of the first 400 miles, except for ties, has been brought by boat up the Missouri to Omaha. Native timber will be used for ties. The construction crew

will average only a mile a week in the beginning stages.

19. Louisiana governor Madison Wells tells residents of his state to take the oath of allegiance to the federal government that President Lincoln called for in 1863, or they will lose their voting rights.

20. James Butler "Wild Bill" Hickok and former Union soldier Dave Tutt quarrel verbally over a poker game in Springfield, Missouri.

21. The first recorded Western "showdown," or duel, is fought between "Wild Bill" Hickok and Dave Tutt.

24. Following a three-day march, Red Cloud, Crazy Horse, Roman Nose, Young Man Afraid, and their followers camp near Fort Casper in present Wyoming and plan their next battle.

■ In Montana Territory, Helena's first church is dedicated—a Methodist house of worship with A. M. Hough as minister.

25. The Fight at Platte Bridge begins near Fort Casper, Wyoming. Troops don't fall for Crazy Horse's decoy party of Sioux; instead of following them into certain ambush, the soldiers return to the fort just ahead of 3,000 warriors.

26. The fight at the Platte Bridge ends, a major disap-

THE FIRST SHOWDOWN
JULY 21, 1865

In an incident that later became a standard plot device for western movies, James Butler "Wild Bill" Hickok and Dave Tutt squared off at 6:00 P.M. on the main street of Springfield, Missouri. The confrontation was the culmination of a feud that began over a woman, one Susanna Moore. A disagreement over a poker game the night before, in which Tutt accused Hickok of cheating, was the last straw. During that dispute, Tutt grabbed Hickok's pocket watch and refused to return it.

A large crowd gathered the next day to observe the fight. When Tutt positioned himself about 75 yards from Hickok, Wild Bill shouted, "Don't come any closer, Dave!" Tutt fired first and missed; Hickok's shot landed squarely in Tutt's chest. Tutt died instantly. Hickok retrieved his watch and surrendered to authorities, who cleared him of manslaughter charges. Soon after, Bill made an unsuccessful run for mayor of Springfield.

pointment for Crazy Horse, as his 3,000 warriors have taken only eight scalps; most of the troops remain inside Fort Casper.

■ Indians kill Caspar Collins on the Platte Bridge near Fort Casper, Wyoming.

28. The *Brother Jonathan* sails from San Francisco for Oregon. On board is Brigadier General George T. Wright, hero of the Indian wars in Florida, and his wife.

30. The *Brother Jonathan* runs into rocks and sinks near the California-Oregon border; 190 on board are killed, including General and Mrs. Wright.

Also in July 1865:

The bloodiest stagecoach robbery in Idaho's history occurs near Fort Hall, in Bingham County, when six armed desperados stop a coach driven by Frank Williams. Eight passengers open fire on the robbers, who return the fire with shotguns. Three passengers and the driver die; the bandits get away with $60,000 in bullion.

Current estimates for freighting goods by wagon reveal that rations for 28 men for 60 days cost $768.62.

The steamboat fare from St. Louis to Fort Benton, Montana, varies from $150 to $200.

San Diego school teacher Mary Walker is fired for having dinner with a black student.

National Headlines/July 1865:
8. FOUR LINCOLN CONSPIRATORS HANGED

AUGUST

2. The "California," the first locomotive constructed in that state, is built by Donahue, Booth and Company at the Union Iron Works in San Francisco.

4. Colonel Thomas F. Meagher is appointed Montana's territorial secretary.

7. During a skirmish with the Paiute chief Black Rock Tom on the Quinn River in northern Nevada, Colonel Charles McDermit is ambushed and killed.

8. George A. Custer and his troops depart Alexandria, Louisiana, for Texas, where they will enforce the federal government's reconstruction policies for one year.

11. The Paiute chief Black Rock Tom is captured and shot by soldiers near Unionville, Nevada.

15. The United States signs a treaty with Comanches, Kiowas, Arapahos, and Kiowa Apaches at the mouth of the Little Arkansas River in Kansas.

26. The first book published in Montana, *The Vigilantes of Montana, or Popular Justice in the Rocky Mountains,* by Thomas J. Dimsdale, appears in the *Montana Post.*

31. Mining begins at Lincoln Gulch, Montana.

Ambushes of settlers increase in the wake of the Sand Creek Massacre. (Library of Congress)

SEPTEMBER

3. Colonel Cole leads a unit of General Connor's command in defeating some 3,000 Sioux, Arapahos, and Cheyennes at the Dry Fork of the Powder River in Wyoming. The battle will last three days.

12. Colorado voters ratify a state constitution.

14. The *Daily Alta* reports on San Francisco's famed canine: "Bummer [is] in a bad way" after being kicked by a drunkard. "His body is now swollen to twice its usual size, and the poor old fellow appears to be at death's door."

19. U.S. Commissioner D. N. Cooley signs a treaty with the Osage Indians at the Canville Trading Post in Neosho County, Kansas.

23. Denver witnesses the arrival of the first Butterfield Overland Mail stagecoach.

24. In San Francisco, James Cooke walks a tightrope from Cliff House to Seal Rocks.

29. William F. Cody's Company H of the 7th Kansas Volunteers is disbanded.

OCTOBER

3. Chief Little Hill addresses the U.S. Senate on the condition of the Winnebagos in Nebraska.

8. An earthquake shakes San Francisco. The *Daily Alta's* headlines read:

> THE GREAT SENSATION OF THE SEASON. SAN FRANCISCO GETS A SHAKE-UP WHICH MAKES THINGS CRACK. THE WHOLE TOWN MORE SCARED THAN HURT.

11. Fort Fletcher is established southeast of present Hays, Kansas, to protect railroad construction and to guard the Smoky Hill Trail to Colorado.

14. Representatives of the Cheyennes and the Arapahos sign a treaty with U.S. Commissioners John B.

Sanborn, William S. Harney, Thomas Murphy, Kit Carson, William W. Bent, Jesse H. Leavenworth, and James Steele at a camp on the Little Arkansas River in Kansas. The Indians cede their Colorado lands, but none of the parties to the treaty will abide by its terms.

- The first stagecoach mail service to Helena, Montana, is established.

17. President Andrew Johnson appoints Alexander Cummings, the founder of the *New York Daily World*, as the 3rd territorial governor of Colorado.

- Representatives of the Kiowa-Apache, Cheyenne, and Arapaho tribes sign a treaty with the U.S. commissioners who signed an earlier treaty, on the 14th, at the camp on the Little Arkansas River.

18. U.S. commissioners at the camp on the Little Arkansas sign another treaty, this one with representatives of the Kiowas and the Comanches.

23. Federal troops retake Fort McIntosh from Confederate forces in Laredo, Texas.

Also in October 1865:

The *Council Grove* (Kansas) *Press* announces the "death of Leavenworth," killed by railroads.

Since July, the Butterfield Overland Dispatch has freighted over 7,000 tons of cargo through Arizona, Nevada, New Mexico, Montana, Idaho, Utah, and Colorado.

California banker Louis McLane travels from San Francisco to Salt Lake City in three days and 17 hours.

NOVEMBER

2. Bummer, the famous dog of gold-rush San Francisco, expires at the Hayes Valley Farm. Concerned citizens had taken him there because of its quiet atmosphere following last month's earthquake. The *Bulletin* writes: "Bummer was not a dog to resort to tricks at any period of his life, or for any purpose. He died as he lived, open and above board. Bummer by name, bummer by nature, no more, no less." From Nevada, in Virginia City's *Territorial Enterprise,* Samuel Clemens will write that the renowned dog departed "full of years, and honor, and disease, and fleas." Bummer will be honored in the same way that Lazarus, his departed companion, was: Together again through the wonders of taxidermy, they will appear in saloons and museums for more than 40 years. It is believed they were in a janitor's storage closet on April 18, 1906, and disappeared in the great San Francisco earthquake.

9. Troops at Montana's Fort Owen ship 12,000 pounds of cabbage to mine workers.

18. Mark Twain's yarn about a California frog appears

in New York's *Saturday Press* as "The Notorious Jumping Frog of Calaveras County." For a country reeling from Civil War and presidential assassination, it is a welcome bit of comic relief.

25. By the close of the season on the busy Santa Fe trail, a total of 5,197 men, 4,472 wagons, 1,267 horses, 6,452 mules, 38,281 oxen, 112 carriages, and 13,056 tons of freight have passed over the toll bridge at Council Grove, Kansas, since May 21.

National Headlines/November 1865:

10. CAPT. WIRZ HANGED FOR ATROCITIES AT ANDERSONVILLE

DECEMBER

2. In Bannack, Montana, sugar sells for $1 a pound, flour for $28 a sack.

11. Captain Simon Snyder and a detachment of the 5th Infantry kill four Apaches near Peoples Ranch in Arizona.

12. Hostlers in San Francisco go on strike for higher pay.

15. The *Radiator,* a newspaper, begins publishing in Virginia City, Nevada.

20. Lyne Barret drills the first oil in Texas; his backers are skeptical, refusing to believe there can be much oil in the state.

22. Frank Finley Merriam, the 28th governor of California (1934–1938), is born in Hopkinton, Iowa.

25. Chicago's Union Stockyards open.

27. In Washington, D.C., Secretary of the Treasury Hugh McCulloch authorizes a committee of three Nevadans—Abe Curry, F. Rice, and John Mills—to approve a location for what will become the Carson City mint.

29. The landscape artist Peter Tofft sketches in Montana.

31. Some 2.5 million acres of western land have been claimed under the 1862 Homestead Act.

- Wells Fargo records a net profit of $221,704.36 for 1865.

National Headlines/December 1865:

18. 13TH AMENDMENT RATIFIED; SLAVERY ABOLISHED IN U.S.

Also in 1865:

Charles Durkee becomes Utah's territorial governor; he will serve until 1869.

Charles Farrar Browne publishes *Artemus Ward, His Travels.*

Apache leader Victorio tells a U.S. government representative that he has become tired of his hit-and-run lifestyle: "I and my people want peace. We are tired of war. We are poor and have little for ourselves and our families to eat or wear. . . . I have washed my hands and mouth with cold fresh water, and what I said is true." He and another chief, Nana, are told they will live on the barren Bosque Redondo Reservation, covering 40 square miles on the Pecos River in eastern New Mexico. Rather than accept the dismal offer, many of Victorio's followers scatter; some join Cochise, while others retreat into Mexico.

Bret Harte's first published book is an anthology of poetry which he edited, called *Outcroppings: Being Selections of California Verse.*

The Civil War was a boon for the arms business. Samuel Colt's weapons factory went from sales of $237,000 to over $1 million a year. For the war alone, the company manufactured 387,017 pistols, 113,980 muskets, and 7,000 rifles.

The Central Pacific Railroad employed 2,500 Irish and 7,000 Chinese workers. The Union Pacific Railroad laid 40 miles of track.

1866

"Kill the buffalo, kill the Indians."

—General Philip Sheridan

JANUARY

1. There are 172 Wells Fargo offices in operation.

4. Fort Richardson, Texas, is established.

12. Troops under Captain George Conrad kill 34 Indians at Fish Creek, Nevada; five soldiers are wounded.

27. Hundreds of fortune seekers return to Helena, Montana, after rumors of gold being discovered on the Sun River prove to be false.

31. The Marks and Brands Act, an attempt to establish rules in the wide-open cattle trade, is signed into law in Montana.

Also in January 1866:

Joaquin Miller becomes the judge of Grant County, Oregon. While a resident of Canyon City, Miller will publish his first two volumes of verse, *Specimens* (1868) and *Joaquin et al.* (1869).

The U.S. government reports that the Kansa tribe is "completely destitute."

Catherine McCarty lives in Marion County, Indiana, with her sons Joseph and Henry, the future "Billy the Kid," age 7. The year before, she met Indianapolis store clerk William Antrim.

FEBRUARY

5. Ben Holladay incorporates as the Holladay Overland Mail and Express Company.

9. Colorado's territorial legislature approves the creation of Las Animas county.

11. Jacob Moses, the father of 5-year-old Phoebe Ann Moses (Annie Oakley), dies of pneumonia.

13. The James boys rob their first bank.

BIRTH OF THE JAMES GANG
FEBRUARY 13, 1866

America's first peacetime bank robbery occurred at the Clay County Savings and Loan in Liberty, Missouri. Historians argue whether Jesse was even there—he may have been recuperating from a bullet wound. Two masked men entered the bank while 10 others stood guard. The heist garnered $15,000 in gold and $45,000 in securities. College student George Wymore was gunned down as the gang thundered away. A letter of apology to his parents was sent by the sensitive Frank James.

---

15. Major S. P. Smith leads the 2nd Cavalry against Indians at Rock Canyon in Guano Valley, Nevada. Reported casualties: 96 Indians killed, 15 wounded, 19 captured. One enlisted man is killed.

16. Infantrymen and Oregon troops defeat Indians near Jordan Creek.

23. In another fight at Oregon's Jordan Creek, Captain J. H. Walker reports 18 Indians killed and two wounded; one soldier is killed.

Also in February 1866:

Richard King raises more than 80,000 head of cattle on his 146,000-acre King Ranch in Texas.

General George A. Custer is mustered out of the volun-

JESSE WOODSON JAMES
SEPTEMBER 5, 1847—APRIL 3, 1882

1847: Jesse is born near Kearney, Missouri, the second surviving child of Robert and Zerelda James. His older brother is Frank, age 4.

1850: His father dies in California of pneumonia while searching for gold. Jesse's mother, Zerelda, weds Benjamin Simms, who is generally described as "mean to the boys."

1857: Benjamin Simms dies. Zerelda weds the doctor and farmer Reuben Samuel, who establishes a good relationship with Frank and Jesse.

1863: Jesse is flogged by Union soldiers who come to harass the family for Frank's alleged guerrilla activities.

1864: Jesse rides with the raiders of William Clarke Quantrill, then joins Bloody Bill Anderson for the raid on Centralia, Missouri.

1865: He attempts to surrender in Lexington, Missouri, when amnesty is offered to "irregulars," but takes a bullet in the lung in the process. He recuperates by plotting criminal acts with his brother Frank.

1866: The James gang robs its first bank, although Jesse may not have participated.

1867: Jesse robs a Richmond, Missouri, bank, killing three persons.

1868: With Frank and the Youngers, Jesse robs the Southern Bank of Kentucky in Russellville.

1869: He murders cashier John Sheets while robbing a bank in Gallatin, Missouri.

1870: Jesse, along with Frank, has a $3,000 price on his head.

1871: He robs the Corydon, Iowa, bank of $40,000.

1872: He robs the Columbia Kentucky Deposit Bank, killing a teller. Jesse steals $4,000 from the Savings Association Bank in Ste. Gene-vieve, Missouri. He also steals the gate receipts from the Kansas City Fair.

1873: The James gang robs its first train: the Jameses and the Youngers derail a Rock Island train in Adair, Iowa, killing an engineer, John Rafferty, and several passengers.

1874: Jesse robs the Concord Stagecoach in Malvern, Arkansas. Smaller train and bank robberies follow. He weds his cousin, Zee Mimms.

1875: Jesse escapes when Pinkerton agents firebomb the home of his mother and father. Zerelda loses an arm while Jesse's 8-year-old half-brother Archie Samuel is killed. In Texas, Jesse robs a stagecoach of $3,000.

1876: The James gang steals $75,000 from a Missouri-Pacific Express train near Otterville, Missouri. The gang is decimated in the Great Northfield Minnesota Bank Raid: the Youngers are captured, while Frank and Jesse escape.

1879: After a three-year hiatus following the botched raid in Northfield, Frank, Jesse, and a new gang rob $35,000 from the Chicago and Alton Express outside Glendale, Missouri.

1881: Jesse robs a Riverton, Iowa, bank of $5,000. He also robs a train near Winston, Missouri, killing an engineer and a passenger. A $10,000 reward is placed on his head. He commits his last train robbery outside Glendale, Missouri.

1882: Jesse is killed at his Missouri home by gang member Robert Ford, who shoots him in the back of the head while Jesse is standing on a chair to adjust a wall hanging.

teer service following a mutiny by his 3rd Michigan Cavalry, whose members objected to his frequent use of the lash to discipline soldiers. He reverts to the army rank of captain, although he will be referred to as "General Custer" by many.

National Headlines/February 1866:
12. FIRST FORMAL OBSERVANCE OF LINCOLN'S BIRTHDAY

MARCH

1. Near Arizona's Fort Buchanan, William Wrightson, the publisher of the *Arizonian,* and Gilbert Hopkings of the territory's first Board of Regents are killed by Indians.

2. Captain J. F. Millar and Assistant Surgeon Benjamin Tappan are killed during a fight between the 14th Infantry and Indians at Cottonwood Springs, Arizona.

3. Congress creates the Colorado River Reservation in Arizona for tribes living along the river and its tributaries.

6–9. Lieutenant Thomas Ewing of the 1st Arizona Infantry reports 20 Indians killed in a fight in the area between Fort McDowell and Palos Blancos.

6. William F. Cody (Buffalo Bill) marries Louisa Frederici in St. Louis.

8. Mini-Aku, Spotted Tail's daughter, is buried at Fort Laramie, in present Wyoming.

12. The Holladay Overland Mail and Express Company, incorporated on February 5, 1866, purchases all of Ben Holladay's personally owned mail and express lines west of the Missouri River, some 2,670 miles, and property owned by the Overland Dispatch Company for a grand total of $3 million. Holladay also sells his mail contracts and stock for $1.5 million.

20. Capital for the Holladay Overland Mail and Express Company is increased to $10 million.

20–25. Lieutenant P. Cervantes of the 1st Arizona Infantry reports 22 Indians killed in a fight on the Salt River.

23. Emanu-El Synagogue in San Francisco is consecrated.

28. Captain Nicholas Hodt of the 1st New Mexico Cavalry reports one Indian killed and six wounded at Rita Mangas, New Mexico.

30. John McDougall, the second governor of California (1851–1852), dies in San Francisco.

31. Infantrymen and Indian scouts kill 25 Indians and capture another 16 northeast of Pimos Village, Arizona. Lieutenant J. D. Walker reports one soldier killed and two wounded.

Crow agency in Dakota Territory around 1866. (Library of Congress)

APRIL

1. Western Union absorbs the U.S. Telegraph Company, increasing its capital to $40,000,000. Western Union now enjoys the first complete nationwide monopoly.

2. The Confederate insurrection is declared officially ended in Louisiana and Arkansas.

6. Lincoln Steffens, the journalist who will specialize in uncovering political corruption, is born in San Francisco.

9. Congress adopts the Civil Rights Act, under which all native-born Americans are granted citizenship regardless of their race. The measure does not apply to untaxed Native Americans.

■ The first Montana constitutional convention opens in Helena.

11. Two companies of the 1st Arizona Infantry kill 16 Indians between Forts Lincoln and Whipple in Arizona.

13. Robert LeRoy Parker, the future outlaw "Butch Cassidy," is born in Beaver, Utah.

ROBERT LEROY PARKER—BUTCH CASSIDY
APRIL 13, 1866–1908 OR 1937

1866: Robert LeRoy Parker is born near Beaver, Utah.

1879: He moves with his family to a ranch near Circleville, Utah.

1882: He idolizes the Utah bandit Mike Cassidy and leaves home at age 16 to ride with him. Parker becomes an expert rustler.

1887: He participates in an aborted train robbery in Colorado.

1889: Parker pulls his first holdup in Telluride, Colorado, and returns to Hole-in-the-Wall country in Wyoming.

1892: He works at a butcher shop in Rock Springs, Wyoming, where he gets the nickname "Butch." He is arrested for rustling on a warrant sworn out by rancher Otto Franc.

1894: Butch begins an 18-month jail sentence in Laramie for rustling.

1896: He heads for the Hole-in-the-Wall region, meets Harry Longabaugh (the
(continued)

(continued)

"Sundance Kid"), and forms the Wild Bunch. More than five years of train robbing begins.

1897: The gang's first holdup in Utah occurs.

1899: The Wild Bunch robs a train near Wilcox, Wyoming.

1901: The last robbery in the United States by the Wild Bunch occurs near Wagner, Montana.

1902: Butch travels to New York City and then to South America with the Sundance Kid and Etta Place. The boys rob banks in South America.

1907: With the Sundance Kid, Butch begins a series of robberies in Bolivia.

1908: Butch is reported killed by Bolivian cavalrymen, although rumors persist that it was the Sundance Kid who died and that Butch returned to the United States and married Gertrude Livesay in Adrian, Michigan.

1910: Supposedly living under the alias William Thadeus Phillips, Butch is thought to relocate to Spokane.

1925: He allegedly returns to Hole-in-the-Wall country in search of buried loot.

1934: Butch again allegedly returns to Wyoming to search for buried booty. He is said to attempt to market a manuscript, *The Bandit Invincible.*

1937: Butch allegedly dies of cancer in Spangle, Washington, near Spokane.

---

16. A nitroglycerin explosion damages the Wells Fargo office in San Francisco.

22. Captain Edmond Butler leads a large group of cavalrymen and infantrymen in a fight with Indians at Canyon de Chelly, in present Arizona; 26 Apaches are killed, 30 are wounded, and nine are captured.

23. The Holladay Overland Mail receives authorization to establish assaying offices in Montana, Idaho, and Utah.

29. A wagon from Confederate Gulch, Montana, arrives at Fort Benton, carrying 2.5 tons of gold dust worth approximately $1.5 million.

National Headlines/April 1866:

9. CIVIL RIGHTS ACT PASSED OVER JOHNSON'S VETO

30. RACE RIOTS LEAVE 47 DEAD IN MEMPHIS

MAY

3. Congress proposes admitting Colorado to the Union, based on the territory's 1865 constitution, despite allegations that the actions of the second constitutional convention might have been illegal.

5. Fort Fletcher, in Kansas, is abandoned.

6. Father De Smet departs St. Louis for Montana aboard the steamboat *Ontario.*

15. President Johnson vetoes the Colorado statehood bill because of doubts about the legality of the territory's constitution. Other factors in his decision are the decline in the territory's population following the initial gold strikes, and the activity of hostile Indians in the area.

■ Wells Fargo pays Hop Cik a total of $755.75 for the loss of his opium.

27. Major L. H. Marshall's 2nd Batallion of the 14th Infantry kills seven Indians and wounds another 12 on Idaho's Owyhee River. One soldier is reported killed.

Also in May 1866:

Range cattle in Texas sell for $3 to $4 a head. Butchers in northern and eastern markets are paying $30 to $40 a head.

Cholera again ravages the West: St. Louis often reports 200 deaths a day from the disease.

National Headlines/May 1866:

10. SUSAN B. ANTHONY OPENS 11TH WOMAN'S RIGHTS CONVENTION

JUNE

1. The Holladay Overland Mail announces a 25 percent fare reduction for ministers.

7. Chief Seattle, believed to be 78, dies at the Port Madison Reservation near present Bremerton, Washington.

13. Talks between representatives of the United States and the Brulé and Oglala Sioux led by Red Cloud are held at Fort Laramie in present Wyoming. While the government attempts to secure safe passage along the Bozeman Trail from the fort to Montana's mines, Colonel Henry B. Carrington arrives at the fort with 700 troops after a long march from Fort Kearny, Nebraska. Carrington, unaware of the nature of the talks, announces that he is under orders to construct forts along the Powder River. Says

Fort Phil Kearny is built in July 1866 despite Red Cloud's threat: "I will kill any white who comes into Indian country." (Denver Public Library, Western History Department)

one Sioux in attendance, "Great Father sends us presents and wants new road, but white chief goes with soldiers to steal road before Indian say yes or no." An insulted Red Cloud storms out of the meeting, grumbling, "I will kill any white who comes into Indian country."

20. A civilian train of 25 wagons journeys on the Bozeman Trail from Fort Laramie to Virginia City, trading sugar and flour for goods along the way. It reports no problems with the Indians. Notes one diarist, "the Indians led the way around for us to cross another bad stream, and rode along with us nearly all the forenoon trying to swap."

28. Colonel Henry B. Carrington's regiment comes to the aid of two companies of soldiers skirmishing with Indians on the Powder River. The area will be secured and named Fort Reno.

Also in June:

Nelson Story, a Virginia City, Montana, businessman, is in Texas purchasing cattle and hiring 22 cowboys. Accounts differ on the size of the herd—some say it is 600, others 1,000, others 3,000. Whatever the total, he plans to drive them to Montana.

JULY

4. Superintendent of Indian Affairs Thomas Murphy signs a treaty with the Delaware Indians at their agency in Kansas.

9. The first permanent army post in Montana, Camp Cooke, is established near the mouth of the Judith River.

13. Colonel Henry B. Carrington and his 18th Infantry Regiment make camp between the forks of the Little Piney and Big Piney Creeks in present Wyoming, and construction begins on Fort Phil Kearny. Red Cloud smokes with a series of chiefs, including the Oglala Crazy Horse, and Black Shield and High Backbone of the Minneconjous. Over the next six months, 154 soldiers and citizens will be killed in 51 skirmishes. A total of 306 cattle, 304 mules, and 161 horses will be stolen.

- Kentucky congressman Green Clay Smith is named as 2nd territorial governor of Montana.

16. A delegation of 40 Cheyenne chiefs and warriors including Two Moon, Black Horse, and Dull Knife, visit the site of Fort Phil Kearny to parley with the "Little White Chief," Colonel Henry B. Carrington. A demonstration of a howitzer prompts the Cheyennes to agree to a "lasting peace with the whites and all travelers on the road," meaning the Bozeman Trail.

17. The Red Cloud War begins in the Powder River region, as Red Cloud's Oglala Sioux stampede the horses and mules, some 175 animals, of the 18th Infantry Regiment on the construction site of Fort Phil Kearny. Soldiers pursue the attackers on a 15-mile chase in which two of the soldiers are killed and three are wounded. Shortly after this attack, Red Cloud's warriors happen upon the party of traveling sutler Louis Gazzous and kill six.

- In a separate incident, Captain Henry Haymond's 18th Infantry battalion suffers one dead and four wounded in an attack by Indians at Reno Creek, Dakota Territory.

- Capt. J. H. Walker and a detachment of the 14th Infantry kill three Indians and wound five in Oregon's Steins Mountains.

18. The mint selection committee receives Federal permission to begin construction of a new U.S. mint in Carson City, Nevada.

- Lieutenant R. F. Bernard and a company of the 1st Cavalry kill 11 Indians in a fight near Oregon's Snake Creek. Bernard reports one soldier killed.

21. A detachment of the 18th Infantry under Captain T. B. Burrowes is attacked by Indians on the Crazy Woman's Fork in Dakota Territory. Lieutenant N. H. Daniels and an enlisted man are killed.

24. Colonel Henry B. Carrington writes for reinforcements for Fort Phil Kearny.

29. Corporal F. R. Neale's 1st Cavalry detachments kill two Indians and capture five near Owen's Lake, California.

- Three soldiers are killed in an Indian attack near Camp Cady, California.

30. A race riot in New Orleans reportedly results in 200 deaths.

31. One enlisted man is killed in a fight with Indians near Fort Rice, Dakota Territory.

Also in July 1866:
George A. Custer is appointed lieutenant colonel in the newly organized 7th Cavalry.

AUGUST

1. The U.S. Army is ordered by the War Department to train Indian scouts who will be used "in the territories and Indian country" and "who shall receive the pay and allowances of cavalry soldiers." Within a year, the number of scouts will reach 474.

▪ The Union State Central Committee, meeting in San Francisco, issues resolutions calling for equal rights for all men, regardless of race.

2. By presidential proclamation, the Confederate insurrection is declared officially ended in Texas.

3. Colonel Henry B. Carrington sends two of his seven infantry companies, 150 men, from Fort Phil Kearny in present Wyoming to establish Fort C. F. Smith, in present Montana 90 miles to the north on the Bighorn River, in order to protect traffic along the Bozeman Trail.

4. The Santa Fe *New Mexican* reports: "On the eastern mail route the time has been reduced to ten days for eight months of the year and twelve days for four months."

6. San Francisco's journeymen plasterers go on strike for an eight-hour workday.

11. In Montana, the *Helena Gazette* publishes its first issue.

13. Federal and Arizona troops kill 33 Indians and wound 40 at Skull Valley, Arizona. One enlisted man is reported killed.

17. One Indian is killed and one is captured by troops on Arizona's Salt River.

23. Johnny Grant sells his ranch at Deer Lodge, Montana, to Conrad Kohrs for $19,000.

24. Arizona infantrymen capture two Indians in Arizona's San Francisco Mountains.

26. Federal and Oregon troops kill seven Indians on Idaho's Owyhee Creek.

Also in August 1866:
The U.S. government reports that the Kansa tribe is in a "very destitute condition."

Nelson Story and his 22 cowboys begin driving a large herd of cattle from Texas to Montana.

SEPTEMBER

1. James J. "Gentleman Jim" Corbett, the heavyweight boxing champion from 1892 to 1897, is born in San Francisco.

2. Hiram Warren Johnson, the 23rd governor of California (1910–1917), is born in Sacramento.

10–16. Captain W. J. Fetterman reports two soldiers killed and two wounded in a Sioux attack near Fort Phil Kearny.

14. One Indian is killed and another is captured by cavalrymen near Camp Watson, Oregon.

16. The Holladay Overland Mail and Express Company borrows $100,000 from Wells Fargo.

18. The cornerstone for the new Carson City mint is dedicated and laid by the Grand Masonic Lodge of Nevada.

20. Captain N. C. Kinney reports two soldiers killed in an attack near Fort C. F. Smith in Montana.

▪ The $1,000 prize for the best seawall design for San Francisco goes to Lewis and Allardt.

22. One soldier is wounded in an Indian attack on Dunder and Blitzen Creek, in Idaho.

28. One soldier is wounded in a scrape between the 2nd Cavalry and Indians on Montana's La Bonte Creek.

29. Captain W. J. Fetterman records one soldier lost during an Indian attack near Fort Phil Kearny, in present Wyoming.

30. Mark Twain returns to Virginia City, Nevada, to lecture at Pipers Opera House.

Also in September:
Nelson Story, his cattle herd and cowboys, on a drive from Texas to Montana, reach Fort Laramie.

OCTOBER

2. Mark Twain delivers the first lecture at Maguire's Academy of Music in San Francisco.

3. Arizona governor McCormick reports bad news to the third territorial legislature convening today in Prescott. The Territory has a population of 5,526 and no stagecoach lines, the Apaches are on the warpath, and in the last year the territory collected $355 in taxes.

▪ Cavalry and infantry under Captain G. B. Sanford kill 15 Indians in Arizona's Cedar Valley; another 10 are taken captive.

▪ A company of cavalrymen under Lieutenant J. F. Small kills 10 Indians in Nevada's Long Valley.

▪ Major A. J. Alexander leads a division of cavalrymen and citizens against Indians near Trinidad, Colorado. Thirteen Indians and one soldier are killed.

5. The 1st Oregon Infantry, under Lieutenant H. B. Oatman, kills four Indians near Fort Klamath, Oregon.

6. The first armed robbery of a train in U.S. history is committed by the Reno brothers, John and Simeon, who hit an Ohio and Mississippi Railroad express in Jackson County, Indiana.

11. In Kansas, Fort Fletcher, which was abandoned the previous May, is reoccupied.

13. Texas becomes the first state to reject the proposed 14th amendment to the U.S. Constitution regarding rights for all born and naturalized citizens.

14. Captain E. M. Baker reports that his 1st Cavalry killed three Indians and captured eight in Oregon's Harney Lake Valley.

15. The 1st Oregon Infantry under Lieutenant H. B. Oatman kills 14 Indians near Fort Klamath, Oregon. Oatman reports that another 20 Indians were wounded, while his unit suffered only two wounded.

21. Construction is completed on Fort Phil Kearny in present Wyoming.

23. The 2nd Cavalry under Lieutenant G. A. Armes kills four Indians near Fort Sedgwick, Colorado, on the north fork of the Platte River. Another seven Indians are reported wounded.

26. Near Oregon's Lake Albert, Lieutenant J. F. Small's 1st Cavalry and Oregon infantrymen kill 14 Indians and capture seven. Small reports two soldiers wounded.

28. Roy Bean, who will gain fame as the "Law West of the Pecos," marries Virginia Chavez in San Antonio, Texas.

30. The Jameses and Youngers rob $2,011.50 from the Alexander Mitchell Bank in Lexington, Missouri.

▪ Captain R. F. O'Beirne reports his 23rd Infantry's success against the Indians in Malheur Country, Oregon: two were killed, eight were wounded, and eight were taken prisoner.

31. Wells Fargo pays a dividend of 3 percent, making a total of 22 percent for 1866. The company now has 196 offices.

NOVEMBER

1. The "Great Consolidation" occurs when Wells Fargo assumes control of the Holladay Overland Mail and Express Company and becomes Wells, Fargo and Company, which now controls every stagecoach line between the Mississippi and California. Under the complicated deal, the U.S. Express Company will discontinue service west of the Missouri in return for $447,500 in cash, and American Express will soon quit the same area for $400,000

THE GREAT CONSOLIDATION
NOVEMBER 1, 1866

The interests of the Holladay Overland Mail and Express Company were consolidated with the Overland Mail Company, Wells, Fargo and Company, and other express companies into one large enterprise that will control every stagecoach line between the Mississippi and California. The name Wells Fargo was retained because of its financial position. Under the complicated deal, the U.S. Express Company discontinued service west of the Missouri for $447,500 cash. American Express quit the same area for $400,000 cash. Holladay received $1.5 million in cash and $300,000 in Wells Fargo stock. Shareholders of Wells Fargo retained 59% of the shares of the new conglomerate, while Overland Mail Company shareholders received 15%. New brochures indicated the enormous changes: "GREAT OVERLAND MAIL ROUTE," Pacific and Atlantic States, Wells, Fargo & Co. Sole Proprietors."

in cash. Holladay receives $1.5 million in cash and $300,000 in Wells Fargo stock.

▪ Following its takeover of the Butterfield Overland Mail in 1865, the Holladay Overland Mail and Express Company now services some 5,000 miles of the West with 20,000 vehicles and 14,000 employees.

▪ Captain J. H. Walker reports that his 23rd Infantry killed four Indians and wounded three at Trout Creek Canyon, Oregon.

▪ Brevet Lieutenant Colonel William J. Fetterman arrives at Fort Phil Kearny and proudly announces: "Give me 80 men and I would ride through the whole Sioux Nation."

2. Telegraph communication links Virginia City, Nevada, with Salt Lake City.

11. Fort Fletcher in Kansas is renamed Fort Hays in honor of General Alexander Hays, who was killed at the Battle of the Wilderness.

12. The board of directors named in the "Great Consolidation" of November formally approve the name of Wells, Fargo and Company.

17. Captain G. B. Sanford reports that six Indians were killed and five were taken prisoner by his 1st Cavalry at Sierra Ancha, Arizona.

18. Three Indians are killed and one is wounded by a company of the 1st Cavalry on John Day's River in Oregon.

21. The artist Albert Bierstadt marries Rosalie Osborne Ludlow, who was recently divorced from Bierstadt's western traveling companion, the author Fitz Hugh Ludlow. Bierstadt has just completed *A Storm in the Rocky Mountains—Mt. Rosalie,* which is based on his sketches of the Idaho Springs area. A financially strapped Bierstadt will sell the painting to an Englishman in 1896. The painting will be misplaced and thought lost until 1976, when it will be discovered in a London warehouse. The Brooklyn Museum will pay $600,000 in cash and art for what the publication *Mainliner* called "the summit of American nineteenth-century art at its most intense and rapturous."

Also in November 1866:

Navajo leader Barboncita and 21 of his followers surrender at Fort Wingate, New Mexico.

Myra Maybelle Shirley (Belle Starr), 18, weds the hoodlum James C. Reed.

One of Denver's newly elected lawmen is six-foot, three-inch Dave Cook. Among his outlaw-busting rules: "Never hit a prisoner over the head with your pistol, because you may afterwards want to use your weapon and find it disabled." Also: "It is better to kill two men than to allow one to kill me."

DECEMBER

3. Fourteen Indians are killed and five are taken captive by a company of the 1st Cavalry near Camp Watson, Oregon.

▪ Members of San Francisco's fire department will henceforth be paid for their work.

▪ Nelson Story, his cowboys and herd, arrive in the Gallatin Valley near Bozeman in present Montana, having completed the first Texas-to-Montana cattle drive. They chop some trees and begin building a corral.

6. Chief Red Cloud observes the decoy tactics of the Oglala Sioux braves Crazy Horse, Yellow Eagle, and High Back Bone two miles from Fort Phil Kearny. Warriors taunt soldiers who are out guarding woodcutters, lead a chase, and then swoop down on the soldiers from their rear. Two soldiers are killed and several are wounded. The chief is convinced that if a large number of soldiers could be lead out of the fort's gates, a thousand warriors could wipe them out.

9. Nelson Story, having just completed the first cattle drive from Texas to Montana, rides proudly into

Red Cloud (Makhpiya-Lúta) (c. 1822–1909). First in war. (Denver Public Library, Western History Department)

Virginia City with some of his livestock. The drive covered 2,500 miles.

11. A soldier is killed by Indians on Arizona's Grief Hill.

14. Lieutenant W. H. Winters leads the cavalry and infantry in killing three Indians in Arizona's Pinal Mountains.

15. The now-established author Mark Twain leaves the West, sailing out of San Francisco Bay and bound for New York. Before departure, Twain arranges to publish in the *Alta California* letters he will write on his upcoming tour of the Holy Land. In addition to increasing the author's visibility, the letters will become the foundation of his novel *The Innocents Abroad* (1869).

16. Arta Cody, the daughter of William F. Cody, is born in St. Louis.

17. General Patrick E. Connors commands that Indians living north of the Platte River "must be hunted like wolves." He issues orders stating that every male Indian over the age of 12 should be killed on sight.

20. At Fort Phil Kearny, Captain William J. Fetterman and Captain Fred Brown ask Colonel Henry Carrington to lead an offensive against Red Cloud.

21. The Fetterman Massacre, also known as the "Battle of the Hundred Slain," takes place.

21–24. A blizzard engulfs Fort Phil Kearny shortly after the Fetterman affair. Colonel Carrington calls for a volunteer to ride 236 miles south to Fort Laramie for reinforcements. John Phillips, the "Portugee," volunteers, even though the thermometer reads −30°. After battling 20-foot snowdrifts through the Big Horn Mountains, at dawn on the 23rd at Horse Shoe Station, 190 miles from Fort Phil Kearny, he wires his message to Laramie but cannot get through. Phillips trudges the remaining miles and arrives at the fort on Christmas Eve. He will take weeks to recover from his ordeal, which will become known as the "Ride of the Portugee."

24. Two Indians are killed by the 4th Cavalry on Mud Creek, near Fort Clark, Texas.

24–25. A battle at Dakota's Fort Buford claims three Indians.

26. Lieutenant Colonel George Crook leads a company of the 1st Cavalry against Indians on Idaho's Owyhee Creek. Thirty Indians are killed and seven are taken prisoner; one soldier is killed.

28. The first Presbyterian services in Arizona are held in Prescott.

31. The China and Japan Steamship Line begins operations in San Francisco.

■ Since August 1, Sioux have killed 154 persons at or near Fort Phil Kearny in 51 attacks.

Also in 1866:

In the period 1864–1866, the Holladay Overland Mail and Express Company posts a half-million-dollar loss due to Indian raids alone. Still, the express business as a whole enjoyed a good year. For example, Adams Express paid a 500 percent dividend— $300 in stock and $200 in cash—and showed capital of $12 million.

There are 200,000 head of cattle in Arizona valued at $3 million.

Five years after Ben Holladay entered the Denver market, he ends his express service altogether to spite those who complained of his high rates. The *Rocky Mountain News* predicts that Holladay will be hanged if he is ever spotted inside the city's limits. City officials change the name of McGaa Street, a well-known alley of prostitution, to "Holladay" to embarrass the transportation tycoon. (The street will later be renamed "Market" following protests from Holladay's heirs.)

The first school in Butte, Montana, opens.

The first hospital in Helena, Montana, opens.

The U.S. government surveys Montana.

The first band of sheep in Montana is in Prickly Pear Valley.

The black entrepreneur Barney Ford opens two restaurants in the West, one in Denver and one in Cheyenne. Aside from being one of the wealthiest men in the region, he organized a school for black children in a church basement in Denver. When a railroad refused him a ticket to return to the East, he leased an entire car and took several friends with him.

Perhaps for old time's sake, African American scout Jim

THE FETTERMAN MASSACRE
DECEMBER 21, 1866

Outside Fort Phil Kearny, Red Cloud attacked a group of woodcutters. Captain William J. Fetterman assembled a force of 48 infantry soldiers, 27 cavalry troops, and some volunteers, a total of 80 men, but he was ordered by Colonel Henry Carrington not to cross Lodge Trail Ridge.

Not far from the fort, the 2nd Cavalry and 27th Infantry soldiers encountered a group of decoys, including Crazy Horse. The braves taunted the bluecoats, calling them "sons of bitches" in English. Two howitzer blasts from the stockade sent the Indians running in mock fear for Lodge Trail Ridge. Fetterman charged after them into a valley behind Lodge Trail Ridge, where his troops were met by the Cheyenne Little Horse and 2,000 Cheyenne, Arapaho, and Sioux warriors. Fetterman and his entire troops were wiped out in the worst defeat for the army thus far in the Indian wars. Some 200 Indians were killed, many by the civilians James Wheatley and Isaac Fisher, who used new 16-shot repeating rifles.

George Armstrong Custer wrote that the news of the Fetterman disaster was received "with universal horror and awakened a bitter feeling toward the savage perpetrators." In a telegram to President Johnson, General William Tecumseh Sherman said: "I do not understand how the massacre of Fetterman's party could have been so complete. We must act with vindictive earnestness against the Sioux, even to their extermination, men, women, and children. Nothing less will reach the root of this case."

Beckwourth joins some Crow Indians for a hunting trip from which he never returns. Some accounts say he simply became ill, others suggest he probably died of food poisoning after feasting on dog. His body is placed in a tree, and his spirit will be remembered as that of a great warrior.

In Texas, bars and saloons are ordered closed on Sundays.

Oliver F. Winchester opens the Winchester Repeating Arms Corporation in Connecticut. His first Model 1866 is a 17-shot, lever-action rifle that fires .44-28 rimfire ammunition.

The Goodnight-Loving Trail is blazed from Texas to New Mexico.

Mark Twain publishes *The Celebrated Jumping Frog, and Other Sketches*.

General Philip H. Sheridan reports 100 million buffalo in Kansas and in Indian Territory. Sheridan also believes the "Indian problem" can be solved if the buffalo is exterminated.

Captain George A. Custer declines an offer to become a colonel in the Negro 9th Cavalry.

The Union Pacific lays down 250 miles of track.

The Chisholm Trail opens. It will become a well-traveled cattle route from Texas, through Indian Territory, to the railroads in Kansas.

1867

"Stripped of the beautiful romance with which we have been so long willing to enve-
lope him, transferred from the inviting pages of the novelist to the localities where we
are compelled to meet with him, in his native village, on the war path, and when raiding upon our frontier settlements and lines of travel, the Indian forfeits his claim to the
appellation of the 'noble red man.' We see him as he is, and, so far as all knowledge
goes, as he ever has been, a savage in every sense of the word; not worse, perhaps,
then his white brother would be similarly born and bred, but one whose cruel and ferocious nature far exceeds that of any wild beast of the desert."

—George Armstrong Custer

JANUARY

1. In a report to the Secretary of the Treasury, J. Ross Browne will estimate that from January 24, 1848, until today, $1,205,000 worth of gold and silver have been dug out of the nine Western states and territories.

■ A detachment of cavalrymen kills five Indians near Fort Stanton in New Mexico.

2. The Santa Fe *New Mexican* reports on the hanging of Colonel Thomas Means:

> Means who was a desperate character, has for a long time been a terror to his family and the town, and the community at last became so enraged at his actions that his presence was no longer to be tolerated . . . he attempted to murder Judge Blackwood . . . he attempted to take the life of his wife . . . he was too drunk to be examined, was placed . . . in the court house, under a guard of two men to be held till morning. About 12:00 that night a party of some twenty men, masked, broke open the door and demanded him . . . Means seeming to see at a glance his fate, said, "I sup-pose you have come to kill me." These were his last words, as he was immediately strung up, to the rafters in the center of the court house, where his body was left dangling until the next day.

■ Tom Hodges leads 14 Arizona Rangers in a surprise attack on Apaches at Rock Springs; 21 Indians are killed.

6. Gutzon Borglum, the artist who will realize his dream of carving giant busts of four American presi-dents on South Dakota's Mount Rushmore, is born in Bear Lake, Idaho.

■ A party of Indian scouts kills 26 Indians and cap-tures eight on Oregon's Crooked River.

8. The 1st Cavalry reports killing five Indians on Idaho's Owyhee River.

9. Lieutenant Colonel George Crook leads the 1st Cavalry against Indians on Oregon's Malheur River, capturing 30.

17. The Northwestern Railroad becomes the first to reach Council Bluffs from the east.

18. A group of Denver pioneers, aware that the Union Pacific's decision to bypass their city could end their hopes for an empire, organizes the Denver Pacific Railway and Telegraph Company. The intent of the officers—Bela Hughes, L. Kuntz, F. M. Case, John Pierce, W. F. Johnson, and David H. Moffat—is to link Denver to the transcontinental railway by laying track to Cheyenne.

■ Two Indians are reported killed by the 8th Cavalry at Eden Valley, Nevada.

David Moffat in his later years. Connecting Colorado to the rest of the world by rail is his main priority. (Denver Public Library, Western History Department)

19. Two Indians are reported killed by the 4th Cavalry on the Nueces River in Texas.

25. Elizabeth Garrett, mother of Sheriff Pat Garrett, dies.

26. In Washington, D.C., Senator James Doolittle's congressional investigation of the Indian depopulation problem reports:

> 1. The Indians . . . are rapidly decreasing in numbers from various causes: By disease; by intemperance; by wars, among themselves and with the whites; by the steady and resistless emigration of white men into the territories of the west. . . .
>
> 2. . . . In a large majority of cases Indian wars are to be traced to the aggressions of lawless white men, always to be found upon the frontier. . . .
>
> 3. . . . [Other factors include] the loss of their hunting grounds and the destruction of that game upon which the Indian subsists.

27. The *New Mexican* reports on the appearance yesterday in Santa Fe of a delegation of Hopis complaining of outrages by whites and Utes: "The whites, while ostensibly hunting Apaches, stole seven hundred sheep and goats, murdered seven men and carried off to Abiquiu eleven children and one woman."

29. Lieutenant Colonel George Crook leads the 1st Cavalry against Indians on Oregon's Owyhee River, killing 60 and capturing 27. One citizen is re-

ported killed and three soldiers are reported wounded.

■ President Johnson vetoes Colorado's second attempt at statehood.

31. Congress extends voting rights to males 21 years of age and over in the U.S. territories.

Also in January 1867:

A grand public funeral takes place in Virginia City, Nevada, for the popular prostitute queen, Julia C. Boulette, who was found strangled to death in her bed with her jewelry missing. The Metropolitan Brass Band plays "The Girl I Left Behind Me."

The Locomotive Engineers' Monthly Journal, a union newsletter, publishes its first issue.

Colorado is represented at the Paris World Exposition by a mineral exhibit.

FEBRUARY

1. In San Francisco, bricklayers return to work with an eight-hour-workday contract.

7. Laura Elizabeth Ingalls, who will become the author Laura Ingalls Wilder of "Little House" fame, is born near Pepin, Wisconsin. She is the second child of Charles Philip Ingalls and the former Caroline Quiner.

■ The 1st Cavalry clashes with Indians at Vicksburg Mines, Nevada.

12. Acts of violence against Chinese take place in San Francisco. Laborers excavating a lot on Townsend Street are driven from the site by a mob, and their provisions and shacks are demolished. The mob then marches to the rope works of Tubbs and Company, scatters its workers and burns their homes.

15. The 8th Cavalry clashes with Indians in Nevada's Black State Mountains. Six Indians are reported killed.

16. The 1st Cavalry under Captain S. Munson fights Indians at Surprise Valley, California. Five Indians are killed and two are captured.

18. The Sac and Fox Treaty cedes new Indian lands to the United States.

20. Anti-Chinese meetings in San Francisco receive heavy public support.

■ Oil is discovered in Deer Lodge County, Montana.

21. The Deseret Telegraph Company is organized in Utah.

23. The 1st Cavalry fights Indians in Arizona's Meadow Valley.

27. Indians kill three soldiers in a hunting party near Fort Reno, future El Reno, Oklahoma.

LAURA INGALLS WILDER
FEBRUARY 7, 1867—FEBRUARY 10, 1957

In 1930, a 63-year-old Missouri farm wife acted on an idea she had been nurturing for some time. She wanted to pass on the pioneer experience, then unknown, to modern youth. Thought Laura Ingalls Wilder, "I wanted the children now to understand more about the beginnings of things . . . what it is that made America as they know it."

With that goal and a mind full of memories, she sat down with tablet and pen and began one of America's most fascinating literary careers: "Once upon a time, sixty years ago, a little girl lived in the Big Woods of Wisconsin, in a little gray house made of logs."

Laura Ingalls Wilder's fiction sprang from real-life experiences on the rugged frontier. Born Laura Elizabeth Ingalls on February 7, 1867, near Pepin, Wisconsin, she was the second child of Charles Philip Ingalls and the former Caroline Quiner. Like thousands of other settlers, Charles was always chasing elusive dreams, always on the move.

Laura was just over a year old at the time of the family's first migration, to Missouri in 1868. A year later the Ingallses pushed westward to Indian Territory in present Kansas. Laura and her older sister Mary were joined by a third child, Caroline, born in Montgomery County in 1870. But the Ingallses and other families soon discovered that the lands they were cultivating legally belonged to the Osage Indians, so the family packed its worldly belongings and headed back to Wisconsin.

By 1874, "Pa," as he would become known to future readers, felt it was again time to relocate. The little house in the big woods and the property on which it sat were sold for $1,000. This time, the family migrated to the banks of Plum Creek in Walnut Grove, Minnesota, where Laura's brother, Charles Frederick, was born on November 1, 1875. Two grasshopper invasions later, they set out for Burr Oak, Iowa, where Laura's father had found employment running a hotel. Young Charles died en route. About the time Laura's father was souring on his role as innkeeper, another child, Grace Pearl, was born.

In 1878, the Ingallses returned to Walnut Grove. There the family was stricken with scarlet fever. Mary suffered a stroke that claimed her sight. "The last thing Mary ever saw," Laura would write,

"was the bright blue of Grace's eyes, as Grace stood holding the chair looking up at her."

In 1879, Laura's aunt Docia told Charles of a job at her husband's store at the Silver Lake railroad camp in Dakota Territory. There, the Ingalls family became a part of the fledgling community of De Smet. During the long winter of 1880–1881, Laura's attention was caught by the farm boy Almanzo Wilder, who helped bring supplies into the little town on the prairie during a grave shortage.

Laura worked briefly as a seamstress, helping the family earn enough money to send Mary to a special school. At age 15, Laura received her teaching certificate and began instructing at the Bouchie school, some 15 miles away. Every weekend, Almanzo appeared with a wagon to take her home. The courtship had begun in earnest.

Laura and Almanzo, whom she called "Manly," were married on August 25, 1885. Their first four years together were an emotional roller coaster. From the birth of their first child, Rose, on December 8, 1886, until the death of a newborn son in 1889, they experienced a succession of crop failures followed by a fire that destroyed their home.

After spending a year in Westville, Florida, the Wilders returned to De Smet. Then, in 1894, they relocated to Mansfield, Missouri, where they farmed successfully. Laura became a popular speaker at farmers' gatherings. Once, when she was too ill to attend a meeting, her speech was delivered by another speaker. In the audience was the *Missouri Ruralist* editor John Case, who invited Laura to submit an article for his magazine. Her "Favors the Small Farm Home" appeared in 1911.

The Wilders' daughter, Rose, had become a staff journalist at the *San Francisco Bulletin*. She encouraged her mother to submit articles to other periodicals. In 1919, Laura sold a story to *McCall's*, and her byline next appeared in the *Country Gentleman*. Her spurt of literary activity was interrupted when she took a secretary-treasurer job at the Mansfield Farm Loan Association.

With more prodding from Rose, Laura again took up the pen. Her manuscript "When Grandma Was a Little Girl" was tentatively accepted by the book publisher Alfred A. Knopf. When complications
(continued)

(continued)

arose with that house's children's department, the manuscript was submitted to Harper and Brothers, who wired their acceptance on Thanksgiving Day 1931. The newly titled *Little House in the Big Woods* was published the following spring.

In April 1932, as a main selection of the Junior Literary Guild, *Little House* became a sensation. Encouraged, Wilder wrote *Farmer Boy,* the story of Almanzo. As it was being published in 1933, she began work on a series of books based on her frontier life.

Little House on the Prairie appeared in 1935, followed by *On the Banks of Plum Creek* (1937), *By the Shores of Silver Lake* (1939), *The Long Winter* (1940), *Little Town on the Prairie* (1941), and *These Happy Golden Years* (1943). Also during this period, she penned *The First Four Years,* the story of her early married life, but decided not to publish it.

The "Little House" books became instant classics, in large part due to Wilder's "word pictures"—a term she coined for the descriptions she provided her sightless sister—coupled with a strong love of hope, home, and family. The honors that were heaped upon her only solidified the notion that she had succeeded in providing that all-important human link with the past.

Following Almanzo's death in 1949, Laura's writings ceased. She spent her final years in failing health, yet warmed by the daily fan letters she continued to receive. The Laura Ingalls Wilder Award was established by the Association for Library Services in 1954, with Wilder as the first recipient. She died at age 90 on February 10, 1957.

The First Four Years was finally published in 1971, and was followed by *West from Home,* the letters she had written during her visit to the 1915 San Francisco World's Fair. In 1974, *The Little House on the Prairie* began its long and successful run on television. Purists argued that the series was only loosely based on Laura Ingalls Wilder's books, but there was no denying that it made millions of Americans more aware of the unique gift that was the Wilder West.

Also in February 1867:

The mining boom that began in Colorado's California Gulch in 1860 is largely over; some 400 die-hard miners remain.

MARCH

1. Nebraska enters the Union as the 37th state. Its name is derived from "Nibthaska," an Omaha Indian word meaning "flat water." The new state's population is "as high as 40,000," according to President Andrew Johnson. The capital moves from Omaha to Lancaster, which will be renamed Lincoln.

■ Farmers fear for their crops as young grasshoppers appear near Leavenworth, Kansas.

2. Congress authorizes the War Department to establish the "King Survey," the Geological Exploration of the Fortieth Parallel. The results of the survey will appear in seven volumes from 1870 to 1880. Also, the General Land Office is directed to conduct the Geological and Geographical Survey of the Territories, which will become known as the Hayden Survey; its results will appear in several volumes from 1867 to 1883. In another action, peonage, or debt servitude, is abolished.

11. A pony express-type route is established between Helena, Montana, and Minneapolis, Minnesota.

■ The 1st Cavalry reports killing a dozen Indians in California's Coso Mountains.

12. Captain J. A. Wilcox leads the 4th Cavalry against Comanches on the Pecos River in Texas. One soldier and 25 Indians are reported killed.

18. Arizona Territory's military headquarters are transferred to Tucson from Prescott.

19. The *Atchison Champion* claims there are 6,866 Indians in Kansas, and that treaties have resulted in the acquisition of 1,071,946 acres of former Indian land in the state.

28. The 8th Cavalry fights Indians on Oregon's Murderers' Creek.

29. The Workingmen's Convention begins in San Francisco.

Also in March 1867:

Congress authorizes a Peace Commission in the wake of last December's Fetterman Massacre. A plan is afoot to move all the plains Indians onto two reservations, one in the Black Hills for the northern tribes, and one in Indian Territory for the southern tribes.

National Headlines/March 1867:

29. FIRST NEWS STORY ON KKK IN TENNESSEE
30. U.S. AGREES TO PURCHASE "SEWARD'S FOLLY," ALASKA

APRIL

1. Blacks vote in Colorado elections for the first time; there is no opposition.
2. The Kansas Pacific Railroad sells Delaware Indian land at Lawrence, Kansas.
3. Captain Guildo leads the 14th Infantry in a fight with Indians in Arizona's Tonto Valley; three Indians are killed and one is captured.
5. Alonzo Erastus Horton arrives in San Diego. After following through on his idea of building a new city on the waterfront, he will be credited as being the founder of the present city.
7. Major General Winfield Scott Hancock arrives at Fort Larned, Kansas, on the south bank of Pawnee Creek, six miles west of the Arkansas River, for a conference with local Indian chiefs. He is currently organizing a 1,400-soldier campaign against the southern plains tribes; Hancock's chief field commander is Lieutenant Colonel George A. Custer. Agent E. W. Wynkoop sends runners to summon Cheyenne, Apache, and Arapaho chiefs to the conference.

■ The journalist Henry M. Stanley, 25, arrives in Kansas to cover Hancock's campaign for the *St. Louis Missouri Democrat.* Stanley will make $15 a week from the *Democrat,* but will manage to earn a total income of approximately $90 a week by freelancing for other newspapers, including the *New York Times* and *New York Herald.*

8. The 8th Cavalry reports 30 Indians killed in a fight on the Rio Verde in Arizona.

■ A Kansas blizzard prevents Indian chiefs from assembling for a conference at Fort Larned.

10. The 8th Cavalry reports three Indians killed in a fight in Arizona's Black Mountains.
12. Major General Winfield Scott Hancock confers with Cheyenne chiefs at Fort Larned. He tells the Cheyennes to abide by the treaty of 1865 and to stay on their lands south of the Arkansas River, or his soldiers will make war.
15. One soldier is reported wounded in a brush with Indians near Fort Lyon, Colorado.
16. The 8th Cavalry under Captain J. M. Williams reports 20 Indians killed in a fight in Arizona's Black Mountains.
19. The 7th Cavalry under Lieutenant Matthew Berry reports six Indians killed in a fight near Fort Dodge, Kansas.
23. San Francisco's Cosmopolitan Hotel burns; the damages total $150,000.
24. The 8th Cavalry reports five Indians killed and five captured in a fight near Arizona's Fort Mojave.

General William Tecumseh Sherman (1820–1891): "We must act with vindictive earnestness against the Sioux." (Library of Congress)

■ An earthquake at 2:45 P.M. is felt in eastern Kansas and western Missouri.
27. The 1st Cavalry reports six Indians killed in a battle on Oregon's Silvies Creek.
29. Trains arrive for the first time in Salina, Kansas.
30. Burton C. Mossman, the future rancher and first captain of the Arizona Rangers, is born near Aurora, Illinois. Before he retires in 1944, a million head of cattle will wear his brand.

Also in April 1867:

General William Tecumseh Sherman sets in motion his plan to drive Indians out of the path of the transcontinental railroad. Cavalry and infantry under General Winfield S. Hancock conduct raids across western Kansas, including at Pawnee Fork, where some 250 Cheyenne lodges are put to the torch.

National Headlines/April 1867:

9. U.S. PAYS $7 MILLION FOR ALASKA

MAY

1. A soldier in the 2nd Cavalry is killed in an Indian attack near La Prelle Creek, Dakota Territory.

5. The 1st Cavalry reports one Indian killed in a fight near Camp Watson, Oregon.

6. The 14th Infantry defends against an Indian attack on a pack train in Arizona's Mazatal Mountains.

■ Two companies of infantrymen report two Indians killed in fighting in Arizona's Mazatal Mountains.

10. City builder Alonzo Erastus Horton buys 960 acres of San Diego waterfront property for 27 cents an acre. Construction begins on "Horton's Addition," or "New San Diego."

13. Workers in San Francisco demand an eight-hour workday.

14. Wells Fargo buys the Western Transportation Line from a Mr. Creighton for $50,000 in cash and $15,000 in stock.

22. The Hughes and Mason Bank in Richmond, Missouri, is robbed of $4,000 in gold by the James gang, which kills three persons, including Mayor Shaw.

25. *Harper's Weekly* publishes a pictorial on Fort Dodge, Kansas.

23. Two soldiers are killed in an Indian attack near Bridger's Ferry, Dakota Territory.

27. Alexander C. Hunt is appointed territorial governor of Colorado by President Johnson.

■ Captain Myles Keogh of the 7th Cavalry reports a fight with Indians near Pond Creek Station, Kansas.

30. The 8th Cavalry reports 15 Indians killed in fighting near Beale Station, Arizona.

■ Indians kill a soldier herding cattle near Fort Reno, Dakota Territory.

31. Two enlisted men, members of an escort from Fort Dodge, are slain by Indians near Bluff Ranch, Kansas.

Also in May 1867:
In Texas, cholera afflicts the Wichita and Caddo tribes.

JUNE

1. Lieutenant Colonel George A. Custer departs Fort Hays, Kansas, with 350 troops "to hunt out & chastise the Cheyennes, and that portion of the Sioux who are their allies, between the Smoky Hill & the Platte."

■ In Cass County, Texas, Cullen Baker kills a shop owner when the latter complains about Baker's bills.

■ A member of the 4th Infantry is killed in an Indian attack near Fairview, Colorado.

3. More than 2,000 laborers take to the streets of San Francisco to demonstrate in favor of an eight-hour workday.

6. General William Tecumseh Sherman arrives in Julesburg, Colorado, just ahead of the approaching Union Pacific Railroad, and wires Colorado governor Hunt:

> I am here now and Gen. Augur is across the Platte on the line of the Union Pacific Railway. The Indians are everywhere. Ranchers should gather at stage stations. Stages should bunch up and travel together at irregular times. I have six companies of Cavalry and General Custer is coming up from the Smoky Hill Route.

7. In Kansas, torrential rains make Big Creek overrun its banks, flooding Fort Hays. The commanding officer, Lieutenant Colonel George. A. Custer, had moved the residents, including his wife, Elizabeth, to high ground before he departed on a mission, but that was not enough. She writes that "seven men were drowned near our tent, and their agonizing cries, when they were too far out in the current for us to throw our line, are sounds that will never be stilled."

8. Indians clash with the 7th Cavalry under Lieutenant H. J. Nowlan at Chalk Bluffs, Kansas.

11. A member of a detachment of the 7th Cavalry is killed by Indians while escorting mail near Big Timbers, Kansas.

12. Old Man Afraid (also known as Man Afraid of His Horses), representing 200 Oglala Sioux lodges, meets with whites at Fort Laramie to discuss peace. When he requests ammunition, negotiations are broken off.

■ A member of the 2nd Cavalry is killed in an Indian attack near Fort Phil Kearny in present Wyoming.

■ Indians attack the 7th Cavalry near Fort Dodge, Kansas; one soldier is wounded.

13. Sunday schools in Kansas have 10,000 students enrolled and more than 1,000 teachers.

14. The 8th Cavalry reports 20 Indians killed and nine captured in fighting at Arizona's Peacock Springs.

15. The 3rd Infantry clashes with Indians at Big Timbers, Kansas. Two soldiers are killed and one is wounded; there is no estimate of Indian casualties.

■ Businessmen in North Platte, Nebraska, are reported "ready to pull up and go to the new rail terminus [at Julesburg, Colorado], anticipating a rich harvest of business spoils."

16. The 3rd Cavalry fights Indians in the Gallinas Mountains of New Mexico, killing one and capturing two.

19. Building westward from Kansas City, Missouri, the Kansas Pacific Railroad reaches Fort Ellsworth, Kansas.

■ The first train tracks are laid in the state of Colorado (the exact date is uncertain).

- A detachment of Indian scouts kills 12 Indians and captures two near Steens' Mountains, Oregon.
20. Major Frank North leads a company of Pawnee scouts against the Sioux on the Union Pacific rail line at the foot of the Black Hills.
21. Lieutenant J. M. Bell reports two soldiers killed in a fight with Indians near Fort Wallace, Kansas.
- Lieutenant E. J. Harrington reports that his cavalry and infantry killed three Indians and captured six near Calabases, Arizona.
22. Two enlisted men of the 37th Infantry are wounded in a brush with Indians near Goose Creek Station, Colorado.
- Lieutenant H. J. Nowlan and a detachment of the 7th Cavalry report a skirmish with Indians near Fort Wallace, Kansas.
24. Lieutenant Colonel George A. Custer reports a fight between Indians and five companies of the 7th Cavalry on the north fork of the Republican River in Kansas. One soldier is wounded; there is no estimate of Indian casualties. Captain L. M. Hamilton, with a detachment of the 7th Cavalry, reports two Indians killed elsewhere on the Republican.
- News reports state that Union Pacific trains will begin running to Julesburg, Colorado, the next day. A stagecoach can then take passengers from Julesburg to Denver in 33 hours.
- Grasshoppers are reported moving into Colorado.
25. Union Pacific rails reach Julesburg, 377 miles west of the Missouri River. Julesburg will be the only railroad town in Colorado Territory for two years. (Note: The Julesburg of 1867 was five miles west of present Julesburg).
26. Corporal D. Turner and a detachment of the 38th Infantry kill five Indians near Wilson's Creek, Kansas.
- Lieutenant S. M. Robbins and a detachment of the 7th Cavalry engage Indians on the south fork of the Republican River in Kansas, killing five. Two soldiers are reported wounded.
- Captain Albert Barnitz of the 7th Cavalry reports six soldiers killed and six wounded in a fight with Indians near Fort Wallace, Kansas.
27. The Bank of California opens in San Francisco.
30. Fort Shaw is established in Montana Territory.
- Captain W. P. McCleery and the 18th Infantry battle Indians near Fort Phil Kearny.

JULY

1. Thomas F. Meagher, Montana's territorial secretary, drowns after falling from a steamboat at Fort Benton.

- The Northern Overland Pony Express begins operation. Serving about 500 miles of Montana and 450 miles of Dakota Territory, it promises 14-day delivery.
3. Civilian contractor J. R. Porter arrives at Fort Phil Kearny to provide a supply of wood for the coming winter. Porter's wagon contains a healthy arsenal, specifically, 700 new breech-loading Springfield rifles and 100,000 rounds of ammunition.
- The 3rd Infantry, on escort duty from Fort Wallace, Kansas, reports one soldier wounded by Indians near Goose Creek, Colorado.
4. Following last month's disastrous flood, Fort Hays, Kansas, is relocated to the south of what will soon become Hays City.
5. Lieutenant Colonel George Crook leads two companies of the 1st Cavalry against Indians on Dunder and Blitzen Creek, Oregon, killing five and capturing three.
7. The 8th Cavalry reports one soldier wounded in action against Indians at Arizona's Beale's Springs.
8. Captain E. M. Baker and the 1st Cavalry kill two Indians and capture 14 near the Malheur River in Oregon.
- The 8th Cavalry clashes with Indians near Truxton's Springs, Arizona. The army reports one officer and one enlisted man killed, and three Indians dead.
- Two detachments of the 3rd Cavalry battle Indians near Fort Sumner, New Mexico. Five soldiers are killed and four are wounded.
10. The weapons brought to Fort Phil Kearny on July 3 are issued to soldiers.
12. The first town lot in what will become Cheyenne, Wyoming, is sold for $150 by James Whitehead, the realtor for the Union Pacific Railroad. The first residents, six men and two women, will arrive soon.
13. Lieutenant G. A. Goodale and the 23rd Infantry report five Indians killed and two captured on Oregon's Malheur River. One enlisted man is reported killed.
15. The Merchant's Exchange opens in San Francisco.
- George A. Custer leaves his command without permission in order to search for his wife among the forts of Kansas.
18. Margaret Tobin, the "Unsinkable Molly Brown" who will "refuse" to go down with the *Titanic* in 1912, is born in Hannibal, Missouri.
19. Construction of Fort Fetterman is begun near the North Platte River in present Wyoming.
- Captain E. M. Baker and the 1st Cavalry report two Indians killed and eight captured in a fight in Oregon's Malheur River country.

- "Vast quantities" of grasshoppers are reported in Utah.
20. President Andrew Johnson signs an act establishing peace with certain hostile Indians.
21. The town of Cheyenne is established in Dakota Territory; it is laid out by General Grenville Dodge of the Union Pacific Railroad.
- One Indian is reported killed in a fight with the 6th Cavalry at Buffalo Springs, Texas.
- The San Francisco City Gardens open.
22. The Kidder Massacre takes place.
25. Construction is completed on Cheyenne's first house.
27. Lieutenant Colonel George Crook and three detachments of the 1st Cavalry engage Indians between Forts C. F. Smith in Montana and Harney in Oregon. Forty-six Indians are reported "killed and wounded."
28. Lieutenant Colonel George A. Custer is arrested. His pending court-martial will be for desertion, for overmarching his troops, and for cruel treatment of deserters.
- Captain Albert Barnitz writes in a letter about the state of affairs at Fort Wallace, Kansas: "We are becoming very fashionable out here! We are having the cholera just like other people, and are beginning to feel quite as important as city folks! Only think, seven dead men in an evening."
29. The 8th Cavalry fights Indians near Willows, Arizona.

Also in July 1867:

A two-month plague of grasshoppers begins in Colorado.

After covering General Winfield Hancock's actions against the Kiowas and Comanches, the journalist

Henry M. Stanley writes: "They [the Indians] move us by their pathos and mournful dignity. But half a continent could not be kept as a buffalo pasture and hunting ground."

AUGUST

1. The Hayfield Fight takes place in Montana Territory.
- Montana's *Helena Daily Herald* begins publication.
2. The Wagon Box Fight occurs.
- The 10th Cavalry under Captain G. A. Armes engages Indians on the Saline River in Kansas; Armes is wounded and one soldier is killed.
4. The destruction of Fort Union, Dakota Territory, begins as the steamship *Miner*'s crew destroys the kitchen for fuel. The post was originally established in 1828 by the American Fur Company.
8. A Mr. Cave of the British Parliament visits the camp of the Oglala chief Big Mouth near Julesburg, Colorado. As a gift, the chief offers Cave a new bride, his 17-year-old daughter, but Cave politely declines and assures the chief he wishes to remain monogamous.
- General Alfred Terry reports one citizen wounded in a 31st Infantry engagement with Indians near Fort Stevenson, Dakota Territory.
12. Denver newspapers advertise that town lots in Cheyenne, Dakota Territory, are now being sold by the Union Pacific Railroad.
13 Captain H. B. Freeman reports three enlisted men

THE KIDDER MASSACRE
JULY 22, 1867

A major fight developed at Beaver Creek, Kansas, between a detachment of 10 soldiers of the 2nd Cavalry under the command of Lieutenant Lyman S. Kidder. Kidder's group was transporting an important dispatch to the 7th Cavalry. Pawnee Killer led 300 Sioux against Kidder's group and killed all its members, including their Indian guide, the Sioux Red Bead. Their mutilated bodies were discovered by George A. Custer and his men.

THE HAYFIELD FIGHT
AUGUST 1, 1867

Some 500 Cheyennes, led by Dull Knife and Two Moon, attacked Second Lieutenant Sigismund Sternberg, 30 soldiers, and civilians in a Montana Territory hayfield. The Sternberg party, armed with new repeating rifles, took shelter inside a makeshift corral about two miles from Fort C. F. Smith. One warrior made it into the log structure and was killed. Stymied by the rifles, the attackers set fire to the tall grass around the corral. The fire closed in but was then extinguished by the wind. The Cheyennes retired, having suffered 20 warriors dead and some 30 with serious wounds. Although the fight was seen from the fort, no help was given. Four in Sternberg's group were killed, including Sternberg.

THE WAGON BOX FIGHT
AUGUST 2, 1867

Red Cloud and Crazy Horse led 1,000 Sioux against Major J. W. Powell's 32 infantrymen guarding woodcutters near Fort Phil Kearny in present Wyoming. Some 3,000 other Indians, mostly women and children, lined the horizon to watch the show. Powell and his men had circled 15 wagons into a minifortress from which they repulsed three charges.

The breech-loading .50 caliber Allin-Springfield rifles that Powell's men had were a distinct advantage over the muzzle-loaders that Red Cloud initially believed the soldiers possessed. About 500 mounted warriors launched the first charge and met the new technology head-on. "Instead of drawing ramrods and losing precious time," Sergeant Sam Gibson would recall, "we simply threw open the breech-blocks of our new rifles to eject the empty shell and slapped in fresh ones." Red Cloud's nephew next led a foot charge by 700 warriors clad only in warpaint; he died in the first volley.

The battle then erupted into hundreds of simultaneous incidents over three hours. Archers arced their arrows to come down almost vertically inside the corral, giving the battle scene the appearance of a giant wooden porcupine. Fire arrows zipped through the air, igniting dung heaps. The Indians at last fell back into the hills at about 1:00 P.M. when the fort's howitzer was heard in the distance and Major Benjamin F. Smith approached with a relief column of 100 soldiers.

Powell lost only seven men; another three were wounded. Red Cloud and his chief warriors—Crazy Horse, American Horse, and Crow King—amassed 200 dead, although other estimates ranged from as low as 60 to as high as 1,137. Official army estimates counted 60 Indians killed and 120 wounded. Red Cloud will say that he lost the "flower of his fighting youth" that day.

wounded in a fight between the 27th Infantry and Indians at O'Connor's Springs, Dakota.
14. Indians kill a member of the 27th Infantry at Chalk Springs, Dakota.

- Lieutenant F. F. Whitehead and the 18th Infantry engage Indians near Fort Reno, Dakota Territory.
16. Two citizens are reported killed by Indians near Fort Reno, Dakota.
17. Pawnee scouts under Captain James Murie kill 15 Indians and capture two near Plum Creek, Nebraska.
20. Utah inventor Anson Mills patents the army cartridge belt.
12. Captain G. A. Armes leads a company of the 10th Cavalry and a detachment of the Kansas Infantry against Indians at Prairie Dog Creek, Kansas. The army reports eight soldiers killed and 35 wounded, and 150 Indians dead.
22. Two members of the 4th Cavalry are killed in an Indian attack near Fort Chadbourne, Texas.
- Chief of Scouts Archie McIntish and his Boise Indian Scouts report two hostile Indians killed and seven wounded in a fight in California's Surprise Valley.
23. Several soldiers of the 4th Cavalry are killed by Indians near Fort Concho, Texas.
28. One soldier is wounded in an encounter with Indians near Camp Goodwin, Arizona.
30. Lieutenant Gustavus Schreyer reports two members of the 6th Cavalry killed by Indians near Fort Belknap, Texas.

Also in August 1867:
Construction is completed on the great Tabernacle in Salt Lake City, Utah.
In Nevada, timber costs $60 per thousand board feet in Virginia City and $140 per thousand board feet in Belmont.
Long's Peak in Colorado is scaled for the first time.
The first white woman scales Oregon's Mount Hood.

SEPTEMBER 1867
4. Arizona's fourth territorial legislature convenes in Prescott.
5. The first rail shipment of cattle, 20 Kansas Pacific Railroad cars filled with Texas longhorns, leaves Abilene, Kansas, bound for the East Coast. Abilene will become a major terminal for cattle shipping, thanks to Chicago cattleman J. G. McCoy. Cattle are herded from Texas to Abilene along the Chisholm Trail, named after the half-breed Cherokee Jesse Chisholm.
6. Five Indians are captured and one is killed by the 1st Cavalry under Lieutenant J. F. Small near Silver River, Oregon.
8. The 1st Cavalry reports 23 Indians killed and 14 captured near Silver River, Oregon.

Jesse Chisholm (1805–1868). Of Scottish and Cherokee descent, he blazes the world's greatest cattle trail and will die broke. (Oklahoma Historical Society)

- The Army delivers the first triweekly mail from the East to Tucson.
9. Construction begins on the initial section of San Francisco's seawall.
10. General William Tecumseh Sherman arrives in Denver.
16. "Chinese Mary," the first Asian to be set on fire by whites, dies from her burns in Helena, Montana. She was set ablaze for her gold.
- Sergeant C. H. Davis reports a fight between the 10th Cavalry and Indians on the Saline River in Kansas. His report states: "Two citizens killed."
19. Lieutenant Mason Carter reports one soldier killed and three wounded in a fight between the 5th Infantry and Indians at Walker's Creek, Kansas. It is estimated that two Indians were killed.
- The *Cheyenne Daily Leader* becomes the first newspaper to publish in Cheyenne, Dakota Territory.
22. San Francisco's Trinity Church is consecrated.
23. John Avery Lomax, ballad hunter extraordinaire, is born in Goodman, Mississippi. The founder of the

Texas Folklore Society, he will "discover" such trail tunes as "Git Along, Little Dogies," "The Old Chisholm Trail," and "Home on the Range" and publish them for the first time in *Cowboy Songs and Frontier Ballads* (1910).
- Lieutenant Ephraim Williams is reported wounded by Indians in 5th Infantry action on the Arkansas River, 9 miles west of Cimarron Crossing in present Kansas.
25. Oliver Loving, the cattle industry pioneer and partner of Charles Goodnight, dies of gangrene at Fort Sumner, New Mexico. He had recently suffered wounds in a battle with Indians.
26–28. Lieutenant Colonel George Crook reports a fight between Indians and the 1st Cavalry, the 23rd Infantry, and the Boise Scouts at Infernal Caverns, near California's Pitt River. Casualties: one officer, six enlisted men, and one citizen killed, and 11 enlisted men wounded; 20 Indians killed, 12 wounded and two captured.
27. Wild Bill Hickok appears for the first time in a dime novel as "Wild Bill the Indian-Slayer" in *De Witt's Ten Cent Romances.*
- The *John L. Stephens,* the first ship to sail from California to Alaska, departs San Francisco.
28. In a letter to John Sherman, General William T. Sherman writes: "Whether right or wrong, those railroads will be built, and everybody knows that Congress, after granting the charts and fixing the routes, cannot back out and surrender."
29. Two members of the 37th Infantry are wounded by Indians at a camp near Fort Garland, Colorado.

Also in September 1867:

A peace commission composed of Generals William T. Sherman, Alfred Terry, William S. Harney, and four civilians takes a Union Pacific train from Omaha to North Platte, Nebraska, to meet with Sioux and Cheyenne leaders. Red Cloud is not present, but Spotted Tail, Standing Elk, Pawnee Killer, and Man Afraid of His Horses are there. The journalist Henry M. Stanley covers the event for St. Louis and New York newspapers. Says Sherman: "You must submit and do the best you can. If you continue fighting you will all be killed . . . live like white men, and we will help you all you want."

Following a freak accident in which he was nearly blinded, John Muir, 29, sets out from Louisville, Kentucky, on a journey through the cradle of the Civil War, with a vague idea of reaching the Gulf of Mexico before venturing on to the wilds of South America. The one highwayman who stops him returns Muir's gear: comb, brush, towel, soap, a New Testament, Milton's *Paradise Lost,* underwear, and a notebook inscribed "John Muir, Earth-planet, Universe."

The court-martial of George A. Custer begins at Fort Leavenworth, Kansas. The charges against him are numerous: being absent without leave from his command, using troopers as an escort while on unauthorized personal affairs, abandoning two men on the march, failing to recover two bodies, sending a party to find deserters and shoot them dead, and unjustifiable cruelty to three wounded troopers.

The Colorado Agricultural Society holds its first fair.

OCTOBER

1. Indians attack soldiers escorting the mail near Howard's Well, Texas. Two members of the 9th Cavalry are reported wounded.

6. Seven Indians are reported killed by the 8th Cavalry near Trout Creek, Arizona.

10. The 14th Infantry reports killing an Indian near Camp Lincoln, Arizona.

■ The outlaw Cullen Baker holds up a government supply wagon in Cass County, Texas. The driver is killed.

■ The *Pacific Hygienist* begins publication in San Francisco.

17. Sergeant W. A. F. Ahrberg reports three Indians killed and one captured by detachments of the 6th Cavalry near Deep Creek, Texas.

■ City lots in Cheyenne sell for $400 to $1,200.

18. Captain F. H. Wilson reports "25 or 30 Indians killed or wounded" by the 3rd Cavalry at Sierra Diablo, New Mexico.

19. The *Cheyenne Daily Leader* reports that the city's 125 school-age children are in need of a school.

20. One Indian is reported killed by troops at Crazy Woman's Fork, Dakota Territory.

21. The Medicine Lodge Talks take place in Kansas.

25. Lieutenant A. B. Wells reports that his 8th Cavalry killed an Indian at Truxell Springs, Arizona.

26. Captain J. P. Baker reports Indian action near Camp Winfield Scott, Nevada; three Indians were killed and four were captured.

■ Sensing a need for a toll bridge to connect Denver with the new rail city of Cheyenne, the Denver-Cheyenne Platte Bridge Company is incorporated.

28. U.S. commissioners sign treaties with Cheyenne and Arapaho representatives at Medicine Lodge, Kansas. These treaties call for relocating the tribes to land between the Cimarron and Arkansas Rivers in Indian Territory.

TALKS AT MEDICINE LODGE
OCTOBER 21, 1867

U.S. Commissioners Nathaniel G. Taylor, William S. Harney, C. C. Augur, Alfred H. Terry, John B. Sanborn, Samuel F. Tappan, and John B. Henderson signed a treaty with the leaders of some 7,000 Kiowas, Comanches, and Kiowa-Apaches, including Satanta, Black Kettle, and Stumbling Bear, at the Medicine Lodge Creek council camp in Kansas. The Comanches and Kiowas received some 3 million acres in western Indian Territory between the Washita and Red Rivers. Quanah Parker, who refused the terms of the treaty, said: "Tell the white chiefs that the Quohadas are warriors and will surrender when the bluecoats come and whip us."

---

31. Dakota Territory's first museum opens in Cheyenne.

Also in October 1867:

William F. Cody obtains a contract from the Union Pacific Railroad to begin supplying its workers with buffalo meat. He is directed to kill a dozen buffalo a day along the Kansas Pacific route for a payment of $500 a month. In eight months, Cody will kill more than 4,000 buffalo.

National Headlines/October 1867:

18. ALASKA TRANSFERRED TO U.S.

NOVEMBER

1. Tucson becomes the second capital of Arizona Territory, a distinction it will hold for a decade.

■ Building westward from Kansas City, Missouri, the Kansas Pacific Railroad reaches Ellis, Kansas.

3. Lieutenant Patrick Hasson reports that his 1st Cavalry detachment killed 32 Indians at Willow Grove, Arizona.

4. Ninety kegs of gunpowder are set off on San Francisco's Telegraph Hill to open a section of seawall.

■ Montana Governor Smith estimates that 99 percent of federal taxes are being collected in his territory, far ahead of the 30 percent of territorial taxes he is collecting.

■ The army reports that Lieutenant E. R. P. Shurly was wounded and one enlisted man was killed in Indian action at Goose Creek, Dakota.

5. Captain E. W. Kingsbury defeats Wild Bill Hickok in the election for sheriff in Ellsworth County, Kansas.

■ Indians ambush Lieutenant J. C. Carroll of the 32nd Infantry "and one citizen" near Camp Bowie, Arizona. Carroll is killed, his partner is wounded.

7. Lieutenant Patrick Hasson and cavalrymen report a fight with Indians near Willows, Arizona. Six soldiers are wounded; 19 Indians are killed and 17 are captured.

11. Attorney Jacob Downing sues John M. Chivington of Sand Creek fame for $3,055 in legal fees for services rendered from February 9 to May 27, 1865.

12. A Fort Laramie conference begins to discuss "Indian problems" as well as negotiations with the Sioux.

13. The Union Pacific's rails reach Cheyenne, whose population has increased from eight to more than 4,000 in four months. Some 200 businesses are already established in the town.

■ Lieutenant O. I. Converse is reported wounded in an Indian attack near Aqua Frio Springs, Arizona.

14. Cheyenne holds a major celebration in honor of the arrival of the Union Pacific's tracks.

14–14. Indian scouts report a fight at Tonto Creek, Arizona, in which four Indians are killed and nine are wounded.

15. Cheyenne residents welcome the first train to enter their town.

17. Thirty-two Denver civic leaders, including General Bela Hughes and David Moffat, file papers to create the Denver Pacific Railway, whose purpose will be to construct track from Denver to Cheyenne. General F. M. Chase begins the first survey for the new railroad.

■ The 37th Infantry and Indians clash near Fort Sumner, New Mexico.

20. Lieutenant Oscar Elting reports two Indians killed near Fort Selden, New Mexico.

21. It was a lousy wedding day for Carry Amelia Moore, 21. The groom, a very drunk Dr. Gloyd, arrives an hour late for the Missouri ceremony. His drinking problem will worsen, and Carry will leave him after a year and a half and one baby. Her wedding will become just one of the early bad experiences with booze for the future Carry Nation.

■ The *Deseret Evening News* begins publication in Salt Lake City.

22. Captain D. S. Gordon of the 2nd Cavalry reports one Indian killed and three wounded at De Schmidt Lake, Dakota Territory.

25. The court-martial of Lieutenant Colonel George A. Custer ends at Fort Leavenworth, Kansas.

CUSTER'S COURT-MARTIL
NOVEMBER 25, 1867

Lieutenant Colonel George A. Custer was found guilty on eight counts, including being absent without leave from his command and ordering deserters to be shot without trial. Particularly damning was Captain Frederick Benteen's testimony:

> It was like a buffalo hunt. The dismounted deserters were shot down, while begging for their lives, by General Custer's executioners: Major Elliot, Lieutenant Tom Custer, and the executioner-in-chief, Lieutenant Cooke. . . . Three of the deserters were brought in badly wounded, and screaming in extreme agony. General Custer rode up to them, pistol in hand, and told them if they didn't stop making so much fuss he would shoot them to death.

Custer's sentence was "to be suspended from rank & Command for one (1) year, and to forfeit his pay proper for the same time."

---

26. William F. Cody is in town, according to the *Leavenworth Daily Conservative,* which reports the group as "Capt. Graham . . . Buffalo Bill and other scouts." (Cody will tell the artist R. Farrington Elwell years later that Graham's group was the first to call him by his famous nickname). In the same article, the paper notes that "Buffalo Bill, with fifteen or twenty citizens volunteered to go out and look for" a Judge Corwin, who has strayed from an Ohio hunting party. Corwin will be found about five miles from Fort Hays, exhausted but otherwise in good condition.

29. A dispatch from Fort Phil Kearny reports four Indians killed by soldiers at Shell Creek, Dakota.

Also in November 1867:

Two months into his nature walk, John Muir comes down with malaria at Cedar Key, Florida. He decides the dry air of the West is what he needs. He travels by ship to Cuba, then to Panama, crosses the isthmus, and sails for San Francisco.

DECEMBER

2. Sergeant G. Gillaspy reports one soldier killed and three wounded, as well as "43 citizens wounded," in Indian action at Crazy Woman's Creek, Dakota.

4. The Grangers, the Patrons of Husbandry, is founded

---

in Washington, D.C.; the group seeks to control railroad rates.

5. Democrat Henry H. Haight becomes California's governor.

9. The capital of Colorado Territory is relocated from Golden to Denver.

12. Interpreter D. C. Pickett reports that he and Indian Scouts killed seven Indians on Oregon's Owyhee River.

14. Two woodcutters are killed by Indians in an attack near Fort Phil Kearny.

18. The Kansas Pacific's rails reach Coyote (later called Collyer), Kansas.

23. A treaty with Senecas, Shawnees, Quapaws, and other tribes guarantees their removal from Kansas to Indian Territory.

26. Captain W. T. Frohock reports that his detachment of the 9th Cavalry engaged Indians near Fort Lancaster, Texas. Three soldiers and 20 Indians are dead.

27. The Virginia City Masonic Temple is dedicated in Nevada.

30. There are 523 miles of railway in Kansas.

31. Silver production at the Comstock mining area in 1867 is valued at $16 million.

■ Wells Fargo's net operating income for 1867 is $199,362.86.

Also in December 1867:
The California Steam Navigation Company announces that dividends totalling $162,500 were paid in 1867.

Also in 1867:
This is the peak year for steamboat traffic on the upper Missouri: 71 ships ply the waters during the heavy season; a record 37 go all the way to Fort Benton.

Bret Harte publishes his second book, *The Lost Galleon and Other Tales.*

George Ward Nichols, writing about Wild Bill Hickok for *Harper's New Monthly Magazine,* paints a vivid picture of pioneer life in Springfield, Missouri. Nichols describes the people as "strange, half-civilized," with "men and women dressed in queer costumes; men with coats and trousers made of skin."

Alexander Cameron becomes Colorado's 4th territorial governor, a position he will hold until 1869.

Barnard Taylor publishes *Colorado: A Summer Trip.*

The Cherokee National Council passes a law requiring cattlemen to pay 10 cents a head for cattle passing over Indian lands. Other tribes follow suit.

Gaslights and iron water mains are installed in Los Angeles.

Gold is discovered in the Moreno district of New Mexico's Colfax County.

The Irish novelist Mayne Reid, a Mexican War veteran living in England, publishes his most popular work, *The Headless Horseman,* about a Texas legend.

There are 220,000 head of cattle in Arizona, with a net worth of $3.5 million.

The Union Pacific Railroad lays 240 miles of track.

1868

"As brave men and as the soldiers of a government which has exhausted its peace efforts, we, in the performance of a most unpleasant duty, accept the war begun by our enemies, and hereby resolve to make its end final. If it results in the utter annihilation of these Indians it is but the result of what they have been warned again and again, and for which they seem fully prepared."

—William Tecumseh Sherman

JANUARY

1. Work begins on the Colorado Central and Pacific Railroad.

3. Ground-breaking ceremonies for the Colorado Central and the Pacific Railroad attract 250 to Golden City, Colorado.

4. Interpreter D. C. Pickett reports that he and Indian Scouts killed one Indian and captured 15 on Oregon's Owyhee River.

6. The first school building in present Wyoming is dedicated in Cheyenne.

11. The *Leavenworth Daily Conservative* reports: "Bill Cody and [his horse] Brigham started on a hunt Saturday afternoon and came in Tuesday. The result was nineteen buffalo totalling 4,000 pounds of meat, which he sold for .07 a pound, making $100 a day for his labor."

14. Captain S. B. M. Young and the 8th Cavalry report a fight with Indians at Difficult Canyon, Arizona. Casualties: 16 Indians killed, six wounded; two soldiers wounded.

■ Troops under Lieutenant J. D. Stevenson report five Indians slain near Beale Springs, Arizona.

18. The New Idea Theater opens in San Francisco.

27. The Chinese Theater opens in San Francisco.

29. The names of Great Salt Lake County and Great Salt Lake City are changed to Salt Lake County and Salt Lake City.

30. Grant County is established in New Mexico.

Also in January 1868:

George A. Custer receives a telegram from General Philip Sheridan, informing him that he will be reinstated before his year's suspension is completed and that he will be given command of a regiment around October 1, with the mission of moving against Indians in Indian Territory.

FEBRUARY

1. James Parks goes to work as a bridge carpenter for the Union Pacific Railroad. He will ascend to become the railroad's supervisor of bridges and buildings in Colorado in 1871, a position he will hold for 32 years.

10. The editor William Allen White the "Sage of Emporia" is born in Emporia, Kansas. White will buy the *Emporia Gazette* in 1895 and win the Pulitzer Prize for his editorial "To an Anxious Friend" (1922) and a posthumous Pulitzer for *The Autobiography of William A. White* (1946).

■ The German Savings and Loan is incorporated in San Francisco.

11. The Union Pacific completes the laying of tracks to Coyote (present Collyer), Kansas.

13. The cornerstone of the Alhambra Theater is laid in San Francisco.

26. The Chicago and Northwestern Railroad sends 1,600 carloads of iron to the Union Pacific's construction crews.

Also in February 1868:

The U.S. government reports that the Kansa Indians are "completely out of blankets and food . . . have disposed of all saleable property and have exhausted their credit."

National Headlines/February 1868:

24. PRESIDENT JOHNSON IMPEACHED BY HOUSE

MARCH

2. Forts Phil Kearny, Reno, and C. F. Smith are ordered abandoned by President Andrew Johnson as part of the agreement with Red Cloud for ceasing hostilities. Under the treaty's terms, no whites will be "permitted to settle upon or occupy any portion of the territory, or without the consent of the Indians to pass through the same." Negotiations are set for April at Fort Laramie.
4. Jesse Chisholm, whose name is immortalized on the most famous of the Western cattle trails, dies penniless in Oklahoma of food poisoning. A monument, placed on Chisholm's grave in 1939 reads:

JESSE CHISHOLM
Born 1805
Died March 4, 1868
No One Left His Home
Cold or Hungry

4. The *Omaha Herald* reports that at least five trains a day are arriving from Chicago loaded with iron, and that a square mile of the Union Pacific's grounds is covered with the shipments.
5. Major W. F. Johnson, the president of the Denver Pacific Railway, dies. He will be succeeded by John Evans.
6. Sergeant C. Gale reports 13 settlers killed and one child captured by Indians at the headwaters of the Colorado River in Texas.
■ Captain A. R. Chaffee reports seven Indians killed by cavalrymen at Paint Creek, Texas.
12. The Northern Overland Pony Express suspends operations and declares bankruptcy.
14. Troops under Lieutenant Colonel George Crook engage Indians at Dunder and Blitzen Creek, Oregon; they report 12 Indians killed and two captured.
18. The 18th Infantry reports one enlisted man killed in an Indian attack on a sawmill near Fort Fetterman, Dakota Territory.
19. Crazy Horse attacks the Horsecreek Station, Dakota.
20. A dispatch from Fort Fetterman reports three citizens killed by Indians at Horsecreek Station and Twin Springs Ranches, Dakota.
■ Vigilantes in Cheyenne hang two alleged criminals.
21. Jesse and Frank James, Jim and Cole Younger, and four accomplices rob the Southern Bank of Kentucky in Russellville. Jesse shoots and wounds the bank's president, Nimrod Long, as the gang gallops away with $14,000.
■ Corporal D. Troy reports that two enlisted men in an escort were killed by Indians near Camp Willow Grove, Arizona.
23. The Unites States government grants a yearly subsidy to Wells Fargo for a daily mail service to California.
■ The University of California at Berkeley is chartered.
24. The survey for a Denver Pacific Railway line from Denver to Cheyenne is completed by General Case.
25. Captain Guido Ilges reports one Indian killed and two wounded by the 14th Infantry near Cottonwood Springs, Arizona.
28. Wild Bill Hickok and Buffalo Bill supervise prisoners being relocated from Fort Hays to Topeka, Kansas.
31. The steamer *China* docks in San Francisco Bay; on board is the staff of the Chinese Embassy.

Also in March 1868:

Phoebe Ann Moses (Annie Oakley), age 8, shoots her first squirrel. "It was a wonderful shot," she will recall years later, "going right through the head from side to side. My mother was so frightened when she learned that I had taken down the loaded gun and shot it that I was forbidden to touch it again for eight months."

The first smelter in Blackhawk, Colorado, is constructed by Nathaniel Hill.

APRIL

2. The Topeka *Weekly Leader* reports: "BAND OF ROAD MEN CAPTURED—W. F. Cody, government detective, and 'Wm. Haycock'—Wild Bill Hickok—deputy U.S. Marshal, brought eleven prisoners and lodged them in our calaboose on Monday last."
3. A woodchopping party near Rock Creek, Wyoming, is attacked by Indians. One woodcutter is reported killed.
■ The horse known as Comanche, a survivor of the Battle of the Little Bighorn in 1876, is purchased for the military by an army quartermaster from a civilian horse trader in St. Louis.
5. Captain David Perry commands cavalrymen, infan-

trymen, and Indian scouts in a battle against Indians at Malheur River, Oregon: 32 Indians are reported killed and two are taken captive.

7. Brigham Young, 67, marries Anna Eliza Webb, 23, his 51st bride.

11. In Dakota Territory, word arrives at Fort Berthold that the Hunkpapa Sioux under Sitting Bull have joined in an alliance with the Miniconjoux and Blackfeet.

17. At Nexmith's Mills near Tularosa, New Mexico, Sergeant Glass and a detachment of cavalrymen and citizens kill 10 Indians and wound 25.

■ Captain G. K. Brady reports that the 23rd Infantry killed five Indians and captured three near Camp Three Forks, Idaho.

18. The Society for the Prevention of Cruelty to Animals (SPCA) is founded in San Francisco.

22. Indians attack cowboys and a herd of cattle near Fort McPherson, Nebraska, killing six citizens.

26. Josefa Jaramillo Carson dies 10 days after giving birth to her last child by her husband, Kit Carson.

27. The Denver Pacific Railway buys 40,000 railroad ties for a dollar apiece to construct its first 20 miles of track.

■ Union Pacific tracks reach Oakley, Kansas; the railroad has laid 376 miles of track.

28. The Chinese Embassy is honored at a grand banquet given by San Francisco merchants.

■ Negotiations begin at Fort Laramie to end "Red Cloud's War." Commissioners had sent Red Cloud a peace offering of tobacco and asked him to come to Laramie to negotiate in the spring. Red Cloud thanked them for the gift and said he would talk peace upon the departure of the soldiers from the Powder River region. General William Tecumseh Sherman arrives at the conference with orders from Washington to abandon the posts that had been established in the region, in return for the cessation of Indian raids. With this visit, Sherman receives only the signatures of minor chiefs.

Also in April 1868:

John Muir arrives in San Francisco and asks directions to "any place that is wild." Traveling through the April flowers in Central Valley, California, he makes his way toward the "range of light." In the Yosemite Valley, he writes: "it seems to be not clothed with light, but wholly composed of it, like the wall of some celestial city." His writings will soon attract national attention when they are published in the *New York Tribune*.

MAY

1. The Denver Pacific Railway's president, John Evans, is called to Washington, D.C. His post is taken by General John Pierce.

■ Captain E. G. Fechet reports six Indians killed and four captured in action with the 8th Cavalry near Camp Grant on the Gila River in Arizona.

4. In Arizona, Yavapai County supervisors establish a new election precinct called Phoenix.

6. The first annuities are paid by the U.S. government to the Crow Indians in Montana.

9. The Central Pacific Railroad holds a public auction for real estate at Lake's Crossing, Nevada; 200 lots are sold in the city, which will boom as a result of the railroad passing through it. The city is renamed Reno for General Jesse Lee Reno.

10. The horse Comanche, purchased by the army last month in St. Louis, arrives at Fort Leavenworth and receives a "US" brand. Shortly thereafter, the horse will be purchased from the government for $90 by Captain Myles W. Keogh, who is in need of a second mount.

16. Realizing that the transcontinental railroad is being built, Wells Fargo's directors authorize the selling of all of the company's stagecoach lines as long as their express shipping privileges are retained by the company.

17. Camp Cooke, on Montana's Judith River, is attacked by some 2,500 Sioux.

18. Ground-breaking ceremonies for the Denver Pacific Railway are held just northeast of Denver, with Governor William Gilpin addressing a crowd of 1,000. The Denver band strikes up "The Railroad Gallop," volunteers rush for the tools, and by sunset a mile of track has been laid.

■ Fort Morgan in Colorado is abandoned; its soldiers are sent to Dakota's Fort Laramie.

■ Lieutenant Robert Carrick reports that the 8th Cavalry killed six Indians at Rio Salinas, Arizona.

19. Brigham Young agrees to allow Mormons to work on the construction of Union Pacific Railroad.

21. The Kansas Pacific Railroad's rails reach Sheridan, Kansas; that town, 405 miles west of Kansas City and 235 miles east of Denver, will remain the railroad's terminus until October 1869.

22. The Alhambra Theater opens in San Francisco.

23. Kit Carson, 59, dies at Fort Lyon, Colorado. Under Dr. H. R. Tilton's care for a thoracic aneurysm, Carson underwent chloroform treatments in his final days. In a letter written years later, Tilton said: "I explained to him the probable mode of termination of his disease, that he might die from

Bodies of women and children lie scattered in the aftermath of a surprise Indian attack on an Idaho village.
(Library of Congress)

suffocation or, more probably, the aneurysm would burst and cause death by hemorrhage. He expressed a decided preference for the latter mode." Today, Carson calls out, "Doctor, compadre, adios," and then dies as blood pours from his mouth.

27. U.S. Commissioner N. G. Taylor signs a treaty with Osage Indians at the Drum Creek agency in Kansas.
29. Sergeant H. Miller leads cavalrymen and Indian scouts against Indians near Idaho's Owyhee River; they report 34 Indians killed.

Also in May 1868:

William F. Cody, now known as Buffalo Bill, concludes his service supplying buffalo for the Union Pacific's Eastern Division workers when the line reaches Sheridan, Dakota. Cody's universally accepted estimate of the number of buffalo he killed is 4,280, although a more reasonable number would be around 2,928.

JUNE

1. U.S. and Navajo representatives sign a treaty creating Arizona's Navajo Indian Reservation. School facilities are guaranteed, along with mandatory education for residents 6 to 16 years of age. The Indians are promised clothing and other items for the next 10 years.
4. Cheyennes attack Kansa Indians in Kansas.
6–13. Lieutenant Deane Monahan of the 3rd Cavalry reports three Indians killed and 11 taken captive near Apache Springs, New Mexico.
8. General William T. Sherman orders the Navajos at Bosque Redondo in New Mexico back onto a reservation in their native country.
9. Corporal J. Moan of the 23rd Infantry reports three Indians killed in Idaho's Snake Canyon.
10. Red Cloud is still refusing to come to Fort Laramie to negotiate. His recently delivered message appears in the *Omaha Weekly Herald:* "We are on the mountains looking down on the soldiers and the forts. When we see the soldiers moving away and the forts abandoned, then I will come down and talk."
▪ In the past month, 100 houses have been built in Reno, Nevada.
13. The Union Pacific advertises in the *New York Tribune* it has completed 600 miles of track.
16. Sergeant Lemon reports that four members of the 1st Cavalry were killed in an Indian attack on a mail escort at Arizona's Toddy Mountain.
19. Wells Fargo signs a contract worth almost $1.4 million a year to operate mail service between Cheyenne and Virginia City, Nevada.
22. Arkansas is readmitted to the Union.
24. Captain J. J. Coppinger reports that the 23rd Infantry killed eight Indians and captured three near Battle Creek, Idaho.
25. Louisiana is readmitted to the Union. Also, under the terms of the Omnibus Bill passed today over President Andrew Johnson's veto, North Carolina, South Carolina, Louisiana, Georgia, Alabama, and Florida are granted representation in Congress. Texas is the only state without congressional representation.
26. Ben Thompson begins a two-year sentence at the Huntsville Penitentiary in Texas, having been found guilty of "intent to kill."

27. The first 46 miles of the Denver Pacific's rail line from Denver to the Platte River are graded.
30. The Union Pacific's "way and local business" for the fiscal year ending today totals more than $4 million.

Also in June 1868:

Catharine McCarty tells the compilers of the Indianapolis City Directory that she is the widow of Michael McCarty and resides at 199 North East Street with her two sons, Joseph and Henry, the latter being the future Billy the Kid.

National Headlines/June 1868:

1. FORMER PRESIDENT BUCHANAN DEAD AT 77
25. CONGRESS PROVIDES 8-HOUR WORKDAY

JULY

2. In a second agreement signed at Fort Bridger, the Washakies of the eastern Shoshone tribe agree to a reservation to be located on the Wind River northeast of South Pass.
11. Congress authorizes a geographical and geological survey of the Rocky Mountain Region to be conducted by John Wesley Powell.
21. Republican presidential candidate General Ulysses S. Grant, joined by General William T. Sherman and Philip Sheridan, arrives in Denver after a 170-mile stagecoach trip from Cheyenne Wells.
25. President Andrew Johnson signs the Organic Act, creating Wyoming Territory from portions of Dakota and Utah Territories.
■ Captain J. B. Sinclair reports that his 23rd Infantry captured 41 Indians on Idaho's Big Salmon River.
26. Action is reported between the 23rd Infantry and Indians at Idaho's Juniper Canyon; five Indians are killed and four are captured.
27. The *Cheyenne Daily Leader* is the only newspaper in Wyoming receiving telegraphic dispatches.
28. The door is open for unrestricted Chinese immigration under the terms of a treaty signed by William Seward, the secretary of state, and Anson Burlingame, the head of the U.S. diplomatic mission to China. It is believed that most of the new arrivals will be laborers for the western railroads.
29. Fort C. F. Smith, on the Bozeman Trail in southern Montana and established in 1866 by Colonel Henry B. Carrington, is abandoned in the wake of the Red Cloud War.
30. Red Cloud allows his celebrating warriors to burn the vacant Fort C. F. Smith to the ground.

Also in July 1868:

Sitting Bull refuses Father Pierre Jean De Smet's invitation to a peace conference at Fort Rice in present North Dakota. Instead, he sends Gall, a Sioux war chief, with the following message: "Move out the soldiers, and stop the steamboats and we shall have peace." From this comes the Treaty of 1868, guaranteeing the Sioux the land between the North Platte, the Missouri, and the Yellowstone Rivers.

Shorter A. M. E. in Denver becomes the first African Methodist Episcopal church founded in Colorado; it has a congregation of 28.

Laura Ingalls, age 1, migrates with her parents from Wisconsin to Missouri. She will grow up to be the author of the "Little House" series.

The proprietor of the Harnisch and Baer Ice Cream Parlour in San Antonio, Texas, claims to have made the world's first ice cream soda.

National Headlines/July 1868:

9. DEMOCRATS NOMINATE SEYMOUR AT NYC
28. 14TH AMENDMENT RATIFIED; NO VOTE FOR INDIANS

AUGUST

10. Cheyenne outrages are reported at Spillman Creek, Kansas.
12. Captain Fredrick W. Benteen of the 7th Cavalry reports that Indians killed 17 civilians at Solomon River, Kansas.
13. Captain Benteen reports that the 7th Cavalry killed three Indians and wounded 10 at Saline River, Kansas.
■ Final peace treaties are negotiated with the Nez Perce by the Indian Peace Commission.
14. Indian raids continue along the Republican and Saline Rivers in Kansas; 10 settlers are reported killed.
15. Madame Schiller stars in *The Pearl of Savoy* at the Ming Theatre in Helena, Montana.
18. In Arizona, Mary A. Gray is believed to be the first white woman to arrive in the valley just north of the Salt River.
20. The Union Pacific advertises in the *New York Tribune* that it has completed 750 miles of track. Some 20,000 men are now employed by the railroad, which predicts "It is now probable that the whole line to the Pacific will be completed in 1869."
■ Captain C. J. Dickey reports three members of the 31st Infantry killed in an Indian attack at Fort Buford, Dakota.

- Two civilians are killed at Comstock's Ranch in Kansas during an Indian raid.
23. Indians reportedly kill three members of the 31st Infantry in an attack near Fort Totten, Dakota. Another eight settlers are reported killed between Pond Creek, Kansas, and Lake Station, Colorado.
- Edgar Lee Masters, the future poet (*Spoon River Anthology*), is born in Garnett, Kansas.
24. General Philip Sheridan reports that Indians have killed 20 citizens of Kansas and wounded many more. He advocates the Indians' forcible removal to reservations.
27. The 38th Infantry reports three Indians killed in New Mexico's Hatchet Mountains.
28. Indians kill three settlers near Kiowa Station, Kansas.

Also in August 1868:
Bret Harte's "The Luck of Roaring Camp" is published in the San Francisco periodical *The Overland Monthly*. The story of an illegitimate baby being raised by earthy miners takes prudish readers by surprise. Harte will later write of his article: "Christians were cautioned against pollution by its contact; practical business men were gravely urged to condemn . . . this picture of California society that was not conducive to Eastern immigration."

The Santa Fe Company buys 338,766 acres of the Potawatomi Reservation for $1 an acre.

Fort Phil Kearny is abandoned. Red Cloud gives the honor of burning it to Little Wolf and his Cheyennes.

National Headlines/August 1868
11. THADDEUS STEVENS DIES AT 76

SEPTEMBER
1. Indians kill nine settlers near Spanish Fort, Texas.
- San Francisco's *Morning Chronicle* begins publication.
2. Indians attack a mail escort at Little Coon Creek, Kansas; three soldiers are wounded and three Indians are killed.
3. The army captures a Santee Sioux village at White Stone.
- Indians kill four settlers at Colorado City, Colorado.
6. Montana's first territorial fair is held in Helena.
6–7. A report to the secretary of war states that 25 citizens of Colorado Territory have been slain in recent attacks by Indians.
7. At Fort Hays, Kansas, General Philip Sheridan sends General Alfred Sully on a mission south of the Arkansas River to make war on the Cheyennes and the Arapahos. He tells Sully to kill any Indians he sees along the route of the Kansas Pacific Railroad.
8. A skirmish between seven Sioux warriors and members of the Gros Ventre, Ree, and Mandan tribes occurs near Fort Berthold, Dakota, when the Sioux fire shots from across a river. Members of what are also known as the Three Affiliated Tribes give chase and catch one Sioux warrior, whom they kill and scalp.
- Indians reportedly kill 17 settlers in a raid at Cimarron Crossing, Kansas.
- The grading of the first 20 miles of Denver Pacific track from Cheyenne begins.
10. Captain W. H. Penrose of the 7th Cavalry reports four Indians and two soldiers killed in action on the Rule Creek of Colorado's Purgatory River.
- Lieutenant Rufus Somerby reports that the 8th Cavalry killed four Indians and captured eight near the Lower Aqua Fria in Arizona.
11–15. General Alfred Sully, on the mission begun September 7 from Fort Hays, reports that his 7th Cavalry and 3rd Infantry engaged Comanches at Sand Hills in Indian Territory. Casualty reports list 22 Indians killed, 12 wounded, and three soldiers killed. Captain Myles Keogh's horse takes an arrow in the right hindquarter during a fight on the 13th, but doesn't complain. The wound isn't discovered until the men return to camp. Keogh names the horse "Comanche."
14. Lieutenant Patrick Cusack of the 9th Cavalry reports 25 Indians killed and another 25 captured at Horse Head Hills, Texas.
15. Indian action is reported on the Big Sandy Creek River in Colorado: Captain G. W. Graham states that the 10th Cavalry killed 11 Indians and captured 14.
17. The 7th Cavalry reports three Indians killed and five wounded on the Saline River in Kansas.
17–25. The Battle of Beecher's Island takes place.
19. A grading crew informs Denver Pacific Railroad engineers that it is ceasing operations until it is better protected from Indians.
25. Colonel L. H. Carpenter leads 70 black troopers in reinforcing Forsyth's volunteers on Beecher Island. The few remaining Indians around the island scatter when they hear the approaching bugle. Carpenter is equipped with a badly needed field ambulance.
- Arizona becomes a Roman Catholic diocese.

THE BATTLE OF BEECHER'S ISLAND
SEPTEMBER 17–25, 1868

This conflict is also known as the Battle of the Arikaree or "the fight when Roman Nose was killed." During the campaign against the Southern Plains Indians, 50 soldiers under Major George A. Forsyth and Lieutenant Frederick Beecher were attacked in eastern Colorado by some 500 Sioux and Cheyenne warriors.

The summer of 1868 had been long and hot. Western Indians, in a rage over the advancing railroads, had wiped out teams of railway workers. Raids on 40 homesteads had resulted in the deaths of 99 white settlers. Wives and children had been dragged away screaming.

Civil War General Philip H. Sheridan, commander of the Department of the Missouri, boomed, "I am here to clean up the savages!" Major George A. "Sandy" Forsyth, 30, was ordered to recruit "50 first-class hardy frontiersmen" to go lesson-teaching in Indian country. Lieutenant Fred Beecher of the 3rd Infantry, a nephew of the abolitionist clergyman Henry Ward Beecher, was named second-in-command. Thirty volunteers, many in their teens, signed up at Fort Harker, the rest at Fort Hays.

On August 30, 1868, Forsyth and his men marched toward Fort Wallace, near present Wallace, Kansas. They met no resistance and arrived on the evening of September 5. Five days later, a band of Cheyennes killed three teamsters and stole livestock in an attack near Sheridan, 13 miles to the east. Forsyth and his volunteers arrived on the scene in seven hours, only to find the tracks of 30 ponies leading north toward the Republican River. For two weeks he followed the Indian party, which, the trail showed, had become larger.

Late in the afternoon of September 16, Forsyth came to the Arikaree River in eastern Colorado, 17 miles southeast of present Wray. Rations were low and the men and horses were tired. At the bottom of a grassy valley, a sandbar 40 yards wide and 150 yards long rose from a nearly dry riverbed.

That night, while his men slept near the river, Forsyth was unable to rest. His worst fears had come true: his presence was well known to the Indians. For three days, a force of 4,000 Cheyennes, Arapahos, and Sioux, including 1,500 warriors, had been aware of his every move.

At dawn a group of young braves, trying to impress their elders, unintentionally saved the volunteers from being wiped out in their sleep. Whooping and shooting, the youths tried to stampede the troops' horses but only succeeded in doing so with a half dozen. Forsyth's men awoke to the battle cries of 600 attackers. "My God," gasped Chief Scout Sharp Grover, "look at the Indians!" Forsyth thought, "The ground seemed to grow them."

The men were ordered to the island, where they dug trenches in the sandy earth. Bullets and arrows came from three directions. By 9:00 A.M. every army horse and mule was dead; their bodies would provide a certain amount of cover, but now there was no means of escape.

At 9:30, an estimated 300 mounted warriors, riding 60 abreast in five ranks, tried to ride the volunteers down. At the last instant, Forsyth commanded his men to fire their Spencer seven-shot rifles. The repeating weapons broke the charge, as the Indians galloped around but not over the island. Indian women and children watched in horror from a nearby hill.

In the encounter, Forsyth was struck by bullets in both legs. When Roman Nose did a death waltz, the commanding officer could only marvel at his would-be conqueror, who, "save for a crimson silk sash knotted around his waist, and his moccasins on his feet, was perfectly naked." "He drew his body to its full height and shook his clenched fist defiantly at us," recalled Forsyth. "He . . . gave tongue to a war cry that I have never yet heard equaled."

Again the rifles broke a charge of hundreds. As the riders swept by on either side of the island, one scout stood up and blasted Roman Nose with a .52 caliber slug in the back at point-blank range. By day's end, Roman Nose was dead and the attackers had been driven back. Forsyth's men rejoiced in the late afternoon rain.

But the day had not been without toll. Lieutenant Beecher had been killed, as had army surgeon Dr. John Mooers, who was shot in the head while tending to Beecher. Forsyth had been shot again, grazed in the head. That night, Jack Stillwell and

(continued)

(continued)

Pierre Trudeau volunteered to try to make it to Fort Wallace, 85 miles to the southeast.

Action on the "island of death" lasted for eight days. The Indians still charged, though their organization deteriorated seriously after the death of Roman Nose. The volunteers' provisions ran out quickly—they were forced to eat horseflesh and wild plums for the better part of a week.

After a series of dramatic close calls, Stillwell and Trudeau made it back to Fort Wallace. A hundred black soldiers, Troop H of the 10th U.S. Cavalry, were sent to rescue Forsyth's command. They arrived on September 26. By then, most of the Indians had moved on, leaving behind a small force to try to starve out the defenders. The Indians quickly dispersed at the sound of the approaching bugle.

Ten men had died on the island and another 20 had been seriously wounded. Forsyth refused to have his infected leg amputated, but he eventually made a full recovery. Indian casualties were difficult to determine: Forsyth said 35 were killed, whereas another soldier counted at least 50; perhaps as many as 200 were wounded.

Technology was the true winner at the Battle of Beecher Island. With repeating rifles and Colt pistols, a small band of frontiersmen had beaten what a few years earlier would have been considered insurmountable odds. In one of the West's most hellish encounters, the conflict on the plains had taken on newer, deadlier dimensions.

OCTOBER

3. Two die in the wreck of the *D. M. Hall* near Coos Bay, Oregon.

5. William F. Cody, "Buffalo Bill," joins the 5th Cavalry as chief of scouts.

9. Major A. J. Alexander reports 13 Indians killed in a fight with cavalrymen, infantrymen, and scouts at Salt River and Cherry Creek in Arizona.

■ General Philip Sheridan from Fort Hays calls on the governor of Kansas to provide an Indian-fighting regiment.

■ Clara Blinn and her 2-year-old son are captured by Cheyennes and Arapahos on the Arkansas River below Fort Lyon in Colorado. She manages to send a plea for help that reads in part: "Whoever you may be, if you will only buy us from the Indians with ponies or any thing, and let me come and stay with you until I can get word to my friends, they will pay you well; and I will work for you also, and do all I can for you."

13. Four civilians are killed and one is wounded by Indians in the Solomon Valley of Kansas. Two women are carried away as captives.

15. General William Tecumseh Sherman writes to General Philip Sheridan: "I will say nothing and do nothing to restrain our troops from doing what they deem proper on the spot, and will allow no mere vague general charges of cruelty and inhumanity to tie their hands, but will use all the powers confided to me to the end that these Indians, the enemies of our race and of our civilization, shall not again be able to begin and carry on their barbarous warfare on any kind of a pretext that they may choose to allege."

18. Captain L. H. Carpenter reports 10 Indians killed in action with the 10th Cavalry at Beaver Creek, Kansas.

■ Vigilantes in Laramie, Wyoming, hang four persons and shoot two.

19. Lieutenant Rufus Somerby reports that the 8th Cavalry killed seven Indians on the Dragoon Fork of Arizona's Verde River.

■ Mrs. Bassett and an infant child are captured by Indians on the Solomon River in Kansas.

21. An earthquake jolts San Francisco; damage is estimated at $3 million.

25–26. Major E. A. Carr reports 30 Indians killed in action with the 5th Cavalry between Beaver and Prairie Dog Creeks in Kansas.

30. Work begins on the Atchison, Topeka, and Santa Fe Railroad in Topeka, Kansas.

Also in October 1868:

The *San Diego Union* begins publication.

A strange story is told about the future artist Charles M. Russell, age 4, of Missouri. Lost for a short period of time, Charles is found following a man with a trained bear by his frantic family. That night, little Charley scrapes the mud from his boots and fashions it into a shape that uncannily resembles the bear.

National Headlines/October 1868:

1. *NY TIMES* APOLOGIZES TO READERS FOR INCREASING FROM 8 TO 12 PAGES TO ACCOMMODATE ADVERTISING

NOVEMBER

3. Arizona's first U.S. land office opens in Phoenix.

6. The "Red Cloud War" officially ends.

7–15. Major W. R. Price reports 11 Indians killed, two wounded, and 20 captured by the 8th Cavalry near Willow Grove, Arizona.

10. Arizona's fifth territorial legislature convenes in Prescott.

11. Lieutenant A. B. Wells reports 15 Indians killed and 40 captured by the 8th Cavalry near Squaw Peak, Arizona.

13. Telegraph poles to be installed between Denver and Cheyenne begin arriving in Denver. It should take 10 days to construct the telegraph line.

20. Fort Omaha is established in Nebraska.

23. Lieutenant Colonel George A. Custer leads the 7th Cavalry from Camp Supply, in present Oklahoma, toward Black Kettle's Cheyenne encampment on the Washita River in Indian Territory as part of Major General Philip Sheridan's plan to snap the Indians' pattern of war in summer and peace in winter, and to herd them onto a reservation near Fort Cobb. Custer's offensive is in response to two months of Indian raiding throughout Kansas and Texas: 147 settlers have been killed and 57 wounded, 14 women have been raped, 426 women and children have been taken captive, 24 ranches have been burned, and 11 stagecoaches have been attacked.

24. Composer Scott Joplin, the creator of ragtime music, is born in Texarkana, Texas. He will be best known for his "Maple Leaf Rag" and the opera *Tremonisha*.

25. William Ellsworth "Elzy" Lay, a member of Butch Cassidy's Wild Bunch, is born in McArthur, Ohio.

26. San Francisco's first baseball game is played on an enclosed field.

27. The Battle on the Washita takes place in Indian Territory. Captain Lewis [Louis] M. Hamilton, 24, the grandson of Alexander Hamilton, is killed in the battle. George A. Custer will acquire many nicknames; after today, the Cheyennes will call him "Squaw Killer."

29. After receiving Custer's scouts, General Philip Sheridan sends this dispatch to Custer: "The Battle of the Washita River is the most complete & successful of all our private battles and was fought in such unfavorable weather & circumstances as to reflect the highest credit on Yourself & Regt."

PEACE AT FORT LARAMIE
NOVEMBER 6, 1868

Red Cloud and his entourage of warriors made a grand entrance to Fort Laramie to sign the peace that ended the "Red Cloud War." He had refused to negotiate at the original meetings that began April 29, 1868, until soldiers had left the Powder River region, and Forts C. F. Smith, Phil Kearny, and Reno had been vacated. That having been accomplished, he signed the agreement that stated: "From this day forward all war between the parties to this agreement shall forever cease. The government of the United States desires peace, and its honor is hereby pledged to keep it. The Indians desire peace, and they now pledge their honor to maintain it." Representing the United States at the signing was General William Tecumseh Sherman.

THE BATTLE ON THE WASHITA
NOVEMBER 27, 1868

Lieutenant Colonel George A. Custer and an 800-man force from the 7th Cavalry launched a four-pronged attack against Black Kettle's Cheyenne village on the north bank of the Washita River in Indian Territory (about 14 miles northwest of present Cheyenne, Oklahoma). The Indians were camped on reservation grounds and had been guaranteed safety by the commander of Fort Cobb. This mattered little to Custer, who ordered the dogs of the 7th Cavalry killed the night before to keep his campsite quiet. The assault began in a dawn snowstorm, lasted until 10:00 A.M., and was played out to the strains of a bugler blowing "Garryowen." Black Kettle, 67, was killed, along with his wife and 101 other men, women, and children. Some 53 women and children were taken prisoner. Custer ordered a bonfire for 241 saddles, 47 rifles, 35 revolvers, 573 buffalo robes, and all the other possessions of Black Kettle's band, as well as the slaughter of 800 Indian ponies. Realizing he had attacked only one of a series of villages, he ordered his men away from the battle site. His official report cited two officers and 19 soldiers killed in action and 16 wounded.

Some of Custer's prisoners after the action on the Washita. Black Kettle, 67, a survivor of the Sand Creek Massacre, does not survive Custer's attack. (Library of Congress)

National Headlines/November 1868:
3. ULYSSES S. GRANT ELECTED PRESIDENT

DECEMBER

1. A temporary bridge across the Missouri River in Omaha is completed. Some 550 railcars of supplies for the Union Pacific will cross over the bridge in the next 48 hours.
3. High water and ice destroy two spans of the Missouri River bridge in Omaha.
10. On a −18° day, George A. Custer conducts a tour of the Washita battle site for General Philip Sheridan. During the tour, Custer's men find the bodies of an 18-man detachment of his troops who never returned from the battle because of his negligent orders; the bodies are found mutilated near a dry tributary of the Washita River.
▪ Repairs are underway on the bridge across the Missouri in Omaha while 1,000 freight cars wait on the bank.
13. The 8th Cavalry reports eight Indians killed and 14 captured at Walker Springs, Arizona.
14. John Evans is elected president of the Denver Pacific Railway.
16. George A. Custer is interviewed at length in the *Cheyenne Daily Leader.*
▪ Albany and Carbon Counties are established in Wyoming.
24. Captain Albert Barnitz, wounded in the Battle on the Washita, writes to his wife about how a mass of tissue has been removed from the wound.
25. A posse mistakes 17-year-old "Wild Bill" Longley—

who had been hiding out on a Karnes County, Texas, ranch after two suspicious murders—for a horse thief and gives chase. Longley turns in his saddle and puts a bullet between the posse leader's eyes.
▪ Cavalry and infantry under Major A. W. Evans engage Indians at Elm Creek, Indian Territory; 25 Indians are reported killed.
30. In Omaha, the bridge over the Missouri is repaired; some 1,248 freight cars have crossed it since December 1.
31. Wells Fargo, which moved its headquarters from New York to San Francisco this year, announces a net operating income of $176,516.61.

Also in December 1868:
Ambrose Bierce become the editor of the weekly *San Francisco News-Letter.*

National Headlines/December 1868:
25. JOHNSON ISSUES UNCONDITIONAL PARDON AND AMNESTY FOR CIVIL WAR PARTICIPANTS

Also in 1868:
Captain Jack Harvey, a good friend of Wild Bill Hickok, dies in Ellsworth, Kansas.
The California Steam Navigation Company announces dividend payments of $375,000.
There are 235,000 head of cattle, valued at $3.7 million, in Arizona Territory.
Among those coming west to work on the Union Pacific Railroad are the brothers Virgil and Wyatt Earp of Monmouth, Illinois, who arrive in Wyoming.
A traveling circus playing in Evergreen, Texas, refuses free admission to "Wild Bill" Longley, 17. The youth punches out the owner of the show, shoots holes in the tent, and makes the clowns "dance" to the beat of his .45.
Fort Supply is established in Oklahoma.
From Louisiana's Avery Island, Edmund McIlhenny, a New Orleans banker, begins the bottling and selling of Tabasco sauce.
John Younger, 15, pistols whips to death a man who hit him across the face with a wet fish. Younger is acquitted on the grounds of self-defense.
A record stagecoach run is made when a Wells Fargo coach travels 503 miles from Salt Lake City to Helena, Montana, in 3.5 days.
The Union Pacific Railroad lays 430 miles of track.
The U.S. commissioner of Indian affairs estimates that the government is spending $1 million for each Indian killed in the wars in the West.
In his journal, General Regis de Tobriand records these

impressions of what became Dakota Territory during the past 30 years:

> If theft, deceit, murder, and war have come since those days, the fault is definitely that of the whites alone. . . . The great profits from the trade bred rivalries among the traders; these rivalries resulted in stratagems of all sorts . . . each made great efforts to attract the Indians and to turn them away from competitors. So to harm one another, the whites began to stir up the Indians . . . encouraged them to steal. . . . Whiskey was introduced among them to encourage them in evil and to despoil them more easily. Pandora's box was opened on the plains. And the vice, injustice, bad treatment sown by the whites produced this bloody harvest, which . . . has cost so much in blood and money.

1869

"The last rail is laid. The last spike is driven. The Pacific railroad is finished."
—Telegram from Promontory Point

JANUARY

1. The Denver Pacific Railway and Telegraph Company's telegraph line to Cheyenne is completed. Denver's Mayor William Clayton wires Cheyenne's Mayor Murrin.

3. Construction begins on a 900-foot Denver Pacific Railway bridge across the South Platte near present Evans, Colorado.

6. The outlaw Cullen Baker is tracked down and killed in southeastern Arkansas by Thomas Orr, a schoolteacher whom Baker had picked on once too often.

8. General Philip H. Sheridan establishes Camp Wichita on Medicine Bluff Creek in present Oklahoma.

16. Lincoln County is established in New Mexico; the county seat is Carrizozo.

18. The California Theater opens in San Francisco.

19. Eugene Manlove Rhodes, the author of *Good Men and True* (1910), is born in Tecumseh, Nebraska.

25. With a futile estate fight behind him, 18-year-old Pat Garrett departs Claiborne Parish, Louisiana, to seek a new start in the West.

■ Colfax County is established in New Mexico.

28. The 7th Cavalry reports six Indians killed and 10 wounded in action on the Solomon River in Kansas.

■ The first recorded triplets born in Montana are to Mrs. Samuel Hardesty.

Also in January 1869:

As Comanche chief Tosawi (Silver Brooch) surrenders to General Philip Sheridan at Fort Cobb, Missouri, he reportedly says, "Tosawi good Indian." Replies Sheridan, "the only good Indians I ever saw were dead." Lieutenant Charles Nordstrom hears the remark and passes it on for posterity as "the only good Indian is a dead Indian."

National Headlines/January 1869:

19. FIRST NATIONAL WOMEN'S SUFFRAGE CONVENTION CONVENES IN WASHINGTON

FEBRUARY

2. James Oliver patents a plow that can handle the difficult western sod.

4. The 1st Cavalry reports eight Indians killed and eight captured in action in the Hulalapai Mountains of Arizona.

■ A women's suffrage convention opens in Topeka, Kansas.

5. Apaches raid the Portrero, Arizona, ranch of Pete Kitchen, driving his sheep away. Kitchen chases after the attackers.

10. Nat Love, about 15 years old, gives half of the $100 he won in a raffle in his home state of Tennessee to his mother and with the remaining $50 heads West. Outside the future Dodge City, Kansas, he will obtain employment with the Duval cattle outfit from Texas, after a wild audition on Good Eye, a foul-tempered bronco.

15. The University of Nebraska is chartered in Lincoln.

■ The first school in Laramie, Wyoming, opens.

18. Wells Fargo's directors vote to reduce the company's capital stock from $10 million to $5 million.

28. James Butler Hickok leaves his position as an army scout at Fort Lyon, Colorado.

Also in February 1869:

The U.S. government reports that Kansa chiefs are asking, "Shall we starve?"

Fighting Indians is one of the lowest-paying jobs in the Old West. U.S. Army privates earned $16 a month, from which a dollar is deducted for pay at the end of service and 12½ cents are taken to support the Soldier's Home, leaving a monthly earning of $14.87½.

Crazy Horse weds Black Shawl.

National Headlines/February 1869:

6. FIRST "UNCLE SAM" APPEARS IN *HARPER'S*

MARCH

1. A Union Pacific Railroad train crosses the newly constructed Devil Gate Bridge in Utah.
3. Congress cuts the size of the military from 54,641 to 37,313 enlisted men.
4. In his inaugural address, President Ulysses S. Grant speaks about "civilizing Indians."
6. Construction of the Denver Pacific Railway's South Platte Bridge is completed. It is 984 feet high.
▪ Some 20 soldiers from Arizona's Camp Lowell go on a drinking binge, ride into Tucson, and start shooting. One citizen is wounded.
8. The Union Pacific's rails reaches Ogden, Utah.
9. The Union Pacific's temporary bridge across the Missouri River in Omaha is removed.

National Headlines/March 1869:

4. GRANT INAUGURATED 18TH U.S. PRESIDENT

APRIL

4. The Central Pacific and Union Pacific Railroads continue grading their railways in Utah at a furious pace as their labor camps move closer together.
6. Anson P. K. Safford is named territorial governor of Arizona
7. The 13th Infantry reports nine Indians killed on the Musselshell River in Montana.
▪ The Union Pacific's tracks cross Bear River near Corrinne, Utah.
8. Montana territorial governor Green Clay Smith resigns.
10. The Board of Indian Commissioners is created by Congress.
13. The first annual meeting of the National Grange, which was founded in 1867 to organize farmers, is held in Washington, D.C.
15. In *Texas v. White,* the Supreme Court rules that secession from the Union is unconstitutional.
16. Snow slows the work of Union Pacific and Central Pacific construction crews.

18. A team of Californians wins the First International Cricket Match to be held in San Francisco.
20. In Arizona, one hundred soldiers from Camp Grant surround a large Apache encampment and kill 27 Indians.
21. President Grant names Brigadier General Ely Samuel Parker, a Tonowanda-Seneca chief, commissioner of Indian affairs, a position he will hold until December 1871.
23. The Union Pacific's tracks reach Blue Creek, Utah.
▪ James Rolph, the 27th governor of California (1931–1934), is born in San Francisco.
24. Union Pacific and Central Pacific tracks are reported to be 20 miles apart.
25. The playwright Paul Armstrong (*Alias Jimmy Valentine,* 1909) is born in Kidder, Missouri.
26. The "Picnic Special," the first official run of the Atchison, Topeka, and Santa Fe Railroad, travels over seven miles of track.
▪ In Arizona, Indians steal the mail from an express rider at Apache Pass for the third time since February.
28. Central Pacific workers lay 10 miles of track in one day.
▪ Clement Calhoun Young, the 26th governor of California (1926–31), is born in Lisbon, New Hampshire.
29. Major John Green reports that Indians clashed with cavalrymen, infantrymen, and scouts in Arizona's Turnbull Mountains; 28 Indians were killed and eight were wounded.
30. Union Pacific tracks reach Promontory Point, Utah.

TEN MILES IN A DAY
APRIL 28, 1869

A Central Pacific construction crew put on an incredible display on a bet. Construction supervisor Charles Crocker had boasted to Union Pacific vice president Thomas Durant that his crew could lay 10 miles of track in one day. Durant wired back: "Ten thousand dollars that you can't do it before witnesses."

Beginning at 7:00 A.M. on April 28, 14 miles outside of Promontory Point, Utah, a crew of Chinese and eight husky rail carriers began the attempt. Before the sun set, the crew lifted 3,520 rails and 25,800 ties weighing a quarter of a million pounds to lay a total of 10 miles and 56 feet of track.

MAY

1. The Central Pacific's work crew reaches the summit of Promontory Point, Utah. The first true connection of the two segments of the transcontinental railroad occur when the Central Pacific's track meets the Union Pacific's.

2. The last bridges needed to complete the transcontinental rail line are under construction.

4. A railroad tie made of laurel wood and the ceremonial Golden Spike leave San Francisco on a special car heading for Utah. Ceremonies marking the completion of the transcontinental railroad are slated for May 8.

5. Devils Gate bridge, 84 miles from Promontory Point, is reported to be impassable. A repair crew leaves at 4:00 A.M. on the newly constructed track and arrives at Devils Gate at 8:00 A.M.

6. Grading of the Denver Pacific Railway's track is completed.

7. Captain G. W. Smith reports that 14 Indians were killed by infantrymen and scouts at Paint Creek, Texas.

8. As construction crews repairing the Devils Gate bridge work through a driving rainstorm, Union Pacific chief engineer Major General Grenville Dodge sends a telegram stating that the ceremonial joining of the rails will be delayed until May 10; Dodge neglects to cite the reason for the delay.

9. Repairs are completed on Devils Gate bridge. VIP cars and sleeping cars begin passing over the bridge, en route to the ceremony at Promontory Point.

■ The Union Pacific has laid 120 miles of track since January 1, 1869. Since January 1868, the Union Pacific has laid 555 miles of track, for a grand total of 1,086 miles since the first tracks were installed in July of 1865. The Central Pacific has spent $23 million on its 690 miles of track—much of which was laid through the Sierra Nevada—and employed an average of 12,000 men per day during construction.

10. The Golden Spike is driven at Promontory Point, Utah. Railroad historians will point out that, the ceremonial driving of the Golden Spike notwithstanding, the transcontinental railroad was not yet a continuous railway crossing the entire country from west to east. There was no bridge spanning the Missouri River at Omaha and Council Bluffs, nor was there any other railroad bridge that crossed that river.

11. The transcontinental railroad cuts the travel time from San Francisco to New York from three months to eight days.

Rails west.   (Library of Congress)

13. Major E. A. Carr reports four men of the 5th Cavalry lost in action at Beaver Creek, Kansas; 25 Indians are killed and 20 are wounded.

16. Wells Fargo, having moved its main headquarters from New York to San Francisco in 1868, sells its

THE DRIVING OF THE GOLDEN SPIKE

MAY 10, 1869

The Golden Spike, symbolic of the final link in the transcontinental railroad, was driven at Promontory Point, Utah, 53 miles northwest of Ogden.

A huge celebration erupted around the joining of the rails of the Union Pacific and the Central Pacific, the completion of the first transcontinental railroad. The Union Pacific had constructed 1,086 miles of track from Omaha, and the Central Pacific had built 690 miles of track from Sacramento.

The Central Pacific's *Jupiter 90* and the Union Pacific's *119* faced each other as the spike was laid in a predrilled hole by California governor Leland Stanford. The spike itself was attached to a telegraph wire so that the world would "hear" it being driven in. Stanford missed on his first attempt to strike the spike. After other failed attempts, and the hootings and catcalls of the workers attending the event, the spike was eventually driven by Grenville Dodge of the Union Pacific at 2:47 P.M. Eastern Time.

In celebration of the driving of the Golden Spike, the Liberty Bell was rung in Philadelphia and 7,000 Mormons celebrated at their Tabernacle. San Francisco offered a 220-cannon salute. The text of the telegram from Promontory Point read:

> The last rail is laid. The last spike is driven. The Pacific railroad is finished.

The Golden Spike used in the ceremony was made by Schultz, Fisher and Machling of San Francisco; it was cast from $20 gold pieces and weighed 18 ounces, with a six-inch gold nugget fixed to its head. On it is this inscription:

> The Last Spike
> as this railroad unites the two
> great oceans of the world.
> May God continue the unity of our country.

A lithograph of the joining of the rails. (Colorado Historical Society)

New York building at 84 Broadway to D. N. Barney for $130,000.

17. Ground-breaking ceremonies are held in Ogden for the Utah Central Railroad.

20. William F. Cody and the 5th Cavalry arrive at Fort McPherson, Nebraska, after skirmishing with Tall Bull.

22. An earthquake rocks Helena, Montana.

24. Major John Wesley Powell's party of nine embarks on an exploratory voyage down the Green and Colorado Rivers. Leaving from Green River Station, Wyoming, the party will travel 1,048 miles in 98 days. "More than once have I been warned by the Indians not to enter this canyon," Powell will write. "They consider it disobedience to the gods and contempt for their authority and believed that it would surely bring upon me their wrath."

25. Indians kill six settlers in Jewell County, Kansas.

26. The first circus to travel on the transcontinental railroad is "Dan Castello's Great Show, Circus, Menagerie, and Abyssinian Caravan," which plays in Omaha today.

28. Cheyennes destroy Union Pacific track at Fossil Creek, Kansas, temporarily severing the transcontinental railroad.

29. William F. Cody sees his first circus (Dan Castello's) in North Platte, Nebraska.

30. Maria Weichel and Susanna Allerdice are captured by Cheyennes during a raid on a settlement at Spillman Creek, Kansas.

Also in May 1869:

Laura Ingalls, age 2, migrates with her parents from Missouri to Indian Territory, in present Kansas, a setting she will use in *Little House on the Prairie* (1935).

Golden Spike ceremonies at Promontory Point, Utah. The Central Pacific Railroad's chief engineer, S. S. Montague (left center), shakes hands with Grenville Dodge of the Union Pacific. One era ends, another begins. (Union Pacific)

James Butler Hickok, 31, arrives at Hays City, Kansas, where he will begin his law enforcement career.

John C. Frémont is ruined financially when the Memphis and El Paso Railroad fails.

Missouri dentist Dr. William Newton Morrison describes how he placed the first gold crown on a tooth in this month's issue of the *Missouri Dentist Journal.*

National Headlines/May 1869:
FRENCH FINISH SUEZ CANAL

JUNE

1. Indians kill 13 civilians in raids on settlements on the Solomon River in Kansas.

3–4. Captain G. B. Sanford reports cavalrymen and infantrymen fought Indians in Arizona's Pinal Mountains, killing 20, including Chief Squirrel Rifle.

6. The first circus to play Denver reports that 10,000 attended its four performances. The traveling show came in wagons from Cheyenne.

7. Colonel Ranald Mackenzie reports two Indians and one enlisted man killed on the Pecos River in Texas.

■ A treaty is signed at Fort Bridger, Wyoming.

15. President Grant appoints Edward M. McCook territorial governor of Colorado.

17. Secretary of State William H. Seward arrives in Denver.

19. A detachment of the 7th Cavalry reports four Indians killed and 12 wounded near Sheridan, Kansas.

■ Lieutenant A. B. Curtiss reports seven Indians killed by an 8th Cavalry expedition that began today and will last for three weeks in Arizona's Red Rock Country.

■ Denver's City Council passes an ordinance banning the tossing of "any wrapping paper, old clothes, books, boots, shoes, hats, or any combustible matter" into streets and alleys.

27. Captain S. B. M. Young of the 8th Cavalry reports three Indians killed at Great Mouth Canyon, Arizona.

30. The transcontinental railroad is officially completed when a rail bridge across the Missouri River in

Kansas City opens. Forty thousand people turn out to watch as the bridge is tested by five locomotives.

Also in June 1869:

The one-year-old Edgar Lee Masters migrates with his family from Kansas to Illinois.

Some 1,400 unemployed Chinese overwhelm the San Francisco job market; many were recently laid off after the completion of the transcontinental railroad.

JULY

2. Camp Wichita in Indian territory, present Oklahoma, is renamed Fort Sill in honor of General Joshua W. Sill.
3. Lieutenant A. B. Curtiss reports four Indians killed by the 8th Cavalry at Hell Canyon, Arizona.
■ Brigham Young marries Elizabeth Jones, 56, his 52nd bride.
4. In Kansas City, the first railroad bridge across the Missouri River is opened by the Burlington Railroad.
■ The *New York Times* carries a story about the Central Pacific laying 10 miles of track in one day just before the transcontinental railroad was linked at Promontory Point, Utah.
■ In one of the first rodeos ever held, at Deer Trail, Colorado, cowboy Emilne Gardenshire wins a new suit and the title "champion bronco buster of the plains."
6. Lieutenant William McCleave reports that cavalrymen killed nine Indians and wounded 10 in Arizona.
8. A military telegraph line links Santa Fe, New Mexico, and Fort Leavenworth, Kansas.
11. The Battle of Summit Springs takes place in Colorado Territory.
13. In an expedition that begins today and will conclude on August 19, Major John Green reports that his detachment of cavalrymen and infantrymen killed 11 Indians, wounded two, and captured 13 in Arizona's White Mountains.
■ Anti-Chinese riots are reported in San Francisco.
15. General J. M. Schofield and his staff arrive in Denver to tour Colorado.
24. William F. Cody is officially "discovered."
25. The first shipment of ore from Utah's Monitor and Magnet mine is shipped to San Francisco at $32.50 a ton.
26. The first circus to travel on the transcontinental railroad, "Dan Castello's Great Show, Circus, Menagerie, and Abyssinian Caravan," plays in San

Francisco. The show has now played on both coasts in the last six months.

28. The explorer John Wesley Powell names the Dirty Devil River in present Arizona. About the Grand Canyon, he writes:

> Stand at some point on the brink of the Grand Canyon where you can overlook the river, and the details of the structure, the vast labyrinth of gorges of which it is composed, are scarcely noticed; the elements are lost in the grand effect, and a broad, deep, flaring gorge of many colors is seen. But

---

THE BATTLE OF SUMMIT SPRINGS
JULY 11, 1869

Tall Bull's Cheyenne "Dog Soldiers" were attacked by the 5th Cavalry under General Eugene Carr in Colorado Territory (about 10 miles north of present Sterling), in an attempt to free two captives, Maria Weichel and Susanna Allerdice (see May 30). Allerdice was killed and Weichel was rescued. Tall Bull and 51 of his warriors were killed, while 15 Indians were captured.

This was the last major battle against Indians in Colorado. William F. Cody, a scout at Summit Springs, will work the battle into his future Wild West performances.

A WESTERN STAR IS BORN
JULY 24, 1869

On this date Ned Buntline, at $20,000 a year the highest-paid writer in America, met William F. Cody at Fort McPherson, Nebraska. Buntline had come west to interview Major Frank North and hoped to find a hero for his dime novels. When Buntline described what he was looking for, North admonished him, saying that "real men" did not brag about their exploits. He pointed to Cody, 23, sleeping off a hangover. "If you want a man to fill that bill," said North, "he's over there under a wagon." The old hack and the young scout hit it off immediately and spent 10 days drinking and swapping stories.

The Grand Canyon, as seen by John Wesley Powell in 1869. "A stairway from the gloom to heaven." (National Archives)

stand down among these gorges and the landscape seems to be composed of huge vertical elements of wonderful form. Above, it is an open, sunny gorge; below it is deep and gloomy. Above, it is a chasm; below, it is a stairway from gloom to heaven.

Also in July 1869:

Dr. F. V. Hayden, the head of the U.S. Geological Survey, arrives in Denver to begin a preliminary examination of the Rocky Mountains.

John Muir spends his first summer in the Sierra Nevada.

AUGUST

5. Spanish Fork, Montana, is renamed Deer Lodge.
10. Indians kill four settlers near Fort Buford, Dakota Territory.
11. Mark Twain receives the first printed copy of *The Innocents Abroad*.
21. The *San Diego Weekly Bulletin* begins publication.
23. The first rail freight from Boston, a carload of boots and shoes, arrives in San Francisco in 16 days.
■ Locals persuaded J. B. Hickok to run for sheriff of Ellis County, Kansas. Today, he is elected to fill an unexpired term.
24. In Hays City, Kansas, a drunken soldier, John Mulrey, sometimes referred to as Bill Molvey, resists arrest by Sheriff J. B. "Wild Bill" Hickok, who in turn shoots him. It is Hickok's first day on the job.

25. The soldier John Mulrey dies in Hays City, Kansas, of a bullet wound he received from Sheriff Wild Bill Hickok the night before.
■ Lieutenant Robert Carrick reports that the 8th Cavalry killed six Indians and captured one at Tonto Station, Arizona.
■ Lieutenant Rufus Somerby reports that the 8th Cavalry killed nine Indians and wounded seven on Arizona's Santa Maria River.
28. Three members of Major John Wesley Powell's first party of explorers traveling down the Colorado River—Seneca Howland, O. G. Howland, and William H. Dunn—having endured enough thrills and danger for one summer, decide to separate from the group and return home. They climb the north rim of the Grand Canyon, where they are killed by Paiute Indians.
29. Major John Wesley Powell and the five remaining members of his party, which is presumed lost, complete the first journey down the Green and Colorado Rivers; they emerge at the mouth of the Virgin River in Arizona, where Mormon rescuers are fishing with nets for the party's remains.
30. The first rail shipment of tea to the West Coast—90 baskets from Chicago's Williams, Butters and Company—arrives in San Francisco.

Also in August 1869:

Grasshoppers are reported to be numerous in Utah.

S. Bowles writes about health conditions among the Ute Indians in the newly published *The Switzerland of America:*

> Coughs are frequent, and dyspepsia; sickness and deaths are quite common among the children. The incongruous mixture of white man's food and raiment and life with their own . . . is sapping their vitality at its fountains. . . . To make matters worse, they have got hold of our quack medicines.

Bret Harte's short stories appear in book form for the first time in *The Luck of Roaring Camp and Other Sketches.*

SEPTEMBER

2. Esther Morris holds a tea party in South Pass City, Wyoming.
3. A woodcutter's camp near Fort Stanton, New Mexico, is raided by Indians. Probate Judge Murphy is reported to be "too busy" to organize a posse.
5. Troops and Indians clash near Fort Stanton, New Mexico. Three Indians are reported killed and seven wounded; two enlisted men are wounded.
6. Three Montanans, David Folsom, C. W. Cook, and

Esther Morris (1814–1902): The "mother of women's suffrage," and America's first female judge.   (Denver Public Library, Western History Department)

William Peterson, set out to dispel the rumors about the hot springs wonders of Yellowstone. In a six-week tour, they visit Yellowstone Lake, Fountain Geyser, and some of the 10,000 thermal springs in the area. According to the historian Hiram Chittenden, the Montanans were later "unwlling to risk their reputations" by recounting what they had seen.

13. The rails of the Denver Pacific are connected with those of the Union Pacific in Cheyenne, Wyoming.

14. Catherine McCarty, Billy the Kid's mother, buys a town lot in Wichita, Kansas.

22. The Cincinnati Red Stockings, one of the first sports teams to travel across the country by rail, arrive in San Francisco for some exhibition games.

23. Lieutenant T. W. Gibson reports that the 8th Cavalry killed 18 Indians on Arizona's Red Creek.

24. During frenzied trading in New York, the price of gold rises to $162 an ounce before the U.S. government puts $4 million in gold on the market.

26–27 Samuel Strawhim leads a pack of drunken teamsters who bust up Oderfeld's Saloon in Hays City, Kansas. Sheriff Wild Bill Hickok arrives on the scene after midnight and orders the party stopped, but all hell breaks loose. Hickok blows Strawhim's head off and the trouble stops immediately. Hickok's deeds are cleared as "justifiable homicide."

Also in September 1869:

Nathan C. Meeker, an employee of Horace Greeley, begins a two-month trip by rail and stagecoach through Kansas and Colorado.

National Headlines/September 1869:

24. BLACK FRIDAY—GOLD PANIC ON WALL STREET

OCTOBER

4. The Omaha Conference takes place.

■ The Denver Pacific's track, being laid toward Denver, crosses the Wyoming-Colorado border some nine miles south of Cheyenne.

5. The *Cheyenne Leader* reports that the Denver Pacific is laying rail at the rate of a mile per day.

8. Lieutenant W. H. Winters reports that the 1st Cavalry killed 12 Indians at Arizona's Chiricahua Pass.

9. About 25 miles from Apache Pass in present Arizona, Apaches attack a mail train and the army detachment guarding it, killing six members of the group.

■ Gold is discovered on Cedar Creek near Superior, Montana.

10. Wild Bill Hickok prevents a lynching in Hays City, Kansas.

11. Wyoming's first territorial legislature convenes in Cheyenne.

12. A number of Wells Fargo stagecoach lines are sold; the deals will take effect on designated dates during the next year. Gilmer and Company buys the Salt

THE OMAHA CONFERENCE
OCTOBER 4, 1869

William G. and Charles Fargo, along with Wells Fargo president A. H. Barney, met with financier Lloyd Tevis and his colleagues behind locked doors in Omaha, Nebraska.

Tevis pointed out that he owned a controlling interest in Wells Fargo as well as a 10-year express contract with the Central Pacific Railroad. Under the terms of a new agreement, the Pacific Express turned over its business to Wells Fargo and then disbanded, in return for $5 million in Wells Fargo stock. Pacific Express paid Wells Fargo 3.3 percent of $500,000 in cash. All assets previously owned by Wells Fargo in excess of 3.5 percent on its $10 million capital stock were to be distributed to the shareholders, reducing the company's working capital to $5 million. In effect, Tevis assumed control of Wells Fargo.

Lake–Uintah line for $22,500; J. P. Cope and Company purchases the Argenta to Austin route for $15,000; and John Hughes and Company the Colorado lines, including the one from Cheyenne to Georgetown, for $106,000.

14. The Denver Pacific's tracks cross Lone Tree Creek, Colorado.

20. A few celebrities arrive by stagecoach in Denver: Cyrus W. Field, who has been in the headlines recently because of his telegraph cable across the Atlantic Ocean; Kansas Pacific Railroad official General W. J. Palmer; and *New York Tribune* editor Nathan Meeker, making an exploratory tour of the West for Horace Greeley.

■ Captain R. F. Bernard reports that the 1st Cavalry killed 18 Indians at Arizona's Chiricahua Pass; two soldiers are reported killed.

21. The Denver Pacific's track is nearing its goal: it is now 24.5 miles from Cheyenne.

■ The first rail shipment of oysters from Baltimore arrives in San Francisco.

23. In Arizona, a mail route is established between Camp McDowell, Phoenix, Florence, Fort Grant, and Tucson.

25. Stagecoach service links Denver and Evans, Colorado.

26. The Denver Pacific Railroad and Telegraph Company operates four telegraph stations—in Denver, Cheyenne, and Evans, and one mobile station on a railroad car.

28. William F. Cody, the chief of scouts for the 5th Cavalry, returns to Fort McPherson, Nebraska, for the winter. In the past year and 23 days, he has participated in seven expeditions against Indians and in nine battles.

28–29. Captain J. M. Bacon reports that cavalrymen and infantrymen killed 50 Indians and captured seven at the headwaters of the Brazos River in Texas; eight troopers are reported wounded.

31. William F. Cody is discharged as an army scout in Nebraska.

Also in October 1869:

Joseph Becker, 28, a field artist for *Frank Leslie's Illustrated Newspaper,* begins a seven-month tour of the West by train. His sketches will help to increase the newspaper's circulation to 70,000.

Passenger service begins on the transcontinental railroad.

The Cardiff Giant is big news back in the East. Soon the giant will be revealed as a hoax: Instead of being a prehistoric petrified man, the "giant" is actually a figure made of gypsum mined in the area around Fort Dodge, Iowa.

National Headlines/October 1869:

8. FORMER PRESIDENT PIERCE DIES AT 64

NOVEMBER

2. Wild Bill Hickok is unsuccessful in his bid to be re-elected sheriff of Ellis County, Kansas; the vote is 114 to 89.

4. The Masonic Savings and Loan is incorporated in San Francisco.

6. A murder occurs in Evans, Colorado. Jack Carr, dissatisfied with the dinner served at Daniel Steele's hotel, becomes loud and abusive to Steele and his wife and daughter. Carr's money is refunded and he is asked to leave. Insulted beyond measure, Carr returns with a loaded revolver and shoots Daniel Steele dead. A crowd assails Carr, but cooler heads prevail. A trial is arranged, witnesses' statements are recorded, and the jury returns a guilty verdict. The crowd then grabs Carr and hangs him from the nearest tree.

10. Wells Fargo stockholders receive a letter from company president A. H. Barney explaining the terms of the Omaha Conference (October 4).

■ The 8th Cavalry reports four Indians killed in the Tompkins Valley of Arizona.

11. The Denver Pacific's rails reach Ault, Colorado.

14. Wyoming's first Masonic Lodge is established in South Pass City.

15. Free postal delivery begins in San Francisco.

21. William Henry David "Alfalfa Bill" Murray, the controversial Oklahoma governor (1930–1934), is born in Toadsuck, Texas.

23. The first of Ned Buntline's tales about William F. Cody, "Buffalo Bill, the King of Border Men," appears in installments in Street and Smith's *New York Weekly*.

▪ The Denver Pacific's rails reach the future Greeley, Colorado, but the crews run out of iron before they reach the site of the depot.

25. George Wallace, the Kansas Pacific's track construction superintendent, dies in Sheridan, Kansas. The last station he helped to construct will be named Wallace.

26. As the tracks of the Denver Pacific Railway reach closer to Denver, the last four-horse Concord stagecoach run between Denver and Cheyenne is completed at 1:30 P.M.

27. Cyrus W. Fisher is appointed superintendent of the Denver Pacific Railway at Evans, Colorado.

30. The Wyoming Senate passes a bill giving women the right to vote; the bill now goes to the territory's House.

Also in November 1869:

An article by George A. Custer, titled "The Hunt on the Plains," appears in *Turf, Field and Farm*. He concludes the article with a tear-inducing poem to his dog Maida, who was killed by a soldier.

National Headlines/November 1869:

▪ RUTGERS-PRINCETON FIRST FOOTBALL GAME SUEZ CANAL OPENS

DECEMBER

1. Uinta County is created in Wyoming.

4. Nathan Meeker announces in Horace Greeley's *New York Tribune*: "I propose to unite with the proper persons in the establishment of a colony in Colorado Territory." Meeker's new settlement will be called Greeley.

5. Fritz Heinze, the Montana copper king, is born in New York.

▪ Ellis Parker Butler, the humorist and author of "Pigs Is Pigs" (1905), is born in Muscatine, Iowa.

6. The Wyoming House passes the bill giving women the right to vote.

7. The Daviess County Savings Bank of Gallatin, Missouri, is hit by Frank and Jesse James and Cole Younger. Jesse, posing as a customer, kills cashier John Sheets, with whom the boys allegedly have had a grudge since the Civil War. The gang gets away with only $500.

▪ The first commercial freight to be shipped on the Denver Pacific Railway leaves Cheyenne for the future Greeley, Colorado; it is addressed to Salomon Brothers.

8. Construction of the first 32 cells at Colorado's Canon City penitentiary is completed.

9. The Denver Pacific's rails are extended to the depot site in what will become Greeley, Colorado.

10. Wyoming governor John Campbell signs the bill passed by the territorial legislature granting women the right to vote as well as the right to hold public office. Wyoming becomes the first state or territory in the nation to grant women these rights. Toasts one lawmaker: "To the lovely ladies, once our superiors, now our equals."

▪ Lieutenant G. B. Sanford reports that the 1st Cavalry killed 11 Indians at Chillson's Creek, Arizona; one soldier is wounded.

13. The Denver Pacific's tracks reach Evans, Colorado. A major celebration is held in the first town in Colorado to be reached by rail. Evans will be the railroad's terminus until May 1870, when track construction will resume.

15. The Samuel farmhouse in Clay County, Missouri, is surrounded by a small posse of four, but Frank and Jesse James manage an escape. Deputy Sheriff John Thomason and his boys feel the $3,000 reward slip through their fingers.

▪ The 200-ton brig *Ida D. Rogers* is a total loss on the Coos bar, Oregon.

19. Two Hughes and Company stagecoaches, running daily to Evans from Denver, make it possible to travel from Denver to Chicago in 2.5 days.

23. Nathan Meeker hosts the first meeting of his would-be colonists at Cooper Institute in New York City. The name "Union Colony" is chosen for the new settlement, and some basic plans are made for a migration to Colorado in May 1870.

25. At a poker game in Towash, Texas, John Wesley Hardin, 16, kills James Bradley for supposedly cheating.

31. The Kansas Pacific's track reaches just west of Sunland, Kansas, about 12 miles from the Colorado line.

Also in December 1869:

The California Steam Navigation Company announces that it has paid dividends totaling $250,000 in 1869.

Echoing the sentiments of many, California governor Henry Haight says: "The Chinese are a stream of

John Wesley Harding (1853–1895), perhaps the deadliest gunman of all. (Library of Congress)

"Pilgrims on the Plains," by Theodore R. Davis, from an 1869 Harper's. (Harper's Weekly)

filth and prostitution pouring in from Asia, whose servile competition tends to cheapen and degrade labor."

The 140-ton schooner *Alaska* runs aground off the coast of Oregon with a shipload of lumber destined for Hawaii.

The Union Pacific freights 36 carloads of Chinese and Japanese silkworm eggs destined for France.

National Headlines/December 1869:

1. HAWAII NOW PROTECTED UNDER MONROE DOCTRINE

24. STANTON DIES 4 DAYS AFTER BEING NAMED TO SUPREME COURT

Also in 1869:

In the last 10 years, publisher Hubert Howe Bancroft has collected more than 40,000 books, mostly on travel and history. He houses them in a five-story building at 721 Market Street in San Francisco, along with his multifaceted business. In addition to books and stationery, he sells pianos, sheet music, and business forms. A chugging steam engine runs a basement printing press, which one season prints 20 million color labels for salmon cans. Wondering what to do with all his books, Bancroft decides to publish a massive history of the American West, one that a staff of 600 will eventually help to write. Indexing the books by subject will cost $35,000, but the "History Factory" is becoming a reality.

Silver production at the Comstock Lode totals $7.5 million.

Four businesses in California failed.

There are 250,000 head of cattle in Arizona Territory, valued at just over $4 million.

Wells Fargo opens 61 new offices, for a total of 293. The company's net operating income is $170,778.12.

Trout sell for $6 apiece in Laramie, Wyoming.

The German Colonization Society forms in Chicago to establish settlements in Colorado.

The first railroad in Los Angeles is built to ship wine, fruit, wheat, and other products to Wilmington.

Surviving Navajos of the Kit Carson displacement of 1866 return to Canyon de Chelly in Arizona.

Piegan Indians kill Malcolm Clark in Montana.

Alexander K. McClure publishes *Three Thousand Miles Through the Rocky Mountains,* about his 1867 journey in the West.

Edwin Higgins becomes acting governor of Utah Territory.

Arabella Mansfield is admitted to the Iowa bar, becoming America's first female lawyer.

It is believed that Belle Starr and her first husband, Jim Reed, live in the Los Angeles area from 1869–1871.

The University of California is chartered in Oakland.

1870

"I don't want any more such men sent out there, who are so poor that when they come out there their first thoughts are how they can fill their own pockets."

—Red Cloud

Red Cloud. (International Portrait Gallery)

JANUARY

1. A gold rush of sorts begins when a Mexican miner appears in San Diego with nuggets he claims to have found 60 miles south of the border.

▪ The *Weekly Tribune* begins publication in Salt Lake City.

6. Nathan C. Meeker's group of about 800 colonists reports that a committee is about to start for Colorado in search of a location for the colony.

8. The U.S. mint in Carson City, Nevada, officially opens for the receipt of bullion.

▪ Edmund Davis becomes the first Republican governor of Texas.

9. The transcontinental railroad is officially open. A press release by D. C. Dodge of the Northwestern Railroad in Denver reads:

> The ice bridge across the Missouri River at Omaha was completed and five hundred freight cars crossed on Friday, Jan. 7, 1870. Now for the first time are the Atlantic and Pacific oceans connected by a continuous band of iron rails from shore to shore.

10. The last spike is driven on the Utah Central Railroad. A crowd of 15,000 watches as Brigham Young does the honors.

23. The Baker Massacre occurs in Montana.

25. The third railroad in Colorado is the Kansas Pacific, whose tracks cross into the future state about four miles west of Weskan, Kansas.

THE BAKER MASSACRE
JANUARY 23, 1870

Colonel Eugene M. Baker and troops from Fort Ellis were on the trail of Blackfeet Piegans who had killed a fur trader when they happened upon an encampment of Indian smallpox victims on the Marias River in north-western Montana. Baker ordered a charge and slaughtered 175 Indians, including Chief Heavy Runner. Some men, but mostly women and children, were clubbed and shot. Baker reported 40 Indians wounded and 140 captured, and one enlisted man killed. At a later court-martial, Baker will be cleared of any wrong-doing.

27. A thousand-mile journey on the Kansas Pacific costs $45.
28. U.S. troops destroy Cochise's Apache camp in Arizona. Captain R. F. Bernard reports that the 1st Cavalry killed 13 Indians and captured two in the Dragoon Mountains.
29. The University of Colorado is organized in Boulder.
30. A petition on women's suffrage circulated in west Denver nets 72 signatures and two refusals.

Also in January 1870:
Four rail lines now cross Iowa.

National Headlines/January 1870:
10. ROCKEFELLER ORGANIZES STANDARD OIL

FEBRUARY
1. The Kansas Pacific's tracks reach Arapahoe, Colorado.
2. Utah becomes the second territory to grant women the right to vote.
■ The Union Colony search committee, headed by Nathan C. Meeker, departs New York for Colorado.
4. The Colorado legislative council passes the women's suffrage bill, which will die in the House.
5. Wells Fargo orders all of its offices west of the Missouri River to send their correspondence and remittances to San Francisco rather than New York.
9. The Denver Pacific's president, John Evans' reports that the last $1.5 million in bonds have been sold in London; he promises that the railroad to Cheyenne will be completed perhaps as early as June.

11. Bent County is established in Colorado.
14. The Wild West comes to Broadway as *Kit the Arkansas Traveler,* by T. B. DeWalden, premieres.
15. Construction begins on a second transcontinental railroad at Lake Superior in Duluth, Minnesota. Because of the Panic of 1873, the Northern Pacific will not be completed for 13 years.
16. Esther Morris becomes the first woman to be appointed justice of the peace in the United States; she serves in South Pass City, Wyoming.
■ Nathan Meeker and his committee of colonists arrive in Denver via stagecoach from Evans, Colorado, and stay at the Broadwell House.
22. The anti-Chinese group known as the Industrial Reformers is organized in San Francisco.
24. In Colorado, a band of Indians drives a Kansas Pacific crew from its work area near Arapahoe Station.
28. A telegraph exchange opens in Denver.

Also in February 1870:
Levi Strauss abandons making overalls and pants from canvas in favor of the tough cotton cloth from Nimes, France, called *serge de Nimes.* Strauss dyes the cloth blue and is responsible for the birth of blue jeans.

MARCH
1. A Union Pacific ticket office opens in Denver.
2. It is reported that the only bridge across the Missouri River, at Kansas City, cost $1,200,000 to build and earns $13,000 in tolls each month. Also, General Grenville Dodge has resigned as the Union Pacific's chief engineer, to be replaced by T. E. Sickles.
■ Orders from military headquarters in St. Louis require all Kansas Pacific track-laying workers from Fort Harker westward to arm themselves against Indian attacks.
3. The Kansas Pacific's tracks reach Cheyenne Wells, Colorado.
4. The *Laramie Sentinel* predicts that Nathan Meeker's Union Colony will locate in Wyoming's Bear River valley.
7. For the first time, a woman is chosen for jury duty in Laramie, Wyoming.
9. Sergeant Francis Brannon reports that the 8th Cavalry killed four Indians at Reno Road, Arizona.
■ It is reported that several undesirables left Sheridan, Kansas, after a massive coil of rope addressed to the "Vigilance Committee" arrived at the train depot.
14. The word blizzard originally meant "a blow . . . by

the fist." Today, an Iowa newspaper uses the word for the first time to describe a violent snowstorm. By 1880, the word will be picked up by newspapers in New York and Canada, and it will acquire a new definition in the dictionary.

22. The town of Pueblo, Colorado, is established. An earlier settlement was wiped out by Utes in 1841. Zebulon Pike built a cabin there in 1806.

28. The Kansas Pacific's tracks reach Kit Carson, Colorado, population 333.

29. Telegraph poles are constructed alongside the Kansas Pacific tracks, which are expected to reach Denver by April 15.

30. Military rule in Texas ceases; the state is readmitted into the Union.

31. Denver awaits a visit from the man the city was named after, General J. W. Denver, now a Washington lawyer.

Also in March 1870:
There are 14 million bison in North America, down from 15 million in 1865.

National Headlines/March 1870:
30. 15TH AMENDMENT GUARANTEES VOTING RIGHTS REGARDLESS OF RACE OR COLOR

APRIL

1. Nathan Meeker's list of potential colonists has 442 names. Fewer than 200 will settle in Colorado.

2. Indians kill six settlers at the headwaters of the Sweetwater River in Wyoming.

4. Nathan Meeker and leaders of the Union Colony meet with *Rocky Mountain News* editor William Byers on the Cache la Poudre River, where they pick the site for the future town of Greeley; 70,000 acres will be purchased for $1 an acre.

■ The War Department issues an order to arm the Arizona militia and to furnish rations for the military.

■ Golden Gate Park is established in San Francisco.

6. Lieutenant W. R. Harmon reports that the 10th Cavalry killed one Indian and captured 10 at Clear Creek, Texas.

8. Violence erupts between competing Chinese cigarmakers in San Francisco.

■ The Iowa legislature approves the construction of a new statehouse.

16. William Stanley is found dead after a train ran over him in Denver. Authorities believe he was murdered and that his body was placed on the tracks by the perpetrator.

17. The Kansas Pacific's telegraph line reaches Denver. Two buggies reportedly get tangled in the wire, but there is no damage.

20. After Nathan Meeker declines to have the Union Colony named after him, the name Greeley is chosen. On April 23, Meeker will leave his son George, 22, in Colorado while he returns to New York to pick up the rest of his family. Three days later, George Meeker will die of pneumonia.

27. The last to swing from the "Hangman's Tree" in Helena, Montana, are J. L. Compton and Joseph Wilson, who were found guilty of robbery and murder.

30. Captain G. B. Sanford reports that infantry and cavalry killed 11 Indians and captured four in Arizona's Pinal Mountains.

Also in April 1870:
The city of Tucson, Arizona, is reported to have a hotel, a newspaper, a brewery, two doctors, many saloons, and a bathtub.

National Headlines/April 1870:
27. RICHMOND SUPREME COURT FLOOR COLLAPSES KILLS 61 IN VIRGINIA

MAY

1. The first 50 families of the Union Colony, heading for Greeley, Colorado, depart Omaha, Nebraska, on the Union Pacific Railroad.

3. The 297-ton *Occident* runs aground on Coquille bar in Oregon.

4. Captain D. S. Gordon reports that seven Indians were killed and one was wounded at Miner's Delight, Wyoming. Lieutenant C. B. Stambaugh was killed in the fight.

■ The Kansas Pacific begins laying track westward from Kit Carson, Colorado.

■ The 50 Union Colony families depart Cheyenne, Wyoming.

5. San Diego's Chamber of Commerce publishes a pamphlet to attract more residents, *Climate Resources and Future Prospects of San Diego.*

7. The Denver Pacific begins building track from Evans to Denver.

8. Brigham Young, 68, is sealed to Lydia Farnsworth, 62, his 53rd and final bride.

9. The Denver Pacific Railway sends the first train, the Union Pacific's *Number 28,* across the bridge over the South Platte River in Evans.

10. It is reported that houses are being purchased in Evans, Colorado, and moved to Greeley.

- The Englishman Jem Mach claims the world heavyweight boxing crown by defeating Tom King near Kennersville, Louisiana.
11. The population of Greeley, Colorado, is 250.
12. A head-on train crash in Eureka, Missouri, kills 19 persons.
13. An Indian attack on a Kansas Pacific Railroad construction crew near Kit Carson, Colorado, leaves 11 dead and 19 wounded; 500 head of livestock are also driven away. The attack, launched from 10 different directions, occurred at 9:00 A.M.
14. A stagecoach arriving in Kit Carson, Colorado, reports 30 killed by Indians between there and Lake Station.
- The Union Pacific is reportedly constructing a second telegraph wire from Omaha, Nebraska, to Ogden, Utah.
16. Ten workers on the Kansas Pacific Railroad are reported slain by Indians.
- General Philip Sheridan begins a four-day visit to Helena, Montana.
17. Indians are reported to have torn down the Union Pacific water tank near Kit Carson.
19. Some 35 Kansas Pacific tracklayers go on strike for higher wages.
20. The Kansas Pacific's tracks reach Gilcrest, Colorado.
23. A transcontinental railroad excursion, the first of its kind and organized by the Boston Board of Trade, departs Boston for San Francisco. The travelers pack a printing press and publish their own paper, *Trans-Continental*, en route to San Francisco.
24. The Kansas Pacific's tracks are some 35 miles from Denver.
25. Captain G. B. Sanford reports that the 1st Cavalry killed 21 Indians and captured 12 in the Tonto Valley of Arizona.
26. The Seven Sisters of St. Joseph, an order of nuns, completes its journey from San Diego to Tucson.
- Grading for the Kansas Pacific's track in Denver begins north of the city's fairgrounds.
27. The Indians who attacked a Kansas Pacific construction crew near Kit Carson, on the 13th of this month are reported to have crossed the Union Pacific tracks at Antelope, Wyoming, with General Forsythe's four cavalry companies in hot pursuit.
28. Gill and Company signs a contract to build the Denver Pacific's freight depot in Denver for $5,794 and to complete it by June 15.
- Two settlers are killed by Indians near Fort Supply in Indian Territory.
30. Red Cloud visits the "Great Father," President Grant, in Washington, D.C.
31. The transcontinental railroad excursion organized

by the Boston Board of Trade arrives in San Francisco.
- Sergeant James Murray reports that the 3rd Infantry killed five Indians and wounded two at Bear Creek, Kansas. Two soldiers reported killed.

Also in May 1870:

An organ is installed in the Mormon Tabernacle in Salt Lake City; the instrument has 27 pedals, 2,638 pipes, and 35 stops.

The artist Joseph Becker's impressions of San Francisco's Chinese quarter appear in *Frank Leslie's Illustrated Newspaper*.

The first train to travel from the Atlantic to the Pacific, the Trans-Continental Excursion sponsored by the Boston Board of Trade, makes the Boston–San Francisco trip in eight days in heralded Pullman "hotel cars." The train does not make the trip entirely by rail; its cars are ferried across the Niagara, Detroit, and Missouri Rivers.

JUNE

1. One month after becoming a town, Greeley, Colorado, has a population of 460 living in 70 houses.
2. The Denver Pacific's track is one mile north of Fort Lupton, Colorado.
4. Wild Bill Hickok takes the oath of office as marshal of Abilene, Kansas.
5. Lieutenant H. B. Cushing reports that the 1st and 3rd Cavalry killed 30 Indians in the Apache Mountains of Arizona.
- The Denver Pacific's tracks reach Hughes Station, the present Brighton, Colorado; it is reported that 76 miles of track have been laid in the past eight months.
- The *Salt Lake Daily Herald* begins publication.
6. The first train track in Indian Territory is laid just across the Kansas border by the Missouri, Kansas, and Texas (the Katy) line.
7. Dogs are being used by Kansas Pacific construction crews (now 17 miles from Denver) to bark at stray Texas cattle that have hampered workers.
8–9. William F. Cody leads the 5th Cavalry on a 120-mile, two-day march after Indians stole horses from Fort McPherson and local ranches in Nebraska. Most of the horses are recovered, but Cody's prize mount, Powder Face, is ridden away by a Sioux brave.
10. A canal to supply water to Greeley is completed.
11. Lieutenant Colonel A. D. Nelson reports that cavalry and infantry killed six Indians and wounded 10 near Fort Supply in Indian Territory.
12. Captain C. B. McLellan reports that the 6th Cavalry

killed 15 Indians on the Little Wichita River in Texas. Two enlisted men were killed.

13. A cavalry detachment reports killing three Indians and wounding 10 near Grinnell Station, Kansas.

16. The Kansas Pacific has laid 15 miles of track west of Kit Carson, Colorado.

17. The *Rocky Mountain News* reports that the first locomotive whistle has been heard in Denver: the Denver Pacific's tracks are only 7.5 miles outside of town.

■ A silver spike is being crafted in Georgetown, Colorado, for the ceremony that will mark the Denver Pacific's arrival in Denver.

■ The showman P. T. Barnum arrives in Denver and delivers a lecture. Tomorrow, he will leave for Georgetown and another speaking engagement.

18. "Nearly every tall building in Denver had some one on its roof yesterday looking at the inbound engine," according to one account. The Denver Pacific's track runs to within one-half mile of Sand Creek.

22. The Denver Pacific Railway's track reaches Denver's city limits at R (26th) Street and Broadway at 11:00 A.M. The line from Cheyenne is completed at approximately 3:30 P.M., and the first train from Cheyenne arrives at 7:30 P.M. One John S. Campbell predicts that Denver will become the capital of the United States by 1920.

■ *The Daring Buffalo Chase of the Plains,* featuring Wild Bill Hickok, together with a host of western characters, Indians, and real buffalo, opens and closes in Niagara Falls, New York. No tickets were sold for the performance, which was held in a vacant lot, and Bill's attempt to pass the hat yields little. Finally, Hickok sells six bison to a Niagara Falls butcher in order to pay the train fare home for those Indians who want out of show business. The first Wild West show is thus a miserable failure.

23. The first passenger train from Denver to Cheyenne departs at 6:45 A.M. and is expected to arrive at 11:45 A.M.

24. A ceremony marks the completion of the Denver Pacific Railway, and the cornerstone for Denver's Union Station is laid. A tinsel-covered iron spike is used instead of the silver one from Georgetown. It seems the men in charge of bringing the spike to Denver became intoxicated en route and did not arrive until 24 hours after the ceremony.

25. The Kansas Pacific's tracks are 30 miles west of Kit Carson.

27. Lieutenant R. H. Young reports that the 2nd Cavalry killed 15 Indians at Pine Grove Meadow, Wyoming.

28. The first transcontinental rail excursion, returning from San Francisco, is forced to forego its planned side trip to Denver when grasshoppers covering the tracks delay the journey to Cheyenne by 19 hours.

29. A round-trip ticket for travel between Denver and Greeley on the Denver Pacific costs $5.

30. The steamboats *Robert E. Lee* and *Natchez* begin the "great race" up the Mississippi from New Orleans to St. Louis.

■ Two train cars filled with Denver school children make the round-trip to Greeley as an outing.

Also in June 1870:

The first Ghost Dances are performed in Nevada's Mason Valley. Tavibo, a Paiute shaman, predicts that the ritual will return fallen warriors from the dead and that great holes will open in the ground to swallow the white man. The dances spread to California and Oregon, but the prophecy never materializes.

The Denver Pacific brings 1,037 passengers to Denver and takes away 788.

In Wyoming, the Union Pacific hires Chinese to work for $32.50 a month rather than pay the $52 that white laborers are demanding.

After a visit to Salt Lake City's three-story Lion House, the residence of Brigham Young and several of his wives, J. H. Beadle writes: "Over the pillared portico in front is a stone lion, a sad misapplication of the emblem . . . as that royal brute is ever content with one mate. The bull would have been more appropriate."

JULY

2. The Kansas Pacific begins laying track eastward from Denver.

■ Denver's *Rocky Mountain News* switches from being an evening paper to a morning paper.

4. The *Robert E. Lee* defeats the *Natchez* in their 1,100-mile steamboat race up the Mississippi from New Orleans. The *Robert E. Lee* arrives in St. Louis at 11:24 A.M. after a trip of three days, 18 hours, and 14 minutes. The *Natchez* arrives at approximately 6:00 P.M.

■ A major 4th of July celebration takes place in Greeley, Colorado: 1,000 people attend a rally at Island Grove Park on the Cache La Poudre River.

10. Professors from Vassar College enjoy a picnic in Lake Station, Colorado, the western terminus of the Kansas Pacific line, and regret that the tracks are still some 90 miles from Denver.

11. The Kansas Pacific's tracks from the east reach the site of future Limon, Colorado.

12. Captain C. B. McLellan and 54 members of the 6th Cavalry battle about 100 of Kicking Bird's Kiowas on the Little Wichita River in Texas. Kicking Bird, recently accused of cowardice by his peers, is eager to redeem himself. His forces defeat, and Kicking Bird himself rides into the soldiers and slays one with a spear. McLellan lists two enlisted men killed and nine wounded; he reports 15 Indians slain.

16. On his eastern trip to visit President Grant, Red Cloud delivers a speech at Cooper Union, in New York, on the conditions at his reservation: "I don't want any more such men sent out there, who are so poor that when they come out there their first thoughts are how they can fill their own pockets." Soon, Grant will give control of Indian agencies to a dozen different Christian denominations instead of to the Army.

17. An intoxicated Wild Bill Hickok takes on five drunken members of the 7th Cavalry in a saloon brawl in Hays City, Kansas. Private John Kile is killed and Private Jeremiah Lanigan is wounded. Wild Bill leaves town shortly after the episode.

18. Wells Fargo publishes in the *New York Times* and the *Rocky Mountain News* its intention to reduce its capital stock from $15 million to $5 million.

20. H. A. W. Tabor operates stores and post offices at Upper and Lower Oro City, Colorado.

23. According to one Denver newspaper: "Fear of Indians should not discourage rail travel in Colorado. Both the Denver and Kansas Pacifics are well guarded and the redmen know it."

24. The first train to travel the transcontinental railroad from San Francisco arrives in New York City.

■ Texas cattleman Charles Goodnight, 34, weds Mary Ann Dyer of Tennessee.

25. The San Francisco Board of Supervisors forbids the renting of rooms that have less than 500 cubic feet of air per person for the purpose of sleeping.

27. Kit Carson, Colorado, reports that its artesian well is down to 1,100 feet, and still no water has been found.

28. The Denver Pacific announces an excursion rate between Denver and Omaha: Beginning on August 1, a round-trip ticket will cost $66.95.

30. Milton H. Straight and Dan O'Connell are the latest deceased in Kit Carson, Colorado. Straight, a rail worker employed on the city's new water tank, killed O'Connell when the latter tried to get some water. Straight was held in custody in the Greenwood County courthouse until a mob of 75 people came for him and hanged him from a railroad bridge.

30. The Kansas Pacific's rails are now 54 miles from Denver.

31. The Kansas Pacific's rails reach Deer Trail in Arapahoe County, Colorado.

Also in July 1870:
Stagecoach service to Des Moines, Iowa, is suspended.
A southern visitor to southwestern Utah writes: "I believe we were close to hell, for Dixie is the hottest place I ever was in."

National Headlines/July 1870:
16. NAPOLEON III DECLARES WAR ON PRUSSIA

AUGUST

1. In a U.S. territory where women's rights are often a matter of bitter controversy, the women of Utah become the first in the United States to vote.

■ Lieutenant H. B. Cushing reports a fight between Indians and the 3rd Cavalry in Skirmish Canyon in the Apache Mountains of Arizona. Six Indians and one soldier are listed as killed.

■ The first fresh fruits from California arrive in Denver—pears and peaches picked three days ago in Sacramento.

3. Members of the Industrial Workers of the World riot in Wheatland, California, over itinerant farmworkers' conditions.

7. In Arizona, 10 settlers are reported slain in Indian raids during the last 11 days.

9. Two trains collide on the Kansas Pacific tracks under construction near present Bennett, Colorado. The brakes go out on a construction train, which rams into cars being boarded, killing six and injuring eight.

■ The gap in the Kansas Pacific's tracks is now 24.5 miles, from Peoria to Manila, Colorado.

11. The Kansas Pacific's tracks reach Bennett, Colorado.

12. A three-day discussion on polygamy, between Reverend J. P. Newman, chaplain of the U.S. Senate, and Elder Orson Pratt of the Mormon Twelve Apostles, begins at the New Tabernacle in Salt Lake City.

13. The Kansas Pacific's tracks reach Byers, Colorado.

15. The Kansas Pacific Railroad is completed.

16. The first eastbound through train from Denver to St. Louis and Chicago departs.

17. The last ox-powered wagon train bearing Kansas Pacific freight arrives in Denver.

18. The last stagecoach arrives in Denver.

19. San Diego obtains telegraph service.

30. Work begins on the Colorado Central Railroad, which will connect Denver with nearby Golden.

■ An all-Pullman "palace-car" train leaves St. Louis for Denver.

Also in August 1870:

Gold deposits in Virginia City, Montana, have just about been exhausted; the city's population is down to 2,555.

National Headlines/August 1870:

14. ADMIRAL FARRAGUT DEAD AT 69

SEPTEMBER

1. This is the day on which Calamity Jane will claim she married Wild Bill Hickok in a ceremony performed by two itinerant ministers on the prairie.
6. The first woman to cast a vote in Wyoming is Louisa Swain; she will be joined on this day by 1,000 other women of the territory.
7. N. P. Langford completes the first detailed map of what will become Yellowstone National Park.
8. The total value of gold shipped from Helena, Montana, this summer is $500,000.
10. U.S. Commissioners J. D. Lang, John V. Farwell, and Vincent Colyer sign a treaty with Osage Indians at the Drum Creek agency in Kansas.
18. Montana's surveyor general, Henry D. Washburn, leads a party of eight to "Old Faithful," a geyser in Yellowstone. The discovery will become big news.
20. A first run of crude gold bullion at Utah's first smelter, six miles south of the Great Salt Lake, takes place.
21. Governor Safford of Arizona has personally led

the Arizona militia on a punitive campaign against Apaches between the San Pedro and Santa Cruz Rivers. The party returns today after 26 days, having failed to sight even one Apache.

22. The Colorado Central Railroad, running from Denver to Golden, is completed.
27. Henry Comstock, 50, the discoverer and seller of the Comstock Lode, is found dead in Bozeman, Montana. Comstock, in ill health and broke, committed suicide.
30. The first passenger train from Golden arrives in Denver. The fare for the trip is $1.50.

Also in September 1870:

Thomas Mooney, a major San Francisco savings and loan figure, takes a vacation in the Orient, supposedly for his health. When he does not return, his California Building, Loan and Savings Society is found to be in deep financial trouble, with Mooney as the culprit. He remains in the Orient.

OCTOBER

3. Utah governor J. Wilson Shaffer dies; he will be succeeded by Vernon Vaughn.
7. A lynch mob led by Clay Allison hangs accused murderer Charles Kennedy in Elizabethtown, New Mexico. Allison decapitates the body and displays the head in a saloon.
11. Horace Greeley, the *New York Tribune* editor who is on his second visit to the Rockies, arrives in Denver on the Kansas Pacific Railroad.
12. The Southern Pacific Railroad Company is formed when the Central Pacific takes over the Southern Pacific as well as the San Francisco and San Jose Railroads.

■ Horace Greeley visits his namesake city, Greeley, Colorado.

15. The first issue of the *Arizona Citizen* is published in Tucson by congressional delegate Richard McCormick.
20. Citizens outline the townsite of Phoenix, Arizona.
22. The Greeley Lyceum Debating Society is organized.
24. The Kansas Pacific announces lower fares starting in November: six cents per mile.
29. Captain Harrison Moulton reports that the 1st Cavalry killed four Indians in Arizona's Pinal Mountains.

■ General Palmer, who headed the Denver Pacific's construction of track to Denver, departs the Mile High City for a honeymoon trip to Europe.

30. One of the settlers in the new town of Greeley, Colorado, is Fritz Neymeyer, who has opened a saloon. Tonight the saloon is burned by community

leaders who want to rid the town of that type of business. Six persons will be charged with arson and riot, and two will be put on trial.

National Headlines/October 1870:
12. ROBERT E. LEE DIES AT 63

NOVEMBER

1. There are 352 houses in Greeley, Colorado.
2. In the Greeley saloon-burning trial, W. R. Norcross is charged with arson and Ralph Meeker with rioting.
- Bear River Tom Smith is shot and killed near Abilene, Kansas.
4. The Central Pacific's No. 1, from Oakland, California, to Ogden, Utah, carrying silver and gold bullion as well as a cash payroll for a Virginia City mine, is stopped in Verdi, Nevada. Seven masked men make off with $42,000 in gold and silver.
5. Only 20 hours after being robbed in Verdi, Nevada, the Central Pacific's No. 1 is robbed again, about 385 miles from Verdi. Bandits take $4,000 in gold and silver.
- Sleet downs telegraph lines in Evans, Colorado.
8. Denver newspapers report that an unidentified Kickapoo was killed after he tied one end of a lasso around his waist and tossed the loop over the smokestack of a Kansas Pacific train traveling at 40 miles per hour.
11. The Union Pacific's annual report states that the 1,032 miles of track the railroad constructed from Omaha, Nebraska, to Ogden, Utah, cost $111,074,000 or some $100,000 per mile. Operating costs for the year were $5,600,000, while gross earnings were $8,406,000.
16. The first issue of the *Greeley Tribune* is published.
17. The site of present Tempe, Arizona, is established when Charles Hayden begins his Hayden Milling and Farming Ditch Company on the south side of the Salt River.
24. The first through freight car from New York arrives in Denver after a 13-day trip, carrying wines, liquor, and cigars. For the return trip, it is loaded with 22,300 pounds of silver ore from Central City.
- Susan James marries Allen H. Palmer, the former Quantrill raider, against her brother Jesse's wishes.
26. Kit Carson Cody, the first son of William F. Cody, is born. Cody will later recall that he wished his son's name to be "Elmo Judson, in honor of Ned Buntline, but the officers and scouts objected." According to Cody, "Major Brown proposed that we should call him Kit Carson, and it was finally settled that this should be his name."

Also in November 1870:
One of the Verdi, Nevada, train robbers is apprehended when the wife of a tavern keeper, sitting on one side of an outhouse, peeps through a crack in the wall and sees the robber examining a boot full of $20 gold pieces.
In Los Angeles, there is one saloon for every 50 persons.
There are 1,738 farms in Colorado.

DECEMBER

5. The first homestead claim in Wyoming is filed.
6. William S. Hart, the silent-screen actor (*Hells Hinges,* 1917; *Tumbleweeds,* 1925) is born in Newburgh, New York.
10. Wyoming governor John Campbell signs a bill passed by the territorial legislature that confers on women the right to vote and to hold office.
16. A blizzard blocks the Kansas Pacific's rails in Colorado for nearly two weeks, until December 30. Fifteen-foot drifts also develop between Box Elder and Wilson, Kansas.
25. Christmas is celebrated by passengers on four Kansas Pacific trains blocked by the snow, two eastbound ones in Kit Carson, Colorado, and two westbound ones in Wallace, Kansas. Soldiers from Fort Wallace provide the passengers with fresh buffalo meat.
- The Chinese Mission Institute is dedicated in San Francisco.
27. In Wyoming, the Cheyenne National Bank is organized.

Also in 1870:
There are 250,000 head of cattle, valued at $4.2 million, in Arizona.
Washington Territory lists the value of its industrial products as $2,851,042, and the value of its agricultural products as $2,111,902.
In their first full year of operation, the Union and Central Pacific Railroads carry 32,241 westbound passengers and 23,795 eastbound passengers.
The Indian population in California has dropped from 100,000 to 30,000 since 1849.
The California Steam Navigation Company pays dividends totalling $225,000.
There are some 4,000,000 settlers in the trans-Mississippi West.
Two hundred and seventy businesses failed in California.
This country's Native American population reaches an all-time low of 300,000.
William G. Fargo becomes president of Wells Fargo;

Lloyd Tevis is named vice president. The company's operating income drops to $133,526.52.

In California, an all-white school refuses to enroll the child of a black couple; a court upholds the school's decision in *Ward v. Flood*.

Congress passes the first appropriations bill for Indian education; the bill includes $100,000 for federal schools for industrial education.

Bret Harte writes *Plain Language from Truthful James.*

Frances Fuller publishes her most notable book, *The River of the West,* a history of Oregon that focuses on the life of Joseph L. Meek, whom she interviewed.

The Kiowa tribe is introduced to peyote, probably by the Comanches, who learned about it from Mexican Indians.

Alice Ivers (the future "Poker Alice"), 19, weds mining engineer Frank Duffield in Lake City, Colorado. Their life is happy and includes much social card playing. After Duffield is killed in a mining accident, Alice decides to support herself by dealing faro.

The Spanish Santa Fe Archives of New Mexico, partially destroyed in 1680, are sold as wastepaper by the administration of Governor William A. Pile. About 25 percent of the documents will be recovered.

1870 CENSUS

Arizona	9,658
Arkansas	484,471
California	560,247
Los Angeles	5,614
San Francisco	149,473
Colorado	39,864
Denver	4,759
Dakota Territory	14,000
Idaho	15,000
Iowa	1,194,000
Kansas	364,000
Louisiana	727,000
Minnesota	440,000
Missouri	1,721,000
Montana	20,595
Nebraska	123,000
Nevada	42,000
New Mexico	91,874
Oregon	91,000
Texas	818,579 (35 percent growth during last 10 years)
Utah	87,780
Washington	23,955
Wyoming	9,000

The population center of the United States is 48 miles northeast of Cincinnati, Ohio.

1871

"Always remember that your father never sold the country. You must stop your ears whenever you are asked to sign a treaty selling your home. My son, never forget my dying words. This country holds your father's body. Never sell the bones of your father and your mother."

—Tuekakas (on his deathbed,
as dictated to his son, Chief Joseph)

JANUARY

1. Captain R. F. Bernard reports that the 1st and 3rd Cavalries killed nine Indians near Arizona's Gila River.

2. The city of Golden, Colorado, is incorporated.

11. Arizona's sixth territorial legislature convenes; it reports that the territory is out of debt but that there are no public schools in operation.

17. The cable-operated streetcar is patented in San Francisco.

19. A campaign against Apaches in Arizona Territory is begun by General George Stoneman.

21. Denver's first gaslights burn outside the city's gasworks.

■ President Lincoln's private railroad car passes through Denver. Purchased by the Union Pacific as an officer's car, it is on its way to Omaha for repainting.

24. The Denver and Boulder Valley railway is completed; it stretches from Denver to the Erie coalfields in Boulder County, Colorado.

25. The first meeting of the California Women's Suffrage Society is held in San Francisco.

FEBRUARY

3. In Denver, the First National Bank and the Colorado National Bank are lit by gas, as are some streetlights.

10. Montana's first successful homestead application is that of D. D. Carpenter of Helena.

12. Captain William Kelly reports that the 8th Cavalry killed 14 Apaches and wounded 20 in Arizona's Chiricahua Mountains.

13. San Diego's *Daily Bulletin* begins publication.

15. Denver jewelers announce that they will obtain daily by telegraph Chicago time, which they intend to use to regulate their timepieces. Until now, each watchmaker used his or her own time, as did each of the three railroads.

■ Arizona's first school for Indians is begun by Reverend Charles Cook at Sacaton.

17. Governor George Woods, named to succeed Governor Vernon Vaughn, arrives in Salt Lake City.

18. Indians attack a government train near Fort Dodge, Kansas, killing three persons.

21. Frank Cross, 21, is apprehended while trying to ship himself from Denver to Boston in a box. According to one account: "The hitch came when the [Wells Fargo] agent refused to accept the box unless the expressman would either pay or guarantee payment of the $20 express charges. Unable to find the owner of the box, the expressman turned it over to the police. Cross got a trip to jail instead of to Boston." A Denver saloon owner will purchase the box and then charge patrons a quarter to look at it.

28. Phoenix becomes the county seat of Maricopa County, Arizona.

Also in February 1871:

"Shoo Fly, Don't Bother Me" becomes a popular song among miners in Montana.

Denver has only three buildings that are three stories tall.

In Wichita, Kansas, William H. Antrim acquires town lots that adjoin those of Catherine McCarty, whom he met in Indianapolis.

MARCH

3. Congress passes the Indian Appropriation Bill, which states that no tribe will be considered as a sovereign power or an independent nation, thus ending the practice of making treaties with the Indians. Less formal agreements will supersede treaties.

■ The *Arizona Miner* appeals to the U.S. government for protection against the Indians; it prints three columns of names of settlers slain since 1864.

■ The Chicago–Colorado Colony is reported to have purchased 55,000 acres of railroad and U.S. lands in Colorado, lying between Big Thompson Creek and Saint Vrains. A town, as yet unnamed, has been staked out.

15. An item in the *Wichita Tribune:* "The City Laundry is kept by Mrs. McCarty, to who we recommend those who wish to have their linen made clean." Mrs. McCarty's 11-year-old son will achieve fame as Billy the Kid.

20. San Diego's *Daily Union* becomes the city's first daily newspaper.

27. The University of Arkansas is founded in Fayetteville.

28. The opening reception for the San Francisco Art Association is held.

Also in March 1871:

General George Crook is thrust into the national spotlight when he is chosen by President Grant to head the army's Department of Arizona and to deal with the Apaches, the tribe that Crook calls "the tiger of the species." The man whom the Apaches dub "Gray Wolf" will choose not to fight them conventionally.

Work begins on the construction of the Denver and Rio Grande rail system.

APRIL

10. The colonists in Greeley, Colorado, celebrate their first anniversary. The population includes 674 men and 421 women.

11. The light from Denver's gaslit streets can be seen from Ward, Colorado, 50 miles away.

12. Lieutenant H. B. Cushing reports that 27 Indians

THE CAMP GRANT MASSACRE
APRIL 30, 1871

Federally protected Apaches were massacred by a mob at Camp Grant in Arizona Territory. A group of 140 Americans, Mexicans, and Papago Indians, led by William S. Oury, shot and clubbed to death 83 women and children. Another 30 children were stolen for the Mexican slave trade. An outraged President Grant called the incident "pure slaughter," but a jury will acquit every perpetrator. This incident will set off a 15-year war between settlers and Apaches.

---

were killed in a fight with the 3rd Cavalry in Arizona's Apache Mountains.

■ In Minneapolis, Minnesota, Charles Pillsbury receives title to the flour mill that he will use to begin Pillsbury and Company.

15. Wild Bill Hickok is appointed marshal of Abilene, Kansas, at a salary of $150 a month. He will serve in that post until the end of the year.

■ The *Daily Tribune* begins publication in Salt Lake City.

16. Some 90,000 head of cattle are being driven from Texas to Abilene, Kansas. The Kansas Pacific Railroad is preparing to load and ship four trainloads of cattle a day.

■ The Diamond R. Company promises eight-day freight service on the 480-mile stretch from Helena, Montana, to Corinne, Utah.

21. The double murderer John Boyer is executed in Laramie, Wyoming; his is the first legal hanging in the territory.

23. Blossom Rock in San Francisco Bay is dynamited by officials who perceive it as a traffic hazard.

30. Apaches are massacred at Camp Grant, Arizona.

Also in April 1871:

The sod house of rancher Henry L. Sitler becomes the first home to be built on the eventual site of Dodge City, Kansas.

MAY

1. Ground-breaking ceremonies are held for the Utah Southern Railroad.

5. A detachment of the 3rd Cavalry is defeated by Cochise's warriors at Bear Springs, Arizona. His Chiricahua Apaches surprise the soldiers in the

Cattle being shipped to the East from Abilene, Kansas, in 1871.   (Library of Congress)

Whetstone Mountains, and in fierce fighting Lieutenant H. B. Cushing and 10 of his 22 men who had been chasing the famous chief are killed. Thirteen Indians are also reported killed.

12. Troops from Fort Sill, Oklahoma, report killing three Indians and wounding four near the Red River. Seven citizens are also reported killed.

17. The baseball club of Kit Carson, Colorado, challenges Denver's club to a match on May 26 to determine the baseball champions of Colorado Territory.

■   Town lots go on sale in Tucson, Arizona.

18. The "Warren Massacre" takes place at Salt Creek, Texas, when the Kiowa Satanta leads a charge of 150 Kiowas and Comanches against a wagon train: wagon master Nathan Long and six members of the 10-wagon train freighting grain from Weatherford to Fort Griffin are killed.

19. Members of the 4th Cavalry discover the mutilated bodies of Nathan Long and his wagon train crew at Salt Creek, Texas.

22. Major John Wesley Powell begins his second expedition on the Green and Colorado Rivers.

24. William F. Cody scouts for the 5th Cavalry as

Lieutenant Hayes leads 30 soldiers against a band of Sioux camped on Birdwood Creek in Nebraska. Six Sioux are killed and 60 horses are recovered. Cody is cited for "conspicuous and gallant conduct."

26. In Colorado, the Kit Carson club throws in the sponge after the Denver club scores 12 runs in the 9th inning with no one out. The final score: Denver 66, Kit Carson 31.

29. Lieutenant A. P. Caraher reports that 22 Indians suspected of being cattle thieves were killed at Kiowa Springs, New Mexico.

■   Greeley, Colorado, is incorporated.

JUNE

1. A group of cowboys led by John Wesley Hardin arrives in Abilene, Kansas. Ben Thompson tries to convince Hardin to gun down the town's marshal, Wild Bill Hickok; Hardin declines.

■   A major celebration is held in Utah for Brigham Young's 70th birthday.

3. The James gang robs the bank in Corydon, Iowa.

8–9. Lieutenant Charles Morton reports that 56 Indians were killed and eight were wounded in a running fight with the 3rd Cavalry near Arizona's Verde River.

16. Catherine McCarty sells her land in Wichita, Kansas.

■ A huge tornado does significant damage to El Dorado, Kansas.

20. Cotton from Texas arrives in Parsons, Kansas.

24. Susan B. Anthony "thrills an overflow audience" at a lecture in Denver. One newspaper predicts an end to all wars if women are given the vote.

■ The cornerstone of Denver's Arapahoe Street school is laid.

One of the first photographs of Old Faithful, by William Henry Jackson. (Denver Public Library, Western Historical Collection)

27. A surveying party departs Denver to stake out the city of Colorado Springs, which was founded by William J. Palmer.

■ Track laying for the Denver and Rio Grande Railroad begins at the foot of Denver's 15th Street.

Also in June 1871:
Dr. F. V. Hayden, with $40,000 in funding, leads a team of 34 on the first scientific tour of the Yellowstone region.

JULY

3. The acting governor of Utah forbids the militia to celebrate the 4th of July.

5. Satanta and Big Tree are sentenced to hang by a cowboy jury in Jacksboro, Texas, for their part in the killing of seven men in raids in Texas. Satanta had bragged of the killings at Fort Sill, Oklahoma, and was arrested on the spot. A third warrior, Setangya, was killed during the arrest.

7. In Bluff City, Kansas, the Mexican cowboy Juan Bideno is shot dead while lunching at a saloon. Bideno had killed cowboy Bill Cohron near Newton, and was on the run from a group of Cohron's friends that included John Wesley Hardin. Hardin walked into the Bluff City saloon, put a bullet through Bideno's forehead, and then produced an arrest warrant naming his victim as a fugitive. Hardin deposited $20 for Bideno's burial and rode out of town.

13. Captain H. M. Smith reports that the 21st Infantry killed 15 Indians at Clenega de Los Pinos, Arizona. One soldier was killed.

17. The steamer *H. C. Nutt,* ferrying a Pullman car across the Missouri River in Omaha, is swept off course and collides with the pier of a railroad bridge. The car's passengers receive a hard jolt, but no injuries are reported.

19. The Hayden expedition sees its first wonder in Yellowstone, Devil's Slide on Cinnabar Mountain. Joining the expedition is the artist Thomas Moran and the photographer William Henry Jackson.

20. The members of the Hayden expedition become the first "white men" to view the Mammoth Hot Springs in Yellowstone.

25. Thomas Moran sketches Yellowstone's 156-foot Tower Falls.

26. In Texas, the first issue of the *Austin Statesman* appears.

28. The first spike of the Denver and Rio Grande Railroad is driven at Denver's Union Depot. It marks the laying of the first narrow, three-foot-gauge track on the continent.

Thomas Moran (1837–1926), the first trained artist to visit Yellowstone. (Denver Public Library, Western History Department)

Also in July 1871:
The first edition of the *Book of Mormon* to be published in Utah, 2,500 copies, is printed in Salt Lake City.

National Headlines/July 1871:
8. BOSS TWEED FRAUD EXPOSED
12. 52 KILLED IN NYC IRISH RIOTS

AUGUST

11. On election day in Kansas, lawmen Mike McCluskie and William Wilson are assigned to keep order during the voting in Newton. In the evening they argue about who will buy the drinks at the Red Front Saloon. They take their argument to the street, where McCluskie guns down Wilson. McCluskie then leaves town to avoid Wilson's companions.

15. The first run of a passenger train on narrow-gauge track in the United States begins in Denver, as the train leaves Union Depot and travels three miles to the end of the Denver and Rio Grande's tracks.

19. Mike McCluskie returns to Newton, Kansas, and proceeds to get drunk at Tuttle's Saloon.

20. Newton's General Massacre takes place.

22. The Denver and Rio Grande's tracks reach Littleton, Colorado.

23. The Utah Northern Railroad is created to build track from Ogden, Utah, to Soda Springs, Idaho.

25. Captain Frank Stanwood reports that the 3rd Cav-

"NEWTON'S GENERAL MASSACRE"
AUGUST 20, 1871

Cowboy Hugh Anderson avenged the August 11 death of his friend, William Wilson (Billy Bailey).

By 2:00 A.M. on August 20, Wilson's murderer, Mike McCluskie, was fairly drunk in Perry Tuttle's saloon. Anderson barged in with a group of Texas cowboys and they opened fire on McCluskie, who fell dead. One T. Riley, a youthful but consumptive friend of McCluskie, picked up the latter's six-shooter and the fight was on. Riley killed three of the Texans, and three others were wounded, including Anderson. One reporter wrote: "It was worse than Tim Finnegan's wake."

---

alry killed five Indians in Arizona's Arivaypa Canyon.

26. Ground-breaking ceremonies for the Utah Northern Railroad are held in Brigham City.

Also in August 1871:
In Texas, the death sentences of Satanta and Big Tree are commuted to life imprisonment at the request of Indian Agent Lawrie Tatum.
John Wesley Hardin leaves Abilene, Kansas.

SEPTEMBER

3. The town of Green River, Wyoming, is planned by the Union Pacific Railroad.

6. The Denver and Rio Grande Railroad's tracks reach Plum Creek (present Sedalia), Colorado.

8. Halfway up Pike's Peak, a four-room tourist house is under construction, it will be called the Half-Way House.

9. Newton, Kansas, becomes the western terminus of the Atchison, Topeka, and Santa Fe Railroad.

13. The *Pick and Plow,* the first newspaper in Bozeman, Montana, is renamed The *Avant Courier.*

15. The Denver and Rio Grande's tracks reach Castle Rock, Colorado.

16. The Teller House, a hotel, is under construction and "going up fast" in Central City, Colorado.

20. The Colorado Territorial Fair is under way in Denver.

22. General Philip Sheridan arrives at Fort McPherson, Nebraska. His party will leave tomorrow for Fort

Hays, Kansas, expecting to arrive there in 10 days with its guide, William F. Cody.

- Denver's City Council meets in its new chambers on Holliday Street. The mayor and four councilmen adjourn the meeting after one minute to attend the grand ball at the fairgrounds.
23. The *Enterprise,* a labor journal, begins publication in San Francisco.
28. General Philip Sheridan and his companions go on a buffalo hunt near Wallace, Kansas.
29. The Denver and Rio Grande's tracks reach Palmer Lake, Colorado.

Also in September 1871:

Satanta and Big Tree leave their prison in Texas to go on an escorted trip to St. Louis, where they will meet with a delegation of Kiowas; the latter had demanded the meeting as a condition for their upcoming trip to Washington, D.C.

OCTOBER

1. Of 28 gravestones in the cemetery in Laramie, Wyoming, 19 read "killed."
2. Brigham Young, 70, and other Mormon leaders are arrested on charges of "lascivious cohabitation"—polygamy. Lower courts will convict them, but the U.S. Supreme Court will overturn the convictions, citing the courts' lack of jurisdiction.
3. The *Boulder News,* unhappy that no Colorado rails have yet to reach the city, announces that visitors may walk along the new railroad grade from Erie for free.

- In Denver, the "Delmonico of the West" restaurant has its grand opening at 1540 Larimer Street.
5. While putting down a disturbance by 50 Texas cowboys, Abilene, Kansas, sheriff Wild Bill Hickok accidentally shoots his friend Mike Williams dead. Enraged at what he has done, Hickok then shoots cowboy Phil Coe, whom he believed had started the row. Hickok takes the mistake badly.

- San Francisco's Occidental Skating Rink burns to the ground.
8. San Francisco's business community is greatly affected by a devastating fire in Chicago: thanks to the transcontinental railroad, local insurance companies took the opportunity to write policies for many Chicago buildings. Insurance companies in San Francisco will pay out $1.5 million in cash, all withdrawn from San Francisco banks.

- After lingering for three days with two bullets in his belly, Phil Coe dies of wounds he suffered at the hands of Sheriff Wild Bill Hickok in Abilene, Kansas.

James Butler "Wild Bill" Hickok (1837–1876): A reluctant legend. (Denver Public Library, Western History Department)

9. The bandit Coal Oil Jimmy and accomplices known only as Taylor and Burns stop the Elizabethtown U.S. Mail and Express Coach in New Mexico and take some $500 from the strongbox.
10. The Union Pacific and the Kansas Pacific Railroads announce that they will ship all relief supplies to Chicago free of charge.
11. San Franciscans contribute $25,000 to aid Chicago's fire victims.
12. San Diego acquires its first fire truck.
18. A freight car carrying 600 kegs of gunpowder for the Colorado Central Railroad explodes six miles out of Cheyenne, Wyoming; no one is injured.
20. Coal Oil Jimmy, Taylor, and Burns rob a stagecoach near Vermejo, New Mexico.
21. Coal Oil Jimmy, Taylor, and Burns rob another stagecoach, this time near Trinidad, Colorado.

- The Denver and Rio Grande's tracks reach Colorado Springs, Colorado.
23. Regular rail passenger service begins between Denver and Colorado Springs. The 70-mile trip takes five hours at an average speed of 15 miles per hour.
24. The "Chinese Massacre" riots erupt in Los Angeles when residents lynch 19 Orientals after one allegedly killed a white man.
28. The mayor of Salt Lake City, Daniel H. Wells, is arrested and charged with murder, based on the testimony of Bill Hickman, a reputed outlaw.
31. The stagecoach robbers Taylor and Burns are killed by bounty hunters near Fort Union, New Mexico.

Also in October 1871:
Several tribes report that whites are invading sacred burial grounds to steal Indian bones for use in making buttons.

National Headlines/October 1871:
8. GREAT PESHTIGO FIRE IN WISCONSIN KILLS 600
8–11. CHICAGO FIRE KILLS 250; 17,450 BUILD-INGS DESTROYED; 98,500 HOMELESS

NOVEMBER

5. The "Wickenburg Massacre" takes place in Arizona.
9. The medical scientist Florence Sabin is born in Central City, Colorado. She will pursue a medical career after graduating Phi Beta Kappa from Smith College in 1893. During her 23-year career at Johns Hopkins University, she will write *Atlas of the Medulla and Mid-Brain*. Her tuberculosis research will provide radical new ways of treating that disease. *Good Housekeeping* will name her one of "America's 12 greatest women" in 1931. After World War II, she will work for healthcare reform in Colorado. Hers will be one of two statues of Coloradans in the National Statuary Hall in Washington, D.C.
■ The White Mountain Reservation is established in Arizona.
10. Nathan Bowers files the first homestead claim in Arizona at Prescott.
■ The author Winston Churchill (*The Crisis,* 1901) is born in St. Louis.
■ Mollie Shepherd, a survivor of the "Wickenburg Massacre," dies of an infected wound in her arm.
15. Boulder, Colorado, is incorporated.
17. A public school operates in Colorado Springs.
18. Grand Duke Alexis of Russia arrives in New York aboard the frigate *Svetlana;* his visit to the United States will include a wild buffalo hunt in the West.
21. The bodies of the outlaws Taylor and Burns are brought to Cimarron, New Mexico. A letter published in the *New Mexican* reads: "This community now breathes free. The notorious highwaymen who for the past month have kept our people in constant apprehension, were this morning brought into town stiff and stark, with ghastly bullet holes through their heads."
23. At a White House dinner for Russia's Grand Duke Alexis, the first Romanov to visit America, General Philip Sheridan assures the guest that there is plenty of excitement west of the Mississippi. The seed for a "grand buffalo hunt" is planted.
27. The Summit County Railroad Company is organized in Utah.

THE WICKENBURG MASSACRE
NOVEMBER 5, 1871

A stagecoach running between Wickenburg and La Paz was attacked without warning by Apaches, or Mexicans disguised as Apaches, in Arizona's Vulture Mountains. Driver John Lanz and five passengers were killed almost immediately, leaving two passengers, a Mr. Kruger and Mollie Shepherd, who was wounded. The two made it from the coach to cover, thanks to Kruger's six-shooter, and the next La Paz–Wickenburg stagecoach picked them up two hours later.

Also in November 1871:
Construction begins on the state capitol building in Des Moines, Iowa.
New Mexico reports that it is $74,000 in debt.

National Headlines/November 1871:
10. STANLEY FINDS LIVINGSTON ON LAKE TAN-GANYIKA

DECEMBER

4. The Denver Pacific Railway train that left Denver for Cheyenne, Wyoming, this morning is forced to stop two miles from its destination because of drift-ing snow. Sleighs from Cheyenne pick up the pas-sengers.
5. Bill Pickett, the rodeo star who will invent the sport of bulldogging, is born near Austin, Texas.
6. A large ball is held in Tucson to celebrate today's arrival of the military's telegraph line.
7. Thousands of buffalo reportedly surround Kit Car-son, Colorado, ranging some 200 miles farther west than usual. Local Indians say this is a sign that a bad winter is approaching.
8. Republican Newton Booth is elected governor of California.
10. The sale of town lots in Phoenix is authorized.
13. Cheyenne's hotel for railroad passengers burns to the ground. The Union Pacific has no insurance on the $23,000 structure.
■ Wild Bill Hickok is dismissed as sheriff of Abilene, Kansas, by the City Council, which states that it has no further need for his services.
16. The Helling Mill in Phoenix supplies flour to many Arizona settlements and military posts.

---

17. Two miles of Denver and Rio Grande track through Denver are completed.

■ The Denver Horse Railroad, organized in 1867 as a local transit service, begins operation as the Denver City Railway Company.

18. Snow blocks the tracks of the Denver Pacific, Kansas Pacific, Union Pacific, Rio Grande, and Boulder Valley Railroads.

25. Ambrose Bierce weds Ellen Day in San Francisco.

28. The first stone of San Francisco's new City Hall is laid.

■ The Teller House, a hotel in Central City, Colorado, is completed.

31. One-horse open streetcars begin operating in Denver.

Also in 1871:

Fort Smith is abandoned as a military post in Arkansas.

Colt revolvers are redesigned for greater long-range effectiveness.

San Diego whalers make 55,000 gallons of whale oil.

Eleven years after she was recaptured by whites from the Comanches, Cynthia Ann Parker, despondent over the death of her daughter, starves herself to death.

The last recorded lynching in Los Angeles takes place.

There are 265,000 head of cattle, valued at $4.2 million, in Arizona.

Eighty-nine businesses in California fail.

Wells Fargo's net operating income is $227,902.90; the company has 436 offices.

Two collections of Joaquin Miller's poetry are published: *Pacific Poems* and *Songs of the Sierras.*

George L. Woods becomes governor of the Utah Territory; he will serve in that post until 1874.

Frontier price check: coffee—$4 a pound; brandy—$40 a gallon; soap—50 cents a bar; broom—$6.

1872

"The flower-fed buffaloes of the spring
In the days of long ago,
Ranged where the locomotive sing
And the prairie flowers lie low."
—Vachel Lindsay, *The Flower-Fed Buffaloes*

JANUARY

1. There are 121 newspapers in Kansas.
3. The "horse railway" system started in December 1871, has its official opening in Denver, using 12 horses and six cars. Service is on the half-hour; the fare is 10 cents.
9. The Colorado Stock Growers' Association is formed.
10. The Denver Water Company begins supplying the city from Holly, Colorado.
11. The party of Russia's Grand Duke Alexis departs St. Louis for a western buffalo hunt.
12. Grand Duke Alexis and his entourage are joined at the Omaha, Nebraska, train depot by George Armstrong Custer.
13. Grand Duke Alexis and his party arrive by train in North Platte, Nebraska, where they are greeted by one of their guides for the upcoming buffalo hunt, William F. Cody. Another personality joining the entourage is Texas Jack Omohundro, a friend of Cody.
■ Buffalo are reported to be present "as far as the eye can see" from Kit Carson to Kiowa, Colorado.
14. Grand Duke Alexis, celebrating his 21st birthday on a wild-west buffalo hunt, kills his first buffalo. After the duke's first six shots with an engraved Smith and Wesson miss their mark, Buffalo Bill Cody hands him his famed "Lucretia Borgia".50 caliber rifle. Alexis gets within 10 feet of his mark and scores a bull's-eye. "Very soon the corks began

to fly from the champagne bottles," wrote Cody. Later in the afternoon, when Alexis accidentally slays a buffalo cow with a pistol, bottles appear. Wrote Cody: "I was in hopes that he would kill five or six more before we reached camp, especially if a basket of champagne was to be opened every time he dropped one." *Frank Leslie's Illustrated Newspaper* described George A. Custer's "warpaint" for this expedition: his face was "illustrated with setting suns, anatomical dogs, and primitive canoes."
15. On his royal buffalo hunt, Grand Duke Alexis is sent shimmying up a telegraph pole to escape a wounded bison. The party of hunters records 56 kills today.
17. Grand Duke Alexis arrives in Denver; his party occupies 15 rooms in the American House.
18. The "biggest social event in Denver's history" occurs as the Grand Ducal Ball is held at the American House, with Alexis as the guest of honor. At the ball, a fiddler tells George A. Custer that there is good hunting in the area of Kit Carson, Colorado.
20. The California Stock Exchange is formally organized in San Francisco.
21. Alexis hunts buffalo near Kit Carson, Colorado. Excited by his first kill of the day, the grand duke hugs and kisses George A. Custer. A total of 50 kills are reported by the party, including three by Custer.
22. Grand Duke Alexis arrives in Topeka, Kansas, on

George Armstrong Custer and Russia's Grand Duke Alexis take time out from the rigors of royal buffalo hunting to pose at a Kansas portrait studio. (Denver Public Library, Western History Department)

the Kansas Pacific Railroad, and is received by the Kansas legislature.

■ The Society of Colorado Pioneers Association is founded in Denver.

FEBRUARY

1. Montana's legislature enacts limits on big-game hunting.
7. Snow has blocked the Union Pacific's trains from entering Denver from Cheyenne via the Denver Pacific's rails since December 20.
8. John J. Valentine becomes the new superintendent of Wells Fargo's express department.
13. George Buck and Matilda Murray become the first Americans to wed in Phoenix, Arizona.
22. The cornerstone of San Francisco's new City Hall is laid.
23. The 120-member Grand Embassy of Japan, blocked by snow in Salt Lake City, is reported to be "having a grand time."
29. Denver's Union Station, a passenger train depot, is completed.

Also in February 1872:
A roller skating rink opens in Cheyenne, Wyoming. The proprietor calls it "a moral and exciting diversion."

MARCH

1. President Ulysses S. Grant signs a bill designating Yellowstone the nation's first national park. The park contains more than 3,000 geysers and covers 2,221,772 acres in Wyoming, Idaho, and Montana. Bear, moose, and elk are plentiful within its boundaries.
■ The Kansas Pacific purchases the Denver Pacific Railway, which has been financially weakened by the snow blocking its traffic. The deal calls for the Kansas Pacific to buy 60 percent of the Denver Pacific's $2.5 million in stocks.
2. Utah Territory's constitutional convention draws up a new constitution and petitions the federal government for admission to the Union as a state.
4. In Arizona, Tucson's first public school opens.
10. The *Arizona Sentinel* begins publishing in Yuma.
12. The former mountain man Jim Bridger is reported to be visiting Denver.
20. The Denver Hotel and Restaurant Keepers' Association publishes a list of all local deadbeats. The debtors on the list are incensed and organize to fight the action.
22. The rail bridge over the Missouri River between Omaha, Nebraska, and Council Bluffs, Iowa, is completed.
24. Four outlaws are lynched in Tucson.
26. At 2:25 A.M., an earthquake at Lone Pine, California, kills 27 people and injures 60.
■ The Denver and Rio Grande Railroad begins laying track from Colorado Springs to Pueblo, which it hopes to reach in May.
27–28. Sergeant William Wilson reports that the 4th Cavalry killed two Indians, wounded three, and captured one near Fort Concho, Texas.

Also in March 1872:
The Grange endorses the newly formed Montgomery Ward Company, which pledges to sell products at a lower price by mail.

The author Ambrose Bierce and his new bride depart San Francisco for a three-year stay in England.

The U.S. government reports that the Kansa Indians are "absolutely destitute . . . living on a little corn and dead animals they can find lying around."

APRIL

4. A post office is established in Loveland, Colorado.
5. American wolfers and Assiniboine Indians clash in Montana's Sweet Grass Hills, near the Canadian border, resulting in the first Cypress Hills Massacre.
6. The "state of Deseret" elects as senators W. H. Hooper and Thomas Fitch, who would serve in

Washington, D.C., in the event the state were admitted to the Union.

10. In Nebraska, Arbor Day is celebrated for the first time in the United States.

15. The U.S. Supreme Court overturns all judicial decisions reached in Utah during the last 18 months.

18. The completion of a bridge across the Missouri River is cause for a major celebration in Leavenworth, Kansas. A crowd of 30,000 attends.

20. Fire destroys much of San Diego's Old Town.

■ Lieutenant F. R. Vincent is mortally wounded in a fight with Indians near Howard's Mills, Texas; six Indians are reported killed.

■ The San Francisco Bar Association is organized.

23. A major tornado strikes Coffeyville, Kansas.

26. William F. Cody and Company B of the 5th Cavalry fight Indians at the South Fork of the Loup River in Nebraska. Cody claims he killed six Indians, whereas the official report notes three.

29. Frank and Jesse James, Cole Younger, and Clell Miller rob the Columbia Kentucky Deposit Bank of $600 and kill teller R. A. Martin.

Also in April 1872:

Among those hunting buffalo at the Salt Fork of the Arkansas River, in clear violation of treaties with Indians, are Wyatt Earp and Bat Masterson.

MAY

2. The new constitution of the "state of Deseret" is presented to both houses of Congress.

10. Nathaniel Pitt Langford is appointed Yellowstone National Park's first superintendent.

11. Passengers of the Kansas Pacific protest against the senseless killing of buffalo from railroad cars. Animal carcasses are said to be lining the tracks.

12. Jim Antrim, brother of William, is appointed an assistant marshal in Wichita, Kansas.

15. The Santa Fe Railroad reaches Wichita, Kansas.

■ Buffalo Bill Cody tracks and kills four Indians who committed depredations near North Platte, Nebraska.

16. San Francisco's Metropolitan Gas Company lights its first lamps.

■ Henry M. Teller is named president of the Colorado Central and Pacific Railroad.

17. The Denver and Rio Grande's tracks are reported to be 20 miles from Pueblo, but the railroad's workers have run out of iron.

■ San Francisco's Bohemian Club is founded.

20. Ground-breaking ceremonies are held in Utah for the American Fork Railroad.

22. William F. Cody is awarded the Medal of Honor for his bravery in the battle against Indians on April 26. An act of Congress in 1916 will rescind the honor "on the ground that at the time of the act of gallantry he was neither an officer nor an enlisted man, being at that time a civilian."

23. Jesse James teams with Cole and Bob Younger and Bill Stiles to rob the Savings Association Bank of Ste. Genevieve, Missouri, of $4,000.

25. Ned Buntline's "Buffalo Bill's Best Shot or The Heart of Spotted Tail" begins serialization in the *New York Weekly*.

■ The Salt Lake City Gas Works is founded.

National Headlines/May 1872:

4. LIBERAL REPUBLICANS NOMINATE GREELEY AT CINCINNATI

JUNE

1. Shipping a carload of freight from San Francisco to Omaha costs $350; to send it all the way to New York costs $325.

■ The journal *Woman's Exponent* begins publication in Utah.

5. Congress creates a reservation for the Flathead Indians in Montana. In another action, the Bitterroot Valley, in the region that will become the Montana-Idaho border, is opened to homesteading.

6. President Grant's appointee as associate justice of the New Mexico Supreme Court, Warren Bristol, arrives in New Mexico.

8. Denver's first pipe organ is being installed in the First Presbyterian Church.

9. Marshal William L. Brooks is wounded three times while trying to arrest Texas cowboys in Newton, Kansas.

10. Congress authorizes a geographical survey west of the 100th meridian; the Wheeler Survey will be published in 1875–1889.

■ The Atchison, Topeka, and Santa Fe Railroad is completed to Hutchison, Kansas.

12. The population of Denver is 12,000.

14. Fort McKeen is established south of present Bismarck, North Dakota.

17. As the Atchison, Topeka, and Santa Fe Railroad nears, rumors have been spreading that a town will be built on the site of Fort Dodge, Kansas. These rumors were heard by the Canadian George M. Hoover, 24, who got an idea. Because U.S. military jurisdiction reaches to the 100th meridian, five miles west of Fort Dodge, Hoover carefully measured the distance. Here, he and John G. McDonald erect a tent, unload their whiskey, and open the first "saloon" in the future Dodge City at 8:00 A.M.

19. The Denver and Rio Grande's tracks reach Pueblo, Colorado.

20. The first train enters Pueblo, Colorado. According to an eyewitness report: "Mexicans and Indians lined up along the tracks, broke and ran when the monster approached. Some jumped into Fontaine Creek."

24. Settlers erect a bridge on the Little Colorado River and name their settlement St. Johns.

26. The village of Tucson, Arizona, comes into being as deeds are issued following the completion of a survey by S. W. Foreman.

National Headlines/June 1872:

7. GOP NOMINATES GRANT IN PHILADELPHIA

JULY

1. Salt Lake City's street railroad formally opens.

2. A special excursion train takes Denverites to Pueblo for a banquet and ball celebrating the arrival of the Denver and Rio Grande Railroad.

4. An old-fashioned cabin raising for Ohio native Brewster M. Higley, M.D., takes place on Beaver Creek in Smith County, Kansas. At 38, he will homestead a claim and contemplate with quiet verse. In the fall of 1873, he will write:

> Oh, give me a home where the buffalo roam,
> Where the deer and the antelope play,
> Where never is heard a discouraging word
> And the sky is not clouded all day.

■ Wild-steer riding is included in the competition at an early rodeo in Cheyenne, Wyoming.

8. Ned Buntline's *Buffalo Bill's Last Victory, or Dove Eye, the Lodge Queen* begins serialization in the *New York Weekly*.

13. Lieutenant W. P. Hall reports that the 5th Cavalry killed four Indians in the Whetstone Mountains of Arizona.

16. Control of Fort Collins, Colorado, is transferred from the War Department to the Interior Department.

HOME ON THE RANGE

As recognizable as "The Star Spangled Banner" or "America the Beautiful," "Home on the Range" offers its own brand of western nostalgia as soon as anyone starts to sing, "Oh, give me a home. . . ." Still, the fuss that was made over "Home on the Range" was hardly deer-and-antelope play. The legal squabble over the song's authorship ended up in New York law offices, far from where the buffalo roam.

During the summer of 1908, University of Texas professor John Lomax was in San Antonio pursuing his life's passion, the exploration of American folk music. Appearing in the Buckhorn Saloon with his clunky Edison recorder, he explained his mission to the startled proprietor, who in turn offered a lead. Running a small beer saloon beyond the Southern Pacific Railroad depot was an old black man who had been a cook on the Chisholm Trail.

Lomax found the old-timer, and on a sweltering afternoon in a mesquite grove, "Home on the Range" was resurrected from oblivion. "It was the first time I ever heard the melody," remarked Lomax, who included it, along with 111 other trail tunes he had rediscovered, in his 1910 collection, *Cowboy Songs and Other Frontier Ballads*.

Over the next 20 years, the song appeared in other folk anthologies. It became a campfire favorite, an American tune known round the world. Admiral Richard Byrd even used a recording of the song, which he played on an old phonograph, to serenade the penguins at the South Pole in 1929: "I gave myself daily concerts, always playing the song that tells about the land of sunshine where the sky is not cloudy all day."

Franklin Delano Roosevelt, on the night he was first elected president in 1932, commented that "Home on the Range" was his favorite song. That innocent remark vaulted the tune into the national spotlight. Pop singers included it in their repertoires. By 1934, it had reached the "top ten" on radio's *Hit Parade*. Because the song was not covered by copyright, there was no need to pay royalties.

The public domain received a jolt in June 1934, when William and Mary Goodwin of Tempe, Arizona, filed suit in U.S. District Court in New York, claiming that they had written and copyrighted "Home on the Range" as "An Arizona Home" on February 27, 1905. NBC was among the 35 defendants in the suit, including publishing houses, radio networks, and film producers. The Goodwins wanted a half-million dollars.

(continued)

(continued)

The song was pulled from broadcast, and all publication ceased. The Music Publishers Protective Association took over the legal defense. Manhattan attorney Samuel Moanfeldt was called upon to research the validity of the Goodwins' claim. If they did not write "Home on the Range," who did?

The *Leadville Herald Democrat* in Colorado claimed to know the answer: the song was written in nearby California Gulch during the winter of 1885 by a group of miners. From the cabin they dubbed "Junk Lane Hotel," a group consisting of Bob Swartz, Bill McCabe, Bingham Graves, and Jim Fouts made up a song called "Colorado Home" that went: "Oh give me the hill, and the ring of a drill, / In the rich silver ore in the ground. / And give me the Gulch, where the miners can sluice, / And the bright yellow Gold can be found."

Moanfeldt tracked down the barkeep who first sang the song for Lomax. The old man claimed tohave heard it from cowboys. Meanwhile, letters had been arriving from Kansas, from other old-timers who had first heard the song on the open range.

Clearly, it was time for Moanfeldt to head west. In Dodge City, Kansas, he found people who remembered singing the tune before 1880. A newspaper there ran a dispatch over the Associated Press wires about Moanfeldt's inquiries and drew a big response. In one letter, Florence Pulver of Osborne said her mother sang a song by a Dr. Higley.

Pulver directed Moanfeldt to her childhood home of Gaylord, in Smith County. At the county seat of Smith Center, he met the editor of the *Smith CountyPioneer*, A. L. Headley, who produced the smoking gun. In an 1873 reprint of the newspaper were the words to "My Western Home":

Oh, give me a home where the buffalo roam,
Where the deer and the antelope play,
Where never is heard a discouraging word
And the sky is not clouded all day.

Ohio native Brewster M. Higley, M.D. was a three-time widower by 1871. His fourth marriage had dissolved, probably because of his drinking, while he lived in Indiana. At 38, he moved to Smith County, Kansas, and homesteaded a claim on Beaver Creek, where an old-fashioned cabin raising took place on July 4, 1872.

During the following autumn, Higley penned his poem, stuck it between two books on his shelf, and forgot about it. L. T. Reese brought an injured friend to the doctor's cabin during the spring of 1873, discovered the verse while browsing through the bookshelf, and commended Higley.

Higley next showed the poem to Dan Kelley, a member of the Harlan Brothers Orchestra. Kelley worked out the melody on his violin. In April 1873, at a social event in Harlan, Kansas, Kelley's singing brother-in-law, Clarence "Cal" Harlan, gave the song its public debut.

The song was printed in the aforementioned newspaper later that year, and again in 1876 in the *Kirwan Chief*. From there, it traveled the path of a folk tune. Many versions were invented to suit the local surroundings.

Higley continued to live the life of a frontier doctor. One year, he treated 86 typhoid cases. He took a fifth wife in 1875, and they moved to Arkansas in 1886, then to Shawnee, Oklahoma, in 1893; he died there at age 87 on May 10, 1911.

Dan Kelley was 30 when he wrote the tune to Higley's words. He listed his occupation as carpenter, though he was also an amateur inventor. He moved to Waterloo, Iowa, in 1889, where he passed away at age 62 on October 23, 1905. It is highly probable that Higley and Kelley never knew of the popularity their song had achieved, or that it was ever published. They never saw any royalties.

Before he left Gaylord, Moanfeldt got an added bonus. Taken to the home of 86-year-old Cal Harlan, he was treated to a creaky rendition of the song from the man who had first sung it. When Moanfeldt was asked if he had gathered sufficient evidence during his research trip, the attorney quipped, "I have everything but the quill the song was written with."

Indeed, Moanfeldt's findings were enough to send the Goodwins packing—their case was dismissed in 1935. Still, legends die hard, and as late as 1944, Colorado was still claiming to be the real home of "Home." Congressman Robert Rockwell even told the story of the singing miners on the floor of the U.S. House of Representatives, as if getting it printed in the *Congressional Record* would make it true. To prevent a border war, the state of Kansas decided to take matters one step further. In 1947, "Home on the Range" was made the state's official song.

25. San Diego's *Daily Word* begins publication.
28. C. W. Penrose, editor of the Ogden, Utah, *Junction*, is beaten by the "pettifogging lawyer Keithly," who had received some bad press.
30. In San Francisco, a corporation is formed to explore the "diamond fields" of the West; it is the beginning of a major hoax.

Also in July 1872:

A crowd of 5,000 greets the first train to arrive in Dallas, Texas, a Houston and Texas Central. Within a year, the city's population will increase from 3,000 to 6,000.

Applying for a position with Horace Greeley's presidential campaign is none other than stagecoach driver Hank Monk, who gave Greeley such a rousing ride back in 1859. Greeley's response: "I would rather see you ten thousand fathoms in hell than give you a crust of bread."

National Headlines/July 1872
9. DEMOCRATS NOMINATE GREELEY

AUGUST

8. According to the Santa Fe *New Mexican:* "If some men about the plaza, would go to the trifling expense of constructing a suitable place to receive and conceal their offal and swill, it would be a move towards decency, and give less offense to the feet and nostrils of those who are compelled sometimes to pass by their doors."
14. Major E. M. Baker reports that the 2nd Cavalry and the 7th Infantry were involved in action against Indians near Prior's Fork, Montana. Casualty estimates: two Indians, one soldier, and one civilian killed; 10 Indians and five soldiers wounded.
15. Captain William McCleave reports that the 8th Cavalry killed four Indians and wounded eight on Palo Duro Creek in New Mexico.
18. Dr. F. V. Hayden's U.S. Geological Survey expedition camps at Geyser Basin in Yellowstone.
19. "The Great Diamond Fields of America" are reported in the Laramie *Daily Independent.* Cousins Philip Arnold and John Slack of Kentucky have salted a secluded mesa in Colorado with uncut diamonds that they purchased in Europe. Their scam will reach dizzying proportions and involve some very influential people before it is exposed by Clarence King, the future head of the U.S. Geological Survey.
22. "Diamond excitement" grips New Mexico and Arizona as false rumors of gem fields abound.
23. The first Japanese commercial vessel arrives in San Francisco with a cargo of tea.

26. Indian scouts report six of their ranks killed in an attack near Fort McKeen, Dakota Territory.
27. The Flathead Indians cede their lands in Montana to the United States.
■ Lieutenant R. T. Steward is among the four soldiers killed in an Indian attack on the 5th Cavalry in Arizona's Davidson Canyon.
28. Wild Bill Hickok is not a big enough draw to ensure the success of "The Grand Buffalo Hunt" in Niagara Falls, New York: the show is a financial failure, but Wild Bill's take is larger than the gate receipts.

Also in August 1872:

A town company is established on the site of the future Dodge City, Kansas. Because the population is comprised largely of buffalo hunters anticipating a September arrival of the Atchison, Topeka, and Santa Fe Railroad, the community is unofficially named "Buffalo City." Among the town's population of 2,000 buffalo hunters are men like Tom Nixon, who once killed 120 animals in 40 minutes and claimed 3,200 bison kills in 35 days. Charles Rath and Company, a buffalo clearing house, will ship 2.5 million buffalo hides from 1872 to 1874.

Texas Jack Omohundro finds work as a guide for the Pawnees' summer buffalo hunt.

SEPTEMBER

3. The members of the Santa Fe police force resign, claiming they have to provide their own uniforms and equipment and pay their own medical bills.
4. The *New York Sun* exposes the Credit Mobilier scandal: Vice President Schuyler Colfax, among others, is accused of having received shares of Credit Mobilier of America, a phony company created to absorb profits from the Urban Pacific Railroad.
5. The first public school in Phoenix, Arizona, opens.
19. Denver begins renaming its streets and numbering houses.
22. A report filed at the Military Headquarters of the Pacific by Lieutenant Colonel George Crook cites 154 acts of depredation by Indians in Arizona since September 1871. The acts include the killing of 41 civilians and three soldiers, and the theft of 554 cows.
25. Captain J. W. Mason reports that 40 Indians were killed by the 5th Cavalry at Muchos Canyon on Arizona's Santa Maria River.
■ In an anti-saloon edict, Houston's *Daily Telegraph* proclaims that "Houston is too elegant a city to be afflicted with such places as Smoky Row, Jones' Woods, Hash Row, French Soldier, and Frogtown in Galveston."

26. Jesse and Frank James and Cole Younger grab the gate receipts of the Kansas City Fair from ticket-seller Ben Wallace and make off with $978 (another source says $8,000). In the scuffle, a bullet ricochets and hits a little girl in the leg.

27. At the Kansas City Fair, Wild Bill Hickok refuses to let the band play "Dixie." Texans in attendance are infuriated.

29. Colonel Ranald Mackenzie reports a fight between Indians and the 4th Cavalry, assisted by Tonkawa scouts, on the north fork of the Red River in Texas. Casualty estimates: 23 Indians killed and 120 captured; one soldier killed.

30. Lieutenant Max Wesendorff reports that the 1st Cavalry killed 17 Indians and wounded one near Squaw Peak, Arizona.

Also in September 1872:
The first resident of Boot Hill, a small bluff some 700 feet from Second Avenue and Front Street in Dodge City, Kansas, is Black Jack, who is shot by a gambler called Denver.

OCTOBER

1. The United States enters into peace talks with Cochise near Dragoon Springs, Arizona.

9. The first Southern Colorado Agricultural and Industrial Fair is held.

12. Cochise signs a peace treaty with General O. O. Howard in Arizona.

18. The *New Mexican* reports: "The streets of Santa Fe were never so dirty as now. Hay wagons, bull trains, etc., have been camping about the plaza for more than a week, adding all their filth to the already abundant dust, until the public square presents a shameful appearance."

21. Following the arbitration of Germany's Emperor William I, the United States is awarded the Islands of San Juan in Puget Sound, off the coast of Washington Territory; the islands had also been claimed by England.

■ The penitentiary in Laramie, Wyoming, opens.

30. Mrs. Horace Greeley dies.

NOVEMBER

15. The mayor of San Francisco communicates with the mayor of Adelaide, Australia, in ceremonies honoring the completion of a telegraphic route to Australia through Europe.

19. Dakota Territory's Fort McKeen, four miles south of Bismarck, is renamed Fort Abraham Lincoln.

25. Captain Emil Adam reports that the 5th Cavalry killed 11 Indians and captured four at Hell's Canyon, Arizona; one soldier is reported wounded.

26. The San Francisco *Evening Bulletin* exposes the "great diamond hoax" under a headline that reads: "The Diamond Chimera." The Bank of America's William Ralston returns $80,000 to each of 25 investors, while the men who started the scam, Philip Arnold and John Slack, escape to greener pastures with $600,000 to divide between themselves.

■ In Utah, the American Fork Railroad is completed to Deer Creek.

28. Fighting breaks out between Modoc Indians, led by Captain Jack, and 38 members of the 1st Cavalry under Captain James Jackson. The Modocs have refused to move to Oregon's Klamath Reservation, and when Jackson's men try to move them by force, a battle erupts in the lava beds near Tule Lake, California. The Modocs retreat south, killing a total of 12 civilians along the way.

29. Horace Greeley dies at age 61 in Pleasantville, New York, just 24 days after losing the presidential election to Ulysses S. Grant. The town of Greeley, Colorado, mourns.

■ Captain James Jackson reports that the 1st Cavalry killed eight Indians on Oregon's Lost River; one soldier was killed and seven were wounded.

Also in November 1872:
Sidney Lanier arrives in San Antonio, Texas, seeking a cure for tuberculosis. During his stay, which will conclude next April, he will decide to focus his attentions on poetry and music rather than on law.

National Headlines/November 1872:
5. GRANT RE-ELECTED, DEFEATS GREELEY
9. $75 MILLION BOSTON FIRE
19. BOSS TWEED JAILED

DECEMBER

4. The *New Mexican* confirms the worst about the great diamond swindle: "In thirty days more, but for the complete and timely exposure by Clarence King, no less than twelve million dollars of the stock would have been put upon the market. . . ."

7–8. The 5th Cavalry reports that a dozen Indians were killed in a fight in Arizona's Red Rock country.

11. Pinckney Benton Stewart Pinchback, a veteran of the Union Army during the Civil War, becomes acting governor of Louisiana; as such, he becomes the first black to serve as governor in the United States.

- Lieutenant Thomas Garvey reports that 14 Indians were killed in a fight at Bad Rock Mountain, Arizona.

12. Buffalo Bill Cody and Texas Jack Omohundro arrive in Chicago by train to prepare for their stage debut.

13. Lieutenant W. C. Manning reports that 11 Indians were killed in a fight with troops in Arizona's Mazatal Mountains.

15. The Colorado Central's narrow-gauge railroad is completed to Black Hawk.

16. The first major school building in Arizona opens in Florence.

17. In Chicago, Buffalo Bill and Texas Jack Omohundro make their acting debut in *The Scouts of the Prairie,* written by Ned Buntline, who plays Cale Durg. The epic's heroine, Dove Eye, is played by Giuseppina Morlacchi. Neither Bill nor his costar are able to deliver a single line as written. The action and fight sequences thrill the audience, however, and Cody is a sensation. Says the *Times:*

> On the whole it is not probable that Chicago will ever look upon the like again. Such a combination of incongruous drama, execrable acting, renowned

From left to right: Ned Buntline, William F. Cody, and Texas Jack Omohundro. "On the whole it is not probable that Chicago will ever look upon the like again." (Denver Public Library, Western History Department)

performers, mixed audience, intolerable stench, scalping, blood and thunder, is not likely to be vouchsafed to a city for a second time—even in Chicago.

21. An explosion rocks San Francisco's Hercules Power Works.

22. Texas Jack Omohundro, who is in Chicago with Buffalo Bill and appearing in *The Scouts of the Prairie,* falls in love with Giuseppina Morlacchi, an Italian dancer in the show.

23. The Atchison, Topeka, and Santa Fe Railroad reaches Colorado, 470 miles from Atchison, Kansas.

- In a Dodge City shoot-out, Bill Brooks, the former marshal of Newton, Kansas, kills a Mr. Brown of the Santa Fe Railroad.

25. On Christmas Day, the first southbound passenger train on the Missouri, Kansas, and Texas line completes its journey through Indian Territory and crosses the Red River into Texas.

26. A fire destroys part of Concordia, Kansas.

27. Lord Dunraven, an Irish nobleman and former war correspondent for the *London Daily Telegraph,* arrives in Colorado's Estes Park and writes: "The climate of Colorado is health-giving . . . giving to the jaded spirit, the unstrung nerves, and weakened body, a stimulant, a tone and vigor."

28. The U.S. Army defeats the Apaches at Salt River Canyon, Arizona, in the last big battle with that tribe. Captain W. H. Brown reports that the 5th Cavalry killed 57 Apaches and captured 20, while one soldier was killed and one was wounded.

- George Catlin, 76, the artist who depicted the Indians along the Missouri River in the last days before the white man arrived, dies as a pauper in Jersey City, New Jersey.

- Dodge City saloon keeper Matthew Sullivan is shot dead by an unknown assailant who fired through the saloon's window. Bully Brooks is a popular suspect.

30. The 5th Cavalry reports killing six Indians and capturing two in a clash at the mouth of Arizona's Baby Canyon.

31. In its story on the Sullivan murder in Dodge City, the *Kansas Daily Commonwealth* states: "It is supposed that the unknown assassin was a character in those parts called Bully Brooks, but nothing definite is known concerning the affair, or what led to it."

Also in December 1872:

An earthquake in Washington Territory causes a rock slide that interrupts the flow of the Columbia River.

Also in 1872:

A half-million buffalo hides are shipped from Dodge City.

There are 290,000 head of cattle worth $4.6 million in Arizona.

Colorado crops earn $4.65 million.

Clarence King writes *Mountaineering in the Sierra Nevada.*

In Denver, 237 brick buildings and 447 frame buildings are constructed.

The University of Oregon is chartered in Eugene.

Fifteen killings in Dodge City's first year as a community prompt the construction of Boot Hill Cemetery, just west of the center of town.

Denver ships $1,212,934 in gold bullion, $19,760 in silver, and $62,717 in gold coins.

Before his gambling and gunfighting days begin, Doc Holliday, 20, graduates from the Pennsylvania College of Dental Surgery.

Mark Twain publishes *Roughing It,* which is based on his experiences in the Nevada mining country and on his travels on the Overland Trail.

J. J. McAlester begins developing a four-foot vein of coal in the Choctaw Nation, on the site of the future town that will bear his name in present Oklahoma.

William F. Cody is elected to the Nebraska legislature.

Francis Fuller writes *All Over Oregon and Washington.*

Sisseton Sioux sell 11 million acres of agricultural land in Minnesota's Red River valley to the United States for 10 cents an acre.

1873

"This is the finest fence in the world. It's light as air, stronger than whiskey
and cheaper than dirt!"

—John W. "Bet-a-Million" Gates, Texas barbed-wire salesman

JANUARY

1. The Atchison, Topeka, and Santa Fe's rails cross the eastern boundary of Colorado, moving west.

6. Arizona City's name is changed to Yuma.

7–9 A blizzard strikes the Great Plains; farmers who recently relocated from the East reportedly perish in large numbers in Iowa and Minnesota.

12. Montana Territory's first bank charter is issued to the Missoula National Bank.

17. Nine soldiers are killed and 27 are wounded in a futile attempt, led by Lieutenant Colonel Frank Wheaton, to storm the Modoc Indians and Captain Jack in their natural fortress at California's Tule Lake lava beds.

22. Lieutenant Frank Michler reports that 17 Indians were killed by the 5th Cavalry at Tonto Creek, Arizona.

31. The Utah Northern Railroad is completed to Logan.

FEBRUARY

12. Gold becomes the sole standard for U.S. currency as President Grant signs the Coinage Act. As new deposits of silver are discovered in the West, a political issue will evolve.

20. Troops under Captain C. C. C. Carr reportedly kill five Indians and capture four near Fossil Creek, Arizona.

25. The bandit Tiburcio Vásquez and four members of his gang rob Hoffman's store in Firebaugh, California. Customers in the store are robbed as well.

When the stagecoach pulls into town, the bandits also take the Wells Fargo strongbox.

26. Five Indians are reported killed and seven wounded in an encounter with the 8th Cavalry at Angostura, New Mexico.

27. The House of Representatives censures members James Brooks and Oakes Ames for their part in the Credit Mobilier scandal.

MARCH

1. Catherine McCarty, having moved west in the hope of curing her tuberculosis, weds William Antrim in the First Presbyterian Church in Santa Fe. Her sons, Henry (the future Billy the Kid) and Joe, are witnesses. Soon, the family will move to Silver City, New Mexico.

3. The Timber Culture Act grants individual homesteaders an additional 160 acres of timberland, provided they agree to plant trees on at least 40 acres. This means 65,292 homesteaders will receive 10,000,000 acres of land. Also, the Coal Lands Act makes public domain coal-bearing land available at $10 to $20 per acre; individuals may purchase up to 160 acres, whereas groups may purchase 320 acres.

9. President Grant appoints Samuel H. Elbert governor of Colorado Territory.

19. Fort Lowell is established by the Tucson garrison in Arizona.

■ The 5th Cavalry reports that it killed eight Indians and captured five in a fight in Arizona's Mazatzal Mountains.

Catherine Antrim (c. 1829–1874), Billy the Kid's mother. (Author's Collection)

- A gunfight erupts at the Matador Saloon in Lampasas, Texas, when authorities try to arrest Clint Barkley, alias Bill Bowen. Three lawmen are killed.
25. Sergeant S. M. Hill and a detachment of the 5th Cavalry report killing 10 Indians and capturing three in Arizona's Turret Mountains.
27. Captain G. M. Randall reports that the 5th Cavalry killed 23 Indians and captured 10 in Arizona's Turret Mountains.

National Headlines/March 1873:
4. GRANT TAKES OATH FOR 2ND TERM

APRIL

11. The Modoc War begins.
14. Armed whites massacre many inhabitants of the predominantly black settlement of Colfax, Louisiana.
- The "Easter Blizzard" hits South Dakota, Nebraska, and Kansas. The three-day storm accounts for many deaths among settlers.
25. Captain G. M. Randall is the commanding officer at the surrender of Del Chay and his band near Canyon Creek, Arizona.

THE MODOC WAR BEGINS
APRIL 11, 1873

Peace talks with California's Modoc Indians turned violent when Captain Jack produced a hidden pistol and killed Brigadier General E. R. S. Canby. Boston Charley killed Reverend Eleaser Thomas, and former Modoc agent A. B. Meacham was wounded. A thousand soldiers then took up the chase against some 50 Modocs. The official report will list six enlisted men and one civilian killed, and two officers, 13 enlisted men, and two civilians wounded.

26. More fighting between cavalrymen, infantrymen, and Indians occurs at California's Tule Lake lava beds. Captain Evan Thomas and 21 other soldiers are killed.
29. President Grant, on his second trip to Colorado, visits Central City and spends the night at the Teller House.

Also in April 1873:
The song "Home on the Range" has its debut in Harlan, Kansas.
Gordon Lillie, 13, the future "Pawnee Bill," is in the audience for William F. Cody and Wild Bill Hickok's Bloomington, Illinois, performance of *The Scouts of the Plains.*

MAY

2. The first legal hanging in Yuma, Arizona, takes place across the road from the school.
4. The remains of Dr. William York and other murder victims are found on the farm of the Bender family in Labette County, Kansas.
6. Captain Thomas McGregor reports that four Indians were killed by the 1st Cavalry on Arizona's Santa Maria River.
8. The bodies of Captain Thomas and Lieutenant Howe, who were killed in the Modoc War, arrive in San Francisco on their way back east.
10. Captain H. C. Hasbrouck reports a fight with Indians at Lake Soras, California. Two enlisted men are killed and seven are wounded; one Indian is killed and two are wounded.
14. The first railcar of coal is shipped from Coalville, Utah.
17. In the Sutton–Taylor feud, an argument between

the clans of William Sutton and Pitkin Taylor in central Texas, John Wesley Hardin, Taylor's cousin, kills Jack Helm with a shotgun in front of a blacksmith shop in Albuquerque. Hardin will write of the incident: "The news soon spread that I had killed Jack Helms [sic] and I received many letters of thanks from the widows of the men whom he had cruelly put to death. Many of the best citizens of Gonzales and DeWitt counties patted me on the back and told me that was the best act of my life."

18. Colonel Ranald Mackenzie reports that the 4th Cavalry killed 19 Indians, wounded two, and captured 42 in a fight near Remolina, Mexico.

22. Colonel J. C. Davis accepts the surrender of 150 Modocs at Fairchild's Ranch, California.

23. Postcards go on sale in San Francisco for the first time.

27. Lieutenant Jacob Almy is murdered by Indians near Arizona's San Carlos Agency.

28. The home base for Chinese laborers in San Francisco, the Chinese Six Companies, sends a telegram to Hong Kong, advising that emigration to San Francisco cease.

30. Major John Green reports the capture of 33 Modocs—including Scarface Charley, Chonchin, and Boston Charley—in Langell's Valley, California.

■ Eight thousand attend a reunion of Civil War soldiers in Lawrence, Kansas.

Also in May 1873:
John J. Joslin opens his Denver dry goods store.

National Headlines/May 1873:
AROUND THE WORLD IN 80 DAYS SELLS A MILLION COPIES

JUNE

1. Captain David Perry captures Captain Jack and six other Modoc Indians at Willow Creek, California.

2. In San Francisco, ground-breaking ceremonies for the world's first cable-powered street railroad are held on Clay Street.

3. Emma Stanley, a prostitute, is shot in the thigh during an argument with cavalrymen in Delano, Kansas. Dance hall owner Red Beard opens fire, wounding two of the soldiers.

5. Charles E. Bassett is elected the first sheriff of Ford County, Kansas.

9. Some four miles of construction on the Utah Northern Railroad, from Brigham City to Corinne, are completed.

15–17. The 17th and the 6th Infantries report a battle with Indians near Fort Abraham Lincoln, Dakota Territory: four Indians are killed and eight are wounded.

16. The 5th Cavalry engages Indians at Tonto Creek, Arizona, killing 14 and capturing five.

■ President Grant designates the Wallowa Valley in northeastern Oregon as "a reservation for the roaming Nez Percé Indians."

24. The California Savings and Loan is incorporated in San Francisco.

30. The Salt Lake City Gas Works begins producing gas.

Also in June 1873:
The brothers Billy and Ben Thompson open a gambling room in Ellsworth, Kansas.

JULY

1. Major General David Stanley, in charge of a Yellowstone expedition, tells Lieutenant Colonel George A. Custer that he is a troublesome subordinate. Recently, Stanley wrote to his wife about his escort: "I have seen enough of him to convince me that he is a cold-blooded, untruthful and unprincipled man. He is universally despised by all the officers of his regiment excepting his relatives and one or two sychophants."

3. Vigilantes in Phoenix lynch a rustler who stole a widow's cow.

4. The Aquarium at San Francisco's Woodward's Gardens opens.

7. Major General David Stanley orders George A. Custer to get rid of an iron cookstove he has brought along on their Yellowstone expedition. Custer se-

---

THE JAMES GANG SWITCHES TO TRAINS
JULY 21, 1873

In what is believed to have been their first train robbery, the Jameses and the Youngers derailed a Chicago, Rock Island, and Pacific train near Adair, Iowa, killing engineer John Rafferty. The gang took $2,000 from the express car and perhaps as much as $24,000 in cash and valuables from the passengers, many of whom were badly hurt by the derailment. The boys rode away amidst the wails of the injured.

cretly places the stove on another wagon, but Stanley finds out about it and has Custer arrested.

8. The editor W. J. Forbes writes in the last issue of California's *New Endowment:* "I'd like to publish it longer, but the fact is, I didn't bring enough money."

9. George A. Custer writes to his wife, Elizabeth, that Major General David Stanley apologized for the incident involving the cookstove.

21. Jesse James robs his first train.

AUGUST

2. San Francisco's cable cars, devised by Andrew Hallidie, get a trial run in the fog, climbing a 307-foot grade on the Clay Street hill between Kearny and Jones Streets.

4. Captain Myles Moylan reports that the 7th Cavalry under Lieutenant Colonel George A. Custer, protecting Stanley's Yellowstone expedition, had one of its men wounded in a brush with Indians. While Custer's men engaged in the skirmish at the mouth of the Tongue River, a sutler named Baliran and a veterinarian named Honsinger strayed to hunt for fossils. They were discovered by a band of Sioux and were killed.

6. Vigilantes in Tucson lynch four suspected murderers in the city's Court Plaza.

9. In Washington Territory, Tacoma's first newspaper, the *Daily Pacific Tribune,* begins publication.

11. Lieutenant Colonel George A. Custer reports that his 7th Cavalry got into a fight with Sioux while protecting Stanley's Yellowstone expedition. Custer reports that three soldiers were killed and four were wounded. There are no estimates of Indian casualties.

15. Billy Thompson shoots Sheriff Chauncy Whitney in Ellsworth, Kansas.

■ Major General David Stanley's survey of Yellowstone for the Northern Pacific Railroad ends at Pompey's Pillar. George A. Custer will be given command of six companies of soldiers at the recently constructed Fort Abraham Lincoln in Dakota Territory.

18. The first Americans to scale California's Mount Whitney are John Incas, C. D. Begole, and A. H. Johnson. At 14,495 feet in the Sierra Nevadas, Mount Whitney is the country's tallest peak.

20. The citizens of Linn County, Kansas, hang a man named Keller for having murdered his wife, a Mrs. Wood, and her two children, and then setting the Wood home (near Twin Springs) on fire with the bodies inside.

THOMPSON TROUBLE
AUGUST 15, 1873

In Ellsworth, Kansas, Billy Thompson lost money to gambler John Sterling at Joe Brennan's saloon. When Thompson found Sterling at another saloon later in the afternoon, an argument ensued and Sterling struck Thompson in the face. Sterling's companion, a policeman called Happy Jack Morco, drew his pistol on the unarmed Thompson, who was obliged to depart.

When Billy Thompson returned to Brennan's, Sterling and Morco demanded that he get his guns. Thompson left for his hotel room. As he was returning with a Winchester and a six-gun, he met his brother, Ben Thompson, who was carrying a shotgun. The Thompsons were intercepted by Sheriff Chauncy Whitney, who implored them to have a drink and cool off. The Thompsons were then charged by Sterling and Morco. Billy Thompson fired his shotgun at Morco but instead hit Sheriff Whitney, who died immediately. Ben Thompson persuaded his brother to ride out of town and then returned to his hotel.

Ellsworth's three-man police force was fired by Mayor Jim Miller when no one could be found with enough courage to arrest Ben Thompson. A deputy sheriff persuaded Morco to surrender his weapons, at which time Ben Thompson agreed to be placed in custody for questioning. Morco refused to appear in court the next morning. Thompson explained that the fatality was an unfortunate accident, and was released.

24. Colorado's elusive Mount of the Holy Cross is photographed for the first time on glass plates by William Henry Jackson. A topic of rumor and Indian legend, the mountain is secluded in the Rockies near Leadville. On it, a natural crucifix has eroded over thousands of years—deep ravines crossing at a 90° degree angle and protecting snow from sunlight. The crucifix is approximately 1,500 feet tall and 700 feet wide. For the perfect dawn exposure, Jackson's party camped overnight without food or shelter on Notch Mountain.

26. The Tres Pinos Massacre occurs.

William Henry Jackson (1843–1942). His photographs show the Old West as it was to an audience that can only imagine it. (Denver Public Library, Western History Department)

- One of radio's fathers, the inventor Lee DeForest, is born in Council Bluffs, Iowa. He will invent the first electronic sound amplification system, will patent the audion tube, and develop a process for putting sound on film that will revolutionize the motion picture industry.

Also in August 1873:

Satanta and Big Tree are removed from prison in Texas and sent to the guardhouse at Fort Sill, Oklahoma.

Texas Jack Omohundro weds the Italian dancer Giuseppina Morlacchi in Rochester, New York.

SEPTEMBER

2. The Boulder Valley Railroad is completed from Denver to Boulder.

6. David Roberts shoots and kills Peter Welsh and George Summer in front of Cy Goddard's saloon in Hays City, Kansas.

10. The British writer Isabella Bird arrives in Colorado for a tour that will center on the Estes Park region.

Isabella Bird (1831–1904), with her horse Birdie, on her sojourn in Colorado. (Denver Public Library, Western History Department)

THE WEST

She took a train from Cheyenne to Greeley, where she had a meal she remembered for its "greasiness and black flies." Her memoir will be published as *A Lady's Life in the Rocky Mountains.*

11. The Kansas Pacific Railroad extends an additional 42 miles, from Kit Carson to Fort Lyon, Colorado.

■ A buggy takes Isabella Bird from Greeley to Fort Collins. From there, she enlists another wagon to take her to Estes Park.

18. The Panic of 1873 begins when Jay Cooke and Company, a brokerage firm, fails. The Northern Pacific Railroad, whose financial agent was Cooke, suspends construction at Bismarck in Dakota Territory; the work stoppage will last for five years. Some 5,000 businesses will fail during the five-year depression that follows the Cooke affair.

21. George A. Custer's command arrives at Fort Abraham Lincoln in Dakota Territory.

23. The 5th Cavalry reports that 14 Indians were killed and five were captured at Hardscrabble Creek, Arizona.

24. On "Black Friday" in New York, a financial panic begins. In Denver, the news is suppressed until currency arrives from New York, and a bank panic is thereby averted in Colorado.

25. In her memoirs, Calamity Jane claims to have given birth today to Wild Bill Hickok's illegitimate daughter "Janey" in a cave.

Also in September 1873:

Harper's Weekly decides to give its readers a fresh angle on the West by sending two French celebrity journalist-artists, Paul Frenzeny and Jules Tavernier, to the region.

The Patrons of Husbandry achieves its peak membership of 1.5 million.

National Headlines/September 1873:

20. PANIC OF '73; WALL STREET CLOSES 10 DAYS

OCTOBER

3. Captain Jack and three other Modoc Indians, convicted of the murders of General E. R. S. Canby and Reverend Eleazer Thomas, are hanged at Oregon's Fort Klamath.

7. George Cram Cook, the author of *The Chasm* (1911), is born in Davenport, Iowa.

8. The photographer William Henry Jackson, a widower, marries Emilie Painter.

15. Governor Evans hosts a convention on irrigation in Denver.

16. The journalist Eugene Field marries Julia Comstock in St. Joseph, Missouri.

27. Joseph Glidden applies for a patent on barbed wire.

THE BIRTH OF BARBED WIRE
OCTOBER 27, 1873

Galvanized wire was popular before barbed wire was invented—more than 350,000 miles of it were sold between 1850 and 1879—but it was easy for livestock to get through the strands. A public outcry for cheaper, stronger fencing was echoed by one editor, who wrote, "It takes $1.74 worth of fences to keep $1.65 worth of stock from eating up $2.45 worth of crops."

At an 1873 county fair in De Kalb, Illinois, Henry Rose displayed his patented "Wooden Strip with Metallic Points." In essence, it was a slat of wood to which were attached sharpened wire points. His invention would not progress much beyond being exhibited at the fair, but three individuals saw it and began to have ideas of their own.

The farmer Joseph F. Glidden, the lumberman Jacob Haish, and the hardware merchant Isaac Ellwood all began working on prototypes. Glidden used his wife's coffee mill to twist wire into two-pronged points for fitting on a wire fence. Haish developed what would become the S-barb. Ellwood's work proved fruitless, but when he saw what Glidden was up to, he became his partner.

Glidden applied for his patent in October 1873, but it was held up for a year because of Haish's protests. Both inventors eventually received a total of five patents, but Glidden is considered the inventor of barbed wire. Nonetheless, his disgruntled competitor had hung on his house a placard that said: "Jacob Haish, Inventor of Barbed Wire."

At the age of 60 Glidden sold his interest in the business to the Washburn and Moen Manufacturing Company of Massachusetts for $60,000 and a royalty of 25 cents for every one hundred pounds sold. Production reached nearly 3 million pounds in 1876, but power equipment boosted production to 80.5 million pounds by 1880. Hundreds of barbed wire companies were born, and the courts were jammed with claims as to who rightfully owned the patent.

- In Delano, Kansas, the drunken dance hall owner Red Beard wounds the prostitute Anne Franklin. Beard and Joe Lowe, the owner of Rowdy Joe's Bar, then quarrel. Lowe mortally wounds Beard. During the argument, gunfighter William Anderson is blinded when a bullet passes behind his eyes.

28–30. Captain W. H. Brown reports that cavalrymen and infantrymen killed 25 Indians and captured six in Arizona's Mazatzal Mountains.

30. The 8th Cavalry takes 18 Indians captive at Pajarit Springs, New Mexico.

Also in October 1873:

Satanta and Big Tree are released on parole from Fort Sill, Oklahoma.

NOVEMBER

1. The first barbed wire is manufactured in De Kalb, Illinois, by Joseph F. Glidden.

11. Red Beard, the Delano, Kansas, dance hall owner, dies of gunshot wounds he received at the hands of "Rowdy" Joe Lowe.

- A telegraph line is established between Prescott and Yuma, Arizona.

12. San Francisco's Bay District Race Track has its grand opening.

18. Stitzel and Blair, alleged horse thieves, are shot and killed by citizens of Grasshopper Falls, Kansas.

22. The boundaries of the Colorado River Indian Reservation are expanded.

28. Frank Phillips, the oil magnate, is born in Scotia, Nebraska.

Also in November 1873:

The author Helen Hunt, 42, visits Colorado for the first time. She describes Denver as "blank, bald, a pitiless gray, under a gray November sky."

DECEMBER

1. Violence breaks out in a Prescott, Arizona, courtroom. During a water-rights hearing, the attorney general and the district attorney come to blows. The defendant in the case produces a knife and stabs two of the litigants before he himself is killed.

- In Lincoln, New Mexico, the Ben Harrell gang kills constable Juan Martinez. Incensed friends of the constable in turn kill Harrell, Jack Gylam, and Dave Warner.

2. Henry Starr, the train robber, actor, and horse thief, is born at Fort Gibson in Indian Territory. On February 25, 1921, he will become the last "old West style" bank robber to be shot to death while

FRANK PHILLIPS
NOVEMBER 28, 1873–AUGUST 23, 1950

Frank Phillips was born too late for the gold rush and just missed the silver rush, but the idea of coaxing riches out of the ground appealed to him. When the oil boom began, Phillips made sure he was not left behind again.

Born in Scotia, Nebraska, on November 28, 1873, Frank was the third of 10 children. His parents, Lewis and Lucinda Phillips, had come from Iowa to seek a future in the virgin West. An army of grasshoppers ended those dreams shortly after Frank's birth. When he was a year old, his family relocated to a farm near Conway, Iowa.

As the oldest son, Frank spoke with authority from an early age. His childhood heroes included Horatio Alger and Buffalo Bill Cody, both wildly successful in fiction and in reality. At 14, he was ready to strike out on his own. Phillips trained as a barber and worked in nearby Creston. For three years, he soaked up the world of lather, leather, and men with big ideas.

In 1890, the 17-year-old tonsorial artist rode a Union Pacific train to Denver and then made his way to the silver diggings in Aspen. In three years of employment at the Silver Dollar Barber Shop, Phillips saw the boom turn to bust. In the Silver Panic of 1893, he migrated to Ogden, Utah, then to Terrace, a nearby railroad camp. After a brief stint as a brakeman, he returned to Iowa.

With savings, he purchased the Climax Barber Shop, located in a Creston bank, the first of what became a chain of three shops. In 1897, Phillips married a local banker's daughter, Jane Gibson. Shortly after the birth of their first child the next year, Phillips sold his barbershops and became a bond and securities salesman. Within a few months, he earned a $75,000 commission selling bonds for the Chicago Coliseum Company.

Always scanning the horizon for new opportunities, Frank Phillips attended the Louisiana Purchase Exposition in St. Louis in 1903. There, he met an old friend, Reverend C. B.

(continued)

(continued)

Larrabee, who had just returned from Indian Territory, where he had witnessed the beginnings of the oil rush. Phillips wanted to see it for himself.

With the sale of Osage tribal lands in Kansas, the U.S. government had purchased some 1.5 million acres for the Osage from the Cherokees in present Oklahoma. Many had believed that the land—with its mucky soil and grimy waters—was undesirable. The oil explosion would change that thinking.

At Bartlesville, Oklahoma, Phillips began by investing in speculative oil leases. There, with his younger brother L. E. and $100,000 in capital, Frank organized the Anchor Oil Company in 1903. Within two years, he moved his family to the boomtown and began drilling into the earth in search of the black gold.

His initial strike, on June 23, 1905, at Holland No. 1, proved to be a small pocket that was exhausted quickly. His second and third attempts were dreaded "dry holes." Phillips had enough money for one last try.

On September 6, 1905, on Delaware Indian land belonging to 8-year-old Anna Anderson but leased to Phillips through her grandfather, a flood of oil shot high into the Oklahoma skies—enough crude to fill 250 barrels a day. The rig was named Anna Anderson No. 1, after what was now one of the wealthiest children in Indian Territory.

From there, Phillips's success grew upon itself. Frank and L. E. drilled a whopping string of 81 consecutive oil wells without a "duster" in the bunch. On March 23, 1917, the 43-year-old wildcatter made front-page headlines with a 1,000-barrel-a-day gusher on Osage Lot 185. That summer, the brothers incorporated as the Phillips Petroleum Company, listing their assets at $3 million.

Research and development led Phillips into natural gas. Airplane fuel was another area of interest, as was the process that Phillips started and called thermal polymerization, the converting of waste products into gasoline. By 1927, when the first "Phillips 66" filling station opened in Wichita, Kansas, Frank Phillips was worth about $40 million.

The creativity he brought to the oil business sparked Phillips's other interests. At his Woolaroc Ranch, 4,000 acres outside of Bartlesville, he provided a reserve for 132 buffalo (at the time the second-largest herd in the country), as well as for camels, kangaroos, and exotic birds. Phillips's collection of Indian and western art became one of the most extensive in the world. He bestowed large contributions on the Boy Scouts and funded the University of Oklahoma's excavations of prehistoric Indian burial mounds. He took special pride in being the first white to be ceremonially adopted into the Osage tribe, which called him Eagle Chief.

In 1930, Phillips Petroleum acquired Independent Oil, a concern that involved Frank's younger brother Waite. The three brothers were now united in a $316 million conglomerate. Still, the Great Depression was taking its toll: net earnings that year were $3 million, down from $21 million in 1926; by 1932, they had dropped to $776,000.

In 1935, the company had a major breakthrough when drilling rights were granted within the city limits of Oklahoma City, where some of their wells produced 20,000 barrels a day. That success, along with a pipeline project, put Phillips Petroleum back on the road to prosperity. On November 28, 1939, "Uncle Frank" celebrated his 66th birthday in grand style: his company was now worth $226 million and employed 30,000.

World War II sparked a major increase in the consumption of petroleum. In 1945, the last year of the war, Phillips Petroleum produced more than 93,000 barrels of crude oil per day and saw an annual profit of $22.5 million. The company's wartime prosperity was further aided by another Phillips development, synthetic rubber.

Frank Phillips remained chairman of his company until 1949. He died in Atlantic City, New Jersey, on August 23, 1950. His last will revealed that he had given away about 75 percent of his wealth to philanthropic causes.

---

plying his trade, attempting to rob the People's National Bank in Harrison, Arkansas. He will claim to have "robbed more banks than any man in America" (unofficial estimates say he hit 43). Newspapers will report that the "last bad Indian" was buried in Dewey, Oklahoma.

3. President Grant urges Congress to grant Colorado statehood.
4. The 5th Cavalry reports that 15 Indians were killed on Arizona's Verde River.
5. The 10th Cavalry reports that four Indians were killed and 16 were captured on Elm Creek in Texas.

- George A. Custer celebrates his 34th birthday with his wife, Elizabeth, at Fort Abraham Lincoln in Dakota Territory. He is putting the finishing touches on his book *My Life on the Plains.*

7. Willa Cather, the author of *My Antonia, O Pioneers!,* and *Death Comes for the Archbishop,* is born near Winchester, Virginia. In childhood, she will move with her family to Nebraska.

8. The 5th Cavalry and Indian scouts under Lieutenant W. F. Rice launch a punitive expedition against Indians from the San Carlos Agency in Arizona. The expedition, which will last until January 20, 1874, will result in 25 Indians being killed and 17 being captured.

10. The 4th Cavalry reports that nine Indians were killed at Kickapoo Springs, Texas.

20. More blood is shed in Lincoln County, Nebraska, as members of the Ben Harrell faction kill Pedro Patron, Juan Candelaria, Isidoro Padilla, and Juan Balagan.

21. The 5th Cavalry reports that six Indians were killed near Ehrenberg, Arizona.

22. The first building in Montana's Judith Basin is erected in Lewiston by Peter Koch.

23. The 5th Cavalry reports that nine Indians were killed and three were wounded at Cave Creek in Arizona.

31. The 5th Cavalry reports seven Indians killed and 11 captured near Fort Reno, Arizona.

Also in 1873:

Father Pierre Jean De Smet dies after a life of service to the Sioux Indians in the Dakota region.

Lily Chin becomes the first Chinese woman born in Colorado, the daughter of the prominent Denver community member Chin Lin Sou.

A major innovation in the denim pants sold in San Francisco by Levi Strauss comes from Nevada tailor Jacob Davis, who has the idea of repairing ripped pockets by studding the stress points with tiny copper rivets. Davis sends a letter to the "gents" at Strauss, his idea is patented under the names of Davis and Strauss, and Levi's "501 Double X" overalls become a western fashion sensation.

Dodge City, Kansas, ships 754,329 buffalo hides.

There are 300,000 head of cattle valued at $4.5 million in Arizona.

The Warm Springs Reservation is established for Mimbreno Apaches near old Fort Cummings, New Mexico.

The poet Joaquin Miller publishes a new collection, *Songs of the Sunlands.*

The "Big Bonanza" strike occurs near Virginia City, Nevada: the vein of silver and gold is 54 feet wide at a depth of 1,167 feet. Another "Big Bonanza" will yield two mines that will produce $1.5 million in ore per month from 1873–1877. Before they are

An afternoon outing at Julietta, Idaho, in 1873. (Library of Congress)

Buffalo hides piled in Dodge City. The boom is nearly over. (Kansas State Historical Society)

exhausted in 1897, the mines will produce ore worth more than $135 million.

The city of El Paso is incorporated in Texas.

The first Aberdeen-Angus cattle are imported to Victoria, Kansas, by George Grant.

The Winchester Company introduces an iron-framed repeating rifle with a stronger mechanism, which allows the gun to fire .44-40 center-fire ammunition from a 15-round magazine. One hundred and thirty-six of the rifles are inscribed "One of One Thousand," certifying that factory tests found the barrel to be exceptional. The Model 1873 will often be referred to as "the gun that won the West."

1874

"The white man goes into his church house and talks about Jesus. The Indian goes
into his tipi and talks *to* Jesus."

—Quanah Parker

JANUARY

4. Eskiminzin leads several Apaches off the San Carlos
Agency in Arizona and attacks a wagon train, killing two.

▪ The 5th Cavalry reports that four Indians were
killed on Wild Rye Creek in Arizona.

5. The physiologist Joseph Erlanger is born in San
Francisco. In 1944, he will win the Nobel Prize for
his studies of nerve impulses.

7. After Clay Allison and Chunk Colbert tie in a horse
race, the two decide to forget their differences over
dinner at an inn in Las Animas, Colorado. As coffee
is being served, Colbert raises his gun, but the
barrel is blocked by the table. Allison shoots Colbert
between the eyes and he calmly finishes his meal,
his guest face down in the soup bowl. Says the
"shootist" (a term it is believed he coined), "I didn't
want to send a man to hell on an empty stomach."

▪ Street car conductors and drivers go on strike in
San Francisco.

▪ In Colorado, *The Golden Transcript* reports that
the Golden Brewery of Adolph Coors is "assuming
permanent form" and will provide "a safe substitute
for drink of a more ardent nature."

9. In Montana, the third major fire in Helena claims
most of the business buildings and 150 homes; total
losses are estimated to be $1 million.

10. The 5th Cavalry reports that four Indians were
killed, three were wounded, and three were captured on Canyon Creek in Arizona.

11. Gail Borden, Jr., the Texas newspaperman and food
industry pioneer, dies of pneumonia at age 72 in
Bordenville, Texas.

15. Frank and Jesse James, Cole and Jim Younger, and
Clell Miller hold up the Concord Stagecoach in
Malvern, Arkansas, netting $4,000 in jewelry and
money.

17. Post–Civil War reconstruction in Texas officially
ends.

20. Welterweight boxing champ Jim Ferns, "the Kansas
Rube," is born in Pittsburg, Kansas.

21. A group of gold prospectors from Utah led by Alferd
Packer reaches the broad valley of the Uncompahgre
River, near present-day Delta, Colorado. Ill-pre-
pared to continue their trip, the prospectors have
run out of food and are surviving on chopped
barley. They are found by Ute Indians and are taken
to Chief Ouray, who replenishes their supplies but
suggests that they stay at his lodge until spring.
Some of the prospectors agree, but others continue
their journey with Packer.

27. President Grant reappoints Edward M. McCook
governor of Colorado.

31. The James gang robs the Little Rock express train
of $22,000 near Gadshill, Missouri.

▪ The Crow Reservation is established in Montana.

Also in January 1874:

The Circuit Rider, a major novel by Edward Eggleston,
is published. It is a tale about a frontier preacher
who delivers his sermons on horseback.

GAIL BORDEN
NOVEMBER 9, 1801–JANUARY 11, 1874

Of all the American industrial success stories of the 19th century, Gail Borden's seems the least likely. Until his 55th year, he was considered by many to be a borderline crackpot whose inventions were more curious than practical. Then Borden milked his creativity for all it was worth.

He was born on November 9, 1801, the first of four sons for farmers Gail and Philadelphia Wheeler Borden of Norwich, New York. In 1815, the family moved overland to the Ohio River and then by barge to present Covington, Kentucky. A year later, they migrated to Jefferson County, Indiana.

There, Gail received his entire education—in one and a half years. Still, it was enough to earn him a teaching job. In 1822, he and his brother Tom journeyed down the Mississippi for New Orleans, intent on becoming colonists in Texas, which had recently been opened for settlement.

Tom went on, but poor health forced Gail to stay behind. For two years he taught school in Amite County, Mississippi, where he also became the county's official surveyor. On September 28, 1828, he married one of his pupils, Penelope Mercer.

All three of his brothers as well as his father by now had migrated to Texas; Borden was eager to follow. In a covered wagon, he and his bride left for Galveston, where the first of their six children was born upon their arrival in December 1829. Soon after, the couple received a 4,428-acre land grant along the Colorado River.

As Texas sped toward its war of independence with Mexico, Borden became embroiled in politics. Choosing pen over sword, he founded the *Telegraph and Texas Register* on October 10, 1835, in San Felipe, with branch offices in Harrisburg, Columbia, and Houston. Less than a year later, Borden wrote his most memorable headline: "REMEMBER THE ALAMO."

On April 14, 1836, Borden escaped just before Santa Anna's troops burned the newspaper's Harrisburg office and dumped the press in the river. As an honor to this journalistic patriot, Borden County was established in northwest Texas, along with its county seat of Gail.

The newspaper continued to be published for 42 years, although Borden left it shortly after the revolution. In 1837, President Sam Houston appointed him collector of customs in Galveston. There, Borden dabbled in real estate, selling $1.5 million in city lots from 1839–1851.

Always the tinkerer, Borden's early inventions were off-center classics. First came the "Locomotive Bath House," a movable structure intended to offer Galveston ladies convenient, fresh-water bathing at the beach. His beloved "Terraqueous Wagon" came next, an amphibious Conestoga whose wheels converted into paddles. At its debut, the wagon rolled across land into the Gulf of Mexico, where it sank like a stone, its crew of disgusted dignitaries managing to swim ashore.

Galveston now was gripped in a deadly yellow fever epidemic, and Borden's 4-year-old son, Stephen Austin Borden, died in March 1844. In September, the disease claimed Penelope. Another son, Morton, followed two years later. In order to provide his surviving children with a mother, Borden married his housekeeper, Azuba Stearns. They divorced in 1854.

Because the epidemic raged in the warm months, Borden thought the citizens of Galveston could be housed in an air-conditioned cubicle, using $12,000 worth of ether to maintain a 40° temperature. He built a prototype, but his plan fizzled.

As always, it was replaced by another, this one geared to gold-seeking 49ers. Borden tried to solve a major problem of the wilderness—food spoilage. He condensed meat, boiling 120 pounds of beef down to 10 pounds of awful tasting muck. He then added flour and baked it. The "meat biscuit," as it became known, still tasted dreadful, but a sale of 600 pounds to a California-bound wagon train represented Borden's first marketing success. The meat biscuit even won a prize at London's International Exhibition. But during the next six years, Borden's savings of $100,000 dwindled. The U.S. Army, which had shown initial interest in the meat biscuit, ultimately rejected it. Sales dropped, and it looked as if he might be finished.

In 1851, on his voyage home from England, where he received a gold medal from Queen Victoria, Borden had witnessed the deaths of four children from drinking contaminated milk. The

(continued)

(continued)

children who survived the trip had wailed because of hunger. This haunting experience cried out to his inventive spirit.

Working in a friend's laboratory in Brooklyn, New York, Borden tried condensing milk by boiling it, but the product had a burnt taste. Adding sugar didn't help. In New Lebanon, New York, he observed members of the Shaker religious sect boiling fruit and maple syrup in airtight vacuum pans. Borden found that milk condensed in this fashion boiled at much lower temperatures and that the burnt flavor disappeared. He applied for a patent in 1853, but it took three years to convince the Patent Office that his process was workable. Finally, patent No. 15,553 was issued for Borden's condensed milk on August 19, 1856. Said Borden: "I shall . . . within one year either be a citizen of the world, known in every civilized country, or I shall be a retired, humble individual in the back woods of Texas."

Borden's milk production began in Burrville, Connecticut, in 1857. With the aid of the financier Jeremiah Milbank, the New York Condensed Milk Company built a plant in Wassaic, New York. By 1859 there were more factories, and sales reached $48,000 a year. Borden married Emeline Church in 1860 and looked forward to his business triumph.

Ironically, while the founder fretted over the Civil War, having sons in both the Union and Confederate Armies, the Union Army's orders reached 25,000 quarts per month. In 1864, that much was being produced on a daily basis, netting the company an annual profit of $145,000. After the war, in 1866, the product first appeared under the label "Eagle Brand."

Borden retired to Texas in 1872. He died of pneumonia at age 72 on January 11, 1874, leaving behind a huge personal fortune and his products in stores nationwide. In the next century, his company would expand into a food and chemical giant. As for Gail Borden he was laid to rest at New York's Woodlawn Cemetery under a milkcan-shaped tombstone inscribed with the epitaph he penned:

> I tried and failed. I tried again and again and succeeded.

The reward for Tiburcio Vásquez stands at $3,000 alive, $2,000 dead.

FEBRUARY

2. Elbert and Grand Counties are established in Colorado.

3. More Apaches leave the San Carlos Agency and launch an attack against the residents of the former Camp Grant in Arizona; five civilians are killed.

5. Construction of the Utah Northern Railroad from Ogden to Brigham City is completed.

■ Lieutenant Colonel G. P. Buell reports that cavalrymen, infantrymen, and scouts killed 10 Indians on the Brazos River in Texas.

7. The Utah Northern Railroad begins operating. According to the *Ogden Junction:* "No formal arrangements were made for the reception, as no official notice had been received of the trip, but the Ogden Brass Band and a number of our citizens assembled at the depot and congratulated the company on completion of this division of the road."

9. The gold seekers Alferd Packer, Shannon Bell, James Humphrey, Frank Miller, George Noon, and Israel Swan leave the safety of Chief Ouray's Ute camp in Colorado to continue their journey and plunge into a blizzard. Chief Ouray had warned that they had too few provisions, adding: "Your journey will end in death."

■ Lieutenant L. H. Robinson is killed by Indians while guarding a pack train near Laramie Peak, Wyoming.

10. Hinsdale, La Plata, and Rio Grande Counties are established in Colorado.

Also in February 1874:

In California, the poet Ina Coolbrith becomes the librarian of the Oakland Public Library, a position she will hold until 1893. During those years, she will influence Bret Harte and Jack London, and raise Joaquin Miller's daughter, Cali-Shasta. In 1915 she will become the poet laureate of California.

MARCH

4. The U.S. Army takes possession of the Fort Laramie–Cheyenne telegraph line because of various acts of sabotage by the Indians. Military news will now be delivered by bull team.

8. Captain G. M. Randall reports that the 5th Cavalry killed 12 Indians and captured 25 in Arizona's Pinal Mountains.

11. William E. Sutton and Gabriel Slaughter are shot dead while standing on the deck of a riverboat docked in Indianola, Texas. They are the last to be killed in the long-running Sutton-Taylor feud, which claimed some 40 lives in DeWitt and Gonzales Counties, Texas, over many years.

- The telegraph embargo between Ft. Laramie and Cheyenne is lifted.

16. Pinkerton agents engage in a shoot-out with the Youngers near Osceola, Missouri. John Younger, 21, is killed, as are agent Louis Lull and St. Clair County sheriff E. B. Daniels.

20. Captain Barbiere arrives in San Francisco with the hot-air balloon *Le Secours*.

23. In Wyoming Territory, a post road is established from Cheyenne, via Fort Fetterman, to Bozeman, in present Montana, then on to the Whetston Agency in Dakota Territory.

- Granger laws regulating maximum rail rates to the benefit of railroad managers and farmers go into effect in Iowa.

25–26. Lieutenant W. S. Schuyler reports that the 5th Cavalry killed 12 Indians and captured two during a regimental return in Arizona's Superstition Mountains.

26. The body of C. M. Manchester, a cowboy for rancher John Iliff who was killed by Indians, is brought to Cheyenne, Wyoming.

28. Captain Barbiere ascends from San Francisco's Woodward's Gardens in the hot-air balloon *Le Secours*.

Also in March 1874:

Camp Robinson, the military post of the Red Cloud Agency, is established in Nebraska.

National Headlines/March 1874:

8. MILLARD FILLMORE DIES AT 74

APRIL

2. Lieutenant A. B. Bache reports that the 5th Cavalry killed 31 Indians and captured 50 at Pinal Creek, Arizona.

- A mail route to the Red Cloud Agency in Nebraska is established.

3–14. The 5th Cavalry reports 14 Indians killed and 28 captured in Arizona's Pinal Mountains.

14. Sixty-six days after leaving Chief Ouray's camp on a wild chase for gold, the only survivor of Alferd Packer's party is Packer himself, who staggers into the Los Pinos Indian Agency near Saguache, Colorado. Some accounts say Packer was ravenous, while others say he gagged at the sight of meat; all witnesses report that he asked for whiskey. Packer's complicated story is of men quarreling and killing

Convicted cannibal Alferd Packer (1842–1907). (Denver Public Library, Western History Department)

each other and then eating the dead's flesh to survive. "Meat cut out of a man's breast is the sweetest I've ever eaten," says Packer. "After having lived on it for nearly two months, I've become very fond of it." The Colorado cannibal will lead a search party to within a half-mile of the crime scene before becoming disoriented and unable to continue.

15. A mini-war breaks out in Arkansas when Joseph Brooks, who lost the gubernatorial election to Elijah Baxter, takes the state capitol by force.

17–18. The 5th Cavalry reports 38 Indians killed and 12 captured during a regimental return in Arizona's Mazatzal Mountains.

19. Fire claims the military barracks on Alcatraz Island in San Francisco Bay.

- A disaster is narrowly averted during the descent of the balloon *America,* with many San Franciscans on board, from an altitude of 3,000 feet. There is much fright but no casualties.

22. The senate ratifies a treaty in which the Utes cede most of the San Juan mining region in Colorado to the United States.

24. Jesse James weds his first cousin, Zerelda Mims, in Independence, Missouri. "Zee," as he calls her, nursed him to health after he was wounded during the Civil War. They had been together for nine years.

28. The 5th Cavalry reports 23 Indians killed and 12 captured in Arizona's Arivaypa Mountains.

National Headlines/April 1874:

22. GRANT VETOES LEGAL TENDER ACT

MAY

4. In *Bartemeyer v. Iowa,* the Supreme Court rules that the 14th amendment does not protect the right to sell liquor.
9. Charles Adams, Indian agent at Colorado's Los Pinos Agency, authorizes a search for the bodies of Alferd Packer's companions.
12. The Helena, Montana, assay office is authorized by Congress.
14. A posse finds Tiburcio Vásquez's hideout near Los Angeles. As Vásquez attempts a getaway, he is wounded by the shotgun of George Beers and surrenders.
21. The 5th Cavalry begins an operation against Indians that will conclude on June 6 near Diamond Butte, Arizona. Nineteen Indians are killed.
26. John Wesley Hardin turns 21.
27. The 5th Cavalry reports four Indians killed and nine captured in Arizona's Sierra Anchas.
29. Construction begins on the National Park Hotel in Yellowstone.

Also in May 1874:

In two years, Britain's Lord Dunraven has worked out a smashing scheme for acquiring land in Colorado's Estes Park region, thanks to the Homestead Act. His British purchasing agent enlists claim filers from among unemployed cowboys and Denver hard cases, pays them to file for Estes lands, and then quietly redistributes the titles to Lord Dunraven. Dunraven currently owns 4,000 acres of Estes Park; his holdings will increase to 15,000 acres before anyone notices his scheme.

Bessie Earp, the wife of James (Wyatt Earp's brother), is fined for prostitution in the Wichita, Kansas, police court.

National Headlines/May 1874:
16. MASSACHUSETTS DAM BURST KILLS 100

JUNE

3. Bessie and Sallie Earp are arrested in Wichita, Kansas, when a citizen complains that they "set up and keep a bawdy house or brothel and did appear and act as Mistresses."
8. Cochise, approximately 62, the chief of the Chiricahua Apaches, dies of natural causes on a reservation

Quanah Parker (1845–1911). He leads his warriors into the buffalo guns of Adobe Walls. (Library of Congress)

HARDIN'S 21ST BIRTHDAY
MAY 26, 1874

John Wesley Hardin celebrated his 21st birthday in Comanche, Texas, by racing horses and winning $3,000. All was going well until Deputy Sheriff Charles Webb appeared, intent on arresting Hardin. Not wishing to fight, Hardin offered to buy Webb a drink. As the men walked side by side toward the saloon, Webb tried to get the drop on Hardin. Someone yelled a warning and Hardin turned to find Webb's pistol half out of his holster. Before the lawman could raise the gun any further, he became another statistic, the 39th man killed by Wes Hardin. The incident prompted Hardin to leave Texas and spend time in Alabama and Florida.

THE SECOND BATTLE
OF ADOBE WALLS
JUNE 27, 1874

About a mile and a half from the ruins of William Bent's 1843 fortress where Kit Carson battled Indians on November 26, 1864, 29 buffalo hunters and one woman gathered in another "fortress" that included Charlie Myers's log store, Jim Hanrahan's sod saloon, Tom O'Keefe's blacksmith hut, and Charles Rath's market.

The Comanche chiefs Quanah Parker and Lone Wolf, and some 700 Comanche and Cheyenne warriors, received yellow "bullet-proof" body paint from the medicine man Isatai (Little Wolf) to help repel the white hunters. At dawn, hunter Billy Dixon saw "hundreds of painted half-naked warriors . . . mounted on their finest horses, armed with guns and lances, carrying heavy shields of thick buffalo hides." The two Shadler brothers, sleeping in their wagons, were scalped, as was their dog. Billy Tyler was also killed, shot through the lung as he attempted to run between buildings at Adobe Walls. Quanah then directed his forces in a head-on assault.

The hunters retaliated with Sharps "Big 50s," .50 caliber buffalo guns that can fell an animal a mile away. On the second charge, Quanah's horse was blasted out from under him. William Olds became a casualty when he accidentally blew his head off with his shotgun while climbing a ladder.

Following the last charge at 4:00 P.M., the remains of 56 horses and 28 oxen were counted. Exactly how many Indians were killed was difficult to tell—perhaps the most notable was the son of the Cheyenne chief Stone Calf. The hunters decapitated 13 Indian corpses that had not been recovered, and stuck the heads on poles outside their stronghold.

The next day Billy Dixon put an end to any possibility of another attack on the settlement. That afternoon, about a dozen Indian scouts appeared on a high bluff across the creek. Dixon took aim and fired. Everyone was sure he had missed. Then, the warrior Tohohkah fell to the ground. Years later, a surveyor measured the distance to be 1,538 yards, 222 yards short of a mile. The episode made Dixon a frontier legend and effectively ended the attacks on Adobe Walls; however, after Quanah's combined forces broke up, they carried out a series of raids in Texas, New Mexico, Colorado, and Kansas that claimed the lives of 80 settlers.

Perhaps the most famous of the Adobe Walls survivors was young Bat Masterson, who later wrote: "So close would they come that we planted our guns in their faces and against their bodies through the portholes, while they were raining their arrows and bullets down on us." On the failure of the Indians' yellow protective paint, Isatai was quick with an excuse: A brave had killed a skunk the morning of the attack, breaking the magic. The Indians who survived tended to ignore him from then on; when asked how to translate his name, they told reporters it meant "Coyote Droppings."

near Apache Pass in the Dragoon Mountains in Arizona Territory.

11. Alferd Packer is being held in custody in Saguache County, Colorado, without charges while authorities search for the bodies of his companions.

17. The *Bismarck Tribune* writes:

> This is God's country. He peopled it with red men, and planted it with wild grasses, and permitted the white man to gain a foothold; and as the wild grasses disappear when the white clover gains a footing, so the Indian disappears before the advances of the white man. Humanitarians may weep for poor Lo, and tell the wrongs he has suffered, but he is passing away. Their prayers, their entreaties, can not change the law of nature; can not arrest the causes which are carrying them on to their ultimate destiny—extinction.

23. Congress authorizes a continuation of John Wesley Powell's surveys in Utah.

24. Bill Tilghman and a group of buffalo hunters retrieve the body of fellow hunter Pat Congers from the saloon in which he was killed in Petrie, Indian Territory. A fight breaks out with Congers's murderer, Blue Throat. When the lights go out, Tilghman and his men escape, and Congers is given a decent burial.

■ Six Indians are killed and 11 are wounded in a fight

with the 6th Cavalry at Bear Creek Redoubt, Kansas.

25. Jane Oswald of Walnut Grove becomes the first postmistress in Arizona.

27. The second Battle of Adobe Walls takes place in Texas.

Also in June 1874:

Lieutenant Frank Baldwin is sent to join General John Pope at Fort Dodge, Kansas.

Annie Ralston, a farmer's daughter from Missouri, writes home: "Dear Mother, I am married and going West." Curiously, she fails to mention that her new husband is Frank James.

JULY

4. The first steel-arch bridge to span the Mississippi River opens in St. Louis. It was designed and built by James B. Eads, 54, over a period of seven years.

■ Captain A. E. Bates reports that the 2nd Cavalry and its scouts engaged Indians on the Bad Water Branch of the Wind River in Wyoming. Casualties: 26 Indians killed and 20 wounded; four soldiers killed and six wounded.

17. Fort Reno is established on the banks of the North Canadian River near present El Reno, Oklahoma.

23. George A. Custer's Black Hills "scientific" expedition, a 1,200-man force, is under way. Supposedly seeking a location for a new fort, Custer leads 10 companies of the 7th Cavalry, two infantry companies, 60 scouts, and a Gatling gun detachment, in Dakota Territory.

24. Floods kill 30 people in Eureka, Nevada.

28. A posse of 150 under Sheriff John G. Davis captures a group of horse thieves in Caldwell, Kansas. Among the rustlers is William Brooks, who may have been Billy Brooks, the onetime marshal of Newton, Kansas. The bandits are taken to Wichita.

30. With regard to William Brooks and the other horse thieves arrested on July 28, the *Sumner County Press* headlines read:

DEAD! DEAD! DEAD!

THE VIGILANTS AT WORK

THREE MEN HANGED BY THE NECK UNTIL THEY ARE DEAD

A FEARFUL RETRIBUTION

THE BEGINNING OF THE END

The newspaper reports that the "prisoners are still confined in the calaboose, which is securely guarded by armed men." A lynch mob forms to see that

justice is applied. Three are hanged, including Billy Brooks, possibly the onetime lawman.

Also in July 1874:

Potato bugs, or "Colorado beetles," which can heavily damage potato crops, were first discovered in the Rocky Mountains. This year, they turn up on the Atlantic coast.

The family of the future author Laura Ingalls Wilder, who is 7 years old, relocates again, this time from its original Wisconsin home to Plum Creek in Walnut Grove, Minnesota.

The grasshoppers are particularly bad on the western plains, from Texas to Canada.

AUGUST

2. Horatio N. Ross and William T. McKay, civilian prospectors with the Custer expedition into Dakota's Black Hills, discover gold on French Creek. Custer sends word back to Fort Laramie with Lonesome Charley Reynolds, a scout.

6. Jim Reed, the husband of Belle Starr, is ambushed and killed near Paris, Texas.

8. In Mohave County, Arizona, Jackson McCracken discovers a silver deposit that will yield $800,000 in ore during the next 30 years.

10. Herbert Clark Hoover, the 31st U.S. president (1929–1933), is born in West Branch, Iowa. The son of the blacksmith Jesse Clark Hoover and Hulda Randall Minthorn, he will grow up in Indian Territory and Oregon.

15. Chief Desaline reports that his Indian scouts killed nine Indians and captured 119 near Arizona's San Carlos Agency.

18. The guide C. E. Cooley reports that Indian scouts killed 13 Apaches at Black Mesa, Arizona.

20. John Randolph, an artist for *Harper's Weekly,* discovers the remains of Alferd Packer's five gold-seeking companions in the Colorado mountains. It seems as if four of the five victims were killed in their sleep, while the fifth struggled before meeting his end. The nearby town of Saguache is in an uproar, but the previously jailed Packer is not around to hear it: he bribed the sheriff's 16-year-old son and has escaped. Packer will remain at large for nearly 10 years.

22. U.S.–Canadian boundaries are set.

■ Guide C. E. Cooley reports that scouts killed 10 Apache in Arizona's Sierra Ancha.

22–23. Lieutenant Colonel J. W. Davidson reports that cavalry and infantry engaged Indians at the Wichita

Agency in Indian Territory, killing 16. He reports four enlisted men wounded.

24. In the "Lone Tree Massacre," a band of Cheyennes kills six government surveyors in Meade County, Kansas.

26. The *New Mexican* reports that New Mexico Territory is at peace:

> They have come and gone. The Indians of this territory are perfectly peaceful and quiet. The settlers have no trouble with them whatever and indeed, they volunteer to assist the troops in endeavoring to defend us against invasion. . . . Having no trouble from our Indians, we must needs suffer invasion and have our people murdered and scalped, and our stock run off by breech clouted whelps, robbers and vagabonds, who come five hundred miles or more to do it.

30. The first battle of what will turn into the Red River War to coax Indians onto a reservation is fought in the Palo Duro Canyon of Texas between forces under Colonel George Miles and a combined force of Cheyennes, Comanches, and Kiowas.

■ George A. Custer's Black Hills expedition returns triumphantly to Fort Abraham Lincoln. The fort's band plays "Garry Owen."

Also in August 1874:

A rich deposit is discovered by a crew building a wagon road from Saguache to the Animas valley above Lake City, Colorado.

Out on parole, the Kiowa leader Satanta and his friend Big Tree witness a huge fight among Indians at the Anadarko Agency in Indian Territory. Afraid that they will be blamed for the fight, they rush to the nearby Antelope Hills.

Some 60 white settlers have been killed by Indians in the past year in the area around Fort Sill in present Oklahoma. The fort itself has never been attacked.

William E. Curtis of the *Chicago Inter-Ocean* files a story reiterating Custer's official report: "It has not required an expert to find gold in the Black Hills, as men without former experience in mining have discovered it at an expense of but little time or labor."

Clay Allison, his mouth raging with toothache, rides into Cheyenne, Wyoming, a city with two dentists. When one dentist accidentally drills the wrong tooth, Allison storms over to his competitor, has the work repaired, and then returns to the first dentist. Allison straps the dentist in the chair, grabs a pair of pliers, and begins practicing outlaw ortho-

dontia. According to the varying accounts, the dentist looses one, three, or all of his teeth.

My Life on the Plains, by George Armstrong Custer, is published.

SEPTEMBER

1. The first telegraph line to the Black Hills in Dakota Territory is completed.

3. The presence of gold in the Black Hills is no secret. According to the *Press and Dakotaian:* "No sensible man will think of going to the Black Hills without first insuring his life." The region is considered sacred by the Sioux.

4. The Brewer's Protective Association incorporates in San Francisco.

11–12. Colonel Nelson Miles reports that two of his men were killed in an Indian fight on McClellan Creek near the Wichita River in Texas.

12. The Battle of Buffalo Waller begins at Hemphill County, Texas, where six men defend against a force of 100 Indians for three days. Scouts Billy Dixon and Amos Chapman and four others are pinned down by Kiowa and Comanche attackers while trying to deliver dispatches. The men take the only available cover, a hollow in the ground where buffalo come to roll. The attackers circle the hole.

14. In New Orleans, the White League clashes with police in a successful attempt to oust the Republican governor, William P. Kellogg, who the Democrats claim was fraudulently elected.

15. Troops arrive to relieve the men pinned down by Indians in Hemphill County, Texas. One of the six scouts died of his wounds; the others will receive Congressional Medals of Honor.

16. Catherine Antrim, 45, dies of tuberculosis in Silver City, New Mexico. She will never hear her son Henry, 14, called "Billy the Kid."

17. The 5th Cavalry reports 14 Indians killed and two captured in a fight at the headwaters of Cave Creek, Arizona; one soldier is killed.

■ Federal troops restore William P. Kellogg as governor of Louisiana.

19. Grasshoppers are reported covering the ground in Kansas, in some places to a depth of two inches.

26–28. Colonel Ranald Mackenzie attacks the Comanche chief Quanah Parker's camp in the Palo Duro Canyon of Texas while the chief is away on a hunt. Mackenzie reports four Indians killed and 1,000 horses captured.

28. The slaughter of 1,000 Comanche ponies in the Palo Duro Canyon of Texas is ordered by Colonel

Ranald Mackenzie, who also orders a 200-mile forced march of captured Indians to Fort Sill, Oklahoma.

■ According to the *Tucson Citizen,* Steven Ochoa has grown the first cotton in Arizona.

29. The Kiowa parolee Big Tree surrenders to federal authorities at the Cheyenne and Arapaho Agency in Darlington, Texas.

Also in September 1874:
Mennonite immigrants from Russia introduce "Turkey Red" wheat to Kansas; the drought-resistant crop will change the face of the land.

OCTOBER

4. The Kiowa leader Satanta turns himself in at the Cheyenne and Arapaho Agency in Darlington, Texas. He and Big Tree will be returned to Fort Sill. Later, Big Tree will be allowed to remain out on parole, but Satanta will be returned to the Texas State Penitentiary.

6. The Gordon party—26 men, one woman, and a 10-

Satanta (1830–1878), "the Orator of the Plains." (Denver Public Library, Western History Department)

Wyatt Earp (1848–1929). His adventures will not be widely known until the 1920s. (Denver Public Library, Western History Department)

year-old boy—depart Sioux City, Iowa, in search of the gold that was discovered by Custer's men in August.

23. Lieutenant Bernard Reilly, Jr., reports that the 5th Cavalry killed 16 Indians on the Little Colorado River in Arizona.

29. Wyatt Earp is first mentioned in print in the *Wichita City Eagle,* which refers to him as "officer" and "Wiatt Erp."

■ Sergeant R. Stauffer reports that the 5th Cavalry killed eight Indians and captured five at Cave Creek in Arizona.

NOVEMBER

3. The prospectors who are flocking to the Black Hills are the subject of a meeting between President Grant and Generals Philip Sheridan and George Crook, Indian Affairs Commissioner Edward P. Smith, and others. The government will have no official policy toward the prospectors.

■ Colonel Ranald Mackenzie reports two Indians

killed and 19 captured by the 4th Cavalry on the Laguna Curato in Texas.

5. The new San Francisco mint is transferred to the control of General O. H. LaGrange.

6. Gray Beard's Cheyenne camp near McClellan's Creek, Texas, is attacked by a detachment of the 8th Cavalry under Lieutenant Frank Baldwin. Julia and Adelaide Germaine, the 6- and 4-year-old daughters of John Germaine who were kidnapped from their wagon train in Kansas the previous spring, are rescued. Four Indians and two soldiers are killed; 10 Indians and four soldiers are wounded.

8. Lieutenant Colonel J. W. Davidson reports that his expedition from Fort Sill that began on October 28 captured 391 Indians.

16. The Colorado River Indian Reservation's boundaries are expanded by executive order.

17. A mild earthquake is reported in Yuma, Arizona.

24. The De Kalb, Illinois, farmer Joseph Glidden is granted a patent on barbed wire.

29. Hawaii's King Kalakaua visits San Francisco.

Also in November 1874:

Following his unsuccessful run for the Missouri Senate, Isaac Parker is offered the position of chief justice for Utah Territory by President Grant. When Parker request a post closer to home, Grant makes him the youngest (at 36) federal judge in the nation, to preside over the newly created Western District of Arkansas, with an annual salary of $3,500. Parker's jurisdiction, the largest of any in the nation's history, will stretch from the Arkansas River in the east to the Colorado line in the west. The region includes Indian Territory, which has become a sanctuary for the worst bandits in the West, a "Robbers' Roost."

National Headlines/November 1874:

17. NEW ZEALAND SHIP FIRE KILLS 468

18. WOMEN'S CHRISTIAN TEMPERANCE UNION FORMS IN CLEVELAND

29. 12 WORKERS KILLED IN PENNSYLVANIA STRIKE

DECEMBER

1. The 5th Cavalry reports killing eight Indians, wounding two, and capturing 14 at Canyon Creek in Arizona's Tonto Basin.

7. Captain A. S. B. Keyes and the 10th Cavalry accept the surrender of 26 Indians at Kingfisher Creek in Indian Territory.

12. Robbers believed to be the James brothers, along

Thomas Coleman "Cole" Younger (1844–1916), the oldest of the four outlaw brothers. (Library of Congress)

with Cole, Bob, and Jim Younger, Bud McDaniel, and Clell Miller, make off with $25,000 after robbing a train in Muncie, Kansas. The James gang is implicated a few days later when Daniel is arrested with $1,000 of the loot and some jewelry taken from the train. Miller is also apprehended but escapes jail before his trial and is shot dead by a Lawrence, Kansas, farmer.

23. The Gordon party, gold seekers from Sioux City, Iowa, reach the area in the Black Hills that they call "Custer's Park," where gold was discovered in August.

26. New Mexico, Arizona, and California residents petition the postmaster general for a daily mail service from San Diego.

▪ The first commercial buffalo hunt in Texas is staged by Joe McComb.

28. Captain A. S. B. Keyes and the 10th Cavalry accept

the surrender of 52 Indians on the Canadian River in Indian Territory.

31. Doc Holliday, 22, has his first brush with the law. According to the *Dallas Weekly Herald:* "Dr. Holliday and Mr. Austin, a saloon keeper, relieved the monotony of the noise of firecrackers by taking a couple of shots at each other yesterday afternoon. The cheerful note of the six-shooter is heard once more among us."

Also in December 1874:

Since August, several hundred Comanches and Kiowas have surrendered at Fort Sill, Oklahoma. As a precautionary measure and as a show of force, at least 72 chiefs are taken to St. Augustine, Florida, in chains.

Wells Fargo, with 609 offices, announces an operating income of $392,000.

National Headlines/December 1874:

7. 70 BLACKS DIE IN VICKSBURG RACIAL VIOLENCE

Also in 1874:

S. B. Axtell becomes governor of Utah Territory; he will serve in that post until 1875.

There are 320,000 head of cattle worth $4.4 million in Arizona.

President Grant creates the Pyramid Lake Reservation in California by executive order, giving Indians fishing rights to one of the country's largest bodies of water.

Bill Tilghman, 19, estimates that he killed 7,500 buffalo during the winter of 1873–1874.

Colorado College is founded in Colorado Springs.

The first Peavey "Blind Horse" Grain Elevator is installed in Sioux City, Iowa; the elevator is powered by a blinkered horse walking around a wheel.

W. H. Jackson discovers Pueblo Indian cliff dwellings on the Mancos River in southwestern Colorado.

The medical discipline of osteopathy is developed by Dr. Andrew T. Still of Baldwin, Kansas.

Francis Fuller writes *Women's War with Whiskey, or Crusading in Portland.*

"Slaughtered for the hide." From 1870–1875, the bison population of North America drops from 14 million to 1 million. (*Harper's Weekly*)

The University of Nevada at Reno is founded in Elko, Nevada.

The first reports about Arizona's "Lost Dutchman Mine" come from Jacob Waltz, 64, who claims it is "a round pit, shaped like a funnel with the large end up." After a few weeks of gold mining, Waltz and two accomplices go to Tucson and convert their ore into $60,000. On their next trip to the mine, only Waltz returns, claiming that his two helpers were slain by Apaches.

Dodge City, Kansas, ships 126,867 buffalo hides, down from 754,329 in 1873.

1875

"Westward the Star of Empire Takes Its Way."
—Banner at the National Railroad Convention, St. Louis, Missouri

JANUARY

2. Montana's acting governor, J. E. Callaway, issues a proclamation recognizing the popular vote in favor of moving the territorial capital from Virginia City to Helena.

■ In an operation that will last until February 23, Captain F. D. Ogilby and the 5th Cavalry kill 15 Indians and capture 122 near Camp Apache, Arizona.

6. Arizona's eighth territorial legislature convenes in Tucson; it offers a $3,000 reward to whomever discovers the first artesian well.

7. The Northern Pacific Coast Railroad from San Francisco to Tomales, California, opens.

9. Indians in Arizona are reportedly stealing cattle from freight haulers and then offering to return them for prices ranging from $2 to $8 a head.

■ Cheyenne, Wyoming, sets a record low temperature of −38°.

14. Congress passes the Specie Resumption Act, an attempt to reconcile the inflationary policy desired in the West with the more conservative monetary policy favored in the East.

23. Molly Wright, who will become Dr. Molly Armstrong, the first female optometrist in Texas and the second in the nation, is born in Bell County, Texas.

25. The commissioner of agriculture is authorized by Congress to distribute $30,000 in seeds and other aid to western farmers who have been devastated by the plague of grasshoppers.

26. Frank and Jesse James escape a firebombing.

28. The Wells Fargo Mining Company of California,

FRANK AND JESSE ESCAPE
JANUARY 26, 1875

Recent events caused Pinkerton security agents to make a bad decision in their hunt for Frank and Jesse James. In late 1874, Pinkerton agent John Whicher took a train to Kearney, Missouri, and upon arrival asked directions to the Samuel farm; his body was found the next day. While the Missouri legislature was appropriating $10,000 for a special task force to combat the James gang, the boys went back to work. On December 12, 1874, they robbed $25,000 from a train in Muncie, Kansas.

On January 26, 1875, Pinkerton agents and railroad operatives gathered outside the Samuel homestead in the darkness. Confident that the boys were inside, they threw an incendiary device, possibly a huge ball of cotton soaked with kerosene, into a window; the official Pinkerton report said it was a flare and was meant to illuminate the interior of the house. Zerelda Samuel, the mother of Frank and Jesse, awakened and scooted the object into the fireplace, where it exploded. Jesse's 8-year-old half-brother Archie Samuel was killed, and Zerelda was forced to have her arm amputated below

(continued)

(continued)

the elbow by her husband, Dr. Samuel. Frank and Jesse were nowhere to be found.

Shortly after this incident, the Missouri legislature took up a bill that would have given amnesty to the Jameses and Youngers. After the bill was defeated by a small margin, the Samuels' neighbor, Dan Askew—whose house had been used as a base for the Pinkerton agents the night of the bombing—was found murdered. Public sympathy for the James brothers increased at the worst time. Farmers throughout the region hid the gang members or otherwise provided cover for their movements.

capitalized at $10,800,000, is incorporated to develop and sell mines in the Virginia City area of Nevada.

31. R. R. Whitney, a member of the Gordon party, illegal gold seekers from Iowa, writes from the Black Hills: "Gold we find in every pan, and it is my opinion that it is as rich here as it ever was in far famed California."

■ The author Zane Grey (*Riders of the Purple Sage,* 1912) is born Pearl Zane Gray in the town founded by his ancestors, Zanesville, Ohio.

Also in January 1875:

At Fort Abraham Lincoln in Dakota Territory, the scout Charley Reynolds reports to George A. Custer that during a Hunkpapa ceremony he observed at the Standing Rock reservation, Rain in the Face had boasted of slaying Baliran and Honsinger on August 4, 1873. An outraged Custer dispatches his brother, Colonel Tom Custer, to make an arrest. On a −54° day and with two feet of snow on the ground, Rain in the Face appears at an agency trading post and is wrestled to the floor by Tom Custer, who then takes the Indian back to Fort Lincoln.

FEBRUARY

10. Congress appropriates an additional $150,000 in aid to western farmers plagued by grasshoppers.

12. Reverend John B. Lamy becomes the archbishop of the newly created Catholic archdiocese of Santa Fe, New Mexico.

15. T. H. Russell, a member of the Gordon party that is illegally searching for gold in the Black Hills, writes: "We are finding gold everywhere we prospect."

18. Two of five recently apprehended cattle rustlers are lynched in Mason County, Texas, by a hooded group of vigilantes who will come to be known as the "Hoodoos," Violence in the "'Hoodoo War" will claim 18 lives over the next 18 months.

27. The hostages Catherine and Sophie Germaine, kidnapped from their wagon train in Kansas in 1874, are freed when Stone Calf's Cheyennes surrender.

Also in February 1875:

Denver lawman Dave Cook solves what he will call his most exciting case. Local con-artists were perpetrating mail fraud with newspaper advertisements offering gold watches for $3. Those who sent in their money received small boxes of Arvada sawdust. A deputy sent to investigate the scam was murdered. Cook and Deputy Frank Smith trail the desperados to Colorado Springs. Unable to obtain fresh horses, the lawmen arrange for a handcar to take them by rail through a blizzard to Pueblo. (The owner of the handcar refused an offer of $30, so Marshal Cook commandeered the vehicle at gunpoint.) Cook and Smith find the culprits, Ike Clodfelter and John W. Johnson, in the snowy streets of Pueblo at six o'clock the next morning and open fire. The gunbattle continues on horseback for 13 miles before the two crooks are apprehended and escorted back to Denver by train.

Native Races of the Pacific States, the first five volumes of Hubert Howe Bancroft's histories of the West, is published.

MARCH

1. The *New York Times* fuels further interest in gold in the Black Hills with a report of a party that "sank 25 prospect-holes and struck gold in every instance." The report also notes that "the party never saw an Indian while in the Hills." What the newspaper fails to mention is the terrible weather: 67 consecutive days of rain will culminate in a snowfall on June 2.

3. President Grant signs the Colorado Enabling Act, which grants the territory statehood. Colorado will become the last state admitted to the Union until the famed Omnibus Bill of 1888. Under the Enabling Act's provisions, Colorado is authorized to hold another constitutional convention in preparation for admission.

■ A homestead law for the desert lands of Lassen County, California, authorizing claims four times larger than those allowed by the 1862 Homestead Act, is passed by Congress.

4. Romauldo Pacheco, a Republican, becomes the first native-born governor of California.

11. A school for black children is founded in Laramie, Wyoming.

15. A. A. McSween, a major figure in New Mexico's coming Lincoln County War, arrives in Lincoln with his wife, Susan.

19. The outlaw Tiburcio Vásquez is hanged in San Jose, California, specifically for murders committed during the "Tres Pinos Massacre," on August 26, 1873. According to one estimate, Vásquez killed as many as 42 men.

22. Silver is discovered in the Pinal Mountains of Arizona, at what will become the Silver King mine. Initial ore assays are $4,300 a ton.

27. The Bank of California suffers a financial collapse, sending the state into economic chaos.

29. Colorado's last territorial governor, John L. Routt, takes office; he was appointed by President Grant.

Also in March 1875:

Former Union soldier Michael Hickey lays claim to a 1,500 foot by 600 foot tract that he calls Anaconda, in Butte, Montana. Although Hickey is looking for silver and has found some, he is literally sitting on a copper bonanza.

James Pattee begins the "Pattee Swindle Lottery" in Wyoming, where he "floods the country with circulars for nonexistent drawings."

National Headlines/March 1875:

1. CIVIL RIGHTS ACT PASSES CONGRESS

APRIL

6. Lieutenant Colonel T. H. Neill reports 11 Indians killed, including Chief Black Horse, near the Cheyenne Agency in Indian Territory; 19 enlisted men are reported wounded.

10. The U.S. Cavalry escorts the Gordon party of illegal gold seekers from its diggings in the Black Hills to Fort Laramie. For the moment, the sacred area that the Sioux call Paha Sapa is free of white men.

18. After three months of incarceration, Rain in the Face escapes from the guardhouse at Fort Abraham Lincoln, Dakota. He will later cite a kind jailer as his benefactor: "The old soldier taught me that some of the white people have hearts." Others believe the escape was arranged by George Custer as a convenient way of avoiding a trial for which he had little evidence.

19. The territorial capital of Montana moves from Virginia City to Helena.

21. Wyatt Earp is hired as a $60-a-month policeman in Wichita, Kansas.

23. The Battle of Sappa Creek occurs in northwestern Kansas. Seventy-five Northern Cheyennes under Little Bull, returning to their homes in the Black Hills, are almost wiped out at their camp by a cavalry company and buffalo hunters under Lieutenant Austin Henely of Fort Wallace. The soldiers bury alive many of the wounded Indians along with the dead. Official reports cite 27 Indians and two enlisted men killed.

26. A financial panic closes San Francisco's Bank of California.

Also in April 1875:

The first literary piece signed "by Buffalo Bill" is published as "The Haunted Valley, or A Leaf from a Hunter's Life" in *Vickery's Fireside Visitor*. It is believed that Cody actually dictated the article to a stenographer. His sister, Helen Cody Wetmore, will describe it as "destitute of punctuation and short of capital in many places," adding that it was the colonel's feeling that "life's is too short to make big letters when small ones will do; and as for punctuation, if my readers don't know enough to take their breath without those little marks, they'll have to lose it, that's all."

MAY

1. The *St. Louis Democrat* charges that a "whiskey ring" of distillers and internal revenue officers is bilking the U.S. government through the nonpayment of taxes.

2. Isaac Parker, the new federal judge for Indian Territory, arrives at Fort Smith, Arkansas, with his wife. When Mrs. Parker sees the unpaved streets and the population of 2,500, which is served by 30 saloons, she remarks that they may have made the wrong choice. "No, Mary," says the judge, "we are faced with a great task. These people need us. We must not fail them."

3. Wells Fargo publishes the following poster:

REWARD!
WELLS, FARGO & CO'S
Express was Robbed this Morning, between
Ione Valley and Galt, by two men, described
as follows:
One elderly, heavy set, and sandy complexion.
The other tall, slim, and dark complexion.
$200 Each and one-fourth of the Treasure recovered, will be paid for the **arrest** and **conviction**
of the robbers.
JNO. J. VALENTINE, Gen Supt.

Judge Isaac Charles Parker (1838–1896). The "Hanging Judge" has a gallows that can accommodate six prisoners at a time for the purposes of "launching [them] into eternity." (Denver Public Library, Western History Department)

4. Wyatt Earp makes his first arrest as a Wichita policeman, nabbing the horse-thief W. W. Compton.
6. William D. Leahy, the future U.S. Navy admiral and personal chief of staff for President Franklin D. Roosevelt, is born in Hampton, Iowa.
10. Judge Isaac Parker presides over his first cases at Fort Smith, Arkansas. Throughout an eight-week session, he will pound the gavel 91 times. Of 15 murder convictions, eight defendants will receive jail terms; the other seven will be sentenced to death. To each of the latter, the judge speaks in tones that would chill a branding iron: "I sentence you to hang by the neck until you are dead, dead, dead!"
12. The James and Younger brothers take $3,000 in a stagecoach heist near Austin, Texas.

16. General William Larimer, 64, the colonist who jumped the claim of the original settlers of St. Charles and renamed the settlement Denver, dies in Leavenworth, Kansas.
25. The city of Denver purchases the ditch of the Platte River for irrigation purposes.
30. The first white child born in Yellowstone Valley is recorded by race, not by name.

Also in May 1875:
The Consolidated Virginia and the California mines are producing some $1.5 million in silver each month.
There are 1 million bison in North America, down from 14 million in 1870.
On the Goodnight-Loving Trail, the cattle route that runs through Texas and New Mexico, is the black cowboy Nat Love, 20, who will write about his experiences in his memoirs: "What man with the fire of life and youth and health in his veins could not rejoice in such a life?"
The convicted murderer "Wild Bill" Longley, in hiding as a farmer in Bastrop County, Texas, learns of the death of his cousin, Cale Longley. Most accounts say the death was an accident, but Bill believes his old friend Wilson Anderson is responsible. Bill rides out to the field and fills Anderson with lead. The dying Anderson asks, "Oh God, what did you shoot me for, Bill?" Longley grins, "Just for luck."

National Headlines/May 1875:
17. FIRST KENTUCKY DERBY HELD
29. GRANT NIXES THIRD TERM

JUNE
1. Denver's first mining exchange opens.
2. The last Comanches to surrender to Colonel Ranald Mackenzie at Fort Sill in Indian Territory are led by Quanah Parker. On September 28, 1874, Mackenzie had found Quanah's secret camp at Palo Duro Canyon in the Texas panhandle; in a surprise attack, Mackenzie had captured 1,000 horses and ordered them slaughtered. Today, Mackenzie and Quanah meet face to face for the first time and say nothing to one another.
■ After 67 consecutive days of rain, snow falls in the Black Hills.
3. Lieutenant Colonel James W. Forsyth carves the name of his steamer, *Josephine*, on Pompeys Pillar, east of Billings, Montana. The rock formation has had thousands of pioneers' names carved into it since William Clark was the first to do so on July 25, 1806.
■ The 4th Cavalry reports one Indian killed at Hackberry Creek, Indian Territory.

5. The Pacific Stock Exchange opens in San Francisco.
13. Miriam Amanda Wallace, the first female governor of Texas, is born in Bell County.
14. Jefferson Davis declines an offer to become the first president of Texas A&M.
19. The U.S. Marine Hospital opens in San Francisco.
27. An expedition of the 8th Infantry begins in the Tonto Basin of Arizona. By the time it ends on July 8, 30 Indians will have been killed and 15 will have been captured.

Also in June 1875:

Flora Wellman Chaney, an unwed mother, tries to commit suicide, first with laudanum, then with a pistol pointed squarely at her forehead. Both attempts fail, and seven months later her son, the future author Jack London, is born. The *San Francisco Chronicle* sums up the story:

"A DISCARDED WIFE"
Driven from Home for Refusing to Destroy her
Unborn Infant.
A Chapter of Heartlessness and Domestic Misery.

Shortly after migrating to Kansas with his family, Gordon Lillie, 15, makes friends with Pawnees in present Oklahoma; this will earn him the sobriquet "Pawnee Bill." The Pawnees call him "Ku-luks-Kitty-butks," or Little Bear.

JULY

1. Corporal R. W. Payne reports that the 2nd Cavalry killed two Indians at the Little Popo Agie River in Wyoming.
5. A Wells Fargo express box on the Latrobe and Fiddletown Stagecoach is robbed of $7,000 in gold. A $2,750 reward is offered.
7. The James and Younger brothers stop a Missouri-Pacific Express train near Otterville, Missouri, and steal $75,000.
■ Lieutenant G. H. Wright reports that three members of the 7th Infantry were killed by Indians near Montana's Camp Lewis.
8. In Montana, Helena's famous "Hanging Tree" is chopped down by the Methodist minister Reverend Shippen.
10. The funniest town in the West is Palisade, Nevada.
12. Swarms of grasshoppers converge on Helena Valley, Montana; crop damage is said to be "light."
26. Black Bart robs the Sonora-to-Milton stagecoach four miles from Copperopolis, near Reynolds' Ferry, in California.

National Headlines/July 1875:
31. ANDREW JOHNSON DIES AT 66

BIG FUN AT PALISADE

Civic reputations in the Wild West were often made by events. Tombstone was tough because of the gunplay at the O.K. Corral; Deadwood gained its reputation because Wild Bill Hickok drew his last hand there; and Coffeyville, Kansas, was valiant because the townspeople rid the world of the Dalton gang.

Palisade, Nevada, gained fame in another way. Indian attacks, gun duels at sundown, "necktie parties" for horse thieves—the lurid hard copy of the "penny dreadfuls"—all came alive on her mean streets. But perhaps the most amazing aspect of this wholesale violence was that it always seemed to occur when the train pulled in with a load of passengers from back East. There was a reason for all this: Palisade was the town too funny to die.

Palisade was born on the banks of Nevada's Humboldt River, one of the many small railroad towns to emerge during the construction of the Central Pacific in the late 1860s. At first, it was an overgrown watering hole with a few scattered corrals used by Elko County ranchers while shipping livestock. Then a discovery in Eureka, some 70 miles to the south, brought into being a new railroading enterprise: the Eureka and Palisade was formed to carry the ore from the mines to the tracks of the Central Pacific in Palisade.

The town boomed. The trappings of society—dry goods emporiums, groceries, a trio of saloons, and a gambling house—sprouted along the main street. A new train depot was constructed, complete with a restaurant. By the mid-1870s, the population had grown to 290.

Exactly who had the idea of putting Palisade on the map as the wildest town in the West is not known. Making eastern "dudes" the target of practical jokes was a popular sport on the frontier. Still, nowhere else has it ever been done on such a grand scale.

The first incident occurred shortly after the noon train chugged into the station one day. The passengers, many of them tourists, had hardly disembarked when they were served a scene of public chaos. The rugged cowboy Frank West—tall, dark, and outraged—was in

(continued)

(continued)

the street, hollering for one Alvin "Dandy" Kittleby to come out and fight like a man. West's "poor sister" had been wronged by the cad, the crowd soon learned through a diatribe of spit and whiskey. The tale of tragedy having been absorbed, Kittleby appeared some 50 feet down the dusty boulevard.

West cussed even louder. The men pulled their six-guns and proceeded to blast away at each other. Suddenly, Kittleby screamed in mortal agony, threw himself into the dirt, kicked like a poisoned cockroach, and died.

At this point, the onlookers came unglued. Some ran for the depot, others back inside the train. In the pandemonium, two citizens' groups appeared, one to carry Kittleby's carcass away, the other to haul West to the hoosegow. Less than a half-hour later, the train pulled away, her passengers ducking safely below window level. West, the miraculously revived Kittleby, and the rest of Palisade watched the locomotive's smoke trail away and laughed their heads off.

The municipal joke was so beloved that during the next three years the people of Palisade pulled off some sort of mock massacre for almost every arriving train. The railroad knew about the hoax and filed the reports of terror in appropriate fashion. Still, the stories of wanton violence in Palisade often made their way into big-city newspapers, usually in high-strung editorials pleading for a cessation of hostilities.

The horseplay soon moved from small gunfights to tiny wars. A band of horsemen would try to knock over a bank, only to be met by a posse. Hundreds of blanks were fired. A group of friendly Shoshones were known to apply war paint and regularly "raid" the town, slaughtering men, women, and children who got in the way.

The Palisade entertainment committee always strived for realism. Indeed, before each performance, buckets of beef blood were obtained from a local slaughterhouse. The entire town got into the act, rotating the killing and dying roles. For more than a thousand times, always a few minutes after the train arrived, all hell broke loose in Palisade. But for all the rootin' tootin' hype, Palisade was otherwise a fairly peaceful place. The crime rate was such that the residents never got around to electing a sheriff.

The "violence" in Palisade subsided considerably toward the end of the 1880s. The town itself continued to exist until the 1930s, when the Eureka and Palisade ceased operations.

AUGUST

9. The first of 24 dime novels to be signed "by Buffalo Bill" is *The Pearl of the Prairies, or The Scout and the Renegade,* which begins serialization in the *New York Weekly.*

17. About 17 miles from Oroville, California, a lone robber stops the Quincy Stagecoach and demands the treasury box.

27. The financier William Ralston drowns in San Francisco Bay shortly after the board of directors of his bank requested his resignation. Whether the death is accidental or a suicide will never be determined.

Also in August 1875:
A party led by Frank Bryant becomes the first to discover gold on the site of the future Deadwood, Dakota Territory.

SEPTEMBER

3. George Maledon, the chief executioner for the "hanging judge" Isaac Parker at Fort Smith, Arkansas, performs his first duty. The convicted murderers Edmund Campbell, Daniel Evans, Samuel Fooy, Smoker Mankiller, James Moore, and John Whittington are escorted to the gallows at 9:30 A.M. by a dozen guards and four ministers. The condemned are dispatched on a king-sized scaffold before a crowd of 5,000.

11. "Deadly Eye, the Unknown Scout," a serial by Buffalo Bill, begins appearing in the *Saturday Journal.*

15. John Riley of the Murphy Company in New Mexico shoots Juan Patron in the back; Patron will recover.

16. J. C. Penney, the dry goods magnate, is born in Hamilton, Missouri. In his 95 years, he will see 1,660 of his stores established nationwide.

20. The Reverend F. J. Tolby is murdered, supposedly for a letter he sent to the *New York Sun* in which he criticized a political group called the Santa Fe Ring. The deed is carried out in New Mexico while the minister is on a wagon trip from Elizabethtown to Cimarron. At the urgings of Reverend O. P. Mains, Cruz Vega is arrested; he will be released

GEORGE MALEDON: THE GRIM REAPER OF FORT SMITH
JUNE 10, 1830—MAY 6, 1911

Officially, he was just doing his job. Still, the broom-bearded figure with the dull shark-eyes sent chills through Fort Smith, Arkansas. In the 21 years that he served as executioner for the court of the "hanging judge" Isaac Parker, George Maledon saw lots of overtime.

The "Prince of Hangmen" was born on June 10, 1830, in Landau, Bavaria. As a baby, he emigrated to Detroit with his parents. Upon completing a rural education, he moved to wild Fort Smith and joined the police force. During the Civil War, he saw action on the Union side as a member of the 1st Arkansas Federal Battery.

Upon the creation of the District Federal Court of Western Arkansas, Maledon became a U.S. deputy marshal. Isaac Parker was appointed judge by President Grant in 1874 and it was he who assigned Maledon to be capital punisher. Shortly after Parker became the country's youngest federal judge, construction of Maledon's stage began.

The gallows at Fort Smith became a symbol of law and order to Wild West outlaws. An extended trap door 30 inches wide and 20 feet long could launch a dozen men into eternity at once, if necessary. Soon, Maledon could be seen dropping dirt-filled feed sacks through the trap, honing the equipment to a professional level.

The first to test Maledon's effectiveness were the convicted murderers Edmund Campbell, Daniel Evans, Samuel Fooy, Smoker Mankiller, James Moore, and John Whittington. At 9:30 A.M. on September 3, 1875, a crowd of 5,000 parted as the condemned were escorted to the scaffold by guards and ministers. Quietly, George Maledon adjusted the Kentucky hemp nooses and then stomped across the platform to the lever. After a gut-wrenching pause, he threw the wooden control. Justice was swift.

The gruff Judge Parker would not be intimidated, not by the eastern press and not by the local thugs. His jurisdiction covered most of Indian Territory, present Oklahoma, a haven for bandits and cutthroats.

During two decades, Maledon publicly hanged 87 of the 88 men that Parker sent to the gallows. The one exception was Sheppard Busby, whom Maledon asked to be excused from terminating because of the convicted's service in the Union Army. When he was not being called upon to spring the economy-sized trap door, Maledon served as a jail guard. During the same two decades, he shot dead a total of five escaping prisoners.

George Maledon believed that each man he dispatched certainly had it coming. At $100 a hanging, the executioner should have cleared $8,700, but he did not. Many who found justice at the end of a rope were never claimed, and Maledon had to cover their burial expenses himself.

About his professionalism, Maledon was candid. "Every one of my hangings has been a scientific job," he once said. "I have dropped as many as six through at one time, and twice have hanged five at one time, and there was no quiver in the entire sixteen, not even a foot moved." When, after several residents reported hearing midnight moans from the area, he was asked if he believed his gallows were haunted, Maledon quipped: "I've never hanged a man who came back to have the job done over. The ghosts of men hanged at Fort Smith never hang around the old gibbet."

Only once was the hangman cheated, and not by any fault of his own. Maledon's 18-year-old daughter was pretty, eligible, and lonely. Perhaps her father's occupation kept the beaus at bay. Regardless, when the alcoholic but handsome gambler Frank Carver wooed, Anne Maledon willingly responded.

Carver took her to Colorado to live in sin. Two years later, upon learning of his drinking, his wife, and his two children, the broken-hearted Anne returned to Fort Smith. There, she rebounded to the dashing Frank Walker, who had "none of the habits" of her first love. On the night of March 25, 1895, an insanely jealous Carver appeared drunk in the streets of town. By chance, he found Anne out for a stroll and gunned her down. Hospitalized with four wounds, she clung to life for three painful months and then expired.

Her father had no comment. He attended the daily sessions of Carver's trial and showed no visible emotion when Judge Parker pointed his long finger at the guilty one and sentenced him to be hanged by the neck until he was "dead, dead, dead."

(continued)

(continued)

Before Maledon could adjust the noose, Carver's attorney, J. Warren Reed, found a series of witnesses who could clear his client, and Reed convinced the Supreme Court to overturn Parker's ruling. A second trial was ordered and Carver was again convicted, but this time he was sentenced to life imprisonment. The disappointment of being denied the opportunity to stretch the neck of his daughter's murderer was something Maledon never got over.

Toward the end of Judge Parker's rule, more and more cases were being reversed in this fashion. The West was no longer what it had once been. But even the land's highest court could not help Rufus Buck, Lewis Davis, Lucky Davis, Sam Sampson, and Maomi July, whose three-day rape and murder spree through the Creek Nation got them an appointment with George Maledon. On July 11, 1896, they were the subjects of the city's last multiple hanging, ending an era. Parker retired that September and died unexpectedly two months later.

For a year after he hung up the ropes, Maledon traveled the lecture circuit with S. W. Harman, author of *Hell on the Border,* speaking on the subject of the unprofitability of crime. The two approached Fort Smith's city council with an offer to buy the famed gallows for their road show. The council was so repulsed by the suggestion that it had the thing burned.

After his lecturing career tapered off, Maledon ran a grocery at Fort Smith and then retired to a local farm. From there, he checked into a soldier's home in Johnson City, Tennessee, where he died on May 6, 1911.

later for lack of evidence. Mains will convince gunslinger Clay Allison of Vega's guilt.

23. In Silver City, New Mexico, Henry McCarty (the future Billy the Kid) is arrested for the first time after a practical joke in which he is left holding a bag of laundry that was stolen from Charlie Sun and Sam Chung.

25. Henry McCarty escapes from the Silver City jail and rides toward Arizona Territory.

26. Eleanor Gates, the author of *Poor Little Rich Girl* (1913), is born in Shakopee, Minnesota.

Also in September 1875:

The Treaty of Fort Laramie is officially broken when the last great Council of the Northern Plains Indians fails in its efforts to have the U.S. government return the Black Hills to the Indians.

The Texas State Legislature consists mostly of Democrats; of its 90 members, six are black.

National Headlines/September 1875:

1. MOLLY MAGUIRES CONVICTED OF MURDER

OCTOBER

2. President Grant visits Cheyenne, Wyoming, where he dines at Barney Ford's Inter-Ocean Restaurant.

7. The task of placing iron pillars along the Canadian–Montana border is completed.

14. San Francisco's Palace Hotel, with 9,000 cuspidors, opens for business.

16. "Prairie Prince, the Boy Outlaw; or Trailed to His Doom," whose authorship is attributed to Buffalo Bill, appears in the *Saturday Evening Post.*

23. The serial "The Prairie Rover, or The Robin Hood of the Border," by Buffalo Bill, begins appearing in the *Saturday Journal.*

27. The 5th Cavalry reports that two Indians were slain in a fight near Buffalo Station, Kansas.

30. Clay Allison and his boys get Cruz Vega to admit that he was present at the September 20 murder of the Reverend F. J. Tolby, but Vega claims that it was Manuel Cardenas who pulled the trigger. Nevertheless, Allison's bunch hangs Vega from a telegraph pole at Cimarron, New Mexico. This will bring the renowned badman Pancho Griego into the territory to seek out his friend Vega's killer.

Also in October 1875:

As gold seekers flock to the Black Hills, the Sioux Indians begin to leave their reservations in Dakota Territory. The influx of whites, strictly prohibited by the Treaty of Fort Laramie, forces the tribe to hunt for food.

The author Helen Hunt marries the future Colorado empire builder William Sharpless Jackson (presently the secretary-treasurer of the Denver and Rio Grande Railroad) in New Hampshire. The couple will move to Colorado Springs.

Tribes to the north of the Platte River refuse to sell their lands to the U.S. government.

The first municipal high school in Texas is established in Brenham.

John B. Pearson finds diggings rich with gold in Deadwood Gulch.

NOVEMBER

1. Clay Allison, the leader of the mob that lynched Cruz Vega on October 30, guns down Pancho Griego in Cimarron, New Mexico. The men were having a conversation in a corner of the St. James Hotel's saloon when Allison shot Griego three times with a Peacemaker. After someone hit the lights, Allison escaped.

2. Lieutenant Andrew Geddes reports that the 10th Cavalry killed one Indian and captured five on the Pecos River in Texas.

4. The steamer *Pacific* sinks off Cape Flattery, Washington Territory, killing 236 people.

9. Sioux followers of Sitting Bull and Crazy Horse are labeled hostile by Indian Inspector E. C. Watkins. He recommends that all Sioux be forced onto reservations by January 31, 1876.

10. Manuel Cardenas, who is being held on charges of murdering the Reverend F. J. Tolby on September 20, is murdered by a mob that storms the Cimarron, New Mexico, jail and fills him full of lead.

■ Near Boise City, Idaho Territory, three highwaymen grab the strongbox from a stagecoach bound for Silver City.

15. In Wichita, Kansas, the *Weekly Beacon* praises the policeman Wyatt Earp, who found a drunken stranger with $500 in his pocket asleep under a town bridge: "He [the stranger] may congratulate himself that his lines, while he was drunk, were cast in such a pleasant place as Wichita, as there are but few other places where that $500 roll would ever have been heard from. The integrity of our police force has never been seriously questioned."

23–25. The National Railroad Convention is held in St. Louis; 31 states and territories are represented by 869 delegates. It is considered to be the largest formal meeting held in the West up to this date.

25. The *Rocky Mountain Husbandman* publishes its first issue in Diamond City, Montana.

27. A dance in Tucson, Arizona, raises $1,675 for the public school.

Also in November 1875:

In New Mexico, A. A. McSween becomes the attorney of John Chisum.

National Headlines/November 1875:

22. VICE PRESIDENT WILSON DEAD AT 63

DECEMBER

1. A lone robber ("Mexican, lightish complexion," says Wells Fargo's wanted poster) robs the Chinese and Copperopolis Stagecoach of $600 in gold dust and coins near Burns Ferry in Tuolumne County.

2. A labor strike in Wyoming's Rock Springs coal mine is settled.

4. Andrew Bryant becomes the new mayor of San Francisco; he will continue his anti-Chinese campaign.

6. The Indian Bureau in Washington, D.C., sets a deadline: Indians found off their reservations after January 31, 1876, will be considered hostile and treated as such.

7. John Clark brings the first flock of sheep into Arizona on Hardy's ferry.

8. Indians stampede 5,000 sheep at Maricopa, Arizona, killing 20 in the process. The Indians then round up the sheep and are given five by the grateful drover.

9. The Democrat William Irwin becomes governor of California.

10. William J. "Buffalo Bill" Wilson, convicted of murder in Lincoln, New Mexico, is sent to the gallows. All does not go well at Lincoln County's first legal execution—authorities have to hang Wilson twice.

16. A solitary road agent robs the San Juan stagecoach near Smartsville, California.

20. The Colorado Constitutional Convention assembles in Denver's First National Bank.

24. San Francisco's Commercial Bank suspends operations.

26. The Spanish American Church is dedicated in San Francisco.

28. In California, Black Bart robs the North San Juan–Marysville stagecoach 10 miles from North San Juan.

Also in December 1875:

The tracks of the Atchison, Topeka, and Santa Fe reach La Junta, Colorado.

Of the 2,953 school-aged children in Arizona, half are illiterate and only 1,213 go to school regularly.

The million-dollar-a-floor Palace Hotel in San Francisco serves a testimonial dinner for Lieutenant General Philip H. Sheridan.

National Headlines/December 1875:

4. BOSS TWEED ESCAPES PRISON

Also in 1875:

Former Indian agent Thomas C. Battey, who taught near present Anadarko, Oklahoma, in 1871, publishes *A Quaker Among the Indians*.

Wells Fargo operates 407 offices, down 202 from last year's figure. Income from transportation charges is

$2,390,000; express service income is $1,206,000. Net income is $409,000.

There are 340,000 head of cattle worth $4.4 million in Arizona.

A presentation of Handel's *Messiah* in Salt Lake City grosses $1,200.

A Yale professor discovers "prehistoric camel and horse" remains at Pawnee Buttes, Colorado.

Luther Burbank establishes a plant nursery in Santa Rosa, California.

Grasshoppers are reported thick on the plains.

George B. Emery becomes governor of Utah Territory; he will serve in that post until 1880.

Gertrude Simmons Bonnin, the Yankton Sioux author, is born at the Yankton Reservation in Dakota Territory. Her articles will appear in *Harper's* and *Atlantic Monthly* at around the turn of the century. She often signed her name Zitkala-Sa.

Brigham Young University opens in Provo, Utah, and Westminster College opens in Salt Lake City.

Colonel Nelson A. Miles estimates that 5,373,730 buffalo have been slaughtered on the plains by white hunters since 1872.

President Grant vetoes a bill to prevent the extinction of the buffalo.

The Indian Herald, a periodical, begins a three-year publishing stint in Pawhuska, the seat of the Osage Agency in Indian Territory.

John Wesley Powell publishes *The Exploration of the Colorado River and Its Tributaries.*

Annie Oakley meets Frank Butler at a Cincinnati shooting contest. The competition is arranged by the owner of the Bevis House, where Butler has been staying. A side wager of $100 makes the contest interesting. Annie (Phoebe Ann Moses), 15, has seen her share of hardship. To support her mother and siblings, she hunted game, selling what she bagged to establishments like Bevis House. When asked if she would like to shoot against the famous Mr. Butler, she was hardly intimidated. Of 25 clay pigeons, Butler hits 24; Annie bags all 25. Far from being dashed by the experience, Butler is infatuated with Annie and their courtship begins in earnest. They will be married a year later.

1876

"We had buffalo for food, and their hides for clothing and for our teepees. We preferred hunting to a life of idleness on the reservation, where we were driven against our will. At times we did not get enough to eat, and we were not allowed to leave the reservation to hunt. We preferred our own way of living. We were no expense to the government. All we wanted was peace and to be left alone. Soldiers were sent out in the winter, who destroyed our villages. Then Long Hair came in the same way. They say we massacred him, but he would have done the same thing to us had we not defended ourselves and fought to the last. Our first impulse was to escape with our squaws and papooses, but we were so hemmed in that we had to fight."

—Crazy Horse

JANUARY

1. The prevaricator John Thomas O'Keefe of the U.S. Signal Corps is ordered to "the foot of heaven," Pikes Peak near Colorado Springs. Almost immediately, strange occurrences there are reported. O'Keefe's bizarre sense of humor will make national headlines.
3. The first meeting in Helena of Montana's territorial legislature takes place.
5. Central, Helena's first multigrade school, opens.
9. Wyatt Earp has a close call when his revolver slips from its holster while the Wichita, Kansas, policeman visits with his cronies at the Custom House saloon. The gun discharges and a bullet passes through the fabric of his coat on its way through the ceiling. The *Wichita Beacon* reports "a lively stampede from the room."
- Captain F. D. Ogilby reports that the 6th Cavalry killed one Indian and captured five near Camp Apache, Arizona.
10. Lincoln County War figure Jesse Evans arrives in Lincoln County, New Mexico.
11. Wells Fargo offers an $800 reward for "George Little, alias Dick Fellows, alias Richard Perkins."

12. The author Jack London is born in San Francisco. His unmarried mother, Flora Wellman Chaney, names him John Griffith Chaney. London's father is the astrologer William H. Chaney, whom he will never meet.
17. Wade's Opera House opens in San Francisco.
22. Lieutenant H. S. Bishop reports that the 5th Cavalry killed three Indians and captured four on the Cimarron River, 125 miles east of Camp Supply in Indian Territory.
24. Molly Brennan is killed by a stray bullet fired by one of two men who were fighting over her in a Mobeetie, Texas, saloon; the men are one Sergeant King and Bat Masterson. Masterson slays King, but not before he is wounded in the upper thigh. Henceforth, Masterson will walk with a cane.
25. In Montana Territory, Sitting Bull attacks Fort Pease, a civilian post near the mouth of the Bighorn River.
- The Hot Springs Railroad, the first rail link serving Arkansas's natural spas, begins operating from Malvern to Hot Springs. Chicago's "Diamond Joe" Reynolds built the railroad so that he would not have to take the stagecoach on the 23-mile trip to the baths.

William Barclay "Bat" Masterson (1853–1921). Dapper and deadly, his career progresses from law enforcement in the Wild West to sports reporting in New York City. (Denver Public Library, Western History Department)

30. An outbreak of smallpox in La Paz, Arizona, forces the steamers on the Colorado River to avoid the settlement.

31. Today is the deadline established by the Indian Bureau for all Indians to be on their reservations; those found off their reservations will be considered hostile.

■ San Juan County is created in Colorado.

FEBRUARY

1. Secretary of the Interior Zachariah Chandler informs Secretary of War William Belknap that Sitting Bull and his followers have failed to report to their reservation and that responsibility for them is being turned over to the War Department "for such action . . . as you may deem proper under the circumstances."

■ Captain F. D. Ogilby reports that Indian scouts

killed four Indians and captured six near Chevelons Fork, Arizona.

2. There are approximately 1,000 white men illegally prospecting in the Black Hills.

■ The first stagecoach bound for the Black Hills departs Cheyenne.

3. Secretary of War William Belknap acknowledges Secretary of the Interior Zachariah Chandler's dispatch of February 1: "I have the honor to inform you that the Adjutant-General has directed the General of the Army to take immediate measures to compel these Indians to remain upon their reservation."

8. General George Crook receives orders from General Philip Sheridan to commence a military operation against the hostile plains Indians. Among the many officers who will take part in the offensive are Brigadier General Alfred H. Terry and Lieutenant Colonel George Armstrong Custer. The operation will commence near the headwaters of the Powder, Tongue, Rosebud, and Bighorn Rivers.

■ A party of prospectors led by California Joe departs for the Black Hills.

10. Brigadier General Alfred H. Terry receives orders to take military action against the Sioux and Cheyennes who remain off their reservations in Dakota Territory.

15. The last constitution of Texas is formally adopted.

22. Troops under Major J. S. Brisbin depart Fort Ellis in present Montana to reinforce Fort Pease, which is besieged by Sitting Bull.

26. The Atchison, Topeka, and Santa Fe's tracks reach Pueblo, Colorado.

MARCH

1. General George Crook leads his men north from Fort Fetterman on a search-and-destroy mission in Dakota Territory.

2. Secretary of War William Belknap resigns after being impeached by the House of Representatives. He was charged with taking bribes in exchange for the sale of trading posts in Indian Territory.

5. Wild Bill Hickok weds an old flame, the show rider Agnes Lake, in Cheyenne, Wyoming.

17. The Battle of Powder River takes place in Dakota Territory.

■ Major J. S. Brisbin reports that six settlers have been killed and eight have been wounded in Indian attacks near Fort Pease, Montana Territory, since February 22.

20. Residents of Tucson, Arizona, defeat a proposal to disincorporate their village.

23. The *Cheyenne Daily Leader* reports that Sitting Bull

THE BATTLE OF POWDER RIVER
MARCH 17, 1876

An advance column of General George Crook's troops under Colonel Joseph Reynolds attacked the peaceful camp of Two Moon's Cheyennes and He Dog's Sioux on the Powder River. Reynolds unexpectedly withdrew and many Indians escaped. Some 800 of the Indians' horses, stolen in the attack were retaken under the cover of darkness by warriors under Crazy Horse. Reynolds listed four soldiers killed and six wounded. Crook was enraged and ordered the troops to return to Fort Fetterman for regrouping.

will surrender in return for a lump payment of $60,000.

24. A telegram from General Alfred Terry to General Philip Sheridan reads:

> THE MOST TRUSTWORTHY SCOUT ON THE MISSOURI RECENTLY IN HOSTILE CAMP REPORTS NOT LESS THAN TWO THOUSAND LODGES AND THAT THE INDIANS ARE LOADED DOWN WITH AMMUNITION.

25. The Buffalo Bill dime novel *Kansas King, or The Red Right Hand* begins serialization in the *Saturday Journal.*

27–28. Indian scouts report killing 16 Indians in Arizona's Tonto Basin.

National Headlines/March 1876:

3. ALEXANDER GRAHAM BELL RECEIVES TELEPHONE PATENT

The Battle of Powder River, March 17, 1876. Crook attacks Crazy Horse. (Harper's Weekly)

APRIL

2. Wichita police officer Wyatt Earp gets into a fistfight with William Smith, a candidate for the post of city marshal. Earp is fined $30 and released from the force.

3. San Francisco's Board of Supervisors is petitioned for protection by the Chinese Six Companies, a group of representatives from the province of Kwangtung.

10. Apaches leave the San Carlos Reservation in present Arizona and slay a couple of Sulphur Springs station keepers and a San Pedro rancher.

13. The 4th Cavalry reports killing six Indians near Fort Sill, Indian Territory.

17. Colonel John Gibbon climbs Pompey's Pillar in Montana, giving himself a good view of the Little Bighorn River, about which he will write in his journal: "afterwards to play so prominent a part in the history of our campaign."

19. The Witchita City Council votes 2 to 6 against reinstating Wyatt Earp to the police force.

21. At Fort Smith, Arkansas, four persons are sentenced by the "Hanging Judge" Isaac Parker to be hanged.

25. Brazil's Emperor Pedro II visits San Francisco.

28. The town of Deadwood, Dakota Territory, is born.

▪ Cornerstone-laying ceremonies for the Arizona Ter-

DEADWOOD

With the human stampede to find gold in Dakota Territory, mining towns proliferated. First there was Custer City, then Elizabeth City and Crook City. The first gold was discovered in August 1875 by a party led by Frank Bryant, near what would become Deadwood. Located at the head of Deadwood Gulch and named for trees felled either by a tornado or by a beaver colony, the town was laid out on April 28, 1876.

Along one of Deadwood's main streets, a mining camp civilization sprang up almost overnight. For every store, there were three saloons. Perhaps as many as 10,000 people populated Deadwood and the surrounding hills. As had been the case with the California and Colorado gold crazes, gamblers and prostitutes were drawn to the mines like magnets.

One of the favorite pastimes in Deadwood was rushing to reported new strikes, with or

(continued)

(continued)

without evidence. The bizarre "Wolf Mountain Stampede" began when livery stable owner Red Clark spread a rumor of a fabulous discovery in the mountains. At least 1,500 prospectors headed for the hills, though no one really knew where to look. Neither the location nor the gold was ever found, but we do know that Clark sold all his horses.

Like all other Wild West locales, Deadwood became known not for its sea of faceless prospectors but for its celebrities. Reverend Henry W. "Preacher" Smith was famous for his street-corner sermons until he was mysteriously murdered on his way to nearby Crook City. Mule skinner Phatty Thompson, noticing the dearth of felines in the town, rounded up a wagonload of cats in Cheyenne and then sold them to Deadwood's prostitutes; many claim the term "cathouse" originated here.

Deadwood's most celebrated personality never left. James Butler "Wild Bill" Hickok, 39, a man long on reputation but short on cash, arrived in the spring of 1876, hoping to strike it rich at the gaming tables. His luck deserted him, however. He even commented to his friend Charley Utter, "I feel this is going to be my last camp, and I won't leave it alive." On the afternoon of August 2, 1876, a drunken saddle bum named Jack McCall put a bullet into the back of Hickok's head as he played poker.

Hickok's death only served to solidify Deadwood's notoriety. In September 1877, *Frank Leslie's Illustrated Newspaper* described the town:

One of the liveliest and queerest places west of the Mississippi . . . , Courts have been established, and the city is policed; but the police happen to be in league with the gamblers who rule the town, and so criminals are apt to go unwhipped of justice. . . . Saloons start up all over the place like mushrooms.

The gold rush subsided in 1879, the same year that fire destroyed Deadwood's entire business district. The town rebuilt and made great strides toward respectability. Incorporation came in 1881, floods devastated many buildings in 1883, and another major fire occurred in 1894.

But Deadwood's reputation stayed intact, and the town attracted the likes of the cigar-chomping Poker Alice Tubbs and Martha Jane Canary. The latter, better known as "Calamity Jane," was buried in Mount Moriah cemetery next to Wild Bill Hickok, her true love, in 1903.

With the 20th century's glamorization of the Old West, Deadwood adapted itself into a popular tourist attraction. Beginning in 1924, a "Days of '76" celebration was initiated, featuring parades, rodeos, and barbecues. Visitors could attend the theatrical "Trial of Jack McCall" and see Wild Bill's "Dead Man's Hand" framed in the saloon where Hickok drew his last breath.

A December 1987 blaze severely damaged Deadwood's 1876 Main Street, a registered national landmark. Yet again, the town's 2,000 residents faced the monumental task of rebuilding.

ritorial Prison are held in Yuma. The prison will open in June and quickly earn the moniker "Hell Hole of Arizona."

Also in April 1876:

The first "Harvey Girls," hostesses in uniform, serve meals to passengers of the Atchison, Topeka, and Santa Fe on their arrival in Topeka. The idea was the brainchild of the Englishman Fred Harvey.

National Headlines/April 1876:

2. 1ST OFFICIAL NATIONAL LEAGUE BASEBALL GAME

MAY

2. A special tax on Chinese laundries in San Francisco is ruled unconstitutional by District Judge S. B. McKee.

8. The Wichita City Council votes to pay Wyatt Earp $40 for the 20 days he worked in April.

14. Violent encounters between Sioux Indians and prospectors at Buffalo Gap in the Black Hills are reported. According to observer Joseph G. Bemis:

A man by the name of Woods . . . on his way to Spotted Tail Agency, lost his life, horse, saddle and scalp. . . . On the same day a party of five persons were killed in Red Canyon, fifty miles south of here, on the Cheyenne road, and two others severely wounded. Among the killed were a Mr. Metz and wife, and Mrs. Mosby. . . . The women were ravished, then filled with arrows and bullets, and their brains beaten out.

■ A telegram from General Alfred Terry to General Philip Sheridan regarding the plains Indians reads:

"It is represented that they have fifteen hundred lodges, are confident and intend making a stand."

15. The boundaries of the Colorado River Reservation are enlarged.

17. Custer begins his expedition against the Indians.

18. The slaying of the Red Cloud Agency's mail carrier is reported in the *Cheyenne Daily Leader*.

22. Denver reports her greatest rainfall in a 24-hour period, 6.53 inches. Cherry Creek overflows its banks.

24. The *Wichita Beacon* reports: "Wyatt Earp has been put on the police force at Dodge City."

■ Henry Plummer's horse, used by the Montana outlaw prior to his execution in 1864, is purchased by Kleinschmidt and Brother in Helena, Montana.

25. The *Pueblo Chieftain* carries the first of the wild tales invented by the "Pikes Peak Prevaricator," John T. O'Keefe, the U.S. Signal Corps member in charge of that mountain's high-altitude weather station: "Attacked by Rats, Terrible Conflict on the Summit of Pikes Peak." The lurid tale concludes with the demise of the prevaricator's two-month-old daughter, Erin O'Keefe: "The rats had found their way to the infant and had left nothing of it but the peeled and mumbled skull." O'Keefe had cooked up the whole story, including the existence of an infant daughter, and even photographed her mock funeral.

THE CUSTER OFFENSIVE BEGINS
MAY 17, 1876

Lieutenant Colonel George Armstrong Custer and 12 companies of the 7th Cavalry moved out of Fort Abraham Lincoln under General Alfred H. Terry's command to deal with Indian resistance in the Yellowstone country. The offensive unfolded along three fronts, with Terry moving west to the Yellowstone River and then upstream, General George Crook approaching from Fort Fetterman, and Colonel John Gibbon working in an easterly direction from Fort Ellis, Montana. Elizabeth Custer will write: "When our band struck up 'The Girl I Left Behind Me,' the most despairing hour seemed to have come. All the sad-faced wives of the officers who had forced themselves to their doors to try to wave a courageous farewell and smile bravely . . . gave up the struggle at the sound of the music."

---

29. General George Crook's troops set out from Fort Fetterman to join forces with those of Custer and Terry in search of Sitting Bull.

31. In a letter to his wife from "ten miles west of the Little Missouri," George A. Custer describes a practical joke in which he fired a gun over the head of his younger brother, Boston Custer, making him think he was under attack by Sioux.

Also in May 1876:

The first Creek Indian Newspaper, the *Indian Journal*, begins publication in Muskogee, Indian Territory, with William P. Ross as editor.

The Polish author Henryk Sienkiewicz (*Quo Vadis*, 1895) is in Anaheim, California, inspecting the area around the future Disneyland as a possible site for a utopian community for his countrymen. Lack of knowledge about farming will doom the project, despite fund-raising performances by the would-be colonist Madame Modjeska. Sienkiewicz will move to Los Angeles in 1878, and back to Poland in 1879.

National Headlines/May 1876:

10. CENTENNIAL EXHIBITION OPENS AT PHILA-DELPHIA

23. JOE BORDEN PITCHES FIRST NO-HITTER

JUNE

2. Black Bart robs the Roseburg, Oregon–Yreka, California, stagecoach nine miles from Yreka.

3. Because of a San Francisco law that says prisoners must have a haircut, a Chinese convict loses his queue.

4. The Transcontinental Express arrives in San Francisco after speeding from New York in just over 83 hours.

8. Officials in Kansas announce that the state will produce $20,000 worth of silk this year, compared with just $7,000 worth in 1875.

10. A new state seal for California is being designed; it will be four and one-half feet high and a foot thick, and made from 41 varieties of native California wood.

15. Perhaps as many as 15,000 Indians congregate on Montana's Rosebud River, where Sitting Bull holds a three-day Sun Dance. During the ceremony, after 50 small sections of skin are cut from his arms, he has a vision in which soldiers wander into the camp and fall head down like grasshoppers.

16. The *Sacramento Bee* announces that "one way has been discovered to utilize and humanize the incipient hoodlum element of the state—an element by the way, that would not exist did our half-grown

Sitting Bull (Tatanka Yotanka, c. 1831–1890), leader and holy man of the Hunkpapa Sioux. (Denver Public Library, Western History Department)

The Battle on the Rosebud was the dress rehearsal for the Battle of the Little Bighorn. General George Crook's 1,325 men stopped for one of the West's more memorable coffee breaks on Montana's Rosebud Creek, 20 miles north of the present Wyoming boundary. Crook was playing cards at 8:30 that morning when a force of 1,500 Sioux and Cheyennes under Crazy Horse fell upon his soldiers. Charging columns divided Crook's command. Crook's earlier decision to camp for eight weeks following the Powder River battle prevented him from joining with Terry and Custer, and thus made Crazy Horse's victory all the more important. Crook counted 57 of his men dead or wounded, although the official report states that nine soldiers were killed and 21 were wounded; 11 Indians are reported killed.

men have means of legitimate employment." The solution is to put the men to work repairing and constructing railroads.

- Custer's expedition passes through an Indian burial ground where corpses are arranged in trees and on platforms. When Custer orders some of the bodies pulled down for examination, his men help themselves to souvenirs; some cut out portions of flesh to use as fish bait.

17. The Battle on the Rosebud takes place.

- A heavy wind collapses a three-story building in San Francisco, killing three.

- Omaha's Deputy Sheriff Mace is shot dead by a man named Hallowell at Plum Creek. Hallowell is apprehended immediately, then taken from his cell at midnight by a mob and lynched.

18. Cunningham Watts commits suicide by overdosing on laudanum while on board the ship *Mary Whiteridge,* which is docked in San Francisco Bay. His cryptic farewell note to his mother reads, "You know the reason."

- At Truckee, California, a mob sets fire to the cabin of three Chinese prospectors. When the residents run outside, one is shot dead while the other two escape.

Artist's depiction of Crazy Horse (Tashunka Witco, c. 1842–1877) at the Battle on the Rosebud, June 17, 1876. (Frank Leslie Illustrated Newspaper)

19. Washakie and 200 Eastern Shoshone warriors arrive at Rosebud Creek too late to aid General George Crook.

- A fire in Virginia City, Nevada, destroys a hotel and 25 buildings.

- James White shoots and kills ferryman John D. Dove on the ferry at Guadalupe, five miles south of Seguin, Texas. It seems that the two were old business partners who believed they had a score to settle.

20. George A. Custer and the 7th Calvary pass in review before General Alfred Terry and Colonel John Gibbon. Custer's men then begin marching toward the Little Bighorn River as the band plays "Garry Owen."

- Scouts inform Custer that the rumored Indian camp does indeed exist on the Little Bighorn, and that it contains between 2,000 and 4,000 warriors.

- Crow and Snake Indians join General George Crook on Goose Creek. Crook's command will begin marching, expecting to strike the combined Sioux forces under Crazy Horse and Sitting Bull within four days. Crow scouts report the presence of a large Sioux village on the Tongue River.

21. Lieutenant Colonel George A. Custer meets with General Alfred Terry and Colonel John Gibbon on board the steamship *Far West* to discuss their strategy against the Indians. Unaware of the Rosebud battle, Gibbon and Terry decide to follow the Yellowstone River to the Bighorn River, and from there to go to the Little Bighorn for a rendezvous with Custer.

- Boston Custer writes: "Armstrong, Tom and I pulled down an Indian grave the other day. Autie Reed got the bow with six arrows and a nice pair of moccasins which he intends taking home."

- In Dakota Territory, the Standing Rock Agency reports that 3,000 Indians are absent from the reservation. It is alleged that those missing are out hunting. A news release from Chicago notes that "persons well informed do not believe that the Indians will attack any settlement east of the Missouri River."

- In St. Louis, the hemp market is reported to be "quiet and unchanged." The price of whiskey is "nominal at $1.11."

22. Lieutenant Colonel George A. Custer takes 675 men, 12 companies of the 7th Cavalry, and splits off from Colonel Gibbon and General Terry, as the search continues for a reported Indian gathering near the Little Bighorn River. Custer's orders are to proceed south up Rosebud Creek, following the trail of the large gathering of Indians. Gibbon is to move south up the Bighorn River. Custer is told that if the trail turns toward the Little Bighorn, he is to continue on his way south and then launch an attack after he converges with Gibbon. As Custer leaves, Gibbon calls out: "Now, don't be greedy, Custer, as there are Indians enough for all of us. Wait for us." Custer's reply is a stutter, "No, I . . . I won't."

- George Custer writes his last letter to his wife:

  Do not be anxious about me. You would be surprised to know how closely I obey your instructions about keeping with the column. I hope to have a good report to send you by the next mail—A success will start us all towards Lincoln. . . .

- Antonio López de Santa Anna, 80, the former ruler of Mexico and commander of the army, dies as an embittered old man in Mexico City.

- A train of 60 wagons is en route from Bismarck to the Black Hills with supplies for the gold miners.

23. George A. Custer's 7th Cavalry begins marching at 5:00 A.M.; it will cover 30 miles of rugged terrain.

- Denver voters reject by 660 to 517 a $75,000 bond issue to pay for changing the course of Cherry Creek, the waterway that runs through the heart of the city and has been known to cause devastating floods.

24. After marching 28 miles (and finding a scalp, believed to be that of Private Augustine Stoeker, secured to a stick), George A. Custer and his men make camp on the upper reaches of Rosebud Creek. At 9:00 P.M., Crow scouts inform the commanding officer that the wide Indian trail they have been following has turned west to cross the divide between the Rosebud and the valley of the Little Bighorn. Custer, having decided to disobey orders and follow the Indians westward, tells his men to prepare to march at 11:00 P.M. Three hours and 10 miles later, the head of the column stops at a wooded ravine.

- The Downieville, Arizona, stagecoach is stopped by two masked men at the foot of Stanfield Hill. A messenger named Hackett produces a shotgun that frightens the would-be highwaymen into a thorny thicket.

- The *Rocky Mountain News* reports: "The Leipsic [sic] bookseller Minde has published a pamphlet which predicts the end of the world will be August 28, 1876. Retail dealers may return unsold copies of the pamphlet until the end of the year."

25. The Battle of the Little Bighorn takes place in Montana Territory.

SHOWDOWN ON THE LITTLE BIGHORN
JUNE 25, 1876

Lieutenant Colonel George Armstrong Custer divided his command at Ash Creek for an expected skirmish with the Indian encampment that was reported to be about 12 miles away. Captain Frederick Benteen and three companies (125 men) were ordered to the west, to scout the bluffs. Major Marcus Reno was instructed to lead three companies (112 men) across the Little Bighorn and then to attack the southern end of the camp from the valley. Another company was sent back to the pack train.

When Custer and his five companies, about 215 men, were spotted by Indians camped in the valley, Custer ordered his last charge. He ran into what was perhaps the largest gathering of tribes in history—15,000 Sioux, Cheyennes, Blackfeet, and Sans Arcs. Hearing that the soldiers were approaching the Little Bighorn, Crazy Horse reportedly shouted, "Hoka-hey! It is a good day to fight! It is a good day to die!" Sitting Bull did not participate in the battle, remaining in the camp.

Custer was outnumbered by at least 2,000, possibly 5,000, warriors led by Crazy Horse. Custer's men never made it to the stream; they were driven back to a slope where they were swarmed over and wiped out in less than half an hour. How Custer died remains unclear. Indians say he died early in the battle and that they lost 22 of their own in what they call the Battle of the Greasy Grass. One of the first to claim to be Custer's killer was Chief Joseph White Bull, a Miniconjou subchief of the Teton Sioux.

Three miles from the tepees, Reno began his first charge on the Indians. A hundred yards from the camp, he saw hundreds of warriors rising out of a ravine to repulse his charge. He ordered his men to dismount, and some were told to go into a grove of cottonwoods while about 80 were instructed to form a skirmish line. In the confusion, Reno desperately communicated in sign language with the scout Bloody Knife. A bullet hit the scout between the eyes, and Reno was splattered with brains. Outnumbered perhaps 10 to 1, it is almost certain that Reno panicked and ordered a retreat from the grove of trees. During the mad dash to "Reno's Hill"—and during two more days of fighting—Reno lost a third of his men.

The official army reports listed 13 officers, 189 enlisted men and four civilians killed. The best known were George Custer, his brothers Boston and Tom, George W. Yates, Myles W. Keogh, Q. W. Cooke, A. E. Smith, James Calhoun, J. E. Potter, H. M. Harrington, J. G. Sturgis, W. V. M. Reiley, Lieutenant J. J. Crittenden, and Assistant Surgeon George E. Lord. One of the Indians who died at the Little Bighorn was Black Moon, killed while defending the Hunkpapa camp.

- In his memoirs, Nat Love recorded that on this day he was on a cattle drive with 2,000 longhorns en route to Deadwood, some 60 miles from the Little Bighorn. Writes Love: "We did not know that at the time or we would have gone to Custer's assistance."
- Calamity Jane reaches Fort Russell in present Wyoming "so blind drunk she couldn't see" (according to Denver's *Rocky Mountain News*), and drives right past to Chugwater, some 50 miles to the north of the Little Bighorn. Later, she arrived at Fort Laramie and "alighted as brisk and cheerful as a harvest grasshopper."
- **26.** Lieutenant James Bradley and his Crow scouts are the first to learn of the Custer debacle from smoke signals sent by several of Custer's Crows, whom he had dismissed before the battle and who were now

A Sioux painting of the Battle of the Little Bighorn, possibly by an eyewitness.   (Library of Congress)

George Armstrong Custer (1839–1876). The Indians call him "Long Hair," "Hard Backsides," and "Son of the Morning Star." (National Archives)

on the other side of the Little Bighorn. The scouts reporting the battle are White Man Runs Him, Goes Ahead, and Hairy Moccasin.

- The members of the 7th Cavalry commanded by Major Marcus Reno remain under attack. As the sun goes down, the Indians end their attack. Reno will report two officers, 46 enlisted men, and one civilian killed, and 46 wounded. It will take the scout Bloody Knife's widow, She Owl, four years to collect the back wages her husband was owed, less than $100.

27. The mutilated bodies of Lieutenant Colonel George A. Custer and his men are found at the Little Bighorn by General Alfred Terry and Colonel John Gibbon.

- The first news of Custer's battle is conveyed to the crew of the ship *Far West,* a half-mile from the mouth of the Little Bighorn, by Curly, Custer's Crow scout.

- The only survivor of Custer's battle on the military side is Captain Myles Keogh's horse Comanche, who is found with seven wounds and is lapping water from the Little Bighorn. The other mounts of

Martha Jane Canary, "Calamity Jane" (1852–1903). She spread her own legend across Kansas, Wyoming, and Montana. (Denver Public Library, Western History Department)

the 7th Cavalry were either slain or hustled away, but the Indians would not come close to Comanche. The Indians thought him enchanted. Keogh had dropped to the ground, holding the reins of his horse with one hand and firing with the other, until he was slain. In an interview years later, the Indian Little Soldier spoke of Keogh still holding his horse in death and said, "no Indian would take that horse when a dead man was holding the reins." Comanche

Comanche (c. 1866–1891), "survivor" of the Little Bighorn battle, the only U.S. Cavalry horse the Indians do not take or destroy. He is shown with handler Gustav Korn and Captain Henry Knowlan. (Denver Public Library, Western History Department)

will never be ridden again and will become a living symbol of the men who fell at the Little Bighorn. He will live the good life at various military posts, enjoying nothing better than a bucket of beer. Comanche will die in 1891.

Also in June 1876:

The *Rocky Mountain News* smells a rat concerning John T. O'Keefe's report of May 25 that rats have invaded the top of Pikes Peak. Scientists state flatly that rodents do not live above the timberline. The hoax is exposed, but the public is unconcerned. Says a *News* reporter, "People are more ready to believe a good story than a dry truth."

Living on his father's ranch less than 200 miles from the Little Bighorn fight is the future idol of silent-screen Westerns, William S. Hart, age 6.

In an interview with the *New York Herald*, President Grant says: "I regard Custer's massacre as a sacrifice of troops, brought on by Custer himself, that was wholly unnecessary—wholly unnecessary. He was

not to have made the attack before effecting the junction with Terry and Gibbon."

National Headlines/June 1876:
16. GOP NOMINATES HAYES
29. DEMS NOMINATE TILDEN

JULY

1. The first news of the Little Bighorn battle reaches Fort Abraham Lincoln: Speckled Cock and Horned Toad, both Crows, arrive at the fort and tell the Indians there of a big fight and of a white leader (Custer) who committed suicide.

- Colorado voters approve a state constitution by a 4 to 1 margin.

- In Arizona, the Yuma Territorial Prison, built on 10 acres on the east bank of the Colorado River where it joins the Gila River, opens to house seven prisoners.

3. The *Far West*, the ship carrying the bodies of George A. Custer and his men, Major Marcus Reno's wounded, and the horse Comanche, begins her journey down the Yellowstone River.

- The first newspaper account of Custer's battle appears in the *Bozeman Times;* the dispatch comes from General Alfred Terry's white scout Muggins Taylor.
- Indians at the Standing Rock Reservation learn of the battle at the Little Bighorn from a runner named Freighter, who will not inform the local whites.

4. In Arizona, immigrants from Boston celebrate the 4th of July near the San Francisco Mountains and name their settlement Flagstaff.

- The first exhibition of electric lighting in San Francisco is put on by Father Joseph Neri from the roof of St. Ignatius College.
- The *Helena Herald* reports the Little Bighorn battle.
- In Deadwood, Nat Love wins a mustang-roping contest and a shooting match. In addition to the prize money, the excited residents bestow upon him the title "Deadwood Dick." In a time when men are known by their buckskin monikers, Love is honored.

5. The *Far West* completes its incredible journey down the Yellowstone and Missouri Rivers—710 miles from the Little Bighorn to Bismarck, Dakota—in 54 hours. Captain Grant Marsh hurries to the telegraph office, where he gives the news of the Custer fight to the *Bismarck Tribune*'s founder, Clement A. Lounsberry. Operator John M. Carnahan telegraphs the bulletin to the *New York Herald,* a feat that takes 22 hours to complete and costs $3,000.

- The wives of the men of the 7th Cavalry congregate at the Custer home at Fort Abraham Lincoln; a feeling described as one of "impending disaster" cuts short the hymn-singing.

6. Captain William S. McCaskey of the 20th Infantry receives a communiqué from General Alfred Terry at 2:00 A.M. He summons his officers and assigns committees to inform 27 widows. Mrs. Elizabeth Custer is awakened at 7:00 A.M. with the news of her husband's death, as well as those of his brothers Tom and Boston, her brother-in-law James Calhoun, and her nephew Henry Armstrong "Autie" Reed. She then accompanies an officer to 25 other doors to inform the widows. Of this day, Mrs. Custer will write: "The sun rose on a beautiful world, but with its earliest beams came the first knell of disaster."

- A *Bismarck Tribune* extra carries the first in-depth account of Custer's battle, with headlines like "No Officer or Man of 5 Companies Left to Tell the Tale," "Squaws Mutilate and Rob the Dead," and "What Will Congress Do About It?" *Tribune* re-

porter Mark Kellogg perished in the battle.

- The *New York Times* prints its first bulletin about the battle at the Little Bighorn.
- Handbills distributed in Monroe, Michigan, inform Elizabeth Custer's hometown of the battle.
- At least one influential American is convinced that Rain in the Face murdered George Custer. Today, Henry Wadsworth Longfellow publishes "The Revenge of Rain-in-the-Face," a verse filled with error:

And Rain-in-the-Face, in his flight
Uplifted high in air
As a ghastly trophy, bore
The brave heart, that beat no more,
Of the White Chief with yellow hair.

7. The first in-depth *New York Times* story on the Custer battle appears:

Rain in the Face (Iromagaja, c. 1835–1905). The Hunkpapa war chief got his name battling a band of Gros Ventres: "I had wished my face to represent the sun when partly covered with darkness, so I painted it half black, half red. We fought all day in the rain, and my face was partly washed and streaked with red and black." (National Archives)

On June 25, Gen. Custer's command came upon the main camp of Sitting Bull, and at once attacked it, charging the thickest part. . . . The soldiers were repulsed and a wholesale slaughter ensued.

12. In Dakota Territory, Will Bill Hickok, 39, rides into Deadwood. Rumored to have killed 21 men in fair fights, he has recently told the journalist Henry M. Stanley that the number is actually closer to 100. Almost upon arrival, Hickok feels his luck shifting. He comments to his friend Charley Utter, "I feel this is going to be my last camp, and I won't leave it alive."

13. The Monroe, Michigan, *Commercial* announces "Our City in Mourning!" and that businesses will close in respect for the men of the 7th Cavalry. A town meeting to form the National Custer Monument Association is scheduled.

14. Apaches kill two prospectors in Pinery Canyon, Arizona.

15. In Congress, bills are introduced to provide a pension for the Custer family. The widowed Elizabeth Bacon Custer is the beneficiary of George's $5,000 life insurance policy, "less 10% if killed in battle." That money will go to pay her husband's debts. Her pension from the army will be $30 a month.

■ "Shooting and yelling," J. J. Dolan's cowboys ride through Lincoln, New Mexico.

16. In Wyoming, Colonel Wesley Merritt, en route to join forces with General George Crook, learns of a large Cheyenne encampment on the White River. Merritt will march his 5th Cavalry 85 miles in 24 hours and surprise 800 Northern Cheyenne warriors at War Bonnett Creek.

■ One of the few accounts of being scalped is told in the *Bozeman Times* by Herman Ganzio, who was also shot in the leg and shoulder by an attacker in the Black Hills. As he was lying on the ground, he says, "All I knew was that I was being scalped; my hair was held tight."

17. William F. Cody, scouting for Colonel Wesley Merritt, slays Yellow Hand as 800 Cheyennes are kept from joining Sitting Bull and Crazy Horse. At War Bonnett Creek, Nebraska, Cody is still in the red and black velvet vaquero outfit he was wearing while appearing in "Scouts of the Prairie" in Wilmington, North Carolina, when he was summoned by telegraph. Cody shoots Yellow Hand (also called Yellow Hair in some sources) twice with a Winchester and then scalps him with a huge bowie knife. According to legend, Cody cries: "The first scalp for Custer!"

18. The *New York Times* reports that a new town in Will County, Illinois, will be named Custer. The *New York Herald* announces a campaign to solicit private funds for a Custer monument; the newspaper contributes $1,000 and promises to print a list of contributors each day.

19. The first illustration of Custer's last battle is W. M. Cary's woodcut "The Battle of Little Big Horn," which runs in the *New York Graphic Illustrated Newspaper*. Although it is inaccurate, it will nevertheless become the model for the many "Custer's Last Stand" portraits that will appear in tabloids and on saloon walls during the next decade.

22. Congress, acting on the public outcry for revenge following Custer's defeat, gives the army temporary supervision of the Sioux reservation in Dakota Territory. All reservation Sioux will automatically become prisoners of war.

■ Another argument for capital punishment: It costs 39 cents a day to feed a prisoner at the territorial prison in Yuma, Arizona.

24. An explosion at the Black Diamond mine in Nortonville, California, kills six.

30. Samuel Axtell becomes New Mexico's territorial governor.

Also in July 1876:

General Alfred Terry writes two accounts of Custer's battle—a glowing one for public release, and another to the secretary of war that questions Custer's judgment. The *Philadelphia Inquirer* obtains a copy of the secret report and publishes it.

Captain Jack Crawford, informed of the Custer disaster by a telegram from William F. Cody, is moved to pen this verse:

> Did I hear news from Custer?
> Well, I reckon I did, old pard;
> It came like a streak of lightnin',
> And, you bet, it hit me hard.
> I ain't no hand to blubber,
> And the briny ain't run for years;
> But chalk me down for a lubber,
> If I didn't shed regular tears.

As the Little Bighorn battle seizes the public imagination, wild theories abound. One of the most remarkable is the rumor that Sitting Bull attended West Point under an alias, thus explaining Custer's mystifying defeat.

National Headlines/July 1876:

4. U.S. CENTENNIAL OBSERVED

AUGUST

1. Former secretary of war William Belknap, having been impeached by the House of Representatives for taking bribes in exchange for the sale of trading posts in Indian Territory, is acquitted in a Senate trial.

- Colorado, a territory since 1861 and with a population of 150,000, enters the Union as the 38th state. President Grant proclaims it the "Centennial State." John L. Routt, Colorado's last territorial governor, will be elected the first state governor. The state's senators will be Henry M. Teller and Jerome B. Chaffee.

2. Wild Bill Hickok is murdered in Deadwood, Dakota Territory.

3. Hickok's funeral notice in Deadwood reads:

> Died in Deadwood, Black Hills, August 2, 1876, from the effects of a pistol shot, J. B. Hickok (Wild Bill) formerly of Cheyenne, Wyo. Funeral Services will be held at Charlie Utter's camp, this afternoon, Aug. 3, at 3 pm. All are respectfully invited to attend.

- Deadwoodites organize a trial to begin at 9:00 A.M., just after the evening performance at McDaniels' Theater. The trial adjourns at 3:00 P.M. for Hickok's funeral. Later, McCall lies when he says that Hickok murdered his brother, Samuel Strawhim, in Hays City in 1869. McCall will be found not guilty. The outraged prosecutor, Colonel George May, claims

---

THE MURDER OF WILD BILL
AUGUST 2, 1876

Early in the afternoon of August 2, 1876, James Butler "Wild Bill" Hickok, 39, sat down to his last game of poker in Deadwood's No. 10 saloon.

A knight-errant with failing eyesight, a celebrity on the verge of poverty, Wild Bill seemed to have been renewed upon his arrival in Deadwood the previous month. When asked about his philosophy, he replied: "When a man really believes the bullet isn't moulded that is going to kill him, what in hell has he got to be afraid of?" At other times he was moody, plagued by rumors that Deadwood's outlaw element, which wrongly believed that he might be there "to clean up the town," was conspiring against him.

Hickok had played poker at Carl Mann's No. 10 saloon on August 1, with his back to the wall, as he preferred. At one point, saddlebum Jack McCall got into the game. Wild Bill may have cursed McCall for being $3.50 short when it was time to settle up. Another account says that the living legend took pity on McCall and gave him breakfast money the next morning. Whatever happened, Hickok went on about his business while McCall seethed over his losses.

The next afternoon, August 2, Hickok returned to the No. 10 to find in progress a game between Carl Mann, Charles Rich, and ex–riverboat captain William R. Massie. They invited Hickok to participate. He said he would if Rich, who had the stool against the wall, would change seats. Rich made a joke that Hickok "wouldn't be attacked." Bill felt a little silly, took the vulnerable chair, and sat down.

From where he sat, Hickok could see the swinging front door, but if he saw the drunken Jack McCall stumble in around 4:15 P.M., he showed no concern. He was losing heavily to Massie. Still, he held two black aces, two black eights, and a jack of diamonds.

McCall inched his way along the bar until he stood two or three feet behind his intended victim. He slipped his dusty old Colt .45 from the holster, leveled it at Wild Bill's 14-inch tresses, and squeezed the trigger. "Damn you, take that," barked McCall.

The bullet ripped through the back of Hickok's skull, exited just under his right cheekbone, and came to rest in Captain Massie's forearm, just above his left wrist. The captain's first thought was that the irked gunfighter had shot him. (Massie soon realized what had happened. He refused to have the slug removed, and carried it until his death in 1910.) For Hickok the lights went out instantly as he slumped to the floor. What would soon come to be known as the "dead man's hand" slipped from his fingers.

McCall turned his pistol on the other eight people in the bar, growling "Come on, ye sons of bitches" as he fled out the rear door. Cries of "Wild Bill is dead!" filled the streets. A half-hour later, McCall was found hiding in a butcher shop.

---

that the jury was bought by the same men who paid to have Hickok slain.

5. The *Cheyenne Daily Leader* ponders America's "bullish" enemies that seem to appear in years ending with "76." The story is called "1776–John Bull, 1876–Sitting Bull, 1976–?"

15. The backlash to the Little Bighorn battle continues. Congress passes a bill that in effect breaks the Red Cloud Treaty of 1868 and ends the rights of the Sioux to the Powder River country of Wyoming and Montana. The bill's backers note that the Indians broke the treaty by going to war. Custer's avoidable disaster becomes the cornerstone of the government's Indian policy.

■ The 6th Cavalry reports killing seven Indians and capturing seven in the Red Rock country of Arizona.

■ The Englishman John Tunstall arrives in Santa Fe, where he intends to pursue a ranching career.

29. Colonel George May tracks Jack McCall to a Laramie bar, where he finds him bragging about the murder of Wild Bill Hickok. May has with him Deputy U.S. Marshal Balcombe, who arrests McCall on the spot. Because McCall's trial took place in Deadwood—a city that was not supposed to be in existence because of the Indian treaties—nothing decided by any court there is legal.

31. In Arizona, the boundaries of the Gila River Reservation are expanded.

Also in August 1876:
General George Crook leads his men on what will become known as the "Horsemeat" or "Starvation March," a fruitless search for the Indians who attacked him in June at Rosebud Creek. During several weeks, the men trek through Wyoming,

The First National Bank of Northfield, Minnesota, as it looks on the day the Jameses and Youngers try to rob it, September 7, 1876. (Library of Congress)

THE GREAT NORTHFIELD, MINNESOTA, RAID
SEPTEMBER 7, 1876

The James and Younger gang's ill-fated robbery attempt on the First National Bank of Northfield, Minnesota, was carried out after much preparation. Following the July 7, 1876, heist of $75,000 in gold from a Missouri-Pacific Express train, Jesse James could afford to research what would become a Waterloo of sorts for him. He and his brother Frank, along with Jim, Bob, and Cole Younger, Clell Miller, Charlie Pitts, and Bill Chadwell, visited 10 Minnesota towns in search of the right bank. They chose Northfield after a worker on the streets of Mankato recognized Jesse and called out to him.

Their plan was flawed at best; the inebriation of Pitts, Miller, and Bob Younger weakened their chances of success. Still, Jesse figured that his gang at its worst could handle this job.

On Thursday, September 7, Jesse, accompanied by Pitts and Bob Younger, rode into town around 2:00 P.M. They tied their horses in front of the bank, then sauntered up the street, stopping to sit in front of a small store. Cole Younger and Clell Miller arrived, walking their horses, and remained in the street to keep watch while Jesse, Pitts, and Bob went into the bank.

Inside, cashier Joseph Heywood had his throat partially slit when he refused the robbers' demands. J. A. Allen, a hardware store owner, noticed what was happening at the bank and advanced toward it. Miller stopped him, holding him off with a pistol. Allen bolted, ran down the street, and sounded the alarm.

At this point Frank James, Bill Chadwell, and Jim Younger rode into town and tried to hold back an instant army of about 40 armed citizens.

Inside the bank, Heywood told the robbers that his safe had a time lock. The situation outside now warranted a quick exit; one of the robbers blew Heywood's brains out upon departure. Jesse, Pitts, and Bob Younger then
(continued)

(continued)

made a deadly run across Division Street as the battle erupted.

Chadwell died, then Miller. Cole Younger was wounded in the arm, Frank James in the leg, and Jim Younger in the face. Townspeople who didn't have guns pelted the gang with rocks. Sensing total defeat, Jesse ordered his men out of town, with a posse numbering in the hundreds following close behind.

The gang split up soon after Jesse suggested that the wounded Bob Younger be put out of his misery. The three Younger brothers were captured by a posse two weeks later, in a gun battle that claimed Pitts. Cole, Jim, and Bob Younger received life sentences in the state penitentiary. Frank and Jesse made slow progress back to Missouri, from where relatives secreted them to Tennessee. There, for the time being, the boys assumed the lives of Nashville farmers.

THE BATTLE OF SLIM BUTTES
SEPTEMBER 9, 1876

In the wake of the battle at the Little Bighorn, the Sioux American Horse, 75, and his band of Oglalas and Miniconjoux had separated from Crazy Horse at the Grand River to turn south for the winter. They camped during an 11-day rain in present South Dakota, only to be discovered by General George Crook's troops under Captain Anson Mills. During the fight, American Horse, four warriors, and 15 women and children were trapped in a cave. Crook appeared on the scene, assumed command, and directed the assault. American Horse received a stomach wound and surrendered his forces. He refused chloroform or any other assistance from army doctors, preferring instead to chew on a piece of wood while waiting for death. Upon his demise, soldiers scalped the corpse.

Montana, and Dakota Territory until they run out of food and have to eat their horses.

A smallpox epidemic ravages parts of New Mexico.

Annie McDougal, the future "Cattle Annie," is born in the Osage Nation near present Pawnee, Oklahoma.

Texas John Slaughter, working as a cowboy for John Chisum, shoots the rustler Barney Gallagher in the thigh after the latter drunkenly threatens him with a sawed-off shotgun. Gallagher dies that night from loss of blood.

SEPTEMBER

2. The San Francisco Society for the Prevention of Cruelty to Children is established.

6. The Southern Pacific's rail line between San Francisco and Los Angeles is completed.

7. The Great Northfield, Minnesota, Raid takes place.

■ Flora Chaney marries truck farmer John London in San Francisco. Her 8-month-old son now become John Griffith London (the future author Jack London).

9. The Battle of Slim Buttes takes place in present South Dakota.

18. Indian scouts report killing five Indians and capturing 13 east of Verde, Arizona.

21. The brothers Jim, Robert, and Cole Younger are arrested for the attempted robbery of a Northfield, Minnesota, bank, in which the James brothers also participated. All three Youngers are given life sentences. Jim and Cole will receive pardons after 25 years, but Robert will die in prison in 1889.

23. The Buffalo Bill dime novel "The Crimson Trail, or On Custer's Last Warpath" begins serialization in the *New York Weekly*. To compete with the *Weekly*, the *Saturday Journal* begins serializing another Buffalo Bill dime novel, "The Phantom Spy, or The Pilot of the Prairie."

Also in September 1876:

A commission from Washington, D.C., arrives at Red Cloud's reservation to inform the chief that his people have lost all rights to the Powder River country of Wyoming and Montana because of the battle at the Little Bighorn. Red Cloud replies: "Tell the eastern people that this is not an Indian War. It is a White Man's War!"

The "Bibulous Babylon of the Frontier," Dodge City, Kansas, provides pioneer editors with a juicy focal point. "A Den Of Thieves And Cut Throats," says the *Yates Center News*, "The Whole Town In League To Rob The UnWary Stranger." The *Kansas City Times* reports: "She awakes from her slumbers about 11 am, takes her sugar and lemon at 12, a square meal at 1 pm, commences biz at 2 o'clock, gets lively at 4, and at 10 pm it is hip-hip-hurrah! 'till 5 o'clock in the morning." "Decency she knows not," huffs the *Hays Sentinel*.

OCTOBER

1. Sergeant John Armstrong of the Texas Rangers attacks a camp of outlaws near Carrizo, Texas, at midnight. Of the four badmen present, three die and the other is shot four times.

3. Colorado's last territorial governor, John L. Routt, is elected the first state governor.

4. The Agricultural and Mechanical College of Texas (Texas A & M), the state's first academy of higher learning, opens in Brazos County.

■ The 6th Cavalry reports killing eight Indians and capturing two in the Tonto Basin of Arizona.

11. William Andrews Clark, builder of Butte's first smelter, first water system, and first electrical plant, speaks at the Montana Day celebration of the U.S. Centennial Exposition in Philadelphia.

19. A fire in San Francisco's Chinese Theater leaves 19 dead.

21. Colonel Nelson A. Miles attacks Sitting Bull's camp on the Big Dry River (Clear Creek) in Montana. Miles reports five Indians killed and two enlisted men wounded.

22. Troops arrive at the Red Cloud Agency in present Nebraska, to drive the Sioux to central camps. Near Camp Robinson, Colonel Ranald S. Mackenzie tells Red Cloud to surrender all ponies and weapons. The old chief and his people are forced to march 20 miles back to their agency. Mackenzie reports that five companies of the 4th Cavalry captured 400 Indians.

23. Red Cloud and Spotted Tail tour possible reservation sites in Indian Territory.

25–26. Colonel Ranald Mackenzie reports that 25 Indians and six soldiers were killed, and 25 soldiers were wounded, in a fight on the north fork of the Powder River.

26. The 276-ton brig *Perpetua* sinks in the choppy seas of Coos Bay, Oregon. Four die; survivors are picked up by the schooner *Rebecca*.

27. Colonel Nelson Miles accepts the surrender of 2,000 Sioux at the Big Dry River in Montana.

Also in October 1876:

Troops from Fort Reno accompany Cheyenne and Arapaho hunters from the Darlington Agency in present Oklahoma on their fall buffalo hunt. The reported kill is 7,000 animals.

In his memoirs, Nat Love will recount an adventure that began this month in Texas, in which his party was attacked by Yellow Dog's warriors. Firing from behind a dead horse, Love was wounded in the thigh and passed out from pain, only to awake in Yellow Dog's camp. According to Love, he was told he was "too brave to die," and plans were made to adopt him. Soon, he was chosen to marry Buffalo Papoose, the daughter of the chief. A month later, with the wedding day fast approaching, Love was well enough to steal a pony and ride 100 miles in 12 hours and return to the ranch where he is employed.

William F. Cody tours in *The Red Right Hand, or Buffalo Bill's First Scalp for Custer*, staged by J. V. Arlington.

NOVEMBER

6. The Englishman John Tunstall arrives in Lincoln. He will become a rancher and play a major role in the Lincoln County War.

7. The arrest of Johnny Ringo and George Glidden signals the end of the "Hoodoo War" in Texas. The blood feud had begun over a year earlier with cattle rustlings. The Hoodoos were night-riding vigilantes who disguised themselves with hoods and boot-black.

■ Culbert L. Olson, the 29th governor of California (1938–1942), is born in Fillmore, Utah.

8. Mary Davis of Tie Siding, Wyoming, becomes the first woman to be elected a justice of the peace in the United States.

25. Dull Knife's village in the Bighorn Mountains near the Red Fork of the Powder River (the present Kaycee, Wyoming) is destroyed by Colonel Ranald Mackenzie's troops in the wake of the Little Bighorn massacre. More than 200 lodges are buried, and souvenirs from Custer's 7th Cavalry are found in the rubble.

29. Nellie Tayloe is born in St. Joseph, Missouri; as Nellie Tayloe Ross, she will become the first female governor in the United States.

Also in November 1876:
Many cases of diphtheria are reported in San Francisco.

National Headlines/November 1876:
7. PRESIDENTIAL ELECTION IN DISPUTE; TILDEN LEADS
23. BOSS TWEED RETURNED TO NY FROM SPAIN

DECEMBER

4. Jack McCall's second trial for the murder of Wild Bill Hickok begins in Yankton, Dakota Territory. When asked why he had not challenged Hickok to a fair fight, McCall answers, "I didn't want to commit suicide."

6. Jack McCall is convicted of murdering Wild Bill

Hickok and sentenced to hang on March 1, 1877.

7. In Wilson County, the Texas Rangers John Armstrong and Leroy Deggs open fire on the murderer John Mayfield at his ranch. Mayfield dies immediately. The Rangers make a quick exit when the deceased's relatives realize what has happened.

15. Charles Goodnight's cowboys complete the first room of a ranch house in the Palo Duro Canyon of Texas.

16. Montana's *Mining Review* estimates that gold worth $110 million has been produced in the territory since 1863.

21. A disturbance at the Olympic Dance Hall in Las Animas, Colorado, brings Deputy Sheriff Charles Faber to restore order. The brothers John and Clay Allison are both drunk, and Faber returns with two deputies and a shotgun. John Allison is seriously wounded and Clay Allison puts a bullet next to Faber's heart, killing him instantly. Thinking that John is dying, Clay drags over Faber's body to show his brother that his death will have been avenged. John will recover, however, and charges against Clay will be dropped.

Charles Goodnight (1836–1929). In 1876, the cattle king moves 1,800 head from Colorado to the Palo Duro Canyon of the Texas Panhandle. (National Archives)

23. Snow halts the construction of Charles Goodnight's ranch house in Texas.

24. On Christmas Eve at the partially completed ranch house of Charles Goodnight, a blizzard is raging. Writes cowboy James T. Hughes: "We all shaved and 'greased up' with bear oil for Christmas—the only thing we could think of doing, as we had run out of all grub except flour; but then flour, bear, buffalo, and turkey is pretty good living."

25. Following a heated argument, Ben Thompson guns down the Austin theater proprietor Mark Wilson, who fired first with a shotgun and missed. In the fracas, Thompson also wounds a bartender. Thompson will be acquitted in the spring of 1877.

Also in December 1876:

At Fort Abercrombie, Dakota Territory, Major Marcus Reno is court-martialed for taking liberties with a captain's wife. He is found guilty of "conduct unbecoming of an officer and a gentleman." Taking Reno's 20 years of service into consideration, President Rutherford B. Hayes will impose a two-year suspension without pay.

The U.S. Army employs approximately 600 Indian scouts.

National Headlines/December 1876:
5. 289 DIE IN NYC THEATER FIRE
6. HAYES DECLARED WINNER OF PRESIDENTIAL ELECTION

Also in 1876:

Mark Twain publishes *The Adventures of Tom Sawyer.*

There are 350,000 head of cattle worth $4.2 million in Arizona.

Thirteen thousand mining claims are recorded in Arizona.

Wells Fargo, operating 438 offices, reports incomes of $2,322,000 from transportation, and $1,117,000 from express services.

The future author Gertrude Horn marries George H. Bowen Atherton in San Francisco, an event she will recall in *Adventure of a Novelist.*

The Winchester Company introduces its Centennial Model, a .47-75 lever-action rifle. Fifty-one of the rifles are inscribed "One of One Thousand," certifying that factory tests have shown their barrels to be exceptional.

Health services for Indians are instituted by the federal government under Treaty No. 6, which reads: "A medicine chest will be kept in the house of the Indian Agent in case of sickness amongst you."

Ann Eliza Webb Young, who is on the lecture circuit

discussing her 1872 divorce from Brigham Young, publishes *Wife No. 19, or The Story of a Life in Bondage* and dedicates it "to the Mormon wives of Utah." (Why she chose the number 19 is unclear—more recent calculations show her to have been either wife No. 27 or No. 55.)

Dan de Quille, the pen name of William Wright, publishes *The Big Bonanza*.

The University of Oregon opens in Eugene.

In Texas, the Sam Houston Normal School, the Prairie View Normal School, and the Industrial College for Negroes open.

1877

"Hear me, my chiefs! I am tired; my heart is sick and sad. From where the sun now stands
I will fight no more forever."

—Chief Joseph

JANUARY

1. Colonel Nelson Miles and his troops begin an eight-day running battle with Sioux and Cheyennes in Montana.

8. Crazy Horse and some 800 Sioux and Northern Cheyennes launch a surprise attack on Colonel Nelson Miles and seven companies of infantrymen in Montana's Wolf Mountains above the Tongue River. Miles's men repel the Indians with howitzer fire and the Indians retreat in a snowstorm. Miles lists three enlisted men killed and eight wounded.

9. Captain G. M. Brayton leads the 6th Cavalry and scouts on an expedition in Arizona's Tonto Basin. By February 5, Brayton will report that they have killed 18 Indians and captured 20.

■ The 6th Cavalry and scouts report killing 10 Indians and capturing one in the Leidendorf Mountains of New Mexico.

11. Arizona's ninth territorial legislature returns the territory's capital to Prescott and empowers the governor to enlist volunteers to stop Indian depredations.

16. In the Pacific, the 246-ton, $20,000 schooner *Oregonian* is a total loss when it runs aground near Oregon's Coquille River.

17. Nez Percés battle the 1st Cavalry under Captain David Pery at White Bird Canyon in Idaho. Lieutenant E. R. Theller and 33 enlisted men are killed.

18. Uncompahgre County is created in Colorado. It will later change its name to Ouray to honor the Ute chief.

29. Routt County is established in Colorado.

FEBRUARY

4. Apaches murder four settlers near Sopori, Arizona.

7. The Arizona territorial legislature recognizes the incorporation of Tucson as a city.

9. In Lincoln, New Mexico, A. A. McSween buys the Murphy store building in order that he and his wife, Susan, may convert it into their home.

12. Arizona governor Safford is given a promise of receiving 500 rifles and bayonets, and 25,000 ball cartridges by the secretary of war.

19. Fort Missoula is established in Montana.

28. Congress ratifies the Manypenny Agreement, the result of an ultimatum to the Sioux to either relinquish the Black Hills or starve. Under the agreement, the Sioux's rights in the Black Hills are given up, as are their rights outside the Great Sioux Reservation.

MARCH

1. Jack McCall, the convicted murderer of Wild Bill Hickok, is hanged in Yankton, Dakota Territory. His last words are, "Oh God."

■ The *Daily Bulletin* begins publication in Tucson, Arizona; by the end of the month, it will be renamed The *Arizona Star*.

3. The Desert Land Act takes effect: the U.S. government will sell 640-acre tracts in arid climates for $1.25 an acre, and accept payments of 25 cents per acre as a down payment. Stipulations include the land being irrigated within three years of purchase.

■ Camp Huachuca is established in Arizona in order to protect the border.

7. Two civilians are reported killed by Indians near Fort Davis, Texas.

9. Custer and Gunnison Counties are created in Colorado.

14. The site for Fort Keogh is established near Miles City, Montana.

22. Three civilians are reported killed by Indians near Fort Clark, Texas.

24. In a letter to the *Tucson Citizen,* Governor Safford blasts General A. V. Kautz for his failure to contain Apache raids in Arizona.

27. The Cheyenne and Black Hills stagecoach is hijacked, probably by the Sam Bass gang; the driver, Johnny Slaughter, is slain. The hijackers are foiled in their attempt to seize $150,000 in gold dust when the stage's horses, frightened by gunfire, run away with the loot.

28. Montana's territorial legislature passes a law prohibiting swine from running at large except in Missoula County.

Also in March 1877:

George W. Hull, a bankrupt prankster who, in 1869, bestowed on the world the great Cardiff Giant—a 2,900-pound gypsum humbug—meets secretly with P. T. Barnum to discuss pulling off a similar stunt out West. In the wake of the furor over Darwin's theory of evolution, Hull has cast a giant man out of $11.45 worth of Portland cement. Barnum likes the idea and contacts a former employee, William A. Conant, now a Colorado railroad agent, to help with the scheme and to plant the giant at an appropriate location. Just to make the discovery look good, Hull casts a petrified turtle and a fish, which will be found with the "Solid Muldoon." The group will show a profit until the hoax is exposed.

National Headlines/March 1877:

5. HAYES SWORN IN AS 19TH U.S. PRESIDENT

APRIL

1. Ed Schieffelin, 29, is prospecting in Apache country in present Arizona. Friends scoffed, saying that the only thing he would find is his tombstone. Today, after striking one of the richest silver veins in the Old West—seven inches wide and 50 feet in length—Schieffelin displays his sense of humor by naming his bonanza Tombstone.

■ Wyatt Earp resigns as a Dodge City, Kansas, police officer to participate in the Black Hills gold rush.

5. John Hoyt is appointed Arizona's 4th territorial governor.

7. A hospital for the insane opens at Warm Springs, Montana.

DODGE CITY: 1877

Sixteen saloons, including the Lone Star, the Alamo, the Alhambra, the Occident, and the Long Branch, served a population of 1,000 in Dodge City this year. The Lady Gay dance hall and theater was opened by Jim Masterson (brother of Bat) and Ben Springer, and headlined stars such as vaudevillian Eddie Foy. John Mueller's Front Street bootery was easily identifiable by its large boot-shaped sign. The Centennial Barber Shop advertised "Shaving, shampooing, and haircutting . . . in the latest fashion." The Dodge City Hotel, or Dodge House, could house 90 people in 38 rooms, and had a U.S. weather observatory. At the Dodge City Market, one could buy bacon, eggs, and dressed chickens, as well as the hides of buffalo, wolves, coyotes, and skunks.

---

15. Captain William Hancock files the first claim in Arizona under the Desert Land Act.

21. U.S. troops and 40 San Carlos Apache scouts led by John Clum cross from Arizona into New Mexico's Hot Springs Reservation, where they raid a Chiricahua Indian camp that is believed responsible for recent depredations. Approximately 427 warriors and their 17 leaders are marched back to the San Carlos reservation, many in chains.

24. Reconstruction officially ends as the last federal troops depart Louisiana.

26. New Mexico's attorney general, William Breeden, threatens to invoke the Territory's "Sunday Law"

Dora Hand entertaining the boys in Dodge City.
(Library of Congress)

---

against those who continue playing baseball on Sundays.

MAY

4. The 10th Cavalry reports killing four Indians and capturing six at Lake Quemado in Texas.

5. Sitting Bull leads his people into Canada, which he refers to as "Grandmother's Land," so named for Queen Victoria.

■ Crazy Horse leads nearly 900 followers to Fort Robinson at the Red Cloud Agency in present Nebraska, having been promised a reservation in the Powder River country.

■ In New Mexico, the cattle conflicts begin to warm when Jerry Dillon kills the unarmed Paul Dowlin at Dowlin's Mill.

6. Crazy Horse, along with approximately 900 warriors, women, and children, surrenders at Fort Robinson in Nebraska's White River valley. Soldiers confiscate 1,700 ponies and 117 rifles and pistols from his people. The Army counts 217 men and 672 women.

7. The Battle of Lame Deer takes place in Montana.

13. The gunman Wild Bill Longley, wanted for many murders, is arrested in Louisiana and taken to Giddings, Texas, where he will be tried and sentenced to hang for the murder of Roland Lay. Longley will convert to Catholicism and repent in local newspapers.

17. The midgets General Tom Thumb (Charles Stratton) and Lavina Warren, his wife, famous for their appearances for P. T. Barnum, perform in Denver's Guard Hall.

28. Nine hundred and thirty-seven Northern Chey-

CRAZY HORSE
1841?–SEPTEMBER 6, 1877

1841: He is believed to have been born on Rapid Creek in Dakota Territory. His father is called Crazy Horse; his mother's name is unknown. He is called Curly.

1853: He earns his own horse by killing a buffalo.

1854: Curly is present at the "Grattan fight," in which Chief Conquering Bear and 30 soldiers are slain.

1855: As a teen, he witnesses the Battle of Blue Water as soldiers attack Little Thunder's camp.

1856: After a three-day fast, Curly has a vision that if he refrains from taking scalps or material possessions from those he kills in battle, he will remain unharmed. The vision also informs him that he will only encounter trouble if one of his people holds his arms.

1857: He receives the name His Horse Looking after a horse-stealing raid against the Omaha Indians.

1859: During a battle with Arapahos, he scalps one of his two victims and is wounded in the leg by an arrow. During his convalescence, his father gives him the name Crazy Horse (the father takes the name Worm). Chips, a medicine man, makes him a good-luck charm and urges him not to act against his vision. Crazy Horse will never take another scalp, and he will go through all of his remaining battles unharmed.

1865: Crazy Horse begins service under Red Cloud during the war against whites.

1866: The Fetterman Massacre takes place near Fort Phil Kearny in present Wyoming. Crazy Horse decoys 81 soldiers into a death trap.

1867: Crazy Horse participates in the Wagon Box Fight, in which 1,000 Sioux attack infantrymen guarding woodcutters near Fort Phil Kearny, Wyoming.

1868: He woos Black Buffalo Woman from her husband, No Water. When No Water learns what has happened, he shoots Crazy Horse in the face. Crazy Horse recovers and weds Black Shawl.

1875: He mourns for three days following the death of his daughter from cholera.

1876: Crazy Horse fights in the Battle of Powder River, the opening conflict of the war for the Black Hills. In the Battle on the Rosebud, he attacks General George Crook and his 1,000 troopers with columns of mounted Sioux and Cheyennes. He serves as one of the field marshals in the Battle of the Little Bighorn.

1877: Crazy Horse surrenders in the White River valley in Nebraska. On September 5, he is murdered while being led to a cramped cell at Camp Robinson, Nebraska.

THE BATTLE OF LAME DEER (OR MUDDY CREEK)
MAY 7, 1877

Colonel Nelson Miles led four companies of cavalry and six companies of infantry at Little Muddy Creek, a tributary of the Rosebud in Montana. Chief Lame Deer's Miniconjou camp was attacked at dawn. Hump, a Miniconjou who had previously surrendered and now accompanied Miles, located Lame Deer and Iron Tail, and persuaded them to surrender. Lame Deer tossed down his gun, shouted "friend" to Miles, and shook his hand. A confused scout approached and shot Lame Deer. The old chief snatched a gun and in turn killed a soldier standing near Miles. Lame Deer then began to run up a slope but was cut down by a volley. Iron Tail was also killed. The official report listed 30 Indians and four enlisted men killed; 20 Indians and one officer wounded; and 40 Indians captured.

ennes are sent by the U.S. government to a reservation in Indian Territory.

31. Colonel Nelson Miles reports that 2,300 Sioux have surrendered at the Red Cloud and Spotted Tail Agencies in northwestern Nebraska in the last two months.

Also in May 1877:

General Oliver O. Howard orders the Nez Percés to vacate Oregon's Wallowa Valley. To show that he means business, Howard jails the prophet Toohoolhoolzote and refuses to free him until Chief Joseph reluctantly capitulates.

John Muir assists in a geodetic survey in the Great Basin.

The Territorial Teachers' Institute is established in Prescott, Arizona.

Various acts of vandalism are reported at Yellowstone National Park.

National Headlines/May 1877:

1. HAYES WITHDRAWS LAST FEDERAL TROOPS FROM SOUTH

JUNE

13. Talks between the U.S. government and the Nez Percés break down when a band of younger war-

riors, to protest their treatment, kill 11 white settlers. Chief Joseph, 36, decides that his best hope now is to gather his 250 fighting men, 450 women and children, and 2,000 horses and attempt a dramatic migration to Canada.

14. Friends and brothers of Clint Barkley run into rival ranchers on the streets of Lampasas, Texas, sparking a major shootout. Frank Mitchell is killed.

15. General Oliver O. Howard reports that four civilians were killed by Nez Percés at John Day's Creek, Idaho.

17. General Oliver O. Howard attacks Chief Joseph's Nez Percé warriors at White Bird Canyon, Idaho. The Nez Percés, outnumbered 2 to 1, repel the attack, killing 34 soldiers in the process.

18. John George Adair partners with Charles Goodnight in a cattle enterprise in the Palo Duro Canyon of the Texas panhandle. During the next six years, they will show a profit of $512,000.

22. John Sallee, Jr., dies in Missouri. One of his best

Chief Joseph (Heinmot Tooyalaket, c. 1840–1904). "I will fight no more forever." (Denver Public Library, Western History Department)

friends, Jesse James, will disguise himself in order to serve as a pallbearer.

23. Jesse Evans, a member of the Murphy-Dolan faction in the Lincoln County War, is acquitted in the murder of Quirino Fletcher at Mesilla, New Mexico.
28. General Oliver O. Howard reports another fight with Nez Percés on the White Bird River in Idaho.

Also in June 1877:

"Measles and fever" are reported among the Cheyenne, Arapaho, Kiowa, and Kiowa Apache tribes in Texas.

William Wright, the true name of the Virginia City, Nevada, *Territorial Enterprise* editor Dan de Quille, publishes *History of the Big Bonanza,* with a foreword written by his former employee, Mark Twain.

National headlines / June 1877:
14. FIRST FLAG DAY OBSERVED
21. TEN MOLLY MAGUIRES SWING FOR MURDER

JULY

1. In Arizona, San Carlos Indian agent John Clum resigns after many conflicts with the military bureaucracy.
1–3. Captain S. G. Whipple reports one officer and 10 enlisted men killed in a fight with Nez Percés at the Cottonwood Ranch on the Clearwater River in Idaho. Two civilians are also listed as killed.
4. General Oliver O. Howard reports a skirmish with Nez Percés at Norton's Ranch, Idaho.
■ Having completed the building of his combination store and residence, A. A. McSween departs Lincoln, New Mexico, for St. Louis on a buying trip.
4–5. Captain David Perry reports that two enlisted men of the 1st Cavalry were wounded fighting Nez Percés at the Cottonwood Ranch on the Clearwater in Idaho.
5. An anti-Chinese convention convenes in San Francisco.
7. The *Dodge City Times* hopes that Wyatt Earp will be rehired by the police force: "He had a quiet way of taking the most desperate characters into custody. . . . It wasn't considered policy to draw a gun on Wyatt unless you got the drop and meant to burn powder with any preliminary talk."
11. The Battle of Clearwater takes place in Idaho.
13. General Oliver O. Howard and his troops again skirmish with Nez Percés, this time at Kamiah, Idaho.
17. Major E. C. Mason's 1st Cavalry and scouts again attack the fleeing Nez Percés, this time at Weippe (Oro Fino Creek), Idaho; one enlisted man and one Indian are reported killed.

THE BATTLE OF CLEARWATER
JULY 11, 1877

General Oliver O. Howard and members of the 1st Cavalry, the 21st Infantry, and the 4th Artillery again attacked fleeing Nez Percés, this time in a 24-hour battle on the Clearwater River in Idaho. Chief Joseph withdrew his people to the 150-mile Lolo Trail that will take them across Idaho into Montana. General Howard reported the following casualties: 13 enlisted men killed and 27 wounded; 23 Indians killed, 46 wounded, and 40 captured.

Following the battle, the Nez Percés' leaders debated what to do next. Joseph wanted to return to Wallowa in Oregon, but the majority sided with Looking Glass, who favored a pilgrimage to the north to join with Crow Indians. Some 150 warriors, 500 women and children, and 2,000 horses would attempt to make it through the wilderness ahead of 1,900 troops.

20. Members of the Seven Rivers gang raid an Indian camp in New Mexico and steal 13 horses.
21. Wyatt Earp is fined $1 for engaging in a public quarrel with "Miss Frankie Bell," who, according to the *Dodge City Times,* "heaped epithets upon the unoffending head of Mr. Earp."
23. John D. Lee is executed. Convicted of the 1857 "Mountain Meadows Massacre," Lee is escorted by federal troops to the scene of the atrocity, where he is photographed sitting on his coffin. He utters his last words, stands, and is shot by a firing squad. His body falls back into the wooden box and is carried away on a wagon to Panguitch for burial.
■ A crowd of 8,000 San Franciscans demonstrate in support of striking Eastern Railroad workers.
24. Angry workers listening to speeches in San Francisco go on a rampage, destroying several Chinese washhouses. Also set ablaze are the Pacific Mail Steamship Company's docks. Firemen are detained by the mob.
25. San Francisco's Chinatown is ransacked by a mob of 5,000 unemployed workers. A lumberyard near the Pacific Mail Steamship Company is put to the torch; rioters prevent firemen from saving it.
■ Fort Missoula volunteers under Captain Charles Rawn set up a barricade to prevent the fleeing Nez Percés from entering Montana. The Nez Percés cross into the territory through Lolo Pass, carefully

THE CHINESE IN THE WEST

From every corner of the globe, immigrants rushed to the American West in search of the dreams that had eluded them. The Chinese were no different, calling the country Gum San, "Land of the Golden Mountains." This land of plenty offered mixed blessings: the lure of riches, the reality of backbreaking labor and racism. It reflected the times, when the Far East met the Old West.

The first Chinese to appear in America probably arrived in 1840. Immigration increased slowly because of an edict from the Ching Dynasty that declared "conniving with rebels" to be punishable by death. These restrictions were not relaxed until the 1860s. But China's internal strife, the droughts of 1847–1850, and the high unemployment following its defeat by the British in the Opium War (1839–1842) made new horizons even more appealing to many Chinese.

Around 1849, a letter home from one Chum Ming on the subject of gold in California unleashed a flood of immigration. Rumors of high wages in America and a transpacific fare of $15 to $50 were reason enough to take a chance. All had heard of the two Chinese who discovered a 240-pound gold boulder worth $30,000 near the Yuba River; the luck seemed most favorable in the United States.

But first, the Chinese had to get here. The journey across the Pacific was hardly a pleasure cruise—500 passengers crowded below in a rickety vessel for 40 days at sea. In 1850, 45 of those ships sailed from Hong Kong. By the following year, some 25,000 Chinese had made the 7,000-mile voyage.

San Francisco became the primary point of debarkation. The Custom House recorded 2,716 Chinese immigrants in 1851 and 18,400 in 1852. A settlement on DuPont Street grew into Chinatown, a thriving cultural center geared to transplanted countrymen. Chinatown's first laundry was started by Wah Lee, who thought it silly that miners had to send their laundry to Hawaii or China. By 1876, 300 such enterprises crowded against each other.

Upon arrival, the "celestials" were greeted by representatives from home. The Chinese Six Companies represented different geographic regions of the province of Kwangtung, from where most of the immigrants came. The companies—Hop-Wo, Kong-Chow, Ning Yeung, Sam Up, Shen Hing, and Yan-Wo—provided lodging and acted as employ-ment coordinators. Competing with these district organizations were deep-rooted Chinese secret societies, or *tongs.*

The Oriental ideal was to strike it rich in America and then return home for a life of luxury and familial glory. Gold found in America was shipped overseas. This differed from the "end of the rainbow" approach taken by many Europeans. By 1855, the 20,000 Chinese in California who worked as miners were objects of torment. They became victims of organized efforts to run them from the mines. Miners in Columbia voiced their hatred of the "long-tailed, horned and cloven-hoofed inhabitants of the infernal regions." Tents were torched in some camps, and "get out of town" notices were posted. New restrictions were designed to make things tough on the Chinese working in the goldfields.

A new way of earning a living soon emerged. The Chinese "rented strength," a term they called *koo lee.* Many "coolies" worked as a type of indentured servant, paying off the Chinese merchants who had funded their voyage and protected them from *fan qui,* or "foreign devils." The system amounted to debt bondage. A seemingly inexhaustible supply of cheap labor for the greening of California toiled in vineyards, lumberyards, and factories.

The 10,000 Chinese who worked on the first transcontinental railroad in 1864 became labor legends. With the Civil War, the gold rush, and a number of other opportunities beckoning, Central Pacific Railroad partner Charles Crocker could not keep men engaged in laying rails for a paltry $40 a month. Consultants assured him that Chinese laborers would not be able to withstand such physical torture. Stunned engineers then witnessed a test crew of 50 Chinese eat rice and cuttlefish, sleep, wake at sunrise, and then lay track like a cooperative machine for 12 hours.

When the supply of labor became depleted, recruiting was done in China. "Crocker's Pets," as they were called, became a study in western heroics, boring through the granite barriers of the Sierra Nevada. During the terrible winter of 1866, with half the crew shoveling snow, they tunneled through Donner Mountain. At one point, they

(continued)

(continued)

covered 7,000 feet of mountain rise in less than a hundred miles. The job of completing the transcontinental railroad, estimated to take 14 years, ended at Utah's Promontory Point in 1869, nine years ahead of the deadline.

Despite their rail triumphs, the Chinese experienced increasing prejudice. Chinese immigration reached an all-time high of 123,201 in the decade ending in 1880. A new fear arose, similar to that during the gold rush wherein the influx of workers was seen as a "Yellow Peril" to the labor force of white America. The most vocal agitator was California's Dennis Kearney, who left history such quotations as "The Chinamen must go. If they don't, by the eternal we will take them by the throat, squeeze their breath out and throw them into the sea."

Twenty-five laundries were burned during the San Francisco riots of July 1877. Lynchings were common and seldom punished. Other cities followed suit. The Denver "Hop Alley" riot took place in 1880.

Politicians also plunged into this racially charged issue. A series of slanted regulations and taxes culminated in the infamous Chinese Exclusion Act of 1882, whereby immigration by laborers was nullified for 10 years. Later regulations denied citizenship and prevented Chinese males from bringing their wives to this country. The Exclusion Act itself was not repealed until 1943.

Eventually, the condition of Chinese-Americans improved. Although their initial treatment could not have been worse, their contributions to the winning of the West were monumental.

guiding their horses through narrow cliffs. The fort earns a new nickname for its misstep, "Fort Fizzle."

26. Montana governor B. F. Potts issues a proclamation calling for the raising of a militia against the fleeing Nez Percés.

■ The Committee of Safety, another vigilante group, forms in San Francisco in an effort to help the police put down anti-Chinese riots.

■ George Hoyt, a rowdy gunfighter in Dodge City, is shot by a group of peace officers that includes Wyatt Earp. Hoy was disturbing the peace and under a $1,500 bond for rustling in Texas.

Also in July 1877:

An outbreak of smallpox occurs among the Mescalero Apaches.

After negotiating Lolo Pass, the Nez Percés trade for supplies and food without incident at Stevensville, Montana.

Horace and Augusta Tabor relocate from Oro City to "Slabtown," the town that will soon become Leadville, Colorado, where they set up that city's first post office and its second store.

AUGUST

3. Black Bart leaves behind his first poem after robbing the stagecoach between Fort Ross and Duncan's Mills, California:

> I've labored long and hard for bread
> for honor and for riches
> But on my corns too long you've tred
> You fine haired Sons of Bitches.
> —Black Bart, the PO8

Charles E. Boles (c. 1830–1917?). Even the years are a mystery for "Black Bart," the highwayman "PO8." (Denver Public Library, Western History Department)

5. A portion of Arizona's White Mountain Reservation is returned to the public domain by executive order.

■ Northern Cheyennes being relocated from Fort Robinson in Nebraska arrive at Fort Reno in Indian Territory following a three-month march. Of the 972 who began the journey, 937 finish it.

■ Shots are fired into the home of A. A. McSween in Lincoln, New Mexico, allegedly by Frank Freeman and Charles Bowdre. John Chisum is in the home at the time, but no one is hurt.

7. Nine hundred and thirty-seven Northern Cheyennes, including Chief Little Wolf, arrive at the Darlington Agency in Indian Territory (present Oklahoma).

9. Chief Joseph's Nez Percés are attacked on the Big Hole River in Montana.

11. Rustlers run horses off the Mescalero Agency near Fort Stanton, New Mexico, and are chased by troops under Lieutenant Davenport.

12. A posse kills rustling suspect Nelson Armstrong near Lincoln, New Mexico.

17. Frank "Windy" Cahill calls Billy the Kid a "pimp" during an unfriendly card game near Camp Grant in Arizona Territory. The 17-year-old Kid calls Cahill a "son of a bitch." Cahill jumps on the Kid, and in the scuffle the Kid yanks Cahill's gun from its holster and shoots Cahill barrel to belly.

18. Frank "Windy" Cahill becomes the first man to die of a gunshot wound administered by Henry McCarty, aka Henry Antrim or Kid Antrim, soon to be known as Billy the Kid. Justice of the Peace Miles Wood conducts a coroner's inquest at which the jury announces that the murder "was criminal and unjustifiable, and that Henry Antrim, alias Kid, is guilty thereof."

■ The Nez Percés now follow Poker Joe as their supreme war chief. Ollikut leads a force of 28 Indians on a raid to drive away 200 of General Oliver O. Howard's pack mules near Camas Creek, Montana. While Howard's force is distracted, the Nez Percés move through Targhee Pass into Wyoming and Yellowstone National Park.

19. Camp Grant's justice of the peace, Miles Wood, arrests Henry Antrim while the Kid breakfasts at Wood's hotel. The Kid is incarcerated in a post guardhouse.

20. Ollikot and 27 Nez Percé sharpshooters keep General Oliver O. Howard's troops under Major G. B. Sanford at bay while the rest of the tribe cuts into Yellowstone National Park; one soldier is killed and seven are wounded. General William Tecumseh Sherman, sightseeing in the park, orders reinforcements.

21. The gunfighter George Hoy dies of gunshot wounds he received on July 26 in Dodge City, Kansas. Wyatt Earp was one of the officers who fired on Hoyt, and he is credited with killing his first man.

23. Although he is far beyond his legal jurisdiction, Texas Ranger John Armstrong arrests John Wesley Hardin on a train in Pensacola, Florida. Armstrong kills Jim Mann in the process and pistol-whips Hardin until he falls unconscious. Armstrong, who also arrests Hardin's three suite-mates, will haul them back to Texas, where Hardin will stand trial for the 1874 murder of Deputy Sheriff Charles Webb.

25. The first recorded duel between two women occurs in Denver. Madam Mattie Silks, upset over the advances that Kate Fulton made toward her beau, Cort Thomson, challenges Fulton to a fight to the death. They choose pistols, square off, and fire. Both shots miss their mark, but Thomson receives a flesh wound in the neck; in the confusion, no one can say which gun shot him. The ladies throw down their guns and charge at one another for a fistfight. Kate receives a broken nose.

■ Montana's Sun River Rangers are organized; their purpose is to protect settlers from cattle thieves, Indians, and prairie fires.

BATTLE AT BIG HOLE
AUGUST 9, 1877

Looking Glass had chosen a camp on the Big Hole (Wisdom) River in Montana for the fleeing Nez Percés including Chief Joseph and his family. They were attacked at dawn on August 9, by Colonel John Gibbon and a force of 198 men from the 2nd Cavalry and the 7th Infantry out of Fort Shaw, many of whom had been assigned burial duty following the Custer debacle. Warriors under White Bird counterattacked and defeated the troops again, killing two officers, 21 enlisted men, and six civilians, and wounding 38 soldiers, including Gibbon.

Nez Percés suffered a total of 89 dead, 50 of them women and children. Among the dead were the inseparable friends Rainbow and Five Wounds, who had vowed they would die in battle on the same day, as well as the wives of Chief Joseph and Ollikot. Joseph was shocked and later wrote: "The Nez Percés never make war on women and children . . . we would feel ashamed to do so."

26. In the wake of her duel yesterday with Mattie Silks, Kate Fulton leaves Denver by stagecoach.

29. The Mormon leader Brigham Young, 76, dies of peritonitis in Salt Lake City. His *New York Times* obituary reads in part: "Cruel, bloody, and vindictive though this man doubtless was, he must be credited with the possession of abilities of a superior order. He seems to have loved power for its own sake. . . . [His death] will be the final blow which shall shatter the monstrous fabric of Mormonism." The $2.5 million estate is divided among the survivors: 17 wives and 48 children. (Young's total number of brides is a matter of historical debate. A conservative estimate is 27, the Mormon Genealogical Society counts 53, and other guesses put the number around 70. He fathered 56 children, the first when he was 24 and the last at 69.)

- In New Mexico, the Lincoln County Bank is established by John Tunstall. As a gesture of goodwill, J. J. Dolan receives a loan of $1,000.

Also in August 1877:

The first silver in Arizona's Bisbee district is discovered by government scout John Dunn.

Shortly after he is jailed, Henry Antrim escapes the Camp Grant guardhouse, possibly with the aid of a soldier. Three shots are fired by a sentry, but the Kid rides off into the night. For his getaway, he selected Cashaw, one of the fastest mounts from nearby Silver City, Arizona.

James Addison Reavis, the "Baron of Arizona," arrives in Tucson with his forged "Peralta Grant," with which he intends to claim ownership of much of Arizona and New Mexico. The Peralta Grant encompasses a rectangular piece of land 75 miles by 235 miles that includes Phoenix, the Salt River Valley, and the Silver King mine—a total of 7,500 square miles, or 12 million acres that he wants to sell to the United States for $250 million.

The newly formed Sam Bass gang has held up the Deadwood stagecoach four times in July and August, making off with a grand total of $50 and a crate of peaches.

After some 17 years of warring with whites, Victorio and his Mimbreño Apaches agree to live peacefully on 600 square miles at the headwaters of the Gila River. The grounds include a choice hunting area known as Ojo Caliente in present Arizona.

The *Telegraph and Texas Register,* the newspaper begun by inventor Gail Borden, ceases publication after 37 years. Its most famous headline appeared in 1836: "REMEMBER THE ALAMO."

SEPTEMBER

1. Fearing an uprising while Crazy Horse is in captivity at Fort Robinson in Nebraska, General Philip Sheridan wires General George Crook: "I think your presence more necessary at Red Cloud Agency than at Camp Brown and wish you to get off at Sidney and go there."

3. In Arizona Territory, Ed Schieffelin records his silver claim on the future site of Tombstone.

4. After Lieutenant William Clark offers $100 to anyone at Camp Rogers, Nebraska, who will murder Crazy Horse, 400 Indians and eight cavalry companies leave for the chief's lodge, six miles away. At the Spotted Tail Agency to obtain medical treatment for his wife, Crazy Horse is persuaded to return home.

5. Crazy Horse is mortally wounded at Fort Robinson, Nebraska.

- The University of Colorado opens in Boulder.

- California voters approve a new state constitutional convention.

THE MURDER OF CRAZY HORSE
SEPTEMBER 5, 1877

Living at the Red Cloud Agency, Crazy Horse, 36, had been suspected of plotting an "uprising" since his surrender in May. Having refused General George Crook's request to meet with President Rutherford B. Hayes in Washington, D.C., the war leader had made few friends among the whites.

When Crazy Horse left Red Cloud to take his sick wife to the Spotted Tail Agency for medical care, Crook, fearing a rebellion, ordered him arrested. On September 5, Crazy Horse was escorted by troops to a cramped cell at Fort Robinson, Nebraska. When he saw the tiny quarters, he attempted to escape. Indian police tried to restrain him, but in the scuffle a soldier named William Gentles stabbed Crazy Horse through the abdomen with a bayonet. Crazy Horse lay in agony in the adjutant's office while his parents were kept outside and prevented from seeing their son. At 11:40 P.M., the Strange Man of the Oglalas expired. His parents, who were not allowed to be with their son when he died, took the body and supposedly buried it somewhere near Wounded Knee in present South Dakota.

6. A dispatch is sent from Fort Robinson, Nebraska:

> Crazy Horse died at midnight. His people took his body, and all is quiet this morning.

8. Captain T. C. Tupper reports that the 6th Cavalry killed 12 Indians and captured 13 on the San Francisco River in New Mexico.

12. Dennis Kearney organizes the Workingmen's Party of California.

13. In Montana, the Battle of Canyon Creek takes place, Colonel Samuel D. Sturgis, with seven companies and two detachments of cavalry—some 350 men from Fort Keogh—attack Nez Percés at Canyon Creek. Warriors fight the troops as women and children escape through the canyon. The troops withdraw after they count three soldiers killed and 11 wounded. The Nez Percés count 21 dead.

14. The poet Whitney Montgomery (*Corn Silk and Cotton Blossoms,* 1928) is born in Eureka, Texas.

15. John Tunstall, returning from a trip to St. Louis, is stricken with smallpox in Las Vegas, New Mexico.

18. Sam Bass and his gang make history by pulling off the biggest train robbery thus far, relieving a Union Pacific train at Big Springs, Nebraska, of $60,000 in gold coins. The gang members fill their saddlebags with $10,000 each and split up. They will be tracked by Charles Bassett and Bat Masterson.

■ In Las Vegas, New Mexico, Jesse Evans and his boys steal horses belonging to John Tunstall, A. A. McSween, and Dick Brewer from the Brewer ranch.

20. Dick Brewer, Charles Bowdre, and Doc Scurlock arrive in Las Cruces, New Mexico, and have warrants issued for Jesse Evans and his gang. The sheriff tells Brewer, Bowdre, and Scurlock that they will not get help from him.

22. Charles Bowdre and Doc Scurlock find the horses stolen on September 18 but are unable to retake them because of the number of men guarding them.

23. The Nez Percés raid an army depot at Cow Island Landing, Montana, in search of food. Sergeant William Molchart reports one enlisted man and two civilians killed.

24. Dick Brewer, Charles Bowdre, and Doc Scurlock return to Lincoln.

25. Major Guido Ilges and civilian volunteers fight Nez Percés at Cow Creek Canyon in Montana. One settler is killed and two Nez Percés are wounded.

■ Two members of the Sam Bass gang, Bill Heffridge and Joel Collins, are killed by soldiers in Gove County, Kansas.

26. J. J. Dolan deeds land in New Mexico to A. A. McSween.

THE BATTLE OF BEAR PAW MOUNTAINS
SEPTEMBER 30, 1877

Colonel Nelson Miles and a force of 600 men from Fort Keogh, including 30 Sioux and Cheyenne scouts and units of the 5th Infantry and the 2nd and 7th Cavalry, engaged Chief Joseph's Nez Percés. Joseph's camp was along the Snake Creek in the Bear Paw Mountains of Montana, barely 40 miles south of the Canadian border and freedom. Nez Percé marksmen kept the soldiers at bay from rifle pits, but the army's howitzers and Gatling guns proved to be too much. In the five-day battle, 24 soldiers died and 50 were wounded in the first charge; 18 Nez Percés were killed (including Ollikot and Toohoolhoolzote) and 40 were listed as wounded. Wrote Chief Joseph: "We fought at close range not more than twenty steps apart, and drove the soldiers back upon their main line, leaving their dead in our hands. We secured their arms and ammunition." The Nez Percés tried to move north but, finding themselves surrounded, dug trenches.

27. The Jesse Evans gang steals more horses in Dona Ana County, New Mexico.

28. The Jesse Evans gang drives away a posse from Santa Barbara.

30. The Battle of Bear Paw Mountains begins in Montana.

Also in September 1877:

Henry (Billy the Kid) Antrim rides 40 miles south of Silver City, Arizona, to the Knight ranch, where he stays two or three weeks. He then asks that Cashaw, the horse he stole in Silver City, be returned to its rightful owner. Sarah Knight gives the Kid a fresh horse.

OCTOBER

1. In Montana, under a white flag, Colonel Nelson Miles sends word to Chief Joseph, asking him to surrender and save his people. Snow has begun to fall; Joseph replies that he will consider the proposal. Meanwhile he hopes that a blizzard might cover a run for the Canadian border. Two Sioux scouts from Miles's division return under a white

flag and convince Joseph of the general's sincerity. Joseph accompanies the scouts and is taken prisoner.

2. Colonel Nelson Miles attacks the Nez Percés again. Chief Joseph refuses to surrender while he is being held prisoner. Nez Percés take an officer prisoner and threaten to kill him if Joseph is not released. Miles frees Joseph. General Oliver O. Howard arrives with reinforcements.

■ Colorado voters reject women's suffrage.

3. Colonel Nelson Miles delivers another ultimatum to the Nez Percés: "If you will come out and give up your arms, I will spare your lives and send you to your reservation."

4. The Nez Percés negotiate their surrender at Bear Paw Mountains.

5. Chief Joseph surrenders the Nez Percés to Colonel Nelson Miles.

7. The small band of Nez Percés with White Bird meets Sitting Bull's tribe in Canada and is taken in.

8. A group of rustlers steals horses belonging to a Colonel Ledbetter in New Mexico's Burro Mountains.

9. President Rutherford B. Hayes gives the Southern Pacific Railroad permission to expand into New Mexico and Arizona.

■ In New Mexico, a Mr. Carpenter meets a party of men who he believes were the rustlers of Colonel Ledbetter's horses; Carpenter could swear that Henry Antrim is among the men.

11. On Wild Bill Longley's hanging day, Bill lights a big black cigar for his last walk. To a crowd of 4,000, he says, "I see a good many enemies around, and mighty few friends." Following a grand oration, he kisses the priest and the sheriff, then bids the crowd farewell. The rope slips the first time the trap door opens—Longley's knees drag the ground. Quickly, he is rehanged, with more-lasting results.

■ Clay Calhoun, the "Outlaw Exterminator," kills the mass-murderer John Allman, who is hiding among Arizona cliff dwellings, and turns in the body at Holbrook. The coroner reports that Allman has four aligned bullet holes in the mouth, chest, stomach, and groin.

13. Reports that a petrified man has been discovered in southern Colorado are received. Rail agent William A. Conant tells the *Colorado Springs Gazette:* "I discovered the curious stones or toes protruding from the ground. Carefully removing the dirt from them, I soon discovered the shape of a human foot. Calling to my son to bring the shovel from the wagon, I proceeded to remove the soil until the

THE NEZ PERCÉS SURRENDER
OCTOBER 4–5, 1877

Negotiations for the surrender of Chief Joseph, 37, and his band of Nez Percés began shortly after another in the series of conflicts that was the Battle of Bear Paw Mountains. The 1,700-mile, 115-day attempt to escape to Canada had come within 40 miles of the border.

Of its 418 prisoners, the army counted but 87 men, of whom half had been wounded in the five-day standoff. Among the dead were Poker Joe, Ollikut, Toohoolhoolzote, and Looking Glass. The army counted 127 soldiers and 50 civilians slain. In the night, while terms of surrender were being discussed, White Bird, Joseph's nephew Little Wolf, and a handful of braves escaped to freedom in Canada.

On October 5, Chief Joseph surrendered his tribe to Colonel Nelson Miles. Joseph's speech, perhaps enhanced by the interpreter, Lieutenant Charles Erskine Scott Wood, was nevertheless recorded for posterity as the most eloquent surrender of a Native American:

"Tell General Howard I know his heart. What he told me before I have in my heart. I am tired of fighting. Our chiefs are killed. Looking Glass is dead. Toohoolhoolzote is dead. The old men are all dead. It is the young men who say yes or no. He who led on the young men (Ollikot) is dead. It is cold and we have no blankets. The little children are freezing to death. My people, some of them, have run away to the hills, and have no blankets, no food; no one knows where they are—perhaps freezing to death. I want to have time to look for my children and see how many of them I can find. Maybe I shall find them among the dead. Hear me, my chiefs! I am tired; my heart is sick and sad. From where the sun now stands I will fight no more forever."

Joseph and the remaining Nez Percés were made prisoners of war and, in direct violation of the surrender terms, hustled to Fort Leavenworth, Kansas.

limbs of a human being were exposed, and finally the full figure."

14. John Tunstall, partially recovered from smallpox, arrives in Lincoln, New Mexico.

15. The author Edward Lytton Wheeler, who has never been west of Pennsylvania, publishes the dime novel *Deadwood Dick, the Prince of the Road, or The Black Rider of the Black Hills* for the house of Beadle and Adams.

16. In New Mexico, rustlers led by a McCabe steal 400 head of cattle from John Tunstall and drive them toward the Texas line.

17. Jesse Evans and his gang are arrested at Beckwith's Seven Rivers Ranch by a posse led by Dick Brewer and Sheriff Brady; they are hauled to the Lincoln County Jail.

20. No sooner are Jesse Evans and his bunch in Lincoln's new $3,000 jail than Dick Brewer organizes another posse, this one to go after the rustlers of Tunstall's cattle.

21. Dick Brewer's fresh posse rides out of Lincoln.

22. George Wilson escapes from the Dodge City jail. Reports the *Dodge City Times*: "When Sheriff Bassett heard that his bird had flown he looked as sorrow-stricken as if he had lost his dearest friend, and immediately sought to find his prodigal and return him to his keeper, but George was still on the wing at last accounts."

23. John Tunstall returns to his New Mexico ranch, where he learns about the theft of his cattle.

25. Dick Brewer's posse catches up with John Tunstall's stolen cattle 10 miles from the Texas line.

Also in October 1877:

Henry "Billy the Kid" McCarty shows up in Pecos County, New Mexico, at the Jones ranch in the Seven Rivers area.

In south Texas, the divorcée Carry Moore, 30, is married again, this time to the part-time preacher David Nation. In 1892, she herself will begin preaching and campaigning against demon rum, hatchet in hand.

As they did last year, troops from Fort Reno accompany Cheyenne and Arapaho hunters from the Darlington Agency, in present Oklahoma, on their fall buffalo hunt. The total kill last year was 7,000; this year it is 219.

NOVEMBER

5. A three-card-monte shark known as Canada Bill is reported dead in Cheyenne, Wyoming.

6. Bat Masterson is elected sheriff of Ford County, Kansas, succeeding Charles E. Bassett.

12. San Francisco's Fidelity Bank suspends operations.

13. The convicted murderer Katarino Romero escapes from the Lincoln jail in New Mexico.

16. An interview with Sitting Bull on the subject of the Little Bighorn battle appears in the *New York Herald*:

> *HERALD*: How did they act? How did they behave themselves?
> *SITTING BULL*: Your people were killed. I tell no lies about deadmen. These men who came with the Long Hair were as good men as ever fought. When they rode up their horses were tired and they were tired. When they got off from their horses they could not stand firmly on their feet. They swayed to and fro—so my young men have told me—like the limbs of cypresses in a great wind. . . . Our young men rained lead across the river and drove the white braves back.
> *HERALD*: Did the whole command keep on fighting until the last?
> *SITTING BULL*: Every man, so far as my people could see. There were no cowards on either side.

17. The jailors in Lincoln learn that they forgot to lock the cell doors the night before. Jesse Evans and his bunch have escaped.

18. Lincoln's Sheriff Brady and John Tunstall argue; Brady accuses Tunstall of encouraging Jesse Evans to escape and threatens to shoot him. A. A. McSween intervenes.

19. The Jesse Evans gang visits the Tunstall ranch at Feliz but steals no cattle.

DECEMBER

5. The installation of the first telephone in San Diego takes place.

15. The *Dodge City Times* reports that "Sheriff Bassett has been appointed by Mayor Kelley to assist Marshal [Edward] Masterson in preserving order and decorum in the city."

18. The A. A. McSweens and John Chisum depart Lincoln for St. Louis.

■ The 6th Cavalry reports 15 Indians slain in a fight in Mexico's Las Animas Mountains.

21. J. J. Dolan has an affidavit issued charging McSween with embezzling.

22. Following their escape from a Lincoln, New Mexico, jail, the Jesse Evans gang stops in Mesilla en route to El Paso.

24. Henry Underwood is arrested for complicity in the Big Springs, Texas, train robbery of September 18, 1877, even though it occurred before he joined the Sam Bass gang. He is jailed in Kearney, Nebraska, from where he will escape before being recaptured and brought to trial.

- A. A. McSween and John Chisum are jailed in Las Vegas, New Mexico, on embezzlement charges.
25. Sam Bass robs the Fort Worth–Cleburne stagecoach of $11.25.
26. The warrants for A. A. McSween and John Chisum have not arrived within the required 48 hours. After spending Christmas in jail, the two are released and then rearrested. Chisum is jailed in Las Vegas, while McSween will be taken to Mesilla to appear before Judge Bristol.

Also in December 1877:

At Fort Griffin, Texas, the gambler Edward Bailey makes the fatal mistake of questioning Doc Holliday's honesty. The good dentist jumps over the table and disembowels Bailey with a bowie knife. Fort Griffin does not have a jail, so the sheriff locks Doc in a hotel room. When Doc's live-in prostitute, Kate Elder, hears that her hero will be lynched before dawn, she acts quickly. As the angry mob moves down the street toward the hotel, she sets the rear entrance on fire. Upstairs, she gets the drop on Doc's guard. While the men put out the fire, Doc Holliday and Katie Elder make hoofprints for Dodge City, Kansas.

Wells Fargo, operating 459 offices in 1877, announces an annual income of $2,150,000 from transportation and $918,000 from express services.

Also in 1877:

Gold and silver mines in Arizona produce ore worth $5.7 million.

The 375,000 head of cattle in Arizona are worth $4.5 million.

Francis Fuller writes *Eleven Years in the Rocky Mountains and Life on the Frontier* and *The New Penelope and Other Stories and Poems.*

The Stock Raisers' Association is organized in Texas.

Santa Fe, New Mexico, is connected by telegraph to San Diego and El Paso.

Madam Mattie Silks opens her house of prostitution in Denver.

John Taylor is chosen to head the Mormon Church.

Texas Jack Omohundro and Giuseppina Morlacchi, now residents of Lowell, Massachusetts, tour with their own stock company in plays such as *Texas Jack in the Black Hills!*

From Fort Dodge, Kansas, Colonel Richard I. Dodge, who said in 1872, "Boys, if I were a buffalo hunter, I would hunt where the buffalo are," now writes that "the buffalo is virtually exterminated." With the coming of the railroad, the food supply of the plains Indians has been transformed into great piles of bleached bones.

1878

"Fly—scatter through the country—go to the Great West. The West is the true destination!"

—Horace Greeley

JANUARY

3. A crowd of 500 unemployed gathers at San Francisco's City Hall, demanding jobs from the mayor.

4. In New Mexico, A. A. McSween is escorted by two deputies from the Las Vegas jail; he will be taken to Mesilla, where he will face Judge Bristol.

5. Indians reportedly kill six settlers in a raid 63 miles northwest of Presidio del Norte, Texas.

6. Robert Frank James, the only child of the outlaw Frank James, is born in Missouri.

7. The 6th Cavalry reports three Indians killed in action near Tonto Creek, Arizona.

10. In Washington, D.C., California senator A. A. Sargent introduces legislation to amend the Constitution: "The right of citizens of the U.S. to vote shall not be denied or abridged by the U.S. or by any state on account of sex."

14. "Slabtown," a small mining establishment near Colorado's Oro City, changes its name to Leadville. New ore discoveries will bring 6,000 settlers to the area this year.

16. Two civilians are reported killed in an Indian raid in Limpia Canyon, Texas.

■ Two civilians are reported killed in an Indian raid in Mason County, Texas.

■ The silver dollar becomes legal tender.

18. John Tunstall writes a letter alleging fraud to the *Mesilla Independent.* Tunstall had paid territorial taxes of $1,543.03 to Sheriff William Brady, received a cancelled check endorsed by "Jno. H. Riley," and then was accused of failing to pay taxes.

Artist's conception of an Indian attack on a pioneer home. (Library of Congress)

In the letter, Tunstall implicates the firm of J. J. Dolan and Company.

21. The first convention of the Workingmen's Party is held in San Francisco.

23. Two civilians are reported killed in an Indian raid near Fort Duncan, Texas.

24. In Texas, the Sam Bass gang robs a Houston and Texas Central train at the Allen station.

- The first long-distance telephone conversation to take place in Wyoming is between participants in Laramie and Cheyenne.

26. The *Salt River Herald* becomes the first newspaper to be published in Phoenix, Arizona.

28. A posse led by Sheriff Bat Masterson captures the outlaw Dave Rudabaugh 24 hours after his gang robbed a pay train near Kinsley, Kansas.

- Escorted by deputies, A. A. McSween arrives in Mesilla.

Also in January 1878:

The Kiowa chief Satanta commits suicide at the Texas State Penitentiary. Jailed without evidence for raids in 1871, he was paroled in 1873. He was returned to prison in 1874 for jumping parole; he fled to the hills when he believed he would be blamed for a fight at the Anadarko Agency. His accomplice, Big Tree, who was allowed to remain out on parole, will live until 1927.

Live Boys, or Charley and Nasho in Texas, the first authentic narrative of a cattle drive from Texas to Kansas, is published by Texas attorney Thomas Pilgrim under the pen name Arthur Morecamp.

In Nebraska, Camp Robinson becomes Fort Robinson.

FEBRUARY

2. In Mesilla, New Mexico, Judge Bristol begins hearing embezzlement charges against A. A. McSween.

4. Judge Bristol transfers A. A. McSween's hearing to Lincoln after McSween requests a grand jury. McSween's bail is set at $8,000.

- An earthquake occurs at Beartooth Mountain, Montana.

5. John Tunstall, who accused the Dolan cattle company of tax fraud, is threatened at Shedd's ranch by a group including J. J. Dolan and Jesse Evans.

9. Pioneer Colorado rancher John Wesley Iliff dies at 46; he had 35,000 head of cattle on the open range.

10. John Tunstall and A. A. McSween reach Lincoln, New Mexico. McSween is still in the custody of Sheriff Barrier, who will not relinquish custody to Sheriff Brady.

11. John Tunstall arrives in Lincoln with William Bonney, Fred Waite, and Robert Widenmann. Deputies George Peppin and James Longwell, working under orders from Sheriff Brady, have attached Tunstall's store. Tunstall remains in Lincoln to work on lifting the attachment, and to help A. A. McSween raise bail.

13. Billy the Kid, who now calls himself William Bonney, along with Robert Widenmann and Fred Waite, departs the Tunstall ranch for Lincoln, to tell Tunstall that a posse led by Billy Mathews and including Jesse Evans plans to attach his cattle. Upon hearing the news, Tunstall rides to John Chisum's ranch to seek advice. Chisum is not there; he is still in jail in Las Vegas.

16. William Bonney, Robert Widenmann, and Fred Waite return to John Tunstall's ranch.

THE LINCOLN COUNTY WAR
FEBRUARY 18, 1878

The complicated range war of New Mexico's Lincoln County took a violent turn with the murder of John Tunstall, 24, an Englishman and ally of A. A. McSween.

Tunstall was driving a small herd of livestock with Robert Widenmann, Fred Waite, Dick Brewer, John Middleton, and William Bonney when Widenmann and Brewer left to hunt some wild turkeys. The remaining men were met about 10 miles south of Lincoln by an 18-man posse that was sympathetic to the cause of cattleman J. J. Dolan. Among them were Jesse Evans, William Morton, and Tom Hill.

Waite and Bonney were driven away from Tunstall, who rode toward a smaller group of adversaries, presumably to surrender his weapon. Morton fired his rifle into the chest of Tunstall, who fell from his horse. Jesse Evans arrived, took Tunstall's pistol from its holster, and fired a bullet into the back of Tunstall's head. Next, he killed Tunstall's mount. When the rest of the posse arrived, Evans presented Tunstall's fired revolver and said that Tunstall was killed while resisting arrest.

That night, the men who rode with Tunstall arrived in Lincoln to tell what they had seen. The Lincoln County War was off to a bloody start.

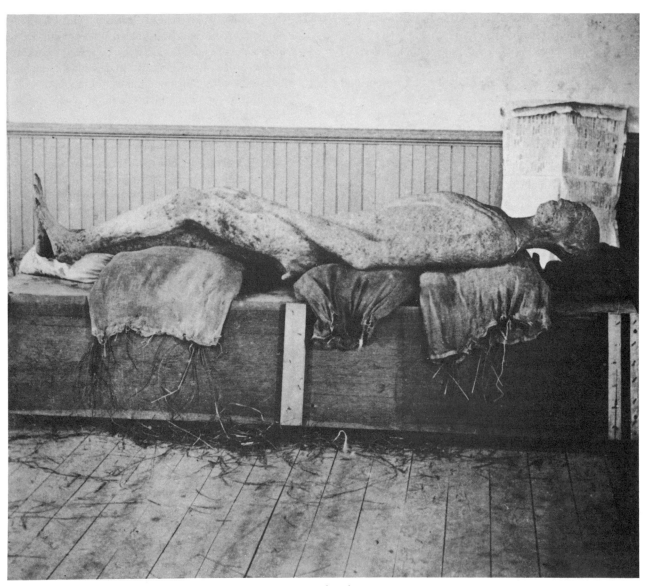

The Solid Muldoon. Colorado's biggest rock star is a cement humbug. (Denver Public Library, Western History Department)

17. John Tunstall arrives at his Rio Feliz ranch at about 10:00 P.M. He learns that Billy Mathews's posse is eight miles away and plans to drive off his cattle.

■ Roving bands of Cheyennes attack cattle camps near Fort Dodge, Kansas, killing many civilians. Fort Supply sends troops.

18. John Tunstall is murdered; the Lincoln County War begins.

19. John Tunstall's body is brought to Lincoln. William Bonney and Dick Brewer swear affidavits in the presence of the justice of the peace. A coroner's jury determines that Tunstall was killed by a party that included J. J. Dolan, Jesse Evans, Frank Baker, George Hindman, Tom Hill, and William Morton.

20. At the request of Constable Martinez, William Bonney and Fred Waite attempt to serve warrants for the murder of John Tunstall on J. J. Dolan and his men at the Dolan store, now protected by soldiers from Fort Stanton. Sheriff William Brady arrests Bonney and Waite for disturbing the peace.

22. William Bonney and Fred Waite are released from jail following Tunstall's funeral.

24. Sam Bass and new members of his gang—Jackson, Seaborn Barnes, and a few others—hit the Houston and Texas Central Express train near Allen and ride away with $3,000.

25. Isaac Ellis is named administrator of John Tunstall's estate. A. A. McSween, still in the custody of Deputy A. P. Barrier, makes out his will.

27. A. A. McSween leaves Lincoln with Deputy Sheriff Barrier; McSween is planning on going to Kansas until things cool off a bit.

28. Congress passes the Bland-Allison Act, which requires the U.S. government to coin between $2 million and $4 million of silver each month. The act is seen as a compromise with Westerners.

Also in February 1878:

The "Solid Muldoon" is exposed in Colorado.

Virginia City, Nevada, now has 50 dry goods stores, 20 laundries, four banks, 18 barbershops, eight dairies, two pawnshops, 20 insurance agents, 35 doctors, six churches, and 150 saloons and houses of prostitution. The city averages 15 funerals a month.

National Headlines / February 1878:

19. EDISON PATENTS PHONOGRAPH

THE SOLID MULDOON
FEBRUARY 1878

The "Solid Muldoon," Colorado's most famous "rock star," was a hoax, according to the *New York Tribune*. Endorsed by no less than Phineas Taylor Barnum ("We have found the missing link which Darwin claims connects mankind with the beast creation. It is certainly the petrified body of a man with a tail"), it was discounted by Darwin himself. Wrote his daughter and assistant, Francis Darwin, upon seeing a stereoscopic photograph: "It is impossible to form a judgment without seeing the specimen. It seems to be a strong probability that the whole thing is an imposture." Returning from the exhumation site, a Pueblo editor wrote: "We were unable to discover that he had ever lived in the neighborhood. . . . In fact, the whole thing is too thin and smells of P. T. Barnum."

Following the Solid Muldoon's tour and a five-week exhibition in New York City, E. J. Cox, a small cog in the "Giant Company," as the promotion firm was called, blew the whistle. Cox, who was not getting what he believed to be his fair share of the $20,000 take, sang like a bird for the *Tribune*.

MARCH

4. The Central City Opera House opens in Colorado.

6. A posse of "Regulators," self-proclaimed justice seekers in the Lincoln County War and mostly consisting of John Tunstall's former employees, including Billy the Kid (William Bonney), is led by Dick Brewer, who arrests William Morton and Frank Baker after a six-mile running fight. The Kid supposedly tells Brewer: "Dick, we've got two of them and they are the worst of the lot. Let's avenge John Tunstall by killing them right now." Brewer rejects the Kid's suggestion and begins taking his prisoners to Lincoln.

8. The Regulators, with the prisoners William Morton and Frank Baker, bunk at John Chisum's South Spring River ranch, where they learn that J. J. Dolan has organized a large posse to search for them. Meanwhile, in Lincoln, Governor Axtell visits J. J. Dolan.

9. In Blackwater Canyon, near John Chisum's South Spring River ranch, Frank Baker, William Morton, and William McCloskey are gunned down in cold blood by a member of the Regulators, possibly Billy the Kid. The details of the incident are unclear: McCloskey perhaps was shot accidentally as the other two were killed trying to escape. It is doubtful that the Kid committed all three murders. The location will henceforth be known as Dead Man's Draw.

■ Governor Axtell voids the Lincoln County commissioner's appointment of John B. Wilson as justice of the peace.

10. J. J. Dolan breaks his leg in Lincoln. According to Dr. Ealy, "one of the worst men in the country broke his leg while trying to shoot an unarmed man."

11. A. A. McSween, accompanied by George Washington, George Robinson, and Dick Brewer, departs Lincoln for John Chisum's ranch on the Pecos River.

13. In the Lincoln County War, Tom Hill is killed and Jesse Evans is wounded during a raid on the camp of John Wagner. Evans goes to Fort Stanton, where he turns himself in and checks into the hospital. A. A. McSween returns to Lincoln.

15. A soldier convicted of murder is hanged in Prescott, Arizona.

18. The Sam Bass gang robs a Houston and Texas Central train in Hutchins, Texas. Express messenger Heck Thomas hides $20,000 until a bullet in the face convinces him to surrender.

26. Colonel N. A. M. Dudley assumes command from Colonel Purington at Fort Stanton, New Mexico.

29. Much shooting is reported in the streets of Lincoln, New Mexico.

31. The A. A. McSweens and John Chisum depart the Chisum ranch and stay the night at a ranch house some 20 miles away.

■ A group of Regulators, including Billy the Kid, rides into Lincoln and spends the night at John Tunstall's store.

APRIL

1. In Lincoln, New Mexico, Sheriff Brady is murdered in a gunfight with Regulators.

4. At Blazer's Mill in Lincoln County, the Regulators engage in a shoot-out with J. J. Dolan's men. Dick Brewer's head is blown off by Jesse Andrews, aka "Buckshot" Bill Roberts. Roberts is then killed by Charles Bowdre. Billy the Kid is grazed in the arm by a bullet.

■ The Sam Bass gang robs a Texas and Pacific train at Eagle Ford, Texas.

5. Captain Charles Porter reports that cavalrymen and infantrymen killed seven Apaches and captured seven in Arizona's Mogollon Mountains.

7. After the Utah Northern Railroad is allowed to default on bonds and interest totaling $1,453,000, the company is officially dissolved at the Salt Lake City courthouse. The Union Pacific Railroad will purchase the property for $100,000.

THE KID GETS BRADY
APRIL 1, 1878

William Bonney (Billy the Kid) and five Regulators ambushed Sheriff Bill Brady, Deputy George Hindman, and three others in Lincoln, New Mexico, just after 9:00 A.M., because they believed the sheriff was on his way to assassinate A. A. McSween. Bonney's group intercepted Brady's on the streets of Lincoln, and shots rang out. Bonney was hit on the inside of his left thigh when he tried to retrieve a rifle that had been confiscated during a previous arrest, a weapon that Brady had carried proudly down the street just minutes before. Hindman and Brady were killed in the gunfight; observers counted eight bullet holes in Brady's corpse. A. A. McSween, who arrived after the shooting, was arrested and taken to Fort Stanton. As soon as he was able, Billy the Kid left town for San Patricio.

---

8. In New Mexico, A. A. McSween, George Washington, Robert Widenmann, and David Shield are released from custody at Fort Stanton. McSween returns to Lincoln, where he is served a warrant for his arrest on charges of embezzlement.

9. Marshal Ed Masterson, Bat Masterson's oldest brother, is shot dead by the drunken cowhand Jack Wagner at the Lady Gay Dance Hall in Dodge City, Kansas.

10. The Sam Bass gang attempts to rob a Texas and Pacific train near Mesquite, Texas. Passengers disrupt the holdup when they pull their curtains and open fire. Gang member Seaborn Barnes is wounded seriously.

13. The grand jury trial of A. A. McSween begins in Lincoln.

■ Billy the Kid is first mentioned in the *Santa Fe Weekly New Mexican* when it describes the murder of Sheriff Brady: "When Brady fell he dropped his rifle; Antrim [the Kid] who it appears was one of the attacking party, ran out to secure it; he was fired on by Matthews and wounded."

14. The world's largest gold brick is cast in Helena, Montana; the "Penobscot" tips the scale at 242 pounds.

16. In another blow to the Mormon Church, the U.S. Supreme Court rules in *Reynolds v. United States* that freedom of religion does not include toleration of "immoral" or "criminal" acts (polygamy).

17. J. P. Tunstall offers a $5,000 reward for the arrest and conviction of his son's murderer.

■ In Texas, four civilians are reportedly killed in Indian raids near Fort Quitman, San Ygnacio, Steele's ranch, and Brown's ranch.

■ The first tornado ever reported in Wyoming touches down near Laramie.

18. A Lincoln County grand jury exonerates A. A. McSween but hands down indictments against Jesse Evans, J. J. Dolan, and Billy Mathews for the murder of John Tunstall, and against William Bonney, Fred Waite, Henry Brown, and John Middleton for the deaths of Sheriff Brady and George Hindman. Charles Bowdre is indicted for the killing of Buckshot Roberts.

■ A meeting of 200 citizens in Lincoln declares that Axtell is unqualified to serve as governor; he is held responsible for the loss of many lives.

■ Four civilians are reported killed in Indian raids at Rancho Soledad and Charco Escondido, Texas.

19. Indians continue to carry out raids in Texas: two settlers die at Quijotes Gordes and Charco Escondido.

---

20. Three civilians are reported killed in an Indian raid at Point of Rocks, Texas.
22. A Lincoln County grand jury indicts J. J. Dolan and Jesse Evans on charges of cattle rustling.
23. J. J. Dolan publishes a notice of the "temporary" suspension of his business.
24. Henry Underwood, a member of the Sam Bass gang, leaves Texas, never to be heard from again.
26. Lawrence Murphy, John Riley, and J. J. Dolan arrive at Fort Stanton, seeking refuge from their enemies as well as from the Lincoln County grand jury.
27. Judge Bristol's appointee, John S. Copeland, is confirmed as interim sheriff of Lincoln County. J. J. Dolan leaves Fort Stanton for Lincoln, where he hopes to persuade Governor Axtell to overturn Copeland's appointment; Dolan believes that Copeland is a McSween sympathizer.
28. During the Lincoln County War, Marion Turner and John Jones organized the Seven Rivers gang to fight John Chisum. On a ride to Lincoln, they kill Frank Macnab, shoot Ab Sanders, and capture Frank Coe.
29. A posse discovers Sam Bass and members of his gang hiding at the home of Jim Murphy near Cove Hollow, Texas. A running gun battle will last for days.
■ San Francisco judge Lorenzo Sawyer rules that Chinese immigrants are ineligible for U.S. citizenship.
30. The Seven Rivers gang, fresh from its April 28 attack on Frank Macnab and his friends, arrives in Lincoln, New Mexico, under cover of darkness. Fearing it is severely outnumbered by A. A. McSween's supporters, the gang splits up. Half of the group hides at J. J. Dolan's store, while the others are housed in the home of Captain Saturnino Baca.

Also in April 1878:
Horace Tabor, the recently elected mayor of Leadville, Colorado, grubstakes the miners August Rische and George Hook with some $64 worth of supplies in return for a share of whatever ore they find. Within a week, the novice miners discover the "Little Pittsburg," one of history's richest silver finds; it will soon produce $20,000 worth of silver ore each week.

The removal of Ute Indians from New Mexico to a Colorado reservation begins; it will conclude in June.

MAY
1. A posse led by J. J. Dolan's man George Peppin surrounds the Issac Ellis house—packed with A. A. McSween supporters—in Lincoln at 3:00 A.M.

Around noon, one of McSween's men, George Coe, is sitting on the roof of the Ellis House with Henry Brown. Coe spies Charles Kruling, a member of the Seven Rivers gang, sitting on a cow skull a great distance away. Coe fires at Kruling and wounds him. Firing from both sides commences. Lieutenant George W. Smith and 15 soldiers, acting on instructions from Sheriff John H. Copeland, arrive at 3:00 P.M. and arrest some 30 members of the surrounding party near the Ellis house; they are allowed to keep their arms for the trip to Fort Stanton.
■ That evening, in connection with the murders of Sheriff Brady, George Hindman, and Buckshot Roberts, A. A. McSween, Isaac Ellis, and 20 others are arrested by soldiers at San Patricio and taken to Fort Stanton.
■ In Texas, Jim Murphy and his father are arrested for harboring the Sam Bass gang. Jim Murphy cuts a deal with a Texas Ranger, Major John B. Jones, in which Murphy will pretend to join the Bass gang and then tip the authorities as to its location. Bass is suspicious when Murphy arrives all smiles, but he is talked out of killing him by Frank Jackson.
3. A. A. McSween, Isaac Ellis, and the others are released from the Fort Stanton guardhouse.
4. A phonograph is exhibited at San Francisco's Grand Opera House.
6. James Longwell and Lawrence Murphy depart with Dolan from Lincoln, heading for Santa Fe.
■ A. A. McSween is arrested again at San Patricio.
10. A murder warrant is issued for William Bonney in Mesilla.
■ J. J. Dolan, Lawrence Murphy, and James Longwell arrive in Santa Fe.
11. "Lost Lulu, or The Prairie Traveler, A Romance of Life and Love in a Frontier Fort," Buffalo Bill's first literary output in two years, begins running in serial form in the *Saturday Journal*.
■ A. A. McSween is released again from Fort Stanton, along with many others who were taken into custody on May 6.
12. Nathan Meeker is appointed Indian agent for the White River Agency, some 200 miles west of Greeley, Colorado. He is joined by his wife and daughter and some of the colonists he has recruited.
■ The cattle "Queen" Ann Bassett is born at Brown's Park, a Colorado canyon near the Wyoming and Utah borders.
14. Regulators, allegedly led by Billy the Kid, steal 27 horses from a ranch on the Pecos River outside Lincoln.
18. The *General Sherman* docks in Miles City, Montana; it is the first of 54 steamboats that will bring sup-

plies this summer for the construction of Forts Custer and Keogh.

19. Denver's Cherry Creek floods, causing extensive damage.
20. Lieutenant E. E. Dravo reports that 17 Indians were captured by the 6th Cavalry near Wickenburg, Arizona.
21. The Colorado Central and Pacific Railroad is completed to Central City.
25. In a letter to the *Santa Fe Weekly New Mexican,* J. J. Dolan writes: "I will here state Wm. H. Antrim, alias 'The Kid' a renegade from Arizona where he killed a man in cold blood." The Kid becomes a larger-than-life figure.
28. John S. Copeland is dismissed as Lincoln County sheriff by Governor Axtell; Copeland is replaced by George Peppin, an employee of J. J. Dolan. A gang headed by John Kinney is deputized to seek out Regulators.
30. General Oliver O. Howard begins a campaign from Fort Boise, Idaho, against Bannock Indians that will last until September. Militant Bannocks had attacked white settlers after leaving the reservation at Fort Hall, Idaho.

Also in May 1878:

Of 1,735 Chippewa Indians who received land allotments in 1871, almost all have either sold their land or been swindled out of it.

En route from Texas to Arizona, "Texas John" Slaughter's wife contracts smallpox and dies.

JUNE

1. The first telephone book to appear in San Francisco is published by the American Speaking Telephone Company.
■ Two herders are killed by Indians near Camp Wood, Texas.
3. Congress passes two acts that directly affect the West. The Timber and Stone Act will offer up to 160 acres of nonagricultural public lands in the far West for $2.50 an acre. The Timber Cutting Act will give settlers free access to public land for timber.
5. Doroteo Arango, better known as Francisco "Pancho" Villa, is born in San Juan del Rio, Mexico. As a military guerrilla leader, he will execute 16 Americans during a raid on Columbus, New Mexico, in 1916.
8. Arizona's fifth territorial governor is John C. Frémont.
■ William Bonney (Billy the Kid) signs an affidavit against the Seven Rivers gang regarding the murder

of Frank McNab for Justice of the Peace John Wilson.

9. The following ad appears in the *Dodge City Times:*

DENTISTRY.

J. H. Holliday, Dentist, very respectfully offers his professional services to the citizens of Dodge City and surrounding country during the summer. Office at room No. 24, Dodge House. Where satisfaction is not given money will be refunded.

13. Gunfire erupts between Texas Rangers and the Sam Bass gang at its Salt Creek camp in Wise County, Texas. The outlaw Arkansas Johnson is killed; the other gang members escape.
15. A military escort takes Jesse Evans from Lincoln to Mesilla, where he will stand trial for the murder of John Tunstall.
17. In Mesilla, Samuel R. Perry names William Morton, Jesse Evans, and Tom Hill as the murderers of John Tunstall.
18. A. A. McSween and his sympathizers depart Lincoln to hide in the hills of San Patricio; Sheriff Peppin and soldiers arrive to catch them but are a little late.
22. John Kinney and 11 members of his gang arrive in Lincoln.
25. Lincoln County authorities are informed that the secretary of war will now limit the use of military forces in aiding civilians in the county.
28. Captain R. F. Bernard reports that the 1st Cavalry killed five Bannock Indians and wounded two at the Silver River in Oregon; three enlisted men were killed and two were wounded.
29. In New Mexico, an arrest warrant is issued for A. A. McSween by Justice Wilson.

Also in June 1878:

In Texas, John Selman and a group of thugs stage a raid on Fred Tucker's wagon train on the Staked Plains and steal several horses.

Horace Tabor's luck continues in Leadville, Colorado. One "Chicken Bill" salts a supposedly worthless mine with ore from Tabor's own Little Pittsburg. Tabor buys the mine for $40,000. Chicken Bill thinks he's had the last laugh, but Tabor does, in fact, find silver deep in the "Chrysolite Mine."

JULY

3. In the Lincoln County War, a posse under J. J. Dolan terrorizes the town of San Patricio, New Mexico, searching for Regulators.
4. Billy the Kid and a group of Regulators have a long-range shoot-out with rival factions of the Seven Rivers gang at John Chisum's South Spring River ranch. No one is injured.

5. Billy the Kid and the Regulators leave the South Spring River ranch.

6. The Denver and Rio Grande Railroad is completed to Alamosa, Colorado.

8. The ranch owned by Ab Sanders and George Coe is raided by John Selman's bunch; horses are stolen and the ranch house is set ablaze.

■ General Oliver O. Howard leads seven companies of cavalry against Bannocks at Birch Creek in Oregon. Howard reports one enlisted man killed and four wounded. There are no estimates of Indian casualties.

12. Captain J. L. Viven and the 12th Infantry report capturing 21 Bannock Indians at Ladd's Canyon in Oregon.

13. Dr. W. F. Carver, who will become a business associate of William F. Cody, shoots 5,500 of 6,211 glass balls at an exhibition in Brooklyn, New York.

14. A. A. McSween and 60 supporters, including Billy the Kid, ride into Lincoln and prepare for battle. The men occupy three homes for defense, those of Isaac Ellis, a neighbor called Montaño, and McSween. Most in the force are in McSween's house, where they barricade windows and doors in preparation for a major battle.

15. The Lincoln County War's "Five Days Battle" begins at A. A. McSween's home. Outside, the forces of J. J. Dolan gather, including John Kinney and the Doña Ana gang, and Marion Turner with the Seven Rivers gang. A horse and a mule are the first casualties; shooting erupts when some cowboys try to make it from the Montaño house to McSween's.

16. Sharpshooters position themselves around the perimeter of A. A. McSween's home, as well as in an "Indian tower" lookout station. In retaliation, riflemen take positions on the roof of Montaño's house. Dolan sends men to the hilltops to return the fire from the Montaño roof. Sheriff Peppin's request for a cannon from Fort Stanton is denied, although Colonel N. A. M. Dudley's replying note states: "In my opinion you are acting strictly within the provisions incumbent upon you as deputy U.S. marshal and sheriff, and were I not so circumscribed by law and orders, I would most gladly give you every man and all the material at my post to sustain you in your present position, believing it to be strictly legal." Private Berry Robinson, bringing the message from the fort, is wounded, probably by one of Dolan's men. Peppin fires off another note to the local military, this one blaming McSween's faction for the shooting.

17. On Wednesday, Charlie Crawford, one of Dolan's sharpshooters, is wounded by Fernando Herrera, who is positioned atop the Montaño house. Crawford and others, frustrated about the duration of the conflict, were leaving their hillside positions to return to the Wortley Hotel. Crawford's wound is serious, and he is taken to a hospital at Fort Stanton, where his condition will worsen.

■ New Mexico governor Axtell wires Washington, requesting a 90-day leave of absence from his duties.

18. Tom Cullens, aka Joe Bowers, is wounded while standing in A. A. McSween's kitchen. In another incident, Ben Ellis is shot in the neck while tending his corral. Otherwise, this is the quietest day in the five-day standoff with the McSween faction.

19. A showdown takes place at McSween's home in Lincoln, New Mexico.

■ "We are on our way to Round Rock to rob the bank. For God's sake get there." So reads a note from Jim Murphy to the Texas Rangers, informing them of the next planned heist by the Sam Bass gang. Bass and the boys ride into town for advance work. Deputy Sheriff A. W. Grimes approaches Bass, asks if he is armed, and is shot dead. The quiet afternoon erupts in gunfire. Seaborn Barnes is slain by Ranger Dick Ware. Bass is mortally wounded but makes it to his horse. Outside of town, Bass has gang member Frank Jackson lay him on a farmer's front porch near Bushy Creek.

■ John Selman, the lawman who will slay John Wesley Hardin in 1895, arrives in the Pecos Valley of New Mexico. His group, "Selman's Scouts," will be involved in cattle rustling.

20. A. A. McSween and the others who were killed during the battle at his home were resisting arrest, according to the coroner's jury. Troops depart Lincoln for Fort Stanton. McSween's funeral is held, but Mrs. McSween does not attend.

■ Lieutenant Colonel J. W. Forsyth reports a fight at John Day's River in Oregon during the campaign against the Bannock Indians; one civilian is reported killed and two cavalrymen are wounded.

■ Sam Bass is found on a farmer's porch at Bushy Creek by Texas Rangers. "I'm shot to pieces and there's no use to deny it," he says. When authorities try to get him to divulge the gang's secrets, he says: "It is against my profession to blow on my pals. If a man knows anything he ought to die with it in him."

21. Sam Bass, 27, dies after the botched robbery at Round Rock, Texas. Although Texas Rangers had filled him with lead, he held on for a couple of days so that he could die on his 27th birthday. His last words are "the world is bobbing around me."

■ The 3rd Infantry reports a fight with Indians at

SHOWDOWN AT McSWEEN'S
JULY 19, 1878

Preparations to storm A. A. McSween's compound in Lincoln, New Mexico, were now in place. Marion Turner demanded that those in the McSween house surrender, shortly after the gunfire began at 7:00 A.M. At about 10:30 A.M., Colonel N. A. M. Dudley arrived from Fort Stanton with 35 enlisted men and a howitzer with 2,000 rounds of ammunition. Seeing this, many in the McSween faction planned their escapes. Notes were exchanged between McSween and Colonel Dudley, who refused the embattled McSween any military protection if he left the house. The men in the homes of Isaac Ellis and Montaño were successfully evacuated.

J. J. Dolan's forces next set fire to the west kitchen of McSween's house. Mrs. McSween and other noncombatants were then allowed to leave. Billy the Kid, Jim French, and Tom O'Folliard stayed put for the moment, but they successfully escaped at around 9 P.M. Harvey Morris was killed in his attempt to get out. A. A. McSween tried to surrender, but he, Bob Beckwith, Vicente Romero, and Francisco Zamora were slain in the confusion. Eugenio Salazar was wounded with them, but he managed to play dead until he could get away. McSween's last words were "I surrender, oh, my God save me. Oh, Lord, Lord save me." J. J. Dolan's men set McSween's body on fire and then ran wild in celebration through the streets of Lincoln.

moned to help quiet a disturbance by Texas cowboys in Dodge City, Kansas. In doing so, he shoots the gunman George Hoyt, who will die in four weeks from an infected wound.

- Chinese ambassador Chen Lan Pan visits San Francisco.
27. The first laundry in Phoenix, Arizona, opens in a home.
28. Black Bart again robs the Quincy–Oroville stagecoach. The masked gunman appears from a clump of bushes and demands: "Throw down the box!" After filling his pockets with $379 in cash, a watch, and a diamond ring, he deposits a poem. The third stanza reads: "Let come what will I'll try it on, / My condition can't be worse; / And if there's money in that box / 'Tis munny in my purse."
- New Mexico's *Grant County Herald* erroneously reports that "Kid Antrim" was killed in the McSween battle.
- Fort Stanton's military court begins investigating the McSween affair.
29. A Lincoln County grand jury indicts Marion Turner and John Jones for murdering McSween and the others.
- Navajo scouts report killing three Indians, wounding three, and capturing one in the Sacramento Mountains of Arizona.
30. Black Bart robs the LaPorte–Oroville stagecoach five miles from LaPorte, California.

Also in July 1878:

The photographer David F. Barry begins a two-year stint running Orlando Goff's studio in Bismarck, Dakota Territory. During this time he will photograph many Sioux.

Horace Tabor and August Rische buy George Hook's share of the Little Pittsburg mine in Leadville, Colorado, for $90,000.

Joe McLane, the brother of a Kansas Pacific Railroad agent, disappears near Cheyenne Wells, Colorado.

Montana's Clearwater River; six Indians are killed, three are wounded, and 31 are captured.
23. At the Fort Stanton hospital, Charles Crawford dies of wounds he suffered on July 17 in the McSween battle.
25. Black Bart robs the Quincy–Oroville stagecoach one mile from California's Berry Creek.
- In Denver, Madam Mattie Silks pays a $3,000 down payment on a house on Holliday Street that she is purchasing from the estate of Nellie French.
- Mrs. McSween pens a letter to John Tunstall's father in London, informing him of more details of his son's death.
26. At 3:00 A.M., Assistant Marshal Wyatt Earp is sum-

AUGUST

3. The *Grant County Herald* reports that "Kid Antrim's real name is W. H. McCarty."
5. Billy the Kid and two other Regulators, Henry Brown and George Coe, are involved in a gun battle with a posse led by Atanacio Martinez. Martinez shoots clerk Morris Bernstein as the battle unfolds near Blazer's Mill. The murder is blamed on the Kid. Colonel N. A. M. Dudley sends troops from Fort Stanton after William Bonney.
6. The Dodge City Council approves the following:

Chas. E. Bassett, salary as Marshal	$100.00
Wyatt Earp, salary as Assis't Marshal	$ 75.00
John Brown's salary as Policeman	$ 75.00
James Masterson, salary as Policeman	$ 75.00

8. Denver records its hottest day so far: 105°.

9. Captain W. E. Dove lists one enlisted man wounded at Bennett Creek in Idaho, in the campaign against the Bannock Indians.

12. The miner John W. Swilling, 47, awaits trial in the Yuma, Arizona, jail on charges of stagecoach robbery and murder. Swilling swears that he is innocent, that at the time of the crimes, he was on a mission to rebury a friend who was killed by Apaches.

13. Having eluded the posse from Fort Stanton, William Bonney appears at one of John Chisum's ranches. Before the month is out, he will demand $500 in back wages from Chisum for his Regulators.

■ Juan Patron and a party of Regulators arrive at Fort Sumner, New Mexico, looking for Selman's cowboys who are calling themselves "Wrestlers."

14. William Bonney and Sam Smith are seen at Fort Sumner.

16. At Henry Beckwith's ranch near Seven Rivers, New Mexico, a huge family argument erupts. Beckwith does away with his son-in-law, William Johnson, with one blast from his shotgun. Beckwith is wounded, shot in the face by Wallace Olinger.

18. Rancher Thomas Gardner requests military protection at Seven Rivers, claiming that it is "full of men of the worst class." Sheriff Peppin hides from Regulators in a slaughterhouse at Fort Sumner.

22. Some 200 head of cattle, the last of John Tunstall's herd, is rustled from the Feliz ranch.

■ John Chisum's daughter Sallie writes in her diary: "Two candi hearts given me by William Bonney. . . ."

Also in August 1878:

Four hundred Bibles are sold in Dodge City, Kansas. The sales, says one local paper, "would bear comparison to towns of lesser note."

National Headlines/August 1878:
21. AMERICAN BAR ASSOCIATION FORMS

SEPTEMBER

1. William Bonney and a small party arrive in Lincoln, New Mexico, to help Charles Bowdre and Doc Scurlock move their families from nearby Ruidoso to Fort Sumner. They feel they may be in danger from opposing gangs.

2. Henry Huntley Haight, the 10th governor of California, dies at age 53 in San Francisco.

4. Colonel Nelson Miles reports a fight with Indians at Clark's Fork, Montana—Captain A. S. Bennett and one civilian are killed and two enlisted men are wounded; 11 Indians are killed and 31 are captured.

■ President Rutherford B. Hayes appoints General Lew Wallace governor of New Mexico, replacing Governor Axtell.

6. In the Lincoln County War, perhaps as many as 80 of John Selman's "Wrestlers" stage a raid, killing one.

7. Charles Fritz's ranch in Lincoln County, New Mexico, is raided by Sam Smith and Joe Bowers; 17 horses and 180 head of cattle are scattered.

9. An epic exodus of Indians begins, caused by poor living conditions, including inadequate food rations and outbreaks of malaria. Chiefs Dull Knife and Little Wolf lead 297 Cheyenne men, women, and children from their agency near Fort Reno, in Indian Territory, in an attempt to return to their northern homelands in the region of the Tongue River in southern Montana and northern Wyoming.

11. William Bonney (Billy the Kid) spends the night at John Chisum's camp.

12. John Charles Frémont, the new governor of Arizona, visits San Francisco.

13. The fleeing Cheyennes led by Dull Knife and Little Wolf have traveled 150 miles since September 9. Today they cross the Cimarron River. Troops under Captain Joseph Rendlebrock intercept them, but Little Wolf tells Rendlebrock's Arapaho guide that they intend to continue their journey northward. The soldiers fire the first shots but are trapped in a series of canyons by return fire.

14. Cheyennes under Dull Knife and Little Wolf slip away from the confrontation with soldiers on the Cimarron River that began yesterday.

16. Henry Beckwith, wounded in a domestic dispute in August, is released from the Fort Stanton hospital into the custody of a deputy sheriff.

19. Outlaws rob a stagecoach near Cold Springs, Wyoming.

22. The cornerstone is laid for the new B'nai B'rith building on San Francisco's Eddy Street.

23. Some 300 Cheyennes under Dull Knife and Little Wolf, attempting to return to their homelands, cross the Arkansas River and the Santa Fe rail tracks east of Dodge City, Kansas. Federal troops are in pursuit.

25. General Lew Wallace departs Crawfordsville, Indiana, for Santa Fe, New Mexico, where he will become the new governor.

27. Violence erupts in New Mexico. Nine Wrestlers, including John Selman, ransack Will Hudgen's saloon in the Fort Stanton area, pistol whip a bystander, and reportedly are abusive toward women.

■ Lieutenant Colonel W. H. Lewis is among six soldiers wounded in an Indian fight at Famished Woman's Fork, Kansas.

28. The town of Snowflake, Arizona, is founded as a Mormon settlement by Erastus Snow and William J. Flake.

■ Lieutenant Colonel W. H. Lewis dies of wounds he received yesterday.

29. J. J. Dolan departs Fort Stanton for Santa Fe. Jesse Evans rides with him.

30. A three-day rampage by Wrestlers concludes in New Mexico. Women are reportedly raped at Bartlett's Mill, and a store at the Bonito-Ruidoso junction is looted. Two men are murdered at the Jose Chavez farm during a horse theft.

■ General Lew Wallace arrives at Santa Fe, having taken a stagecoach from Trinidad, Colorado.

■ In the past two weeks, soldiers from Forts Hays, Wallace, Dodge, and Riley have caught up with Little Wolf and Dull Knife's party of fleeing Cheyennes. The Indians have escaped each time.

General Lew Wallace (1827–1905) juggles his duties as the governor of New Mexico while writing his novel Ben-Hur.
(Denver Public Library, Western History Department)

William Bonney's gang, including Henry Brown, John Middleton, Tom O'Folliard, and James French, steal 150 head of cattle and 15 horses from J. J. Dolan.

Frederic Remington enrolls in the first School of Fine Arts classes offered at Yale and plays line for the university's football squad. His first published drawing, of a battered football player, will appear this year in the *Yale Courant.*

OCTOBER

1. General Lew Wallace is sworn in as New Mexico's territorial governor. When the general is not dealing with the Lincoln County War and Billy the Kid, he will relax by penning the novel *Ben-Hur.*

■ As the reins of power shift in New Mexico, Billy the Kid and his gang hit the Grzelachowski ranch. The livestock will be sold in Tascosa, Texas.

2. Black Bart returns to action, robbing a Wells Fargo stagecoach 12 miles from Ukiah, California.

■ Frederick W. Pitkin is elected governor of Colorado.

3. Just 24 hours after robbing a stagecoach near Ukiah, California, Black Bart robs another Wells Fargo shipment 10 miles from Potter Valley.

4. John Chisum notes that 10 to 12 of his horses were stolen by Wrestlers.

5. Juan Patron is among the members of a posse that engages Wrestlers in the Seven Rivers area, in what some will call a "two-day running fight." Some horses and cattle are recovered.

■ Four civilians are reported slain in an Indian raid at Johnson's Fork, on the Guadalupe River in Texas.

7. President Hayes declares New Mexico's Lincoln County, crippled by a bitter cattle war, to be in a state of insurrection and authorizes the use of federal troops to quell the disturbance.

8. Arizona Territory grants the Southern Pacific Railroad a charter allowing its rails to cross the Yuma military reservation.

9. Beadle's Dime Library publishes the latest Buffalo Bill fiction, "Lost Lulu," as "Death Trailer, the Chief of the Scouts, or Life and Love in a Frontier Fort."

10. Two Wrestlers are killed by Juan Patron's posse near Fort Sumner.

11. General Lew Wallace visits Cimarron, New Mexico.

16. Two women are reportedly raped by Wrestlers near Barendo Flats, New Mexico.

19. The Lincoln County War rages on. Jicarilla Apaches report that 60 of their horses were stolen. Seven sheepherders near the Capitan Mountains claim 5,000 of their sheep were stolen.

■ L. G. Murphy, a Lincoln County cattleman, dies in Santa Fe. The controlling interest in the Dolan cattle business is assigned to T. B. Catron.

23. Earlier in the month, Cheyennes fleeing from Fort Reno split up. Little Wolf took 53 men, 43 women, and 38 children and headed for the Tongue River. Dull Knife led 150 toward Fort Robinson. Today, Dull Knife's band is intercepted by troops under Captain John B. Johnson and informed that the Red Cloud and Spotted Tail agencies have been moved to Dakota. Dull Knife allows his people to be taken to Fort Robinson.

25. Dull Knife's 150 Cheyennes reach Fort Robinson accompanied by 75 troops. Soldiers will provide the Indians with food, medicine, and blankets.

28. Less travel on the Santa Fe Trail since the arrival of the railroad in 1870 has decreased the need for protection from Kansas's Fort Larned, whose garrison is transferred to Fort Dodge.

Also in October 1878:

Since September, yellow fever has been reported by 27,000 residents of New Orleans; 4,046 have died.

National Headlines/October 1878:

15. EDISON FORMS FIRST LIGHT COMPANY

NOVEMBER

10. T. B. Catron resigns as U.S. district attorney in New Mexico.

13. General Lew Wallace issues proclamation offering amnesty to most participants in the Lincoln County War. Billy the Kid is not included.

16. The first brick building in Phoenix, Arizona, is reported to be nearing completion.

17. Grace Abbott, the future public administrator, is born in Grand Island, Nebraska.

28. Fort Rice, in present North Dakota, is abandoned; in its 14 years as an active army post, it was never attacked by Indians.

30. The Atchison, Topeka, and Santa Fe's tracks cross Colorado's southern boundary into New Mexico; they are the first to be laid in that territory.

Also in November 1878:

Horace Tabor is elected Colorado's lieutenant governor under Governor Frederick W. Pitkin; Tabor will serve in that office until 1883.

Since first appearing in New Orleans in May, yellow fever has claimed 14,000 lives throughout the South.

Helen Hunt Jackson publishes *Nelly's Silver Mine,* a popular children's story.

CATTLE ANNIE (1876–d.?) AND LITTLE BRITCHES (1878–1897)

The most famous groupies in the Old West were Annie McDougal and Jennie Stevens, a pair of teenaged girls who found the times woefully lacking in action. Their exploits as followers of outlaws earned them juvenile delinquent status as "Oklahoma's Girl Bandits," Cattle Annie and Little Britches.

Both came from humble farm beginnings. McDougal was born in 1876 near present Pawnee, Oklahoma, which at that time was in the Osage Nation. Two years later, Jennie Stevens (often called by her alias, Jennie Metcalf) was born on a small nearby dirt farm. They became friends in childhood.

Their teen talk rarely was about gingham gowns and parasols. McDougal and Stevens devoured dime novels, the lurid fiction of the day. In their fantasies, the ideal man packed a six-gun and robbed banks and trains for a living.

Their passion to meet real-life outlaws quickly became a reality one night in 1893, at a barn dance in nearby Ingalls. "Cattle Annie" was 17 and "Little Britches" (so named for her unheard-of fondness for men's Levis) was 15. The usual crop of cowhands and farm boys bored the buckskin vixens. When Bill Doolin and a couple of members of his gang—George "Red Buck" Weightman and Charley Pierce—stepped in, their lives were changed forever.

At 29, Doolin was perhaps the most notorious man in Indian Territory. A member of the fabled Dalton gang, he was saved by his common sense when that bunch decided to rob two banks at once in Coffeyville, Kansas, the year before. Most of the Daltons had been wiped out by shotgun-wielding citizens. Doolin had chosen to lag behind.

Now, Doolin was in Oklahoma with his own gang of desperados (the Oklahombres) that included such picturesque thugs as "Dynamite Dick" Clifton, "Bitter Creek" Newcomb, and Arkansas Tom. Their headquarters was near Ingalls, where they spent the loot from their robberies.

The girls danced with Doolin and his friends and became so excited that they quickly made a pact to ride off and join the Doolin outfit. The boys were probably surprised when Cattle Annie and the four-foot, nine-inch Little Britches rode into their camp and announced their intentions. Said the Guthrie *Daily Leader* in a later article, "Soon they were eating with them and in the corral they shook out oats and fodder for their horses." The runaways also were sexually available to the men, whether the trysting place was the Pierce Hotel in Ingalls or a cave out in the boonies. They also participated in rustling raids and in selling whiskey to the Osage Indians.

Law officers had little regard for the girls until Cattle Annie got in their way. On one occasion a posse—out roaming the hills for the Doolins—came upon a "heavily armed" young woman on horseback who visited with them briefly. Annie waited until they were out of sight and then galloped for the Doolin camp. By the time the lawmen found the robbers' roost, Bill Doolin was soaking in the curative waters of Hot Springs, Arkansas.

Officials became annoyed, and Deputy U.S. Marshals Bill Tilghman and Steve Burke were assigned to bring in the cow punkers. Inquiries led Tilghman and Burke to Doolin's hideout, a little ranch house near Pawnee.

When Little Britches saw them coming, she bolted out the back door, leaped onto her horse, and took off in a dust cloud. Tilghman gave chase, leaving Burke behind to get Cattle Annie. Tilghman realized he could easily overtake the gamine gunslinger, but he also knew he could not shoot a woman for fear of his reputation. Nevertheless, the bullets zipping by his ears convinced him that something had to be done quickly. He aimed his rifle and shot her horse out from under her.

Tilghman dismounted, only to find Little Britches reaching for her dropped pistol. When he went for it, she threw a fistful of dust in his face. When he grabbed her, she scratched, bit, and kicked him. Finally, he turned her over his knee and paddled her denim derrière. Following the little spanking on the prairie, they rode back to the ranch on his horse.

Burke had seen Annie, holding a Winchester, lean out the window and watch as Tilghman chased Jennie over the horizon. Before Annie could get back inside, the deputy grabbed her shoulders and pulled her through the window. A huge fight

(continued)

(continued)

ensued, in which Burke received claw marks down his cheek and had substantial amounts of his hair pulled out. Finally, Annie was subdued. The lawmen took their prisoners to nearby Perry, and the Old West was safe again.

After being scrubbed and outfitted in clean clothes by a matron, the girls awaited their fate. Tilghman spoke on their behalf to Judge Brierer. McDougal and Stevens were sentenced to two years in a federal reformatory in Massachusetts. Newspaper accounts sensationalized the adventures of the newly dubbed "criminalettes." A huge crowd greeted the duo when they arrived to begin serving their time.

According to historian Paul I. Wellman (*A Dynasty of Western Outlaws,* Doubleday, 1961), "Neither of them had ever been far from home, and the outside world was a revelation to their starved little minds." They became model prisoners.

Upon release, Annie Dougal returned to Oklahoma, married, and settled into anonymity. Jennie Stevens went to Boston, worked as a domestic, and then did "settlement work" in New York City, aiding the Bowery bums with soup and religion. She died at age 19 in 1897 at Bellevue Hospital, a victim of tuberculosis. Their saga probably would have been forgotten had it not been for Robert Ward's 1977 novel, *Cattle Annie and Little Britches.* The 1980 movie version of the book starred Amanda Plummer as Annie and Diane Lane as Little Britches.

Jennie Stevens, who will become known as "Little Britches," is born on a dirt farm in the Osage Nation near present Pawnee, Oklahoma. She and "Cattle Annie" McDougal will gain fame briefly in 1893 with the Doolin gang.

The cattle baron I. P. "Print" Olive and his men get embroiled in an argument with the families of Ami Ketchum and Luther Mitchell in Nebraska's Custer County. Olive claims they were encroaching on his cattle land. Olive's brother, Robert, is killed in the fracas. Olive then bribes the authorities to turn Ketchum and Mitchell over to him, and near Clear Creek he has them shot and hanged. Olive and Frederick Fisher are then arrested and convicted of murder. After two years of legal maneuverings, Olive will be released from prison.

DECEMBER

7. The first train to enter New Mexico comes from Colorado via Raton Pass.

■ In New Mexico, Jack Long and another cowboy, identified as Barney Mason by some and as William Bonney by others, become involved in a fracas at Bosque Grande in which the postmaster is forced to leave and the mail station is shot full of holes.

■ Mrs. A. A. McSween petitions the court to have Robert Widenmann removed as administrator of the late John Tunstall's estate. She is trying to recover money she alleges was owed to the late Mr. McSween by the late Mr. Tunstall.

10. Henry Wells, the cofounder of Wells Fargo, dies in Glasgow, Scotland, at age 73.

13. A Lieutenant French barges into the home of the widow McSween and is said to be "abusive" about the current cattle war. An employee of hers, identified as Huston Chapman, is supposedly assaulted.

15. Justice Wilson issues an order to arrest Lieutenant French for attempting to murder Chapman.

20. Lieutenant Dawson and a force of 15 enlisted men deliver Lieutenant French to Justice Wilson.

21. J. J. Dolan sells his store in Lincoln for $3,000 to Will Dowlin.

■ Farmers in Tempe, Arizona, report that 10 acres of sugarcane produced a great quantity of syrup and 6,000 pounds of sugar this year.

22. Billy the Kid surrenders to Lincoln County sheriff George Kimball. After a brief time in jail, the Kid will escape and ride toward Las Vegas, New Mexico.

28. According to an unconfirmed rumor, two of the Old West's most famous outlaws meet for the first and only time (some sources say the meeting occurred on January 28, 1879). Jesse James, traveling under the name Thomas Howard, is supposedly introduced to William Bonney (Billy the Kid) in Las Vegas, New Mexico. Jesse asks the Kid to join him but he politely declines, and the two ride off in their separate ways.

30. Wyoming's Camp Brown is renamed Fort Washakie.

Also in December 1878:

F. O. Vaile opens Denver's first telephone exchange; it has 200 subscribers.

There are 339,000 head of cattle valued at $4.6 million in Arizona.

Wells Fargo operates 489 offices and has an income of

$2,113,000 from transportation and $937,000 from express services.

Also in 1878:

John Wesley Powell publishes *Report on the Lands of the Arid Region of the U.S.*

An estimated 100,000 buffalo are killed in Texas.

The Santa Fe Railroad ships 750,000 buffalo hides to the East from Kansas.

There are 532 business failures in California, with $11,600,130 in liabilities.

With an investment of $2,500 and a $30,000 lien, Joseph Pulitzer merges the former *Post* and *Dispatch* into the *St. Louis Post-Dispatch*.

Approximately 40,000 former slaves, the "Exodusters," settle in Kansas.

Brigham Young College is founded in Logan, Utah.

Joaquin Miller publishes *The Danites (First Families in the Sierras, 1875).*

Hubert Howe Bancroft offers Frances Fuller Victor a job in his library, where she will help to write his massive histories of the West. She will write Bancroft's *History of Oregon, History of Washington, Idaho and Montana,* and *History of Nevada, Colorado and Wyoming,* as well as portions of other major works.

1879

"The plow has plowed its way from the Atlantic to the heart of the Rocky Mountains. Speed the plow!"

—Nathan Meeker

JANUARY

1. J. C. Lea becomes the new commissioner of Lincoln County, New Mexico.

3. Captain Henry W. Wessells, overseeing Dull Knife's Cheyennes at Fort Robinson, Nebraska, receives orders from the War Department to return the Indians to Fort Reno in Indian Territory. The order is to be carried out immediately, despite the winter conditions. When informed of the news, Dull Knife responds to Wessells: "Does the Great Father desire us to die? If so we will die right here. We will not go back!" On September 9, 1878, Dull Knife had led nearly 300 Cheyennes north from Fort Reno. Dull Knife's groups have been under military guard at Fort Robinson since they were apprehended by troops in October, 1878.

5. Rations are cut off for Dull Knife's Cheyennes at Fort Robinson, Nebraska, by order of Captain Henry Wessells. The Indians are to be kept in barracks and given no wood for fires. Wessells is pressuring Dull Knife to comply with the order that they be sent back to their reservation in Indian Territory, present Oklahoma.

6. Arizona's 10th territorial legislature convenes to legalize gambling.

9. After four days without food, Dull Knife's Cheyennes at Fort Robinson, Nebraska, break out of their barracks at about 9:45 P.M. Soldiers pursue on horseback and catch up with the fleeing Indians about 10 minutes later. In the fight, soldiers shoot and club to death about half of the escapees, mostly women and children, including Dull Knife's daughter.

10. Soldiers at Fort Robinson, Nebraska, count 65 Cheyenne prisoners from last night's breakout, 23 of them wounded. A total of 38 have escaped, 32 of whom are moving in the hills, pursued by four companies of soldiers. The smaller group includes Dull Knife, his wife, son, daughter-in-law and grandchild, and a Cheyenne boy named Red Bird. This smaller group will make it all the way to Red Cloud's reservation at Pine Ridge in Dakota Territory.

▪ The Gila River Reservation's boundaries are expanded in Arizona.

13. Stung by criticism of his performance at the Battle of the Little Bighorn, Major Marcus Reno had requested a court of inquiry, which convenes in Chicago. In 26 days and 1,300 pages of testimony, eyewitnesses will give their opinions of Reno's behavior in the battle. Two mule packers will say he was drunk, but others will disagree. Lieutenant DeRudio will state that "if we had gone five hundred yards farther, we would have been butchered." Captain Myles Moylan will testify that "if he had continued to charge down the valley he would have been there yet."

21. The schooner *Esther Colos* becomes a total loss when it runs aground on a bar in Oregon's Rogue River.

22. The "Dull Knife Outbreak" ends when soldiers catch up with 32 Cheyennes who escaped from Fort Robinson, Nebraska, on January 9, at Hat Creek Bluffs. The troops fire several volleys and kill 23 Indians. Nine survivors, mostly women and children, are marched back to Fort Robinson. Dull

Knife, who with five others eluded capture, will surrender at the Pine Ridge Reservation in Dakota Territory in early February.

25. Construction of the new San Francisco seawall begins.

Also in January 1879:

The Pima County Bank is the first to open in Tucson, Arizona.

Mrs. A. A. McSween is successful in having Robert Widenmann removed as administrator of the Tunstall estate, and in having herself appointed instead. Mrs. McSween is trying to recover funds the late John Tunstall owed her deceased husband.

FEBRUARY

1. Construction of Denver's Tabor Block, a row of buildings created with the financing of "Silver King" Horace Tabor, is completed.

▪ Lincoln County Sheriff George Kimball receives William Bonney's arrest warrant, dated May 10, 1878.

3. P. W. Peak is shot dead by C. W. Baits in a church in Manhattan, Kansas.

5. In New Mexico, Captain Carrol begins a 20-day search for John Tunstall's cattle in the Pecos River region of Pope's Crossing, west of Lincoln County, New Mexico.

7. Major Marcus Reno's court of inquiry concludes in Chicago. The court exonerates him of any wrongdoing in the Little Bighorn battle of 1876, and declares that he performed to the best of his abilities in a grave situation.

10. San Francisco's California Theater becomes the first in the city to have electric arc lights.

▪ In Colorado, Lake County is renamed Chaffee County to honor Senator Jerome Chaffee. Carbonate County is renamed Lake County.

13. The first passenger train arrives in New Mexico.

15. Sheriff Bat Masterson, Charles Bassett, and other law enforcement officials arrive at Fort Leavenworth to take charge of Cheyenne prisoners. The members of Dull Knife's band are to be taken to Dodge City for trial; they are accused of committing atrocities in incidents that began with the September 1878 outbreak at their agency in Indian Territory.

18. In the Lincoln County War, Houston Chapman, the one-time attorney for A. A. McSween, is murdered in Lincoln, New Mexico, by J. J. Dolan and Bill Campbell, and perhaps Jesse Evans. Dolan had just concluded a "peace talk" with Tom O'Folliard and William Bonney.

▪ The ferryboats *El Capitan* and *Alameda* collide in the fog in San Francisco Bay.

19. The Montana Stockgrowers is established, with 28 members.

20. Sheriff George Kimball asks Lieutenant M. F. Goodwin of Fort Stanton for six soldiers to help him arrest William Bonney.

26. Lieutenant M. F. Goodwin is ordered by Colonel Edward Hatch to arrest Bill Campbell, Billy Mathews, and Jesse Evans for the murder of Houston Chapman. Sergeant Israel Murphy is ordered to arrest Thomas O'Folliard and William Bonney as accessories to the crime.

MARCH

3. Congress establishes the U.S. Geological Survey and names Clarence King its first director.

5. Governor Lew Wallace arrives in London and sends soldiers to arrest Jesse Evans, Bill Campbell, and Billy Mathews at Murphy's Fairview ranch. J. J. Dolan surrenders and is confined at Fort Stanton. Wallace announces a reward for William Bonney, hoping he will testify against Houston Chapman's assailants.

8. Governor Lew Wallace attends a citizens' meeting at the Lincoln County Courthourse.

13. The Cimarron *News and Press* reports that Captain Carroll has returned 138 head of stolen cattle to Mrs. McSween.

▪ Governor Lew Wallace sends a communication to Billy the Kid, asking that the Kid meet with him on March 17. The Kid has already written to Wallace, offering testimony against Houston Chapman's murderers in return for immunity; he signed it "I am called Kid Antrim but Antrim is my stepfather's name—W. H. Bonney."

▪ A fire destroys part of Abilene, Kansas.

17. Billy the Kid and Governor Lew Wallace hold a secret night meeting at the home of John Wilson. The governor suggests a mock arrest. After the Kid testifies, says Wallace, "I will let you go scot-free with a pardon in your pocket."

18. William Campbell and Jesse Evans escape from Fort Stanton.

20. Governor Lew Wallace receives a message from William Bonney via Squire "Green" Wilson, asking whether the escape of Campbell and Evans will change any of the arrangements agreed upon on March 17. Wallace answers: "The escape makes no difference in the arrangements." The deal is this: Bonney will surrender to Sheriff George Kimball at San Patricio and be jailed in Lincoln.

21. As per the arrangement, William Bonney and Josiah "Doc" Scurlock surrender to Lincoln County sheriff George Kimball a mile east of San Patricio.

23. Governor Lew Wallace receives a list of "thieves and murderers" as well as a map of trails used by the "Rustlers" (Wrestlers) from William Bonney.

25. Governor Wallace orders Captain Purington of Fort Stanton to arrest John Slaughter on suspicion of cattle rustling.

■ Lieutenant W. P. Clark captures Little Wolf and 113 Northern Cheyennes at Box Elder Creek in Montana.

26. Miners at Fort Scott, Kansas, pull Bill Howard, a black man convicted of rape, from his cell, hang him from a lamppost, and set him on fire.

27. Little Wolf and his Cheyennes who escaped from Fort Reno in Indian Territory last September surrender to troops under Lieutenant William P. Clark from Fort Keogh. The incident occurs on the Little Missouri River in Montana.

29. Governor Lew Wallace authorizes Captain Purington to release John Slaughter until his cattle can be inspected for ownership by another source, preferably a probate judge.

■ The Wyoming Stock Growers Association is formed in Laramie.

■ The *Saturday Journal* begins serializing "Gold Bullet Sport, or The Knights of Chivalry," the first work in a year "by Buffalo Bill."

31. Governor Lew Wallace asks the federal government to declare martial law in Lincoln County.

Also in March 1879:

A mining camp is established at Los Cerrillos, New Mexico.

Hostilities break out between the Denver and Rio Grande and the Atchison, Topeka, and Santa Fe Railroads.

Doc Holliday has several scrapes with the law in Las Vegas, New Mexico; the charges range from concealing a deadly weapon to keeping a gaming table.

Henry George self-publishes *Progress and Poverty,* a controversial economic text on the downside of progress: wealth for a few, hardships for many.

National Headlines/March 1879:

1. HAYES VETOES BILL TO RESTRICT CHINESE IMMIGRATION

APRIL

5. A major gunfight erupts at Dodge City's Long Branch Saloon, as "Cockeyed Frank" Loving kills Levi Richardson. Says the *Ford County Globe* of the incident: "Loving Comes Out With A Scratch and Richardson Goes to His Grave."

7. In the Lincoln County War, soldiers surround the camp of Bill Campbell and Jesse Evans near Dowlin's Mill. The pair escape, but the soldiers return with an army deserter called "Texas Jack."

10. Eight Indians are reported captured by the 2nd Cavalry near Fort Keogh, Montana.

12. The brewer Adolph Coors weds Louisa M. Weber in Golden, Colorado.

14. A grand jury convenes in Lincoln. William Bonney is ready to testify against Bill Campbell regarding the murder of Houston Chapman, but before that can happen, Bonney will be taken to Dona Aña County, where he will be tried for the murder of Sheriff Brady.

15. Pat Garrett is recommended to Governor Wallace by John Chisum, to "take care of" the bunch running east of Fort Sumner.

17. The 3rd and 7th Infantries report two soldiers killed in a fight with Indians near Careless Creek, Montana; eight Indians are reported killed.

18. Despite assurances that previous murder charges will be dropped, Billy the Kid (William Bonney) sees his negotiations turn sour. The Lincoln County grand jury indicts Bonney, John Middleton, and Henry Brown for the murder of Sheriff Brady.

19. A flood washes away all of the bridges on Montana's Deer Lodge River.

20. The *Santa Fe Weekly New Mexican* mentions "the Kid, a boy who was arrested for stealing horses from Cal Hunter."

21. The U.S. Supreme Court rules that the Denver and Rio Grande Railroad had a prior right to build a railway through Colorado's Royal Gorge. The financially strapped railroad finds little comfort in the decision; it has already leased its 337 miles of track to the Atchison, Topeka, and Santa Fe. The Denver and Rio Grande's president, William Jackson Palmer, prepares to go to court to have the lease declared null and void.

22. The attorney for William Bonney fails to prevent the venue for Bonney's trial from being moved to Dona Aña County.

24. An unknown assailant tries to kill Judge Ira Leonard, Mrs. McSween's counsel, at Lincoln.

30. A Lincoln County grand jury adjourns after returning almost 200 indictments, including those of George Peppin and Colonel Dudley for damaging A. A. McSween's home. Peppin and Dudley plead not guilty and are granted a change of venue to Dona Aña County.

- Tobe and John Hudgens and Robert Henry escape from the Lincoln jail.

Also in April 1879:

A year after the discovery of Little Pittsburg, Horace Tabor's Little Pittsburg Consolidated Mining Company of Leadville, Colorado, is incorporated with a capital investment of $20,000,000.

The Chiricahua Apache leader Geronimo is brought in chains to the San Carlos Reservation in southern Arizona for questioning concerning recent raids. Mimbreño Apache leader Victorio is physically restrained. The latter is told that he must give up the choice Mescalero Reservation and move to the San Carlos Reservation.

William F. Cody appears in the opening-night performance of Prentiss Ingraham's drama *The Knight of the Plains, or Buffalo Bill's Best Trail.*

MAY

1. A travel guide states that Leadville, Colorado, has "19 hotels, 414 lodging houses, 82 drinking saloons, 38 restaurants, 13 wholesale liquor houses, . . . 3 undertakers and 21 gambling houses where all sorts of games are played as openly as the Sunday School sermon is conducted."

- Lucas Gallegos is sentenced in Lincoln to a year in prison for killing Sostero Garcia.

7. California adopts a new state constitution that forbids the hiring of Chinese.

8. The "Night Hell Let Loose" occurs in the mining town of Leadville, Colorado. The *Carbonate Chronicle* will report some of the events in its next day's edition: "Assault & Robbery on Harrison Avenue," "A Tenderfoot Garroted on Capitol Hill," "Arrest of a Notorious Confidence Man," "Murderous Attack Upon Kokomo Freighter," and "Daring Robbery of a Man at the Comique."

9. Construction begins on Fort Assiniboine south of Havre, Montana.

11. In New Mexico, a gang of 15 highwaymen attacks Fort Sumner's mail wagons and steals the mail.

14. Tom Hudgens dies in the guardhouse at Fort Stanton, New Mexico.

17. In Denver, customs agents auction confiscated tins of opium at $2 a can.

25. In Lincoln County, a court of inquiry begins hearing civil charges against Colonel Dudley; he will be cleared.

28. William Bonney testifies at the court of inquiry investigating Colonel Dudley. From the transcript:

Q: What is your name and place of residence?
A: My name is William Bonney. I reside in Lincoln.
Q: Are you known or called Billy Kid, also Antrim?
A: Yes, sir.

30. Twin tornadoes hit Irving, Kansas, within minutes of each other. The second tornado is two miles wide.

- In Grangeville, Iowa, Captain Reube Bernard receives the order to move his 1st Cavalry against the Indians known as the "sheepeaters."

Also in May 1879:

William Bonney, assuming that Governor Lew Wallace's pardon will not be honored, escapes from the loose custody in which he was held in Lincoln to return to cattle rustling in the Fort Sumner area.

JUNE

1. The U.S. government contracts with the American, the United States, and the Wells Fargo express companies to transport coin and bullion between San Francisco and New York.

7. The San Francisco Public Library opens.

10. Judge Thomas M. Bowen of Colorado's Fourth Judicial Court in Alamosa rules that the Atchison, Topeka, and Santa Fe Railroad must turn the operation of the Denver and Rio Grande Railroad back to its original owners; Bowen's ruling comes in the wake of the April 21 decision of the U.S. Supreme Court.

11. The "Royal Gorge War" erupts in Pueblo, Colorado, the result of friction between the Atchison, Topeka, and Santa Fe Railroad and its smaller competitor, the Denver and Rio Grande. The latter's president, William Jackson Palmer, had leased the tracks of his financially strapped company to the Santa Fe; the April 21 ruling of the U.S. Supreme Court gave his company the right to construct a rail line through Royal Gorge. Anticipating yesterday's decision by Judge Thomas Bowen, both railroads had hired gunfighters. Bat Masterson and Luke Short are among those hired by the Santa Fe who are holed up in Pueblo's roundhouse, vowing a fight to the finish with anyone who tries to evict them. One hundred Denver and Rio Grande special deputies storm the roundhouse and overrun it; one of their number, Dodge City's Harry Jenkins, is killed in the fight. Later, it will be rumored that Masterson, the sheriff of Ford County, Kansas, was bribed by the Denver and Rio Grande to work as an inside man. The rumor will never be proven.

14. The Salt River Reservation in Arizona is set aside for the Maricopa and Pima Indians.

17. The Union Pacific Railroad receives legal title to the Kansas Pacific Railroad.
18. Arizona's first ice plant opens in Phoenix.
20. The *New York Times* reports: "The Santa Fe Railroad has received the Sonora land grant which the South Pacific so much coveted, and which, though it gives 15,000 acres of land to the mile, is of even greater moment to the South Pacific, for its passing to another railroad brings a much dreaded rival line to contest the business of the entire Pacific coast."
21. Black Bart robs the LaPorte–Oroville stagecoach three miles from Forbestown, California.
25. Indian scouts reportedly kill six Indians and capture one in Arizona's Tonto Basin.
29. Crow scouts reportedly kill six Indians at Alkali Creek in Montana.

Also in June 1879:

Laura Ingalls, 13, again moves with her family, this time from Walnut Grove to De Smet in Dakota Territory. The new locale will be the setting for her books *By the Shores of Silver Lake* (1939) and *The Long Winter* (1940).

Robert LeRoy Parker (who will later be known as Butch Cassidy), 13, moves with his family from Beaver to Circleville, Utah. It is there that young Cassidy will idolize the rough cowboy Mike Cassidy, who will give him his first gun.

Victorio settles on the Mescalero Reservation in Tula-rosa, New Mexico, where he will be indicted on charges of rustling and murder.

Gold is discovered at White Oaks, New Mexico, where a number of mining camps will spring up.

National Headlines/June 1879:
16. GILBERT & SULLIVAN'S "H.M.S. PINAFORE" PREMIERES IN NY

JULY

1. Railroad tracks reach Las Vegas, New Mexico.
2. Texas Rangers arrest Jesse Evans near Alamito Creek in Texas; he is wanted in New Mexico for the murder of Houston Chapman.
4. California adopts a new state constitution.
5. In New Mexico, Colonel Dudley's court of inquiry comes to an end with no verdict.
7. The artist George Caleb Bingham, whose scenes of the Midwest include *Fur Traders Descending the Missouri* (1844), dies at 68.
8. The steamer *Jeanette* sails out of San Francisco Bay on an ill-fated Arctic voyage.
13. The new B'nai B'rith building is dedicated in San Francisco.
▪ J. J. Dolan takes time out from the Lincoln County War to wed Caroline Fritz.
15. In Colorado, the *Leadville Daily Chronicle* reports that a "Mountain Charley," whose last name is Walworth, is visiting Cloud City. Charley is actually a woman posing as a man; she served in the Civil

Judge Roy Bean (c. 1825–1903). The "Law West of the Pecos" poses for photographers in 1902. (Denver Public Library, Western History Department)

War, speculated in Wyoming real estate, and ran a gambling house.

17. General Nelson Miles's expedition against the Sioux gets under way at Milk River, Montana; he reports three enlisted men killed and three wounded. There are no estimates of Indian casualties.

19. The ex-scout Mike Gordon tries to persuade a Las Vegas, New Mexico, dance hall girl to run away with him. When she turns him down, an enraged Gordon stands in the street and begins firing his gun into the establishment, which is run by Doc Holliday. Holliday storms out, kills Gordon with one shot, and returns to work.

Also in July 1879:

In Texas, Roy Bean establishes a saloon on the northern bank of the Rio Grande, near the Pecos River, and calls the tent village around his saloon "Vinegarroon."

During two years of captivity at Fort Leavenworth, more than 100 Nez Percés have died of malaria and other diseases. Chief Joseph petitions Congress: "I only ask to be treated as other men are treated. If I cannot go to my own home, let me have a home in some country where my people will not die so fast." In another statement, he says: "Let me be a free man—free to travel, free to stop, free to work, free to trade where I choose, free to choose my own teachers, free to follow the religion of my fathers, free to think, and talk and act for myself—and I will obey every law, or submit to the penalty."

AUGUST

3. In Deadwood, the body of Wild Bill Hickok is moved to Mount Moriah.

5. The first high school in Cheyenne, Wyoming, opens.

10. Fast Bull and 56 of his followers surrender to Lieutenant Colonel J. N. G. Whistler of the 5th Infantry near Poplar Creek, Montana.

16. Acting Governor Gosper of Arizona offers a $500 reward for all stagecoach robbers apprehended during the act.

17. In New Mexico, William Bonney eludes a detachment of the 9th Cavalry that was sent to apprehend him.

22. Vigilantes in Phoenix, Arizona, pull two convicted murderers from jail and lynch them in the city's main plaza.

23. In San Francisco, Charles de Young wounds Isaac Kalloch.

26. In Lincoln County, New Mexico, the rustler John Jones kills rancher John Beckwith during an argument over cattle.

29. John Jones is slain by Bob Olinger in New Mexico.

Also in August 1879:

Judge Bristol dismisses all charges connected with the Lincoln County War murder of Houston Chapman against J. J. Dolan.

Until December, the Scottish author Robert Louis Stevenson will live in Monterey, California, selling articles at $2 apiece to the *Monterey Californian* and working on other writing projects, including the novel *Prince Otto* (1885). It is believed that the forests and beaches around Monterey will inspire the settings for another Stevenson novel, *Treasure Island* (1883).

An article by the editor William B. Vickers in the *Denver Tribune* is being widely distributed throughout Colorado under the bold title "The Utes Must Go!" In it, he writes: "The Utes are actual, practical Communists and the government should be ashamed to foster and encourage them in their idleness and wanton waste of property. . . . Honorable N. C. Meeker . . . went to the agency in the firm belief that he could manage the Indians successfully by kind treatment, patient precept and good example. But utter failure marked his efforts and at last he reluctantly accepted the truth of the border truism that the only truly good Indians are dead ones."

William F. Cody publishes *The Life of Hon. William F. Cody.*

SEPTEMBER

1. The post office's free delivery system is first put into operation in Denver.

■ The Colorado State Agricultural College opens in Fort Collins.

3. Apache raids continue to terrorize New Mexico's settlers.

4. Fearing prosecution, Victorio leads a war party of Mimbreños off the Mescalero Reservation in New Mexico.

■ A black man is elected to the Wyoming legislature for the first time.

5. Two buildings collapse in Cheyenne, Wyoming, killing two children.

6. Victorio and his Mimbreño followers attack the 9th Cavalry near Ojo Caliente, New Mexico. Sergeant S. Chapman reports that five troopers and three civilians are slain; Victorio's forces steal 40 horses and will ride first to Mexico and then to Texas.

8. In Dodge City, Kansas, A. H. Webb settles an argu-

Victorio (c. 1825–1880). The Apache military strategist is physically restrained for this photograph and then shipped to the San Carlos Reservation. (Denver Public Library, Western History Department)

ment with B. Martin by delivering a murderous blow to Martin's head with a Winchester. "Dodge City has added another item to her history of blood," notes the *Ford County Globe,* "and rum has found another victim."

9. In his last article for the *Greeley Tribune,* Nathan Meeker notes the Utes' reluctance to embrace "civilization": "The impression is that if the Indians had been free to choose, they would have forbidden another furrow to be turned. This stopping plows by bullets is by no means a new thing . . . the plow has plowed its way from the Atlantic to the heart of the Rocky Mountains. Speed the plow!"

10. Tensions flare between the Utes and Nathan Meeker. Meeker and Quinkent, also known as Chief Douglas, argue because Meeker wants to plow a grassy horse pasture favored by the chief for his ponies. Quinkent offers to clear an area of sageland just west of the field in question, but Meeker refuses. Shadrach Price is told by Meeker to plow the pasture, but when he begins he is confronted by armed young Utes who order him to stop. Price reports the incident to Meeker, who orders him to return to his work. The Utes then fire a warning shot, and Price lays down the plow again. Intimidated by the incident, Meeker requests assistance from Fort Steele, 150 miles away. "This is a bad lot of Indians," he writes. "They have had free rations so long and have been flattered and petted so much, that they think themselves lords of all."

■ Seven settlers are slain in an Indian raid at McEver's Ranch in New Mexico. Two more settlers are reported killed in a similar raid at Arroyo Seco.

11. Nathan Meeker's relations with the Utes are strained further when the medicine man Canalla, Chief Ouray's brother-in-law, voices to Meeker his concerns about the loss of pastureland to the plowing. Meeker replies: "You have too many ponies. You had better kill some of them."

16. The town of Dillon, Montana, is begun by workers of the Utah Northern Railroad.

17. Two settlers are slain in an Indian raid at Black Range, New Mexico.

18. The 9th Cavalry and Victorio's forces clash on New Mexico's Las Animas River; four enlisted men and one civilian are killed, and two enlisted men are wounded.

26. Major Thomas T. Thornburgh's force of 200 soldiers and volunteers is met by five Utes at their camp at the mouth of Elkhead Creek in Colorado. Nicaagat (Chief Jack) protests Thornburgh's plan to enter the Ute reservation, saying all is well there.

27. As Utes move their families away from the White River Agency in Colorado, Nathan Meeker writes to Major Thornburgh of Fort Fred Steele, Wyoming: "Indians consider the troops a declaration of real war. . . ."

28. Major Thornburgh's reply to Meeker comes from his camp outside the Ute reservation on Deer Creek in Colorado: "Our desire is to avoid war . . . we have not come for war."

29. The "Meeker Massacre" takes place in Colorado.

Also in September 1879:

With an invitation to be a "guest poet" at the Kansas Quarter-Centennial Celebration, and with free Pullman passage, Walt Whitman heads west. He takes the train from Philadelphia to St. Louis, stays a night with his brother, then proceeds to Kansas City, Lawrence, and Topeka. A planned speech falls by the wayside, as Whitman finds socializing more to his liking. He then travels by train another 600 miles to Denver, and from there into the mountains. "I have found the law of my own poems," he notes

TROUBLE ON TWO FRONTS
SEPTEMBER 29, 1879

The relations between Nathan Meeker and local Utes that deteriorated over the summer had now broken down completely at the White River Agency in Colorado. On Monday morning, September 29, Major Thomas T. Thornburgh and some 200 soldiers and volunteers were on the way to assist Meeker.

Proceeding down Milk Creek in northwestern Colorado, some 15 miles from the White River Agency, Thornburgh's men entered Red Canyon's 200-foot bluffs about a mile into the reservation. Nicaagat (Chief Jack), Colorow, and their warriors observed them, then the chief went down to confer with Lieutenant Samuel Cherry. Before they could meet, a shot rang out. Nicaagat waved his men to stop fighting, but it was too late. In the fray, Thornburgh, 11 soldiers, three civilians, and 250 mules and horses were killed, and 47 enlisted men were wounded. The battled lasted five days and claimed the lives of 37 of the 300 Utes who surrounded the intruders.

On the afternoon of the 29th, Quinkent (Chief Douglas) arrived at the agency, some 20 miles from the action, to inform Nathan Meeker, 62, of the soldiers' appearance on Ute land. Quinkent told Meeker that he believed there would be a fight, but Meeker disagreed and even invited Quinkent to ride out with him the next morning to meet the soldiers. Shortly thereafter, a dozen armed Utes, filled with tales of the battle, appeared at the agency and began killing workers in the field. Meeker and nine other men were killed that afternoon, while Mrs. Arvilla Meeker, 63, their daughter Josephina, 21, Mrs. F. S. Price, and two small children were taken captive, hustled away to a camp at Piceance Creek. The three women were raped along the way; Arvilla would later claim to have been raped by Quinkent, although no public charges were ever made.

Because of these two actions, the Utes will be forced to move to Utah, and their 12 million acres in Colorado will be opened for settlement by whites.

during a dawn train ride through Platte Canyon to Leadville. Inspired by scenery and a breakfast of trout, eggs, and pancakes, he writes of "far glimpses of a hundred peaks, titanic necklaces, stretching north and south . . . as we dash along, others similar, simple, monolithic, elephantine."

In Colorado, Horace Tabor sells his interest in Little Pittsburg to David Moffat and Jerome Chaffee for $1 million in cash. With the capital, he purchases a half-interest in Denver's First National Bank and then buys Leadville's Matchless Mine for $150,000. Soon, the mine will be producing $80,000 a month in revenue. Later in the year, Tabor will build Leadville's Tabor Opera House for $78,000 and establish the Bank of Leadville. He will also fund a hometown fire department, order a fire engine from San Francisco, and provide the department with red flannel shirts with "TABOR" emblazoned in white across the chest.

OCTOBER

1. News of the "Meeker Massacre" reaches Denver.
2. U.S. troops at Milk Creek, in Colorado, are relieved by a regiment of black cavalrymen led by Captain Francis Dodge.
- The *Nugget* begins publishing in Tombstone, Arizona.
5. Another force of cavalrymen, this one under Colonel Wesley Merritt, arrives at Milk Creek.
6. The Golden Gate Kindergarten Association begins organizing in San Francisco.
7. Frank and Jesse James return to work after a three-year hiatus following their botched raid on a bank in Northfield, Minnesota. They stop a Chicago and Alton Express train outside Glendale, Missouri, and take $35,000.
- Joel Hagglund, who will become known as the Utah union martyr Joe Hill, is born in Gävle, Sweden.
11. Colonel Wesley Merritt and his men discover the bodies of those killed at the White River Agency on September 29.
13. Eleven civilians are reported slain in an Apache raid at Slocum's Ranch, New Mexico.
15. Colorado governor Pitkin directs General Charles Adams, a former Indian agent, to negotiate with the Ute chief Ouray for the return of the women and children who were kidnapped at the White River Agency.
- Bandits stop an express train leaving Las Vegas, New Mexico, and make off with just over $2,000 in bills and time checks.
19. General Charles Adams arrives at Ouray's camp.

20. Lieutenant W. B. Weir is slain by Indians while hunting on Colorado's White River.
22. Chief Ouray agrees to release the White River Agency captives, including Arvilla Meeker and her daughter Josephina, on the condition that Colonel Wesley Merritt cease his advance. Chief Douglas agrees to turn his captives over to Ouray.
24. The released captives arrive at Ouray's camp, where they are tended to by the chief's wife, Chipeta.
25. Black Bart robs the stagecoach that runs between Roseburg, Oregon, and Redding, California, two miles from Bass Station.
27. Black Bart robs the Alturas–Redding, California, stagecoach 12 miles north of Millville.

Also in October 1879:

Major Edward S. Farrow's capture of 388 Indians concludes the Pacific Northwest Indian Wars.

William Bonney, along with Charles Bowdre, Doc Scurlock, and Tom O'Folliard, steals 118 head of cattle from John Chisum's ranch in the Texas panhandle.

Mary Hallock Foote lives in Leadville, Colorado, the locale of her first novel, *The Led-Horse Claim: A Romance of the Mining Camp* (1883).

In Indian Territory, the Darlington Agency does not sponsor a buffalo hunt this year, due to the scarcity of buffalo. Indians are forced to live on government beef rations.

The 30 occupants of Dodge City's Boot Hill are moved to a new cemetery, Prairie Grove, northeast of town.

National Headlines/October 1879:
21. EDISON DEMONSTRATES ELECTRIC LIGHT

NOVEMBER
4. The humorist-journalist-actor Will Rogers is born William Penn Adair Rogers in Indian Territory near what will become Oolagah, approximately 15 miles north of Claremore, Oklahoma.
▪ Kansas City newspapers erroneously report that Jesse James has been killed by a member of his gang.
5. The *Greeley Tribune* reports the arrival by train of Mrs. Meeker and the other White River Agency captives: "A more remarkable event has not been witnessed since the founding of the town. The rescued women had been greeted . . . along the way home . . . from Alamosa to Denver to Greeley."
10. At Fort Meade in the Black Hills, Major Marcus Reno has become hopelessly infatuated with the 20-year-old daughter of his superior officer, Colonel

Samuel Sturgis. The affection is not mutual. To-night, Reno is caught peeping through her parlor window. Sturgis is outraged, his feelings unaided by his grief for his son, who perished with Custer on the Little Bighorn River. Reno will be drummed out of the service with a dishonorable discharge.
29. Prentiss Ingraham's first Buffalo Bill novel, "Buffalo Bill, the Buckskin King, or Wild Nell, the Amazon of the West," begins serialization in the *Saturday Journal.*
30. William Bonney meets with John Chisum at Bob Hargrove's saloon to talk about the recent rustlings.

Also in November 1879:

Approximately 400 undesirables reportedly depart Leadville, Colorado, after two rustlers named Stewart and Frodsham are lynched. The following note is pinned to the latter's body:

> Notice to all thieves, bunko steerers, footpads, thieves and chronic bondsmen for the same, and sympathizers the above class of criminals: This is our commencement, and this shall be your fates. We mean business, and let this be your last warning . . . Vigilantes' Committee. We are 700 strong.

DECEMBER
1. The three Earp brothers—Wyatt (31), James (38), and Virgil (36)—arrive in Tombstone, Arizona.
▪ A mob of about 20 people pulls prisoner Dick Hardeman from the Lincoln, New Mexico, jail and strings him up.
2. Tombstone is reported to have a population of between 1,000 and 1,500.
5. The *Cheyenne Transporter* begins its seven-year publishing history in Darlington, Indian Territory, the site of the Cheyenne and Arapaho agency.
6. In Mesilla, New Mexico, the trial of Colonel N. A. M. Dudley for setting A. A. McSween's house afire in 1878 reopens.
9. Three minutes of jury deliberation in the Dudley trial results in an acquittal.
11. Amon Carter, the entrepreneur and art collector, is born in Crafton, Texas.
17. Beadle's Dime Library publishes Prentiss Ingraham's Buffalo Bill drama *The Knight of the Plains* in dime-novel form as "The Knights of the Overland."
25. Mormon colonists—about 250 men, women, and children—celebrate Christmas at Hole-in-the-Rock in order to establish a settlement in southwestern Utah. The planned six-week trip will actually take six months, with hardships galore and the birth of three babies along the way.

29. Charlie Parkhurst, a Concord stagecoach driver, is found dead in Watsonville, California.

30. John Otto, the father of the Colorado National Monument, is born in Marthasville, Missouri.

31. As the deceased stagecoach driver Charlie Parkhurst is being prepared for burial in Watsonville, California, a startling discovery is made. The examining physician reports that not only was the hard-drinking, hard-swearing Charlie a woman, but she also had been a mother.

Also in December 1879:

Robert Louis Stevenson, 29, moves from Monterey, California, to San Francisco, to be closer to his new love, Fanny Van de Grift Osbourne of Oakland. The author will live in poverty throughout the winter, taking one meal a day at a small French restaurant.

Just after Christmas, Jennie Rogers, a 36-year-old entrepreneur from Missouri, purchases a two-story brick bagnio at 527 Holladay Street in Denver from the famed Madame Mattie Silks for $4,600 in cash. Rogers's girls will charge customers $5 to $30, depending on the services and the time spent.

Also in 1879:

There are 430,000 head of cattle valued at $5.1 million in Arizona.

The number of farms in Texas increased by 185 percent during the 1870s.

Wells Fargo operates 524 offices and has an income of $1,737,000 from transportation and $771,000 from express services.

The tally for Dodge City's peace officers: Bassett (seven arrests, $14 in fees); Wyatt Earp (12 arrests, $24 in fees); J. Masterson (10 arrests, $20 in fees); J. Brown (0 arrests). Total amount of fees collected: $58.

The Bureau of Ethnology in Washington, D.C., is founded by John Wesley Powell to examine Indian history, including art, linguistics, religion, and music. Over a 40-year period, the bureau will compile 225 volumes on various aspects of Indian life.

Frederick W. Pitkin becomes the second governor of Colorado.

In a personal poem, Henry Wadsworth Longfellow writes about the "Mount of the Holy Cross," which was photographed in 1873 by William Henry Jackson:

Days of the open range, c. 1879. The end is already in sight. (Library of Congress)

JOHN OTTO

DECEMBER 30, 1879–JUNE 1952

He sprang into Colorado history on the front page of the *Denver Post*, portrayed as a full-blown nut threatening to assassinate the governor. Before he left the scene, he had become a unique pioneer environmentalist. He was John Otto, the father of the Colorado National Monument.

John Otto was one of seven children of the educator Carl Emil Otto and his wife, Amelia. He was born on December 30, 1879, in Marthasville, Missouri.

Young Otto grew up with an eccentric flair, one that had blossomed fully by the time he left for the West Coast in 1898. After wandering throughout the Pacific Northwest, he labored in a California gold camp. Around this time, he developed a love for what would become a lifelong practice, writing letters to public officials.

Otto became so enthusiastic in his communiqués that he was committed to the Napa State Hospital in 1902, suffering from "acute mania." Upon his release, he left for Denver. Shortly thereafter, Colorado governor James H. Peabody began receiving handwritten diatribes demanding the eight-hour workday and equal rights for women. He turned them over to the Pinkerton Detective Agency.

Believing he was being granted a personal audience by the governor, Otto arrived at the state capitol building on a November afternoon in 1903. Officials handcuffed and hustled him away. "I am an ideal Socialist," Otto stated from his cell, "not the kind of Socialist that grows in foreign countries. I am just as good an American citizen as you are." Two days later, Otto convinced the authorities that he had only meant to advise the chief executive, and he was released as a "harmless crank." He went back to Missouri, returning to Colorado in 1907.

At Fruita, he found employment on a water pipeline construction project, as a "powder monkey," one who works with explosives. Politics and dynamite never mix, and sure enough, Otto was back in the news in February 1908, now threatening to prevent the delivery of a speech by Governor Buchtel. At his third sanity hearing in six years, Otto was again exonerated.

Otto then diverted his energies in a new direction: an all-out campaign to preserve Colorado's Monument Canyon country, some five miles west of Grand Junction, as a national park. When he wasn't praising the wilderness in letters to editors and elected officials, he was clearing trails and building roads. On his infrequent trips into town, he collected spare change for his landscaping and stocked up on bacon, beans, and explosives before returning to his tent under the stars.

Local legislators soon joined the bandwagon forming around the "Hermit of Monument Canyon," and in 1909 the land was withdrawn from the public domain pending consideration of its suitability as a national park. Thrilled by the prospect, Otto scaled the 550-foot Independence Monument and planted an American flag.

President William H. Taft visited Colorado's Grand Valley Peach Festival that year, accepted peaches from the Peach Queen, but did not sign any park bills. Otto waited patiently, then penned a polite reminder that began: "My dear President. Almost a year has passed since you visited our valley. Perhaps you remember the Peach Queen. . . ."

On May 24, 1911, Taft signed a proclamation designating 17,362 acres, including six canyons, as the "Monolithic National Monument." Otto was made the area's first custodian, at a salary of $1 a month; as did many others, however, Otto disagreed with its name. Characteristically, he suggested that the name be changed to "Smith National Park," believing that millions of dollars in revenue could come from all the prospective family reunions.

When the area officially became the Colorado National Monument, Otto offered no argument. Romance had come to him in the form of a 35-year-old Boston socialite and artist, Beatrice Farnham. She had fallen in love with the stone-country stalwart, proclaiming to the press: "Western men like intelligent women . . . they don't care for Eastern dolls with empty brains. I find more culture out West than I ever did in the East."

On June 20, 1911, Otto and Farnham were wed at the foot of Independence Rock. From the start, however, their relationship was as bumpy as the terrain. Farnham's proposed "girl's colony" never materialized, nor did her carving of the Declaration of Independence in rock. By March 1912, she had

(continued)

(continued)

deserted Otto, telling the press, "I couldn't live with a man to whom even a cabin was an encumbrance."

Otto took the rejection in stride and went back to work. By day, he carved picturesque pathways that would become the Corkscrew and Serpentine Trails. Many of the rock formations he named for presidents. A huge flag over Soldiers Canyon honored war veterans. He brought the beginnings of a buffalo herd—two cows and a bull—from Oklahoma in 1925. A granite slab proclaimed the area "P.P.I.E."—"a Permanent Place for the Inhabitants of Earth."

In 1926, Otto got into a dispute with a member of Fruita's Chamber of Commerce, Frank Merriell, over the installation of fences. The National Park Service officially dismissed Otto on February 28, 1927. But he continued his work in an unofficial capacity, challenging the Chamber of Commerce on several matters. Then, without his usual ceremony, Otto departed for northern California in 1931.

On the Klamath River, he first resided in a cave, then in a tent, and finally in a small shelter. Letters promoting "the highest class park project in all Creation" flowed into the offices of newspapers and politicians. In 1951, the *Post*'s "Empire Magazine" received one that read: "How big are the Rocky Mountains? They are as big as my heart. Nobody loves them more." The promoter of man and rock died at his California hermitage at the age of 81 in June 1952.

John Otto's contributions to Colorado were monumental. The Colorado National Monument remains as vast and mysterious as the imagination that inspired its preservation.

There is a mountain in the distant West
That, sun-defying, in its deep ravines
Displays a cross of snow upon its side.
Such is the cross I wear upon my breast
These 18 years, through all the changing scenes
And seasons, changeless since the day she died.

San Francisco's California Electric Company, the world's first company to sell electrical service, is established.

"The Exodus of 1879" occurs when 20,000 to 40,000 southern blacks migrate to Kansas on the rumor that they will be welcomed there. Many have insufficient capital to start a new life there and must turn back.

1880

"How many, though, never finish, but mark the trail with their silent graves, no one can tell. But when Gabriel toots his horn, the Chisholm Trail will swarm with cowboys. Howsomever, we'll all be thar', let's hope, for a happy trip, when we say to this planet, adios!"

—Texas Jack Omohundro

JANUARY

6. Tom Mix, the movie cowboy is born in Driftwood, Pennsylvania.

■ Seattle's worst snowstorm drops 48 inches.

8. Emperor Norton of San Francisco, the street person who has maintained his charade as the self-proclaimed "Emperor of the United States and Protector of Mexico" for 20 years, is found dead at the corner of California and Grant Streets. The cause of death is listed as "sanguineous apoplexy." In Elmira, New York, Mark Twain will read about Norton's death and be inspired to begin anew his novel *Huckleberry Finn,* adding a fresh character who would be king.

■ George C. Perkins is inaugurated as California's governor.

9. A second Pacific storm in three days slams into the Northwest; Olympia, Washington, and Portland, Oregon, report more than 28 inches of snow. Railroads are blockaded.

10. William Bonney kills the roustabout Joe Grant in a saloon at Fort Sumner, New Mexico.

12. Santa Fe's first omnibus begins operating.

14. A double wedding takes place in Anton Chico, New Mexico—Barney Maso marries Juana Madril, while Pat Garrett marries Apolinaria Gutierrez, the sister of his late wife.

17. The name "Bonney" appears in print for the first time in the *Santa Fe Weekly New Mexican:* "Billy Bonney, more extensively known as 'The Kid' shot and killed Joe Grant."

28. The Cheyenne, Wyoming, stagecoach and mail firm of Salisbury, Gilmer and Company operates 5,000 miles of stagecoach lines and uses more than 6,000 horses. The *Daily Leader* boasts that the company's payroll could have run the John Adams administration.

National Headlines/January 1880:
27. EDISON PATENTS INCANDESCENT BULB

FEBRUARY

1. San Francisco's St. Ignatius Church is dedicated.

2. John P. Clum sells the *Tucson Weekly Citizen* and arranges to have a press and other printing essentials carted 75 miles across the desert to Tombstone, Arizona.

9. The South Park Railroad is completed to a point 30 miles south of Leadville, Colorado.

■ An Atchison, Topeka, and Santa Fe Railroad train arrives in Santa Fe, New Mexico, for the first time.

10. The Denver and Rio Grande Western Railroad's rails enter New Mexico Territory from the north.

11. Wickes becomes the only town in Montana to acquire a church before acquiring a saloon.

12. Sergeant T. B. Glover reports a fight between a detachment of the 2nd Cavalry and Indians near Pumpkin Creek, New Mexico. One soldier is killed and one is wounded; one Indian is killed, two are wounded, and three are captured.

- Emery County is created in Utah: it is named for territorial governor George W. Emery.
- President Rutherford B. Hayes threatens to employ get-tough measures against illegal settlers in Indian Territory.

14. "Fancy Frank of Colorado, or The Trapper's Trust," a dime novel "by Buffalo Bill," begins serialization in *Beadle's Half-Dime Library*.

16. In San Francisco and Oakland, wool and other factories lay off some 1,200 Chinese workers.

17. San Juan County, named after St. John the Baptist, is created in Utah.

18. Uintah County, named for the Utes, is established in Utah.

- Anti-Chinese sentiment reigns in California. Says the *San Francisco Examiner:* "Every country owes its first duty to its own race and citizens."

22. In Utah, hoodlums tar and feather a vocal detractor, the Ogden *Morning Rustler* editor Charles King.

Also in February 1880:

Frederic Remington drops out of Yale University following the death of his father, and goes to work as a clerk in the New York governor's office.

MARCH

4. Elizabeth McCourt divorces her husband, Harvey Doe, in Central City, Colorado. Referred to as "Baby Doe" by the miners, she has already set her sights on the rich and powerful Horace Tabor. She will move into a suite provided by Tabor in Denver's Windsor Hotel.

5. Governor Lew Wallace leaves New Mexico for a brief trip; W. G. Ritch will be in charge while he is gone.

8. Captain F. D. Baldwin reports that two soldiers of the 5th Infantry and three Indians were killed on Rosebud Creek in Montana.

9. The Utah Northern becomes the first railroad to reach Montana, entering the territory at Monida Pass.

17. Ferdinand de Lesseps, the Suez Canal's chief construction engineer, visits San Francisco.

18. The Southern Pacific Railroad of Arizona and New Mexico is completed to Tucson, where it connects with the San Francisco and Pacific systems.

20. The first Southern Pacific train arrives in Tucson amidst great hoopla.

Also in March 1880:

There are 395,000 bison in North America, down from 1 million in 1875.

In San Francisco, Robert Louis Stevenson suffers from pneumonia.

At its peak, Virginia City, Nevada (population 30,000), claims to have more than 2,200 buildings, including 110 saloon, 29 groceries, 22 restaurants, 15 butcher shops, 11 dairies, eight drug stores, and three funeral parlors.

APRIL

1. Captain E. L. Hugguns reports one enlisted man killed and five Indians captured at O'Fallon's Creek in Montana.

2. In Las Vegas, New Mexico, the jailer Antonio Lino Valdez is murdered by a group of outlaws that includes Dave Rudabaugh.

6. The future western artist Charlie "Kid" Russell, 16, arrives in Utica, Montana, from St. Louis.

9. Captain T. C. Lebo reports that his 10th Cavalry killed one Indian and captured five at Shakehand Springs in Texas.

16. Captain Charles Steelhammer reports one Indian killed and the surrender of 300 near South Fork, New Mexico.

- Colonel Edward Hatch reports that 10 Apaches were killed in a fight with cavalrymen at the Mescalero Agency in New Mexico.

18. At last 24 tornadoes rip their way northward from Kansas and Arkansas to Wisconsin and Michigan. More than 100 people are killed, 65 of them in Marshfield, Missouri, where an entire house is picked up and carried 12 miles.

20. New Mexico governor Lew Wallace visits New York City.

22. Railroad tracks reach Albuquerque, New Mexico.

27. Colorado's *Ford County Globe* reports: "Ex-Sheriff Chas. E. Bassett, accompanied by Mysterious Dave Mather and two other prospectors, started out last week in search of 'greener fields and pastures new.'" They are headed for the mining fields around Gunnison, Colorado.

28. Cooney, New Mexico, is raided by the Apache chief Victorio.

29. Apache raids in New Mexico reportedly have claimed the lives of 12 settlers since April 20.

Also in April 1880:

Robert Louis Stevenson and his intended, Fanny Osbourne, journey to the area around Calistoga, California. With her son, Lloyd, they move into a cabin on Mount St. Helena, where they will stay until July. Stevenson's notes of the trip will become *The Silverado Squatters* (1883).

MAY

1. In Arizona, the first issue of the *Tombstone Epitaph* is published in a canvas-roofed shed on the corner of 4th and Fremont Streets. The editor, the former Indian agent John P. Clum, says that "Tombstone is a city set upon a hill, promising to vie with ancient Rome upon her seven hills, in a fame different in character but no less in importance."

- The brewer Adolph Coors buys out his partner, Jacob Scheuler, in Colorado.
- Railroad tracks cross the Rio Grande at Isleta, New Mexico.

2. Seven settlers are reported as having been slain by Apaches on New Mexico's San Francisco River.

4. Six settlers are reportedly slain by Apaches at Las Lentes, New Mexico.

THE TOMBSTONE EPITAPH

Covering the "town too tough to die" offered perhaps the wildest journalistic challenge in the Old West. The prospector Ed Schieffelin had been told he would find only his tombstone deep in the heart of Apache country, but his 1877 discovery of silver had proved otherwise. Tombstone, Arizona, quickly boomed into a sagebrush Sodom. To the pioneer editor John Clum's way of thinking, this Tombstone deserved an "epitaph."

John Phillip Clum was born in New York's Hudson River valley on September 1, 1851. As a divinity student at Rutgers University in 1871, he dropped out to recuperate from an illness. Rather than resume his studies, he applied for and received an assignment with the Army Signal Service to observe the weather around Santa Fe, New Mexico. Then, in 1874, the 23-year-old was named an agent for the San Carlos Apache Reservation in Arizona Territory.

Disagreeing with the federal government's hard line with regard to Indians, Clum resigned in 1877. He was admitted to the bar in Florence, Arizona, where he practiced for two years. In 1879, he bought the *Tucson Weekly Citizen,* which he turned into the territory's first daily.

On February 2, 1880, he sold the *Citizen* and arranged to have a press and other essentials carted 75 miles across the desert to Tombstone. In a canvas-roofed shed on the corner of 4th and Fremont Streets, two printers and the frantic editor labored until dawn to print the first issue of the *Tombstone Epitaph,* dated May 1, 1880.

The *Epitaph* was not Tombstone's first newspaper; the weekly *Nugget* had begun publication in 1879. The two papers rarely agreed on anything. When Clum himself ran for mayor, the *Nugget* wholeheartedly supported his opponent. Clum won the election on January 4, 1881, by 367 votes. Together with his appointment as postmaster, he had, in a very short time, become the most important man in town.

Tombstone, with its stagecoach holdups, gunfights, and crimes of passion, never seemed to have a slow news day. In order that violence not become the overriding theme of his beloved clarion, Clum usually confined the cold blood to a column entitled "Death's Doings." Still, when a major story broke—as when "Billy the Kid" Claiborne (a poor imitation of William Bonney) attempted to kill Frank Leslie—it made headlines: " 'BILLY THE KID' TAKES A SHOT AT 'BUCKSKIN FRANK.' The Latter Promptly Replied and the Former Quietly Turns His Toes Up to the Daisies."

Looking past the gore to the everyday, the *Epitaph* offered classic frontier fillers:

- "All ladies attending the Leap Year Reception to be given by the ladies tomorrow night are asked to 'bring a man and a cake.' Refreshments are to be served and the combination is presumably for that purpose."
- "A fallen angel was arrested last Wednesday on a charge of using profane and indecent language and had a hearing before Justice Hawke in the afternoon. The said angel vehemently denied the charge in terms so strong that His Honor turned pale and nearly fainted."
- "Sam Small says there are four degrees of drunkenness—the sociable degree, the money degree, the lion degree and the hog degree. Sam shows suspicious knowledge of drunkenness."

Clum and the *Epitaph* parted company on May 1, 1882, for reasons unknown. Some believe he left town during the reprisal attacks that followed the shoot-out at the O. K. Corral. Others say he became grief-stricken when he lost his wife in child-

(*continued*)

(continued)

birth. He worked briefly as a *San Francisco Examiner* assistant editor, then joined the Post Office Department, for which he set up the postal service in Alaska during the gold rush. By 1915, he had a date farm in Indio, California, and was keeping up his friendship with Wyatt Earp, who had moved to Los Angeles. Clum died in 1932.

The *Epitaph* has seen Tombstone through boom and bust under a variety of incarnations. After becoming the *Epitaph and Republican* in 1884, the *Daily Record-Epitaph* in 1885, and the Sunday edition of the *Tombstone Prospector* in 1886, the original masthead returned in 1887. The *Epitaph* then published daily until 1924, when it became a weekly. In 1974, the *Epitaph* split into a local edition, published by University of Arizona students, and a monthly national edition, which focuses on the history of the West. Today, the *National Tombstone Epitaph* (P. O. Box 1880, Tombstone AZ 85638) is received by about 8,000 subscribers worldwide.

Time has tamed Tombstone, but not her colorful history. With an eye for more than a century of news, the *Epitaph* still covers the past in the style that made it famous.

5. San Francisco's Mayor Kalloch is impeached for corruption and graft.
7. The Denver City Council is petitioned by Madam Mattie Silks, who seeks to build a carriage house in the rear of block 12 on Holladay Street, the city's main avenue of prostitution.
15. Three settlers are reportedly slain by Apaches at Kelly's Ranch in New Mexico.
19. The *Santa Fe New Mexican* reports on Victorio's recent (May 12) raid on the Luna Brother's ranch at Las Lunitas: "The Indians, numbering about one hundred in the band, attacked Luna's ranch . . . killed seven people, two men, three women and two children. They also carried away as captives two girls."
- Robert Louis Stevenson weds Fanny Osbourne in San Francisco.
29. Five settlers are reported slain by Apaches at Cook's Canyon in New Mexico.

JUNE

11. Jeanette Rankin, the first woman to serve in the U.S. House of Representatives (1917–1919, and 1941–1943), is born near Missoula, Montana. She will be the only member of the House to vote against the declaration of war against Japan in December 1941.
15. The Ute Agreement earmarks $3,500 in annual government payments to Colorado's White River Agency for the welfare of former captives and their families involved in the Meeker incident.
18. John Augustus Sutter, on whose property gold was first discovered in California, dies penniless in Pennsylvania at the age of 77.
20. Sue McSween, the widow of A. A. McSween, weds George Barber in Lincoln, New Mexico.
22. Buckskin Frank Leslie escorts May Killeen to a dance in Tombstone, Arizona. Afterward, as they sit on the front porch of a hotel May's husband, Mike, appears from the shadows, firing a pistol and screaming, "Take that, you son of a bitch!" Two shots graze Leslie's head. As he is being pistol whipped by the enraged husband, Leslie reaches for a small pocket pistol and puts two bullets into his assailant.
24. The Union Pacific, the Kansas Pacific, and the Denver Pacific Railroads consolidate under the Union Pacific name.
- Construction begins on Arizona's largest church, one for Catholics, in Phoenix.
27. Mike Killeen, believed to be around 26 years old, dies of gunshot wounds suffered in a fight five days ago with Frank Leslie in Tombstone.
28. Texas Jack Omohundro, the scout and show-business persona, dies of pneumonia in Leadville, Colorado, at the age of 33.
- Montana's Internal Revenue Service collector lists tax receipts of $33,714.17 for 1879.

Also in June 1880:

Items from the *U.S. Census Report*, June 1880:

> James Masterson, age 24, City Marshal of Dodge City, dwelling with Minnie Roberts, age 16, occupation concubine.
> Bat Masterson, age 25, occupation laborer, dwelling with Annie Ladue, age 19, occupation concubine.

National Headlines/June 1880:
8. GOP NOMINATES GARFIELD
22. DEMS NOMINATE HANCOCK

JULY

3–5. In three days of violence in Lincoln, New Mexico, a mob kills two prisoners and a deputy at the Lincoln jail.

4. At an Independence Day horse race, the Arizonan George Warren bets his share in the Copper Queen Mine. Warren's horse loses. His share in the Copper Queen eventually will be worth $20 million.

7–15. General and Mrs. Ulysses S. Grant visit New Mexico.

20. The Denver and Rio Grande Railroad is completed to Leadville, Colorado.

22. Black Bart robs the Wells Fargo shipment on a stagecoach traveling from Point Arena to Duncan's Mills, California.

25. Wyatt, Morgan, and Virgil Earp are recruited by Lieutenant J. H. Hurst to accompany him and his soldiers to the McLaury Ranch to inform the McLaurys of the theft of six government mules.

26. The Denver and Rio Grande Railroad is completed to Manitou, Colorado.

28. The Mimbreño Apache chief Victorio begins a two-week-long series of raids in the region around Eagle Springs, Texas.

29. Commenting on the recent appointment of Wyatt Earp as deputy sheriff of Pima County, the *Tombstone Epitaph* says: "Wyatt has filled various positions in which bravery and determination were requisites, and in every instance, proved himself the right man in the right place."

30. In the pages of the *Tombstone Epitaph,* Lieutenant J. H. Hurst accuses the McLaurys of stealing six government mules.

■ Colonel B. H. Grierson reports that the 10th Cavalry killed seven Indians at Rocky Ridge, Texas; one enlisted man is reported killed and four are reported wounded.

31. Two settlers are reported as having been slain by Indians near Eagle Springs, Texas.

Also in July 1880:
Pat Garrett is nominated for sheriff by the Lincoln County Democratic Convention.

AUGUST

5. In a letter to the *Weekly Nugget,* Frank McLaury blasts Lieutenant J. H. Hurst for accusing him of the theft of the government mules near Tombstone, calling him "a coward, a vagabond, a rascal and a malicious liar."

6. Captain L. H. Carpenter reports that his 10th Cav-

alry killed four Indians at Rattlesnake Canyon in Texas.

■ Buckskin Frank Leslie weds May Killeen, whom he widowed in June, in the lobby of Tombstone's Cosmopolitan Hotel.

7. Prentiss Ingraham's Buffalo Bill novel "Dashing Dandy, the Hotspur of the Hills, or the Pony Prince's Strange Pard" begins serialization in the *Saturday Journal.*

14. The *Tombstone Epitaph* reports that Virgil and Morgan Earp helped a Fort Grant sheriff locate a rustler, and that the thief surrendered "when a six-shooter was run under his nose by Morgan Earp."

17. Sergeant E. Davern reports that two Indians were slain and one was captured by the 7th Cavalry on Montana's Little Missouri River.

20. The Ute chief Ouray, 60 (?), dies at the Southern Ute Agency in Ignacio, Colorado, shortly after his trip to Washington to answer questions at a Senate inquiry. After the inquiry, he had told a reporter: "Agreements Ute make with the United States all the same like buffalo make with hunter."

26. A letter from Jesse Evans, who is being held prisoner at Fort Davis, Texas, is intercepted by Captain Nevill of the Texas Rangers. It is meant for a "friend of Evans calling himself Billy Antrim," and it asks the famous outlaw to spring him.

SEPTEMBER

7. The 4th Cavalry reports one soldier killed and four wounded in a fight with Indians near Fort Cummings, New Mexico.

9. President Rutherford B. Hayes visits San Francisco.

15. The *Hays City Sentinel* estimates around 400,000 head of Texas cattle were driven to Kansas this season.

16. Black Bart robs the Roseburg, Oregon–Yreka, California, stagecoach one mile from the Oregon border.

■ The first railroad tracks are laid in Dillon, Montana.

25. The 350-ton steamer *Gussie Telfair,* used by the Confederacy to run blockades during the Civil War, wrecks on the bank inside Coos Bar, near Rocky Point, Oregon. The wreckage will sell for $550.

OCTOBER

3. President Rutherford B. Hayes, on a national tour, visits Maricopa, Arizona, to meet with Indian chiefs. When a member of the president's party, General William T. Sherman, hears someone comment that "all Arizona needs is less heat and more water," Sherman blurts, "Huh! That's all Hell needs."

■ Journalist and author Damon Runyon of *Guys and*

Dolls fame, born at Manhattan, Kansas. (Many sources put birth year at 1884).

4. The University of Southern California is founded in Los Angeles.

■ John Irwin is named territorial governor of Arizona.

11. Doc Holliday quarrels with John Tyler at the Oriental Saloon in Tombstone. Friends disarm the men, and Tyler departs. The saloon's owner, Milt Joyce, orders Holliday to leave but does not let Holliday take his pistol, which is checked behind the bar. When Holliday returns with another gun, Joyce hits him over the head with a six-shooter. A fight ensues, during which Joyce is shot through the hand. Holliday will be fined for assault and battery.

12. The novelist Peter B. Kyne (*Three Godfathers,* 1912) is born in San Francisco.

14. Chief Victorio is slain in Mexico.

15. Following its victory over Victorio's Apaches, members of the Mexican militia are cheered as they ride through the streets of Chihuahua City waving 28 scalps, 17 of them from women and children.

16. Blizzards paralyze Dakota Territory and Minnesota. Many railroads are blocked for the duration of winter.

26. The *Arizona Gazette,* soon to be called the *Phoenix Gazette,* begins publishing in Phoenix.

27. Marshal Fred White is summoned to arrest the intoxicated Curly Bill Brocius in Tombstone. Curly Bill submits peacefully, but suddenly his pistol dis-

charges, mortally wounding White. Virgil Earp, the other peace officer on hand, hears White say before he dies that the shooting was an accident. Curly Bill will be acquitted of murder.

■ Five members of the 10th Cavalry are slain by Indians in Ojo Caliente, Texas.

■ The Atchison, Topeka, and Santa Fe Railroad agrees to build a rail line that will connect San Diego to the transcontinental railroad.

29. Jim Averill files a claim on choice grazing land on the banks of the Sweetwater River in Carbon County, Wyoming. The land has been used regularly by three large cattle outfits, the UT, the Bar 11 and the Hub and Spoke. Averill and the ranchers will coexist for a few years, but Averill will become an annoying presence, thanks to his letters blasting local cattle barons that find their way into print in the Casper *Weekly Mail.*

30. An anti-Chinese riot breaks out in Denver's Hop Alley.

■ "Our town is getting a pretty hard reputation," writes George Parsons in the *Tombstone Epitaph.* "Men killed every few days—besides numerous pullings and firings of pistols and fist fights."

Violence in Denver's "Hop Alley" on October 30, 1880. The Year of the Dragon erupts into a race riot. (Colorado Historical Society)

THE DEATH OF VICTORIO
OCTOBER 14, 1880

The Mimbreño Apache leader Victorio (age 50?) and some 80 of his followers were killed in a battle with Mexican troops under Colonel Joaquin Terrazas near the Tres Castillos Mountains south of El Paso, Texas. Victorio and his people were fleeing from two detachments of U.S. troops, one from Arizona under Colonel Eugene Carr, the other from New Mexico under Colonel George Buell. Terrazas's force of about 350 Mexicans and Tarahumara Indians took about 78 Apache women and children prisoner.

Accounts vary as to who actually killed the firebrand leader; some say it was an Indian scout with the Mexicans, while legend holds that Victorio committed suicide before he could be reached by the enemy.

THE HOP ALLEY RIOT
OCTOBER 30, 1880

The commotion started in the Chinese section of Denver when a drunken cowboy assaulted a "celestial" with a cue stick. Another Chinese fired a shot in defense of his friend, hitting no one. But rumors spread quickly that a Hop Alley resident had killed a white man, and a mob gathered. Windows were shattered, and many queues were clipped from Chinese heads. The elderly Ling Sing was lynched from a lamppost in front of 17th Street's Markham Hotel.

A moment of valor occurred at a Chinese laundry, where the desperado Jim Moon was retrieving some shirts. Moon unholstered his pistol when the mob reached Wong's laundry, and hollered at the crowd, "If you kill Wong, who in hell will do my laundry?" Moon was credited with saving Wong and 14 other Chinese hiding in the establishment. Another act of heroism was performed by one Officer Ryan, a big man who was able to carry a Chinese businessman out of his establishment under his arm.

Hoses were turned on the mob by the acting police chief, David J. Cook, who, with Sheriff Michael Spangler, put together a large force of instant deputies to quiet the rioters. The lawmen, together with the Chaffee Light Artillery and the Governor's Guard, roped off the area, arrested 50 agitators, and had the town settled down by 10:00 P.M.

Also in October 1880:

Pat Garrett becomes a special deputy U.S. marshal, making $10 a day.

NOVEMBER

2. The newly elected sheriff of Lincoln County, New Mexico, is Pat Garrett, who has promised to apprehend Billy the Kid.

■ Kansas votes for prohibition.

9. Wyatt Earp resigns as deputy sheriff of Pima County, Arizona.

10. The Northern Pacific's rails cross the Dakota–Montana border.

13. *Ben-Hur,* the epic novel by New Mexico governor Lew Wallace, is published in New York by Harper

and Brothers. Wallace wrote his Biblical tale when he was not dealing with the Lincoln County War and Billy the Kid.

17. The United States and China sign a treaty restricting the immigration of Chinese workers.

18. The first electric lights in Montana go on at the Alice Mine in Walkerville.

20. Black Bart robs the Redding, California–Roseburg, Oregon, stagecoach about a mile from the Oregon line.

■ The merchants' Board of Trade is organized in Denver.

21. William Bonney and four accomplices steal eight horses from the Grzelachowski ranch in New Mexico.

22. Coloradans reelect Frederick W. Pitkin as governor.

23. William Bonney loses his horse in a gunfight with George Neil in Coyote Springs, New Mexico; Neil loses his life.

27. One person is reported killed during a stagecoach holdup in Arizona's Black Canyon.

28. Billy the Kid and D. L. Anderson, aka "Billy Wilson," elude a posse of eight near White Oaks, New Mexico. The Kid and Wilson sell their stolen horses and make tracks.

30. Billy the Kid rides into White Oaks with Dave Rudabaugh and Billy Wilson but then departs quickly.

■ Miss Jeffrey-Lewis appears in the play *Diplomacy* in Tombstone, to benefit the cemetery fund.

Also in November 1880:

The *Colorado Springs Gazette* reports as fact U.S. Signal Corps sergeant John O'Keefe's dispatches on volcanic activity atop Pikes Peak, calling them "the most wondrous discoveries ever brought to light in this mountain region." The paper adds: "O'Keefe happened to be on the roof of the signal station and he portrays the majesty of the scene as the grandest that he has ever witnessed, not excepting that of Vesuvius, seen by him in 1822 when he was a lad and before he left his native Italy for America."

National Headlines/November 1880:

2. GARFIELD DEFEATS HANCOCK FOR PRESIDENCY

DECEMBER

1. In White Oaks, New Mexico, Deputy James Carlyle organizes a posse that catches up with William Bonney, Dave Rudabaugh, and Billy Wilson at the Greathouse ranch and trading post. In the ensuing fight, Carlyle is shot dead by a member of the posse; the killing will be blamed on Billy the Kid.

2. The 15th Infantry reports one Indian wounded and four captured in New Mexico's White Mountains.

■ In Kansas, Topeka's Crawford Opera House is destroyed by fire.

4. The *Santa Fe New Mexican* comments on the gas lights tested in town:

GAS BEGOSH!
LET YOUR LIGHTS SHINE BEFORE MEN.
Santa Fe's Great Improvement Stands
Complete and Ready for Work.

■ The town of Dillon, Montana, is established by Union Pacific Railroad crews; it is named for the company's president.

5. Gas lights burn for the first time in Santa Fe.

10. The first rail mail service in Arizona is inaugurated; it runs between Tucson and Los Angeles.

12. William Bonney writes a letter to Governor Lew Wallace, claiming his innocence in the death of Deputy James Carlyle.

13. Governor Lew Wallace offers a $500 reward for the "delivery" of William Bonney, "The Kid."

14. Governor Lew Wallace applies for a 20-day leave of absence.

■ Pat Garrett overtakes the Frank Stewart posse, which is out looking for Billy the Kid. Their joined forces head for Fort Sumner.

15. Charles Bowdre writes a letter to J. C. Lea from Fort Sumner, saying that he is tired of running and is thinking of turning William Bonney over to Pat Garrett in return for his freedom.

■ Governor Lew Wallace reiterates his offer of a reward of $500 to anyone who can turn Billy the Kid (William Bonney) over to the authorities of Lincoln County.

18. Pat Garrett's posse ambushes Billy the Kid and his bunch at Fort Sumner. Tom O'Folliard is shot dead, but the Kid escapes.

22. According to the *Santa Fe New Mexican:* "The first edition of *Ben Hur* has been exhausted, the entire five thousand copies composing the edition having been sold. The publishers, Harper Brothers, will begin to issue the second edition of five thousand copies immediately, having many orders in advance for the second series. And the author smiles."

23. Pat Garrett's posse attacks Billy the Kid and his cohorts at Stinking Spring, New Mexico. Charles Bowdre is killed; William Bonney, Billy Wilson, and Dave Rudabaugh are apprehended.

24. William Bonney, aka Billy the Kid, is put in chains at Fort Sumner.

26. Pat Garrett deposits his prisoners, including William Bonney, in the Las Vegas, New Mexico, jail.

27. Billy the Kid and his fellow prisoners, escorted by Pat Garrett, board a train in Las Vegas. A mob tries to take Dave Rudabaugh, while the Kid offers to fight the throng. When the train stops in Bernalillo, an acquaintance, Dr. Hoyt, recognizes Bonney through the window and boards the train to talk with him. Hoyt identifies himself to Bonney's escort, Bob Olinger, and then asks the Kid if he can do anything for him. "Sure, Doc," Bonney replies, "just grab and hand me Bob's gun for a moment." Olinger retorts: "My boy, you had better tell your friend goodbye. Your days are short." Says the Kid, "Oh, I don't know, there's many a slip 'twixt the cup and the lip." The party of law enforcement officers and prisoners arrives in Santa Fe at approximately 7:30 P.M.; the Kid and the other prisoners are jailed.

28. Pat Garrett learns that food sent from a hotel to his prisoners has been eaten by the jailers.

Also in December 1880:
The southern buffalo herd is nearly extinct. Toward the end of the century, the Atchison, Topeka, and Santa Fe Railroad will ship some 1,350,000 tons of buffalo bones back east to be ground into fertilizer.

Also in 1880:
Ambrose Bierce edits the *Wasp,* a satiric journal, in San Francisco. His column, "Prattle," will contain definitions that will evolve into *The Devil's Dictionary* (1911). Bierce will remain with the *Wasp* until 1885.

Eli H. Murray becomes governor of Utah.

California's San Diego County, with 20,000 hives, is the world's largest producer of honey.

The Union Pacific takes over the Denver Pacific Railroad.

The Hunkpapa Sioux war leader Rain in the Face surrenders at the Standing Rock Agency in Dakota Territory shortly after accidentally shooting himself in the knee.

There are 93,671 miles of railroad track in the United States.

Since 1876, 1 million head of cattle have been shipped from Dodge City, Kansas.

Arizona reports an average daily attendance of 3,854 students in its public schools.

The Indian population in California has dropped from 100,000 to 20,500 since 1849.

Wells Fargo, operating 561 offices, reports an income of $1,754,000 from transportation and $691,000 from express services.

Photographer Charles M. Bell's portrait of Medicine Crow, the Crow warrior, in 1880. (Denver Public Library, Western History Department)

The 475,000 head of cattle in Arizona are worth $5.7 million.

In the Comstock mining district, 2,770 men are employed below ground in the mines; only 770 of them are Americans.

The recently widowed Myra Maybelle Shirley Reed weds Sam Starr and becomes Belle Starr.

The transplanted nobleman Lord Dunraven makes his last hunt in Colorado. His holdings around Estes Park have shrunk from 15,000 acres to some 6,600 acres.

The population of Leadville, Colorado, 14,820, supports five banks, three newspapers, seven schools and churches, 38 restaurants, 118 casinos, 35 brothels, and 120 saloons.

An item from the Fort Sumner–Cedar Springs, New Mexico, 1880 Federal Census:

> William Bonney: Age 25; single; working in cattle, born in Missouri; parents born in Missouri.

1880 CENSUS

Arizona	40,440 (a gain of 319 percent)
Arkansas	802,525
California	864,694
San Diego	11,183
San Francisco	233,959
Colorado	194,327
Denver	35,629
Idaho	32,610
Iowa	1,624,615
Kansas	996,096
Louisiana	939,946
Minnesota	780,773
Missouri	2,168,380
Montana	39,159
Nebraska	452,402
Nevada	62,266
New Mexico	119,565
North Dakota	36,909
Oregon	174,768
South Dakota	98,268
Texas	1,591,749 (of which 1,455,967 is rural)
Utah	143,963
Washington	75,116
Wyoming	20,789

Six cities west of the Missouri qualify for the 1880 census list of 100 principal American cities:

Rank	City	Population
9	San Francisco	234,000
50	Denver	35,000
51	Oakland	35,000
90	Sacramento	21,420
93	Salt Lake City	20,768
96	San Antonio	20,550

1881

"Billy was a bad man
And carried a big gun,
He was always after Greasers
And kept 'em on the run. . . .

But one day he met a man
Who was a whole lot badder.
And now he's dead,
And we ain't none the sadder."

—From *Cowboy Songs,* collected by John Lomax

JANUARY

1. Tombstone, Yuma, and Tucson, Arizona, are connected to the rest of the world by the Southern Pacific's telegraph.

■ William Bonney pens a letter from the Santa Fe, New Mexico, jail to Governor Lew Wallace; the governor is in New York, celebrating the publication of his novel, *Ben-Hur.* The letter reads: "Dear Sir, I would like to see you for a few moments if you can spare time. Yours Respect, W. H. Bonney." Wallace will not see the letter until February.

■ Pat Garrett is officially sworn in as Lincoln County's sheriff.

2. Cavalry and infantry under Major Guido Ilges attack Gall's Sioux in Poplar, Montana. A major surrender follows the fight, which claims the lives of eight Indians: some 324 Sioux lay down their weapons.

3. Arizona's 11th territorial legislature convenes; the counties of Graham, Gila, and Cochise are created.

4. *Tombstone Epitaph* editor John B. Clum is elected mayor of Tombstone, defeating Mark Shaffer. Clum's victory margin is 532 votes to 165. Clum also serves as the city's postmaster. In the same elections, Virgil Earp is defeated by Ben Sippy for the post of city marshal.

8. The historian and poet John G. Neihardt is born on a farm near Sharpsburg, Illinois.

10. The Colorado Telephone Company (later Mountain States Telephone and Telegraph Company) is incorporated.

■ A 75-foot flagpole is erected on the Point Lobos Signal Station in San Francisco.

12. The *Santa Fe New Mexican* reports that Governor Lew Wallace submitted an approved bill of Pat Garrett's to E. A. Fisk for the $500 price on the head of Billy the Kid.

14. Johnny O'Rourke, Tombstone's "Johnny-Behind-the-Deuce," shoots and kills the mining engineer W. P. Schneider following an argument in Charleston, Arizona. The gambler then rides to Tombstone, where he is protected from a lynch mob by Virgil Earp, Marshal Ben Sippy, and Sheriff John Behan. Says the *Epitaph* about Sippy's role: "No one who was a witness of yesterday's proceedings can doubt that for his presence, blood would have flown freely."

JOHN G. NEIHARDT
JANUARY 8, 1881—NOVEMBER 3, 1973

For 90 minutes in 1971, Dick Cavett's talk-show guest held the television audience spellbound. At age 90, John G. Neihardt offered an eyewitness account of yesteryear. In a life that extended from the Indian wars to the moon landings, he had seen much to fuel his poetic furnace. Now, he said, he was completing his autobiography and preparing for "the greatest adventure."

He was born John Greenleaf Neihardt on a farm near Sharpsburg, Illinois, on January 8, 1881. Using the poet's prerogative to adjust words until they are just so, he would later change his middle name to Gneisenau.

The third child of Nicholas and Alice Culler Neihardt would recall a happy childhood, though events might indicate the contrary. His father's quest for odd jobs saw the family move to the Solomon River in Kansas, then to Kansas City, where Nicholas became a trolley driver.

One of John's vivid early memories was of when his father took him to a bluff to witness the flooding Missouri River. As he saw houses being swept away, Neihardt recalled, "there was a dreadful fascination about it—the fascination of all huge and irresistible things. I had caught my first wee glimpse into the infinite. I was six years old."

Four years later his parents separated. Alice took the children to live in her father's one-room sod house in Wayne, Nebraska. Here, young John helped with the farm and attended school. His interest in poetry began with Tennyson, Browning, Virgil, and Homer. In 1892, a dream he had during a bout with fever convinced him that he had been born a poet.

During his teens, his poems "Chalboa" and "Tlingilla" imitated the masters, and a send-up of a revival service, "The Tentiad," was published by the Nebraska *Democrat*. He worked his way through Nebraska Normal College as a school bell-ringer. Upon graduation in 1897, he pulled weeds and read poetry in the local potato fields.

In 1900, Neihardt paid a vanity press $200 to publish *The Divine Enchantment,* an epic poem based on Oriental philosophy. The reviews were polite, but the overall lack of response made the author despondent. He burned every copy he could find.

To support himself, he worked as a reporter for the Omaha *Daily News,* then for the Bancroft, Nebraska, *Blade.* In 1901, he found employment as an Indian agent's assistant on the Omaha reservation near Bancroft. Listening to the elders became a passion and influenced his writing. His "Little Bull Buffalo" became a fixture around the fires.

Neihardt moved onto the reservation and stayed there until 1907. That year, a New York publishing house published a new collection of his lyrics entitled *A Bundle of Myrrh.* The reviews were better this time. The *New York Times* called it "a symphony with the . . . riotous joy of the flesh . . . the birth of the spirit and of vision."

His most enthusiastic reader was a young American, Mona Martinsen, who, at the time, was a sculpting student of Rodin's in Paris. She initiated correspondence, then by ocean liner and Union Pacific rushed to Omaha. The poet of her dreams met her at the station with a marriage license in his pocket. They remained together for 50 years, until Mona's death in 1958, and had four children: Alice, Hilda, Sigurd, and Enid.

Neihardt's output over the next six years included two more poetry collections—*Man Song* (1908) and *The Stranger at the Gate* (1912)—four plays in verse, a stack of short stories, and novels titled *The Dawn Builder* (1912) and *Life's Lure* (1914). *The River and I* (1910) was a true account of his 2,000-mile Missouri River canoe trip from Montana to Iowa in 1908.

At age 31, with his typical dramatic passion, Neihardt launched himself into a project that he believed would take the rest of his life to complete. Every fiber of his being would be dedicated to *A Cycle of the West.* He would do for the American West what Homer had done for the Trojan War. Completion of the work took 30 years, what Neihardt called the "5,000 days." Broken into five "songs," the epic covered the years 1823 to 1890, from the first fur-trading venture up the pristine Missouri to the final bloodbath at Wounded Knee. "The Song of Hugh Glass" appeared in 1915, fol-

(continued)

(continued)

lowed by "The Song of Three Friends" (1919), "The Song of the Indian Wars" (1925), "The Song of the Messiah" (1935), and "The Song of Jed Smith" (1941).

He was named poet laureate of Nebraska in 1921. Two years later, he was appointed professor of poetry at the University of Nebraska. In 1936, he was awarded the medal of honor from the National Poetry Center. He also served as literary editor for the St. Louis *Post-Dispatch* from 1926–1938, and then filled similar positions at the Minneapolis *Journal* and the Kansas City *Journal* until 1948, when he became poet-in-residence at the University of Missouri.

Many would come to know him best through yet another work. In August 1930, Neihardt traveled to the Pine Ridge Reservation in South Dakota. There he met an Oglala Sioux holy man who had witnessed the Battle of the Little Bighorn as a lad and had grown up during the downfall of his people. Until Neihardt arrived, Black Elk had kept his thoughts to himself.

Speaking through his interpreter son, Black Elk said he had had a change of heart. "I can feel in this man [Neihardt] beside me a strong desire to know the things of the Other World. He has been sent to learn what I know, and I will teach him." The following spring, "Flaming Rainbow," as the old man called Neihardt, returned with daughters Enid and Hilda as his transcribers. The fascinating interview resulted in *Black Elk Speaks* (1932), a vision of a "sacred hoop of life" shattered by the white man. Neihardt's most popular book, it finally achieved bestseller status 40 years later, after the author's appearance on Cavett's television program.

Like Black Elk, Neihardt lived into a time when he himself became an eloquent voice from the past. He published the first volume of his autobiography, *All Is But a Beginning,* in 1972, and was at work on the second, when, on November 3, 1973, one of the West's great treasures died of heart failure at age 92 at Hilda's home in Columbia, Missouri.

"Rumors of the flesh and whispers of the spirit alerted me to the fact that I'm approaching a change," he said in one of his last interviews. "I see nothing to fear. I believe in the continuation of life, so there's no letting go."

19. The first services are held in Tombstone's Catholic church.

29. Fifteen Texas Rangers surprise 12 Apache warriors and eight women and children at Sierra Diablo, killing them all. This is the last armed confrontation between whites and Indians in Texas.

- Major Guido Ilges accepts the surrender of Iron Dog and 63 of his people at Poplar River, Montana.

Also in January 1881:

The humorist Edgar Wilson "Bill" Nye begins publishing the *Laramie Boomerang,* a comic newspaper named after his mule.

John O'Keefe, the "Pikes Peak Prevaricator," resigns from his U.S. Signal Corps post shortly after claiming to have dug an artesian well on the mountaintop. O'Keefe also complains that he had to smoke 10 pounds of gunpowder tea after his tobacco supply failed to arrive from Washington, D.C. The town of Colorado Springs throws him a farewell banquet.

FEBRUARY

9. White Eagle, the last major chief of the Gros Ventres, dies on the Judith River in Montana.

11. Phoenix, Arizona, is incorporated; according to the 1880 census, the city has approximately 1,780 residents.

12. Major Guido Ilges accepts the surrender of 185 Sioux in Redwater, Montana.

16. In New Mexico, Dave Rudabaugh enters a guilty plea on a charge of stealing U.S. mail. He is sentenced to 99 years in prison, and is informed that he will face charges of murder in Las Vegas.

18. Congress sets aside 46,086 acres in Arizona, Dakota, Wyoming, Idaho, and Montana for the construction of universities when the territories become states.

19. Prohibition arrives in the West. Kansas becomes the first state to prohibit the consumption of alcohol, except for scientific or medical purposes.

- Dolores County is established in Colorado.

21. Governor John Charles Frémont addresses Arizona's 11th territorial legislature on the subject of border problems with Mexico.

23. Pitkin County is established in Colorado.

25. Luke Short, having recently arrived in Tombstone, Arizona, from Dodge City, Kansas, with his friend Bat Masterson, kills the drunken Charlie Storms in a street duel. Masterson separated the men once,

but Storms comes looking for Short again. Storms tries to shoot Short at close range but, according to one account, Short "stuck the muzzle of his own pistol against Storms' heart and pulled the trigger."

26. Major D. G. Brotherton accepts the surrender of 325 Sioux at Fort Buford, Dakota.

■ Robbers take only $135 from a stagecoach near Contention, Arizona; the passengers are unharmed.

Also in February 1881:
Wyatt Earp, Doc Holliday, and their two partners file water claims in the Huachuca Mountains near Tombstone.

Having found very little silver during the past six years, Michael Hickey sells his Anaconda mine in Butte, Montana, to Marcus Daly for $70,000.

MARCH

1. In Santa Fe, New Mexico, authorities look under William Bonney's mattress and discover he has been trying to tunnel his way out of jail. He is placed in solitary confinement.

2. The Security Savings Bank opens in San Francisco.

■ William Bonney writes another letter to Governor Lew Wallace:

> Gov. Lew Wallace
> Dear Sir:
> I wish you would come down to the jail and see me. It will be to your interest to come and see me. I have some letters which date back two years and there are Parties who are very anxious to get them but I shall not dispose of them until I see you, that is if you will come immediately.
> Yours Respect—
> Wm H. Bonney

4. A mine explosion in Almy, Wyoming, kills 38 people.

■ President James A. Garfield receives an inauguration present from New Mexico governor Lew Wallace— a deluxe-bound autographed copy of *Ben-Hur*.

■ William Bonney writes yet another letter to Governor Wallace:

> Gov. Lew Wallace
> Dear Sir:
> I wrote you a little note the day before yesterday but have received no answer I expect you have forgotten what you promised me this month two years ago, but I have not; and I think you had ought to have come and see me as I have requested you to. I have done everything that I promised you I would and you have done nothing that you promised me I think when you think the matter over you will come down and see me, as I can explain everything to you.

> Judge Leonard passed through here on his way east in January and promised to come and see me on his way back but he did not fulfill his promise. it looks to me like I am getting left in the cold. I am not treated right by Sherman. he lets every stranger that comes to see me through curiosity in to see me, but will not let a single one of my friends in, not even an attorney. I guess they mean to send me up without giving me any show but they will have a nice time doing it. I am not entirely without friends. I shall expect to see you some time today.
> Patiently waiting
> I am very truly yours Respect,
> Wm H. Bonney

9. Governor Lew Wallace sends his letter of resignation to President Garfield.

10. The second transcontinental railroad is completed. The Southern Pacific's tracklayers meet those of the Atchison, Topeka, and Santa Fe in Deming, New Mexico, connecting the first rail route from New Mexico to San Francisco.

■ A telephone company is established in Tucson, Arizona.

15. The Tombstone stagecoach is robbed.

■ Abilene, Texas, is established by the Texas and Pacific Railroad and west Texas cattlemen.

■ In New Mexico, a San Miguel County grand jury indicts William Bonney for cattle rustling.

16. A posse organizes to find the suspected Tombstone stagecoach robbers Bill Leonard, Harry Head, and Jim Crane. Members include Buckskin Frank Leslie,

---

THE TOMBSTONE STAGE ROBBERY
MARCH 15, 1881

The Tombstone stagecoach, carrying $26,000 in silver bullion, was robbed just north of Contention City, Arizona. The robbery was an event that led to the "Gunfight at the O. K. Corral."

During the holdup, a scuffle broke out and shotgun rider Budd Philpot was shot, as was the robber Bill Leonard. Other bandits believed to be Harry "the Kid" Head and Jim Crane fired their guns, killing passenger Pet Roerig. Frightened horses ran away with the coach, which was eventually stopped by driver Bob Paul. Later, Doc Holliday was arrested for this holdup, but the charges were dropped.

Doc Holliday, Bat Masterson, and Virgil, Morgan, and Wyatt Earp. Wells Fargo offers a $3,600 reward for the capture of the bandits.

18. William Bonney learns that he has been indicted by a San Miguel County grand jury on charges of cattle theft. He is told that on March 28 he will be transported to a hearing before Judge Bristol in Mesilla.

19. Tombstone newspapers hint at Doc Holliday's involvement in the recent stagecoach robbery.

21. In New Mexico, Jim Greathouse is arrested and charged with the murder of Deputy James Carlyle.

22. In Rawlins, Montana, Flat-nosed George Manuse (aka "Big Nose" George Parrott) is hauled from jail by a mob and hanged from a telegraph pole. The hide of the suspected killer of Deputy Sheriff Bob Widdowfield will be tanned and made into a pair of moccasins and a tobacco pouch.

■ The *Tombstone Epitaph* moans: "What action if any did the Coroner take looking to an investigation of the human arm which was found on the street the other day? It surely demanded some attention."

■ Another posse, this one including Buckskin Frank Leslie, searches for the Tombstone stage robbers.

24. In Tombstone, it is rumored that the Earps and Doc Holliday are implicated in the recent stagecoach robbery near Contention City. Also, Tombstone resident George Parsons reports that many San Franciscans are arriving to participate in the town's mining boom: "Town filling up with strangers. A boom is upon us."

25. Water is seeping into the silver mines near Tombstone.

27. In Santa Fe, New Mexico, William Bonney writes his last letter of appeal from prison to Governor Lew Wallace:

> Gov. Lew Wallace
> Dear Sir:
>   For the last time I ask. Will you keep your promise. I start below tomorrow. Send answer by bearer.
>
>   Yours Resp.,
>   W. Bonney

28. William Bonney is transferred to Mesilla, where he will be tried for the April 1, 1878, murder of Sheriff William Brady.

31. The bones of Joe McLane, the brother of a Kansas Pacific agent, are discovered 20 miles northwest of Cheyenne Wells, Colorado. He disappeared in 1878.

Also in March 1881:

The city of Grand Junction is founded in Colorado, at the junction of the Colorado and Gunnison Rivers.

A Del Norte stagecoach is robbed in Colorado by "Old Bill" Miner and Stanton Jones. A posse pursues the pair in a four-day running gun battle but turns back after three lawmen are wounded.

National Headlines/March 1881:

4. JAMES A. GARFIELD INAUGURATED 20TH U.S. PRESIDENT

APRIL

6. The trial of William Bonney—Billy the Kid—begins in Mesilla, New Mexico. Two indictments, for murdering Buckshot Roberts and Morris J. Bernstein, are dismissed, thanks to the efforts of the Kid's attorney, Ira E. Leonard. Prosecutor S. B. Newcomb then declares that Bonney should be tried by Judge Bristol in Territorial Court for the murder of Sheriff Brady. Bristol dismisses Leonard as Bonney's attorney, appointing instead Colonel A. J. Fountain (a member of the same Masonic lodge as that to which J. J. Dolan and S. B. Newcomb belong) and John D. Bail. The jury is picked.

8. Colonel A. J. Fountain announces that his client, William Bonney, is ready for trial.

9. Billy Mathews and J. J. Dolan testify against William Bonney at his murder trial in Mesilla.

10. William Bonney, Billy the Kid, is convicted of murdering Sheriff Brady. Judge Bristol instructed the jury to return a verdict either of guilty in the first degree or of not guilty. The jury deliberated for only a short time.

11. Major D. G. Brotherton accepts the surrender of 135 Sioux at Fort Buford, Dakota.

15. William Bonney is sentenced to death by Judge Bristol, who orders that the Kid be remanded to the custody of Sheriff Pat Garrett until the execution date, Friday, May 13, when he is to "be hanged by the neck until his body be dead."

■ William Bonney pens a letter to Santa Fe attorney Edgar Caypless, inquiring about the selling of a mare to pay for further legal expenses. He closes by saying: "Excuse bad writing. I have handcuffs on."

16. The "Battle of the Plaza" takes place in Dodge City, Kansas. Bat Masterson, having departed Tombstone earlier in the month, arrives in Dodge City, supposedly to help his brother Jim in business dealings. Bat steps down from the train, sees the two men he believes have been making life tough for his brother, unholsters his weapon, and commences firing. Al Updegraff is killed. After paying an $8 fine, Bat leaves for Colorado, accompanied by Jim.

■ William Bonney is chained to a wagon and escorted out of Mesilla by seven law enforcement officers.

Before departing, he grants an interview to the *Mesilla News* in which he voices concerns about his safety on the 150-mile trip to Lincoln. He says: "If mob law is going to rule, better dismiss judge, sheriff, etc., and let all take chances alike. I expect to be lynched in going to Lincoln. Advise persons never to engage in killing."

18. Lieutenant Colonel J. N. G. Whistler accepts the surrender of 156 Sioux at Fort Keogh, Montana.

19. President Garfield finishes reading *Ben-Hur* and decides to appoint Lew Wallace as the new ambassador to Constantinople.

22. William Bonney is delivered to Pat Garrett at Lincoln, where he is locked in a bedroom on the second floor of what was once J. J. Dolan's store. Bonney is also chained to the floor.

THE KID ESCAPES
APRIL 28, 1881

The day began with a former clerk of John Tunstall's, Sam Corbet, bringing Bonney a note of one word: "Privy." It seems that Jose Aguayo, a supporter of Bonney's, had hidden a revolver wrapped in a newspaper in the privy behind the courthouse.

Bonney and other prisoners were taken to have a meal at Wortley's Hotel. At some point, Bonney asked Deputy Sheriff James W. Bell if he could use the privy. The Kid found the gun and hid it in his clothes. As Bell led the Kid up the steps of the Dolan store to a makeshift cell, Bonney produced his weapon. Bell tried to run, but the Kid gunned him down. The shackled Kid then hopped down to the armory, where he found the shotgun of Robert W. Olinger, a guard. Bonney positioned himself in the sheriff's office, above the path he knew Olinger would take when he came running from the Wortley.

Olinger appeared, reacting to the gunfire. The Kid called him from the window; when Olinger looked up he was blasted into eternity by his own shotgun.

Bonney then called the courthouse janitor Godfrey Gauss to bring a tool to get the chains off and to saddle a horse. After an hour, and with one leg shackle removed, Bonney decided he should ride out of town. He spent the night at the ranch of a friend, the teacher José Córdova, where he removed the other shackle.

■ Tombstone is embroiled in a controversy over the boundaries of the Gilded Age Mining Company.

27. In an interview with the Las Vegas *Gazette,* Governor Lew Wallace is asked about William Bonney's looking to him to "save his neck." "Yes," says Wallace, "but I can't see how a fellow like him should expect any clemency from me."

28. William Bonney escapes from his cell in Lincoln, New Mexico.

30. William Bonney gets a horse from Bob Davis while he hides at the home of Petronillo Sedillo. He then rides toward Fort Sumner. New Mexico newspapers carry the news of the $500 reward on the Kid's head.

Also in April 1881:
In Tombstone, Wyatt Earp is deputized to help protect the Mountain Bay mine in a claim dispute.

Tombstone's population of 7,000 is served by 110 licensed liquor establishments.

MAY

4. The *Santa Fe Daily New Mexican* erroneously reports that William Bonney killed Billy Mathews.

6. The estate of John Tunstall is sold at a public auction in Lincoln, New Mexico.

■ James Earp leaves Tombstone, Arizona, for a sojourn with his wife in California.

7. Governor Lew Wallace again offers a $500 reward for the capture of William Bonney.

10. Two mail bags are stolen from a stagecoach that is en route from Canyon Diablo to Flagstaff, Arizona. Wells Fargo had $125,000 in gold, silver, and coins stashed in the coach's bag. A U.S. Cavalry detachment happens upon five suspected bandits at Veit Spring and kills them, but no treasure is found. (In 1913, one Short Jimmy McGuire will produce some of the stolen coins, but after having four drinks at Black's Saloon in Flagstaff, he will suffer a massive coronary and die. The loot has yet to be recovered.)

12. A story in today's *Las Vegas Gazette:*

> William Bonney, alias Kid, has been seen near Fort Sumner, riding a horse stolen from Bell's ranch. It is believed Billy is on the lookout for Barney Mason, who was then in Fort Sumner. The Kid never had any great love for Barney, and especially since he assisted in the capture of Billy and party at Stinking Springs. If Bonney remains much longer in Lincoln County, hovering about to pay off old scores, he is likely to be shot when he is not prepared to do his best shooting.

19. The Southern Pacific Railroad, building eastward from San Diego, reaches El Paso, Texas.

24. Captain O. B. Read accepts the surrender of 50 Sioux at the Poplar River in Montana.

26. Major D. H. Brotherton accepts the surrender of 32 Sioux at Fort Buford, Dakota.

■ The *Cimarron News and Press* reports that Pat Garrett is on the verge of resigning as sheriff unless the residents of Lincoln County show "more readiness to support him in the execution of his arduous duties."

Also in May 1881:

The future author Hamlin Garland graduates from the Cedar Valley Seminary in Osage, Iowa.

Virgil, Jim, and Wyatt Earp join their partner R. J. Winders in filing for a patent on the First North Extension of Tombstone's Mountain Maid mine.

Jim Wallace, a Lincoln County War figure, drifts to the mining community of Galeyville, Arizona, where he quarrels with Deputy Billy Breakenridge. When Curly Bill Brocius tells him to apologize, Wallace shoots him. Reports Breakenridge: "The bullet hit him [Brocius] in the cheek and knocked out a tooth coming through his neck without cutting an artery." A group of cowboys want to lynch Wallace, but Breakenridge reasons with them, telling them that if Curley "dies they would hunt Wallace up, and if Curly lived he could hunt him up himself."

Rain in the Face continues to hold celebrity status at the Standing Rock Agency in Dakota Territory, as the rumor persists that he killed George A. Custer. The widow Elizabeth Custer will write in *Boots and Saddles*: "The vengeance of the incarnate fiend was concentrated on the man who had effected his capture. It was found on the battle-field that he had cut out the heart of that gallant, loyal, and lovable man, our brother Tom." Rain in the Face tells one interviewer: "Many lies have been told of me. Some say that I killed the Chief, and others that I cut out the heart of his brother because he had caused me to be imprisoned. Why, in that fight the excitement was so great that we scarcely recognized our nearest friends!"

JUNE

1. Union Station opens in Denver, Colorado.

4. Lionel Shelton succeeds Lew Wallace as New Mexico's territorial governor.

6. Bill Leonard and Harry Head, who were implicated in the March 15 stagecoach robbery near Tombstone, Arizona, are shot and killed in the Hachita Mountains of New Mexico by the two Hazlett brothers, who suspected that the pair was trying to swipe their property. Jim Crane organizes a party to go after the Hazletts. According to the *Tucson Star,* "the Hazlett boys were game . . . made a brave fight, killing two and wounding three of the Crane party, but being over powered and finally killed."

■ According to Wyatt Earp in later years, Bill Leonard lived long enough to confess and thereby absolve Doc Holliday of the Tombstone stage robbery.

■ Virgil Earp becomes Tombstone's interim city marshal in the absence of Ben Sippy.

9. The *Tombstone Epitaph* praises Interim Marshall Virgil Earp for preventing gunfire during yesterday's altercation between Ike Clanton and Denny McCann.

11. The Atchison, Topeka, and Santa Fe Railroad, building down the valley of the Rio Grande, reaches El Paso, Texas.

15. The *Tombstone Epitaph* says of Interim Marshal Virgil Earp: "Mr. Earp is filling the position of Chief of Police with credit to himself and satisfaction to the people. . . . There is no perceptible increase in stature, dignity nor self-importance since his elevation to his present honorable and responsible position."

16. According to the *Santa Fe Daily New Mexican,* "a man who came to Santa Fe yesterday from Lincoln County says that Billy the Kid has got more friends in that county than anybody."

17. The *Abilene Reporter-News* begins publication in Texas.

21. Prentiss Ingraham's Buffalo Bill novel "Gold Plume, the Boy Bandit, or The Kid-glove Sport" begins serialization in *Beadle's Half-Dime Library.*

22. In Tombstone, Arizona, it is 100° in "the town too tough to die." The proprietors of the Arcade Saloon heave a barrel of bad whiskey out to the street, preparing to return it to the supplier. Someone gets too close to the barrel with a match or cigar, and it explodes into flames. Much of Tombstone's business district , including 66 buildings, is destroyed. Damage estimates range from $175,00 to $300,000.

27. Tucson, Arizona, reports many buildings damaged and many windows broken after 30,000 pounds of gunpowder explode at a powder magazine.

28. Development of the Atlanta copper claim begins in Arizona.

■ Virgil Earp is approved by Tombstone's city council as the permanent police chief until the return of Ben Sippy.

Also in June 1881:

Construction is under way on Tabor's Grand Opera House at 16th and Curtis Streets in Denver. As the artist Robert Hopkin works on a mural in the foyer, he hears Horace Tabor bark, "Mr. Hopkins, who is that fellow." "Why, Mr. Tubor," replies the astounded Hopkin, "that's William Shakespeare." Tabor huffs, "What's he ever done for Denver? Take him out and put my picture in its place."

JULY

1. The Atlantic and Pacific Railroad reaches Arizona.

■ The *Tombstone Daily Nugget* reports that "due to the late disastrous fire there will be no general parade" on the 4th of July.

5. In Tombstone, Judge Wells Spicer issues a warrant for the arrest of Doc Holliday. According to the *Nugget* he is charged with "complicity in the murder of Bud Philpot, and the attempted stage robbery near Contention some months ago. . . . The warrant was issued upon the affidavit of Kate Elder, with whom Holliday had been living for some time past." Cochise County sheriff John H. Behan arrests Holliday, who is immediately released on $5,000 bail, with Wyatt Earp and the proprietors of the Alhambra saloon as his guarantors.

6. Lives are saved, thanks to the heroism of Kate Shelley, 15, who crawls across a 696-foot railroad bridge 50 feet above the Des Moines River in a thunderstorm and then runs a mile and a half to the Moingona, Iowa, telegraph station to warn a Chicago and Northwestern passenger train that the Honey Creek Bridge has collapsed.

7. In Tombstone, Kate Elder is fined $12.50 for being drunk and disorderly.

10. In Riverton, Iowa, Frank and Jesse James rob the Davis and Sexton Bank of $5,000.

14. Billy the Kid is slain at Pete Maxwell's ranch at Fort Sumner.

■ The first legal hanging in Arizona's Pima County is held in Tucson.

15. Near Winston, Missouri, Frank and Jesse James rob the Chicago and Rock Island and Pacific Railroad express of $600 and kill the engineer and a passenger. The gang member Jim Cummins falls under suspicion; Jesse thinks he may be working with the authorities.

■ William Bonney's funeral and interment are held in the old military cemetery at Fort Sumner. At the order of Deluvina Maxwell, the Kid's grave will be marked "Duerme Bien, Querido" ("Sleep well, beloved"). He is buried with fellow young guns Tom O'Folliard and Charlie Bowdre under the collective "PALS."

16. The Colorado State Industrial School for Boys opens in Golden.

THE DEATH OF THE KID
JULY 14, 1881

Pat Garrett, on the trail of Billy the Kid, arrived at Pete Maxwell's farm with two deputies, seeking information. While Deputies John Poe and Tip McKinney waited outside, Garrett went into Maxwell's bedroom to talk, Maxwell having already retired for the night.

Meanwhile, William Bonney and his friend Francisco Lobato were at the nearby ranch of Jesus Silva, preparing for a late-night dinner. The Kid asked for a beefsteak, but Silva had none. Bonney was told that if he rode to Pete Maxwell's ranch he could have all he wanted because Maxwell had killed a yearling that morning.

Poe would later recall: "It was probably not more than thirty seconds after Garrett had entered Maxwell's room when my attention was attracted, from where I sat in the little gateway, to a man approaching me on the inside of and along the fence, some forty or fifty steps away. I observed that he was only partially dressed and was both bareheaded and barefooted, or rather had only socks on his feet, and it seemed to me that he was fastening his trousers as he came toward me at a very brisk walk." The Kid asked the men, "*¿Quien es?*" ("who is it" or "who is there"), but they remained silent. Just before midnight, Bonney entered Maxwell's dark bedroom and asked, "*¿Pedro, quienes son estos hombres afuera?*" (Pedro, who are those men outside). Pat Garrett, sitting in the dark, had his guns drawn. Maxwell responded, "That's him," and Garrett fired twice. Billy the Kid, age 21, fell dead.

---

17. Jim Bridger, the mountain man extraodinaire, dies in Missouri at the age of 77.

19. Sitting Bull, along with 187 Sioux, surrenders to Major D. H. Brotherton at Fort Buford, Dakota Territory. He and his people have just completed four years in exile in Canada. Newspapers report that he said upon surrendering, "Let it be recorded that I was the last man of my people to lay down my gun." Witnesses hear no such comment, but they do hear him tell his son Crowfoot, age 8, "If you live you will never be a man in this world because you can never have a gun or a pony."

- Pat Garrett arrives in Santa Fe, saying that he is going to resign as sheriff of Lincoln County.
- Three citizens are reported slain in an Indian raid at Arena Blanca, New Mexico.
- The *San Diego Sun* begins publication.
21. Pat Garrett claims the $500 reward on Billy the Kid, but payment is delayed.
24. Heavy rains cause flooding in Tombstone.
28. Missouri governor Thomas Crittenden offers a $10,000 reward for the capture of Frank and Jesse James.

Also in July 1881:

Frederic Remington, 19, takes his first vacation in the West. Camping in Montana, he notes: "I knew the wild riders and vacant land were about to vanish forever, and the more I considered the subject, the bigger the Forever loomed. Without knowing exactly how to do it, I began to try to record some facts around me, and the more I looked the more the panorama unfolded."

National Headlines/July 1881:

2. PRESIDENT GARFIELD SHOT IN WASHINGTON D.C.; CHARLES GUITEAU SEIZED

Frederic Remington (1861–1909). Recalling his first western experience, camping in Montana, he wrote: "I knew the wild riders and the vacant land were about to vanish forever, and the more I considered the subject, the bigger the Forever loomed." (Denver Art Museum)

AUGUST

1. The University of Texas is established in Austin.
- A U.S. Quarantine Station opens on Angel Island in San Francisco Bay.
- Virgil Earp tells the Tombstone city council that the city is "at present remarkably quiet" and that the police force can be reduced to three men.
5. The Denver and Rio Grande rail line over the Rockies from Chama, New Mexico, to Durango, Colorado, is completed at a cost of $140,000 per mile.
6. A heavy rain in Arizona's Hassayampa Canyon washes away 20,000 pounds of goods being freighted by wagons to businesses in Phoenix.
7. The James brothers rob the Chicago–Alton Express outside Glendale, Missouri, and ride away with $1,500.
11. In Kansas, the *Wichita Weekly Eagle* reports: "Billy the Kid . . . formerly lived in Wichita, and many of the early settlers remember him as a street gamin in the days of longhorns."
12. Captain Charles Parker reports that his 9th Cavalry killed four Indians at Carrizo Canyon in New Mexico; two enlisted men are also killed.
19. Lieutenant G. W. Smith and three enlisted men are killed in an Apache attack at McEvers Ranch in New Mexico.
25. Temple Houston, 21, draws public attention for the first time when he delivers a speech at the unveiling of a monument to the heroes of San Jacinto, where his father won the battle for Texas independence. His Lone Star rhetoric brings tears to the throng. The oration will appear in several newspapers and impress Governor Oran Roberts, who will appoint Houston district attorney for the 35th Judicial District, which includes 27 counties in the wild Texas Panhandle.
30. Captain E. C. Hentig and five enlisted men are killed in a skirmish with Indians at Cibicu Creek in Arizona.
31. Black Bart robs the Roseburg, Oregon–Yreka, California, stagecoach nine miles from Yreka.
- Three soldiers and five civilians are killed in an Apache attack near Fort Apache, Arizona.

Also in August 1881:

The Apache Nana continues his depredations in southern and western New Mexico, causing the government to reactivate Fort Cummings. The scout Sam Bowman reports that White Mountain Apaches are being stirred up by a medicine man named Nakaidoklini, who is predicting that dead Apaches will rise and drive the whites from the Southwest. After

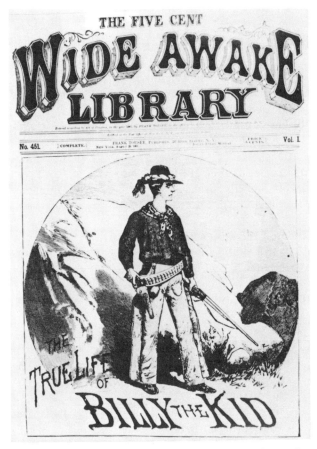

A month after the Kid bites the dust, he's the subject of dime novels. (Library of Congress)

spying on an Indian dance near Fort Apache, Bowman reports: "That kind of dance always meant trouble, and [I] didn't want to get mixed up in it."

The last cattle drives on the Chisholm Trail take place; 2 million head have been driven on the trail since 1866.

"The True Life of Billy the Kid" is published in the *Five Cent Wide Awake Library*.

The con man Soapy Smith operates in Denver. He promises city authorities that he will not hoodwink residents but only tourists at Union Station. His scam: Before a crowd of astonished miners, an accomplice wraps bars of soap with paper money, sometimes with bills as large as $50 or $100; then, the bars are covered with blue paper, and for $5, one can buy a bar and try his or her luck. Of course, the first customer is always Soapy Smith, whose whoop over the discovery of a $100 bill can be heard in the bottoms of the mines. Smith runs the game with picturesque plants—Shoot-Your-Eyes-Out Gray, the Great Gobblefish, Yankee Hank Few-clothes, and Icebox Murph.

SEPTEMBER

1. The Woman's Temperance Union holds its second annual convention at YMCA Hall in San Francisco.

3. San Francisco courts invalidate the city's anti-Chinese ordinances.

4. In Arizona, General Eugene Carr reportedly engages White Mountain Apaches, killing six turncoat scouts and 12 Apaches, including the prophet Nakaidoklini. Apaches in turn attack Fort Apache.

5. Opera debuts in the Rockies as Horace Tabor's Grand Opera House, after 16 months of construction at an estimated cost of $650,000, has its gala opening in Denver. Emma Abbott appears in *Maritana* with her Grand English Opera Company. Approximately 1,500 Denverites pay the hefty ticket price of $2 and slosh through a downpour to attend the opening-night performance.

6. Emma Abbott stars in *Lucia di Lammermoor* at Tabor's Grand Opera House in Denver. In upcoming

The interior of Denver's Tabor Opera House. When the curtain is down, the audience sees a portrait of Rome in ruins, lions roaming through shattered pillars. A verse by Charles Kingsley on the curtain reads: "So fleet the works of men, back to the earth again; ancient and holy things fade like a dream." (Denver Public Library, Western History Department)

performances, she will appear in *Martha, Fra Diavolo,* and *Faust.*

8. James McLaughlin, the Indian agent at Standing Rock, Dakota Territory, writes: "On the day I arrived, Sept. 8, 1881, Sitting Bull and 146 of the more turbulent of his followers were taken down the Missouri River to be held prisoners at Fort Randall . . . and I was left to deal with nearly 6,000 Indians, over half of whom had been out with Sitting Bull in active hostility for several years."

■ The "Sandy Bob" stagecoach is robbed between Tombstone and Bisbee, Arizona; the stage is named for the driver, Charles "Sandy Bob" Crouch. Two bandits make off with $2,500 from the Wells Fargo strongbox and $600 from a passenger.

10. In Tombstone, Deputy Sheriff Billy Breakenridge organizes a posse that includes Morgan and Wyatt Earp, to go after the robbers of the "Sandy Bob" stagecoach. The posse matches the boot prints of Deputy Frank Stilwell with the help of a Bisbee shoemaker, and connects Stilwell with his business partner, Pete Spencer. Stilwell and Spencer are arrested in Bisbee, and their bail, $7,000 each, is met in Tombstone by Ike Clanton. Also today, according to the testimony of Wyatt, Frank McLaury was abusive toward Morgan Earp because of the arrests; McLaury said: "If you ever come after me, you will never take me" and "I have threatened you boys' lives, and a few days ago I had taken it back. But since this arrest, it now goes."

13. In Kansas, the *Ford County Globe* reports that "Charles E. Bassett, ex-sheriff of Ford county and formerly city marshal of Dodge City . . . arrived in the city last Tuesday after an absence of a year and a half. Charley looks as natural as life, wears good clothes, and says Texas is suffering from dry weather."

■ The *Tombstone Epitaph* reasons that if Deputy Frank Stilwell is guilty of the recent stagecoach robbery, "it would seem to be in order for Sheriff Behan to appoint another deputy."

■ Prentiss Ingraham's Buffalo Bill novel "Bison Bill, the Prince of the Reins, or The Red Riders of the Overland" begins serialization in *Beadle's Half-Dime Library.*

16. The citizens of Phoenix demand "Removal or death for the Apache!"

17. Following a matinee of *Chimes of Normandy,* starring Julie Rosewald, at Denver's Grand Opera House, a testimonial is held in the evening for the remarkable Emma Abbott. She performs the serenade scene from *Romeo and Juliet* and the fourth act of *Celecia's Love.*

■ Rustlers reportedly shoot up the town of Gayleville, Arizona.

19. The citizens of Tucson pass a resolution demanding that the U.S. Government remove all Apaches from Arizona to Indian Territory.

23. Dave Rudabaugh escapes from the Las Vegas, New Mexico, jail and makes tracks for Mexico.

30. Forty-seven Apaches surrender at the San Carlos Agency in Arizona.

Also in September 1881:
Lincoln Steffens enrolls at St. Matthew's Hall, a military school in San Mateo, California.

National Headlines/September 1881:
7. POET SIDNEY LANIER DIES OF TB
19. PRESIDENT GARFIELD DIES AT 49 IN NEW JERSEY
20. CHESTER A. ARTHUR SWORN IN AS 21ST U.S. PRESIDENT

OCTOBER

1. Billy "the Kid" Claiborne, a pale imitation of the recently slain icon, kills James Hickey in Charleston, Arizona.

2. Three soldiers are slain in a fight with Indians at Cedar Springs, Arizona.

3–8. The first New Mexico Territorial Fair is held.

4. Deputy Sheriff Billy Breakenridge and a companion discover the body of a wood hauler who was killed by Chiricahuas in Arizona's Dragoon Mountains. In Tombstone, Breakenridge organizes a posse that includes Virgil, Morgan, and Wyatt Earp. At the ranch of Tom and Frank McLaury, they are told that the fleeing Indians stole 27 horses. The three Earps breakfast in Frank McLaury's cabin.

8. A special dispatch to the *Santa Fe New Mexican* from Socorro: "The citizens of this quiet city were surprised this morning in finding the stiffs of Clark and Frenchy, two members of the Ike Stockton gang, the robbers of Browne & Manzanares store at Lamy, a few days ago, and horse thieves on general principles, hanging chained together in a narrow street just off the plaza called 'death's alley,' with a placard on their backs saying: 'This is the way Socorro treats horse thieves and footpads.' "

■ Black Bart robs the Yreka–Redding, California, stagecoach three miles from Bass Station.

11. Black Bart robs the Lakeview–Redding, California, stagecoach two miles from Round Mountain.

■ John C. Frémont resigns as governor of Arizona Territory.

18. A shot is heard outside Tombstone's Alhambra sa-

GUNFIGHT AT THE O.K. CORRAL
OCTOBER 26, 1881

The celebrated gun battle actually took place on a vacant lot in Tombstone, Arizona, when a feud that had been brewing for some time exploded.

Wyatt Earp was told early in the day by Deputy Sheriff Harry Jones that Ike Clanton was "hunting you boys with a Winchester rifle and six shooter." Wyatt, with his brothers Morgan and Virgil, found Ike and physically disarmed him. "I asked him if he was hunting for me," Virgil will testify. "He said he was, and if he had seen me a second sooner he would have killed me." Virgil slammed Ike's head with his six-shooter, and the Earps took Clanton to the recorder's office.

While they waited to be heard, a witness will report Wyatt as having said: "You cattle thieving son of a bitch, and you know that I know you are a cattle thieving son of a bitch, you've threatened my life enough, and you've got to fight." Ike is said to have replied: "Fight is my racket, and all I want is four feet of ground." Morgan offered Clanton his confiscated pistol, saying, "If you want to make a fight right bad, I will give you this one." Another law officer, Campbell, stopped the exchange. Judge Wallace finally heard the disputants and fined Clanton $25.

As Wyatt left the courtroom, he ran into Tom McLaury. After a verbal exchange, Wyatt began to pistol whip McLaury. McLaury reportedly said, "If you want to make a fight, I will make a fight with you anywhere." Wyatt will testify that he responded, "Jerk your gun and use it." When McLaury refused, Wyatt departed for Hafford's Saloon to buy a cigar.

Frank McLaury and Billy Clanton arrived in Tombstone from Antelope Springs at approximately 2:00 P.M. Frank heard about the trouble while trying to get a drink at the Grand Hotel. At this point, Ike and Billy Clanton and Tom and Frank McLaury decided to avoid a confrontation with the Earps, and they headed for the O.K. Corral to retrieve their horses. Sheriff John Behan tried to disarm them, but Frank replied: "Johnny, as long as the people in Tombstone act so, I will not give up my arms. . . . You need not take me, I will go." Ike Clanton and Tom McLaury were unarmed.

Morgan, Virgil, and Wyatt Earp, as well as Doc Holliday, now approached, allegedly to assist Behan in the disarming. The sheriff tried to disarm the Earps and Holliday but was met with a rebuff. Wyatt reportedly addressed the Clantons and McLaurys first: "You sons of bitches, you have been looking for a fight and now you can have it!" Virgil commanded, "Throw up your hands!" Some witnesses reported Tom McLaury as saying that he was already disarmed, and that Billy Clanton pleaded, "Don't shoot me. I don't want to fight." Wyatt Earp will testify that the members of the group went for their guns. The Earps and Holliday then opened fire on the Clantons and McLaurys. Billy Clanton, Frank McLaury, and Tom McLaury were killed; Holliday, Virgil Earp, and Morgan Earp were wounded. Ike Clanton ran away, escaping through a photographer's studio. Wyatt Earp was left without a scratch. Witnesses later claimed that 25 or 30 shots were fired in the 30-second fight.

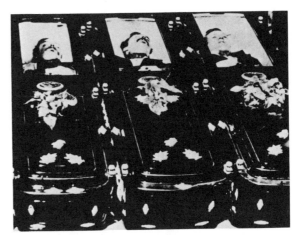

Victims of the O. K. Corral gunfight. From left to right: Frank McLaury, Tom McLaury, and Billy Clanton. Next stop, Boothill. (Arizona Historical Society)

THE STORY

YESTERDAY'S TRAGEDY

Three Men Hurled Into Eternity in the Duration of a Moment.

Stormy as were the early days of Tombstone, nothing ever occurred equal to the event of yesterday. Since the retirement of Ben Sippy as marshal and the appointment of V. W. Earp to fill the vacancy, the town has been noted for its quietness and good order. The fractious and formerly much dreaded cowboys when they came to town were upon their good behavior, and no unseemly brawls were indulged in, and it was hoped by our citizens that no more such deeds would occur as led to the killing of Marshal White, one year ago. It seems that this quiet state of affairs was but the calm that precedes the storm that burst in all its fury yesterday, with this difference in results, that the lightning's bolt struck in a different quarter than the one that fell one year ago. This time it struck with its full and awful force upon those who, heretofore, have made the good name of this country a byword and a reproach, instead of upon some officer in the discharge of his duty or a peaceable and unoffending citizen.

Some time Tuesday Ike Clanton came into town and during the evening had some little talk with Doc Holliday and Marshal Earp, but nothing that caused either to suspect, further than their general knowledge of the man and the threats that had previously been conveyed to the Marshal that the gang intended to clean out the Earps, that he was thirsting for blood at this time, with one exception, and that was that Clanton had told the Marshal, in answer to a question, that the McLowrys were in Sonora. Shortly after this occurred some one came to the Marshal and told him the McLowrys had been seen a short time before, just below town. Marshal Earp, not knowing what might happen and feeling his responsibility for the preservation of the peace and order of the city, staid on duty all night and added to the police force his brother Morgan and Holliday. The night passed without any disturbance whatever and at sunrise he went home and retired to rest and sleep. A short time afterward one of his brothers came to his house and told him that Clanton was hunting him, with threats of shooting him on sight. He discredited the report and did not get out of bed. It was not long before another of his brothers came down and told him the same thing, whereupon he

HISTORY RECORDED

On October 26, 1881, there was a shootout in Tombstone which will be forever famous as the Gunfight at the O.K. Corral. The Tombstone *Epitaph* reported the shooting in its issue of October 27; it reported the testimony at the lengthy hearing to determine if the Earp brothers and Doc Holliday should be tried for murder. And it reported the Judge's decision. Was it a correct one? Read these stories as they appeared in The *Epitaph* ... and judge for yourself.

Direct testimony only, of principal witnesses

got up, dressed and went with his brother Morgan up town. They walked up Allen street to Fifth, crossed over to Fremont and down to Fourth, where, upon turning up Fourth toward Allen, they came upon Clanton, with a Winchester rifle in his hand and a revolver on his hip. The Marshal walked up to him, grabbed the rifle and hit him a blow at the same time on the head, stunning him so that he was able to disarm him without further trouble. He marched Clanton off to the police court, where he entered complaint against him for carrying deadly weapons, and the court fined Clanton $25 and costs, making $27.50 altogether. This occurrence must have been about 1 o'clock in the afternoon.

THE AFTER-OCCURRENCE

Close upon the heels of this came the finale, which is best told in the words of R. F. Coleman, who was an eye-witness from the beginning to the end. Mr. Coleman says: I was in the O.K. Corral at 2:30 p.m., when I saw the two Clantons (Ike and Bill), and the two McLowry boys (Frank and Tom), in earnest conversation across the street, in Dunbar's corral. I went up the street and notified Sheriff Behan,and told him it was my opinion they meant trouble, and that it was his duty, as Sheriff, to go and disarm them; I told him they had gone to the West End Corral. I then went and saw Marshal Virgil Earp, and notified him to the same effect. I then met Billy Allen, and we walked through the O.K Corral, about fifty yards behind the Sheriff. On reaching Fremont street I saw Virgil Earp, Wyatt Earp, Morgan Earp and Doc Holliday, in the center of the street, all armed. I had reached Bauer's meat market; Johnny Behan had just left the cowboys, after having a conversation with them. I went along to Fly's photograph gallery, when I heard

Virg. Earp say, "Give up your arms, or throw up your arms." There was some reply made by Frank McLowry, but at the same moment there were two shots fired simultaneously by Doc Holliday and Frank McLowry, when the firing became general, over thirty shots being fired. Tom McLowry fell first, but raised and fired again before he died. Bill Clanton fell next, and raised to fire again when Mr. Fly took his revolver from him. Frank McLowry ran a few rods and fell. Morgan Earp was shot through and fell, Doc Holliday was hit in the left hip, but kept on firing. Virgil Earp was hit in the third or fourth fire in the leg, which staggered him, but he kept up his effective work. Wyatt Earp stood up and fired in rapid succession, as cool as a cucumber, and was not hit. Doc Holliday was as calm as if at target practice, and fired rapidly. After the firing was over Sheriff Behan went up to Wyatt Earp and said, "I'll have to arrest you." Wyatt replied, "I won't be arrested today; I am right here and am not going away. You have deceived me; you told me those men were disarmed; I went to disarm them."

This ends Mr. Coleman's story which in the most essential particulars has been confirmed by others. Marshal Earp says that he and his party met the Clantons and McLowrys in the alleyway; he called to them to throw up their hands, that he had come to disarm them. Instantaneously Bill Clanton and one of the McLowrys fired, and then it became general. Mr. Earp says it was the first shot from Frank McLowry that hit him. In other particulars his statement does not materially differ from the statement above given. Ike Clanton was not armed and ran across to Allen street and took refuge in the dance hall there. The two McLowrys and Bill Clanton all died within a few minutes after being shot. The Marshal was shot through the calf of the right leg, the ball going clear through. His brother, Morgan, was shot through the shoulders, the ball entering the point of his right shoulder blade, following across the back, shattering off a piece of one vertebrae and passing out the left shoulder in about the same position that it entered the right. This wound is dangerous but not necessarily fatal, and Virgil's is far more painful than dangerous. Doc Holliday was hit upon the scabbard of his pistol, the leather breaking the force of the ball so that no material damage was done other than to make him limp a little in his walk.

Dr. Matthews impaneled a coroner's jury, who went and viewed the bodies as they lay in the cabin in the rear of Dunbar's stables on Fifth street, and then adjourned until 10 o'clock this morning.

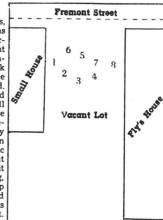

Positions just before the start of the O.K. Corral Gunfight

1. Frank McLowry; 2. Billy Clanton:
3. Thomas McLowry; 4. Ike Clanton:
5. Doc Holliday; 6. Morgan Earp:
7. Wyatt Earp; 8. Virgil Earp.

THE ALARM GIVEN

The moment the word of the shooting reached the Vizina and Tough Nut mines the whistles blew a shrill signal, and the miners came to the surface, armed themselves, and poured into the town like an invading army. A few moments served to bring out all the better portions of our citizens, thoroughly armed and ready for any emergency. Precautions were immediately taken to preserve law and order, even if they had to fight for it. A guard of ten men were stationed around the county jail, and extra policemen put on for the night.

EARP BROTHERS JUSTIFIED

The feeling among the best class of our citizens is that the Marshal was entirely justified in his efforts to disarm these men, and that being fired upon they had to defend themselves, which they did most bravely. So long as our peace officers make effort to preserve the peace and put down highway robbery—which the Earp brothers have done, having engaged in the pursuit and capture, where captures have been made, of every gang of stage robbers in the country—they will have the support of all good citizens. If the present lesson is not sufficient to teach the cow-boy element that they cannot come into the streets of Tombstone, in broad daylight, armed with six-shooters and Henry rifles to hunt down their victims, then the citizens will most assuredly take such steps to preserve the peace as will be forever a bar to further raids.

The Tombstone Epitaph *reacts to the "Gunfight at the O. K. Corral."*   (Tombstone Epitaph)

loon, but no body is found. Says the *Tombstone Nugget:* "disappointed in not having a dead man for breakfast."

22. Milt Hicks is arrested in Tombstone on charges of cattle theft.

23. Says the *Tombstone Nugget:* "We haven't had a man for breakfast for some time, but you can get all the butter, eggs and poultry for breakfast you want at the Boss Store."

24. Milt Hicks, Jim Sharp, and Charlie Thompson escape from the Tombstone jail when a hired boy and a jailer try to remove their dishes. Says Hicks: "We have been in here for some time, come in and try it yourself awhile." The jailers and the prisoners trade places, and the three escapees ride away. A posse that includes Virgil, Morgan, and Wyatt Earp is formed.

25. The Earp–Clanton feud escalates. Around midnight, Doc Holliday challenges Ike Clanton to go for his gun, but Ike, trying to have a meal at the Occidental, refuses. Holliday calls him a "son of a bitch of a cowboy." Morgan Earp, accompanying Holliday, says, "Yes, you son of a bitch, you can have all the fight you want now." Wyatt Earp appears but remains silent. Clanton will later testify that he "walked off and asked them not to shoot me in the back."

■ Prentiss Ingraham's Buffalo Bill novel "Grit, the Bravo Sport, or The Woman Trailer" begins serialization in the *Saturday Journal.*

26. The "Gunfight at the O.K. Corral" takes place in Tombstone, Arizona.

27. Reporting yesterday's gunfight at the O.K. Corral, the *Tombstone Epitaph's* headline reads: "Three Men Hurled into Eternity in the Duration of a Moment." Editor John P. Clum writes: "If the present lesson is not sufficient to teach the cow-boy element that they cannot come into the streets of Tombstone, in broad daylight, armed with six-shooters and Henry rifles to hunt down their victims, then the citizens will most assuredly take such steps to preserve the peace as will be forever a bar to further raids."

■ The *San Francisco Examiner* reports the O.K. Corral gunfight on page 3:

> Desperate Street-Fight in Tombstone.
> Cowboys and a Marshal's Posse the Combatants.
> Three Men Killed and Two Wounded in the Affray.

■ A massive buffalo herd halts a Northern Pacific train near Fairview, Montana.

29. Virgil Earp's appointment as Tombstone's marshal is officially suspended.

30. Says Tombstone's *Nugget:* "The people of this com-munity are deeply indebted to . . . the coroners jury for the valuable information that the three persons who were killed last Wednesday were shot. Some thirty or forty shots were fired, and the whole affair was witnessed by probably a dozen people . . . but people are liable to be mistaken and the verdict reassures us. We might have thought they had been struck by lightning or stung to death by hornets." In the same issue, it is reported that Wyatt Earp and Doc Holliday made bail of $10,000 each on murder charges. Virgil and Morgan Earp, still in their beds recuperating, were spared the serving of papers.

31. In Tombstone, hearings are held to determine whether a grand jury needs to decide the fates of the Earps and Doc Holliday.

Also in October 1881:

The biggest train robbery in Colorado history occurs just north of Colorado Springs, as bandits stop a Colorado and Southern Railroad train that is en route to Denver. The trio of robbers, George Tipton, Gene Wright, and Oscar Witherell, blows open the safe and takes $105,000 in cash and $40,000 in jewelry, and rides off to Corinne, Utah.

NOVEMBER

3. Will McLaury, the brother of two of the deceased participants in the Gunfight at the O.K. Corral, arrives in Tombstone from Fort Worth, Texas. He charges that the murders occurred because Billy Clanton had proof that Doc Holliday had participated in the Tombstone stagecoach robbery.

4. In Tombstone, hearings on the O.K. Corral affair continue with John Behan's testimony.

7. Wyatt Earp and Doc Holliday are jailed in Tombstone in the wake of the O.K. Corral hearings.

8. Colorado voters formally adopt Denver as their state capital.

■ Billy "the Kid" Claiborne offers his testimony at the O.K. Corral hearings: He says he "saw a little shooting."

9. The Texas State Capitol Building is destroyed by fire.

12. Fort Worth's *Daily Democrat* reports: "The trial of the Earps and Holliday for murder is now going on in Tombstone, and public sentiment, which was at first in their favor, has turned now since the evidence shows that it was the gratification of revenge on their part, rather than desire to vindicate law, which led to the shooting."

16. Wyatt Earp takes the stand at the hearings in Tombstone. He testifies: "When Billy Clanton and Frank

McLaury drew their pistols, I knew it was a fight for life and I drew and fired in defense of my own life and the lives of my brothers and Doc Holliday."

19. Virgil Earp testifies at the O.K. Corral hearings.

22. A grand jury convenes in Tombstone to hear the evidence concerning the O.K. Corral incident. One judge complains about "the swearing of certain grand jurors to act as such, because in the cases of Wyatt, Morgan and Virgil Earp and Doc Holliday, there were strong advocates of their actions in cases wherein they would come before the jury."

26. At the O.K. Corral hearings, army surgeon J. B. W. Gardiner testifies about Wyatt Earp's argument with Tom McLaury the day of the shooting.

29. The O.K. Corral hearings conclude in Tombstone. In a separate matter, a grand jury there indicts Billy "the Kid" Claiborne for murder.

30. Tombstone's Judge Wells Spicer hands down his decision in the O.K. Corral hearings: "I cannot resist the conclusion that the defendants were fully justified in committing these homicides—that it is a necessary act, done in the discharge of an official duty. . . . I do not believe that any trial jury that could be got together in this Territory, would, on all the evidence taken before me, with the rule of law applicable thereto given them by the court, find the defendants guilty of any offense."

▪ In Tombstone, John Ringo is arrested for having robbed a poker game in August.

Also in November 1881:

The first telephones in Santa Fe begin operating.

The Sonora stagecoach is robbed in California by "Old Bill" Miner and three accomplices. A posse catches up with Miner, who will be sentenced to 20 years in the San Quentin prison. (Upon Miner's release, he will return to his ways, his last robbery coming in February 1911, in White Sulpher, Georgia. Miner will die in his sleep in 1913.)

DECEMBER

1. In Tombstone, a justice of the peace rules that the brothers Earp acted within their rights as peace officers in the Gunfight at the O.K. Corral.

3. In an incident separate from the O.K. Corral affair, Doc Holliday is arrested and acquitted for firing a pistol inside Tombstone's city limits.

14. Prentiss Ingraham publishes his latest dime novel, "Adventures of Buffalo Bill from Boyhood to Manhood. Deeds of Daring and Romantic Incidents of the Life of William F. Cody, the Monarch of the Bordermen," in the first issue of *Beadle's Boy's Library of Sport, Story and Adventure*.

▪ On the Tombstone theatrical scene, Nellie Boyd's Troupe performs Wilkie Collins's *New Magdalene*.

▪ The editor John Clum boards a Tombstone stagecoach to leave town for the holidays. In his memoirs, he will write: "My greatest probable danger was that, if the rustlers knew I was going, they would pull off a sham stage-robbery, during which they would make it convenient to properly perforate my anatomy with a few of their spare bullets, and thus definitely blot me out of the picture." Sure enough, highwaymen do attempt to stop the stage, which fortunately outruns them.

15. America's third transcontinental railway is completed when the tracks of the Texas and Pacific Railroad meet those of the Southern Pacific Railroad at Sierra Blanca, Texas.

▪ Black Bart robs the Downieville–Marysville stagecoach four miles from Dobbins, California.

16. A grand jury in Tombstone refuses to return indictments against the Earps and Doc Holliday.

18. Bad feelings persist in Tombstone over the Gunfight at the O.K. Corral. An anonymous letter appears in today's *Epitaph*: "TO WELLS SPICER: Sir, if you take my advice you will take your departure for a more genial clime, as I don't think this One Healthy for you much longer. As you are liable to get a hole through your coat at any moment. If such sons of Bitches as you are allowed to dispense Justice in this Territory, the Sooner you Depart from us the better for yourself. . . ."

24. On his last Christmas Eve, Jesse James dresses as Santa Claus at his Missouri homestead, delighting his two children, Jesse, Jr., 6, and Mary, 2.

▪ The 251 school children of Tombstone are greeted by Santa Claus at Schieffelin Hall. The value of their presents "exceeds $300."

25. A peaceful Christmas is reported in Tombstone; many stores are decorated for the season.

26. Disgusted with the legal proceedings concerning the O.K. Corral shoot-out, Will McLaury departs Tombstone.

27. In California, Black Bart robs the North San Juan–Smartville stagecoach.

28. A shotgun ambush on the streets of Tombstone cripples Virgil Earp for life. Earp leaves the Oriental saloon at around 11:30 P.M., and the shot comes from an unfinished two-story building. The assailant is unknown, but the act is believed to be in reprisal for the O.K. Corral gunfight. As doctors tend to Virgil, he tells his wife, "Never mind, I've got one arm left to hug you with."

29. Virgil Earp's elbow joint is removed by physicians in Tombstone.

National Headlines/December 1881:

1. SEC. OF STATE DECLARES HAWAII BELONGS TO U.S. UNDER MONROE DOCTRINE

Also in 1881:

Spotted Tail, the Brulé Sioux leader who aided in the negotiations for the surrender of his people in 1877, is shot dead by Crow Dog in a fight over a woman in Rosebud, Dakota Territory.

The 520,000 head of cattle in Arizona are worth $7.2 million.

The population of Tombstone, Arizona, reaches a record high of 7,000.

Wells Fargo, operating 714 offices, reports incomes of $2,420,000 from transportation and $1,043,000 from express services.

Oil drilling begins in Kansas.

In Colorado, mine owners, claiming an "unjust burden," are able to get the 1877 law that forbade the hiring of children under 14 years of age overturned.

In Colorado, the England-based Prairie Cattle Company becomes the state's largest operation of its kind, grazing 60,000 head on 2 million acres.

Helen Hunt Jackson's *A Century of Dishonor,* a scathing attack on how the U.S. government has dealt with the Indians of the American West, is published.

Denver acquires the first electrical generating plant west of the Mississippi, and becomes the fourth city in the world with electric streetlights.

The brothers Robert and I. P. "Print" Olive establish a ranch near Wray, Colorado.

The first geological survey of the Grand Canyon is completed by Clarence E. Dutton.

1882

"They afterwards took me to a dancing saloon where I saw the only rational method of art criticism I have ever come across. Over the piano was printed a notice: PLEASE DO NOT SHOOT THE PIANIST. HE IS DOING HIS BEST. The mortality among pianists in that place is marvellous."

—Oscar Wilde

The kind of environs Oscar Wilde described in Leadville in 1882. (Harper's Weekly, *June 24, 1854*)

JANUARY

2. Horace Tabor initiates divorce proceedings against his wife of 26 years, Augusta, in Durango, Colorado.

3. On election day in Tombstone, Arizona, the People's Independent Ticket is victorious: Dave Neagle becomes the new city marshal, and John Carr is elected mayor.

4. On the election results, the Tombstone *Daily Nugget* chortles: "EXEUNT EARPS! It is rumored the Earps will take a Holliday."

6. Pony Deal and two accomplices rob the Tombstone–Bisbee stagecoach.

14. San Diego's greatest snowfall is recorded—only a trace of flakes.

16. Margaret Wilson, who will win a Pulitzer Prize for her first novel *The Able McLaughlins* (1923), is born in Traer, Iowa.

22. Marshal George Brown is murdered in Caldwell, Kansas. He will be replaced by Ben P. "Bat" Carr and his assistant, Henry N. Brown.

26. Black Bart robs the Ukian–Cloverdale stagecoach six miles from Cloverdale, California.

27. The Tucson *Daily Star* reprints an article from a "New York newspaper" about wild Tombstone. It says in part: "Few people there die in their beds. . . . A man with good luck and extraordinary vitality may manage to keep out of the tomb long enough to become a citizen, but such instances are rare. Not long since Deputy United States Marshal Earp was found with nineteen bullets in his body and he is alive yet. He seems to be the right sort of man for the place."

28. The Irish writer Oscar Wilde visits San Francisco.

Also in January 1882:

Hubert Howe Bancroft begins an eight-year publishing cycle in which he will reissue in 39 volumes *The World of Hubert Howe Bancroft.*

2.   ROCKEFELLER FORMS OIL TRUST

FEBRUARY

4. There are 370 newspapers and periodicals being published in Kansas.

6. Frederick A. Tritle is appointed Arizona's territorial governor.

13. Wyatt Earp and his common-law wife Mattie mortgage their Tombstone home for $365 and agree to pay 2 percent per month in interest.

18. In New Mexico, Pat Garrett finally collects his $500 reward for killing Billy the Kid.

■   A posse consisting of Wyatt and Morgan Earp and Doc Holliday departs Tombstone to search for the alleged stagecoach robber Pony Deal.

■   Bob Stanley, one of the discoverers of Last Chance Gulch, subscribes to the *Helena Herald,* which will be delivered to his home in England.

26. Frederic Remington's first nationally published illustration, *Cowboys of Arizona,* appears in *Harper's Weekly.*

Also in February 1882:
Roller skating "mania" is reported in Kansas.
There are 26 streams named Bear Creek in Texas.

MARCH

4. Milton Scott Latham, 54, the sixth governor of California, dies in New York City.

9. Garfield County, honoring the assassinated President James Garfield, is established in Utah.

12. Jackson Gregory, the author of *The Splendid Outlaw* (1932), is born.

15. Virgil Earp appears on the streets of Tombstone for the first time since he was shot on December 28, 1881.

18. In reprisal for the Gunfight at the O.K. Corral, Morgan Earp, 30, is shot with a shotgun at 10:50 P.M. while playing pool at Bob Hatch's Billiard Parlor in Tombstone. The shot barely misses his brother Wyatt. Morgan Earp dies within the hour; his last words are: "This is the last game of pool I'll ever play." Morgan's brothers will prepare to avenge his death.

19. In Colorado, Horace Tabor and William Loveland begin organizing the National Mining and Industrial Exposition, which will take place this coming summer in Denver.

20. In the wake of Morgan Earp's assassination, his wounded brother, Virgil, is put on a train bound for California in Tucson by Wyatt and Warren Earp, Doc Holliday, Sherman McMasters, and Turkey Creek Jack Johnson. On the train, the boys find Frank Stilwell, the rumored killer of Morgan. As the conductor clangs his bell, seven shots ring out and Stilwell is dispatched. In 1896, Wyatt will tell an interviewer: "Even at the depot I was forced to fight Ike Clanton and four or five of his friends who had followed us to do murder. One of them, named Frank Stilwell, who was believed to be Morgan's murderer, was killed by my gun going off when he grasped it."

21. The first star of Western films, G. M. "Broncho Billy" Anderson, is born Max Aronson in Little Rock, Arkansas. He will star in the first film of the genre, *The Great Train Robbery* (1903) and will receive a special Academy Award in 1957 for his "contribution to the development of motion pictures."

■   In Rawlins, Wyoming, the suspected thieves known as Lazy Jim and Opium Bill are lynched.

22. The Edmunds Act is passed by Congress. Aimed squarely at the Mormon Church, the act declares polygamy a felony punishable by up to five years in prison and a $500 fine. Unlawful cohabitation becomes a misdemeanor. Those found guilty of practicing polygamy are barred from voting and holding public office. Some 1,300 people will be found guilty of polygamy and serve prison sentences. An appointed presidential board will assume the duties of all registered and elected offices in the territory of Utah.

■   Still seeking revenge for the murder of their brother Morgan, Wyatt and Warren Earp, accompanied by Doc Holliday, Sherman McMasters, and Jack Johnson, return to Tombstone to find Pete Spence. Instead, they find another suspect, Florentino Cruz, and kill him.

24. *The Tombstone Epitaph* reports: "Mrs. James Earp and Mrs. Wyatt Earp left today for Colton, California, the residence of their husbands' parents. These ladies have the sympathy of all who know them, and for that matter, the entire community. Their trials for the last six months have been of the most severe nature."

■   Wyatt Earp's party has a shoot-out with cowboys west of Tombstone, probably in the Whetstone Mountains. The rustler Curly Bill Brocius is killed, although accounts differ wildly as to who did the actual shooting.

■   Horace Tabor is granted his divorce from Augusta in Durango, Colorado.

26. Sheriff Pat Garrett sends a copy of his new book, *The Authentic Life of Billy the Kid, the Noted Desperado of the Southwest, by the Man Who Killed Said Noted Desperado,* to the Library of Congress for copyrighting. The manuscript will arrive on April 17.

■ The entrepreneur Jesse Shwayder is born in Black Hawk, Colorado; he will found the Samsonite Corporation.

27. In regard to what really happened in Wyatt Earp's most recent gunfight, the *Tombstone Epitaph* says: "TWO VERSIONS OF THE FIGHT: YOU PAYS YOUR MONEY AND YOU TAKES YOUR CHOICE."

■ Governor Frederick A. Tritle arrives in Tombstone to examine "the sad state of affairs" there.

■ John Behan's posse rides out of Tombstone, in search of Wyatt Earp and his colleagues.

■ Wyatt Earp's party is denied fresh horses by the rancher Henry Hooker, according to reports out of Tombstone. One rumor is that Hooker paid Wyatt $1,000 for killing Curly Bill Brocius.

28. John Behan's posse arrives at Henry Hooker's ranch after the departure of Wyatt Earp's party. Behan accuses Hooker of "upholding murderers and outlaws." "No sir, I am not," replies Hooker. "I know the Earps and know you; and I know they have always treated me like gentlemen, damn such laws, and damn you, and damn your posse; they are a set of horsethieves and outlaws." Cooler heads prevail, and Hooker serves breakfast to the posse.

■ On his Western tour, the author Oscar Wilde lectures in San Francisco. At the same time, the newspaperman Eugene Field appears in Denver pretending to be Wilde. Field grants interviews and reads poetry. When the real Wilde arrives in April, residents will be confused.

30. Responding to violence in Arizona, President Chester A. Arthur asks Congress for "authority to act against cowboy terrorists."

Also in March 1882:

The famed Indian fighter General George Crook is ordered to Arizona to handle troubles at the San Carlos Reservation. Discovering an atmosphere of paranoia and distrust among the Apaches, Crook writes that they "had not only the best reasons for complaining, but had displayed remarkable forbearance in remaining at peace." Crook advocates an approach of negotiation and honesty toward the Indians. "We must satisfy them that they shall be treated with justice and protected from inroads of white men."

National Headlines/March 1882:
24. LONGFELLOW DEAD AT 75

APRIL

3. Jesse James is murdered.

■ Is Curly Bill Brocius really dead, slain by Wyatt Earp? Both Tombstone newspapers, the *Epitaph* and the *Nugget,* offer rewards to anyone who can provide proof of Brocius's death.

6. Colorado's Senator Henry Teller is appointed secretary of the interior by President Arthur.

7. The *Tombstone Nugget* reports that Turkey Creek Jack Johnson, who has a $2,500 price on his head, is riding with Wyatt Earp's gang.

8. Wyatt Earp's gang rides into Silver City, New Mexico; according to one account, its members are "armed to the teeth."

9. The *San Diego Sun* buys the *San Diego Daily News.*

11. An item in the *San Francisco Daily Exchange:* "It was rumored that the Earp brothers would arrive in Oakland, and the Light Cavalry was immediately put under arms. That gallant and well-trained body resolved that if the two Earps came to Oakland and showed the least disposition to attack them, every man would bite the dust before those redoubtable bandits were allowed the run of the town. Fortunately, the men who were mistaken for the Earps proved to be the Earl brothers, on their way to this city. The joyful news spread like wildfire. Everything is quiet in Oakland now."

12. A lecture on aesthetics is delivered by Oscar Wilde at Denver's Tabor Opera House, where tickets sell for $1.50. The week before, the newspaperman Eugene Field had paraded around town masquerading as the Irish author. Folks thought that the lecture had already been given when the real Wilde arrived. Nevertheless, his lecture is well-attended. The *Denver Times* critic will report that Wilde entered the Opera House in "a languid, dreamy sort of walk such as one would think a lovesick girl would have in wandering through a moonlit garden."

15. Oscar Wilde will recall that before venturing to wild Leadville, Colorado, to deliver another lecture, "I was told that if I went there they would be sure to shoot me or my travelling manager. I wrote and told them that nothing that they could do to my travelling manager would intimidate me."

16. John Allen kills Cockeyed Frank Loving in a shootout in Trinidad, Colorado. The fight begins at the Imperial watering hole and ends at Hammond's Hardware Store. The *Trinidad Daily News* will announce that it will "play down" the numerous gun-

THE ASSASSINATION OF
JESSE JAMES
APRIL 3, 1882

While adjusting a picture on the wall of his St. Joseph, Missouri, home, Jesse Woodson James, 34, was shot in the back of the head and killed by Robert Ford, 19.

The Ford brothers, Charles and Robert, were guests of the Jameses this Monday morning. Their mentor was excited about a new plan to rob the Platte City Bank. With breakfast concluded, Jesse's children went out to play. Noting that a picture on the wall (either a painting or an embroidery of "Home Sweet Home") was dusty or needed straightening, Jesse unbuckled his two gun belts, pulled a chair over to the wall, and stepped up.

The Fords, intent on claiming reward money, looked at each other, numbed by their good fortune. Bob slipped his .45 Smith and Wesson out of its holster and put a bullet through the back of Jesse's head. James turned, looking wild-eyed, and fell to the floor.

When Zee James, Jesse's wife, rushed in, the Fords mumbled something about the gun going off accidentally. The Ford brothers then ran from the house, Bob shouting loudly, "I have killed Jesse James!" Bob then went to a telegraph office and wired Governor Crittenden: "I have got my man."

At the funeral, Jesse's mother became hysterical, wailing, "Jesse! Jesse! They have taken you from me. The miserable traitors!" His body was taken to the Kearney farm and buried beneath the tree from which Yankee soldiers had tried to lynch Dr. Samuel many years before. His gravestone reads: "Jesse

(continued)

Jesse James, posing in his coffin. For most people, this was their first glimpse of the border legend. (Library of Congress)

Fleeting fame for the Ford brothers, as the dime novels cover the deed. (Library of Congress)

W. James / Died April 3, 1882 / Aged 34 years, 6 months, 28 days / Murdered by a traitor and a coward whose name is not worthy to appear here." A heated debate over whether or not the victim was the real Jesse James turned into a true Wild West controversy, especially when the 101-year-old J. Frank Dalton emerged in the 1940s to announce to the world that he was the once and future Jesse. James scholars debunked the old man's story and stuck with the version of events presented here.

Annie Oakley (1860–1926). The West's greatest shot is a woman in show business. (Denver Public Library, Western History Department)

fights around town, so as not to further tarnish civic reputation.

18. The *Albuquerque Journal* complains that the Earp brothers did not pay its office a visit while they were in town.

22. The Texas legislature passes a law that repeals all previous laws granting land for the construction of railroads. Already, the railroads have received 24,453,000 acres or 38,000 square miles (an area larger than Indiana). A problem arose when the state realized that it had issued bonds for eight million acres more than it actually possessed.

23. Apaches attack a detachment of 4th Cavalry and its scouts near Stein's Pass, Arizona, killing four.

24. The Trades Assembly State Convention meets with anti-Chinese organizations in San Francisco.

26. President Arthur orders federal troops into Arizona to deal with "cowboy" terrorists.

27. The Phoenix Guards offer their services to Governor Tritle to help drive the Apaches out of Arizona.

28. Captain T. C. Tupper reports six Indians slain in a fight in New Mexico's Hatchet Mountains.

29. Cheyenne, Wyoming, boasts a population of 5,000.

Also in April 1882:

Augusta Tabor files for separate maintenance against her husband, Horace, who was granted a divorce in Durango, Colorado, last month.

National Headlines/April 1882:

19. CHARLES DARWIN DIES AT 73

27. RALPH WALDO EMERSON DIES AT 79

MAY

1. In Springfield, Ohio, the shooter John Graham falls ill and is unable to perform with his partner, Frank Butler, at a shooting match. In true showbiz fashion, Mrs. Butler, Phoebe Ann Moses, takes Graham's place, and a star is born. Desiring a stage name for the occasion, she chooses "Annie Oakley," for Oakley, Ohio, where she and Butler met in 1875 at a shooting match.

■ The editor John Clum sells the *Tombstone Epitaph,* which he established in 1880. The reasons for his departure from Tombstone are unclear. Some believe that he left town during the reprisal attacks in the wake of the O.K. Corral gunfight; others say he became grief-stricken when he lost his wife in childbirth.

3. Lawlessness in Cochise County, Arizona, prompts President Arthur to threaten to impose martial law.

5. The boundaries of the Gila Reservation in Arizona are expanded.

■ The *Tombstone Daily Nugget,* established in 1879, ceases publication.

6. President Arthur signs the Chinese Exclusion Act into law after Congress overrides his veto; no Chinese laborers will be admitted into the United States until 1892.

9. Voters in Helena, Montana, adopt a proposal to allow black children to attend the city's schools; the vote is 195 to 115.

■ The Telegraph Hill Railroad Company is organized in San Francisco.

10. A survey for the townsite of Sheridan, Wyoming, begins.

16. Shortly after reportedly falling out with Wyatt Earp in Trinidad, Colorado, Doc Holliday is arrested in Denver for the murder of Frank Stilwell. Arizona authorities will try to extradite Doc Holliday for questioning.

17. In Denver, one of Doc Holliday's old acquaintances, Bat Masterson, obtains a writ of habeas corpus on Holliday's behalf.

22. Another saloon fire ignites a major portion of the business district of Tombstone, Arizona.

■ The *Rocky Mountain News* interviews Doc Holliday, describing him as "the terror of the lawless element in Arizona, and with the Earpps [sic] was the only man brave enough to face the bloodthirsty crowd, which has made the name of Arizona a stench in the nostrils of decent men." In the interview, Holliday calls Sheriff John Behan "a deadly enemy of mine, who would give any money to have me killed."

23. The convicted murderer Jesse Evans of Lincoln County War fame, on a work-exchange program with a Texas prison, escapes and disappears from history.

24. In Colorado, the Burlington Railroad completes laying tracks to Barr City, where it meets a crew that has been laying tracks from Denver.

25. In Wyoming, the Cheyenne Opera House, constructed at a cost of $50,000, is dedicated.

27. Virgil Earp is in San Francisco, seeking medical help for his injured arm. Says the *Daily Examiner,* "Virgil Earp is not a ruffian in appearance."

29. Colorado's Governor Pitkin, after a discussion with Bat Masterson, denies Arizona's request for Doc Holliday's extradition.

Also in May 1882:

Whooping cough and malarial fever ravage Indian tribes in Texas, including the Kiowas, the Kiowa-Apaches, the Wichitas, and the Comanches.

National Headlines/May 1882:

15. GREELY EXPEDITION 600 MILES FROM NORTH POLE

JUNE

1. The Pueblo, Colorado, *Chieftain,* commenting on a biography of Doc Holliday that appeared in the *Cincinnati Enquirer,* says: "It was made to appear that he has in his time killed over fifty men, and that Jesse James is a saint compared to him."

3. The *Tucson Citizen* carries the story of Colorado's failure to extradite Doc Holliday to Arizona.

10. The last great buffalo hunt of the Sioux begins, under the auspices of Indian agent James McLaughlin of the Standing Rock Agency in Dakota Territory. Some 2,000 Sioux, 600 of them hunters, were permitted to travel 100 miles west, to Hiddenwood Creek, with the last of the northern herd, about 50,000 bison. Approximately 2,000 buffalo are killed on the first day.

11. Sioux at the buffalo hunt butcher the first day's kill. Writes McLaughlin: "I never have known an Indian to kill a game animal that he did not require for his needs."

12. The last great buffalo hunt of the Sioux ends with the slaying of another 3,000 buffalo. Writes McLaughlin: "The great hunters, head men of the Sioux Nations . . . were all in that hunt and at peace on the banks of the Hiddenwood Creek that night."

14. Black Bart robs the Little Lake–Ukiah, California, stagecoach.

17. A tornado strikes Grinnell, Iowa, and leaves 130 persons dead over a 200-mile path.

18. The first Episcopal services in Arizona are held in Tombstone.

20. Annie Oakley and Frank Butler are issued a marriage certificate in Windsor, Ontario, Canada, although they first tied the knot in 1876. Historians believe that Frank's divorce might not have been final at the time of the 1876 wedding, and that his and Annie's vows were reaffirmed in 1882.

24. A racially motivated street battle erupts between whites and Mexicans in St. Johns, Arizona. Texas cowboys led by Nat Greer start the fight, in which two persons are killed.

Also in June 1882:

Frederic Remington, 21, paint brushes in hand, appears on the old Chisholm Trail. He will also sketch military life at Fort Reno in Indian Territory and Native Americans at the Darlington Indian Agency. Much of this work will appear in *Crooked Trails.*

Isabella L. Bird publishes *A Lady's Life in the Rocky Mountains.*

JULY

4. In a crap game in Pueblo, Colorado, the engineer Henry Arbuckle wins the "Little Emma" railroad engine, which he will use to fight Indians.

- The Telegraph Hill Observatory begins operations in San Francisco.
10. The *Tombstone Epitaph* reports: "About noontime yesterday the remains of the late Kiv Phillips were taken from the undertaker's room on Allen street and started on the journey to San Francisco. The body was not well embalmed and the stench was beginning to get so great it was feared the express company would not ship it."
11. Marshal Ben Thompson of Austin, Texas, decides to settle his two-year gambling feud with Jack Harris, the part-owner of San Antonio's Vaudeville Theatre and Gambling Saloon. Thompson appears in San Antonio, looking for Harris, who is waiting in his office with a shotgun across his lap. Thompson fires through the venetian blinds, wounding Harris, and then steps into the office and finishes him off. Thompson will resign his post following the incident.
- The Denver and Rio Grande's extension of rails from Durango to Silverton, Colorado, is completed.
- The rancher William Reynolds rides into Tombstone, claiming that Buckskin Frank Leslie killed his wife Molly Bradshaw and wounded a hired hand named James Neal the previous night. Reynolds, who found Neal, reports that Leslie is "still on the fight and acting like a crazy man." A Dr. Goodfellow rides out and finds the body of Bradshaw, as well as the wounded Neal.
12. The *Tombstone Epitaph* reports that Johnny Ringo is drunk in Galeyville, Arizona.
13. Black Bart attempts to rob the LaPorte–Oroville stagecoach nine miles from Strawberry Valley, California.
14. The gunfighter Johnny Ringo is found dead in Arizona Territory's Turkey Creek Canyon. Some will claim he was a suicide, but others will find that hard to believe because Ringo was found scalped. Billy "the Kid" Claiborne will claim that Buckskin Frank Leslie is the chief suspect, but a perhaps more reliable source, Pony Deal, will blame Johnny O'Rourke. Ringo's murder will never be solved.
15. There are 457 farms in Wyoming, up from 176 in 1870.
17. Major A. W. Evans directs eight companies of cavalrymen as well as Indian scouts in a battle against Indians at Big Dry Wash or Chevelons Fork, Arizona. One soldier is killed and seven are wounded; 16 Indians are killed.
23. Mormons buy 80 acres of land in Arizona from Charles Hayden for $3,000, and begin the settlement of Tempe.
25. Roy Bean mails to a San Antonio newspaper a postcard announcing the first saloon west of the Pecos River.

Also in July 1882:
"Frank James on the Trail" is published by *Morrison's Sensational Stories*.

AUGUST
2. In Texas, Roy Bean is appointed justice of the peace by the Texas Rangers Captain T. L. Oglesby. Bean resides in Eagle's Nest Springs, but he will soon relocate to nearby Langtry.
3. The Cheyenne Electric Light Company is incorporated in Wyoming.
4. In Kansas, Fort Larned, established in 1859 to protect traders along the Santa Fe Trail, is officially abandoned. (The sandstone ruins can be viewed at the 406-acre Fort Larned National Historic Site.)
- The first post office in Billings, Montana, opens.
5. The Powder River Cattle Company, owned by Moreton Frewen, is incorporated with initial capital of $1.5 million on the London stock exchange.
12. The Northern Pacific Railroad's tracks pass the site of the future Billings, Montana.
19. In Colorado, a feud between Las Animas County undersheriff M. B. McGraw and Trinidad police officer George Goodell erupts into gunfire shortly after McGraw asserts in a letter to the editor of the *Trinidad Democrat* that Goodell and his wife are pimp and prostitute. The fight occurs in Trinidad, in front of Jaffa's Opera House, where Goodell puts six bullets into McGraw.
21. Las Animas County undersheriff M. B. McGraw dies of wounds he suffered in his August 19 duel with George Goodell in Trinidad, Colorado.
23. Two murderers are lynched from a tree on the main street of Globe, Arizona.

National Headlines/August 1882:
3. FEDS RESTRICT IMMIGRATION; BAR CONVICTS, LUNATICS, PAUPERS

SEPTEMBER
1. San Francisco carpenters get their demand—one eight-hour day per week, on Saturdays.
11. In Bisbee, Arizona, miners take a break from their work to lynch an intoxicated murderer.
12. In eastern Kansas, dry winds cause the crops to wither.
14. The Carlisle School, founded in 1879 in Pennsylvania, reports an enrollment of 360 Indian students representing 29 tribes. Sitting Bull's Sioux tribe has 10 students enrolled in the school.

17. Black Bart robs the Yreka–Redding, California, stagecoach 14 miles from Redding.
29. A documented conversation on the streets of Cheyenne: Resident: "All that's needed in Wyoming is water and good society." Tenderfoot: "Why, that's all they need in Hell, isn't it?"
■ Fort Sanders is sold at a public auction at Laramie, Wyoming.
30. Colorado's lieutenant governor, the millionaire Horace Tabor, secretly weds Elizabeth McCourt ("Baby" Doe) three months before his divorce from his wife of 20 years is final.

Also in September 1882:

Jack London enters the first grade at the West End School in Oakland, California. He has already had his first bout with the bottle, an episode he will recall in *John Barleycorn* (1913).

In Kansas, the *Manhattan Enterprise,* published by Alfred Runyan, the father of 2-year-old Damon, folds. The family will begin a series of relocations.

National Headlines/September 1882:
5. FIRST LABOR DAY PARADE IN NYC

OCTOBER
2. Strong winds inflict damage throughout northern California. In the Sacramento Valley, thousands of trees are uprooted.
4. On his 21st birthday, Frederic Remington returns to the West from Albany, New York, this time to a Kansas farm where he will be a cowboy by day and a painter by night.
5. Frank James surrenders in Missouri.
19. Henry N. Brown, the assistant marshal in Caldwell, Kansas, assumes the duties of city marshal while Ben Carr takes a leave of absence.
22. The Cheyenne, Wyoming, telephone exchange lists 135 names, while Laramie's lists 70.
23. Seven dangerous convicts escape from the county jail in Tucson, Arizona.

NOVEMBER
2. The newly elected sheriff of Lincoln County, New Mexico, is John Poe, who replaces Pat Garrett.
3. America's largest county is Custer County, Montana; it covers 36,000 square miles.
6. The British actress Lillie Langtry, who will become Judge Roy Bean's favorite celebrity, makes her American debut at New York's Fifth Avenue Theater in Shakespeare's *As You Like It.*
7. In Wyoming, Fort Laramie experiences an earthquake.

THE SURRENDER OF FRANK JAMES
OCTOBER 5, 1882

The outlaw Frank James surrendered to Missouri governor Thomas Crittenden six months after his brother Jesse was murdered. Before a gathering of the press, Frank said: "I want to hand over to you that which no living man except myself has been permitted to touch since 1861, and to say that I am your prisoner." With that Frank presented the governor his guns and was taken to a jail in Independence.

Frank James was eventually acquitted of his crimes and spent his last 32 years as a laborer. He sold shoes in Nevada and Missouri, and worked for the Mittenthal Clothing Company in Dallas and as a livestock importer in Paris, Texas. From 1894–1900, he was a doorman at a St. Louis burlesque house, and he toured with a theater company from 1901–1905. From age 70 until his death in 1915, James charged tourists 50 cents to view the Missouri cabin in which he and his brother were born.

---

8. Indian scouts report that they killed two hostile Indians at Toullock's Fork in Montana.
13. Billy "the Kid" Claiborne stumbles into Tombstone's Oriental Saloon, where Buckskin Frank Leslie is tending bar. Leslie refuses to serve the drunken Kid and slaps him. Claiborne explodes: "You'd best get your gun and come a runnin', 'cause I aim to shoot you full of holes for this insult, as well as for having a hand in the killing of my friend John Ringo." Leslie tosses him into the street.
14. At 7:30 A.M., the shotgun-toting William F. "Billy the Kid" Claiborne, 22, seeks out Frank Leslie, who has strapped on his .45 Colt Peacemaker. Leslie spots his adversary on a corner of Allen Street, and approaches quietly from behind. When he is within range, he calls out to Claiborne, who wheels around and fires. Leslie returns two quick shots, and Claiborne falls. As Leslie walks toward him, Claiborne says: "Don't shoot again, I am killed." One observer comments that Claiborne "sure weren't no Billy the Kid. Missed with a saddle gun at thirty feet."
15. A telegraph wire connects Deer Lodge with Helena, Montana.

17. Rain in the Face and 500 Sioux surrender at Fort Keogh, Montana.

■ The cornerstone for the University of Texas is laid in Austin.

18. Prentiss Ingraham's Buffalo Bill novel "The League of Three, or Buffalo Bill's Pledge" begins serialization in the *Banner Weekly.*

24. Black Bart robs the Lakeport–Cloverdale stagecoach six miles from Cloverdale, California.

25. San Francisco's Fort Point is renamed Fort Winfield Scott.

Also in November 1882:
Colorado voters elect James Benton Grant governor.

Thomas Moran paints *Cliffs of the Upper Colorado River, Wyoming Territory.*

While working the Anaconda mine, which he purchased last year, for silver, Marcus Daly and his miners hit a vein of solid copper 300 feet below ground; the vein will be found to be 600 feet deep and 100 feet wide. By 1892, the Anaconda mine will be the world's largest copper producer, yielding 100 million pounds annually.

DECEMBER

12. The Gila Bend Indian Reservation is set aside for the Papago Indians of Arizona.

19. The Denver and Rio Grande Railroad is completed to Grand Junction, Colorado.

28. Henry N. Brown, the assistant marshal of Caldwell, Kansas, is appointed city marshal.

30. Josephine Meeker (born in 1857), the daughter of colonist Nathan Meeker, dies in Washington, D.C., of pneumonia. She will be buried next to her father in Greeley, Colorado.

Also in December 1882:
The photographer Alexander Martin relocates his business from Central City to Denver, Colorado. The *Denver Tribune's* editor, Eugene Field, is fascinated by Martin's "ghost photographs" and urges him to hit the lecture circuit.

National Headlines/December 1882:
25. FIRST ELECTRIFIED CHRISTMAS TREE IN NYC

Also in 1882:
The newspaper *Indian Chieftain* is started in Vinita, Indian Territory. Later in the year, it will be taken over by whites and become an exponent of their points of view.

Judge Isaac Parker sentences Belle Starr to a year in a Detroit, Michigan, house of corrections for horse theft.

There are 570,000 head of cattle worth $10.8 million in Arizona.

Wells Fargo, operating 927 offices, reports incomes of $3,045,000 from transportation and $1,314,000 from express services.

The Indian Rights Association is founded.

The Colorado lawman Dave Cook publishes his riproaring memoirs, *Hands Up, or Twenty Years of Detective Life in the Mountains and on the Plains.*

Robert LeRoy Parker, soon to become known as Butch Cassidy, leaves his home in Beaver, Utah, at age 16 to become a bandit.

The author Charles Siringo notes that he sees Clay Allison on the Pecos River in New Mexico with a new bride, looking for a place to settle down.

In Kansas, Fort Dodge is closed. A local editor predicts: "As the homely child becomes a handsome man, so

An El Socorro, New Mexico, saloon, c. 1882. (Library of Congress)

will Dodge, born of ugliness and roughness, mature in brightness and smoothness."

The future artist Charles M. Russell, 18, works as a night wrangler in Montana. He cow punches by night and sketches by day.

Mark Twain returns to Keokuk, Iowa, to gather material for his work in progress, *Life on the Mississippi.*

Helen Hunt Jackson visits San Jacinto, California, where she meets Ramona Lubo, a Cahuilla Indian who will serve as the model for the lead character of her novel *Ramona* (1884).

Fort Benton on the Missouri River in Montana is abandoned.

Sitting Bull's remaining Sioux followers return from Canada.

This is considered as the "last great year" for buffalo hunting in Montana.

1883

"No sight is more common on the plains than that of a bleached buffalo skull."
—Theodore Roosevelt

JANUARY

1. Mayor A. M. Colson and the citizens of Caldwell, Kansas, present Marshal Henry N. Brown with an engraved Winchester.

■ Badger Clark, the cowboy poet and author of *Sun and Saddle Leather* (1915), is born in Albia, Iowa.

4. The Hualapai Indian Reservation is established in Arizona.

5. A fire in Prescott, Arizona, destroys property worth $90,000.

12. Electric lights are turned on in Cheyenne, Wyoming, for the first time.

■ The Montana Wool Growers Association organizes at Fort Benton.

■ On his 7th birthday, Jack London moves with his family from a farm in Alameda, California, to one south of San Francisco, near Colma.

13. Prentiss Ingraham's "Buffalo Bill's Grip, or Oathbound to Custer" begins serialization in *Beadle's Dime Library*.

26. In Colorado, Thomas Bowen is elected to succeed N. P. Hill in the U.S. Senate. Lieutenant governor Horace Tabor is appointed to complete Henry Teller's unexpired Senate term, which will last only 30 days. Tabor will immediately begin planning to publicly wed Elizabeth McCourt ("Baby") Doe in a lavish public ceremony in Washington, D.C. It is not public knowledge that he married her secretly last September. He writes to his young bride, "I am yours from hair to toes and back again."

Also in January 1883:

The remains of the Sac chief Keokuk (who died in 1848) are removed from Franklin County, Kansas, and brought to his namesake city of Keokuk, Iowa, where they are interred beneath a monument.

Augusta Tabor wins a settlement from Horace, noting her ex-husband's desertion of July, 1880, and listing his net worth at $9.5 million with a monthly income of $100,000. The press has a field day. She settles for her home and about $300,000 in mining stock. Her husband's secret marriage to Elizabeth McCourt in Sept. of '82 is still a secret.

National Headlines/January 1883:

10. WORST U.S. HOTEL FIRE CLAIMS 71 IN MILWAUKEE

FEBRUARY

3. The author Clarence Edward Mulford, creator of the character "Hopalong Cassidy," is born.

5. The "Sunset Route" is completed by the Southern Pacific when its tracks from New Mexico reach New Orleans. The railroad benefited when it absorbed the tracks of the Galveston, Harrisburg and San Antonio.

10. Garfield County is established in Colorado.

11. The Colorado legislature makes an initial appropriation for the construction of a state capitol building.

■ Delta, Eagle, and Montrose Counties are established in Colorado.

13. The city of Denver's boundaries are extended to take in an additional 4,625 acres.
14. Mesa County is established in Colorado.
- Temple Houston weds his sweetheart Laura Cross; they will live in Mobeetie, Texas.
23. The University of North Dakota is chartered at Grand Forks.
26. The Rocky Mountain Bell Telephone Company is organized in Utah Territory; it will also serve Montana.

Also in February 1883:

The Fort Union, New Mexico, Dramatic Club is hailed by the *Las Vegas Optic* as a "first class organization . . . entitled to a place on the legitimate stage."

MARCH

1. Colorado lieutenant governor Horace Tabor weds "Baby" Doe in Washington, D.C.
3. Marshal Henry N. Brown resumes his duties in Caldwell, Kansas, following a leave to visit relatives in Missouri. Reports the *Commercial:* "Since his return, the boys are not quite so numerous on the streets at night."
- San Franciscans defeat a new city charter at the polls.
4. A scandal erupts as the public learns of the secret vows made by Horace and Baby Doe Tabor in September 1882. Father P. L. Chappelle, in trouble with his bishop for marrying two divorcés, loudly returns his fee, complaining of a deliberate deception. Moans the *Denver Tribune:*

> He is an utter disgrace to the state. He disgraced it in private life; he disgraced it in public office . . . he is a social and political outcast in all the senses of the word.

11. Homer Croy, the author of *Jesse James Was My Neighbor* (1949) and *He Hanged Them High* (1952), is born in Maryville, Missouri.
13. The suspected cannibal Alferd Packer, on the run from the law for the last nine years, is arrested in a LaPrele Creek, Wyoming, boardinghouse for the incidents of 1874. The fugitive will be returned to Denver, where a thousand people will turn out to greet the "ghoul of the San Juans." In his second confession, Packer will say that Shannon Bell had done all the killing and that he had killed Bell in self-defense before settling down to dine on human flesh. Recalling the end of his fast, Packer will smile and say: "I felt perfectly happy. Slept and slept and slept."

15. In Wyoming, the *Cheyenne Daily Leader* reports the tale of "Cannibal Packer."
- Lillie Langtry plays the Cheyenne Opera House.
17. The Wells Fargo box is taken during a stagecoach holdup between Maricopa and Prescott, Arizona.
18. The *Cheyenne Daily Leader* reports that the tally of executions in that fair city is 37 by the "gunny-sack brigade" and two by legal authorities.
21. Four settlers are reported killed in an Apache raid 12 miles southwest of Fort Huachuca, Arizona, near Tombstone. General George Crook learns that the raid was led by Chato, Chihvahua, and Bonito, and begins plans to follow the Apaches into Mexico.
22. Raiding Apaches reportedly kill three persons at the Total Wreck Mine in Arizona's Whetstone Mountains.
23. Two citizens are reported slain by Indians at Point of Mountain, Arizona.
24. Twenty-four Canadian River cowboys in the Texas panhandle go on strike for a 50-cents-a-day pay raise.
26. The city of Bozeman, Montana, is incorporated.
27. James Addison Reavis appears at the office of Tucson's surveyor general with the claim to his "Peralta Grant," aged Spanish documents that he alleges give him ownership of some 12 million acres in Arizona and New Mexico. While Reavis negotiates with the U.S. government for a settlement on the 235-mile-by-75-mile tract, it will be learned that Reavis went to Spain and Mexico to forge the documents. The "Baron of Arizona" hoax will eventually be exposed.
28. A raiding party of Chiricahua Apaches under chief Chato kills Judge and Mrs. H. C. McComas on the road between Silver City and Lordsburg, New Mexico.

APRIL

11. Alferd Packer takes the stand in his own defense at his Lake City, Colorado, murder trial. District Attorney John C. Bell grills Packer with 318 questions, as the *Silver World* reports, "hoping to confuse the defendant and thereby elicit information not otherwise obtainable, with however, partial success only."
12. Alferd Packer is found guilty of murder in Lake City, Colorado.
- Black Bart again robs the Lakeport–Cloverdale stagecoach, this time about five miles from Cloverdale, California.
14. Captain M. E. O'Brien reports the surrender of 69 Indians at Beaver Creek, Montana.

TABOR AND "BABY" DOE WED
MARCH 1, 1883

Colorado's millionaire lieutenant governor, the "Silver King" Horace Tabor, 52, had, in the last year, divorced Augusta, his wife of more than 20 years, to secretly wed a young Oshkosh divorcée whom Central City miners called "Baby" Doe. Now, as the newly appointed U.S. senator filled a 30-day unexpired term, he publicly proclaimed his love for Elizabeth McCourt Doe, 28, in an opulent Washington, D.C., ceremony. Doe wore a $7,000 white moiré wedding gown. President Chester A. Arthur attended the gala, at which Baby Doe Tabor received a $75,000 diamond necklace. The elated groom presented a case of champagne to each member of both houses of Congress.

For his honeymoon, Horace Tabor wore a pink silk nightshirt trimmed in lace, with buttons of gold. When the *Denver Tribune* columnist Eugene Field heard about the suave attire, he dubbed Tabor "Ex-Senator Night Shirt."

Elizabeth McCourt Doe (1854–1935), the one the miners call "Baby Doe." Dressed to kill, she takes up a spot in the lobby of Leadville's Clarendon Hotel and awaits the Silver King's arrival. (Colorado State Historical Society)

Horace Austin Warner Tabor (1830–1899). Stonecutter, shop keeper, Silver King, pauper. The West's favorite rags-to-riches-to-rags story. (Denver Public Library, Western History Department)

■ About the verdict in Alferd Packer's trial, the *Lake City Silver World* says: "It was one of the fairest criminal trials on record. The prisoner was given every opportunity to prove his innocence and the benefit of every doubt which could possibly be made to favor him."

15. Alferd Packer is sentenced in Lake City, Colorado.

19. The 2nd Cavalry reports two Indians killed in a fight at Wild Horse Lake in Montana.

21. Electric lights are introduced to Denver.

22. Tornadoes tear across Kansas; death and damage are widespread.

23. The state of Texas purchases the Alamo from the Catholic Church and puts it under the control of San Antonio's city government.

30. There is gunsmoke in Dodge City, Kansas. Luke Short and Will Harris own the Long Branch Saloon, where three female entertainers have been arrested by the authorities. Short is angry about the arrests, and on Saturday night he sees City Clerk L. C. Hartman on the streets. "There is one of the sons of bitches," Short tells a friend, "let's throw it into him." Short fires at Hartman, who falls to the ground unhurt, trying to figure out where the shots came from. Short, believing he has killed Hartman, leaves the scene.

Also in April 1883:

Sarah Winnemucca Hopkins becomes the first Indian woman to write a tribal and personal history with the publication of *Life Among the Piutes; Their Wrongs and Claims.*

Annie Oakley and Frank Butler join the Sells Brothers Circus. Frank does the shooting while Annie concentrates on riding. They will tour in *Slocum's Oath,* a play whose script calls for astounding gunplay. Sitting Bull views the performance in St. Paul, Minnesota, and is so impressed by Oakley that he appears backstage to tell her she is blessed; he calls her "Watanya Cicilia," "Little Sure Shot."

MAY

1. Invitations to attend the hanging of Alferd Packer are printed by Sheriff Claire Smith.

■ Captain Emmett Crawford leads a force of 100 troops and 93 Indian scouts into Mexico, searching for Chato's Apaches.

2. A fire destroys most of Livingston, Montana.

8. Captain Emmet Crawford's command is in the Sierra Madres of Mexico, with the permission of that government, seeking Chato's Apaches.

9. The Colorado Supreme Court overturns Alferd Packer's death sentence, according to the *Leadville Democrat,* "because the thick-headed Legislature of 1881 repealed the old murder law. If the Hinsdale County people don't hang the cannibal and two or three members of that legislature they're no good."

14. A Pawnee called Spotted Horse, age unknown, is

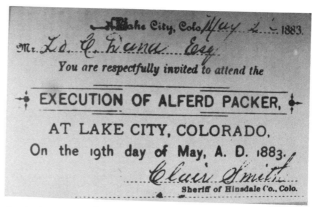

An invitation to the Packer execution that will never happen. (Library of Congress)

shot and killed in a Caldwell, Kansas, grocery store by Marshal Henry Brown. A series of arguments with local merchants prompted Spotted Horse to go for his revolver in the presence of Brown, who delivered four shots, the last one to the center of the Indian's forehead.

15. With permission from the Mexican government, U.S. troops attack Chato's camp. Captain Emmett Crawford and his men, part of General George Crook's expedition, report nine Indians slain and five captured in the Sierra Madres of Mexico.

16. Alferd Packer is secretly moved from the Lake City jail to the Gunnison County jail in Colorado.

17. Buffalo Bill's first touring outdoor extravaganza, "The Wild West, Hon. W. F. Cody and Dr. W. F. Carver's Rocky Mountain and Prairie Exhibition," debuts at the Omaha Fair Grounds in Nebraska.

24. Following the attack on May 15 by Captain Emmett Crawford and his troops, Chato and Nana and 260 other Apaches voluntarily appear at General George Crook's camp wishing to talk peace. They say they are tired of war and promise to return to the San Carlos Reservation in present Arizona.

26. "Wild Bill, the Whirlwind of the West," "by Buffalo Bill," begins serialization in *Beadle's Weekly.*

30. Following another parley with Apache leaders, this time including Geronimo, Naiche, and Loco, General George Crook begins his departure from Mexico. The general has agreed to escort some warriors, the elderly, women, and children back to the reservation and give the warriors time to round up other Apaches as well as livestock. With him go 251 women and children, and 123 warriors, including Loco, Bonito, Chihuahua, and Nana. To their surprise, chiefs Geronimo and Chato are allowed to remain behind to tie up the loose ends.

10. JOSEPH PULITZER BEGINS PUBLISHING "THE WORLD"
25. BROOKLYN BRIDGE OPENS

JUNE

15. Helena, Montana, greets the first eastbound Northern Pacific train.

■ Crow Creek floods great portions of Cheyenne, Wyoming.

18. Various San Francisco laborers meet to organize the Confederation of Building Trades.

23. Black Bart robs the Jackson–Ione stagecoach four miles from Jackson, California.

■ General George Crook's troops, who have been escorting 374 Apaches from Mexico, arrive at the San Carlos Reservation. With them are the old chiefs Nana and Loco.

29. Tualisto, a Creek Indian, is executed at Fort Smith, Arkansas. He was found guilty of robbing and murdering a white man called Cochran. Tualisto is said to have sewn a button to his hatband for each man he killed; four buttons were attached when he went to the gallows.

30. "The Pilgrim Sharp, or The Soldier's Sweetheart," "by Buffalo Bill," appears in *Beadle's Dime Library*.

JULY

1. The stagecoach running through Arizona's Black Canyon is robbed for the second time in three days.

3. In Helena, Montana, a 38-car train departs, carrying 1.2 million pounds of silver bullion worth some $350,000.

4. Buffalo Bill Cody presents an impressive circus of cowboys, Indians, trick riders, and sharpshooters in North Platte, Nebraska. The circus is the prototype of what will develop into his famed traveling Wild West show.

■ Pecos, Texas, claims to hold history's first rodeo.

5. Thus far, 100 million pounds of ore have been extracted from the Gregory mine in Helena, Montana.

6. The Denver and Rio Grande Railroad is completed from Del Norte, Colorado, to Wagon Wheel Gap.

7. Professor Adolph Bandelier of the American Archeological Institute arrives in Santa Fe, New Mexico, after traveling "1,501 miles on horseback."

21. Arizona's Black Canyon stagecoach robbers are apprehended; one is the blacksmith in Gillett.

■ "Liver Eating" Johnson is appointed the deputy of Coulson, the future Billings, Montana.

22. Arson destroys much of Miles City, Montana.

23. The Grand Army of the Republic makes its first national encampment in Denver, with General Logan the hero of the event.

Also in July 1883:
Love in a Colorado mining camp is the subject of Mary Hallock Foote's first novel, *The Led-Horse Claim*.

AUGUST

2. The *Caldwell Journal* reports that the city's two police officers, Henry Brown and Ben Wheeler, have collected $1,296 in fines, or $421 more than their combined salaries.

7. The first Northern Pacific train crosses the Continental Divide at Mullan Pass, west of Helena, Montana.

12. Two stagecoach robberies occur in one night in Arizona, as bandits hit the Prescott–Ash Fork and the Florence–Globe stages. A Wells Fargo agent is killed in the latter incident.

16. The clergyman Henry Ward Beecher lectures in Helena, Montana.

18. "Texas Jack, the Prairie Rattler, or The Queen of the Wild Horses," "by Buffalo Bill," begins serialization in *Beadle's Weekly*.

21. A tornado in Rochester, Minnesota, kills 31 people.

23. President Chester A. Arthur's party tours Yellowstone National Park.

24. The cornerstone of the Garfield Monument is laid in San Francisco.

30. Montana's Territorial Teachers Association holds its first meeting.

Also in August 1883:

In a 48-page pamphlet listing its offices, agents, and correspondents, Wells Fargo claims that it covers 33,000 miles, connecting "nearly every Hamlet, Town, and City in the United States and Canada."

Robert Louis Stevenson writes about his experiences in California in *The Silverado Squatters*.

Undaunted by their marital scandal, Horace and Baby Doe Tabor move into a $54,000 mansion in Denver. A hundred Oriental peacocks play on the lawn. At night, the couple turns heads when it arrives in a splendid coach at Horace's downtown opera house.

SEPTEMBER

3. The Northern Pacific's main rail line, running from Portland, Oregon, to Duluth, Minnesota, is completed.

5. The 4th annual Women's Temperance Union convention is held in San Francisco.

8. The northern transcontinental rail route is completed. Ceremonies at Independence Creek, 60

TALES OF THE TOMBSTONES

In the Wild West, death was a greater certainty than taxes. Some of the graves were marked with crude crosses or simple piles of stones. Others got tombstones inscribed with dates or a bit of verse. Stonecutter poetry ranged from the celestial to the silly, giving the region yet another identifiable trademark. A few examples:

Underneath this stone in eternal rest
Sleeps the wildest one of the wayward west
He was gambler and sport and cowboy too
And he led the pace in an outlaw crew.
He was sure on the trigger and staid to the end
But he was never known to quit on a friend
In the relations of death all mankind is alike
But in life there was only one George W. Pike.
(Famed cattleman George W. Pike, interred in Douglas, Wyoming)

Here lies old Pete with his guts full of lead,
But he was only a bag of wind
And now he is dead.
(Big Pete Sloan's marker in Hays, Kansas)

Joe. F. Kelley
Saloon-Keeper
This One is On Me
(Famed stone of the California Gold Rush)

The following markers in Tombstone's outrageous Boothill cemetery became world-famous for their humor and pathos:

Billy Clanton/Tom McLowery/Frank McLowery/
Murdered on the Streets of Tombstone/1881
(The above-named were killed in the Gunfight at the O.K. Corral by the Earp brothers and Doc Holliday)

Here Lies Lester Moore
Four slugs from a .44
No Les, No More

No graveyard visit would be complete without the following verse, which could be found in many cemeteries:

Remember friends as you pass by
As you are now so once was I
As I am now so you must be
Prepare for death, and follow me.

On a tombstone in the Pioneer Cemetery near Colorado Springs, Colorado, a bit of graffiti was scribbled beneath an inscription:

To follow you I'll not consent.
Until I know which way you went.

---

miles west of Helena, Montana, and attended by former President Ulysses S. Grant, signify the completion of the 1,222-mile Northern Pacific Railroad from Ashland, Wisconsin, to Portland, Oregon. The round-trip journey from the Mississippi to the Columbia River that took Lewis and Clark 2.5 years can now be made in nine days.

13. Railroad tracks reach San Bernardino, California.
15. The University of Texas opens in Austin.
19. The *Cheyenne Daily Leader* reports that "92 men in Dodge City have died with their boots on."

Also in September 1883:

John J. Montgomery, 26, a Santa Clara College professor, flies 100 feet over San Diego, California, in the glider he designed after studying seagulls.

Theodore Roosevelt visits Dakota Territory for the first time, staying at the Maltese Cross Ranch near Medora.

A $500 reward is paid by the Arizona legislature to Felix Hardwick, who grew the first cotton in the territory.

Edgar Watson Howe's *The Story of a Country Town* blasts the traditional sentimental treatment of rural life. The novel, printed on the author's press in Atchison, Kansas, is about the fictional town of Twin Mounds, whose residents one literary observer describes as "futile, argumentative, boastful, discontented, envious, and mean."

OCTOBER

4. In Arizona, a posse shoots it out with stagecoach bandits on the Globe–Florence line. Two robbers are slain.
12. The Eastern Montana Stockgrowers' Association is established.
17–20. While Buffalo Bill's Wild West show plays Chicago, William F. Cody makes plans to jettison his business partner, Dr. W. F. Carver.
24. Orra Maude Cody, 11, the daughter of William F. Cody, dies.
28. At the close of the season, Yellowstone National Park reports 20,000 visitors in 1883.

29. The San Francisco Merchants' and Manufacturers' Association organizes.

Also in October 1883:

The Northern Pacific Refrigerator Car Company opens for business. The brainchild of the Marquis de Mores, of France, the company plans to slaughter beef cattle on the plains and ship them east by rail. The operation is located in the Medora region of the Little Missouri River in Dakota's Badlands. The company employs some 300 cowboys and plant workers. Icehouses now store 6,000 tons of ice cut from the Little Missouri since 1880.

NOVEMBER

3. Black Bart pulls his last stagecoach robbery, on the Sonora–Milton run near Copperopolis, California. A shotgun-wielding youth, 19-year-old Jimmy Rolleri, wings Bart, who leaves behind a handkerchief with the laundry mark "F.X.0.7." The mark will be traced to one C. E. Bolton, aka Charles E. Boles, originally of Decatur, Illinois. James B. Hume of Wells Fargo will finally get his man when he finds the matching laundry mark at the 91st laundry he visits in San Francisco.

■ The U.S. Supreme Court declares Native Americans to be dependent aliens.

17. In San Andreas, California, Charles E. Boles, Black Bart, pleads guilty to the November 3 stagecoach robbery and is sentenced to six years in prison.

18. At noon, railroads operating in the United States and Canada adopt four standard time zones, the dividing lines between them being the 75th, 90th, 105th, and 120th meridians.

28. The steamer *Victoria* runs into a reef between Cape Blanco and Port Orford, Oregon, and is a total loss.

Also in November 1883:

W. J. Sanderson of Sulpher Springs, Arizona, discovers water with an artesian well and collects a reward of $3,000 from the territory.

Hubert Howe Bancroft publishes the first volume of a six-volume work on Mexico.

DECEMBER

1. Violence breaks out in a Prescott, Arizona, courtroom as the attorney general and his aide come to blows with the litigants in a fight over water rights. A defendant named McAteer pulls a knife and wounds two before he is killed.

8. In Bisbee, Arizona, near Tombstone, a botched robbery by five bandits results in the slaying of several Christmas shoppers. A posse is formed, and the bandits will be caught and hanged in Tombstone in March 1884 for the "Bisbee Massacre."

12. In Colorado, Alferd Packer's attorney begins the appeals process on his murder conviction.

15. A disturbance in Caldwell, Kansas, is ended when Marshal Henry Brown slays the gambler Newt Boyce.

26. A bitter cold snap signals the beginning of a treacherous winter that will bring death by starvation to many of Montana's Indians.

National Headlines/December 1883:
18. TYPOGRAPHERS STRIKE NEW YORK TRIBUNE

Also in 1883:

The Arizona Cattle Company is organized under the name of the A. L. Bar outfit by John W. Young, son of Brigham. The ranch building is located at Fort Rickerson, about 10 miles north of Flagstaff.

The 625,000 head of cattle in Arizona are valued at $12.5 million.

Wells Fargo, operating 1,163 offices, reports incomes of $3,507,000 from transportation and $1,518,000 from express services.

The Cherokee Strip Live Stock Association is formed in Caldwell, Kansas. The association consists of some 100 stockmen who own an estimated 300,000 head of livestock. They lease the 6.5 million acres of the Cherokee Outlet in Indian Territory for five years at $100,000 a year.

Lord Dunraven's Estes Park, Colorado, grounds are leased to Theodore Whyte.

John Phillips, the "Portugee" involved in the Fetterman Massacre of 1866, dies.

Mark Twain publishes *Life on the Mississippi*.

The University of Colorado School of Medicine is founded in Boulder.

The last buffalo in the northern herd live near Cannon Ball River in Dakota Territory. Sitting Bull leads his people in one last hunt, killing 1,000 buffalo in a day.

1884

"But I reckon I got to light out for the Territory ahead of the rest, because Aunt Sally she's going to adopt me and sivilize me and I can't stand it. I been there before."

—*The Adventures of Huckleberry Finn,* by Mark Twain

JANUARY

1. Mark Twain publishes *The Adventures of Huckleberry Finn.*
8. The Denver Chamber of Commerce is formed.
■ The "Fence Cutter War," a conflict between open-range enthusiasts and barbed-wire proponents, is a prime topic of discussion in the Texas legislature.
10. Wells Fargo operates more than a dozen railroad lines.
12. Texas Guinan, the nightclub personality, is born in Waco, Texas. During the heyday of the speakeasy, her famous salutation is "Hello, Sucker!"
13. Arizona's Black Canyon stagecoach is robbed near Gillett.
20. Arizona's Wickenburg stagecoach is robbed near Prescott.
22. In Montana, the Bozeman Pass tunnel is completed by the Northern Pacific Railroad.
31. The Arizona Pioneers' Historical Society is organized in Tucson.

Also in January 1884:

Iowa's state capitol building is formally dedicated in Des Moines.

FEBRUARY

7. Arizona citizens meet to challenge recent land claims by the "Baron of Arizona," James Addison Reavis.
14. Back East, the future westerner and president Theodore Roosevelt suffers the deaths of both his wife and mother within a few hours of each other.
22. John Heath, a participant in Arizona's Bisbee Massacre, is taken from the county jail and lynched in Tombstone.
23. "White Beaver, the Exile of the Platte, or A Wronged Man's Red Trail," a dime novel "by Buffalo Bill," begins serialization in *Beadle's Weekly.*
24. Fifty-nine are killed in a coal mine explosion in Crested Butte, Colorado.

Also in February 1884:

Geronimo and Chato return from Mexico as a part of their agreement last May with General George Crook. Geronimo is ordered to relinquish the stolen Mexican cattle he has herded. The livestock will be sold for $1,762.50, with the money going to the Mexican government. Geronimo and Chato are taken to the San Carlos Reservation.

At Atoka, Indian Territory, the first Choctaw newspaper, the *Indian Champion,* begins publication. It will exist for just over a year.

William Sydney Porter, the future O. Henry, 22, works as a clerk at Harrell's Drug Store in the Driskill Hotel in Austin, Texas. He will soon switch to the Morely Brothers Drug Store, where he will work until 1887.

National Headlines/February 1884:

9. TORNADOES RAVAGE SOUTH; CLAIM 700 LIVES

MARCH

5. San Francisco's First National Gold Bank becomes the First National Bank.

6. The city of Sheridan, Wyoming, is incorporated.

■ The first college in Montana, the Montana Collegiate Institute, is renamed the College of Montana. It is located in Deer Lodge.

7. The Diocese of Helena is established as Montana's first Catholic bishop, John Brondel, arrives in the territory.

20. Laramie, Wyoming, is incorporated.

27. In Kansas, the *Caldwell Journal* announces the marriage of Marshal Henry Brown and the former Maude Levagood.

28. Five bandits convicted of the December 8, 1883, Bisbee Massacre are hanged from one gallows. (John Heath, another participant, was removed from his cell and lynched on February 22.)

Also In March 1884:

Ben Thompson arrives in San Antonio, Texas, with Deputy Sheriff King Fisher of Uvalde. After a fair amount of drinking, the pair go to the Vaudeville, where Thompson murdered Jack Harris in 1882. Thompson gets into a squabble with the deceased's business partners, Joe Foster and Billy Sims, and rams his pistol into Foster's mouth. All hell breaks loose. A bartender and a performer appear from nowhere with guns, and bullets fly. When the smoke clears, Fisher and the 40-year-old Thompson lay dead. "It is very doubtful if in his time there was another man living who equalled him with the pistol in a life and death struggle," Bat Masterson will write in 1907. "Others missed at times, but Ben Thompson was as delicate and certain in action as a Swiss pocket watch."

National Headlines/March 1884:

6. SUSAN B. ANTHONY & 100 SUFFRAGETTES GIVE ARTHUR DEMANDS

APRIL

1. Juan Patron, of Lincoln County War fame is murdered, shot in the back by Mitch Maney, a drunken Texas cowboy, at Puerto de Luna, New Mexico.

3. Sierra County is created in New Mexico.

16. Annie Oakley is billed as a markswoman for the first time, as she tours with the Sells Brothers Circus in Columbus, Ohio.

21. Arizona's Black Canyon stagecoach is robbed near Soap Springs.

30. The Caldwell, Kansas, law enforcement officers Henry Brown and Ben Wheeler team up with a

group of Oklahoma thugs and try to rob the bank in Medicine Lodge, Kansas. In the attempt, Brown mortally wounds bank president E. W. Payne; a cashier dies during the robbery. Citizens pursue the bandits out of town and capture them after a two-hour gun battle. At 9:00 P.M., a mob overpowers the guards at the jail, and Brown, 27, who tries to escape, is blown in half by a farmer's double-barreled shotgun. The wounded Ben Wheeler is taken to a tree and lynched, as are the other robbers.

Also in April 1884:

A smelter is built at the Anaconda Copper Company in Montana.

The German count James M. Pourtales, 28, leaves Europe for a tour of Chicago, San Francisco, Denver, and Colorado Springs, where he will visit a French cousin, Count Louis de Pourtales.

The Kansan Thomas W. Stevens departs San Francisco, in an attempt to bicycle around the world.

MAY

1. The town of Caldwell, Kansas, is stunned when it receives a telegram from Medicine Lodge, stating that Marshal Henry N. Brown and his deputy, Ben F. Wheeler, have failed in their attempt to rob a local bank:

> The bank robbers were Brown and Wheeler, marshal and deputy of Caldwell, and Smith and Wesley. All arrested. Tried to escape. Brown killed. Balance hung. Geppert dead. Payne will die.

3. "The Wizard Brothers, or White Beaver's Red Trail," a dime novel "by Buffalo Bill," begins serialization in *Beadle's Weekly.*

6. Fremont County is established in Wyoming.

9. Windows in Phoenix, Arizona, are shattered when a powder magazine on the outskirts of town explodes.

14. The first Arizona Industrial Exposition is organized in Phoenix.

17. Congress determines that the Organic Law in Oregon applies to Alaska.

JUNE

1. Arizona's Black Canyon stagecoach is robbed again.

2. Lillie Langtry plays a return engagement at the Cheyenne, Wyoming, Opera House.

12. Los Angeles records its heaviest June rain ever, .87 of an inch on the 11th and 12th.

14. The *Oklahoma War Chief,* the official organ of the Boomers (supporters of colonization in Indian Territory) and their leader, David L. Payne, is printed in Indian Territory, 25 miles northwest of present

Ponca City, Oklahoma. The periodical, which was published sporadically from 1883–1886, appears for the first time in the areas currently off-limits to white settlement.

- Pasadena, California, reports snow and hail.

25. A cargo of 60,000 pounds of lumber is a complete loss as the *Mose* sinks at Port Orford, Oregon.

28. Shortly after the publication of her novel *Ramona,* Helen Hunt Jackson falls at her Colorado Springs, Colorado, home and fractures her hip.

National Headlines/June 1884:
6. GOP NOMINATES BLAINE
27. BUREAU OF LABOR CREATED

JULY

13. Elizabeth Bonduel Lily Tabor, the first child of Horace Tabor and his wife Baby Doe, is born in Denver. Her diapers are fastened by an $800 diamond solitaire pin.

15. Two settlers are reportedly slain by Indians at Wormington Canyon, Colorado. This is the only Indian battle reported by the military in 1884.

18. Tom Nixon, who recently took "Mysterious Dave"

The Dodge City Democrat *announces a big Fourth of July celebration.* (Kansas State Historical Society)

Mather's job as assistant marshal of Dodge City, Kansas, shoots at Mather, claiming he was drawn upon. Nixon is released on bond.

19. Yellowstone National Park records an attendance of 2,000 for the year thus far.

21. Dave Mather shoots Tom Nixon dead in Dodge City.

24. An antirustler outfit known as Stuart's Stranglers organizes at Granville Stuart's DHS Ranch in Gilt Edge, Montana.

26. "White Beaver's One-arm Park, or Red Retribution in Borderland," a dime novel "by Buffalo Bill," begins serialization in *Beadle's Weekly*

National Headlines/July 1884:
8. DEMOCRATS NOMINATE CLEVELAND

AUGUST

8. Sara Teasdale, the Pulitzer-Prize-winning poet (*Love Songs,* 1917), is born in St. Louis, Missouri.

Also in August 1884:
Doc Holliday's last gunfight occurs in Leadville, Colorado, where one Billy Allen, trying to goad the consumptive dentist into a fistfight, gets a surprise bullet in his arm. Witnesses say that Holliday was trying to kill Allen, but that a bystander grabbed at the gun as it discharged. Holliday will be acquitted on the grounds that he acted in self-defense. The argument that led to the fight apparently involved a $5 loan.

SEPTEMBER

2. A major fire in Missoula, Montana, destroys 22 buildings, including the Missoula National Bank.

11. The Society of Montana Pioneers is established.

17. The Haskell Institute, which provides vocational training for Indians, is dedicated in Lawrence, Kansas. Twenty-two Pawnee children are enrolled on the first day. Within three days, eight Cheyenne and Arapaho chiefs will enroll another 80 students.

Also in September 1884:
The XIT ranch in Texas now encloses 3,050,000 acres.
Miles City, Montana, ships 25,000 head of cattle.
Wyatt Earp, accused of cheating at cards in Lake City, Colorado, is wounded in the arm by a stray bullet in the ensuing fight.

OCTOBER

2. In Montana, Father Anthony Ravalli, 72, dies at St. Mary's Mission, which he built in 1845.

11. Prairie fires rage in North Dakota. Writes one observer: "Millions of acres of burned prairie land and small plowed fields made one continuous field of black for miles and miles and left neither trees, shrubs, nor any other green thing to rest the eye or break the monotony, giving it all the most dismal appearance of anything I have ever seen."

16. With six-guns and a Winchester, Marshal Bill Tilghman convinces a group of drunken and disorderly cowboys to depart Dodge City, Kansas.

18. Arizona's Black Canyon stagecoach is robbed.

■ "Red Renard, the Indian Detective, or The Gold Buzzards of Colorado," a dime novel "by Buffalo Bill," begins serialization in *Beadle's Dime Library*.

19. An amazing feat is performed in San Francisco Bay as D. F. Riehl swims from a cave north of the Cliff House to another on Seal Rocks, and back again.

NOVEMBER

4. Montana voters approve a state constitution backed by the Copper Kings. But the political party balance is so even that statehood will be postponed for 5 more years.

■ Colorado voters elect the Republican Benjamin H. Eaton governor.

26. Montana's Northern Cheyenne Reservation is created from the Crow Reservation by executive order of President Chester A. Arthur.

27. San Francisco's Central Park has its grand opening.

30. In San Francisco, New Mexico, Elfego Baca, 19 and wearing a mail-order badge, arrests a cowboy who is disturbing the peace. When riders come to teach him a lesson, Baca slays the foreman with his Colt revolver.

Also in November 1884:

Wells Fargo issues the following crime report covering the last 14 years: 313 robberies, 34 attempted robberies, 23 burglaries, 4 train robberies, 4 attempted train robberies, 2 Wells Fargo guards killed, 6 Wells Fargo guards wounded, 4 stagecoach drivers killed, 4 stagecoach drivers wounded, 16 stagecoach robbers killed, 7 stagecoach robbers hanged by citizens, 7 horses killed, 14 horses stolen, and 240 convictions. In the same time frame, the company paid $415,312.55 in reimbursements for stolen merchandise, $90,079 in prosecutions, and $326,417 in salaries for guards and special officers. In all, the 355 stagecoach and train robberies (or attempted robberies) cost the company $905,259.55.

National Headlines/November 1884:

4. CLEVELAND DEFEATS BLAINE

DECEMBER

1. A makeshift "trial" finds Elfego Baca's cowboy prisoner, arrested on November 30, guilty and fines him $5.

ELFEGO BACA
FEBRUARY 27, 1865–AUGUST 23, 1945

Elfego Baca was not a man to be trifled with. In his incredible lifetime that linked the frontier with the Atomic Age, Baca was a righter of wrongs, a knight-errant hombre who never lost a showdown.

The charmed life of Elfego Baca began in Socorro, New Mexico, on February 27, 1865—shortly after his mother, Juanita, had competed in a ball game. His father, Francisco Baca, ran a small cattle ranch.

Little Elfego probably slept through most of his first adventure. At the tender age of 1, he was kidnapped by a band of Navajos, only to be returned unharmed two days later. Soon thereafter, Francisco moved his family to Topeka, Kansas, where Elfego and his older brother, Abdenago, received their educations. Following the death of their mother, the boys returned with their father to New Mexico around 1880.

Francisco took a job as a marshal in Beren, while Elfego worked as a cowboy in nearby Socorro. Many accounts suggest that Elfego had a brief friendship with a teenager named Henry McCarty (aka William "Billy the Kid" Bonney). Baca also became a deadly shot at about this time.

At age 17, Baca's legend began in earnest. The trouble started in Las Lunas, where Francisco defeated a local Anglo in a horse race. Indignant cowboys tried to shoot up Beren in retaliation, and Papa Baca shot back; he was overpowered and tossed into the Las Lunas jail. Soon, Elfego and a friend broke into a second-floor window of the jail, sawed a hole in the floor over his father's cell, and pulled off a great escape, taking two other convicts with them.

Two years later, Elfego participated in one of the West's most incredible gunfights. While working as a $20-a-month clerk in a Socorro store, he heard of a great injustice in Frisco (the present Reserve). Rowdy cowboys had castrated a man known as "El Burro" in a saloon, and then had used a local named Martinez for pistol practice. Clad in a Prince Albert coat that covered his two Colt .45s, and wearing a mail-
(continued)

(continued)

order tin star, Elfego Baca became the avenger on horseback.

He arrived in Frisco at the same time that a drunken cowboy was disturbing the peace by taking potshots at dogs, cats, and people. Residents were literally prisoners in their homes, afraid to go outside. The "justice of the peace" inferred that any attempt to arrest the hooligans would only bring reprisals. Having weighed the situation carefully, the cool-headed 19-year-old went to Milligan's wild tavern, arrested the hell-raising cowboy, and marched him to a small hotel. Then Baca announced that he would transport his prisoner to Socorro for trial.

A group of cowboys from the massive John Slaughter ranch heard the news and galloped into town, demanding to know what was going on. Baca stepped out of the hotel and gave them a three count, but before they could react, shots were flying through the air. A frightened horse fell on one of the cowboys, crushing him to death.

Now the word spread like wildfire: A Mexican had killed a Texan. In an effort to avert certain bloodshed, the town held a makeshift "trial" in which Baca's prisoner was found guilty and fined $5. In the meantime, at least 80 bloodthirsty Texans had come for Baca's hide.

Frisco's least popular stranger had by now taken refuge in a small *jacal*, a tiny shack constructed of sticks and mud. At Baca's urging, the occupants had fled to safety. A spokesman for the mob, Jim Herne, pounded on the door, only to be blasted into oblivion by Baca's Colts. During the next day and a half of the furious siege, 80 cowboys tried their hardest to kill one Chicano. When dynamite took off a corner of the flimsy fortress during the night, all were sure that Baca had been killed. The next morning, they awoke to the smell of coffee and beef stew—their target was cooking breakfast.

The authorities arrived and stopped the battle the next day, after 36 hours and 4,000 bullets. Two Texans were dead and at least six others were wounded. When the door containing 300 shell holes was pulled off the shack, Baca emerged without having suffered a scratch. His craftiness had saved him: the ground inside had been dug a foot below street level, so that when the firing got especially heavy, Baca had been able to lie beneath the action. He had hung his sombrero, which drew considerable fire, on a small statue of a saint in the corner.

Two murder trials absolved Baca of any wrongdoing. During one, a cowboy testified that he believed the defendant was immortal—a gun fired at point-blank range had had no effect. Throughout the West, the name of Elfego Baca now struck fear into evil hearts.

When a cousin complained that a herd of the nastiest characters west of the Pecos River was busting up his saloon, Elfego investigated. All he had to do was step inside the swinging doors, and peace reigned. A few of the meek cowboys even shook Elfego's hand on the way out.

At age 20, Baca married Francisquita Pohmer. Sensing that there would be life after the Old West, he began studying law in 1890, and four years later he was admitted to the New Mexico bar. Now he would serve justice from a courtroom. A political fling saw the straight-shooting Republican serving in various positions, including county clerk, district attorney, and mayor of Socorro.

In 1919, Baca was elected sheriff of Socorro County. Though he had put on considerable weight (the author Jack Schaefer said he looked like an "elderly bulldog"), he still managed to uphold the law. During the 1920's, Secretary of the Interior Albert B. Fall directed Baca to Utah to persuade a group of Paiutes to stop interfering with local cattle ranchers.

Baca's indestructible image strengthened even further with the years. He survived being run over by a fire truck, and two stabbings, one by an ice pick-wielding lunatic. During his unsuccessful gubernatorial campaign in New Mexico in the 1930's, Baca was arrested for disturbing the peace because he had beaten a man for stating that "there was no available Spanish-American capable of being governor."

Elfego Baca died peacefully at the age of 80 in Albuquerque, New Mexico, on August 23, 1945, a month after the desert in which he had tracked the worst of the West was used to test the world's first atomic bomb. Although he outlasted his times by many years, his personal code of bravery never went out of style.

2. At Frisco, New Mexico, Elfego Baca begins a standoff against 80 would-be assassins.
8. The Denver National Bank opens.
16. The World Industrial and Cotton Centennial Exposition opens in New Orleans. California's oranges and lemons take first prize and, as a result, a real-estate boom will occur on the West Coast from 1885–1887.
20. John Chisum, the cattle king of New Mexico Territory, dies in Eureka Springs, Arkansas. He will be buried in Paris, Texas.

Also in 1884:

The first windmills in Texas are installed.

Some 415,000 head of cattle are driven from Texas.

There are 690,000 head of cattle worth $14.5 million in Arizona.

Hubert Howe Bancroft's San Francisco "history factory" publishes the first of a two-volume work entitled *North Mexican States and Texas,* the first of a two-volume work entitled *Northwest Coast,* and the first of a seven-volume work entitled *California.*

Wells Fargo, operating out of 1,369 offices, reports incomes of $3,684,000 from transportation and $1,511,000 from express services.

John J. Montgomery completes another of the country's first glider flights, this one in Otay, California, where he travels 600 feet.

Cattle baron Richard King, dying of stomach cancer, makes his last public appearance before the National Convention of Cattlemen in St. Louis. The King Ranch in Texas now covers 1.27 million acres, and its livestock holdings have soared to 65,000 head of cattle, 10,000 horses, 7,000 sheep, and 8,000 goats.

Some 40 percent of the land claims filed in 1884—for 11,082,818 acres—were in Dakota Territory.

Orton's Michigan Circus Trail catches fire en route from Greeley to Fort Collins, Colorado, killing 10 performers.

The last buffalo in the northern herd die.

1885

"The Virginian's pistol came out, and his hand lay on the table, holding it unaimed. And with a voice as gentle as ever, the voice that sounded almost like a caress, but drawling a very little more than usual, so that there was almost a space between each word, he issued his order to the man Trampas—'When you call me that, *smile*.'"

—*The Virginian*, by Owen Wister

JANUARY

4. In a treaty signed with the U.S. government, Oregon's Ahantchuyuk tribe agrees to live on a reservation.

▪ The world's first appendectomy is performed in Davenport, Iowa.

13. Schuyler Colfax, the former vice president of the United States and speaker of the House of Representatives, collapses and dies in Mankato, Minnesota, after walking a mile in freezing temperatures to reach a train.

17. Dr. W. F. Carver, William F. Cody's business associate, begins a six-day exhibition in New Haven, Connecticut, where he will shoot 60,016 out of 64,881 wooden blocks tossed into the air.

21. Colorado voters reelect Henry M. Teller to the U.S. Senate.

21. The blues musician Huddie "Leadbelly" Ledbetter is born in Louisiana.

24. The New Orleans Exposition, a third larger than Philadelphia's Centennial Exhibition, opens.

25. The future author Laura Ingalls, 18, marries Almanzo Wilder in De Smet, Dakota Territory.

30. Interior Secretary Henry M. Teller proposes that settlers be allowed to claim the lands set aside as Indian Territory in present Oklahoma.

Also in January 1885:
Theodore Roosevelt publishes *Hunting Trips of a Ranchman*, written at the Maltese Cross Ranch in Dakota Territory. While there, he also penned a series of articles for the *Century Illustrated Monthly Magazine* that will become *Ranch Life and Hunting-Trail* (1888).

FEBRUARY

1. Following a rough 143-day walk from Cincinnati, the author Charles Fletcher Lummis arrives at the offices of the *Los Angeles Times*. He had agreed to write about his journey in return for employment. During the trip, Lummis broke his arm when he fell from a cliff, and set it himself.

▪ The business of the Mormon Church is being conducted by president John Taylor from several hidden locations in Salt Lake City because of pressure and increased persecution by the federal government over the polygamy issue.

2. Charles Fletcher Lummis is named the first city editor of the *Los Angeles Times*, a position he will hold until 1887. His walk to California from Cincinnati will be recounted in *Tramp Across the Continent* (1892).

12. The Sundance, Wyoming, newspaper reports that it is "so cold chickens are standing on one leg."

13. An avalanche on Friday the 13th kills 16 at Alva, Utah. Another 13 remain buried for 12 hours before being rescued.

21. Montana reports that it paid bounties for the following animals in 1884: 5,410 wolves, 1,621 coyotes, 547 bears, and 143 mountain lions.

25. Congress passes a law prohibiting the unauthorized fencing with barbed wire of public lands in the West.

■ The first broadsword competition (a fencing exhibition using wide-bladed weapons) on the Pacific Coast is held in San Francisco.

Also in February 1885:

One hundred and eighteen Nez Percés, imprisoned at Fort Leavenworth, Kansas, since 1877, are allowed to go to a reservation in Idaho. Chief Joseph and 150 of his followers are considered dangerous and exiled to Washington's Colville Reservation. Each of Chief Joseph's requests to return to Idaho's Wallowa Valley is turned down.

The German-born entrepreneur Count James Pourtales returns to Colorado Springs, where he has fallen in love with his cousin, Countess Berthe de Pourtales, whose marriage is ending badly. He buys a half-interest in William Willcox's Broadmoor Dairy Farm for $25,000.

National Headlines/February 1885:

21. WASHINGTON MONUMENT DEDICATED

28. AMERICAN TELEPHONE & TELEGRAPH IN-CORPORATED

MARCH

1. The Board of Forestry is established in California.

7. Another sign that the free days of the cowboy are numbered: In the wake of an epidemic of hoof-and-mouth disease, the Kansas state legislature makes it illegal to drive Texas cattle through Kansas between March 1 and December 1.

10. Arizona's 13th territorial legislature appropriates $100,000 to build an asylum in Phoenix. Tempe receives $5,000 for a teacher's college, while Tucson gets $25,000 for a university. The legislature will be accused of spending recklessly.

12. The University of Arizona is chartered in Tucson.

■ The Montana legislature bans "pernicious hurdy-gurdy" houses.

13. President Grover Cleveland warns would-be settlers to stay out of Indian Territory (in present Oklahoma).

Also in March 1885:

Benjamin Harrison Eaton becomes the fourth governor of Colorado.

Doc Holliday, acquitted of murder in Leadville, Colorado, is asked to leave town.

In the preface to his first book, *A Texas Cowboy, or Fifteen Years on the Hurricane Deck of a Spanish*

Pony (published by M. Umbdenstock and Company of Chicago), Charles A. Siringo writes: "My excuse for writing this book is money—and lots of it."

National Headlines/March 1885:

4. CLEVELAND INAUGURATED AS 22ND U.S. PRESIDENT

APRIL

3. Some 2.75 million acres in Kansas, Oklahoma, and Dakota Territory are opened for settlement by U.S. Land Commissioner W. A. J. Sparks. The lands had been taken fraudulently by a variety of culprits, including cattlemen, claim jumpers, and railroad corporations.

■ The Montana Stockgrowers' Association organizes in Miles City.

11. More Arizonans band together in Florence to challenge the land claim of James Addison Reavis. His spurious "Peralta Grant" claims he owns most of present Arizona and New Mexico.

14. Archuleta County is established in Colorado.

23. Denver records its greatest snowfall to date, 23 inches in 24 hours. Just to the west, Idaho Springs receives 32 inches.

Also in April 1885:

Elizabeth Bacon Custer pens her book on her husband's time with the 7th Cavalry, *Boots and Saddles, or Life in Dakota with General Custer.*

An often stormy relationship begins when Annie Oakley signs on with Buffalo Bill's Wild West extravaganza. No longer are she and Frank Butler billed as a team; for the rest of his life, Butler will act as her manager and assistant. In negotiations with Cody, Butler informs Buffalo Bill that he cannot own "Missy,"

Annie Oakley poses with her supporting cast. (Library of Congress)

William Frederick "Buffalo Bill" Cody (1846–1917): Buffalo hunter, scout, Indian fighter, actor, showman, and icon. (National Archives)

that indeed she is free to work wherever she pleases between engagements.

MAY

4. In Miles City, Montana, a fire destroys a major city block, including the post office.

7. The actor George "Gabby" Hayes is born in Wellesville, New York.

10. Trouble erupts during a card game in Ashland, Kansas. The gambler "Mysterious Dave" Mather is enjoying a game at the Junction Saloon, playing Seven-Up with grocer David Barnes, 23. Barnes wins two out of three 50-cent games. Mather throws the cards at him and takes the money from the table. "I want my money," says Barnes, who is joined quickly by his brother, John. Mather pushes the brother, at which point David goes for his six-gun and sends a bullet through Mather's hat. Bartender Josiah Mather, the brother of Mysterious

Dave, begins to shoot from behind the bar. Mysterious Dave unholsters his weapon, and the bar fills with smoke. When the shooting stops, David Barnes is dead and the bystanders John Wall and C. C. Camp are suffering from leg wounds. Sheriff Pat Sughrue arrests the Mather brothers, who post a $3,000 bond and ride out of town.

14. John George Adair, the financial partner in Charles Goodnight's Palo Duro cattle operation, dies in St. Louis.

17. One hundred thirty-four Apaches led by Geronimo and Nana escape the San Carlos Reservation in Arizona Territory and begin a series of raids. Geronimo had lived quietly at San Carlos since 1883, but now he decides to break for Mexico after the authorities ban the alcoholic beverage Tiswin. Before the band makes it to the border, some 73 civilians and soldiers will be slain.

Geronimo (Gokhlayeh) (c. 1829–1909). After his fourth surrender in 1886, he is deported to Florida, then to Alabama, and finally to Oklahoma. (National Archives)

22. Captain Allen Smith reports that four members of the 4th Cavalry were wounded in a fight with Indians at Devil's Creek in New Mexico.

27. Lieutenant Britton Davis reports a skirmish with Apaches under the war chief Chihuahua in Mexico.

Also in May 1885:

John Middleton, the reputed lover of Belle Starr, drowns when he is thrown off a stolen horse while crossing a creek in Indian Territory. The horse is wearing one of Belle's saddles. She avoids prosecution for the theft with a solid defense, and celebrates by going on a shopping spree in Fort Smith.

JUNE

5. When asked if he would run for president, General William T. Sherman writes, "If nominated, I will not accept. If elected, I will not serve."

8. Three guards protecting a supply train are slain by Indians at Guadaloupe Canyon in Sonora, Mexico.

23. Captain Emmett Crawford reports that two detachments of cavalry killed one Indian and captured 15 in the Babispe Mountains of Sonora, Mexico.

National Headlines/June 1885:
19. STATUE OF LIBERTY ARRIVES IN NYC

JULY

4. In Salt Lake City, Mormons protest U.S. government policies against them, specifically over the polygamy issue, by flying flags at half-mast.

7. The Albany Hotel opens in Denver.

21. Cornerstone-laying ceremonies for the Cheyenne African Methodist Episcopal Church are held in Wyoming.

22. The author Owen Wister sleeps on the counter of a general store in Medicine Bow, Wyoming. The 25-year-old Philadelphian is on a trip to the West

---

OWEN WISTER
JULY 14, 1860–JULY 21, 1938

The man who invented the modern Western did it with such originality and style that today he is still being imitated. Owen Wister's *The Virginian* offered a profound concept: a cowboy hero who managed to be quite the gentleman. This, combined with the detailed reality of wild Wyoming, elevated the horse opera from the comic book drudgery of dime novels to a respected place in American literature.

Owen Wister, the only child of Dr. Owen Jones Wister and the former Sarah Butler, was born in Philadelphia on July 14, 1860. His maternal grandmother was Fanny Kemble, the most celebrated Shakespearean actress of her time. The Wisters were financially secure; Owen spent many of his early years abroad, receiving his education in the best schools in England and Switzerland. Returning to the United States in 1873, he enrolled at St. Paul's School in Concord, New Hampshire.

His parents believed that young Owen would have a career as a composer. They were pleasantly surprised by the articles he wrote on the Philadelphia Centennial Exhibition of 1876, and the poetry he contributed to his school newspaper. His grandmother, who socialized with such literary personalities as James Russell Lowell, Ralph Waldo Emerson, and Henry Wadsworth Longfellow, might have had some effect on Wister's eventual vocation, but when he enrolled at Harvard his major was music.

In Wister's junior year, his poem on Beethoven was published in the *Atlantic Monthly*. At Harvard, he also came in contact with several notables, including William Dean Howells and Oliver Wendell Holmes (Sr. and Jr.). His best college friend was Theodore Roosevelt, two years his senior, who would play an important role in opening the West to Wister.

Wister published a farcical novel, *The New Swiss Family Robinson,* in 1882, the same year he graduated *summa cum laude*. He went abroad to study musical composition in Paris at the recommendation of Franz Liszt. He returned to the United States a year later at the request of his father. In Boston, he took a boring bank job and began to delve deeper into his fiction.

Health problems arose in 1885. Wister's doctor suggested that a trip might be in order. Roosevelt had preceded him out West, and his sparkling letters had aroused Wister's curiosity. In July, the 25-year-old Owen Wister found himself on a ranch near Kaycee, Wyoming.

The new world—filled with cowboys and cov-
(continued)

(continued)

ered with trail dust—was something Wister had not expected. In the weather-beaten faces of the wranglers, he found heroism. He returned to the East that fall and entered Harvard's law school, but the West stayed with him. He graduated in 1888 and set up a moderately successful practice in Philadelphia. By 1891, he had spent four more summers on the other side of the Mississippi because he "couldn't get Wyoming out of his head."

He filled his diary with what he called "details about pack horses, camps in the mountains, camps in the sagebrush, nights in town, cards with cavalry officers, meals with cowpunchers, roundups, scenery, the Yellowstone Park, trout fishing, hunting with Indians, shooting antelope, white tail deer, black tail deer, elk, bear, mountain sheep; and missing these same animals." "I don't know why I wrote it all down," he said. "I had no purpose in doing so, or any suspicion that it was driving Wyoming into my blood and marrow, and fixing it there."

His first Western story, "Hank's Woman," was published in 1892 by *Harper's Magazine.* More followed, and a collection, *Red Men and White,* was published in 1896. He received encouragement from Roosevelt, who wrote: "I can quite sincerely say that they rank with Bret Harte's and Kipling's pieces. I have long been praying to have somebody arise and write articles of that kind." A novel, *Lin McLean,* came in 1898, followed by *The Jimmyjohn Boss* in 1900.

In 1898, Wister married his cousin, Mary Channing Wister, and settled into a house in Philadelphia, where they eventually raised six children. In 1902, they visited Charleston, South Carolina, the site of their honeymoon, and Wister began to work on a new project. He would take some of his finest tales, compose a few more, and shape them into a novel. In May, he wrote to Oliver Wendell Holmes Jr.: "I set out to draw a man of something like genius—the American genius—and to make the reader feel this by methods other than assuring him of the fact. None of your 'At this point the conversation became both witty and brilliant'; but *action,* sir, action and manifestation."

The Virginian: A Horseman of the Plains, dedicated to Theodore Roosevelt, was published by Macmillan on May 30, 1902. Here was the mysterious and nameless Virginian, winning his own independent West, always with an eye on the pretty schoolmarm Molly Stark Wood. For conflict, there was the evil Trampas, daring to call the Virginian a "son-of-a———" during a card game and, in return, getting one of the great lines of Western fiction: "When you call me that, *smile!*"

The reviews hailed a new genius. "Owen Wister has come pretty near to writing the American novel," said the *New York Times Saturday Review of Books,* Said the *Bookman,* "Mr. Wister has driven into the soil of Wyoming a stake which seems likely to remain for a long time to come."

The status of being an overnight sensation was somewhat of a surprise to Wister, who was soon collaborating with a dramatist on a theatrical version of *The Virginian.* On January 5, 1904, Dustin Farnum debuted in the starring role on Broadway. Stock companies kept the play alive for the next 20 years.

Though his publisher begged for more, Wister never wrote another Western. His other works included biographies of Ulysses S. Grant and Benjamin Franklin. In 1915, he wrote *The Pentecost of Calamity,* a concerned plea for the United States to go to war against Germany. In 1930, he published *Roosevelt: The Story of a Friendship, 1880–1919.*

Owen Wister died of a cerebral hemorrhage at his summer home in Saunderstown, Rhode Island, on July 21, 1938. As a memorial, a mountain in Wyoming's Grand Tetons was named for him.

The Virginian was made into a motion picture four times, with Dustin Farnum (1914), Kenneth Harlan (c. 1920), Gary Cooper (1929), and Joel McCrea (1946) each playing the title role. It also became a hit television series starring James Drury during the 1960s. In the 1970s, the Western Writers of America named the book the best Western novel of all time. Some of Wister's devices—the mail order bride, an order to be out of town by sundown, and the inevitable showdown—have become standard Western plot fixtures.

Why Wister never penned another cowboy tale might be explained better by the times than by the man. Perhaps he believed he had gotten it right the first time. Obviously, he felt no need to fill library shelves with reams of sequels. His tombstone offers a permanent answer for any detractors: "When you call me that, *smile.*"

that was recommended by his doctor. Soon, he will visit the TTT Ranch near Kaycee, Wyoming, where he will take extensive notes for his novel, *The Virginian* (1902).

26. Cherry Creek floods in Denver.

28. Captain Wirt Davis reports two Indians slain by soldiers in the Sierra Madres of Sonora, Mexico.

Also in July 1885:

Following a revolt in western Canada, rebels from a half-breed people known as the Métis take refuge near Helena, Montana. With them is the buffalo hunter Gabriel Dumont, who will achieve fame as a sharpshooter with Buffalo Bill's Wild West.

National Headlines/July 1885:

23. FORMER PRESIDENT GRANT DIES AT 63

AUGUST

7. Captain Wirt Davis reports five Apaches slain and 15 captured by soldiers in the Sierra Madres of Sonora, Mexico.

■ President Cleveland approves legislation ending the fencing of government lands.

12. The author Helen Hunt Jackson, 64, dies of cancer in San Francisco. She had just published *A Century of Dishonor,* about the federal government's bad treatment of Native Americans.

26. J. K. Mullen incorporates his flour mills as the Colorado Milling and Elevator Company.

29. *Harper's Weekly* publishes Rufus F. Zogbaum's painting *Hands Up!,* depicting a stagecoach robbery.

SEPTEMBER

30. In Rock Springs, Wyoming, anti-Chinese riots have claimed 28 lives. Another 15 persons are seriously wounded. Governor Warren appeals to Washington, D.C., for troops in the wake of the "Rock Springs Massacre." President Cleveland orders federal troops to be stationed at Camp Pilot Butte.

Also in September 1885:

Kristofer Janson writes about the Minnesota immigrant experience in *Praeriens Saga* ("Saga of the Prairies").

OCTOBER

14. The humorist Josh Billings dies at age 67 in his hotel room while on a lecture trip at Monterey, California.

18. C. Meyer Zulich is appointed territorial governor of Arizona.

24. The Orange Growers' Protective Union of Southern California is organized.

Also in October 1885:

There are 20,000 bison in North America, down from 395,000 in 1880.

NOVEMBER

3. In Tacoma, Washington Territory, anti-Chinese riots leave 200 homeless.

6. The U.S. Mint in Carson City, Nevada, is ordered to discontinue coinage; it will continue "parting and refining" bullion.

7. President Cleveland orders federal troops to Tacoma, Washington Territory, to quell race riots.

9. In San Diego, the driving of the final spike connects the city to the transcontinental railway via the Atchison, Topeka, and Santa Fe Railroad.

11. Leland Stanford Junior University is founded in Palo Alto, California, by the railroad magnate Leland Stanford, as a memorial to his deceased son.

14. "The Dead Shot Nine, or My Pards of the Plains," a dime novel "by Buffalo Bill," begins serialization in the *Banner Weekly,* which has succeeded *Beadle's Weekly.*

15. After a bitter fight with the Southern Pacific Railroad, which wanted exclusivity in southern California, the Atchison, Topeka, and Santa Fe train departs San Diego.

16. San Francisco's Alcazar Theater opens.

18. Ned Buntline's "Will Cody, the Pony Express Rider, or Buffalo Bill's First Trail" begins serialization in the *Banner Weekly.*

21. The first transcontinental train arrives in San Diego.

29. The final statistics on steamboats stopping at Fort Benson, Montana, this season: 45 boats, carrying 1,110 arriving passengers and 948 departing passengers.

National Headlines/November 1885:

25. VICE PRESIDENT HENDRICKS DIES AT 66

DECEMBER

4. Alferd Packer, the convicted cannibal, files a petition with the Colorado Supreme Court, requesting a writ of habeas corpus and his release from jail because "more than two terms of court" have passed without his being granted a new trial.

5. The Colorado Supreme Court rejects Alferd Packer's petition for his release from jail.

8. President Cleveland calls for a suspension of the mandatory coinage of silver dollars.

9. Lieutenant S. W. Fountain reports two Indians killed by the 8th Cavalry at Littie's Ranch, on Clear Creek in New Mexico.

19. Indians attack the 8th Cavalry at Little Dry Creek,

New Mexico, killing five soldiers and wounding two.

31. Temperatures plunge across the West, as the plains are raked by ice and snow. Six-foot drifts are reported in Nebraska.

Also in December 1885:

General George Crook and his troops chase Geronimo into Mexico.

Arizona reports an average daily public school attendance of 3,226. The number of children not attending is 4,151.

The proprietor of Wade Morrison's Old Corner Drug Store in Waco, Texas, begins selling a new concoction of his that he claims is a "tonic, brain food and exhilarant." Morrison names the product "Dr Pepper," after his true love's father, who had forbidden their marriage.

Also in 1885:

The *Los Angeles Times* reports: "Los Angeles people do not carry arms, Indians are a curiosity, the gee string is not a common article of apparel here, and Los Angeles has three good hotels, twenty-seven churches, and 350 telephone subscribers."

Wells Fargo reports incomes of $4,007,000 from transportation and $1,600.000 from express services. Fifteen holdups account for $2,600 in losses, most of which are recovered.

There are 750,000 head of cattle valued at $15 million in Arizona.

Washington Matthews becomes one of the first Navajos to record sand paintings.

President Cleveland withdraws troops guarding the borders of Indian Territory.

Mark Twain's *The Adventures of Huckleberry Finn* is banned by the public library in Concord, Massachusetts, as "trash and suitable only for the slums."

The first paper mill to use ground wood is established in Camus, Washington Territory.

Missoula and Billings, Montana, are incorporated.

John Stetson organizes his John B. Stetson Company in Philadelphia with a capital of $3 million, as production reaches 150 dozen hats a day. His idea for "felting" hats came during a fruitless search for gold in Colorado's "Pikes Peak or Bust" rush. Stetson struck gold of another kind.

Scott Joplin relocates from Texarkana to St. Louis and begins playing piano in nightspots on Market and Chestnut Streets.

1886

"Once I moved about like the wind. Now I surrender to you and that is all."
—Geronimo

JANUARY

1. The Valley Hunt Club sponsors the first Tournament of Roses Parade in Pasadena, California. The club's founder, Charles Frederick Holder, had suggested that carriages be adorned with the natural flowers of California.

2. Food prices in Topeka, Kansas: butter—20 cents a pound; eggs—20 cents a dozen; prunes—18 pounds for $1; sugar—14 pounds for $1; coffee—8 pounds for $1.

3. Organized criminals in Wichita, Kansas, order Charley Sings to close his laundry and get out of town. The local police promises him protection.

6. A blizzard pounds the Midwest as the "Great Die-Up"—the winter that will kill thousands of cattle on the open range—continues.

9. In Dakota Territory, Fargo records a temperature of −27° at noon; in Bismarck, the mercury drops to −35°. A Clark County, Kansas, newspaper observes: "Blessed is he who has plenty of shelter and feed for his stock and coal for fuel for these times, but woe unto him that hath them not."

10. Captain Emmet Crawford's troops, part of General George Crook's force pursuing Geronimo, engage Mexican troops in a confusing fight near the Aros River in Sonora, Mexico. Crawford is wounded.

11. In Kansas, the *Dodge City Globe* reports: "The water holes are frozen over, the grass is snowed under and the weather is cold, with every prospect of more snow. . . . A gentleman from a ranch south of here reports seeing cattle . . . that were still standing on their feet, frozen to death."

14. Residents of Wichita report Indians on the doorsteps of many homes, begging to be let in from the cold.

18. Captain Emmet Crawford dies of wounds he suffered on January 10.

30. The *Salt River Valley News* begins publication in Tempe, Arizona.

■ Many stoves in Kansas are reportedly burning corn due to shortages of coal.

Also in January 1886:

Count James Pourtales buys the first two cows for his Broadmoor Dairy Farm in Colorado Springs.

The Iowa state capitol building in Des Moines is finally completed after 15 years of construction. The total cost is $2,873,294.59.

Wovoka, the son of the Paiute shaman Tavibo, has a vision in which he is taken to heaven to meet the dearly departed. God tells Wovoka there must be peace—no stealing, no fighting; a new day is coming.

FEBRUARY

4. The last "legal public hanging" in Prescott, Arizona, occurs as Dennis W. Dilda is executed for murdering a Yavapai County deputy sheriff. His last meal is a breakfast of spring chicken in cream sauce, tenderloin steak smothered in mushrooms, fried oysters, lamb chops, potatoes, green peas, pancakes, bread, jelly, and coffee. Captain William "Buckey" O'Neill faints when Dilda drops through the door of the scaffold.

6. "Montebello, the Magnificent, or The Gold King of Colorado," a dime novel "by Buffalo Bill," begins serialization in the *Banner Weekly*.

7. Anti-Chinese riots erupt in Seattle, Washington Territory. Property is destroyed, five "celestials" are shot, and another 200 are forced on board ships headed for San Francisco.

8. William F. Cody and Buck Taylor appear in *The Prairie Waif* at the Grand Opera House in Topeka, Kansas.

■ The Tempe Normal School opens in Arizona.

11. The Building Trades Council, comprised of unions representing painters, plumbers, and plasterers, and the Laborers' Protective Benevolent Association are founded in San Francisco.

14. The first California oranges to be shipped to the East leave Los Angeles by train.

18. Frederick W. Pitkin, the governor of Colorado from 1879 to 1883, dies in Pueblo at age 49.

Also in February 1886:

Cattlemen are finally able to begin taking stock of the losses to their herds from the bitter winter—some losses are as high as 40 percent. "As I drove over the prairies from Kansas into Texas," wrote the cowboy Charles J. "Buffalo" Jones, "I saw thousands upon thousands of carcasses of domestic cattle which had drifted before the chilling, freezing norther. Every one of them had died with its tail to the blizzard, never having stopped except at its last breath, then fell dead in its tracks."

MARCH

2. The first rails of the Kansas, Nebraska, and Dakota Railroad are laid near Fort Scott, Kansas.

3. The ornithologist Nathaniel S. Goss returns to Kansas from a trip to Central America, with 43 new species of birds valued at $100,000.

4. The University of Wyoming is chartered in Laramie.

6. In Colorado, Alferd Packer's murder conviction has been reversed by the Supreme Court, and a new trial on a lesser charge of manslaughter has been ordered. Today, Packer's new attorney, Thomas Brown, files a request for a change of venue from Lake City, Colorado, saying that it is "impossible to find a single person who does not think Packer guilty."

13. In Kansas, Dodge City saloons are closed by order of Bat Masterson.

■ The *Fort Abercrombie Herald* begins publication in Dakota Territory.

15. William Irwin, the 13th governor of California (1876–1880), dies.

Geronimo and Natchez (c. 1857–1921), photographed by Camillus S. Fly in the Sierra Madre, March 27, 1886. From left to right: White Horse (son of Geronimo) holding the infant daughter of Nahi, Geronimo, Natchez (son of Cochise), and Fun. (Oklahoma Historical Society)

16. A census fraud in Leavenworth, Kansas, is discovered. Some 7,268 names have been added to the correct count of 22,000, in order to enchance real-estate opportunities and to secure more representation in the state legislature.

22. Seattle obtains electricity from a steam plant devised and built by Fred Sparling and Sidney Mitchell.

■ Electric lights burn in Abilene, Kansas, for the first time. Says the *Abilene Reflector*, "Time will tell whether it will be to the interest of the city to use the same to any extent."

25. Apache chiefs, including Geronimo, meet with General George Crook south of the Mexican border at Cañon de los Embudos, and agree to surrender.

29. In Arizona, Geronimo reconsiders his recent surrender to General George Crook and escapes with Naiche and some 20 warriors a few miles from Fort Bowie. They ride toward Mexico.

GERONIMO
1829?–FEBRUARY 17, 1909

c1829: The son of Taklishim and Juana, Geronimo is born along the upper Gila River, a Chiricahua Apache called Gokhlayeh ("the one who yawns").

1839: His childhood is spent in the region of the Gila River in present Arizona.

(continued)

(continued)

1858: Mexican soldiers slay Geronimo's mother, wife, and children in an attack on the Apache camp while the men are away hunting.

1860s: He fights under Cochise, and is given the name Geronimo by his Mexican enemies.

1874: Geronimo assumes leadership of the Chiricahuas after the death of Cochise.

1876: Geronimo escapes the reservation after it is moved to San Carlos, and disappears into Mexico. He later allows himself to be arrested by the agent John P. Clum.

1877: He is returned to the San Carlos Reservation.

1881: He leaves the San Carlos Reservation again to go on the warpath.

1882: Along with Juh, Naiche, Chato, and 74 others, he participates in a raid on the San Carlos Reservation.

1883: He surrenders again, this time to General George Crook in Mexico.

1885: After the reservation bans tiswin, an Apache alcoholic beverage, Geronimo leads 100 Apaches in an escape. They terrorize the Southwest.

1886: Geronimo surrenders to General Nelson A. Miles and is transported by rail to Florida, where he is imprisoned.

1887: He is relocated to Mount Vernon Barracks in Alabama.

1894: He accepts an offer from the Comanches and the Kiowas to share a reservation in Indian Territory; he and the remaining imprisoned Apaches are shipped to Fort Sill.

1903: Geronimo joins the Dutch Reformed Church and appears at the St. Louis World's Fair.

1905: He attends Theodore Roosevelt's inauguration.

1906: He dictates his memoirs, *Geronimo's Story of His People,* to S. M. Barrett.

1909: Still a prisoner of war, Geronimo dies of pneumonia at age 80 in Oklahoma.

---

30. Striking railroad laborers in Atchison, Kansas, damage 30 Missouri Pacific Railroad engines.

Also in March 1886:
In Wyoming, cattle outnumber sheep 3 to 1.

APRIL

1. Cheyenne County, Kansas, is created.

3. Nana, Clothia, and Josamie, with nine Apache braves and 60 women and children, arrive at Fort Bowie in present Arizona under military escort.

■ A Kansas National Guard regiment is sent to Parson, Kansas, where striking rail workers are threatening violence.

6. An "anti-dude" club is formed in Newton, Kansas, and its members set fines for various infractions: carrying a cane—$5; wearing kid gloves and a plug hat—$10; parting one's hair in the middle—$20.

9. A first-class rail ticket from Kansas to California costs $12; a second-class ticket is $7.

12. Following a reprimand from the War Department over the escape of Geronimo, General George Crook is replaced as head of the Apache campaign by General Nelson Miles, who arrives today at Fort Bowie in present Arizona. Almost immediately, Miles will have at his disposal 5,000 soldiers as well as 500 Apache scouts and 1,000 irregular civilian militiamen.

14. A tornado kills 74 people in a 25-mile run through Minnesota; eleven are killed at a wedding party in Rice. Witnesses report that they could see the Mississippi River's bottom as the tornado crossed it.

15. The San Diego Street Car Company is incorporated.

23. In Arizona, fire destroys a city block of Phoenix's business district.

30. Fire destroys part of Hubert Howe Bancroft's San Francisco "History Factory," including six sets of printing plates, 2,000 printed volumes, all but one copy of the Spanish and English edition of *Life of Porfirio Díaz,* and all but two copies of the first volume of *Oregon.*

■ *Harper's* magazine publishes "Cattle Raising on the Plains," by the Salina, Kansas, writer Frank Wilkeson.

Also in April 1886:
Count James Pourtales buys 80 cows for his Colorado Springs dairy farm. He also purchases land along Cheyenne Creek, and construction begins on his $20,000 home.

MAY

4. The workers' strike against the Missouri Pacific Railroad ends when an agreement is reached in St. Louis.

10. The U.S. Supreme Court rules in *Santa Clara County v. Southern Pacific Railroad* that the 14th Amendment's due process clause extends to corporations the same rights that persons have under the Constitution.

11. The largest labor parade in San Francisco takes place, as 10,000 union members gather in the streets.

12. A fire in Tombstone, Arizona, consumes the Grand Central Pump House. Mining operations are suspended because the mines are flooded.

14. The *Police Gazette,* a publication known for its lurid crime tales, is banned in Kansas.

18. Socialist labor leaders are arrested in San Francisco for agitating workers.

21. The city of Tucson, Arizona, demands that Governor Zulich provide protection from Geronimo, whose band has reportedly claimed 100 lives.

26. Prentiss Ingraham's "Buffalo Bill's Bonanza, or The Knights of the Silver Circle" begins serialization in *Beadle's Dime Library.*

28. Strawberries in Parsons, Kansas, sell for 4 cents a quart.

■ In Kansas, the military cemeteries at Forts Larned and Dodge are abandoned.

30. A crowd of 6,000 attends the dedication ceremonies for the National Military Cemetery at Leavenworth, Kansas.

Also in May 1886:

Competition between the Atchison, Topeka, and Santa Fe Railroad and the Southern Pacific has lowered

Spring floods in Los Angeles. (Library of Congress)

prices to the point where one can buy a Kansas City–Los Angeles ticket for $1.

Los Angeles is ravaged by flooding.

National Headlines/May 1886:

1. 100,000 WORKERS OUT ON STRIKE

5. BOMB EXPLODES AT LABOR RALLY IN HAYMARKET SQUARE, CHICAGO

15. EMILY DICKINSON DIES AT 56

JUNE

6. In Rawlins County, Kansas, an angry mob lynches Patrick Fleming, the former county attorney, for the murders of five homesteaders.

10. The Missouri Pacific's tracks reach Salina, Kansas. Approximately 1,500 persons celebrate the event.

16. Montana's *Great Falls Leader* begins publishing as a weekly.

19. The first newspaper to appear in the "No Man's Land" area of Indian Territory is the *Beaver City Pioneer,* whose slogan is "Westward the Star of Empire Takes its Way."

26. In Kansas, a team from Topeka defeats one from Emporia in a cricket match.

Also in June 1886:

Charles Siringo reprints *A Texas Cowboy, or Fifteen Years on the Hurricane Deck of a Spanish Pony* with the publishing concern "Siringo and Dobson." The second edition contains a 30-page addendum on "how to get rich and go broke in the cattle business."

In an interview with the *New York Sun,* Doc Holliday is asked if it is true that he killed 30 men. Says Holliday, "I claim to have been a benefactor to the country."

National Headlines/June 1886:

3. CLEVELAND FIRST PRESIDENT TO MARRY IN WHITE HOUSE

JULY

4. An incident on this date is described in Theodore Roosevelt's *Ranch Life and the Hunting-Trail:*

> One evening at Medora a cowboy spurred his horse up the steps of a rickety "hotel" piazza into the bar-room, where he began firing at the clock, the decanters, etc., the bartender meanwhile taking one shot at him, which missed. When he had emptied his revolver he threw down a roll of bank-notes on the counter, to pay for the damage he had done,

and galloped his horse out through the door, disappearing in the darkness with loud yells to a rattling accompaniment of pistol shots firing out of pure desire to enter into the spirit of the occasion—for it was the night of the Fourth of July, and all the country round about had come into town for a spree.

6. Construction begins on the Colorado state capitol building in Denver.

16. Hundreds of women and children are reportedly working in the silk-cocoon industry in Kansas.

19. Alferd Packer and his attorney, Thomas Brown, appear before Judge Melville Gerry at Gunnison, Colorado, in an attempt to have a new judge assigned for Packer's manslaughter trial. Gerry agrees to let Judge William Harrison hear the case.

20. The cornerstone for the new Union Pacific depot is laid in Cheyenne, Wyoming, on the city's 19th anniversary.

21. In Colorado, attorney Thomas Brown again tries unsuccessfully to have his client, Alferd Packer, released from the Gunnison County jail, where he has been housed on charges of manslaughter since May 24, 1883. His motion before Judge William Harrison contends that more than two terms of court had elapsed without his having been placed on trial. The motion is denied.

22. The newspaperman A. L. Runyan, the father of the future author Damon Runyon, buys an interest in the Wellington, Kansas, *Press*.

23. A petition for Alferd Packer's release on grounds of habeas corpus is denied in Gunnison, Colorado.

24. Crops are reportedly drying up in Kansas; the city of Lawrence has seen no precipitation since June 26.

30. The steamship *Kansas Miller* completes a trip from Arkansas City, Kansas, to Fort Smith, Arkansas, with a shipment of 100,000 pounds of flour.

31. In Colorado, Alferd Packer's attorney, Thomas Brown, files a motion arguing that the statute of limitation for manslaughter has run out with regard to his client. The motion is denied. Packer then pleads "not guilty" to five grand-jury indictments of manslaughter, charges that stem from his ill-fated 1874 mining expedition. Members of that party had been discovered dead, their bodies cannibalized.

Also in July 1886:
Mark Twain visits his mother in Keokuk, Iowa.
To prove to the Paiutes that he has had a vision of peace,
Wovoka (also known as Jack Wilson) performs a "miracle" in Nevada's Walking River by making ice appear, but it is a trick: his white brothers threw the ice into the water upriver.

AUGUST

2. Alferd Packer's manslaughter trial begins in Gunnison, Colorado. A jury is seated and various witnesses recount the 1874 incident for which Packer is charged, a mining expedition that ended in murder and cannibalism.

3. Alferd Packer takes the stand in his own defense at his second murder trial. According to the *Rocky Mountain News*: "Packer's manner while on the stand was very excited. He detailed his trip, his act of cannibalism, his arrival at Los Pinos Agency, his arrest and subsequent escape from Saguache, his wanderings up to 1883, and his final capture at Fort Fetterman, in a wild, incoherent manner, standing in his shirt-sleeves, waving his mutilated hand in the air and haranguing the jury in broken sentences. He frequently cursed his enemies in very plain words and refused to be governed by his counsel. Replying once to a remonstrance on their part, he said, 'You shut up. I'm on the stand now.'"

▪ Wyoming's first county fair is held in Johnson County.

4. In Gunnison, Colorado, Alferd Packer is found guilty on five counts of manslaughter.

5. Alferd Packer professes his innocence at his sentencing: "You will see this whole mystery will come out." Judge Harrison sentences him to 40 years in the penitentiary in Canon City, Colorado.

6. Summing up the events of the Alferd Packer trial, Denver's *Rocky Mountain News* reports: "thus thirteen years after his crime Alfred Packer, 'the cannibal,' 'the monster' is disposed of, and from now on he is, as he himself said, dead to the world."

7. The *Topeka Daily Capital* announces that 44 fairs will be held in Kansas in the coming year.

14. Prentiss Ingraham's "Buffalo Bill's Swoop, or The King of the Mines" begins serialization in *Beadle's Dime Library*.

19. A major hurricane destroys the town of Indianola, Texas, killing 176 people.

22. Amos Lawrence, the pioneer for whom Lawrence, Kansas, was named, dies in Nahant, Massachusetts.

25. A fire does $100,000 in damages to the business district of Phoenix, Arizona.

31. Gordon Lillie (the future showman "Pawnee Bill")

Gordon William "Pawnee Bill" Lillie (1860–1942) and May Manning (c. 1864–1936) on their wedding day, right after her graduation from Smith, August 31, 1886. The Lillies compete with Cody's Wild West, then merge their show with his in 1908 to form "Buffalo Bill's Wild West and Pawnee Bill's Great Far East." (Oklahoma Historical Society)

weds May Manning upon her graduation from Smith College.

Also in August 1886:

The first scientific digs in New Mexico and Arizona are conducted by the Hemenway Southwestern Archaeological Expedition. Ethnologist Frank Hamilton Cushing leads a group in uncovering prehistoric sites in the Salt River Valley near Phoenix. They are funded by Boston philanthropist Mary Hemenway.

Theodore Roosevelt, living on his Elkhorn Ranch in Dakota Territory, writes the biography *Thomas Hart Benton* (1887).

SEPTEMBER

2. The Kansas Conference of the African Methodist Episcopal Church meets in Topeka.

4. Geronimo and 38 of his band of Apaches surrender to General Nelson A. Miles at Skeleton Canyon, 65 miles southeast of Arizona's Fort Bowie. The terms of the surrender specify that the Indians will be relocated to Florida. Following his last surrender, Geronimo and many of his followers will be shipped in chains to Fort Marion, Florida. More than 100 will die enroute of "consumption." The government will send the Apache children to the Indian school at Carlisle, Pennsylvania.

9. Ground-breaking ceremonies take place in Cheyenne for Wyoming's state capitol building.

13. *Annals of Kansas 1541–1885*, by Daniel Wilder, is published. At 1,196 pages, it is the longest book ever printed in Kansas. The sale price is $5.

15. The first Wyoming Territorial Fair is held in Cheyenne.

25. Major Frederick W. Benteen, of Little Bighorn fame, is found drunk while on duty at Fort Du Chesne, Utah.

27. P. T. Barnum's "Greatest Show on Earth" draws a crowd of 20,000 in Topeka, Kansas.

Also in September 1886:

Count James Pourtales leaves his thriving Colorado Springs dairy farm in the care of his partner and returns to Germany.

The first Dallas Fair is held.

OCTOBER

1. The Carson City Mint is reopened as an assay office for deposits.

4. The first women's suffrage convention in Kansas is held in Leavenworth.

10. Some 5,000 men are at work constructing the Chicago, Kansas and Nebraska (Rock Island) Railroad.

12. Floods along the Texas Gulf Coast claim at least 200 lives.

16. The first electric lights in Miles City, Montana, are turned on.

17. In Topeka, Kansas, a steam-powered brickyard is producing 50,000 bricks a day.

18. Captain C. L. Cooper accepts the surrender of eight Apaches in Arizona's Black River Mountains.

28. STATUE OF LIBERTY DEDICATED IN NEW YORK

NOVEMBER

2. Colorado voters elect the Democrat Alva Adams governor.
6. "Daredeath Dick, King of the Cowboys, or In the Wild West with Buffalo Bill," by Julius Lewis, begins serialization in the *Banner Weekly*.
8. Sam Purple kills his wife and two children in Jetmore, Kansas. A mob hangs him.
11. At Fort Du Chesne, Utah, commanding officer Major Frederick W. Benteen has a public outburst that will result in his court-martial.
15. There are 56 inmates on death row in the penitentiary in Leavenworth, Kansas.
26. One thousand men are employed as laborers by the Rock Island Railroad near Hutchinson, Kansas.
27. Various ceremonies commemorate California's first Arbor Day.
29. The first Kansas, Pacific and Western train reaches Pratt, Kansas.

Also in November 1886:

The last cattle slaughter by the Northern Pacific Refrigerator Car Company takes place in North Dakota. For a variety of reasons, the creative enterprise of the French Marquis de Mores never prospered.

National Headlines/November 1886:
18. FORMER PRESIDENT ARTHUR DIES IN NYC

DECEMBER

2. A 45-inch coal vein is discovered in Cato, Kansas.
6. The first Kansas, Nebraska and Dakota train arrives in Topeka, Kansas.
7. A 40-inch coal vein is discovered in Clyde, Kansas.
18. Glendive, Montana, records a temperature of 50°.
20. In Kansas, you can pay for your subscription to the *Cedar Vale Star* with coal, stove wood, vegetables, apples, or chickens. Cash is also accepted.
21. A boiler explodes on the steam tug *Escort* near Marshfield, Oregon.
23. The Missouri Pacific Railroad absorbs the Topeka, Salina and Western as well as the Kansas and Colorado Railroads.
25. The temperature in Glendive, Montana, drops to −35°, an 85° swing in one week.

Also in December 1886:

At a Christmas hoedown in Indian Territory, Sam Starr, the husband of Belle Starr, 38, quarrels with the lawman Frank West. The two men shoot each other dead. Following the incident, Cherokee authorities will attempt to confiscate Belle's property because she is no longer married to an Indian. She will solve that problem by entering into a common-law marriage with Bill July, a 24-year-old Creek Indian whom she will rename Bill July Starr.

The New Mexico Educational Association is established in Santa Fe.

Also in 1886:

New Mexico's new capitol building in Santa Fe is completed.

Hubert Howe Bancroft publishes the first volume of a two-volume work, *Oregon,* as well as the one-volume *Alaska.*

The Denver Union Stockyards is established as the country's largest sheep market.

I. B. "Print" Olive is slain in Trail City, Colorado; he was shot in the head by the cowboy Joe Sparrow because of a $10 debt.

Wells Fargo has an income of $4,025,000 from its express service.

Quanah Parker, the Comanche chief who surrendered in 1875, becomes a judge on the Court of Indian Offenses in Indian Territory for the Wichitas, Kiowas, Apaches, and Comanches. He will hold the position until 1898, when he will be dismissed for polygamy. He will have five wives by then.

Fort Ellis in Montana is abandoned.

Caleb W. West becomes governor of Utah; he will serve in that office until 1889.

All Hallows College is established in Salt Lake City, Utah.

A delegation of Apaches, including Chato, Loco, and Alchesay, visits Washington, D.C. Its meeting with President Cleveland to prevent the removal of Apaches to Florida is unsuccessful.

A 10-year depression in the cattle industry begins. Wyoming, which this year has nine million head, will see that number shrink to three million by 1895 due to disease and harsh winters.

The Denver and Rio Grande Railroad is completed to Glenwood Springs, Colorado.

There are 800,000 head of cattle worth $15.2 million in Arizona.

The number of bison in the American West drops to approximately 1,000.

1887

"Everything is decided in Washington by the majority, and these people come out west and see that the Indians have a big body of land they are not using, and they say 'We want the land.' "

—General George Crook

JANUARY

1. Another ceremony to drive a golden spike occurs, this one in Arizona, as Governor Zulich presides over the completion of the Prescott and Arizona railroad.

■ Commodore Perry Owen assumes the office of sheriff of Apache County, Arizona.

4. The Dodge City Cowboy Band accepts an invitation to perform at the inaugural ceremony for the governor of Colorado.

5. John L. Sullivan boxes at an exhibition in Topeka, Kansas.

6. Black voters petition the Kansas legislature to strike the word "white" from a provision concerning the state militia in the state's constitution.

8. A ceremonial spike is driven at 10:00 P.M. in Espanola, New Mexico, linking the tracks of the Denver and Rio Grande with those of the Santa Fe and Northern, thereby connecting the capitals of Colorado and New Mexico.

■ Preston Leslie, Kentucky's former governor, is appointed Montana Territory governor.

■ Washington Bartlett is inaugurated as California's governor.

9. During the second bitter winter of the "Great Die-Up," snow falls at the rate of one inch per hour for 16 hours over much of the Midwest. Temperatures across the Midwest plummet to −46°.

12. Boston Corbett of Cloud County, Kansas, is elected third assistant doorkeeper of the U.S. House of Representatives. In 1865, Corbett shot Abraham Lincoln's assassin, John Wilkes Booth.

■ Maria E. DeGeer becomes the first woman admitted to the Kansas bar.

16. The schooner *Parallel,* with a cargo of gunpowder, explodes near the Cliff House in San Francisco Bay.

19. In Flagstaff, Arizona, two murderers are hauled from jail and killed by an angry mob.

20. In Hawaii, Pearl Harbor is leased by the U.S. government as a naval station.

21. St. Xavier Mission, on Montana's Crow Reservation, is founded by Fathers Prando and Bandini.

28. Arizona's first train robbery occurs 17 miles east of Tucson, as two masked bandits make off with $20,000 from a Southern Pacific passenger train.

29. Prentiss Ingraham's "Buffalo Bill's Secret Service Trail, or The Mysterious Foe" begins serialization in *Beadle's Dime Library.*

30. Richard Wood, a black man jailed in Leavenworth, Kansas, on charges of raping a white girl, is pulled from his cell by a mob of masked farmers, tied to a horse, and dragged to his death.

■ In San Francisco, Thomas Baldwin accomplishes a record-breaking parachute jump from a balloon.

Also in January 1887:

The Kansan Thomas W. Stevens returns to San Francisco after having bicycled around the globe since April 1884.

Cochise County, Arizona, sheriff John Slaughter kills

The Cody legend is the stuff dreams and dime novels are made of. (Library of Congress)

the bandit-murderer Geronimo Baltierrez near Fairbank, Arizona. Slaughter found his victim with a woman inside a tent outside of town. When Slaughter ordered him to surrender, Baltierrez slit a hole in the tent and ran. Slaughter chased him until he was close enough to deliver twin shotgun blasts.

FEBRUARY

2. The court-martial trial of Major Frederick W. Benteen, who was found drunk on duty last year at Fort Du Chesne, Utah, begins.

4. Leavenworth, Kansas, has 200 saloons, one for every thirty families.

5. The biggest snowstorm in San Francisco's history leaves 3.7 inches downtown and 7 inches in the hills west of the city.

8. The Dawes Severality Act is passed by Congress.

■ An argument over a business interest in a Fort Worth, Texas, saloon erupts in gunfire. Luke Short had bought a one-third interest in Jake Johnson's White Elephant Saloon. Short and Johnson were

THE DAWES SEVERALITY ACT
FEBRUARY 8, 1887

Named for its originator, Massachusetts senator Henry Laurens Dawes, the Dawes Severality Act (or General Allotment Act) was seen as an attempt to "civilize" existing Indian tribes and as a means to open more land to white settlement.

By signing the act, President Grover Cleveland dissolved Indian tribes as legal entities (except for the Five Civilized Tribes) and assumed the power to divide tribal lands, giving heads of Indian households 160 acres, single persons 80 acres, and minors 40 acres. Those Indians who accepted land grants received automatic U.S. citizenship. Under the terms of the act, the Indians would agree to farm their allotted land and could not sell it to whites for 25 years. After making the allotments, the government would have the opportunity to open surplus lands to white settlement.

A subject of heated debate, the Dawes Act was seen by many whites as an "emancipation" of the Indians, while Native American authorities protested the breaking up of tribal ownership, another cornerstone of Indian culture. In response to those concerns, J. D. C. Atkins, the commissioner of Indian affairs, said: "Idleness, improvidence, ignorance, and superstition cannot by law be transformed into industry, thrift, intelligence, and Christianity. Thus the real work remains to be done."

Problems will arise from the measure, including the states' refusing to provide basic public services on the tracts of allotted land, and the issue of multiple heirs resulting from the prohibition on the sale of the land. Subsequent legal steps will change and weaken the act. Still, from 1887 to 1934, Indian land holdings will decline from 138 million acres to 47 million acres.

then approached by the gunfighter Longhaired Jim Courtright, who offered protection for a price. Short was unhappy with the arrangement, and when he sold his interest in the saloon on February 7, Courtright issued him a threat through Johnson. Today, Short, accompanied by Bat Masterson, confronts Courtright at a shooting gallery. Courtright goes for his gun when he believes Short is reaching for one. The hammer of Courtright's gun catches on Short's watch chain, giving Short the split second he needs to reach for his own revolver. Short shoots Courtright five times—once through the heart—and Courtright dies. Short will be exonerated for having acted in self-defense.

9. Washington County is established in Colorado.

15. Sixty percent of Montana's cattle have reportedly frozen to death.

■ Boston Corbett, the newly named doorkeeper of the U.S. House of Representatives, is dismissed after threatening to shoot several individuals. He will later be declared insane and institutionalized.

20. W. P. Ricketts writes in his memoirs, *Fifty Years in the Saddle*: "From the last days of November [1886] until the 20th day of February [1887] the mercury ranged from ten to twenty below zero. . . . Ginger, the cook . . . was cranky and so much so I often had it in mind to hit him over the head with a mallet and put him in an ice pack until spring."

23. Moses Harman and his son are arrested by the authorities in Valley Falls, Kansas, and charged with circulating obscene literature through the mail. The publication, described as a "free love" newspaper, is called *Lucifer, the Light Bearer*.

24. The Missouri Pacific Railroad buys the Kansas, Nebraska and Dakota Railroad.

25. Logan County is established in Colorado.

27. San Juan County is established in New Mexico.

28. The establishing of Fort Logan, in Colorado, is authorized by Congress; General Phillip H. Sheridan will choose its location later this year.

Also in February 1887:

Many cattle companies, reporting cattle losses as high as 70 to 90 percent, fold in the face of a second disastrous winter. The Continental Land and Cattle Company reports a near total loss of 30,000 head. The Scottish Swan Land and Cattle Company finds only 100 of its 5,500 three-year-olds alive. The Stuart-Kohrs Company of Montana has lost two-thirds of its 23,000 head of cattle, prompting Granville Stuart to quit the business: "I never wanted to own again an animal that I couldn't feed or shelter," he will write.

One individual who is financially ruined by the bad winter is Theodore Roosevelt, who will return to the East to renew his political career.

MARCH

1. The Lewis Opera House opens in San Diego, California.

2. Congress passes the Hatch Act to develop the science of agriculture.

3. Congress passes the Edmunds-Tucker Bill, which empowers the U.S. government to confiscate and administer property of the disincorporated Mormon Church. Much of the property that will be seized under this law will not be returned to the church until 1896.

■ Women's suffrage is abolished in Utah.

■ The American Protective Association—an anti-Catholic, pro-isolationist group—is founded in Clinton, Iowa.

4. William Randolph Hearst, 24 and recently expelled from Harvard, takes over as publisher of the *San Francisco Examiner*. Soon he will visit Ambrose Bierce at the latter's Oakland, California, apartment, to offer a job that will be eagerly accepted. Bierce will continue his "Prattle" column until 1896.

■ The residents of Tacoma, Washington Territory, who were charged with expelling Chinese in 1855 are found innocent by a grand jury.

6. The Southern Pacific announces a new fare for a one-way trip between Missouri and California: $12. Price wars will drive the fare down to as low as $1 for a time, filling California with immigrants.

8. Factions in the sheep and cattle industry in Arizona

Terrorists hit a sheep herd; artist's conception from Harper's Weekly. *(Harper's Weekly)*

prepare to square off after cowboys stampede 20,000 sheep in the Tonto Basin.

- A special Santa Fe Railroad train makes the 65-mile trip from Topeka to Kansas City in one hour and 45 minutes.

- Henry Ward Beecher dies. In 1856, he was a strong advocate for a free Kansas, and published a pamphlet in which he called for guns and money to fight slavery. The pioneers he inspired became known as the Beecher Bible and Rifle Company; their Sharps rifles were called "Beecher's Bibles."

- James Eads, 67, the builder of the first steel-arch bridge across the Mississippi River in St. Louis, dies in the Bahamas.

10. Arizona's 14th territorial legislature hears Governor Zulick announce that the territory now has 130 school districts.

11. Lieutenant Seward Mott dies from a wound he suffered yesterday in an ambush by Indians during a regimental return at Arizona's San Carlos Agency.

- The *Cheyenne Daily Leader* reports that Calamity Jane is in town.

- Major Frederick W. Benteen is discharged from military service after being court-martialed for conduct unbecoming an officer and a gentleman. Benteen, who was assumed to be intoxicated at the time, entered a store at Fort Du Chesne, Utah, where he was in command. He quarreled with civilians, cursed, removed part of his clothing, and exposed himself.

18. Edwin Booth, the brother of John Wilkes Booth, plays the title role in *Hamlet* in Cheyenne, Wyoming.

19. The *Tombstone Epitaph* comments on the new "seduction law": "It provides that if the victim is under the age of 18, her seducer can escape the penitentiary by marrying her. If however the wronged woman has passed the eighteen year milestone on life's journey, her betrayer has not the choice between marriage and the bastile, but upon conviction goes to the penitentiary will he nil he."

Also in March 1887:

From Colorado Springs to Germany, Count James Pourtales's business partner wires news of a series of catastrophes that have befallen the Broadmoor Dairy: financial ruin, contagious abortion among the cows, plummeting milk prices. The count will return, expand the farm to 2,400 acres, sell the sick cows, and replace them with 200 healthy ones, five prize Swiss bulls, and 2,000 sheep. A cheese expert will be hired from Philadelphia's Darlington Dairy.

Damon Runyan, 6, relocates with his family to Pueblo, Colorado, where his father, Alfred, will work for the *Pueblo Chieftain*. At age 13, young Damon's prose will appear in print for the first time in the *Pueblo Advertiser*, where, due to a typographical error, his name will be spelled "Runyon," a spelling he will adopt.

APRIL

4. Susanna Medora Salter of Argonia, Kansas, is elected America's first female mayor.

- Eighteen persons die in a mine disaster in Savannah, Oklahoma.

27. The Southern Pacific's westbound No. 20 train is robbed near Pantano Station, Arizona. The bandits make off with about $3,000, although the messenger Charles F. Smith manages to stash another $5,000 in the potbellied stove of the Wells Fargo car.

Also in April 1887:

Hubert Howe Bancroft publishes a two-volume history of vigilantism called *Popular Tribunals,* and the one-volume work *British Columbia.*

The Apache Kid, a scout for the U.S. Army, is left in charge of scouts at the San Carlos Agency while Chief of Scouts Albert Sieber is away. Another Apache is murdered, allegedly by the Kid and his cohorts as revenge for the murder of the Kid's father.

MAY

1. The gunfighter Clay Allison is killed when he falls from the wagon he is driving some 40 miles from Pecos, Texas. His skull is fractured by a wagon wheel.

12. A volcanic eruption and an earthquake in Arizona's Dragoon Mountains are reported by the *Tombstone Epitaph.*

15. A large funeral is held in Arkansas City, Kansas, for Chief Wasiki, the former Ponca Indian leader.

19. Halley's electric light plant begins operating in Idaho.

20. U.S. Senator John James Ingalls of Kansas explains his vote against women's suffrage during a speech in Abilene: "Women are women and their place is in the home."

- Bicycle enthusiasts meet at the 8th annual convention of the American Wheelmen in St. Louis.

21. In Montana, the *Rose of Helena,* a steamboat, completes a run from Gates of the Mountains to Great Falls, traveling 112 miles at a speed of 12 miles of an hour.

25. John Taylor, the president of the Mormon Church

since Brigham Young's death in 1877, and who has been presiding over the church in hiding for the past two years because of federal pressure to end polygamy, dies in Salt Lake City at age 79.

27. Jim Thorpe, the Olympic and professional athlete, is born near Shawnee, Oklahoma. A Sak and Fox, his Indian name is Wa-Tho-Huck, which means "Bright Path."

28. In New Mexico, a procession of 502 Jicarilla Apaches passes through Santa Fe's plaza en route to a new reservation in Rio Arriba County.

■ San Francisco registers its warmest May temperature to date: 97°.

Also in May 1887:

Tuberculosis is something Doc Holliday, 35, cannot shoot. He checks into a sanatorium in Glenwood Springs, Colorado, to begin a series of cures.

Many large cattle concerns in the Midwest call it quits following the last two devastating winters.

The Harvard philosopher Josiah Royce writes *The Feud of Oakfield Creek.*

William Jennings Bryan, a 27-year-old lawyer, moves his family from Jacksonville, Illinois, to Lincoln, Nebraska.

National Headlines/May 1887:

3. AMERICAN CATTLE TRUST FOUNDED IN CHICAGO

JUNE

13. The St. Paul and Manitoba Railroad's tracks cross the eastern boundary of Wyoming.

14. Oliver Edwards, a farmer in Doniphan county, Kansas, who reportedly put four male and eight female carp in his pond in 1885, estimates that the carp now total 50,000.

16. The interpreter C. Cacely reports that scouts from Fort Custer killed one Indian and captured one at Pompey's Pillar on Montana's Yellowstone River.

■ The townsite of Glasgow, Montana, is staked out.

20. Buffalo Bill's Wild West performs before Queen Victoria in London, England. Her Majesty pronounces Annie Oakley, 27, "a wonderful little girl!"

21. A fire does $200,000 worth of damage to the business district of Leavenworth, Kansas.

22. The Missouri Pacific's tracks reach Fort Scott, Kansas.

26. In Kansas, the *Wichita Eagle* reports that the "wealthiest Indian in the United States," Mathias Spitlog, has been swindled to the tune of $140,000. Says the *Eagle,* "Mr. Spitlog isn't worried, he still has $864,000."

30. San Francisco's Orpheum Theater opens.

Also in June 1887:

Buck Taylor breaks his leg during a Wild West performance in England.

The city of Amarillo, Texas, begins as a construction camp for workers of the Fort Worth and Denver City Railroad in Potter County. The land on which the camp is built is owned by Jess Jenkins; it is distinguished by buffalo-hide huts, and is called Ragtown.

At the age of 5, Sam Rayburn, the future speaker of the U.S. House of Representatives, relocates with his family from Tennessee to Texas.

JULY

1. William Sydney Porter, the future author O. Henry, elopes with Athol Estes, 17, in Austin, Texas. She will encourage his writing and insist that he submit it to eastern presses.

3. The Maricopa and Phoenix Railroad opens for business; it is the first railroad in Phoenix, Arizona.

8. The former stagecoach magnate Ben Holladay, 68, dies in Portland, Oregon. The *New York Times* obituary misspells his name.

12. The *Tombstone Epitaph* reviews last evening's performance of "serio comic vocalist" Ella Gardiner at the Bird Cage: "She received several encores and the gratified audience like the preacher's daughter kept crying for more."

■ The Rock Island Railroad's tracks reach Hutchinson, Kansas.

13. An item in the *Tombstone Epitaph:* "Several complaints have reached us lately from merchants on Allen street, stating that it was impossible for ladies to visit their stores to do their trading from the amount of empty beer barrels on the sidewalks. The city tax collector should see that the obstructions are removed."

23. The largest individual gold nugget ever found in Colorado is discovered at the Gold-Flake Mine in Summit County. It weighs 156 ounces and is valued at $3,700. The Chicago World's Fair's commissioners will purchase the nugget and several smaller ones for $15,000.

31. Scribner's publishes *Around the World on a Bicycle,* by the Kansan Thomas Stevens.

AUGUST

3. In Kansas, claims resulting from William Clarke Quantrill's raid on Lawrence in August, 1863, are still being processed. Today, the auditor receives a claim from Shalor Eldridge for $60,000, for the burning of his hotel, the Eldridge House.

6. Prentiss Ingraham's "Buffalo Bill's Big Four, or Cus-

ter's Shadow" begins serialization in *Beadle's Dime Library.*

9. Harry Longabaugh, the "Sundance Kid," is convicted of grand larceny in Sundance, Wyoming.

10. The Southern Pacific's westbound No. 20 train is robbed again near Pantano Station, Arizona. The robbers obstruct the track and derail the train, injuring several passengers. The Messenger Charles F. Smith is told that hiding the money in the stove will not work this time, as it did on April 27.

11. The St. Paul and Manitoba Railroad's workers set track-laying records as they work through Milk River Valley, Montana.

12. The Santa Fe's rail line from Santa Ana to Oceanside, California, is completed.

15. Edna Ferber, the author of *So Big* and *Cimarron,* is born in Kalamazoo, Michigan.

■ Walter Stanley Campbell, who will pen works of biography, poetry, and Old West history under the name Stanley Vestal, is born in Severy, Kansas.

19. The last Indian battle in Colorado occurs as state troopers under Major Leslie clash with Utes near Rangely.

■ The first train arrives in Santa Barbara, California.

20. Atchinson, Kansas, reports hailstones 10 inches in diameter.

SEPTEMBER

2. In Pleasant Valley, Arizona, Andy Blevins leads a group of cowboys in an attack on the sheepman John Tewksbury, killing him and William Jacobs. Tewksbury's men hold the attackers off, then slip away under cover of darkness. Blevins is so angry, he turns hogs loose to eat the corpses of Tewksbury and Jacobs.

3. May Leslie divorces her husband, Buckskin Frank Leslie, charging that he physically abused her and was unfaithful. Testimony revealed Frank's strange foreplay: Before they made love, he would stand May against the wall and trace her outline with blasts from his .45. A shocked judge grants the divorce to the newly dubbed "Silhouette Girl."

4. Violence breaks out in the wake of the murder of the Arizona sheepmen John Tewksbury and William Jacobs. Gunfire erupts as Apache County sheriff Perry Owens arrives at a cabin near Holbrook to arrest the cattleman Andy Blevins. Owens kills Blevins, wounds his brother John, then kills Blevins's brother-in-law Mose Roberts, a Texan. Finally, Sam Houston Blevins, 16, makes his last mistake when he runs out of the cabin waving a revolver. He is shot dead.

5. Oregon becomes the first state in the nation to make Labor Day a legal holiday. By 1894, 32 other states will have followed suit.

6. The University of Wyoming opens at Laramie.

8. In Arizona, two members of the Tewksbury sheepmen's faction are killed by the Grahams, rival cattlemen, in revenge for Sheriff Perry Owens's actions on the 4th.

10. Miles City, Montana, is incorporated.

12. California governor Washington Bartlett dies at age 63.

13. Following the death of Governor Washington Bartlett, Robert W. Waterman becomes governor of California.

18. The violence continues in the Pleasant Valley War in Arizona. The Grahams attack the Tewksbury home, and three Grahams and two Tewksburys are wounded.

28. The tracks of the St. Paul and Manitoba Railroad reach Fort Benton, Montana.

29. A silver spike is used in ceremonies marking the completion of the St. Paul and Manitoba Railroad in Fort Benton, Montana.

■ The Southern Pacific's tracks reach the Colorado River in Yuma, Arizona.

Also in September 1887:
In Tempe, Arizona, the *Salt River Valley News* changes its name to the *Tempe News.*

OCTOBER

14. In Kansas, the *Atchison Times* editor John Reynolds is fined $200 and sentenced to 19 months in prison for mail fraud.

25. The St. Paul and Manitoba's tracks reach Great Falls, Montana.

27. Ground-breaking ceremonies are held in Tucson for the University of Arizona.

NOVEMBER

2. The Denver and Rio Grande Railroad is completed to Aspen, Colorado.

5. Brigadier General T. H. Ruger and his troops kill seven Indians, wound 10, and take nine as prisoners at Montana's Crow Agency. Ruger reports one soldier killed and two wounded.

8. John Henry "Doc" Holliday, 35, dies of tuberculosis in Glenwood Springs, Colorado. He had checked into a sanatorium there last May and taken mineral-water cures, but it was too little, too late. His last words—"That's funny"—were uttered when he noticed that he was not dying with his boots on; he then tossed down a toot of whiskey and expired. A *Rocky Mountain News* obituary recalled an interview in which the wildest dentist in the West was asked if his conscience ever bothered him. "No," said Doc. "I coughed that up with my lungs long ago." Wyatt Earp once remarked: "Doc was a dentist whom necessity had made a gambler; a gentleman whom disease had made a frontier vagabond; a philosopher whom life had made a caustic wit . . . the most skillful gambler and the nerviest, speediest, deadliest man with a six-gun I ever knew."

- General Nelson Miles receives a hero's welcome in Tucson following the recent campaign against the Apaches.

10. The construction of an oil pipeline from Omaha, Nebraska, to Casper, Wyoming, is proposed.

15. The artist Georgia O'Keefe is born in Sun Prairie, Wisconsin.

19. The Montana Central Railroad, between Helena and Great Falls, is completed.

- Six workers at a Prescott, Arizona, sawmill die when the boiler explodes.

21. The first Montana Central train arrives in Helena in a snowstorm.

- The St. Paul and Manitoba's tracks reach Helena, Montana.

- Nostalgia from the *Santa Fe Daily New Mexican:* "Billy the Kid was once a distinguished citizen of this country, but through the unerring air of Pat Garrett's pistol, he was rendered an extinguished citizen."

24. The cartoonist Thomas Nast lectures at the Crawford Opera House in Topeka, Kansas.

27. U.S. Marshal Frank Dalton, the "only good Dalton," is slain in the line of duty while trying to apprehend a Kansas bootlegger.

National Headlines/November 1887:
11. THREE ANARCHISTS HANGED IN CHICAGO FOR HAYMARKET RIOT

DECEMBER

2. The U.S. Department of the Interior reports that one of every 15 marriages in Kansas ends in divorce.

5. Rose Wilder Lane, the first child of Almanzo and Laura Ingalls Wilder, is born in De Smet, Dakota Territory.

10. In England, *Beeton's Christmas Annual* runs "A Study in Scarlett," the first Sherlock Holmes story written by Arthur Conan Doyle. One of the locales of the story is Salt Lake City:

> From the Sierra Nevada to Nebraska, and from the Yellowstone River in the north to the Colorado upon the south, is a region of desolation and silence. . . . It comprises snowcapped and lofty mountains, and dark and gloomy valleys. There are swift-flowing rivers which dash through jagged canyons; and there are enormous plains, which in winter are white with snow, and in summer are grey with saline alkali dust. They all preserve, however, the common characteristics of barrenness, inhospitality and misery.

An inviting Kansas promotion piece from 1887. (Library of Congress)

11. Green River City, Wyoming, changes its name to Green River.

22. The first musical group to organize in Butte, Montana, is the Butte Miners Band.

■ In Kansas, the *Leoti Transcript* estimates that there are 852 newspaper editors in the state. Says the paper: "This is an appalling statement coming as it does upon the verge of what promises to be a severe winter."

26. The *Ocean King* catches fire off Cape Blanco, Oregon. The $50,000 ship, weighing 2,434 tons and carrying 3,850 tons of coal, sinks, but all hands are rescued by the schooner *Angel Dolly*.

29. The first Rock Island passenger train passes through Dodge City, Kansas.

Also in 1887

The first orphan's home in Texas opens in Corsicana.

There are 875,000 head of cattle valued at $15.9 million in Arizona.

The real-estate boom continues in Los Angeles County: transactions in 1887 are valued at $100,000,000. In a matter of months, land prices have soared from $100 to $1,500 an acre.

Wells Fargo reports an annual income of $4,107,000.

Elizabeth Bacon Custer publishes *Tenting on the Plains*.

Alva Adams becomes Colorado's 5th governor.

Bauxite is discovered near Little Rock, Arkansas.

Latter Day Saints University is founded in Salt Lake City, Utah.

Theodore Roosevelt publishes the first volume of *The Winning of the West* and proposes a "Boone and Crockett Club" for the protection of big game in the United States.

Annie Oakley leaves Buffalo Bill's Wild West after its last performance in London, to tour with Pawnee Bill's Frontier Exhibition.

A request by Rain in the Face to attend school at the Hampton Institute is noticed by the poet John Greenleaf Whittier, who writes in the *Atlantic Monthly*: "What voice is beseeching thee / For the scholar's lowliest place? / Can this be the voice of him / Who fought on the Big Horn's rim? / Can this be Rain-in-the-Face?" Permission will be denied because tuition would have cost the government $230 a year.

1888

"Without stopping to qualify the averment, the Old World has had the poems of myths, fictions, feudalism, conquest, caste, dynastic wars, and splendid exceptional characters and affairs, which have been great; but the New World needs the poems of realities and science and of the democratic average and basic equality, which shall be greater."

—Walt Whitman, "A Backward Glance O'er Travel'd Roads"

JANUARY

5. Sacramento, California, sets an all-time snowfall record of 3.5 inches in 24 hours.

6. In Atchison, Kansas, fire claims the Union Depot; the loss is valued at $125,000.

10. Street cars begin operating in Cheyenne, Wyoming.

12. A massive cold front chills the entire area between Dakota Territory and Texas during a 24-hour period.

■ Fire destroys the $25,000 home of Kansas senator Ingalls in Atchison.

12. Writes an observer of the terrible blizzard in Dakota Territory: "I saw ice cut from the Pipestem River at Sykeston that month that measured 63 inches in diameter."

13. At Fort Keogh, near Miles City, Montana, the Signal Corps' thermometer records −65°.

17. Tucson, Arizona, receives its first Pullman cars.

23. Public schools in Prescott, Arizona, close for lack of funds.

Also in January 1888:
Frances Courtenay Baylor writes *Juan and Juanita.*

National Headlines/January 1888:
13. NATIONAL GEOGRAPHIC SOCIETY FORMS IN WASHINGTON

FEBRUARY

7. Fire destroys part of the offices of the *Cheyenne Daily Leader* as well as the Cheyenne Opera House.

11. Wichita, Kansas, experiences a smallpox epidemic—47 cases are reported, along with two deaths.

13. The Reverend John Baptist Lamy, the archbishop of Santa Fe, New Mexico, for nearly 40 years, dies in Santa Fe.

20. The Bowersock Flour Mill in Lawrence, Kansas, is destroyed by high water and ice.

22. A train robbery in Arizona's Stein's Pass sets off a bizarre series of events. Frustrated Southern Pacific and Wells Fargo officials offer a $2,000 reward for the capture of the robbers. The sheriff of Cochise County follows the highwaymen into Mexico, where he is arrested and jailed for two weeks.

28. A ferryboat blows up in San Pablo Bay, California.

Also in February 1888:
During the winter, Pawnee Bill plans on going into competition against his idol, Buffalo Bill. The "Pawnee Bill's Wild West" will feature 150 horses and mules, 84 Indians, 50 cowboys, and a score of trappers, warriors, scouts, and settlers. (In 1908, the two show-business legends will collaborate in "Buffalo Bill's Wild West and Pawnee Bill's Great Far East.")

MARCH

1. The Kansas State Historical Society reports that 72 daily papers are being published in the state.

10. In Walnut City, Kansas, armed men seize the records of Rush County and move them to La Crosse, which was chosen by voters as the new county seat last August.

12. Under the terms of a treaty signed today by Secretary of State Charles Bayard and the Chinese minister, Chinese laborers are excluded from entering the United States for 20 years.

■ In response to a shortage of coal in Kansas, the *Garden City Herald* reports that "several young society gents were seen on their way to the residence of their best girls last night carrying a bucket of coal."

19. Three guards from Arizona's Vulture Mine are robbed and murdered en route to Phoenix; bars of gold are reported missing.

■ With all the newspapers being published in the region, the Indian Territory Press Association organizes.

24. Ella Watson, a 26-year-old prostitute, files claim number 2003, for property located about a mile from Jim Averill's spread in Wyoming. Construction begins on a log-cabin bordello, and a large corral. Soon, she and Averill will dabble in stolen cattle.

28. A joint announcement of the Union Pacific, the Missouri Pacific, the Atchison, Topeka, and Santa Fe, and the Rock Island Railroads states that "reasonable amounts" of grain and seed will be carried free of charge for Kansas farmers.

29. A mine in Rich Hill, Missouri, explodes, killing 24.

■ The construction of Wyoming's capitol building is completed in Cheyenne.

Also in March 1888:

The Denver, Texas and Fort Worth Railroad is completed, with connections to New Orleans, Louisiana, and Galveston, Texas.

National Headlines/March 1888:

14. BLIZZARD PARALYZES EAST COAST; 200 DIE IN NEW YORK

16. LOUISA MAY ALCOTT DEAD AT 56

APRIL

11. A U.S. District Court in Topeka, Kansas, throws out the grand jury indictments against Moses Harman and E. C. Walker, who were charged with sending "obscene, lewd and lascivious publications" through the mails. The publication in question is the "free love" newspaper, *Lucifer, the Light Bearer.*

13. In Topeka, Edwin Booth appears in a production of Shakespeare's *Othello.* Says the *Topeka Daily Capital*: "The attraction was too rich for the virgin blood which courses through the veins of this community."

18. Willys Hedges acquires the title to the first homestead in Great Falls, Montana.

24. The town of Liberal, Kansas, a prairie just two weeks ago before the Rock Island Railroad's tracks arrived, now boasts of more than 100 buildings.

Also in April 1888:

Refrigerated railroad cars transport food from the West Coast to the East, including San Joaquin Valley lettuce, Sacramento strawberries, and grapefruits, dates, and figs from southern California.

The American West is just one of the many topics covered in the Englishman James Bryce's book, *The American Commonwealth.*

MAY

3. A major fire destroys much of San Diego's business district; losses will be valued at $200,000.

■ Wells Fargo asks the secretary of the treasury to designate it a common carrier.

9. Natrona County is established in Wyoming.

11. Colorado's warmest temperature ever is recorded in Bennett: 118°.

15. In Des Moines, Iowa, Belva Anne Lockwood, the first woman to argue a case before the U.S. Supreme Court, is nominated to head the presidential ticket of the Equal Rights Party.

17. The United Labor Party nominates W. H. T. Wakefield, the editor of the Council Grove, Kansas, *Anti-Monopolist,* as its candidate for vice president.

26. Boston Corbett, the man who shot John Wilkes Booth and was recently discharged as doorman of the U.S. House of Representatives, escapes from the insane asylum in Topeka, Kansas, where he has been held for the last 15 months.

Also in May 1888:

Wells Fargo and the Santa Fe Railroad approve a contract that will allow the express company straight San Francisco-to-Chicago access without having to do business with the Union Pacific. Wells Fargo guarantees to pay $160 a mile on the main lines, and $60 a mile on the branch lines, including the Gulf, Colorado and Santa Fe lines in Texas, the Chicago, Kansas and Western, and the California Southern.

Hubert Howe Bancroft publishes two volumes of social analysis, *California Pastoral* and *California Inter Pocula.*

JUNE

1. "Politics" is the unofficial reason given for the deaths of Pete Gabriele and Joe Phy at a Florence, Arizona, watering hole; they got into an argument on the topic and killed each other.
5. The Democratic National Convention convenes in St. Louis, where it will nominate President Grover Cleveland for another term as president, and Allen G. Thurman of Ohio for vice president.
6. Wichita, Kansas, celebrates its 18th birthday with a five-mile parade.
7. Cochise County, Arizona, sheriff John Slaughter, his deputy, Burt Alvord, and two Mexicans track another gang of robbers into the Whetstone Mountains. Again, Slaughter and company appear at the bandits' camp at dawn, order the sleepers to surrender, and then open fire. When the robber Guadalupe Robles leaps to his feet, Slaughter kills him with one shot. Another bandit escapes, despite Slaughter's orders to Alvord: "Burt, there is another son of a bitch. Shoot him!"
9. Prentiss Ingraham's "Buffalo Bill's Double, or The Desperado Detectives" begins serialization in the *Banner Weekly*.
13. Dr. John Sullivan, a Tombstone dentist, is reported to be the inventor of the "Dental Electric Vibrator," battery-operated forceps that, according to the *Tombstone Epitaph,* cause "the tooth to spring from the jaw without any perceptible effort on the part of the dentist, and without causing the patient any greater pain than would be caused by the prick of a pin."
24. Kingman, Arizona, the seat of Mohave County, is totally destroyed by fire.
28. Robert Louis Stevenson, 38, has his 95-foot yacht *Casco* towed out of San Francisco Bay and past the Golden Gate, to begin a round-the-world trip that will end with his death in Samoa in 1894.

National Headlines/June 1888:
25. GOP NOMINATES HARRISON

JULY

1. A fire in Prescott, Arizona, claims 13 buildings.
2. The Pawnee Bill Frontier Exhibition opens at Gloucester Beach, New Jersey, with Annie Oakley as the headliner.
3. Mattie Blaylock, the former common-law wife of Wyatt Earp, is found dead in the mining town of Pinal, Arizona, with liquor and laudanum bottles near her bedside.
■ The Rock Island's rails reach Goodland, Kansas.
4. Prescott, the territorial capital of Arizona, sponsors

BILL TILGHMAN
JULY 4, 1854–NOVEMBER 1, 1924

The last of the great Old West sheriffs was the tough Bill Tilghman, who handled outlaws in two centuries. In his time, he encountered some of the West's worst, from saddle-sore bank robbers to cocaine dealers, and still found time for politics and show business.

William Matthew Tilghman, Jr., was born on the Fourth of July in 1854, at Ford Dodge, Iowa. Little Billy was still in diapers the first time someone shot at him: The family was living at Fort Ridgely, Minnesota, when it was attacked by Sioux, and a flying arrow hit his mother in the arm as she held him. In 1856, the family moved to Atchison, Kansas.

Tilghman became the man of the family early, when his father went to fight in the Civil War. At age 16 in 1870, he was strong and willful enough to leave home to become a buffalo hunter, joining that league of high-caliber plainsmen who would deplete the species at an alarming pace. During the winter of 1873, Tilghman alone accounted for 7,500 buffalo kills.

These were wild, busy times. He met his lifelong friend Bat Masterson in 1874, just after the Battle of Adobe Walls in Texas where 37 hunters had held off more than 700 Indians. That same year, Tilghman was involved in a major gunfight while successfully retrieving the body of the murder victim Pat Congers in Petrie, Indian Territory.

With the bison population decreasing, Tilghman got involved in various illegalities, including stealing horses from Indians in Kansas. In 1878, he was twice in court for rustling and train robbery, only to be found innocent.

Perhaps these brushes with the law made him think seriously about on which side of the law he would reside. He became a respected citizen of Dodge City, Kansas, married, raised cattle on the outskirts of town, and ran two saloons. From 1884–1886, he served as marshal of that fabled cow capital, a task for which he was given a badge pounded out of two $20 gold pieces.

An active participant in the Gray County
(*continued*)

(continued)

Seat War of 1889, Tilghman and his buddy Wyatt Earp fought side by side when county records were forcibly removed from Cimarron. That battle behind him, Tilghman looked for greener pastures and found them in the Oklahoma Land Runs. At Guthrie, a town that had boomed literally overnight, he became a peace officer. In 1891, he made the second "run," staking a claim near present Chandler. He also became a deputy United States marshal that year, a job he would hold until 1912.

It was during this time that Tilghman, along with the lawmen Heck Thomas and Chris Madsen, organized the manhunt for Bill Doolin, the leader of the robbing conclave known as the "Oklahombres." On September 1, 1893, Tilghman and a dozen associates converged on the gang while its members played cards at a brothel in Ingalls, near present Stillwater, Oklahoma. Doolin escaped in a hail of bullets, with Tilghman tight on his trail.

During the pursuit, Tilghman captured the bandit groupies Annie McDougal and Jennie Stevens (aka "Cattle Annie" and "Little Britches"), as well as another gamine gunslinger called the Rose of Cimarron, who surrendered when Tilghman shot her horse out from under her. In 1895, his posse captured the gang member Bill Raidler near Elgin, Kansas.

"Uncle Billy," as the desperados called him, finally tracked Doolin to a Eureka Springs, Arkansas, bathhouse in January 1896. Dressed as a country preacher, Tilghman took Doolin after a struggle in the steam. Doolin had once saved the marshal from being shot in the back; now, Tilghman allowed his prisoner to ride the train to Guthrie, Oklahoma, without the cuffs. At the depot, they were greeted by a crowd of 5,000. (Doolin escaped six months later; he was tracked down and slain by Marshal Heck Thomas.)

In 1898, a mob attacked and burned to death two Indian teens who had been wrongly accused of raping and murdering a white woman. In an unprecedented action, Tilghman went after the instigators, winning convictions and sentences for eight of them. He then learned the identity of the true culprit and apprehended him.

From 1900–1904, Tilghman served as the elected sheriff of Lincoln County, Oklahoma. Following the death of his first wife, he remarried in 1903. At the request of President Theodore Roosevelt in 1905, he went to Mexico to return a fugitive. He was elected a state senator in 1910, a position he resigned in 1911 in order to serve as Oklahoma City's police chief until 1913.

At about this time, Tilghman became involved in the blossoming motion picture industry when he was contacted by the photographer J. B. Kent and the reformed outlaw Al Jennings to help film a staged bank robbery in Cache, Oklahoma. Shooting was interrupted briefly while Tilghman explained to the frightened townfolk that it was "only a movie."

Seeing himself nab criminals on the silver screen inspired Tilghman to begin work on his own flick, one that would show the West as it really was. With the lawman E. D. Nix, he formed the Eagle Film Company in 1915, and began production on *The Passing of the Oklahoma Outlaws*.

Tilghman insisted that his film be authentic. The locations included Ingalls and the Eureka Springs, Oklahoma, baths. Production was halted on the afternoon of March 27, 1915, when Henry Starr, a relative of the late "bandit queen" Belle Starr, robbed two banks at nearby Stroud. Tilghman put down his director's megaphone, strapped on his .45s, and joined the posse. He eventually captured one of the robbers.

The movie wrapped that summer, and Tilghman took it on the road, appearing at each showing to answer questions and reminisce. In September 1915, Tilghman projected his masterpiece at Denver's Tabor Palace. Soon after, he took it to Los Angeles, where he met with his aging friend Wyatt Earp.

But the years were catching up with Tilghman as well. Figuring that he would spend his retirement making movies, he was surprised in 1924 when Oklahoma governor M. E. Trapp asked him to become marshal of the wild city of Cromwell. Friends and family tried to discourage him, but the 71-year-old Tilghman had yet to shirk a duty.

In his first three months there, Tilghman cleared Cromwell of the bad guys and busted a cocaine dealer. On November 1, 1924, while eating in Murphy's Restaurant, he heard shots. In the street, he found, of all things, a drunken prohibition agent named Wiley Lynn, whom Tilghman quickly disarmed. But on the way to jail, Lynn produced a concealed weapon and shot Tilghman twice. The old marshal was helped to a couch in a furniture store, where he died with his boots on.

an organized rodeo, which it claims to be history's first. The event will evolve into the modern Frontier Days Rodeo.

10. The first steel bridge on the Pacific Coast is opened in Oregon by the Union Pacific Railroad.

28. Thomas Carney, the governor of Kansas from 1863–1865, dies in Leavenworth.

Also in July 1888:

Greeley, Colorado, completes a 900,000-acre irrigation project.

AUGUST

1. An Emancipation Day celebration in Atchison, Kansas, is attended by 5,000 African Americans.

2. San Francisco's Bijou Theater uses incandescent lamps for the first time.

6. A Kansas state bicycling record is set by Joseph Henley of Wichita, who travels five miles in 18 minutes and 45 seconds.

15. Three persons are lynched in Holbrook, Arizona, following the Pleasant Valley War.

16. Ross Santee, the author and illustrator of *Cowboy* (1928) is born in Thornburg, Iowa.

21. Kansas climbers L. D. Washburn and Victor Murdock reportedly set a new record for the ascension of Pikes Peak in Colorado.

28. Vaida Montgomery, the poet and editor of the *Kaleidoscope,* is born in Childress, Texas.

Also in August 1888:

The author Rex Stout begins living on a farm in Wakarusa, Kansas, just south of Topeka.

SEPTEMBER

9. The Kansas State House closes for the funeral of David Ware, who served as its janitor since 1862. Ware, who was born a slave, came to Kansas from Missouri in 1861.

26. J. Frank Dobie, the historian and author of *A Vaquero of the Brush Country* and *Coronado's Children,* is born in Live Oak County, Texas.

OCTOBER

1. President Cleveland signs the Scott Act, which excludes Chinese laborers from entering the United States for an indefinite period. The law also forbids Chinese laborers who have left the United States to return.

4. Great Falls, Montana, is incorporated.

6. The *Philadelphia Times* carries an account of a recent shooting match that ended in a tie between Annie Oakley and British champion Miles Johnson.

Before the match, Oakley had torn the flesh between the fingers of her left hand when a spring on a trap malfunctioned.

17. Horace Joseph Tabor, the second child of Horace Tabor and Baby Doe, dies 10 hours after being born in Denver.

20. The abolitionist Reverend Pardee Butler dies at age 74 in Farmington, Kansas. A resident sine 1855, he was twice the victim of proslavery mobs: Once he was tarred and feathered, the second time he was set adrift on a raft on the Missouri River.

23. The bandits who rob the Jerome stagecoach in Arizona get away with very little—the six passengers have $30 among them.

24. White Chief becomes the first Native American to attend college in Kansas; he enrolls at the University of Kansas.

31. Federal agents quarantine the border between Arizona and Sonora, Mexico, driving up the price of Arizona beef. The Arizona Territorial Cattle Association had convinced the U.S. government that the Mexican cattle were disease-ridden.

▪ The *Queen Bee,* a feminist newspaper published in Denver since 1882, announces that it has the largest circulation of any weekly paper published between Kansas City and San Francisco.

Also in September 1888:

L. Frank Baum becomes editor of Dakota Territory's *Aberdeen Saturday Pioneer;* he will hold the job until the newspaper fails in 1891.

NOVEMBER

3. Prentiss Ingraham's "Silk-ribbon Sam, the Mad Driver of the Overland, or Buffalo Bill's Twelve" begins serialization in the *Banner Weekly.*

6. Fraud and violence mark the Arkansas gubernatorial election. Democrat James P. Eagle defeats Union Labor Party candidate Dr. Charles Norwood.

▪ Coloradans elect Republican Job A. Cooper governor.

▪ Kansans elect Republican Lyman Humphrey governor.

7. Eighteen Kansas newspaper have women as editors.

9. A mine disaster in Frontenac, Kansas, kills 40.

10. Tom Carter defeats William Clark for Congress in Montana, setting off the "War of the Copper Kings."

17. In the first municipal election in Great Falls, Montana, Paris Gibson is elected mayor.

20. In Wichita, Kansas, a convention to promote white settlement in Indian Territory attracts 500 people from various states.

22. Near Florence, Arizona, bandits rob stagecoach passengers of $26 and take the Wells Fargo box.

26. Members of the Helena Salvation Army are arrested for disturbing the peace.

Also in November 1888:

Topeka, Kansas, has more churches than any city of its size in the nation; it also has no saloons.

National Headlines/November 1888:

6. HARRISON DEFEATS PRESIDENT CLEVELAND

DECEMBER

3. In his search for the remains of ancient man, Richard Wetherill discovers the Cliff Palace in Cliff Canyon, a branch of Mancos Canyon in southwestern Colorado.

18. A convention in Baxter Springs, Kansas, calls for the settlement of Indian Territory by whites. Delegates from the territory agree to the dissolving of tribal relations that would have made Indians citizens and the territory a state.

22. Annie Oakley appears back East in *Deadwood Dick, or the Sunbeam of the Sierras.*

24. In another stagecoach robbery in Arizona, the mail is taken from the Solomon–Bowie stage.

■ *Kate Adams,* a Mississippi steamboat, catches fire, killing 25.

26. The *John H. Hanna,* a Mississippi steamboat, catches fire, killing 30.

29. The first issue of the *Oklahoma City Times* is published in Wichita, Kansas, some five months before the run to open the unassigned lands of Indian Territory to white settlement. After the editors, who were sending their copy by messenger, are ejected by the military from the area that is about to open, the newspaper will be published in Purcell, just south of the unassigned area across the South Canadian River.

Also in 1888:

The Cherokee Strip Live Stock Association renegotiates with Indians its lease of the 6.5 million acres of the Cherokee Outlet in the northern portion of present Oklahoma; it will increase its payment from $100,000 a year to $200,000.

Arizona produces $3 million in gold and silver, and $5.3 million in copper.

Wells Fargo earns $5,982,000 from its express services.

Denver's Charity Organization Society, a forerunner of the United Way, raises $21,700 for 22 charities.

The 925,000 head of cattle in Arizona are valued at $16.2 million.

The *Muskogee Phoenix,* a newspaper, is founded in Indian Territory by Dr. Leo E. Bennett.

The *Indian Arrow,* a newspaper, is founded at Fort Gibson, Indian Territory, by a Cherokee stock company. The editor is William P. Ross.

The Texas state capitol building is completed and dedicated.

The realities of pioneer life. A little house on the prairie in Custer County, Nebraska, in 1888.   (New York Public Library)

The Chicago and the Rock Island Railroads reach Colorado Springs.

Utah State University is established in Logan.

Since 1855, there have been 106 counties organized in Kansas.

A major outbreak of whooping cough is reported along Puget Sound in Washington Territory.

One of the big western books of the year is credited to William F. Cody, although it is unclear whether he wrote it. Nevertheless, the 766-page *Story of the Wild West and Camp-Fire Chats by Buffalo Bill (Hon. W. F. Cody), A Full and Complete History of the Renowned Pioneer Quartette, Boone, Crockett, Carson, and Buffalo Bill* is a blockbuster.

Theodore Roosevelt publishes *Ranch Life and the Hunting Trails*, with illustrations by Frederic Remington.

1889

"The land may be had for the asking and retained at the muzzle of a Winchester."
—*Chicago Tribune*

JANUARY

1. The Ghost Dance religion begins in Nevada with an eclipse.

2. In Kansas, the communities of Cimarron and Ingalls battle over which will be the seat of Gray County. Residents of Ingalls hire a band of Dodge City gunfighters, including Bat Masterson's brother, Jim, and Bill Tilghman, to raid the Cimarron courthouse for the county's records. As the group empties the courthouse, Cimarron's citizens open fire. Some of Ingalls's hired gunfighters escape, but four, including Masterson, are left stranded on the second floor of the courthouse. Cooler heads prevail when a telegram is received from Bat Masterson, who urges the people of Cimarron to free his brother or he will "hire a train and come in with enough men to blow Cimarron off the face of Kansas." The four gunfighters will be tried for the death of Cimarron's J. W. English, but acquitted.

7. Cowboys kill three Mexican sheepherders in a gunfight near Solomonville, Arizona.

17. Kansas City witnesses something it has not seen in years—a buffalo stampede. A heard of 25 bison belonging to C. J. Jones is removed from a train to graze; before it can be reboarded for the trip to Garden City, the herd takes off.

18. Charles Curtis, a future vice president, completes two terms as the attorney for Shawnee County, Kansas. During his time as county attorney, he lost only five criminal cases and won every case involving liquor.

29. Arizona's 15th territorial legislature meets in Prescott. It will vote to move the capital to Phoenix.

THE DANCE OF THE GHOSTS—THE DAY THE SUN DIED
JANUARY 1, 1889

An eclipse of the sun was taken by the Paiute Wovoka—sick with a fever in Nevada—as a sign to begin the Ghost Dance, the religion that would make departed ancestors rise from the dead and drive the white man from the West. Wovoka's credibility was helped by his having "predicted" the eclipse, with a little help from an almanac.

According to Wovoka: "Pretty soon now, the earth shall die, but Indians must not be afraid, because earth will come alive again. Just like sun died and came alive again. . . . The game be thick everywhere. All dead Indians come back and live again. They all be strong just like young men, be young again. Old blind Indian see again and get young and have fine time."

Wovoka's vision targeted the spring of 1890 for when the Indians would go to the mountains, just ahead of a Noah-like flood that would wash the white scourge from the face of the earth. In order for Indians to fulfill the terms of the prophecy, they must not war among themselves, and they must turn away from the ways of the white man, especially from his liquor.

(continued)

(continued)

Most importantly, the Indians had to Ghost Dance. This ceremony saw men and women joining hands in a circle, then dancing to exhaustion in order to fulfill the prophecy. "Indians who don't dance, who don't believe in this word, will grow little, just about a foot high," said Wovoka. "Some of them will be turned into wood and be burned in fire." According to the Great Spirit, God would run heaven, President Benjamin Harrison would rule the East, and Wovoka would reign in the West, with power over rain and snow.

Kicking Bear noted Sioux warriors firing Winchesters at the sky during the eclipse, trying to wake the sun. He and Short Bull and nine other Indians had come to Nevada on a pilgrimage, and it was their interpretation of the dance that spread among the Washoes, the Bannocks, the Mohaves, and the Navajos. The Arapahos taught it to the Cheyennes. The Caddos passed it to the Osages, Otoes, and Cherokees. Then the dance was performed by Shoshones and Sioux, whose interpretation included the wearing of white muslin "Ghost Dance Shirts" that would make Indians impervious to the bullets of the "blue coats."

Belle Starr (1848–1889) poses with Blue Duck at Fort Smith. Her notoriety begins shortly after her assassination. (Oklahoma Historical Society)

30. The University of Idaho is chartered in Moscow.

Also in January 1889:

The Rock Island Railroad is completed to Colorado Springs.

Eugene Field publishes *A Little Book of Western Verse.*

National Headlines/January 1889:

28. TRANSIT STRIKE CRIPPLES NYC

FEBRUARY

3. Belle Starr is murdered in an ambush near Eufala, Indian Territory. Riding her horse home after accompanying her husband, Bill July, part of the way to Fort Smith, she is felled by a shotgun blast to her back. Her murderer is never found. Her tombstone in Porum, Oklahoma, will read:

> Shed not for her the bitter tear
> Nor give the heart to vain regret.
> Tis but the casket that lies here.
> The gem that filled it sparkles yet.

4. Harry Longabaugh, the Sundance Kid, is paroled in Wyoming.

- A large group of Boomers—whites intending to settle illegally in Indian Territory—departs Wichita, Kansas, in 25 wagons.

7. Arizona's 15th territorial legislature reconvenes in the new capital, Phoenix.

10. San Francisco's first Unitarian Church opens.

11. The U.S. Department of Agriculture becomes a cabinet department; the first secretary of agriculture is Missouri's Norman J. Coleman.

16. John Phillips becomes the first Denver policeman killed in the line of duty.

17. Haroldson Lafayette (H. L.) Hunt, the future Texas oil billionaire, is born in Vandalia, Illinois.

19. Morgan County is established in Colorado.

22. The Southern Pacific's No. 17 train is robbed two miles outside of Pixley, California, in the San Joaquin Valley. Bandits use dynamite to get into the express car. At first, the robbery is believed to be

the work of the Dalton brothers, but it will later be attributed to John Sontag and Chris Evans.

- According to the *Topeka Capital-Commonwealth*, "the deadly cigarette is killing off a good many promising boys in various parts of the country."

22. The Omnibus Bill, signed today by President Grover Cleveland, will admit Washington, Montana, North Dakota, and South Dakota into the Union later in the year.

23. McKinley County is created in New Mexico.

25. Chaves and Eddy Counties are created in New Mexico.

- Blacks in Kansas petition the state legislature to end discrimination in public schools.

27. Marsh Murdock of the *Wichita Eagle* loudly protests the assertion by the *Oxford Mocking Bird* that whiskey is not a cure for snakebite. Murdock grouses: "A man who would preach that doctrine would tell children there is no Santa Claus."

28. New Mexico governor Edmund G. Ross signs a bill creating three institutions of higher learning: a university in Albuquerque, a school of mining in Socorro, and an agricultural college in Las Cruces.

Also in February 1889:
Century Magazine runs the following ad:

> If you want to send money to any point, get a WELLS, FARGO & CO'S EXPRESS Money Order. It is cheap, safe and handy, and can be bought at any office of the Company, and is payable everywhere. If you want to forward packages, goods or valuables to the West, to Mexico or Europe, WELLS, FARGO & CO'S EXPRESS will serve you well, and at low rates.

In Tombstone, Arizona, Deputy Burt Alvord shares drinks with two associates, Fuller and Fortino. When the pair gets into an argument, Fuller grabs Alvord's weapon and shoots Fortino dead. Fuller then departs. Sheriff John Slaughter arrives and reprimands Alvord for being involved with such thugs.

MARCH

2. The last of the Indian claims are settled, as Congress transfers the unassigned lands in Indian Territory into the public domain. With the passage of the Springer Bill, the territory will be opened for colonization.

- An Atlantic and Pacific train is robbed of its express box in Canyon Diablo in Arizona.

- Kansas becomes the first state to pass legislation regulating trusts.

9. Ben White is inaugurated as Montana's last territorial governor.

13. Montana's last territorial legislature adjourns in Helena.

15. Yuma County is established in Colorado.

16. "Buffalo Bill's Band, or Cody to the Rescue," by Julius Lewis, begins serialization in the *Banner Weekly*.

23. President Benjamin Harrison announces that a part of Indian Territory will be opened for settlement; immigrants from all over the globe will converge on Indian Territory. "Harrison's Hoss Race," in which land will be offered on a first-come, first-served basis, is coming soon.

24. The Santa Fe Railroad announces daily train service from Topeka to Chicago, departing at 3:40 P.M. and arriving at 10:30 the next morning.

25. Cheyenne, Otero, and Rio Blanco Counties are established in Colorado.

27. Phillips County is established in Colorado.

29. Marcus Reno, 54, the scapegoat of the Battle of the Little Bighorn, dies in Washington, D.C., following an operation for cancer of the tongue. He will be buried in an unmarked pauper's grave in Washington's Glenwood Cemetery.

Also in March 1889:
The Belle Starr legend begins with a truthless yarn penned by Alton Meyers in the *Police Gazette*.

A sign on the side of a wagon bound for Indian Territory reads,

> CHINTZ-BUGED IN ILLINOY
> SILICONED IN NEWBRASKY
> WHITE CAPED IN MISSOURY
> PROHIBITED IN KANSAS
> OKLAHOMY OR BUST

National Headlines/March 1889:

4. BENJAMIN HARRISON INAUGURATED 23RD U.S. PRESIDENT

APRIL

1. Arkansas City, Kansas, reported the arrival of some 100 carloads of freight, ready for shipment into Indian Territory on April 22, the day the unassigned lands will open for settlement.

2. Three weeks prior to the opening of Indian Territory's unassigned lands, the *State Capital*, a newspaper edited by Frank Hilton Greer, begins publishing in Winfield, Kansas. After the run of April 22, it will move to Guthrie and be published from a tent.

9. Lewis Wolfley is appointed territorial governor of Arizona.

- Sedgwick County is established in Colorado.

11. Kiowa, Kit Carson, Lincoln, and Prowers Counties are established in Colorado.

12. Governor Wolfley vetoes a bill that would create Coconino County in Arizona. He is burned in effigy in Flagstaff.

■ Buffalo Bill's Wild West departs New York aboard the *Persian Monarch* for a tour of France.

15. The artist Thomas Hart Benton (*Cotton Pickers, Lonesome Road*) is born in Neosho, Missouri.

16. Baca and Montezuma Counties are established in Colorado.

20. Among the multitude of settlers awaiting the run for the unassigned lands in Indian Territory—and not to claim land but to gamble—is "Poker Alice" Ivers, 38.

22. The first Oklahoma Land Run takes place.

25. The drifter Jim McCarthy robs the Collins and Sons Bank in Ventura, California. He emerges with a teller's tray of money, only to discover that his horse, tied to a wagon wheel, has taken some steps and wedged its reins under the wheel. McCarthy unsuccessfully tries to free them, at which time he is approached by Sheriff A. J. Snodgrass. "I give up," sighs McCarthy.

28. The *Topeka Capital-Commonwealth* changes its name to the *Topeka Daily Capital*.

29. The first newspaper in what will become Oklahoma Territory is the *Guthrie Getup*. Its first issue announces:

> The Guthrie Getup prances into the promised land at the head of the procession. . . . Praise God all ye good people, and let these prairies resound to the measured strokes of our job press. Ah, there is the rub, if you do not give us job work we will have to go back to our wife's folks. This would place us in a hell of a fix, as we are not married. Our last statement is especially directed to single ladies who hold corner lots.

THE FIRST LAND RUN
APRIL 22, 1889

The spectacle of the first of the Oklahoma Land Runs was unprecedented in the history of the West. Thousands of people, responding to President Benjamin Harrison's proclamation, gathered on April 22 to race for free land on a first-come, first-served basis.

Former Seminole and Creek lands in Indian Territory totaling 1,920,000 acres had been purchased by the United States for $4 million. Some 50,000 to 60,000 people assembled on the borders of the "Unassigned Lands," ready for the traffic to rush in. Each person could claim 160 acres by driving a stake into the ground. Townsites and farmlands had been sectioned off in the three weeks between the proclamation (March 3) and opening day. Still, with nearly 2 million acres to be opened, only a fraction of the participants could hope for any success in staking a claim.

On hand were $500 race horses, purchased especially for the event. Families were crowded into covered wagons. Some would-be settlers rode bicycles, while another was seen straddling an ox. The Santa Fe Railroad offered train service into the territory at 15-minute intervals; men were seen clinging to the sides of railcars with one hand, clutching a red claim flag in the other.

The opening gun was fired at noon. According to the *St. Louis Republic,* "Shrill cries rose from the boomers, their whip lashes resounded, the horsemen among them shot forward impetuously, the teams tugged at the rattling harnesses, and the whole motley crowd swept forward in gathering motion."

One of the bigger problems of the day was the "Sooners," those who had placed their claims prior to the opening: One man, for example, was found working land that had four-inch-high onions. When asked how this could be, he praised the rich soil, wryly commenting that he had planted the onions just 15 minutes earlier.

By 9:00 P.M., most of the land had been claimed, certainly all of the choice plots. President Harrison had previously hinted that Guthrie might become the capital of the new territory; its first-day population bulged to 12,000. Oklahoma City (the capital since 1910) started the new era with a population of 10,000. Other new cities included Norman, Kingfisher, and Stillwater.

Homesteaders celebrated in their tents on the outskirts of the new social centers. In 1890, Congress will create the territory of Oklahoma, with Guthrie as its capital.

Guthrie, Oklahoma, just after the run. (New York Public Library)

Also in April 1889:

Count James Pourtales, the owner of the Broadmoor Dairy in Colorado Springs, marries his distant cousin Berthe and organizes the Cheyenne Lake, Land and Improvement Company. Two thousand new trees are planted at "Broadmoor." The 10-acre Cheyenne Lake is excavated and then formed by an earthen dam at a cost of $10,000, which increases the count's four-year investment to $180,000. Before embarking on his European honeymoon, Pourtales leaves William Willcox in charge of the books, and hires Duncan Chisolm to oversee the operation.

Annie Oakley rejoins Buffalo Bill's Wild West after a year of touring with Pawnee Bill. She will remain with Cody, off and on, for another 10 years.

National Headlines/April 1889:

29. GEORGE WASHINGTON INAUGURAL CENTENNIAL OBSERVED

MAY

9. The *Oklahoma Times* begins publishing in Oklahoma City. To avoid confusion with the *Oklahoma City Times,* the second issue will be called the *Oklahoma Journal.* The *Journal* will buy out its rival by the end of the year, at which time it will become the *Oklahoma City Times-Journal.* Other newspapers will appear in the new territory this year: the *Daily Oklahoman* and the *Evening Gazette.*

- Spokane, a Twin Bridges, Montana, horse owned by Noah Armstrong, wins the Kentucky Derby in the record time of 2 minutes, 34½ seconds.

11. A military escort under Major J. W. Wham is ambushed by masked cowboys as it takes a $26,000 army payroll to Fort Thomas, Arizona. Eight soldiers are wounded and eight of the attackers are arrested.

13. The new California Theater opens in San Francisco.

15. The Territorial Insane Asylum opens in Cheyenne, Wyoming, with 15 inmates.

Also in May 1889:

Buffalo Bill's Wild West opens in Paris. Says one reviewer: "I have seen many first performances during the last couple of years in Paris, but never have I seen one at which there was such a splendidly representative gathering of all the city."

National Headlines/May 1889:

31. JOHNSTOWN FLOOD KILLS 2,295

JUNE

2. Captain H. W. Sprole accepts the surrender of 34 Sioux on the Missouri River in Dakota Territory.

4. In Topeka, Kansas, a mob lynches Nat Oliphant. Alonzo Rodgers had come home to find Oliphant burglarizing his home; Oliphant killed him and also harmed Mrs. Rodgers.

6. Fire erupts from an overturned gluepot in Seattle, Washington; the town's entire business district, covering 64 acres, is destroyed.

■ James J. Corbett defeats Joe Choyniski in a San Francisco prizefight staged on a barge in the bay.

10. The United Confederate Veterans is organized in New Orleans.

21. The last luxury steamboat to arrive at Montana's Fort Benton is the *Rosebud*.

27. The *Rocky Mountain News* reports a bank robbery in Telluride, Colorado, that is believed to be the work of Butch Cassidy and his gang. According to the *News,* as the clerk "was bending over the desk examining the check this party grabbed him around the neck, pulling his face down on the desk, at the same time admonishing the surprised official to keep quiet on pain of instant death." The three robbers then mounted horses in the street. "When they had ridden a couple of blocks," says the *News,* "they spurred their horses into a gallop, gave a yell, discharged their revolvers and dashed away."

30. The *Oklahoma Journal* becomes a daily newspaper.

Also in June 1889:

The first two volumes of *The Winning of the West,* by Theodore Roosevelt, are published; they examine the development of the frontier from the time of Daniel Boone to that of Davy Crockett.

Robert Leroy Parker, "Butch Cassidy" (1866–?). In the ultimate Western getaway, he gives history the slip. (Library of Congress)

The Pecos Valley Irrigation and Investment Company begins operating in New Mexico.

JULY

1. The coinage department of the Carson City Mint is reopened, but the equipment is in poor shape and cannot complete the task of making new coins.

4. The Montana Constitutional Convention convenes in Helena.

10. In Tombstone, Arizona, Buckskin Frank Leslie returns home to his current wife, the former prostitute Mollie Williams ("Diamond Annie"), and finds her sitting on the porch with teen ranch hand James Neal. Accusing them of perversion, Leslie storms inside for his six-shooter, returns, and shoots Mollie dead. He then puts the gun to the boy's ribs and pulls the trigger. Thinking he has killed them both, Leslie retires. Neal makes it back alive to Tombstone. Leslie will be charged with Mollie's murder.

10–14. Rudyard Kipling visits Colorado. He travels from Gunnison to Denver over Marshall Pass in a narrow-gauge train. About Denver, he writes: "The pulse of that town was too like the rushing mighty wind in the Rocky Mountain tunnel. It made me tired because complete strangers desired me to do something to mines which were in mountains, and to purchase building blocks upon inaccessible cliffs; and once, a woman urged that I should supply her with strong drinks."

13. An editorial in the *Wyoming Weekly Main* claims that the local court's failure to convict thieves might result in "stockmen taking the law into their own hands."

20. Cattle Kate is lynched in Wyoming.

23. Merchants in Prescott, Arizona, boycott rail lines because of high freight charges.

Also in July 1889:

Wyatt Earp has been managing a bar in San Francisco for the last three years.

Pedro Arondondo is shot between the eyes by Red Ivan, who accused him of cheating at cards, in a duel in Canon City, Colorado. Two days before the gunfight, Arondondo had consulted his tarot cards and then had had a headstone inscribed "Pedro Arondondo, born 1857–died 1889, from a bullet wound between the eyes fired by Red Ivan."

National Headlines/July 1889:

23. JOHN L. SULLIVAN KO'S JAKE KILRAIN IN THE 75TH ROUND

THE END OF CATTLE KATE
JULY 20, 1889

The lynching of Ella Watson, aka "Cattle Kate," and Jim Averill near Independence Rock, in Wyoming Territory, was the latest in the saga of vigilante bravura in the West. It also earned Watson the dubious distinction of being the only woman ever hanged in Wyoming.

The events that preceded this particular incident began on October 29, 1880, when Averill filed a claim on choice grazing land on the banks of the Sweetwater River in Carbon County. The land was used regularly by three large outfits, the UT, the Bar 11, and the Hub and Spoke. Over the years, Averill had opened a general store and become the area's postmaster. He often registered his opinions on the conflicts between cattle barons and ranchers in editorials written for the *Casper Weekly Mail.*

Blasting the barons in print was not enough for Averill. Rumors flew that he dabbled in the rustling trade. New cowboys arrived daily to help with the herd adjustments. With an eye toward even greater commercial success, Averill decided to expand his operations by hiring a quality prostitute. In Rawlins, Wyoming, he found Ella Watson and unveiled his business plan, suggesting a new form of payment for the world's oldest profession. On March 24, 1888, Watson filed claim number 2003 about a mile from Averill's emporium. Construction began on a log-cabin bordello and a large corral.

During the following year, Averill and Watson grew bolder. One stockman found 20 of his mavericks in her corral before she ran him off at riflepoint. A "get tough" attitude was voiced at local smokers. An editorial in the July 13, 1889, *Casper Weekly Mail* hinted that the court's failure to convict thieves might result in "stockmen taking the law into their own hands."

Rancher A. J. Bothwell decided to do just that, shortly after 50 head of his stock appeared among Watson's herd. On the afternoon of July 20, 1889, he rode with six cowhands to Cattle Kate's abode.

Her 14-year-old stable boy watched in horror as Kate was loaded into a wagon, swearing and kicking as she went. Bothwell and his band then galloped to Averill's property and picked him up.

As they would later testify, the members of the self-appointed posse meant only to "throw a scare" into their adversaries. The wagons traveled about four miles to Spring Creek Gulch. Suddenly, Jim Buchanan, one of Averill's men who had trailed them, opened fire on the group. Kate yelled, "Shoot the bastards, every one of them!"

Buchanan was driven off with return fire. Then, almost as an afterthought, the group completed what it had set out to do. Amateurs at proper execution, Bothwell and his men tossed the first rope over a low branch, put the noose around Averill's neck, and then pushed him off a large rock. As he kicked and writhed, slowly strangling, they grabbed Cattle Kate and did the same to her.

When law enforcement officials arrived at the gully the next morning, they found the bodies, according to the *Mail,* "swaying to and fro by the gentle breeze which wafted the sweet odor of the prairie flowers across the plains." "A Cattle Thief and His Paramour Swing from a Cottonwood Branch," read one account, and another professed that "The Man Weakened But the Woman Cursed to the Last."

No charges were ever brought against anyone. The witness, Buchanan, disappeared, returned briefly, and then vanished for good. The stable boy died of Bright's disease. A grand jury was dismissed on October 14, 1889, having failed to issue an indictment because of lack of evidence.

Recalled one old-timer, years after the fact: "This was a horrible piece of business, more especially the lynching of the woman, and in many ways indefensible; yet, what is one to do? Just sit still and see your property ruined, with no redress in sight?"

AUGUST

3. More than 11 million acres of Dakota Territory are ceded to the U.S. government by the Sioux.

4. Fire devastates the business section of Spokane, Washington, doing $10 million in damage. Only two persons die in the blaze.

8. Arlee, the Flathead chief, dies in Jocko Valley, Montana.

13. Denver's "Queen of the Tenderloin," Jennie Rogers, marries her long-time boyfriend, Jack Wood. Her "House of Mirrors," the most famous brothel in the West, is so successful that the *Rocky Mountain News* reported earlier this year that a city council meeting had to be canceled for a lack of a quorum "because most of the members were attending the opening of a new and more fashionable den of prostitution."

Also in August 1889:

Rudyard Kipling fishes in Oregon, gaining experience that he will write about in *From Sea to Sea* (1899).

Fort Laramie, "Old Bedlam," is abandoned in Wyoming.

Richard Fox publishes *Belle Starr, the Bandit Queen, or The Female Jesse James.*

At a meeting in Salem, Oregon, the Knights of Labor, the Farmers' Alliance, and the Grange hold a convention and form the Union Party.

SEPTEMBER

3–21. New Mexico's constitutional convention drafts a new constitution for the proposed state.

4. The *Anaconda Standard,* the forerunner of the *Montana Standard,* publishes its first issue.

16. Robert Younger, 35, dies of tuberculosis in Minnesota at the Stillwater Penitentiary, where he was

Robert Younger (1853–1889). On September 16, 1889, the youngest Younger dies in prison of tuberculosis. (Library of Congress)

serving a life sentence for his part in the Northfield, Minnesota, bank robbery of September 7, 1876.

■ The Great Northern Railway is organized by Jim Hill in Minnesota.

19. Stiffer laws against robbery go into effect, including federal rewards of $1,000 for the arrest and conviction of armed attackers of stagecoaches or trains carrying government mail.

28. Prentiss Ingraham's "Buffalo Bill's Brand, or The Brimstone Brotherhood" begins serialization in the *Banner Weekly.*

National Headlines/September 1889:

14. JANE ADDAMS OPENS HULL HOUSE IN CHICAGO

OCTOBER

1. After four months of repairs and servicing, the Carson City Mint commences the coinage of gold and silver. Coin production will continue until June 1, 1893.

■ Montana voters approve the proposed constitution and elect officers for the new state, which will be created in November. Joe Toole will be the first state governor.

14. A Wyoming grand jury is dismissed, having failed to indict anyone for the lynchings of Jim Averill and Ella Watson because of a lack of evidence.

20. Oil is discovered in Douglas, Wyoming.

21. In Butte, Montana, a funeral procession becomes lost in thick smelter smoke. The group winds up at the Centennial Brewery.

30. The Chicago, Burlington, and Quincy's rails reach Wyoming.

Also in October 1889:

The Wyoming humorist Edgar Wilson "Bill" Nye, who has practiced law and journalism in Laramie since 1876, relocates back East for health reasons.

NOVEMBER

1. The Apache Kid, an outlaw and former U.S. Army scout, and seven other Apache Indians are sent to Yuma Prison in present Arizona on a trumped-up charge of murdering a whiskey peddler.

■ Since 1879, the population of Dakota Territory has increased from 135,000 to more than 500,000.

2. North Dakota and South Dakota are granted statehood. They enter the Union as the 39th and 40th states, with Bismarck and Pierre as the state capitals. North Dakota has a population of 190,983 and covers an area of 70,655 square miles. South Dakota has a population of 328,808 and an area of 77,116 square miles. President Harrison's proclamation is greeted with whistles and fireworks in communities throughout the two states. So that there can be no bragging rights as to "which was first," the president requests that both statehood documents be covered with a blank sheet of paper, leaving the bottoms exposed for his signature.

2. On their way to the penitentiary in Yuma, Arizona, the Apache Kid and his seven followers turn on Sheriff Glenn Reynolds and Deputy Sheriff W. A. Holmes. They kill the lawmen and ride away.

4. The first state officials are installed in office in North and South Dakota.

8. Montana becomes the 41st state, with Helena as its capital. A territory since 1864, Montana covers 147,046 square miles. Its population has increased from 25,000 in 1870 to more than 350,000.

9. North Dakota's flour millers form a state association.

11. Washington, with a population of 350,000 (it had 25,000 in 1870), enters the Union as the 42nd state. Its capital is Olympia, and the state's area is 68,139 square miles.

12. A state irrigation committee organizes in North Dakota.

17. The Union Pacific begins daily service between Chicago and Portland, Oregon, as well as between Chicago and San Francisco.

18. The schooner *Parkersburg* runs aground on the Oregon coast, a mile south of the Coquille River.

19. North Dakota's first state legislature convenes in Bismarck.

21. San Francisco's Mutual Savings Bank is incorporated.

23. Montana's first state legislature convenes in Helena.

26. Prentiss Ingraham's "The Hercules Highwayman, or The Mounted Miners of the Overland" appears in *Beadle's Half-Dime Library*.

27. The first prohibition bill is introduced in the North Dakota legislature.

Also in November 1889:

An outbreak of influenza is reported among the Cheyenne and Arapaho tribes in Texas.

National Headlines/November 1889:

14. NELLIE BLY BEGINS HER ATTEMPT OF AN 80-DAY TRIP AROUND THE WORLD

DECEMBER

4. Cambria, Wyoming, ships its first load of coal.

6. Jefferson Davis, 81, the former president of the Confederate States of America, dies in New Orleans.

10. Buckskin Frank Leslie, found guilty of murder and sentenced to 25 years of hard labor at the prison in Yuma, Arizona, begins his sentence as Inmate 632. Observes the *Tombstone Epitaph*: "Leslie showed cowardice from the time sentence was pronounced, and this weakness remained with him until prison doors closed upon him." He will be pardoned on November 17, 1896.

11. North Dakota's commissioner of agriculture is ordered to investigate destitution in parts of the state and to distribute relief. The study will find 4,000 needy North Dakotans.

■ Marias Pass, the route that will be used by the Great Northern Railroad, is discovered in Montana by John Stevens.

17. Rosemary Echo Silver Dollar Tabor, the second daughter of Horace and Baby Doe, is born in Denver. Her father will call her "Honeymaid."

21. Prentiss Ingraham's "Buffalo Bill's Boys in Blue, or The Brimstone Band's Blot-Out" begins serialization in the *Banner Weekly*.

24. Butch Cassidy, 23, pulls his first holdup at the San Miguel Bank in Telluride, Colorado. (According to one story of how Telluride, Colorado, was named, it is short for "To hell you ride.")

25. In Vance, Texas, Rangers Ira Aten and John Hughes and Deputy Sheriff William Terry silently approach the yuletide campfire of the suspected murderers Will and Alvin Odle, and open fire. The Odles are quickly dispatched.

Also in December 1889:

Variations of the Ghost Dance are seen among the Washoes, the Bannocks, the Mohaves, and the Navajos.

Also in 1889:

The first oil to be discovered in Indian Territory is found west of Chelsea by Edward Byrd, who had obtained a lease from the Cherokee Nation. His first well is dug to a depth of 36 feet.

Wells Fargo reports an income of $6,525,000 from express services. For the first time, the company issues an official statement on the total number of miles its service covered in the past year—45,780.

J. W. Stanford drives the first automobile in California.

California's Orange Country is created from part of Los Angeles County.

Fort Hays is abandoned in Kansas.

There are 980,000 head of cattle worth $14.7 million in Arizona.

Hubert Howe Bancroft publishes the one-volume work

Arizona and New Mexico, the one-volume *Nevada, Colorado, and Wyoming,* and the one-volume *Utah.*

The *Talequah Telephone* is the first daily newspaper in Indian Territory.

Job Adams Cooper becomes Colorado's 6th governor.

John and Max Kuner open a pickle factory in Greeley, Colorado.

Amy Lewis Carpenter, a Teton Sioux who is believed to be the granddaughter of Captain Meriwether Lewis, is born.

Arthur L. Thomas becomes governor of Utah Territory.

The University of New Mexico opens in Albuquerque.

Weber State College opens in Ogden, Utah.

The last four members of the southern herd of buffalo are killed on the Staked Plains of Texas. There are now 1,091 bison in North America, down from 20,000 in 1885.

1890

"It can hardly be classed as the white man's proudest hour."
—Senator Karl Mundt, on Wounded Knee

JANUARY

2. In its first year as Arizona's territorial capital, Phoenix has acquired newly constructed buildings worth $488,000.

6. The Montana State Supreme Court convenes for the first time.

7. Prentiss Ingraham's "Butterfly Billy, the Pony Rider Detective, or Buffalo Bill's Boy Pard" appears in *Beadle's Half-Dime Library*.

11. Monte Blue, the Western film star of *Geronimo* (1940) and *Cheyenne* (1947), is born in Indianapolis, Indiana.

12. Judge Warren Bristol, of Lincoln County War fame, dies in Deming, New Mexico.

17. The old Del Mar Hotel in San Diego goes up in flames.

20. Train robbers believed to be John Sontag and Chris Evans hold up passenger train No. 19 on the Southern Pacific line in Goshen, California—about 40 miles south of Fresno—and get away with $20,000.

21. Frank Chester Robertson, the author of *Back to the West* (1935), is born in Moscow, Idaho.

22. John "X" Beidler, 58, the Montana pioneer and vigilante, dies in Helena. His funeral at the Ming Opera House draws 1,200.

23. Nellie Bly, on her round-the-world journey, passes Lamy Junction in New Mexico at 11:25 P.M., sound asleep. She traveled from San Francisco to Albuquerque—some 1,135 miles—in just over 36 hours. The Atchison, Topeka, and Santa Fe will claim the fastest time for an American train when it whisks her from La Junta, Colorado, to Chicago at an average speed of 78.1 miles per hour.

27. President Harrison nominates John E. Haggard to be U.S. Marshal of North Dakota.

28. North Dakota's state senate passes a women's suffrage bill as well as a measure that lowers the attorney general's annual salary from $2,000 to $100.

▪ Harvey Fergusson, the author of *The Blood of the Conquerors* (1921), is born in Albuquerque, New Mexico.

29. Residents along Arizona's Gila River report an outbreak of spotted fever.

30. Angie Debo, the historian, educator, and author, is born in Beattie, Kansas.

▪ Hawaii's King Kalakau visits San Francisco.

▪ The North Dakota State Senate appropriates $5,000 for relief to the needy.

31. The owners of Arizona's Empire Ranch, disgusted by high freight charges, begin a 1,000-head cattle drive to California.

Also in January 1890:

At Fort Smith, Arkansas, Jim July, a suspected horse thief, dies of bullet wounds he suffered in a fight with Deputies J. R. Hutchins and Bud Trainor. July was also a chief suspect in Belle Starr's murder.

National Headlines/January 1980:
23. UNITED MINE WORKERS ESTABLISHED

FEBRUARY

2. A flu sweeps through Arizona. The *Tombstone Prospector* notes that it knows of no Indian who has gotten the disease who has ever recovered.

The Dodge City Cowboy Band in 1890. (Kansas State Historical Society)

3. Idaho's Test Oath Law of 1885 is upheld by the U.S. Supreme Court. It allows for Mormons to be disenfranchised in that territory.

9. General George Crook's plan to relocate Apache prisoners from Alabama to Indian Territory is formally protested by the Arizona Pioneers' Society.

10. The last Indian treaty goes into effect, as half of the Great Sioux Reservation in South Dakota—some 22 million acres between the White and Cheyenne Rivers—is relinquished.

■ Utah voters elect many members of the non-Mormon Liberal Party.

11. President Harrison declares the Great Sioux Reservation in South Dakota open for settlement.

15. The bandit "Three Fingers Jack" is killed by a wounded express messenger when he and four others attempt to hold up a Southern Pacific train near Fairbank, Arizona.

18. The schooner *Rosalind* sinks just north of Oregon's Rogue River.

■ Prentiss Ingraham's "Butterfly Billy's Man Hunt, or One More Trail" appears in *Beadle's Half-Dime Library*.

21. Rain floods Arizona's Granite Creek, disrupting much train traffic.

22. Rain bursts the Hassayampa River's Walnut Grove Dam in Arizona, causing at least 50 deaths.

26. Montana's first state legislature adjourns, having failed to organize.

28. The "Baron of Arizona," James A. Reavis, attempts to claim all the water in the Gila River below Mineral Creek with his forged "Peralta Grant."

Also in February 1890:

In his new novel *The Bridge of the Gods,* Frederic Homer Balch writes of the area on the Columbia River around Cascade Locks, Oregon.

National Headlines/February 1890:

18. NATIONAL AMERICAN WOMEN SUFFRAGE ASSOCIATION FORMS IN WASHINGTON; CADY STANTON FIRST PRESIDENT

FEBRUARY 1890

MARCH

2. Members of the 7th Infantry leave Fort Laramie, Wyoming, for the last time; the fort will soon be abandoned as a military post.

3. In Italy, Buffalo Bill's Wild West plays Rome; Cody has an audience with Pope Leo.

8. Gene Fowler, the journalist and author of *Timberline* (1938), is born in Denver.

11. Lieutenant J. W. Watson reports two Indians slain and three captured in a fight with the 4th Cavalry at Salt River, Arizona.

12. The North Dakota senate rejects a state lottery.

13. Grand County is established in Utah.

15. Prentiss Ingraham's "Buffalo Bill's Buckskin Braves; or The Card Queen's Last Game" begins serialization in *Beadle's Half-Dime Library*.

16. Andrew Carnegie donates $25,000 for a library to be built in Tucson, Arizona.

21. General George Crook, 61, the man William Tecumseh Sherman called "the greatest Indian fighter and manager the army of the United States ever had," dies of heart failure while weight lifting at his Chicago headquarters. In his later years, Crook became a human-rights activists, campaigning for Indian rights. Says Red Cloud: "He, at least, never lied to us. His words gave the people hope. He died. Their hope died again. Despair came again."

30. A fire destroys a major portion of the business district of Flagstaff, Arizona.

Also in March 1890:

William Michael Harnett paints *The Faithful Colt.*

APRIL

1. Prentiss Ingraham's "Butterfly Billy's Bonanza, or The Spectre Soldier of the Overland" appears in *Beadle's Half-Dime Library.*

25. The first North Dakota state bonds go on sale at 11.6 percent interest.

MAY

1. Denver's Elitch Gardens, the largest zoological exposition in the West, has its grand opening.

2. Congress passes the Oklahoma Organic Act, creating the territory of Oklahoma, which covers roughly the western half of the present state. When asked by the commissioner of affairs what the new territory should be called, the Reverend Allen Wright, a Choctaw, replied "Oklahoma," a combination from his native tongue of the works "ukla" (person) and "huma" (red). Cherokees who believe they should have first choice in naming the state are offended.

16. Weston County is established in Wyoming.

18. Chinook, Montana, boasts a population of 135, along with six stores, two hotels, one newspaper, and only one saloon.

19. The Edmunds-Tucker Act is sustained by the U.S. Supreme Court; the decision is another setback for Mormons of Utah. Under its terms, the church is essentially dissolved.

25. Montana's first electric street railway is opened by Charles A. Broadwater in Helena.

28. An Indian industrial school is designated for Fort Totten, North Dakota, by the U.S. Interior Department.

31. The Butchertown section of San Francisco burns.

Also in May 1890:

Richard Harding Davis travels by rail from Denver to the silver mines of Creede, Colorado, an expedition that he will recount in *The West From a Car Window* (1892).

The future author Jack London's formal education ends in San Francisco at age 14, when he becomes a drop-out to help his family financially with odd jobs.

National Headlines/May 1890:

1. BANK OF AMERICA FAILS

JUNE

2. A new series of anti-Chinese ordinances containing various racially based restrictions is passed in San Francisco.

6. North Dakota farmers begin selling their wheat in Canada's Manitoba Province. Even after paying a duty of 15 cents per bushel, the farmers are able to make 6 to 7 cents more per bushel than they would by selling at home.

7. Prentiss Ingraham's "The Three Bills—Buffalo Bill, Wild Bill and Band-box Bill, or The Bravo in Broadcloth" begins serialization in the *Banner Weekly*.

8. Robbers halt a Northern Pacific train in New Salem, North Dakota; they open the safe but find nothing inside.

12. The *Batchelor* is the last major cargo boat to arrive at Montana's Fort Benton.

JULY

1. Prohibition goes into effect in North Dakota.

3. Idaho, with a population of 89,000, becomes the 43rd state to enter the Union. Its capital is Boise, it covers an area of 82,751 square miles.

4. The 20-ton cornerstone for the Colorado State Capitol is laid in Denver.

7. High winds in Fargo, North Dakota, kill nine persons and injure several others.

- San Diego acquires a new courthouse at a cost of $200,000.
10. Wyoming, with a population of more than 60,000 and Cheyenne as its capital, enters the Union as the 44th state. The right to vote is retained by women, making Wyoming the first state to allow women's suffrage. The state's total area is 97,809 square miles.
13. The explorer and politician John C. Frémont dies at age 77 in New York City.
14. President Harrison signs the Sherman Silver Purchase Act, which requires the U.S. Treasury to buy 4.5 million ounces of silver each month and to issue notes, redeemable in gold or silver, in order to pay for the silver purchases.
- A fire in Prescott, Arizona, destroys much of the town, including the Prescott Bank, a handful of hotels, places of business, and private dwellings.
17. Elizabeth B. Custer is reportedly enjoying a brief visit with a friend in Helena, Montana.
22. Thunderstorms in Trail County, North Dakota, kill five.
23. Fort Abraham Lincoln in North Dakota begins its last year of operation.
- Buffalo Bill's Wild West opens a month-long stay in Berlin, Germany.
24. A fire in Yuma, Arizona, destroys eight buildings.
31. The Deer Lodge, Montana's longest-operating women's club, organizes.

Also in July 1890:
The Wyoming humorist Edgar Wilson Nye publishes *Bill Nye and Boomerang, or The Tale of the Meek-Eyed Mule, and Some Other Literary Gems.*

National Headlines/ July 1890:
2. SHERMAN ANTI-TRUST ACT PASSED

AUGUST
12. The Brown Palace Hotel has its grand opening in Denver.
14. A horse thief, age unknown, is killed in Prescott, Arizona. Citizens drag into the town the body of the man they believe has been helping himself to the local cattle.
18. New Mexico's constitution is amended.
30. Prentiss Ingraham's "The Texan's Double, or Buffalo Bill's Secret Ally" begins serialization in the *Banner Weekly.*

Also in August 1890:
The first territorial legislature in Oklahoma convenes in Guthrie.

Steamboat traffic on the Montana portion of the Missouri River ends.

National Headlines/August 1890:
6. FIRST ELECTRIC CHAIR USED IN NY

SEPTEMBER
12. Police are called to put down the violence at the Democratic Territorial Convention in Phoenix. Several fistfights broke out on the floor.
- The first state election is held in Wyoming.
13. Lieutenant John Pitcher reports two Indians slain by the 1st Cavalry at the Tongue River Agency in Montana.
22. A severe hailstorm strikes Strawberry, Arizona. Five days later, the stones will still be in drifts 1.5 feet deep.
25. The Mormon Church denounces polygamy. Bowing to government pressure, the Latter-day Saints will no longer sanction the practice begun by Joseph Smith and Brigham Young. In his Manifesto, church president Wilford Woodruff urges all members to obey federal law, and he officially outlaws plural marriages.
- Congress establishes Yosemite National Park in California.

Also in September 1890:
In the last 200 years, Karankawan, Akokisa, Bidui, and Coahuiltecan tribes have become extinct in Texas. Other tribes have decreased in number as follows: Tonkawan (1,600 to 56), Caddo (8,500 to 536), Wichita (3,200 to 358), Kichai (500 to 66), Lipan Apache (500 to 60), Mescalero Apache (700 to 473), Comanche (7,000 to 1,598), Kiowa (2,000 in 1780, to 1,140), Arapaho and Cheyenne (6,500 in 1780, to 5,630).
A free public school system is established in Utah.
The future author Willa Cather enrolls at the University of Nebraska in Lincoln.

OCTOBER
1. Yosemite National Park, comprising 761,320 acres, is dedicated in California. Among its spectacular sights are America's tallest waterfall, mountains, glacial formations, beautiful gorges, and three redwood groves.
4. John N. Irwin is appointed territorial governor of Arizona.
6. The Mormon Church in Salt Lake City officially discontinues its sanctioning of polygamy.
7. The amended New Mexico constitution is rejected by popular vote.

9. The Ghost Dance is performed for the first time at Sitting Bull's camp on the Standing Rock Agency in South Dakota. Sitting Bull learned of the dance from his nephew, Kicking Bear, who saw the new messiah, Wovoka, in Nevada. Sitting Bull does not believe dead warriors can be reborn, but the dance itself seems to rile the white authorities and, therefore, cannot be all bad. He will not discourage his people from dancing the dance of the ghosts. To Sitting Bull's interpretation of the dance however, Kicking Bear has added a fatal twist—specially decorated white muslin "ghost shirts" that supposedly make the Sioux invulnerable to bullets.

14. Dwight David Eisenhower, the 34th president of the United States is born in Denison, Texas, where his father works for the M-K-T Railroad. Eisenhower will spearhead the Allies' World War II D-Day invasion of France in 1944 before serving as president from 1953–1961.

16. In South Dakota, Kicking Bear is escorted by the military from the Standing Rock Agency. H. D. Gallagher, the agent at the nearby Pine Ridge Reservation, wires Washington:

> INDIANS ARE DANCING IN THE SNOW AND ARE WILD AND CRAZY . . . WE NEED PROTECTION AND WE NEED IT NOW.

19. Highwaymen, said to be Mexicans, rob Arizona's Bowie and Solomon stagecoach.

20. General Nelson A. Miles issues a recommendation that the U.S. government turn its abandoned forts and military posts into schools or reservations.

■ The Pikes Peak Railroad is completed.

■ Construction begins in Havre, Montana, on the Great Northern Railway's tracks to the Pacific Coast.

28. Buffalo Bill's Wild West concludes its European tour in Strasbourg, France.

Also in October 1890:
Adolph Bandelier writes one of the finest Western novels, *The Delight Makers.*

Buck Taylor, America's first cowboy hero, buys a ranch in the Sweetwater region of Wyoming.

One of the largest cattle-shipping points in the world is Amarillo, Texas.

NOVEMBER

3. Los Angeles reports a high temperature of 96°, a November record that will stand until 1966.

6. Fort Bridger in Wyoming is officially abandoned as the last troops depart.

11. The *Arizona Republican* begins publishing in Phoenix.

15. The black journalist Jerry Nashville Walker begins publishing the *African Advocate* in Denver, in an effort to inform Colorado about the "back to Africa" movement. His reasons include:

> Because we can never hope to rise to the level socially, morally, politically or otherwise of our oppressors, the Caucasian race, so long as we remain here. Because we will always lack race pride, patriotism and manhood so long as we remain the subservient tools of the whites in this country. Because in Africa our children will be born 'free and equal' and will need no constitutional amendments or man-made laws to make us the equals of our fellow citizens.

■ The May Company in Denver advertises overcoats for $15; derbies for $1.98; and "Ladies Bright Dongola Button Boots," slashed from $2.50 to $1.39.

Wovoka (Jack Wilson, c. 1856–1932). His new religion is the "Ghost Dance," based on the belief that dead warriors will rise up to defeat the white man. (Denver Public Library, Western History Department)

Buffalo Bill and some members of his Wild West cast in Venice, 1890. (Denver Public Library, Western History Department)

- Colorado University loses the first football game it ever played to the Denver Athletic Club, 34–0.
17. A possible Indian uprising in Mandan, North Dakota, is reported.
22. Prentiss Ingraham's "Gentleman Jack, the Man of Many Masks, or Buffalo Bill's Peerless Pard" begins serialization in the *Banner Weekly*.
27. San Francisco's first police signal box is put into service.

National Headlines/November 1890:
29. 1ST ARMY–NAVY GAME: NAVY 24, ARMY 0

DECEMBER

2. Bill Pickett, the cowboy and rodeo innovator, weds Maggie Turner in Taylor, Texas.
4. Fear of an Indian uprising continues to grip the Dakotas and Nebraska. Congress passes a joint resolution to furnish residents of those states with $5,000 in arms and ammunition.

12. In South Dakota, the followers of Kicking Bear and of Short Bull unite and move northwest, to a corner of the Pine Ridge Reservation called the Stronghold, where they Ghost Dance. Short Bull has brought his people from the Rosebud Reservation. Kicking Bear, the nephew of Sitting Bull, has been invited by his uncle to come to Pine Ridge to demonstrate the Ghost Dance. Troops from Forts Keogh and Abraham Lincoln are sent after Kicking Bear and Short Bull.
14. Indian agent James McLaughlin orders Sitting Bull's arrest following the latest influx of Ghost Dancers at South Dakota's Pine Ridge Reservation.
15. Sitting Bull is murdered in Grand River, South Dakota.
17. Many of Sitting Bull's followers who have left the Standing Rock Agency reach the Cherry Creek camp of the Miniconjoux chief Big Foot with the news of their leader's murder. The aging Big Foot faces an immediate dilemma. His people are making

an 85-mile journey to Fort Bennett to collect their treaty-guaranteed supplies. Already, he has explained their purpose to Colonel E. V. Sumner of the 8th Cavalry, who believed they might be breaking out from their designated lands. Sumner has let them proceed, but now Big Foot fears they may be ambushed at the fort. He decides to return home to Deep Creek, and is joined by Sitting Bull's Hunkpapas.

22. Big Foot and his people return to their Deep Creek log cabins. On the trip home, they are intercepted by Colonel E. V. Sumner, who has been ordered by General Nelson Miles to arrest the leader for taking in Sitting Bull's Hunkpapas. Big Foot explains that he could not turn them away cold and hungry.

Sumner sees Big Foot's point, and orders cattle slaughtered to feed the 333 Hunkpapas and Miniconjoux. On the freezing trip home, Big Foot contracts pneumonia.

- Captain J. H. Hurst reports the surrender of 294 members of "Sitting Bull's band" at Cherry Creek, South Dakota.

23. Colonel E. V. Sumner and his men arrive at the Deep Creek camp and declare Big Foot's people prisoners; they will be marched to Fort Meade the next morning. The sick chief protests. Sumner decides that if Big Foot would show up the next morning at Camp Cheyenne—where the soldiers are stationed—with the 38 Hunkpapas, they will talk.

- Luke Short's last gunfight occurs shortly after a gambling dispute in Fort Worth, Texas. Short is ambushed on the street by saloon owner Charles Wright, who fires a shotgun at Short from behind and hits him in the leg. Short returns fire with his revolver, breaking Wright's wrist with a bullet; Wright runs away. Short will recover and live until 1893; he will die in Geuda Springs, Kansas, where he will be taking mineral treatments for dropsy, the former term for edema.

24. Fearing treachery by the army, Big Foot has decided to follow the will of his council and heads for the Pine Ridge Reservation in the predawn hours. Sumner learns of this and wires General Miles, who in turn telegrams an alert to a battalion of the 7th Cavalry in Rapid City. The 7th erroneously believes that Big Foot participated in the Battle of the Little Bighorn in 1876. "If we get far enough from headquarters," Colonel James W. Forsyth is heard to say, "there'll be no strings tied to any of us."

28. On Porcupine Creek, Big Foot's tattered caravan encounters four Oglala Sioux scouts from the U.S. Army encampment at Wounded Knee Creek, 10 miles to the east. Two Oglalas ride back to relay word of the discovery. Two hours later, Major Samuel Whitside and his men find Big Foot waving a white flag. Through bloody coughs, the chief tells Whitside he wants only peace. The Sioux agree to follow the soldiers to Chankpe Opi Wakpala, Wounded Knee Creek. At the campsite, they are given hardtack and bacon. A soldier counts 120 men and 230 women and children. Big Foot stays in an army ambulance. As a precaution, Whitside has two rapid-firing Hotchkiss guns positioned on overlooking bluffs. At 8:30 P.M., Forsyth and four troopers of the 7th Cavalry arrive with two more Hotchkiss guns. The Indians call them "twice-shooting guns" because of their two-pound fragmentation shells.

- The last Northwestern stagecoach leaves Deadwood, South Dakota.
29. The Wounded Knee Massacre takes place in South Dakota.
30. Captain J. S. Loud reports an Indian attack on a wagon train near the Pine Ridge Reservation; one soldier is killed.
- Colonel J. W. Forsyth reports a fight with Indians at White Clay Creek, South Dakota; he lists one soldier killed and seven wounded.

Also in December 1890:

The aftermath of the events at Wounded Knee will see Colonel J. W. Forsyth court-martialed for the massacre of noncombatants as well as for positioning his men in their own line of fire. He will be declared innocent of all charges, over the objections of General Nelson Miles.

A quote from Wovoka, the reclusive messiah in Nevada, when he hears of Wounded Knee: "Today I call upon you to travel a new trail, the only trail now open—the white man's road."

Also in 1890:

The first immigrants from the then Russian province of Georgia—15 riders for Buffalo Bill's West—arrive in the United States.

Elizabeth Bacon Custer publishes another memoir of her life with her husband, *Following the Guidon*.

Wells Fargo reports annual earnings of $6,516,000 from express services, and 39,600 miles traveled this year.

MASSACRE AT WOUNDED KNEE
DECEMBER 29, 1890

The last major conflict of the Indian wars began shortly after 8:00 A.M., when Colonel James W. Forsyth called the Indian men to a meeting and explained why he was disarming them. The warriors grumbled and then turned in a small stack of battered rifles. Forsyth remained unsatisfied, as he had seen new Winchesters among the Indians. A search was ordered, in which soldiers retrieved knives, cooking tools, axes, tent stakes, and more. The Sioux complained: Some wanted to sell their rifles for money; others had tales of ancestors who turned over their weapons only to be killed. Amidst the confusion, the medicine man Yellow Bird chanted the Ghost Dance myth: "There are lots of soldiers and they have lots of bullets, but the prairie is large and the bullets will not go toward you."

Black Coyote, a deaf Sioux, objected when a soldier attempted to take his weapon. Two soldiers held him, and his gun fired into the air. Some young warriors then raised their rifles at the men of K troop, and the order was given to soldiers to open fire. Big Foot lifted himself to see the commotion and took a bullet in the head. As he died, Wounded Knee erupted into fighting. Hand-to-hand struggles gave way to the cracking of carbines. The Hotchkiss guns sat silent, unable to fire without hurting soldiers. Then, as warriors broke free to run for their families, the shell-a-second machine guns engaged. Exploding projectiles hit tepees, and fires were started. Women and children fled in all directions, some to the safety of a nearby ravine, others into the raking bullets.

In the initial volley, 52 of Big Foot's 106 male followers were slain. Shouts of "Remember Custer!" echoed through the explosions. Inside her lodge, Big Foot's wife was wounded from one of the deflected bullets that flew every time a soldier rode by to put another slug in the chief. Beneath the truce flag, a baby nursed at its slain mother's breast. Indians camped within a 20-mile radius of Wounded Knee heard what they will later describe as the continuous sound of a great blanket tearing.

The exact body count at Wounded Knee has eluded history. Only four men and 47 women and children arrived with the soldiers at Pine Ridge. The killing ground itself yielded the corpses of 84 men, 44 women, and 18 children. Many of the wounded crawled into the hills to die. As many as 150 persons may have died during the attack. Army records reported "128 killed, 33 wounded." Of the 25 dead and 39 wounded soldiers, many had been shot by their own men. One of the soldiers killed at Wounded Knee was Gustav Korn, the Army blacksmith who had cared for Comanche, the horse that survived the Little Bighorn battle of 1876.

A blizzard postponed burials for many days. When the soldiers returned, they found the corpses—including that of Big Foot—frozen into hellish contortions.

The first labor strike at Adolph Coors's brewery in Colorado is called off when the owner agrees to "10 hours labor for a day's work and 30 cents per hour for overwork."

The University of Arizona opens its agricultural school in Tucson.

There are 16,389 farms in Colorado.

Quanah Parker is relieved of his duties as judge for violating the codes of the Courts of Indian Offenses, specifically, for taking too many wives.

Hubert Howe Bancroft publishes an account of his massive undertaking in publishing—*Literary Industries.* Bancroft also publishes a one-volume work, *Washington, Idaho, and Montana.* Since 1874, he has put his name on 40 volumes of history.

A total of 539 outlaws have lived in New Mexico since 1865, according to the historian Peter Hertzog.

Charles H. Hoyt's play, *A Texas Steer,* becomes the source for much stereotyping of Texans.

The 984,000 head of cattle in Arizona are valued at $13.9 million.

The federal government's first complete census of American Indians shows that there are 248,000 Native Americans in the United States. Ten years later, that number will be 237,000. The Indian population in California has dropped from 100,000 to 18,000 since 1849.

The U.S. population is 62,979,766, twice what it was at the beginning of the Civil War. With some 11,000,000 settlers in the trans-Missouri West, the Census Bureau declares that the U.S. no longer has an unsettled frontier.

1890 CENSUS

Arizona	88,243
Arkansas	1,128,179
California	1,213,398
Los Angeles	50,395[a]
San Francisco	298,997[b]
Colorado	413,249
Idaho	88,548
Iowa	1,912,297
Kansas	1,428,108
Louisiana	1,118,588
Minnesota	1,310,283
Missouri	2,679,185
Montana	142,924
Nebraska	1,062,656
Nevada	47,355
New Mexico	160,282
North Dakota	190,983[c]
Oklahoma	258,657[d]
Oregon	317,704
South Dakota	348,600
Texas	2,235,527[e]
Utah	210,779
Washington	357,232
Wyoming	62,555

[a] The Los Angeles population has increased from 11,000 in 1880 to more than 50,000. By 1900, it will exceed 100,000.

[b] The West Coast's largest city, San Francisco ranks eighth in the nation.

[c] The state with the largest gain over the last decade—394 percent.

[d] The first census of the Five Tribes area in Oklahoma yields the following results: 109,393 whites, 50,055 Indians, 18,636 black.

[e] The rural population is 84.4 percent.

EPILOGUE:

1891—Present

"The frontier is gone."
—Frederick Jackson Turner

January 6: The last recorded Sioux attack on a wagon train occurs not far from the site of the Wounded Knee Massacre in South Dakota.

January 14: General Nelson A. Miles reports that the Sioux are returning to their Dakota reservations.

March 5: Officials in Phoenix, Arizona, offer a $200 reward for any dead Indian.

March 14: The worst lynching in American history occurs in New Orleans, where a mob of angry citizens removes from the city jail 11 Italian immigrants acquitted of murder and kills them.

April 7: Nebraska adopts the eight-hour workday.

May 9: A train robbery occurs in the Cherokee Strip of Indian Territory, as the Dalton Gang hijacks the Sante Fe Limited.

May 17: Relics—including cash—left behind by the ill-fated Donner party during the winter of 1846–1847 are discovered near Truckee, California.

June 30: The first passenger train ascends Pikes Peak in Colorado. In 1806, Zebulon Pike guessed that no one would ever climb the mountain.

September 22: Sak, Fox, and Potawatomi lands—some 900,000 acres—are opened for settlement in Oklahoma.

October 17: The human rights advocate Sarah Winnemucca, 48, dies in Bozeman, Montana.

October 25: Jacob Walzer, the "Dutchman" of "Lost Dutchman Mine" fame, dies, his secret unrevealed.

November 6: Comanche, the only horse of Custer's 7th Cavalry to survive the 1876 Battle of the Little Bighorn, dies.

"The Great Hostile Indian Camp," formed by 4,000 Oglalas and Blue Sioux in the wake of the Wounded Knee Massacre, is photographed by C. H. Grabill in 1891. (National Archives)

THE RIDDLE OF THE LOST DUTCHMAN

Whether or not Arizona's Lost Dutchman Mine is a hidden fact or an abused myth has become a moot point over the years. Truth has yielded to hearsay. This beguiling mystery began some 40 miles east of Phoenix, Arizona, in the foreboding Superstition Mountains.

History records two accounts of the mine's discovery. In the first, a poor, jilted lover from Chihuahua, Mexico, stumbled upon the mine while jogging through Arizona; he returned home with the gold, got the girl back, and lived happily ever after. In the other, more credible account, Don Miguel Peralta obtained a stone map from a Jesuit priest in Arizpe, Sonora, Mexico. Peralta and his two brothers then found a gold mine. They returned home to organize a party of a hundred, their intention being to go for more gold before the 1848 Treaty of Guadalupe Hidalgo made the area part of the United States.

The entire Peralta party—estimates say between 70 and 400 people—was wiped out by Apaches, who were furious at finding the Mexicans in their holy haunts. Indian women then filled in the mine with dirt. Don Miguel's son-in-law, Ramón Peralta y Gonzales, located the scene of the massacre while searching for the mine in the 1870s. Another Peralta, the son of the ill-fated leader, went on to form a partnership with a "Dutchman."

Jacob Waltz (also referred to as Waltzer, Walzer, and Wolz) was not from Holland but from Germany, born in Prussia around 1810. He arrived in New York in 1839 and made his way West. Gold fever lured him to Sacramento in 1850. In 1861, he became a naturalized citizen in Los Angeles. The next year, at age 52, he relocated to Arizona and registered his first claim near Prescott.

Lost treasure in the Superstition Mountains was hardly a fresh topic of discussion at this time. Dr. Abraham D. Thorne of New Mexico claimed that, following an act of kindness toward the Apaches, he was blindfolded and led some 20 miles from the Salt River to a secret canyon. When the eye cover came off, he be-
(continued)

(continued)

held a gold-studded canyon floor, which he was allowed to comb.

Exactly how Waltz gained access to the hidden domain is part of the devilment. One account had him living in Phoenix with an Apache woman who led him to the "thunder god's gold" in 1874. Another suggests that he and partner Jacob Weiser met Don Miguel Peralta II by chance in Mexico, and learned of the nuggets deep in the heart of Apache country.

In return for a piece of the action, Waltz (the one the Indians called "Snowbeard") and Weiser accompanied Peralta to the mine. Waltz called it "a round pit, shaped like a funnel with the large end up." After a few weeks of gold mining, the three went to Tucson and converted their ore into $60,000.

Foul play occurred on their next excursion to the mine. Waltz said his partners were killed by Apaches, but he was widely suspected of having taken the lives of his comrades in order to keep the fortune for himself. Popular legend has it that Waltz danced into the Superstition Mountains regularly, taking great care to cover his trail.

If that is the case, the reality is even more puzzling than the myth. After 1877, the "Dutchman" retired to a Phoenix chicken ranch. In 1878, the 68-year-old Waltz entered into an agreement with a young local wherein he agreed to sign over all of his possessions in return for lifelong care. The written agreement listed 160 acres, two horses, chickens, and $50—hardly the inventory of a Midas.

In 1890, however, Waltz pulled $1,400 out of thin air to help Julia Thomas, the owner of a local restaurant, pay off her creditors. Thomas said he arrived at her home with gold stuffed in tin cans. One year later, Thomas nursed him after he was caught in a flood. Dying of pneumonia, he told her about his incredible mine.

It was located, he said, in the vicinity of the tall rock structure known as Weaver's Needle. "From the mouth of my mine I can look down and see people on the old military trail, but they can't see my mine," Waltz declared before dying on October 25, 1891.

Thomas fruitlessly sought to locate the mine during the rest of her life. Privately, she wondered if it had been sealed off by an 1887 earthquake. Before she died in 1917, she sold many "guaranteed" maps to the mine for $7 apiece.

Another odd twist to the mystery came at the turn of the 20th century, when Geronimo, a prisoner of war at Fort Sill, Oklahoma, tried to bribe a guard with a million dollars in gold from his Arizona "treasure mine." "From my cave," the Apache allegedly boasted, "I can see the soldiers on the military trail below, but they can't see me." This tantalizing connection is probably more fantasy than not.

However, it is indisputable that a number of people have disappeared in the canyon mazes of the Superstitions. In 1931, a Washington, D.C., government employee, the 65-year-old Adolph Ruth, brought a map his son had obtained from someone associated with the Peraltas. His decapitated skull, with two bullet holes in it, was found six months later.

The skeleton of the Lost Dutchman Mine's 20th known victim, the Phoenix photographer James A. Cravey, was also beheaded when it was discovered in February 1948. Tucson's Charles Massey had been shot between the eyes when his body was located on February 24, 1955. One year later, Brooklyn's Martin Zywotho met a similar fate. The headless skeleton of an Australian exchange student was found in 1960. Others who went into the mountains simply never came out.

Then there are those who have claimed to have located the Lost Dutchman Mine. A Los Angeles bra salesman said he did so in 1949, as did an Oklahoma City private investigator in 1966. Charles Kentworthy struck gold using the "Peralta Stone Maps" in 1980. The computer technician Michael Bilbry added his name to the list of those who found gold in 1983.

A lost mine, gold, secret maps, ancient curses, modern murders. . . . And, at the heart of the legend, Jacob Waltz, a mysterious old codger who just might have invented the whole story. Buzzards circle over the Superstition Mountains. The Lost Dutchman Mine remains one of the West's most tantalizing enigmas.

Also in 1891:

Charles M. Russell sketches the last Ghost Dances at the Pine Ridge Indian Reservation in South Dakota.

The first "Del Monte" canned goods are produced in California by the Oakland Preserving Company.

Many Kansas farmers are reportedly falling into bankruptcy. Some 18,000 covered wagons are counted moving back to the East.

A gold rush occurs in Cripple Creek, Colorado, following a discovery by Robert Wommack at Poverty Gulch.

The U.S. government purchases 6 million acres from the Oklahoma Cherokees for $8.5 million. The land will come to be known as the "Cherokee Strip" and will be opened to settlers in 1893.

1892

January 16: A miner's strike takes place at the Coeur D'Alene mines in Idaho.

February 26: N. C. Creede discovers silver in Colorado.

April 3: The Johnson County War, a Wyoming conflict over cattle, rages.

April 15: The Sisseton Indian Reservation in South Dakota is opened to settlers; some 3,000 claim land.

April 18: The Cheyennes hold their last Ghost Dance in Oklahoma.

April 19: Three million acres in Oklahoma that were formerly owned by the Cheyenne and Arapaho tribes are opened to settlers by proclamation of President Benjamin Harrison; 30,000 homesteaders stream in to stake their claims.

May 25: A Mississippi River flood kills 250 in St. Louis, Missouri.

May 26: The Idaho Populist Party is organized in Boise by members of the Farmers' Alliance and the Knights of Labor.

June 8: Robert Ford, the murderer of Jesse James, is slain by a shotgun-toting glory seeker, Edward O'Kelly, in Creede, Colorado.

July 23: The sale of liquor on all Indian lands is banned by Congress.

September 7: James J. "Gentleman Jim" Corbett KO's the boxing champion John L. Sullivan in the 21st round in New Orleans.

October 15: The Dalton gang is decimated when it attempts to rob two banks in Coffeyville, Kansas. The bodies of Bob and Grat Dalton, Bill Powers, and Dick Broadwell are displayed on the town's main street. Although Emmet Dalton survives, he will spend 14 years in prison.

Oklahoma's "Cherokee Strip" is opened by run on a scorching September afternoon in 1893. Photographers had missed the run of 1889. For this opening, the photographer built a platform. (Oklahoma Historical Society)

Also in 1892:

Joseph S. Duncan invents the Addressograph, which prints mailing labels, in Sioux City, Iowa.

The Sierra Club is founded in California by John Muir.

The American School of Osteopathy is founded in Kirksville, Missouri, by Andrew Still.

The University of Idaho opens in Moscow.

1893

August 2: The Osage tribe refuses to sell to the United States 2 million acres near the Cherokee Strip in Oklahoma.

September 1: A major gunfight between law enforcement officials and the Bill Doolin gang erupts in Ingalls, Oklahoma, in the Cherokee Strip. Doolin holes up in the Ransom and Murray Saloon, from which he tells the authorities to go to hell. Three of 13 marshals are killed in the battle. Roy "Arkansas Tom" Daugherty is arrested. Bill Doolin escapes.

September 16: The Cherokee Strip, or Outlet, a 5-million-acre tract of land, is opened to settlers in north-central Oklahoma. Some 50,000 people will claim land in the 165-mile-by-85-mile area in the largest of the Oklahoma land runs.

November 1: With the repeal by Congress of the Sherman Silver Purchase Act, the United States returns to a gold standard and the government withdraws from the silver market. The "Panic of 1893" will begin when Colorado silver producers close their mines and smelters, and the price of silver drops to 77 cents an ounce. A dozen Denver banks will close within two days. Ruined in the panic will be the ex-empire builder Horace Tabor, who finds himself $2 million in debt overnight.

November 7: Colorado becomes the second state to grant women the right to vote.

November 8: The author Francis Parkman (*The Oregon Trail*) dies at age 70.

Also in 1893:

The educator Katharine Lee Bates is inspired to write "America, the Beautiful," following a trip up Pikes Peak in Colorado.

The Great Northern Railroad from Minnesota to the Pacific Northwest is completed.

Frederick Jackson Turner, 31, reads his paper "The Significance of the Frontier in American History" at the World Columbian Exposition in Chicago. In his address, he announces: "The frontier is gone."

Rain in the Face appears at Chicago's World Columbian Exposition, standing in front of the cabin that Sitting Bull lived in at the time of his murder in 1890.

A well that is being dug for water in Corsicana, Texas, strikes oil.

The size of the North American buffalo herd drops to 1,090.

1894

February 17: John Wesley Hardin, after spending 16 years at hard labor, is pardoned by Texas governor Jim Hogg. Hardin was convicted in 1877 for the 1874 murder of County Deputy Sheriff Charles Webb at Comanche, Texas.

March 14: Denver's "City Hall War" occurs when members of the fire and excise commissions, along with some 200 armed sympathizers, occupy the massive City Hall building. Governor Davis "Bloody Bridles" Waits calls out the national guard, and the confrontation ends without a shot being fired.

April 17: Percival Lowell founds the Lowell Observatory near Flagstaff, Arizona.

June 21: William Jennings Bryan, a member of the U.S. House of Representatives from Nebraska, proposes free silver as a solution to America's economic woes.

December 27: A famous argument ends when Harvey Logan, Kid Curry, kills Pike Landusky at a saloon in Landusky, Montana.

Also in 1894:

A hurricane destroys Hinckley, Minnesota, killing 500.

Drought ravages the Great Plains during the summer months.

John Muir writes *The Mountains of California*.

The first commercial chili powder is marketed by the German-American cafe owner William Gebhardt of New Braunfels, Texas.

Prehistoric ruins are discovered in Santa Cruz, New Mexico.

President Grover Cleveland pardons and restores civil rights to all who were disenfranchised in Utah by the antipolygamy laws.

Colonel James W. Forsyth, having been cleared of any wrongdoing in the Wounded Knee massacre of 1890, is promoted to brigadier general.

1895

January 8: John Wesley Hardin weds Callie Lewis; their marriage lasts only a few hours.

February 1: The film director John Ford is born Sean O'Feeney in Cape Elizabeth, Maine. His westerns will include *Stagecoach, Fort Apache, She Wore a Yellow Ribbon,* and *The Searchers*.

March 31: The author Vardis Fisher (*Children of God*) is born in Annis, Idaho.

May 8: Utah's sixth attempt to achieve statehood includes a proposition that would prohibit polygamy.

June 2: Kid Curry robs the Union Pacific's Overland Flyer in Wilcox, Wyoming.

July 1: Alcatraz Island in San Francisco Bay is designated as a U.S. Disciplinary Barracks for the military.

July 25: Bannock Indians surround 250 settlers near Jackson Hole, Wyoming, until they are dispersed by the 9th Cavalry.

August 19: John Wesley Hardin, 41, is shot to death by John Selman in El Paso, Texas.

October 28: F. G. Bonfils and Harry H. Tammen purchase Denver's *Evening Post* for $12,500 and rename it the *Denver Post*.

Also in 1895:

Edgar S. Paxson begins painting *Custer's Last Stand*.

James Addison Reavis is jailed when his 12.8 million-acre claim to New Mexico and Arizona is declared fraudulent.

The mining magnate Winfield S. Stratton, of Cripple Creek, Colorado, is worth $10 million.

Less than 1,000 bison remain on the North American continent, down from 1,091 in 1889.

1896

January 1: The Leadville Ice Palace, a 450-foot-by-350-foot castle made of blocks of ice weighing a total of 5,000 tons, opens in Colorado.

January 4: Utah, with a constitution that provides for women's suffrage, becomes the 45th state in the Union.

February 21: Judge Roy Bean hosts the Maher-Fitzsimmons heavyweight boxing championship fight on an island in the Rio Grande.

May 11: The author Mari Sandoz (*Old Jules* and *Cheyenne Autumn*) is born in the Niobrara River region of Nebraska.

May 27: A tornado kills more than 500 people and does $13 million in damage to St. Louis.

July 11: In Arkansas, Rufus Buck, Lewis Davis, Lucky Davis, Sam Sampson, and Maomi July, sentenced by "Hanging Judge" Parker for their three-day rape-and-murder spree through the Creek Nation, are executed in Fort Smith's last multiple hanging.

August 12: Gold is discovered in Canada's Klondike, near Alaska.

August 25: The outlaw Bill Doolin is killed by a posse led by Heck Thomas in Oklahoma. A posse member, Bill Dunn, fires the fatal shot—one blast from his shotgun fills Doolin with 21 holes.

September 15: The "Crash at Crush" occurs in Texas; it is a staged railway accident that injures two of the 50,000 spectators who pay to see two engines traveling 90 miles per hour ram into each other.

Also in 1896:

Blackfeet, Assiniboines, and Gros Ventres sell all their mineral rights to the U.S. government for $350,000.

In Denver, the Tabor Grand Opera House and the Tabor Block are sold to cover a $476,990 judgment against Horace Tabor.

1897

January 11: The editor and historian Bernard Augustine De Voto is born in Ogden, Utah.

January 19: A miners' strike in Colorado ends after seven months.

February 6: In Texas, a posse captures the remnants of the Dalton gang, killing two of the gang's members and taking one prisoner.

March 17: Bob Fitzsimmons defeats "Gentleman Jim" Corbett in their heavyweight championship bout in Carson City, Nevada.

April 28: The Dawes Commission reaches an arrangement with the Chickasaw and Choctaw Nations that will abolish their tribal governments and divide their lands into 40-acre homesteads.

November 2: J. Edward Harriman assumes control of the Union Pacific Railroad.

Also in 1987:

President Cleveland establishes the Bitterroot Forest Reserve in northern Idaho.

The first Cheyenne Frontier Days celebration is held in Wyoming.

The first oil strike in Oklahoma occurs in Bartlesville.

1898

January 23: The actor Randolph Scott is born in Orange County, Virginia.

February 26: The Lincoln County War figure J. J. Dolan dies in New Mexico and is buried at the Fritz South Spring Ranch south of Lincoln.

February 28: The U.S. Supreme Court upholds a Utah law that limits workdays in the mines to eight hours.

June 5: William Boyd, the "Hopalong Cassidy" of television and motion picture fame, is born in Cambridge, Ohio.

July 1: In the Spanish-American War, Theodore Roosevelt leads western "Rough Riders" up Cuba's Kettle Hill.

July 8: The con man Soapy Smith is shot dead in Skagway, Alaska.

July 24: The aviator Amelia Earhart is born in Atchison, Kansas.

Also in 1898:

Ernest Thompson Seton writes *Wild Animals I Have Known*.

Gertrude Atherton publishes *The Californians*.

In Denver, Horace Tabor's old cronies, upon discovering that the 67-year-old ex-Silver King is working 10-hour shifts at a smelter, have him appointed the city's postmaster.

J. C. Penney moves from Colorado to Wyoming.

Jack London, 22, sells his first story to the *Overland Monthly*.

1899

January 15: The poet Edwin Markham publishes "The Man With the Hoe."

April: A labor war erupts at Idaho's Coeur d'Alene mine.

April 10: The former Silver King Horace Tabor dies in Denver. In his last conversation with his wife, Baby Doe, he reportedly tells her to "hang on to the Matchless," his worthless mine in Leadville.

May 10: The first automobile in Denver is delivered to David Brunton.

May 30: America's last stagecoach robbery is committed by a woman in Arizona. Pearl Hart and her boyfriend, Joe Boot, are apprehended.

June 2: Butch Cassidy, the Sundance Kid, and other members of the Wild Bunch steal $30,000 in cash from a train near Wilcox, Wyoming.

August 23: The first ship-to-shore wireless telegraph message is received at San Francisco's Cliff House.

September 23: U.S. Supreme Court Associate Justice Thomas Campbell Clark is born in Dallas, Texas.

October 5: Ned Green drives the first automobile in Texas, traveling from Dallas to Terrell.

October 15: The Overland Limited railway begins its first run from Chicago to Oakland, California.

Also in 1899:

Mount Rainier National Park is established in Washington.

In Texas, the Brazos River floods, killing 284 people.

1900

February 16: Radical prohibitionist Carry Nation destroys her first whiskey barrel at a saloon in Kansas.

April 3: Irrigation begins in California's Imperial Valley, bringing water from the Colorado River.

April 11: The *Denver Daily News* reports the death of Cort Thomson, the lover of Mattie Silks, citing "the combined effects of whiskey and opium."

April 17: Flatnosed George Currie is killed while rustling steers in Thompson, Utah.

May 26: Harvey Logan, Kid Curry, kills two members of a posse near Thompson, Utah.

June 25: Oliver Lippincott drives a car to the top of Glacier Point in California's Yosemite National Park.

September 8: America's worst hurricane disaster occurs in Galveston, Texas: 6,000 residents drown, and $100 million in property is destroyed.

Also in 1900:

Bubonic plague is reported in San Francisco.

In Wyoming, sheep outnumber cattle by 8 to 1.

Jack London writes *The Son of the Wolf*.

John G. Neihardt publishes his first epic poem, "The Divine Enchantment."

Tom Horn kills the cattle rustler Matt Rash in Routt County, Colorado. Horn follows that deed with the murder of the black rancher Isom Dart.

Washakie, the chief of the Eastern Shoshones since 1843, dies.

1901

January 7: In Colorado, Alferd Packer, is pardoned after a vigorous campaign on his behalf by the *Denver Post*. The "cannibal" had been serving time for manslaughter.

January 10: In Texas, oil is discovered at the Spindletop claim in Beaumont.

January 13: The author A. B. Guthrie (*The Way West, The Big Sky*) is born in Bedford, Indiana.

April 2: Lawmen slay the Wild Bunch member William Carver in Sonora, Texas.

April 26: "I'll be in Hell before you start breakfast. Let her rip!" are the last words of train robber Tom "Black Jack" Ketchum as he is hanged in Texas.

May 7: The actor Gary Cooper, star of *High Noon* (1952), is born in Helena, Montana.

July 3: The last robbery committed by the Wild Bunch on U.S. soil occurs near Wagner, Montana, where a train is stopped by Butch Cassidy, Harry Longabaugh ("the Sundance Kid"), Harvey Logan, and Camilla Hanks. Longabaugh kills Sheriff Griffith of Great Falls. The gang nets a profit of $65,000 in unsigned bank notes.

July 14: Jim and Cole Younger, imprisoned since 1876 for their part in the James gang's attempted bank robbery in Northfield, Minnesota, are released from the Stillwater Penitentiary in Minnesota.

July 18: Hired gun Tom Horn goes gunning for sheep

Butch Cassidy's Hole-in-the-Wall gang poses in a Fort Worth parlor. From left to right: Harry Longabaugh (the Sundance Kid), Will Carver, Ben Kilpatrick, Harvey Logan (Kid Curry), Robert Leroy Parker (Butch Cassidy). (Denver Public Library, Western History Department)

rancher Kels Nickell in southern Wyoming, but mistakenly kills the man's son, the 14-year-old Willie Nickell.

July 25: In Montana, Harvey Logan (Kid Curry) avenges the 1896 death of his brother Johnny. Curry waits in Jim Winters's corral all night, then shoots his foe when he steps out on the front porch the next morning to brush his teeth.

September 14: Theodore Roosevelt becomes president of the United States after President William McKinley is assassinated.

October 28: Annie Oakley is critically injured in a train wreck while touring with Buffalo Bill's Wild West near Lexington, Kentucky.

December 12: Ben Kilpatrick, a member of the Wild Bunch, is sentenced to 15 years in prison in Atlanta, Georgia.

December 13: Kid Curry is arrested in Knoxville, Tennessee.

1902

February 9: The artist Fred Harman, creator of the comic strip "Red Ryder," is born in St. Joseph, Missouri.

April 2: The Wyoming suffragist Esther Morris dies at the age of 88.

April 14: J. C. Penney opens the "Golden Rule Store" in Kemmerer, Wyoming.

May 5: The author Bret Harte dies at age 65 in New York City.

May 22: Crater Lake National Park is established in Oregon.

May 28: Macmillan publishes the first serious western, Owen Wister's *The Virginian: A Horseman of the Plains.*

July 25: The author Frank Waters (*Book of the Hopi*) is born in Colorado Springs, Colorado.

September 23: The explorer John Wesley Powell dies at age 69 in Haven, Maine.

October 19: The former gang member Jim Younger, 54, commits suicide in St. Paul, Minnesota. He had recently completed a 25-year stay in prison.

November 30: Harvey Logan (Kid Curry) is convicted of a 1901 train robbery in Montana and sentenced to 20 years of hard labor. He is also fined $5,000.

Also in 1902:

Calamity Jane is jailed in Billings, Montana, for disturbing the peace.

New Mexico's Mimbres River floods.

The first oil and gas leases on Indian Territory in Oklahoma are issued by the U.S. secretary of the interior.

The first showing of pornographic movies in the West takes place in Denver.

North America's buffalo population numbers 1,940, up from fewer than 1,000 in 1895.

1903

February–March: Conflicts between factions of sheep and cattle ranchers continue in Wyoming.

March 16: Judge Roy Bean, approximately 78 years old, dies of heart and lung disease in the Jersey Lilly, the saloon he named for his fantasy girl, Miss Lillie Langtry.

May 14: The naturalist John Muir guides President Theodore Roosevelt's party at Yosemite National Park in California.

July 4: Following the laying of the first transpacific telegraph cable from San Francisco to the Philippine city of Manila, President Roosevelt sends the first telegraph message around the world from San Francisco. The message circles the globe in 12 minutes.

July 7: A shootout near Parachute, Colorado, on July 5 ends in the suicide of a man the authorities claim is Harvey Logan, aka Kid Curry.

August 1: Martha Jane Canary, "Calamity Jane," dies of pneumonia at age 51 near Deadwood, South Dakota.

August 10: A major labor dispute erupts in Colorado as Cripple Creek miners go on strike.

August 14: Jim Jeffries defeats "Gentleman Jim" Corbett in a boxing match in San Francisco.

September 15: The country music entertainer Roy Acuff is born in Maynardsville, Tennessee.

October 22: In Montana, 10,000 workers are laid off as the Amalgamated Copper company shuts its operations.

November 20: Tom Horn, 42, is hanged in Cheyenne, Wyoming, after being convicted of the murder of Willie Nickell, 14. Horn thought he was shooting Willie's father, Kels Nickell.

Also in 1903:

Andy Adams writes *The Log of a Cowboy.*

Buffalo Bill's Wild West plays London, England, again.

Jack London writes *The Call of the Wild.*

The Great Train Robbery is filmed and released.

In *Lonewolf v. Hickok,* the U.S. Supreme Court upholds the authority of Congress to break Indian treaties.

Walter Woods writes the play *Billy the Kid.*

Wind Cave National Park is established in South Dakota.

1904

April 30: The $31.5 million Louisiana Purchase Exposition opens in St. Louis, Missouri.

June 8: Six striking union members are slain by the Colorado Militia in Dunnville.

September 21: In Washington, Chief Joseph, approximately 64 years old, dies of what Colville Reservation officials diagnose as "a broken heart."

Also in 1904:

The worst floods in New Mexico history occur.

1905

February 15: Lew Wallace, 78, the former New Mexico governor and author of *Ben-Hur,* dies in Indiana.

March 3: Approximately 1.5 million acres of Wyoming's Wind River Reservation are opened for settlement.

April 13: The Wyoming Wool Growers's Association is established.

May 11: A tornado in Snyder, Oklahoma, kills 100 people.

May 16: The actor Henry Fonda is born in Grand Island, Nebraska.

June 1: The Lewis and Clark Centennial Exposition opens in Portland, Oregon.

June 30: An explosion at the Union Pacific Coal Company's Mine Number One in Hanna, Wyoming, kills 169.

September 14: Rain in the Face, approximately 70 years old, dies, adding further confusion to the "who killed Custer" debate. Rain had denied that he was the culprit, but on his deathbed he said: "Yes I killed him. I was so close to him that the powder from my gun blackened his face."

September 24: Of Louis Gantz's 7,000 sheep in Basin, Wyoming, 4,000 are shot or clubbed to death by cattlemen. No one will be prosecuted.

November 5: The actor Joel McCrea is born in Los Angeles.

December 19: The author Dorothy M. Johnson (*The Hanging Tree*) is born in Iowa.

THE GREAT TRAIN ROBBERY
1903

The Great Train Robbery was a flickering, grainy western that changed motion picture history. In a time when the infant medium was comfortable with its own novelty, this 1903 tale of armed robbery, pursuit, and capture boldly dared to do something no film had done—to tell a sequential story.

Often credited as the first western—even as the first motion picture—it was actually neither. Brief movement studies such as *The Kiss* and *The Sneeze* had come before. *Cripple Creek Bar Room,* a four-minute plotless tableau shot in 1898 by Thomas Edison's company, was the first movie to have a western theme. But these facts hardly detract from the monumental importance of *The Great Train Robbery.*

The film was the brainchild of Edwin Stanton Porter. Born in Connellsville, Pennsylvania, in 1870, his introduction to film had come with a job as a projectionist in 1896, operating Edison's Vitascope for astounded New Yorkers. After touring with the contraption in South America and the West Indies, Porter went to work at Edison's East Twenty-third Street studio in Manhattan, where he advanced quickly from cameraman to head of production.

The germ of the idea for story movies came when Porter decided to show a fireman at work and at home. *The Life of an American Fireman* (1902) required 500 feet of film, 10 times the standard amount for the then-current film fare. The rescue of a child from a towering inferno electrified audiences. Porter realized he was on to something. "Encouraged by the success of this experiment," he wrote, "we devoted all our resources to the production of *stories,* instead of disconnected and unrelated scenes."

In September 1903, he went to work on a promotional film for the Delaware, Lackawanna and Western Railroad in New Jersey. The theme would depict the clean cars that the film's heroine, "Phoebe Snow," could travel in without soiling her whitest ruffles. Porter established a rapport with the railroad's officials, an important factor in his upcoming project.

In 1903, the Old West was still kicking. Bat Masterson was a New York City sportswriter. Wyatt Earp was a Colorado prospector. Geronimo was a prisoner of war in Oklahoma. Cole Younger, having completed a 25-year prison sentence, was out preaching the evils of outlawry. Tom Horn was jailed in Cheyenne, awaiting his November 20 hanging. Butch Cassidy and the Sundance Kid were robbing Argentine banks. Calamity Jane and Judge Roy Bean died that year. Therefore, *The Great Train Robbery,* unlike every "oater" that would follow, was not so much a longing for the good old days as a drama based on current events. But its historical significance escaped Porter. Looking for action, he quickly jotted the script on a legal pad.

The vaudevillian George Barnes was hired away from Huber's Museum to play a robber. Frank Hanaway was chosen for his riding skills, which he had acquired in the U.S. Cavalry. Marie Murray ("Phoebe Snow") would be in the dance hall scene. A 21-year-old male model/salesman, Max Aronson (who had recently changed his name to Anderson) was hired as a rider for 50 cents an hour, though he did not know how to ride.

Shooting began in the countryside around wild West Orange, New Jersey. The director and his cast mounted up at a livery stable, then galloped to Essex County park. When they arrived, Porter noticed that Anderson was missing. Porter's budget wouldn't allow for a star search at this point, so he would have to double for Anderson on this day.

The next day, Anderson made it to the set but kept falling off his horse. Rather than fire him, Porter thought such dramatic tumbles might be crowd pleasers. Besides, there were other production problems to worry about.

Near Paterson, New Jersey, the first fight scene atop a moving train was filmed. At a strategic point, just before the train reached the Passaic River bridge, a dummy was tossed from the coal car and landed on a trolley track below. The train's engineer gasped and pulled the emergency brake. Passengers screamed, and many fainted. When the stuffed stuntman was discovered, tempers flared.

In spite of the setbacks—which included an irate New Jersey merchant appearing on the set brandishing a loaded .45, sure that a real robbery was in progress—Porter managed to bring his film in for under $150. Quite by accident, he began as-

(continued)

(continued)

sembling his 14 scenes, not in the order in which they were shot but in the order of the sequence of the story. Another important first had been stumbled upon—the principle of film editing.

The finished product was action-packed. It began with desperados holding up a telegraph office. The operator was bound, and a train was forced to make an unscheduled stop. Passengers were escorted out. The mail car was relieved of money bags. The outlaws galloped away, although one kept falling off his horse. Meanwhile, back at the telegraph office, the operator's daughter discovered her father and set him free. He warned the townspeople, a posse formed, and a chase ensued. The bandits were caught in a wooded area and gunned down.

The finished product astounded ragtime filmgoers. Advertisements proclaimed, "SENSATIONAL AND STARTLING HOLD UP OF THE 'GOLD EXPRESS' BY FAMOUS WESTERN OUTLAWS." A box office smash like no other before it, *The Great Train Robbery* quickly became the most exhibited film in the country. Edison sold prints of the 740-foot-long epic for $11 apiece.

At the end of the film, a mustachioed Barnes appeared in a close-up, firing his pistol point blank at the camera. According to John Tuska in *The Filming of the West,* "women screamed or fainted away; men were terrified or fell to marveling." The scene was strictly for shock value; according to the Edison catalogue, it could be shown at the beginning or the end of the 11-minute film.

Just like modern blockbusters, *The Great Train Robbery* was quickly imitated. Porter himself shot *The Great Bank Robbery* and, in 1905, a disappointing sequel, *The Little Train Robbery,* in which children hijacked a toy train.

Porter remains an enigmatic figure in film history. He never again showed similar genius. One critic noted that when Porter directed Mary Pickford in 1908's *Tess of the Storm Country,* "his technique hadn't progressed one iota." After leaving Edison in 1909, Porter formed two film companies before retiring from production in 1915. He died in 1941.

As for the hapless Anderson, he moved to the West and took riding lessons in Hastings, Nebraska. After persuading a Chicago producer that westerns should be filmed out West, he shot a 1909 film in Golden, Colorado. In 1910 in Oakland, California, he changed his name to Broncho Billy Anderson. In more than 375 westerns over the next seven years, he became the first star of the silver screen. Not only did he introduce the archetypal western hero, he also initiated the star system, much to the chagrin of motion picture producers. From then on, movie actors would command big salaries.

During an autumn romp in the New Jersey woods, of all places, the movies and westerns were changed forever. The cinematic story became a given form. All of the complex issues involved in the winning and losing of the West were distilled into a simple struggle between good and bad guys. *The Great Train Robbery* not only defined a genre, it laid the very foundation for the future of screen entertainment.

December 24: The industrialist Howard Hughes is born in Houston, Texas.

December 30: Idaho's ex-governor Frank Steunenberg is assassinated by a bomb at his home in Caldwell as revenge for the labor problems in the Coeur d'Alene mines in 1899.

Also in 1905:
Las Vegas, Nevada, is founded.
The American Bison Society is established.

1906

April 18: San Francisco is jolted by a massive earthquake and fire that kills 700 and does more than $500 million in damage, destroying 28,000 buildings and burning more than 3,000 acres, including 520 city blocks. Writes Jack London, "Surrender was complete."

May 21: The United States and Mexico agree to share equally the waters of the Rio Grande.

June 16: President Theodore Roosevelt signs the Enabling Act, which will combine Indian Territory and Oklahoma Territory into a single state. Citizens had voted to name their state Sequoyah, after the inventor of the Cherokee alphabet, but were overruled by Congress.

August 1: The only diamond deposit in North America is discovered by John Huddleston in Murfreesboro, Arkansas.

September 24: Wyoming's Devils Tower is designated as the first National Monument.

Also in 1906:

Jack London publishes *White Fang.*

Mesa Verde National Park is established in Colorado.

The first National Western Stock Show is held in Denver.

The U.S. government turns the Blue Lake region in New Mexico—sacred Taos Indian lands—into a national park.

Thomas Hornsby Ferril publishes his first poem, "A Mountain Thought."

William Vaughn Moody writes *The Great Divide.*

1907

January 23: Charles Curtis of Kansas is sworn in as the first Native American U.S. senator.

February 27: Zane Grey moves to Arizona to see if a change of scenery will have any bearing on his writing.

April 23: Alferd Packer, the "cannibal" of the ill-fated 1874 mining expedition, dies in Littleton, Colorado.

May 26: The actor John Wayne is born Marion Morrison in Winterset, Iowa.

September 29: The actor-singer-executive Gene Autry is born in Tioga, Texas.

November 16: Oklahoma, with a population of 1,414,000, becomes the 46th state.

November 19: The author Jack Schaefer (*Shane*) is born in Cleveland, Ohio.

Also in 1907:

Nat Love publishes his memoirs, *The Life and Adventures of Nat Love: Better Known in the Cattle Country as "Deadwood Dick"—By Himself.*

The Neiman-Marcus department store opens in Dallas, Texas.

New Mexico's Gila Cliff Dwellings are designated a National Monument.

O. Henry creates the Cisco Kid in *Heart of the West.*

Samuel F. Cody of Birdville, Texas, flies an engine-operated dirigible from Farnborough to London, England, a distance of some 40 miles.

1908

February 7: The author Fred Gipson (*Old Yeller*) is born in Texas.

February 29: Former Lincoln County sheriff Pat Garrett, the killer of Billy the Kid, is shot dead by Wayne Brazil during a landlord-tenant argument on a desert road near Las Cruces, New Mexico.

March 22: The author Louis L'Amour (*Hondo*) is born in Jamestown, North Dakota.

March 28: A massive cave-in occurs at the Union Pacific Coal Company's Mine Number One in Hanna, Wyoming, killing 59.

May 10: Carl Albert, the speaker of the U.S. House of Representatives (1971–1976), is born in McAlester, Oklahoma.

May 20: The actor James Stewart is born in Indiana, Pennsylvania.

July 7: The Democrats nominate William Jennings Bryan at their national convention in Denver.

August 27: Lyndon Baines Johnson, the 36th U.S. president, is born in Gillespie County, Texas.

October 5: The first flight in an airplane over British soil is accomplished by Texan Samuel F. Cody.

October 23: The last rat carrying bubonic plague in San Francisco is caught.

November 19: The author Frederick Dean Glidden, better known by his pen name Luke Short (*King Colt*), is born in Kewane, Illinois.

December 16: The Moffat Road rail route to Steamboat Springs, Colorado, is completed.

Also in 1908:

Muir Woods in California is designated as a national monument.

Natural Bridges National Monument is established in Utah.

Pinnacles National Monument is established in Utah.

The Grand Canyon in Arizona becomes a national monument.

The National Conservation Commission is created.

Tumacacori National Monument is created in Arizona.

1909

January 23: A mining disaster claims 149 lives in Primero, Colorado.

February 17: The prisoner of war Geronimo, 80, dies in Lawton, Oklahoma.

February 19: The Enlarged Homestead Act provides for homesteads of up to 320 acres in many western states.

March 3: In his last act as president, Theodore Roosevelt converts 2.5 million acres of Indian lands into national forests.

March 24: The outlaw Clyde Barrow is born in Teleco, Texas.

May 10: Maybelle Addington, "Mother Maybelle Carter" of country music fame, is born in Nickelsville, Virginia.

May 22: President William Howard Taft authorizes the

opening for settlement of 700,000 acres in Idaho, Montana, and Washington.

September 9: The Union Pacific Railroad magnate Edward Harriman dies at age 71.

October 17: Jennie Rogers the former Denver madam, dies at age 66.

December 26: The artist Frederic Remington dies at age 48 in Connecticut.

Also in 1909:

Enos Mills writes *Wild Life on the Rockies*.

Red Cloud dies at age 87.

The last railroads to link to form a transcontinental railway are the Milwaukee Road and the Western Pacific.

The Navajo National Monument is created in Arizona.

The Texas Folklore Society is founded.

The Yuma Territorial Prison in Arizona is abandoned.

William F. Cody and Gordon Lillie merge their rival shows to form "Buffalo Bill's Wild West and Pawnee Bill's Far East" touring show.

1910

February 1: Louis Paulhan becomes the first person to fly an airplane over Denver.

March 1: Two trains are tossed down a canyon during a storm near Wellington, Washington, killing 96.

March 21: A Rock Island train derails in Iowa, killing 55.

April 20: The author Samuel Clemens—Mark Twain—who predicted he would exit with Halley's Comet, dies in Florida, Missouri, at the age of 74, three days after the comet looped around the sun.

June 20: Congress passes the Enabling Act that will allow separate statehood for Arizona and New Mexico.

July 5: William Sidney Porter—the author O. Henry—dies at age 47.

August 20: Fires in Idaho claim 85 lives and 3 million acres.

October 1: A bomb explodes at the *Los Angeles Times* building, killing 21 people. J. B. and J. J. McNamara will be convicted of the crime.

October 1: The outlaw Bonnie Parker is born in Rowena, Texas.

November 6: Roy Daugherty, "Arkansas Tom" of the Doolin-Dalton gang, is paroled in Lansing, Michigan.

November 8: An explosion at a mine in Delagua, Colorado, claims 79 lives.

Also in 1910:

Charles Siringo publishes *A Pinkerton Cowboy Detective*.

John Lomax publishes *Cowboy Songs and Frontier Ballads*.

The federal government forbids the Sun Dance, citing the self-torture of the dancers. The dance is performed by 26 plains Indian tribes, including the Arapaho, Cheyenne, and Oglala. Some tribes perform the early summer rite with dancers driving skewers through their chests or back muscles and then tearing them out, or allowing themselves to be suspended from beams built especially for the ceremony.

The Rainbow Bridge National Monument is established in Utah.

Over the last 20 years, the American Indian population has shrunk to less than 250,000.

1911

February 6: Ronald Reagan, the 40th U.S. president, is born in Tampico, Illinois.

February 11: Zerelda James, 87, the mother of Frank and Jesse, dies in Missouri.

February 22: Quanah Parker, age 66(?), the last chief of the Comanches, dies of pneumonia in Oklahoma.

March 18: The Roosevelt Dam begins operating on Arizona's Salt River.

May 6: George Maledon, the chief executioner for the "Hanging Judge" Isaac Parker at Fort Smith, Arkansas, dies in Johnson City, Tennessee.

June 9: Carry Nation dies at age 64 in Leavenworth,

Theodore Roosevelt (1858–1919). The future president as Westerner. (T. Roosevelt Collection, Harvard University)

Kansas, on the eve of her dream coming true—national prohibition.

August 21: President Taft approves the entry of Arizona and New Mexico into the Union as states.

December 5: The first transcontinental airplane flight ends in Pasadena, California; the flight from New York took 82 hours and four minutes.

Also in 1911:

Alphonso Steele, the last survivor of the 1836 Battle of San Jacinto, dies.

The Society of American Indians is founded.

1912

January 6: New Mexico, with a population of 325,000, becomes the 47th state.

February 14: Arizona, with a population of more than 200,000, becomes the 48th state.

April 15: Denver's "unsinkable" Molly Brown survives the sinking of the Titanic.

July 7: The Native American Jim Thorpe wins four of five pentathlon events at the Olympic Games in Stockholm, Sweden. He will be stripped of the medals the following year, when it is learned that he played semi-pro baseball.

July 14: The folksinger Woody Guthrie is born in Okemah, Oklahoma.

August 24: Alaska becomes a U.S. territory.

October 31: The actress Dale Evans is born in Uvalde, Texas.

November 5: The actor and singer Roy Rogers is born Leonard Slye in Cincinnati, Ohio.

Also in 1912:

John G. Neihardt begins his epic poem that will take 30 years to complete: *A Cycle of the West.*

John Muir writes *The Yosemite.*

The Four Mothers Society is formed by Chickasaws, Choctaws, Creeks, and Cherokees who unite against the allotment system of land disbursement.

The last cattle from the Texas XIT ranch are sold.

Zane Grey writes *Riders of the Purple Sage.*

1913

January 9: The 37th president, Richard M. Nixon, is born in Yorba Linda, California.

March 23: A tornado in Omaha, Nebraska, kills 94 and does $3.5 million in damage.

May 19: The California Land Act bars Japanese ownership of agricultural land.

July 10: California's Death Valley experiences the warmest temperature ever recorded in the Western Hemisphere, 134°.

September 3: The actor Alan Ladd is born in Hot Springs, Arkansas.

October 23: Police fire into a crowd in Trinidad, Colorado, killing three striking miners.

December 2: In Texas, the Brazos River floods, drowning 177.

Also in 1913:

"Buffalo Bill's Wild West and Pawnee Bill's Far East" fails financially. Cody joins the *Denver Post*-owned Sells-Floto Circus; he also directs and stars in a film with a $50,000 budget provided by the *Denver Post.* Also starring in the film is General Nelson A. Miles. Indian actors protest when the battle at Wounded Knee is filmed on the graves of their ancestors. No complete prints of the film are known to exist.

Production of the "Buffalo" nickel begins.

The Cabrillo National Monument is established in California.

The last horse-drawn cable cars in San Francisco are retired.

Willa Cather writes *O Pioneers!*

1914

January 10: The labor activist Joe Hill is arrested and charged with murdering a Salt Lake City grocer.

January 10: Mounted national guardsmen charge into a crowd of a thousand women protesting the illegal incarceration of labor advocate Mother Jones in Trinidad, Colorado.

February 9: The country western star Ernest Dale Tubb is born in Texas.

February 16: Silas Christofferson makes the first airplane flight from San Francisco to Los Angeles.

April 20: The Ludlow Massacre occurs in Colorado. Striking miners and their families, camped in small tents in Ludlow to protest the labor practices of the Colorado Fuel Iron Company, are attacked by 200 company guards. Shots are fired, tents are set ablaze, 20 people are killed, and another 100 are wounded.

June 8: Lassen Peak, a California volcano believed dormant, begins to erupt.

August 3: The Panama Canal opens.

September 14: The actor Clayton Moore, TV's "the Lone Ranger," is born in Chicago.

October 24: The actor Richard Widmark is born in Sunrise, Minnesota.

November 3: Montana women get the right to vote as voters pass the suffrage amendment.

December 24: The naturalist John Muir dies at age 76 in Los Angeles.

Frank James (1843–1915), Jesse's smarter brother, outside his outlaw homestead in his last year of life. (Missouri Historical Society)

1915

January 25: The first transcontinental telephone conversation takes place between Alexander Graham Bell in New York and Thomas Watson in San Francisco.

January 26: Rocky Mountain National Park is established in Colorado.

February 16: The Panama-Pacific Exhibition opens in San Francisco.

February 18: Frank James, 72, dies in Clay County, Missouri.

November 19: The labor activist Joe Hill is executed by a firing squad in Utah. He was convicted on a 1914 charge of double murder.

Also in 1915:

Charles Siringo publishes *Two Evil Isms: Pinkertonism and Anarchism.*

Congress authorizes the Bureau of Indian Affairs to purchase land for Indians in California.

The Dinosaur National Monument is established in Colorado and Utah.

Edgar S. Paxson completes his painting *Custer's Last Stand.*

John G. Neihardt publishes the first of his "Cycle" poems, "The Song of Hugh Glass."

Automobiles are allowed to enter Yellowstone National Park for the first time.

1916

January 1: Prohibition goes into effect in Arkansas and Colorado.

February 21: Cole Younger, 72, a former member of the Younger gang, dies in Lee's Summit, Missouri, where he was born in 1844.

March 9: Pancho Villa raids Columbus, New Mexico.

VILLA RAIDS COLUMBUS
MARCH 9, 1916

On March 9, 1916, the United States of America was invaded for the first time since the War of 1812, when a gang of Mexican raiders leveled the small town of Columbus, New Mexico. The legendary bandit Pancho Villa was blamed by President Woodrow Wilson as well as by the press, and the fallout plunged Mexican-American relations to a post-Alamo low.

Francisco "Pancho" Villa had earned his reputation through a revolutionary career. Born Doroteo Arango in the Mexican state of Durango on June 5, 1878, his fugitive days began around 1894, when he killed a man who allegedly raped his sister, Mariana Arango. He joined and eventually led a gang of mountain outlaws, and by 1908 had established a Robin Hood reputation as a fighter, lover, and sadistic killer.

Militarily, Villa supported Francisco I. Madero's successful revolution against the dictator Porfirio Díaz from 1910–1911. Following the assassination of Madero, Villa joined Venustiano Carranza in overthrowing the government of General Victoriano Huerta in 1914. Villa became provisional governor of Chihuahua, the most important general in northern Mexico, and a champion of the people. Within a month, he had begun constructing 40 schools.

A rift over reform developed between Villa and Carranza. The rebel leader joined forces with Emiliano Zapata for the occupation of Mexico City. Following military defeats at Celaya and León in 1915, Villa and his band of Villistas withdrew to Chihuahua for small-scale raiding.

Exactly why he chose to strike at sleepy Columbus, New Mexico, is a historical mystery. Villa is often portrayed as wanting to punish President Wilson for recognizing Carranza in October 1915. In any event, tensions grew on January 10, 1916, when a train carrying 17 American engineers en route from El Paso to Chihuahua was stopped at Santa Isabel. Passengers reported men claiming to be Villistas robbing, and then executing the engineers; Villa denied any involvement in the incident. Like

(continued)

(continued)

wise, his whereabouts during the raid on Columbus are equally confounding.

At 2:30 A.M. on Thursday, March 9, 1916, Columbus, New Mexico, slept while 400 Mexican irregulars crossed the border into the United States west of Palomas, three miles away. Columbus's 300 inhabitants had built a community of adobe dwellings, small houses, assorted businesses, and two hotels. Well aware of Villa's raiding, the town had sought security from Colonel Herbert Slocum's 13th Cavalry, 120 soldiers bivouacked at Camp Furlong, south of the railroad track.

First Lieutenant John Lucas awoke in his house just after 4:00 A.M. to the sounds of soldiers riding past his window. A moment later, the sentry on duty, Private Fred Griffin of K Troop, shouted a halt. He was answered with a bullet in the stomach. Before he fell dead, he took three raiders with him. The shots roused the camp; the battle was on. Shouts of "Viva Villa!" filled the air.

The marauders broke into two columns, one to engage the camp, the other to ransack the business district. Horrified townspeople were caught in the center, awakened by gunfire and the smell of their town burning. The Commercial Hotel went up in flames, and many guests were trapped.

Two soldiers fired machine guns from a second-story window of the Hotel Hoover, inflicting serious damage before they were overwhelmed. Theirs and three other such weapons would eventually fire 20,000 rounds in less than two hours.

Although the attackers retreated with the dawn, the world was already learning about the incident, thanks to telephone operator Susie Parks's eyewitness account to her counterpart in Deming. The southwest's scoop of the year was then transmitted by El Paso's Associated Press bureau chief, George Seese, whose sources convinced him to take a telegraph operator to Columbus.

Major Frank Tompkins and 32 riders gave chase to Villa's men. Before the soldiers were halted, they had driven well into Mexico and killed 70 of the banditos. Another 67 who were killed in the foray into Columbus made for a huge funeral pyre on the outskirts of the town. The Americans who died numbered 17, including nine civilians.

President Wilson was furious. A militia of 150,000 was called upon to protect the border. An unprecedented punitive expedition was launched—essentially the sending of 6,000 soldiers into a foreign country in search of one man. From March 16, 1916, until the First World War called him away on February 5, 1917, General John J. "Black Jack" Pershing led a fruitless search through a highly offended Mexico for Pancho Villa. American taxpayers got the tab—$130 million.

Villa evaded capture and resumed his war on Carranza. Following that leader's overthrow in 1920, Villa was given amnesty and a rancho near Chihuahua City. He himself was assassinated at Parral in 1923.

What Pancho Villa did or did not do at Columbus, New Mexico, remains a mystery. At the time, he was believed to have directed the attack from a small hillside outside of town. But his biographer, Edgcumb Pinchon, says that Villa was 200 miles to the south, at Casas Grandes, chuckling at reports that an eyewitness had him blowing a bugle. Another report places him at Sabinas, 500 miles distant.

More recent findings suggest that the raid on Columbus may have been an act of German sabotage, a complicated provocation to engage U.S. military forces far from the Western Front in Europe. The spy Luther Wertz was hanged in 1918, right after he swore that Villa had had nothing to do with the Santa Isabel robbery or the assault on Columbus.

Pancho Villa is remembered in Mexico as a hero, but is usually portrayed as a villain by Americans. Even his steadfast supporters agree he was no saint. Nevertheless, his true role in the Columbus raid has evaporated into folklore, where it remains as untraceable as an outlaw's trail through the Sierra Madres.

March 21: A devastating fire in Paris, Texas, destroys 1,500 buildings while doing $14 million in damage.

May 1: The actor Glenn Ford is born in Quebec, Canada.

July 22: Ten persons are killed and 40 are injured by a bomb at San Francisco's Preparedness Day parade.

November 22: The author Jack London, 40, commits suicide in Glenn Ellen, California.

December 9: The actor Kirk Douglas is born in Amsterdam, New York.

December 29: Revision of the Stock Raising Homestead Act allows homesteads of up to 640 acres.

Also in 1916:

The Bandelier National Monument is established in New Mexico.

The National Park Service is established.

1917

January 10: William F. Cody, "Buffalo Bill," 72, dies penniless at his sister's home in Denver.

January 28: General Pershing is ordered home from his chase after Pancho Villa in Mexico.

March 4: Jeanette Rankin of Montana, the first woman to serve in Congress, begins her term of office in the U.S. House of Representatives.

June 8: A fire at the Speculator Mine in Butte, Montana, claims 162 lives.

July 2: Race riots in St. Louis leave 39 dead; injuries number in the hundreds.

July 15: The author William Eastlake (*The Bronc People*) is born in Brooklyn, New York.

August 1: Frank Little, labeled an agitator for the Industrial Workers of the World, is lynched in Butte, Montana.

September 4: First Lieutenant William Fitzsimmons of Kansas becomes the first American officer killed in World War I.

December 1: Father Edward J. Flanagan founds Boys Town, his home for homeless boys, in Nebraska.

Also in 1917:

Katherine Stinson sets a nonstop distance record when she flies 610 miles, from San Diego to San Francisco, in nine hours, 10 minutes.

Simon Bamberger becomes the first non-Mormon governor of Utah.

Kansas City's Union Station, the nation's second-largest train station, opens.

The Papago Reservation in Arizona becomes the last to be established by presidential order.

What will become known as the Gerber-Covington oil pool is discovered east of Enid, Oklahoma.

Indian births exceed Indian deaths for the first time in 50 years.

1918

January 24: The evangelist Oral Roberts is born in Ada, Oklahoma.

February 15: The actor Tim Holt is born.

February 22: The Montana Sedition Law, which will become a model for the federal Sedition Act, is passed.

February 28: The Texas state legislature passes a prohibition law.

March 2: The historian Hubert Howe Bancroft, 85, dies in Walnut Creek, California. His priceless collection of books, some 60,000 titles, will go to the University of California.

June 13: The actor Ben Johnson is born in Foreaker, Oklahoma.

June 14: Billy the Kid's friend D. L. Anderson (aka "Billy Wilson"), the sheriff of Terrell Country, Texas, is shot dead by the drunken Ed Valentine, who is lynched an hour later.

July 22: A single lightning bolt kills 504 sheep in Utah's Wasatch National Forest.

August 30: The singer Kitty Wells is born in Nashville, Tennessee.

Also in 1918:

Warner Brothers Pictures is incorporated in California.

The Casa Grande Ruins in Arizona are designated a National Monument.

The Native American Church is incorporated in Oklahoma.

Willa Cather writes *My Antonia*.

1919

January 16: With Nebraska's approval of the 18th Amendment on prohibition—it is the 36th state to do so—the amendment becomes part of the U.S. Constitution.

February 6: A general strike paralyzes Seattle, Washington: 60,000 stay home from work.

February 26: Grand Canyon National Park, covering 657,575 acres, is established in Arizona.

May 26: The actor Jay Silverheels ("Tonto" on television's *The Lone Ranger*) is born in Canada.

June 14: The actor Gene Barry, TV's "Bat Masterson," is born in New York City.

June 29: The actor Slim Pickens is born Louis Bert Lindley in California.

July 4: Colorado's Jack Dempsey defeats Jess Willard of Kansas to win the World Heavyweight Boxing Championship in Dayton, Ohio.

September 25: President Wilson suffers a stroke and collapses during a speech in Pueblo, Colorado.

October 2: Utah ratifies the 19th Amendment granting women the right to vote.

Also in 1919:

The first brand name for fruit, "Sunkist," is used in California by that state's Fruit Growers Exchange.

Charles Siringo publishes *A Lone Star Cowboy*.

John G. Neihardt publishes "The Song of Three Friends."

Will Rogers writes two books, *Roger-isms: The Cowboy Philosopher on the Peace Conference* and *Roger-isms: The Cowboy Philosopher on Prohibition*.

Zion National Park is established in Utah.

1920

February 18: The actor Jack Palance is born in Lattimer Mines, Pennsylvania.

July 29: The first transcontinental airmail arrives in San Francisco from New York.

August 26: The 19th Amendment, which gives women the same voting rights as men, becomes a part of the Constitution.

November 11: The Industrial Workers of the World agitator Wesley Everest is removed from his cell in Centralia, Washington, castrated, and then lynched by American Legionnaires.

Also in 1920:

Charles Siringo publishes *History of Billy the Kid*.

The Sioux Jurisdictional Act authorizes the U.S. Court of Claims to adjudicate the legal claims of Sioux against the U.S. government.

1921

February 22: The outlaw and actor Henry Starr, 47, is shot dead while trying to rob a bank.

March 4: Hot Springs, Arkansas, becomes a national park.

April 21: The first helium production plant opens in Fort Worth, Texas.

June 20: In Pueblo, Colorado, 120 are reported killed or missing in the wake of a flood along the Arkansas River.

October 25: Bat Masterson, 67, dies in New York City. In his obituary, Damon Runyon will call him a "100 per-cent 22-karat real man."

Also in 1921:

Airmail can now travel coast to coast in 48 hours.

The cowboy and author Nat Love, 67, dies in Los Angeles.

Hamlin Garland's *A Daughter of the Middle Border* wins the Pulitzer Prize.

John G. Neihardt is named poet laureate of Nebraska.

1922

January 17: The Clackama, Umpqua, and Rogue River tribes meet in Portland, Oregon, to file a suit against the United States for $12.5 million, alleging the misappropriation of tribal lands.

February 15: John Slaughter, 80, dies in Douglas, Arizona.

April 7: The Teapot Dome scandal begins when Secretary of the Interior Albert B. Fall leases Wyoming's Teapot Dome oil reserve to Mammoth Oil's Henry Sinclair.

December 18: The Denver Mint is robbed of $200,000.

December 24: Will Rogers's first column appears in the *New York Times*.

Also in 1922:

Dude ranches appear in the West.

Lehman Caves, Nevada, is designated a national monument.

Oil is discovered on Navajo land in New Mexico.

Timpanogos Cave in Utah becomes a national monument.

1923

May 23: Curley, the Crow who scouted for Custer's 7th Cavalry at the Little Bighorn, dies and is buried in the National Cemetery of the Custer battlefield in Montana.

May 26: The actor James Arness, "Matt Dillon" in television's *Gunsmoke,* is born in Minneapolis, Minnesota.

June 4: The U.S. Supreme Court reverses laws in Iowa, Nebraska, and 19 other states that make the teaching of foreign languages in schools illegal.

August 2: President Warren G. Harding dies of ptomaine poisoning in San Francisco.

August 20: The singer Jim Reeves is born in Galloway, Texas.

September 10: Some 75 riders reenact the old Pony Express, covering 2,180 miles in 158 hours.

September 17: The singer Hank Williams is born in Georgiana, Alabama.

Also in 1923:

Willa Cather wins a Pulitzer Prize for *One of Ours.*

The attorney Ralph Case files 24 Sioux compensation claims in the U.S. Court of Claims.

Bryce Canyon National Park is established in Utah.

Carlsbad National Monument is established in New Mexico.

The Committee of One Hundred is formed by the U.S. Department of the Interior to examine Indian policy.

Hovenweep National Monument is established in Utah and Colorado.

New Mexico's Aztec Ruins are designated a national monument.

The Pipe Spring National Monument is established in Arizona.

The American Indian Defense Association is formed.

1924

February 8: In Carson City, Nevada, Gee Jon becomes the first person in history to be executed by lethal gas.

June 2: Native Americans born within the boundaries of the continental United States are granted American citizenship with the passage of the Snyder Act.

August 16: The former Doolin-Dalton gang member Roy Daugherty (Arkansas Tom) is killed in a shootout with Missouri authorities.

November 24: Sheriff Bill Tilghman, 71, is slain in the line of duty in Cromwell, Oklahoma.

Also in 1924:

Mount Hood National Forest is created out of Oregon National Forest.

The Craters of the Moon National Monument is established in Idaho.

In Washington, the Division of Indian Health is created.

Wupatki National Monument and Chiricahua National Monument are established in Arizona.

1925

January 5: America's first female governor, Nellie Tayloe Ross of Wyoming, is sworn in.

January 9: The actor Lee Van Cleef is born in Somerville, New Jersey.

January 24: Maria Tallchief, the first Native American ballerina to win widespread acclaim, is born in Fairfax, Oklahoma.

March 5: The country's first old-age pension laws are enacted by Nevada and Montana.

March 31: The Texas cattle baroness Henrietta King, 92, dies.

June 29: An earthquake destroys a portion of Santa Barbara, California.

August 16: The actor Fess Parker, television's "Davy Crockett" and "Daniel Boone," is born in Fort Worth, Texas.

September 26: The singer Marty Robbins is born in Glendale, Arizona.

November 28: The first Grand Ole Opry broadcast is heard from Nashville, Tennessee.

December 12: America's first motel opens in San Luis Obispo, California.

Also in 1925:

John G. Neihardt publishes the poem "The Song of the Indian Wars."

The Lava Beds National Monument is created in California.

The Miller Brothers' "101 Ranch Real Wild West" show makes a triumphant return to performing.

1926

May 18: The evangelist Aimee Semple McPherson disappears in Los Angeles.

October 24: The artist Charlie Russell, 62, dies in Great Falls, Montana.

November 3: The sharpshooter Annie Oakley dies at age 66 in Greenville, Ohio.

November 23: Frank Butler, 75, the husband and business manager of Annie Oakley, dies in Detroit, Michigan.

Also in 1926:

The National Council of American Indians is founded.

Thomas Hornsby Ferril wins the Yale Younger Poets Award for *High Passage.*

Walter Noble Burns writes *The Saga of Billy the Kid.*

Will James writes *Smokey the Cow Horse.*

1927

January 29: The author Edward Abbey is born in Home, Pennsylvania.

February 18: The Moffat Tunnel, an $18 million, six-mile hole through the Continental Divide, is completed in Colorado.

February 28: The Teapot Dome scandal concludes with the U.S. Supreme Court declaring that the oil leases issued by Interior Secretary Albert Fall to Edward Doheny are invalid.

March 7: The U.S. Supreme Court declares invalid a Texas law prohibiting blacks from voting in Democratic primaries.

August 10: President Calvin Coolidge dedicates Mount Rushmore in South Dakota, where Gutzon Borglum intends to carve the busts of four presidents.

Also in 1927:

Charles Siringo publishes *Riata and Spurs.*

Mourning Dove's *Co-ge-we-a* becomes the first published novel by an Indian woman.

Willa Cather writes *Death Comes for the Archbishop.*

The Academy of Motion Picture Arts and Sciences is founded in Los Angeles.

Archaeologists discover Stone Age spear points near Folsom, New Mexico; one, found in a 10,000-year-old bison skeleton, dissolves the theory that man first appeared in North America only 4,000 years earlier.

1928

February 26: The Moffat Tunnel, Colorado's train link through the Rocky Mountains, is formally dedicated.

March 4: Andrew Payne, a Cherokee from Oklahoma, wins the first cross-country footrace; he ran from Los Angeles to New York—3,422 miles—in 573 hours.

March 13: The St. Francis Dam bursts, dumping 12 billion gallons of water into Los Angeles and Ventura Counties; 451 people are killed and $12 million in damage results.

September 15: Bryce Canyon National Park is established in Utah.

October 19: The author Charles Siringo, 73, dies in Venice, California.

Also in 1928:

The Merriam Report, undertaken by the Brookings Institution, declares the Indian allotment system a failure due to excessive taxation and government corruption.

Vardis Fisher writes *Toilers of the Hills.*

1929

January 7: Madam Mattie Silks, 81, dies in Denver.

January 13: Wyatt Earp, 80, dies in Los Angeles.

February 26: Grand Teton National Park is established in Wyoming.

March 4: Charles Curtis becomes America's first Native American vice president.

March 30: Mexican rebels attack Naco, Arizona, wounding one.

June 5: The Colorado brewer Adolph Coors, 82, is killed in a fall from a hotel window.

August 12: The singer Buck Owens is born in Sherman, Texas.

December 13: The cattle pioneer Charles Goodnight, 93, dies in Texas.

Also in 1929:

Colorado's Mount of the Holy Cross is designated a national monument.

J. Frank Dobie writes *A Vaquero of the Brush Country.*

The Virginian, a motion picture with Gary Cooper, is released by Paramount.

1930

February 18: The planet Pluto is discovered by Clyde Tombaugh at the Lowell Observatory in Arizona.

■ The first cow to fly in an airplane is Elm Farm Ollie, a St. Louis Guernsey.

February 28: The gambler "Poker Alice" Tubbs, 79, dies in Rapid City, South Dakota. Reports the Associated Press: "Poker Alice Tubbs coppered her last and biggest bet today—and lost."

March 26: Sandra Day O'Connor, the first woman to serve on the U.S. Supreme Court, is born in El Paso, Texas.

May 6: Tornadoes in Texas kill 82 and cause $2.5 million in damage.

May 31: The actor and film director Clint Eastwood is born in San Francisco.

July 4: A bust of George Washington—the first presidential likeness to appear on South Dakota's Mount Rushmore—is dedicated.

August 12: The country music singer Porter Wagoner is born in West Plains, Missouri.

September 17: Construction begins on Boulder Dam in Nevada.

December 28: North Dakota's state capitol building in Bismarck is destroyed by fire.

Also in 1930:

Carlsbad Caverns is designated a national park.

Edna Ferber publishes *Cimarron.*

J. Frank Dobie publishes *Coronado's Children.*

Joseph Antrim, the brother of Billy the Kid, dies in Denver.

Katherine Anne Porter publishes *Flowering Judas.*

Max Brand publishes *Destry Rides Again.*

Sunset Crater National Monument is established in Arizona.

1931

January 31: The Tombstone lawman William "Billy" Breakenridge, 84, dies in Tucson, Arizona.

February 2: *Primitive Mysteries,* a modern dance based on southwestern Indian and Spanish rites, is staged in New York by Martha Graham.

February 9: *Cimarron,* the first Western to win the Academy Award for Best Picture, is released by RKO/Radio.

March 19: Gambling is legalized in Nevada for the first time since 1910.

July 27: An invasion of grasshoppers is reported to be causing devastation in Nebraska, Iowa, and South Dakota.

September 12: The singer George Jones is born in Saratoga, Texas.

November 22: Ferde Grofé's "Grand Canyon Suite" has its world premiere in Chicago.

Also in 1931:

Lincoln County War figure Sue McSween Barber dies.

Lyn Riggs writes *Green Grow the Lilacs.*

Stuart Lake writes *Wyatt Earp, Frontier Marshal.*

The Miller Brothers' "101 Ranch Real Wild West" show fails.

The *New Mexico Review* begins publishing.

Zane Grey's *Riders of the Purple Sage* is released as a motion picture by Fox.

1932

February 26: The singer Johnny Cash is born in Kingsland, Arkansas.

April 2: The recognized inventor of bulldogging, Bill Pickett, 60, dies after being kicked in the head by a horse.

April 14: The singer Loretta Lynn is born in Butcher's Hollow, Kentucky.

July 16: Colorado's Central City Opera House reopens after a 50-year hiatus.

July 30: The Olympic Games open in Los Angeles.

September 8: The singer Patsy Cline is born in Winchester, Virginia.

Also in 1932:

Colorado's Great Sand Dunes are designated as a national monument.

The film *Destry Rides Again,* with Tom Mix, is released by Universal.

Dust bowl conditions continue to destroy land across the Great Plains.

John G. Neihardt writes *Black Elk Speaks.*

John Joseph Mathews writes *Wah' Kon-Tah.*

Laura Ingalls Wilder writes *The Little House in the Big Woods.*

Millions of dollars in liens on Indian lands are freed by the Leavitt Act.

The Paiute Wovoka dies in obscurity in Walker Lake, Nevada.

1933

January 5: Construction begins on San Francisco's Golden Gate Bridge.

January 18: White Sands, New Mexico, becomes a national monument.

January 30: *The Lone Ranger,* a radio show, debuts on Detroit's WXYZ.

February 2: The *Denver Post*'s founder, F. G. Bonfils, dies in Denver.

February 11: Death Valley in California becomes the nation's largest national monument, with 2,067,627 acres.

March 1: Saguaro National Monument is established in Arizona.

March 2: Black Canyon National Monument is established in Colorado.

March 10: An earthquake in Long Beach, California, kills 120 people and does $50 million in damage.

April 6: Elizabeth Bacon Custer, the widow of George Armstrong Custer for 57 years, dies in New York City.

April 10: The Civilian Conservation Corps is created.

April 30: The singer Willie Nelson is born in Abbot, Texas.

May 26: The singer Jimmie Rodgers, 35, dies of tuberculosis.

July 23: The Texan Wiley Post completes an eight-day flight during which he became the first person to solo around the globe.

August 23: Cedar Breaks National Monument is created in Utah.

September 1: The singer Conway Twitty is born Harold Jenkins in Friars Point, Michigan.

October 12: Alcatraz Island, in San Francisco Bay, is designated a federal prison.

November 5: The speakeasy celebrity Texas Guinan dies.

December 5: Prohibition is officially repealed as Utah becomes the 36th state to ratify the 21st Amendment.

Also in 1933:

Robinson Jeffers writes *Give Your Heart to the Hawks.*

The last Buffalo Bill dime novel appears; some 1,700 have been published by various authors since 1869.

1934

February 27: The author N. Scott Momaday is born in Oklahoma.

March 23: The outlaws Bonnie Parker, 24, and Clyde Barrow, 24, are killed by lawmen in an ambush in Louisiana.

June 18: The Indian Reorganization Act updates the Dawes Act of 1887; it reverses the policy of forced assimilation and grants to tribes more control over their internal affairs.

July 29: Forest fires ravage portions of Idaho, Montana, and Washington.

August 31: The transfer of $3 billion in gold bullion from the San Francisco Mint to the Denver Mint is concluded.

October 22: Oklahoma's notorious outlaw "Pretty Boy" Floyd, 30, is killed by agents of the Federal Bureau of Investigation (FBI) on an Ohio farm. His funeral in Oklahoma will attract 20,000 people.

October 30: Hunger marchers in Denver are clubbed by the police.

November 10: The former Wild Bunch member William Ellsworth "Elzy" Lay, 71, dies in Los Angeles.

Also in 1934:

An Oklahoma road construction crew unearths the remains of Black Kettle, slain at the Battle on the Washita in 1868.

Thomas Hornsby Ferril writes *Westering.*

1935

January 11: Amelia Earhart embarks on the first solo flight by a woman from Hawaii to California.

March 7: Baby Doe Tabor, 80, the widow of Horace Tabor is found frozen to death at the Matchless Mine in Leadville, Colorado.

April 25: The Oregon state capitol building in Salem is destroyed by fire.

June 20: Big Bend National Park is established in Texas.

August 15: Will Rogers and Wiley Post are killed in a plane crash in Point Barrow, Alaska.

August 26: Indian tribes are granted the right to judicial review in cases involving alleged treaty violation.

September 26: The cowboy and author Andy Adams, 76, dies in Colorado Springs.

September 30: President Franklin D. Roosevelt dedicates Boulder Dam in Nevada.

Also in 1935:

California's *Overland Monthly* goes out of business.

Dust bowl conditions continue to spread across the Great Plains.

John G. Neihardt publishes the poem *The Song of the Messiah.*

Laura Ingalls Wilder writes *The Little House on the Prairie.*

Mari Sandoz writes *Old Jules.*

The Texas Rangers merge with the Texas State Highway Patrol.

1936

February 5: The National Wildlife Federation is established.

February 8: Charles Curtis, the first Native American senator and a former vice president, dies at age 76.

March 23: The singer Roy Orbison is born in Vernon, Texas.

April 18: Gene Autry records "Back in the Saddle Again."

June 3: The author Larry McMurtry (*Lonesome Dove*) is born in Wichita Falls, Texas.

June 12: The Kansan Alf Landon becomes the Republican presidential nominee.

August 12: The warmest temperature ever recorded in Texas occurs in Seymour, where the mercury hits 120°.

August 30: A bust of Thomas Jefferson, the second to be carved on Mount Rushmore, is dedicated in South Dakota.

September 7: The singer Buddy Holly is born in Lubbock, Texas.

October 9: The first electricity in Los Angeles is generated at Boulder Dam.

December 21: The first luxury ski resort at Sun Valley, Idaho, opens.

Also in 1936:

The Joshua Tree National Monument is established in California.

Lynn Riggs's *Cherokee Night* becomes the first play written by an Indian on an Indian subject.

Oklahoma's Indian Welfare Act organizes Indians without tribes.

1937

February 27: Floods in San Bernardino, California, kill 87 people and do $79 million in damage.

March 18: A natural gas explosion in a school in New London, Texas, kills 57 people.

April 11: Gunfire claims nine lives during a labor confrontation at the International Mine, Mill and Smelter Workers' Union in Galena, Kansas.

May 27: The Golden Gate Bridge, the world's longest suspension bridge, opens between San Francisco and Marin County, California.

July 13: Emmett Dalton, the last surviving member of the Dalton Gang, dies at age 66.

September 17: A bust of Abraham Lincoln becomes the third presidential likeness to be dedicated at Mount Rushmore in South Dakota.

September 28: The Bonneville Dam on Oregon's Columbia River is dedicated by President Franklin D. Roosevelt.

Also in 1937:

Conrad Richter writes *The Sea of Grass.*

Laura Ingalls Wilder writes *On the Banks of Plum Creek.*

In *Shoshone v. United States,* the U.S. Supreme Court rules that the 5th Amendment requires Congress to pay compensation for the taking of tribal lands.

The Plainsman, a film starring Gary Cooper as Wild Bill Hickok, is released.

1938

June 6: The first academic degree in dude ranching is awarded to Donald Ellsworth Smith by the University of Wyoming's School of Agriculture.

June 29: Olympic National Park is established in Washington.

October 16: Aaron Copland's ballet *Billy the Kid* opens in Chicago.

November 6: "Red Ryder," a western-themed comic strip by Fred Harman, appears.

1939

July 2: In South Dakota, dedication ceremonies are held at Mount Rushmore for the bust of Theodore Roosevelt, the fourth and final presidential likeness to be carved on the mountain under the supervision of Gutzon Borglum.

July 25: Tuzigoot National Monument is created in Arizona.

October 21: The author Zane Grey, 69, dies of a heart attack.

Also in 1938:

J. Frank Dobie writes *Apache Gold and Yaqui Silver.*

The film *Jesse James,* with Tyrone Power, is released.

John Ford directs John Wayne in the film *Stagecoach.*

John Steinbeck writes *The Grapes of Wrath.*

Katherine Anne Porter writes *Pale Horse, Pale Rider.*

Laura Ingalls Wilder writes *By the Shores of Silver Lake.*

1940

January 19: Idaho senator William E. Borah dies.

May–November: The Coronado Cuarto Centennial celebrates the 400th anniversary of the Coronado expedition in New Mexico.

October 12: Tom Mix, the star of more than 400 western films, dies at age 60 in a one-car accident near Florence, Arizona.

Also in 1940:

Laura Ingalls Wilder writes *The Long Winter.*

Ronald Reagan plays George A. Custer in *The Santa Fe Trail.*

Walter Van Tilburg Clark writes *The Ox-Bow Incident.*

Woody Guthrie writes the song "This Land Is Your Land."

1941

March 6: Gutzon Borglum, the sculptor of presidential likenesses on South Dakota's Mount Rushmore, dies at age 73 of a heart attack.

March 22: Construction of the Grand Coulee Dam on Washington's Columbia River begins.

May 11: Jane Hickok McCormick, 68, claims that she is the daughter of Wild Bill Hickok and Calamity Jane.

December 7: Japanese forces attack U.S. naval and air forces at Pearl Harbor in Hawaii; the United States will enter World War II the following day.

Also in 1941:

J. Frank Dobie writes *The Longhorns.*

John G. Neihardt completes *A Cycle of the West* with "The Song of Jed Smith."

Laura Ingalls Wilder writes *The Little Town on the Prairie.*

Pit dweller relics from A.D. 450 are discovered in New Mexico's Apache National Forest.

1942

February 19: President Franklin D. Roosevelt authorizes the relocation of Japanese-Americans in California, Arizona, Washington, and Oregon to inland camps.

March 16: The singer Jerry Jeff Walker is born in Oneonta, New York.

November 28: The matinee idol Buck Jones dies in a massive fire at Boston's Coconut Grove.

Also in 1942:

Frank Waters writes *The Man Who Killed the Deer.*

Mari Sandoz writes *Crazy Horse.*

The Sioux-initiated Black Hills claim is rejected by the U.S. Court of Claims.

1943

January 5: The agricultural chemist George Washington Carver dies at age 79.

March 31: The Richard Rodgers and Oscar Hammerstein musical *Oklahoma!* opens on Broadway.

June: The Zoot Suit Riots rock Los Angeles.

Also in 1943:

Laura Ingalls Wilder writes *These Happy Golden Years.*

The Manhattan Project is created to develop an atomic bomb; it is headquartered in Los Alamos, New Mexico.

Smog appears in Los Angeles for the first time.

1944

January 9: The lawman Chris Madsen, 93, dies following a fall in Guthrie, Oklahoma.

May 11: Frederick Faust, aka the author Max Brand, 51, is killed in battle while working as a news correspondent with the 88th Infantry in Italy.

July 6: Annie Ralston James, the widow of the outlaw Frank James, dies at age 91.

July 17: Two munition ships in San Francisco Bay's Port Chicago explode, killing 321 people.

December 15: The Colorado native and band leader Major Glenn Miller is killed when his airplane is lost over the English Channel.

Also in 1944:

Federal Indian policy is investigated by the House Indian Affairs Committee.

J. Frank Dobie writes *A Texan in England.*

The National Congress of American Indians is organized in Denver.

1945

January 26: World War II's most decorated soldier, the Texan Audie Murphy, 20, kills or wounds 50 Nazi soldiers in battle near Holtzwihr, France.

February 23: Ira Hayes, a Pima Indian from Arizona, helps to raise the American flag on the Pacific island of Iwo Jima.

February 28: Fritz Truan, a rodeo star who shouted "Let 'er buck!" when his craft landed on Iwo Jima, is killed in action.

July 16: The first atomic bomb is tested at Trinity base in New Mexico.

August 23: The lawman Elfego Baca dies at age 80 in Albuquerque, New Mexico.

Also in 1945:

Luke Short writes *And the Wind Blows Free*.

1946

May 16: Irving Berlin's *Annie Get Your Gun* opens on Broadway.

June 23: The film cowboy William S. Hart, 75, dies in Los Angeles.

July 16: The U.S. Bureau of Land Management is established.

August 13: The Indian Claims Commission Act is passed by Congress.

December 10: The writer Damon Runyon, 66, dies of throat cancer in New York.

Also in 1946:

Frank Waters writes *The Colorado*.

The Virginian, a film starring Joel McCrea, is released by Paramount.

1947

April 16: The *Grand Camp*, a French freighter, explodes in Texas City, Texas, killing 500.

April 24: The author Willa Cather dies at age 73.

October 14: Chuck Yeager, flying from Muroc Air Force Base in California, becomes the first person to break the sound barrier.

November 2: Howard Hughes's "Spruce Goose," at 140 tons the largest aircraft in history, makes a one-mile flight across California's Long Beach Harbor.

Also in 1947:

A. B. Guthrie writes *The Big Sky*.

Gene Autry becomes a popular TV cowboy.

The Theodore Roosevelt National Memorial Park is established in North Dakota.

1948

April: The Native American Maria Tallchief, of Oklahoma, becomes the principal dancer of the New York City Ballet.

May 15: The Boy's Town founder Father Flanagan dies in Berlin, Germany, where he was on a mission to assist war orphans.

May 25: Television is seen in San Francisco for the first time.

May 28: Oregon's Columbia River floods, killing 26 at Vanport City.

November 21: The last surviving member of the Outlaw Exterminators, Clay Calhoun, dies at age 87.

Also in 1948:

A federal court in Santa Fe, New Mexico, rules a constitutional provision invalid and grants Indians the right to vote.

Courts force Arizona to grant Indians voting rights.

Bernard De Voto wins a Pulitzer Prize for *Across the Wide Missouri*.

Red River, a film starring John Wayne and Montgomery Clift, is released by United Artists.

1949

February 24: The first rocket to reach outer space is launched from the White Sands Proving Ground in New Mexico.

May 26: The singer Hank Williams, Jr., is born in Shreveport, Louisiana.

September 15: *The Lone Ranger,* starring Clayton Moore, debuts on television.

Also in 1949:

A. B. Guthrie wins the Pulitzer Prize for his novel *The Way West*.

Jack Schaefer writes *Shane*.

She Wore a Yellow Ribbon, a film starring John Wayne and directed by John Ford, is released by Argosy/RKO.

The Hoover Commission on the Reorganization of Government suggests the termination of the government-Indian trust.

Effigy Mounds National Monument is established in Iowa.

1950

May 15: Congress rescinds the "national monument" designation for Colorado's Holy Cross after erosion has made the cross formation nearly unrecognizable.

June 27: A small bear cub rescued from a New Mexico forest fire becomes Smokey the Bear.

July 13: The Ute tribe is awarded $31.7 million for its

lands in Utah and Colorado that were taken from it in 1891–1938.

Also in 1950:

A Black Hills claim is filed with the Indian Claims Commission by attorney Ralph Case, on behalf of the Sioux.

Frank Waters writes *Masked Gods.*

Mabel Young Sanborn, the last survivor of Mormon leader Brigham Young's 56 children, dies at age 87.

The Navajo Rehabilitation Act clears the way for federal aid to the tribe.

The population of Adobe Walls, Texas, is 15.

1951

January: A public ground-breaking for one of the nation's first family fallout shelters takes place in Los Angeles.

March 26: The attorney Jesse Edward James, the son of Jesse James, dies at age 75 in California.

September 4: The nation's first transcontinental television broadcast—President Harry Truman's address to the Japanese Peace Treaty Conference—originates from San Francisco.

September 22: The last white survivor of the Battle of the Little Bighorn, Jacob Horner, 96, dies. A member of the 7th Cavalry, he was left behind because there were not enough horses. He had worked as an advisor for Hollywood westerns.

November 12: *Paint Your Wagon* opens on Broadway.

November 29: The first underground test of an atomic bomb takes place in Nevada.

December 30: *The Roy Rogers Show* debuts on the NBC television network.

Also in 1951:

Hopalong Cassidy is seen on 63 television stations across the nation.

O. Henry's "The Cisco Kid" becomes a popular TV western.

Uranium mining gets under way in New Mexico.

1952

April 22: The first telecast of an atomic bomb test originates in Nevada.

November 4: Dwight D. Eisenhower, born in Texas and raised in Kansas, is elected the 34th U.S. president.

November 12: The Coronado National Monument is established in Arizona.

Also in 1952:

Bernard De Voto writes *The Course of Empire.*

Edna Ferber writes *Giant.*

High Noon, a film starring Gary Cooper, is released by United Artists.

J. Frank Dobie writes *The Mustangs.*

The Bureau of Indian Affairs creates the Voluntary Relocation Program.

Walter Prescott Webb writes *The Great Frontier.*

1953

January 1: Hank Williams, Sr., dies of a heart attack at age 29.

March 28: The Native American athlete Jim Thorpe dies of a heart attack at age 65.

May 11: A tornado in Waco, Texas, kills 114 people and does $50 million in damage.

August 3: The Texas Ranger Ira Aten dies at age 89 in Burlingame, California.

Also in 1953:

Indian prohibition laws are officially repealed by Congress.

Louis L'Amour writes *Hondo.*

Mari Sandoz writes *Cheyenne Autumn.*

Shane, a film starring Alan Ladd, is released by Paramount.

1954

March 19: The first rocket-driven sled on rails reaches a speed of 421 miles per hour in tests in Alamogordo, New Mexico.

April 1: Colorado Springs is chosen over 400 other locations as the site for the U.S. Air Force Academy.

November 3: California's Linus Pauling receives the Nobel Prize in chemistry.

December 15: Walt Disney airs "Davy Crockett, Indian Fighter," the first installment of a television series that will create a $100 million merchandising business by the end of 1955.

Also in 1954:

Alan Le May writes *The Searchers.*

Frederick Manfred writes *Lord Grizzly.*

Mari Sandoz writes *The Buffalo Hunters.*

During the next eight years, Congress strips 61 Indian tribes and communities of federal services and protection.

The Indian Claims Commission rejects the Sioux's Black Hills claim, filed in 1950.

Wild Bill Hickok, starring Guy Madison, is a popular TV western.

1955

January 26: Walt Disney airs the second part of his TV blockbuster, "Davy Crockett Goes to Congress."

February 23: Walt Disney's Davy Crockett saga ends with "Davy Crockett at the Alamo." The TV series will enjoy such popularity that Disney will film two more episodes.

May 28: *Billboard* magazine reports that "The Ballad of David Crockett," the most popular tune in the country, has sold 18 million copies in various versions during the last 18 months.

June 17: Disneyland, an amusement and theme park, opens in Anaheim, California.

September 6: *The Life and Legend of Wyatt Earp* premieres on television.

September 10: The first episode of *Gunsmoke* is aired on television.

September 24: President Eisenhower suffers a heart attack in Denver. He will be released from Fitzsimons Army Hospital in 49 days.

November: The Oglala Sioux chief Iron Hail, the last surviving participant in the Battle of the Little Bighorn, dies at age 98 at the Pine Ridge Reservation in South Dakota.

November 1: John Gilbert Graham plants a bomb in his mother's suitcase as she departs Denver's Stapleton International Airport. She and 43 others die when the plane explodes over Longmont, Colorado.

November 11: The Cowboy Hall of Fame is dedicated in Oklahoma City, Oklahoma.

Also in 1955:
Indian health and medical care is made the responsibility of the U.S. Public Health Service.

1956

June 30: America's worst air disaster to date occurs when two commercial airliners collide over the Painted Desert in Arizona, killing 128 people.

July 7: Colorado's Central City Opera House premieres *The Ballad of Baby Doe,* by Douglas Moore.

October 15: Former Oklahoma governor "Alfalfa Bill" Murray dies at age 86.

November 24: The movie *Giant* is released by Warner Brothers.

Also in 1956:
The Bureau of Indian Affairs establishes an Adult Vocational Training Program.

Edward Abbey writes *The Brave Cowboy.*

Fred Gipson writes *Old Yeller.*

1957

February 10: Laura Ingalls Wilder, who began her writing career at age 63, dies at age 90.

February 26: The underworld figure Bugs Moran dies of cancer at Leavenworth Penitentiary in Kansas.

May 22: A 42,000-pound hydrogen bomb accidentally falls 1,700 feet from a bomber just south of Albuquerque, but does not explode. News of the incident will be officially suppressed until 1986.

July 6: Vandals steal the 560-pound headstone from Wyatt Earp's grave at a cemetery in Colma, California.

October: Two major league baseball teams go west—the New York Giants move to San Francisco, while Brooklyn's beloved Dodgers move to Los Angeles.

November 1: Buddy Holly and the Crickets, from Lubbock, Texas, make their national TV debut on *The Ed Sullivan Show.*

Also in 1957:
A full one-third of TV's primetime fall schedule is taken up by programs set in the trans-Mississippi West of the 1870s and 1880s, adding up to approximately 64 hours of westerns each week. The new programs include *Have Gun Will Travel, Maverick, Sugarfoot, Tales of Wells Fargo, Wagon Train,* and *Zorro.* Shows leaving the air include *The Lone Ranger* and *The Roy Rogers Show.*

Dorothy M. Johnson writes *The Hanging Tree.*

1958

February 1: Airliners collide over Los Angeles, killing 48.

April 7: Frank Eaton, aka "Pistol Pete," dies at age 97 in Anadarko, Oklahoma.

April 13: The Texan Van Cliburn wins the Tchaikovsky Piano Competition in Moscow.

May 23: Charlie Starkweather is convicted of mass murder in Nebraska.

July 24: In Dallas, Jack Kilby of Texas Instruments designs the world's first silicone chip.

November 4: A B-47 bomber carrying a nuclear bomb catches fire over Texas and crashes. The bomb does not detonate.

Also in 1958:
Navajos receive $70 million in oil leases from the Four Corners region on their reservation.

1959

January 31: Alaska becomes the 49th state.

February 3: Buddy Holly, 22, is killed in a plane crash near Clear Lake, Iowa. Also killed in the crash are Ritchie Valens and the Big Bopper.

April 7: Oklahoma becomes the last state to repeal prohibition.

August 21: Hawaii becomes the 50th state.

November 15: Lincoln, Nebraska, records the coldest November day in U.S. history, 53° below zero.

November 18: Robert Frank James, the only offspring of Frank James, dies at age 81.

December 19: The last surviving veteran of the Civil War, the Confederate Texan Walter Williams, dies at age 117.

Also in 1959:

The new television season sees the debuts of *Bonanza, Bat Masterson,* and *Rawhide.* There are 28 Westerns on TV, with a combined budget of $50 million. Toy manufacturers estimate that cap guns and other cowboy toys account for a $125 million market. Says the *New Yorker* about the glut of westerns on TV: "Among the 1959 Westerns, the signs of Byzantine decay are unmistakable. Overcivilization is rampant."

1960

February 13: Twenty-nine U.S. oil companies, on trial in Tulsa, Oklahoma, on charges of price fixing, are exonerated by a judge.

February 18: The eighth Winter Olympics open in Squaw Valley, California.

May 2: Caryl Chessman dies in the San Quentin, California, gas chamber after a legal battle that lasted a dozen years. Convicted on 17 counts of robbery, kidnapping, sexual abuse, and attempted rape, he wrote four books in prison, professing his innocence.

November 5: The singer Johnny Horton, 33, is killed in a car accident in Texas.

Also in 1960:

Koshare, by the Cherokee-Sioux Louis W. Ballard, becomes the first American Indian ballet.

Los Angeles becomes the third largest city in the United States.

Santa Fe, New Mexico, celebrates its 350th anniversary.

The Crow tribe is reimbursed $11 million for lands taken in an 1851 treaty with the U.S. government.

1961

March 13: The actor Gary Cooper dies of cancer at age 60.

July 2: Ernest Hemingway, 61, commits suicide in Ketchum, Idaho.

November 16: Sam Rayburn of Texas, the speaker of the U.S. House of Representatives for 21 years, dies at the age of 79.

Also in 1961:

The Life and Legend of Wyatt Earp, Bat Masterson, and *Wanted, Dead or Alive* air for the last time on television.

The American Indian Charter Convention is held in Chicago.

The National Indian Youth Conference is held in New Mexico.

The U.S. Commission on Civil Rights reports that Indians live in deplorable conditions.

1962

April 10: Major league baseball comes to Texas as the Houston Colt .45's beat the Chicago Cubs 11–2.

May 22: Forty-five people die when a Boeing 707 explodes in the air over Centerville, Iowa.

December 9: The Petrified Forest National Park is established in Arizona.

Also in 1962:

California takes the "most populous state" title from New York.

Edward Abbey writes *Fire on the Mountain.*

Katherine Anne Porter writes *Ship of Fools.*

On television, a host of westerns leaves the air, including *Maverick* and *Tales of Wells Fargo. The Virginian,* based on Owen Wister's novel, debuts, and Ronald Reagan begins a four-year tenure as host of *Death Valley Days.*

The singer Garth Brooks is born in Tulsa, Oklahoma.

The National Farm Workers Association is organized by César Chávez.

The U.S. government forces New Mexico to grant Indians voting rights.

1963

January 14: Texas returns to Mexico 630 acres that were uncovered when the Rio Grande changed course in 1864.

March 5: The singer Patsy Cline, 30, is killed in a plane crash in Camden, Tennessee.

May 15: The astronaut Leroy Gordon Cooper of Oklahoma orbits the earth 22 times in 34 hours in his *Faith 7* spacecraft.

August 2: The author Oliver La Farge dies at age 83.

November 22: President John F. Kennedy is assassinated in Dallas, Texas; Vice President Lyndon B. Johnson assumes the office of president.

Also in 1963:

Frank Waters writes *Book of the Hopi.*

Jack Schaefer writes *Monte Walsh.*

Cheyenne and *Have Gun, Will Travel* air on TV for the last time.

The Texan Billy Sol Estes is convicted of selling $24 million in mortgages on nonexistent fertilizer tanks.

1964

July 16: Arizona's Senator Barry M. Goldwater becomes the Republican nominee for president.

July 31: The singer Jim Reeves, 41, is killed in a plane crash.

August 31: The U.S. Census Bureau makes it official: California has the largest population of any state.

September 3: The National Wilderness Preservation System comes into being as the Wilderness Act becomes law.

September 12: Canyonlands National Park is established in Utah.

December 19: *Cheyenne Autumn,* the screen version of the Mari Sandoz novel, is released by Warner Brothers.

Also in 1964:

Bonanza becomes TV's top-rated show, a ranking it will hold for three years.

J. Frank Dobie writes *Cow People.*

Mari Sandoz writes *The Beaver Men.*

Sam Shepard's first off-Broadway play is *Cowboys.*

The Capital Conference on Indian Poverty held in Washington, D.C.

The National Indian Youth Council conducts "fish-ins" in the state of Washington in support of the fishing rights of local tribes.

Thomas Berger writes *Little Big Man.*

1965

June 16: Colorado's Platte River floods, resulting in $500 million in damage to the state.

June 28: The Pecos National Monument is established in New Mexico.

August 11–16: Los Angeles is rocked by riots in the city's Watts district. The violence claims 35 lives and $40 million in damage.

September 8: César Chávez and his National Farm Workers Union go on strike against California grape growers.

October 28: The Gateway Arch is completed in St. Louis.

Also in 1965:

Mari Sandoz writes her last book, *The Battle of the Little Bighorn.*

Vardis Fisher writes *Mountain Men.*

The Western Literature Association organizes.

Simpson Mann, the last surviving white to see action in the Indian wars, dies at age 98. He served in the army from 1876 to 1891, and fought at Wounded Knee, South Dakota.

1966

March 10: The author Mari Sandoz dies at age 64 in New York City.

July 11: Major electric power outages occur in South Dakota, Wyoming, and Nebraska; the problems result from excessive demand due to air conditioning during warm weather.

August 1: After murdering his mother and wife, Charles Whitman of Austin, Texas, ascends to the top of a University of Texas campus tower and kills 13 others with a high-powered rifle.

August 29: The Beatles play their last concert in San Francisco.

October 15: The Guadalupe Mountains in Texas becomes a national park.

October 15: A tornado in Belmond, Iowa, destroys 75 percent of the city's businesses and does $11 million in damage.

Also in 1966:

Frank Waters writes *The Woman at Otowi Crossing.*

Larry McMurtry writes *The Last Picture Show.*

Special programs are instituted under the White House Task Force on Indian Health.

The Coleman Report studies Indian education.

Thomas Hornsby Ferril writes *Words for Denver.*

1967

January 4: Jack Ruby, the convicted slayer of Lee Harvey Oswald, the alleged assassin of President Kennedy, dies in a Texas prison at age 65.

January 14: Approximately 20,000 gather in San Francisco's Haight-Ashbury district to hear music of rock groups such as Quicksilver Messenger Service, Jefferson Airplane, and the Grateful Dead.

June 5–11: Armed Hispanic-American rebels free 11 comrades from the Rio Arriba County Courthouse at Tierra Amarilla, New Mexico. A running battle with lawmen ensues in the mountains.

September 9: Marcus Reno is posthumously restored to the rank of major, and his discharge from the army is changed to "honorable." His remains will be reburied at the site of the Battle of the Little Bighorn in Montana.

September 20: Hurricane Beulah inflicts $1.5 million in damage and kills 13 people in Texas.

October 3: Woody Guthrie dies at age 55 in Queens, New York.

Also in 1967:

The Indian Resources Development Bill is defeated in Congress.

1968

May 3: A Braniff Airlines plane crashes in Dawson, Texas, during a snowstorm, claiming 88 lives.

May 24: Chief, the last surviving horse of the U.S. Army Cavalry, dies.

June 4: New York senator and presidential candidate Robert F. Kennedy is shot in Los Angeles after winning the California Democratic primary election; he will die the next day.

July 9: The author Vardis Fisher dies at age 73.

October 2: Redwood National Park is established in California.

November 6: Richard Nixon of California is elected the 37th U.S. president.

Also in 1968:

A National Council on Indian Opportunity is advocated by President Lyndon Johnson.

Congress creates the National Trail System.

Congress passes the Indian Civil Rights Act, extending many constitutional rights to reservation dwellers.

Dr. N. Scott Momaday wins the Pulitzer Prize for his first novel, *House Made of Dawn.*

Edward Abbey writes *Desert Solitaire.*

The American Indian Movement (AIM) is founded in Minneapolis, Minnesota.

The Navajo Community College is chartered in Arizona.

1969

January 26: Landslides in Los Angeles kill 95 and cause $138 million in damage.

January 28: Hundreds of thousands of gallons of oil are dumped into the Pacific Ocean in the wake of an oil-well blowout in California's Santa Barbara Channel.

March 12: The Levi Strauss Company begins producing bell-bottom jeans.

July 21: Two American astronauts walk on the moon for the first time.

August 9: Members of the Charles Manson "family" go on a murder spree in California, killing the actress Sharon Tate, 26, and four of her friends in Benedict Canyon outside Los Angeles.

November 20: Indians protest government policies by seizing Alcatraz Island in San Francisco Bay. The occupation will last for nearly two years.

Also in 1969:

AMERIND is founded to protect Indian rights.

Frank Waters writes *Pumpkin Seed Point.*

The National Council on Indian Opportunity is created.

Robert Redford and Paul Newman star in the film *Butch Cassidy and the Sundance Kid.*

The Kennedy Report on Indian Education suggests more participation by Indians.

Vine Deloria writes *Custer Died for Your Sins.*

1970

July 19: It is disclosed that the Air Force has deployed Minuteman missiles and MIRV warheads in Minot, North Dakota.

October 2: Thirty people are killed when an airliner carrying the Wichita State football team crashes near Silver Plume, Colorado.

October 23: A new land speed record is set at Bonneville Salt Lake Flats in Utah: Gary Gabelich travels 622 miles per hour in a rocket sled.

November 11: Peter MacDonald becomes the first college graduate to lead the Navajos, the nation's largest tribe.

December 15: Some 8,000 acres of land in New Mexico, taken in 1906 by the U.S. Forest Service, is returned to the Taos Indians.

Also in 1970:

Pit River Indians in California protest development by the Pacific Gas and Electric Company.

The federal policy of Indian self-determination is put into effect.

The National Indian Youth Council is organized.

1971

February 9: An earthquake in southern California kills 62 and causes $1 billion dollars in damage in Los Angeles.

April 13: Patience Latting becomes mayor of Oklahoma City, Oklahoma; she is the first female mayor of an American city with a population of more than 200,000.

June 11: Federal marshals recapture Alcatraz Island from Indians who have occupied it for 19 months.

August 20: The first electronic pocket calculator, priced at $149, is introduced by Texas Instruments.

October 10: London Bridge, disassembled block by block, is moved to Arizona, and reassembled as a tourist attraction at Lake Havasu.

November 12: Arches National Park is established in Utah.

November 25: The skyjacker "D. B. Cooper" bails out of a passenger airliner over the Pacific Northwest with thousands of dollars extorted from the airline; he is never seen or heard from again.

December 18: The Capitol Reef National Park is established in Utah.

Also in 1971:

Frank Waters writes *Pike's Peak*.

Josiah Red Wolf, believed to be the last Native American survivor of the Indian wars, dies at age 98 in Lewiston, Idaho. A Nez Percé, he was 4 years old when Chief Joseph made his famous "I will fight no more forever" speech at his surrender in Montana's Bear Paw Mountains in 1877.

1972

May 20: Approximately 21,000 acres of tribal lands in the state of Washington are returned to the Yakima Indians.

September 12: William Boyd, the television cowboy "Hopalong Cassidy," dies at age 77.

October 21: Hohokam Pima National Monument is created in Arizona.

October 23: Fossil Butte National Monument is created in Arizona.

November 7: President Richard Nixon of California is reelected in a landslide.

November 2–8: American Indian Movement demonstrators, organized under the Trail of Broken Treaties Caravan, march on Washington, D.C., and occupy the Bureau of Indian Affairs.

Also in 1972:

The Indian Education Act is passed by Congress.

White vigilantes in Gordon, Nebraska, beat Raymond Yellow Thunder to death. A court ruling that his death is a suicide fuels a protest by 1,000 Pine Ridge Reservation Sioux. When the case is reopened, two of his killers are convicted.

1973

January 16: An estimated audience of 400 million in 90 countries view the last original telecast of *Bonanza*.

February 27: Indians begin a protest at Wounded Knee, South Dakota. American Indian Movement members and some 200 Oglalas begin a 71-day occupation of the site of the 1890 massacre.

March 27: The actor Marlon Brando turns down the Academy Award for Best Actor to protest the treatment of American Indians. His statement is read at the award ceremonies by Sacheen Little Feather.

May 29: Thomas Bradley is elected the first black mayor of Los Angeles.

June 18: The last official veteran of the Indian wars, Fredrak Fraske, dies at the age of 101. He was with the 17th Infantry in 1894, when it was sent to quiet a disturbance in Idaho, but there was no fighting.

June 22: The U.S. Department of the Interior is ordered to pay more than $100,000 in legal costs to the Paiute tribe for its lawsuit blocking the diversion of water from Pyramid Lake in Nevada.

November 3: The poet John G. Neihardt dies of heart failure at age 92 in Columbia, Missouri.

1974

January 24: Shirley Plume becomes the first Native American to be appointed superintendent of the Bureau of Indian Affairs.

February 4: In California, the newspaper heiress Patricia Hearst is kidnapped by the Symbionese Liberation Army.

August 9: President Nixon resigns in the wake of the Watergate scandal.

September 11: The works of Laura Ingalls Wilder become familiar to a new generation with the first telecast of *Little House on the Prairie*.

October 12: The Texas Big Thicket, 85,850 acres, is designated a national preserve.

November 13: Karen Silkwood, 28, is killed in an Oklahoma auto crash en route to a meeting with a *New York Times* reporter to discuss the improper safety procedures of her employer, the Kerr-McGee Cimarron Plutonium Plant near Crescent, Oklahoma.

Also in 1974:

John Nichols writes *The Milagro Beanfield War*.

Sioux tribes are awarded $17.5 million for the federal government's seizure of the Black Hills in 1877.

The Indian Financing Act is passed by Congress.

The International Treaty Council organizes.

1975

January 9: The grizzly bear is placed on the list of "threatened" species by the U.S. Department of the Interior.

March 13: The singer Bob Wills dies in Texas.

June 16: Oregon becomes the first state to prohibit aerosols with chlorofluorocarbon propellants.

June 25: Two FBI agents are killed in a shoot-out with American Indian Movement members on the Pine Ridge Reservation in South Dakota.

September 1: The last telecast of *Gunsmoke* completes a 20-year run for the series.

September 5: President Gerald R. Ford is the target of a failed assassination attempt by Lynette Alice "Squeaky" Fromme, 26, in San Francisco.

September 18: Patricia Hearst is captured by police in San Francisco.

September 22: President Ford is the target of another assassination attempt in California, this one by Sarah Jane Moore.

Also in 1975:

Eighteen tribes receive 346,000 acres of land that the federal government has held since 1933.

Edward Abbey writes *The Monkeywrench Gang*.

Russell Means and Dennis Banks of the American Indian Movement are convicted on riot and assault charges stemming from the 1973 Wounded Knee incident.

The Indian Self-Determination Act is passed by Congress.

1976

April 5: The billionaire recluse Howard Hughes dies at age 72, on a flight from Mexico to Texas.

June 5: Idaho's Teton River Dam breaks; 4,000 homes are lost and nine people die.

June 6: The Texas oil billionaire J. Paul Getty, 83, dies in Surrey, England.

August 1: On Colorado's 100th birthday, a flood in the Big Thompson River Canyon kills 139 people and does $30 million in damage.

September 24: Patricia Hearst is sentenced to seven years in prison for bank robbery.

November 8: Smokey the Bear dies in Washington, D.C.

December 14: Lame Deer, the great grandson of the Sioux chief Lame Deer who was present at the Battle of the Little Bighorn, dies. In 1972, he published a book about his experiences as a medicine man called *Lame Deer, Seeker of Visions*.

1977

January 17: The convicted murderer Gary Gilmore is executed by firing squad at Utah State Prison.

March 17: Nevada's AFL-CIO president, Al Bramlet, 60, is found shot to death 40 miles outside of Las Vegas.

April 18: Leonard Peltier of the American Indian Movement is found guilty of killing two FBI agents on the Pine Ridge Reservation in 1975, and is sentenced to life in prison. Peltier is believed by many to be innocent, singled out for his involvement with AIM.

July 24: The Utes and Comanches settle a 200-year-old squabble over hunting rights in Ignacio, Colorado.

December 19: Nellie Tayloe Ross, America's first female governor, dies at age 101 in Cheyenne, Wyoming.

Also in 1977:

The Oklahoma Human Rights Commission reports on race relations between whites and Indians.

1978

April 29: Antinuclear demonstrators begins a series of protests at the Rocky Flats nuclear weapons facility near Denver.

June 11: Joseph Freeman, Jr., becomes the first black Mormon priest.

June 21: A forest fire destroys 12,000 acres in New Mexico.

August 17: Three New Mexicans become the first to cross the Atlantic in a hot-air balloon.

November 10: Badlands National Park is established in South Dakota.

November 27: Dan White, a disgruntled former San Francisco supervisor, shoots to death San Francisco mayor George Moscone and city supervisor Harvey Milk.

December 15: The actor Chill Wills dies at age 76.

Also in 1978:

New legislation aimed at Native Americans is passed by Congress, including the American Indian Freedom of Religion Act, the Indian Education Act, and the Indian Child Welfare Act.

Native American activists stage the "Longest Walk" on Washington, D.C.

The Indian Claims Commission disbands, having distributed some $800 million to Native American tribes since 1946.

The Ottawas, Modocs, Wyandots, and Peorillas are restored to trust status by Congress.

WARN (Women of All Red Nations) is established.

1979

May 6: Gasoline rationing, on the basis of odd–even license plate numbers, begins in California.

June 11: The actor John Wayne dies of cancer at age 72 in Los Angeles.

June 13: The U.S. Court of Claims awards the Sioux $105 million for the federal government's seizure of the Black Hills in 1877.

July 13: Nevada introduces legislation to claim 49 million acres from the U.S. Bureau of Land Management.

December 16: The sound barrier is broken on land by Stan Barret, in a rocket car at Edwards Air Force Base in California.

1980

February 3: Authorities regain control over the state prison in Santa Fe, New Mexico, ending one of the nation's bloodiest prison riots that left 33 dead and 89 wounded.

March 5: California's Channel Islands are designated a national park.

May 18: Washington's Mount St. Helens, a volcano, erupts, killing 22 and devastating 122 square miles of surrounding lands.

September 30: The copper smelter at Anaconda, Montana, is closed by the Atlantic Richfield Company.

November 4: Ronald Reagan of California is elected the 40th U.S. president.

November 21: A fire at the MGM Grand Hotel in Las Vegas, Nevada, kills 84 and injures hundreds.

Also in 1980:
Sam Shepard's play *True West* opens.
The American Indian population is 1,418,195.
The population in the western half of the United States has grown 24 percent since 1970.

1981

April 18: The federal government settles a long-standing land dispute between the Hopi and Navajo tribes in Arizona.

July 17: Two suspended walkways at Kansas City's Regency Hotel collapse, killing 111.

August 17: The skeleton of a 65-million-year-old Tyrannosaurus rex is found near Haystack Butte, South Dakota.

Also in 1981:
Frank Waters writes *Mountain Dialogues*.
The Reagan administration announces cutbacks in programs for Native Americans.

1982

January 18: In Nevada, an accident at a Las Vegas airshow claims the lives of four Air Force "Thunderbirds" pilots.

January 26: Oglala Sioux Indians in South Dakota file a $6 billion lawsuit against the Homestake Mining Company, which has operated a gold mine in the Black Hills for a century.

July 15: Flooding in Colorado's Big Thompson Canyon kills three.

November 2: Peter MacDonald is unseated as chairman of the Navajo tribe following accusations of official improprieties. Peter Zah fills the post.

November 22: President Reagan proposes to deploy 100 MX missiles near Cheyenne, Wyoming.

Also in 1982:
The merger of the Western Pacific, the Missouri Pacific, and the Union Pacific Railroads is authorized by the Interstate Commerce Commission.

1983

June 26: Flooding at Grand Junction, Colorado, leaves 1,200 homeless.

August 18: Hurricane Alicia ravages Texas, killing 21 while doing $1.6 billion in damage to Houston and Galveston.

Also in 1983:
Jim Thorpe's Olympic medals, which he won in 1912, are reinstated posthumously.
The buffalo population in North America is 50,000.

1984

February 22: Houston's "boy in the bubble," David, dies after two weeks of freedom from the plastic shell he was housed in for 12 years because of a disease; he dies of a build-up of fluid around his heart and lungs.

March 26: The western author Louis L'Amour becomes the first novelist to be awarded the Presidential Medal of Freedom.

April 13: Following a week in outer space, the space shuttle *Challenger* lands at Edwards Air Force Base in California.

April 23: The photographer Ansel Adams dies at age 82 in Carmel, California.

April 24: An earthquake in San Jose, California, registers 6.2 on the Richter scale.

July: More than 1,000 artifacts from the Battle of the Little Bighorn are recovered by the National Park Service's Midwest Archaeological Center in Lincoln, Nebraska.

July 18: The unemployed security guard Oliver Huberty kills 20 people at a McDonald's restaurant in San Ysidro, California. He is killed by the police.

July 28: The 23rd Summer Olympic Games open in Los Angeles.

August 30: Fires in Montana destroy some 250,000 acres, jumping such natural barriers as the 100-yard-wide Missouri River.

September 6: The singer Ernest Tubb dies at age 70.

December 19: A fire at the Utah Power and Light Company's mine near Orangeville, Utah, kills 27.

Also in 1984:
The Commission on Indian Reservation Economies says that the Bureau of Indian Affairs is managed improperly.
Vicki Piekarski edits *Westward the Women: An Anthology of Western Stories by Women*.

1985

August 1: Wyoming's worst flash flood kills 12 and does $65 million in damage.

September 19: An earthquake in Mexico City kills 5,000.

November 19: A Texas jury orders Texaco to pay $10.53 billion to Pennzoil for interfering with Pennzoil's agreement to acquire Getty Oil.

Also in 1985:

Levi Strauss Company becomes the world's largest clothing manufacturer.

The first federal legislation to return the Black Hills to the Indians is introduced by Senator Bill Bradley of New Jersey.

The National Tribal Chairmen's Association rejects the 1984 findings of the Commission on Indian Reservation Economies.

Larry McMurtry writes *Lonesome Dove*.

American Indian Movement figure Dennis Banks surrenders to authorities on charges from a 1973 protest at Custer, South Dakota. He will serve 18 months.

1986

January 6: One worker dies and 100 are hospitalized in Gorek, Oklahoma, when an overfilled cylinder of nuclear material bursts after being heated improperly at a Kerr-McGee plant.

March 6: The artist Georgia O'Keefe dies at age 98 in Santa Fe, New Mexico.

July 17: The largest bankruptcy in U.S. history is declared by the LTV Corporation of Dallas, Texas.

July 29: Phoenix, Arizona, surpasses Denver, Colorado, as the largest city between St. Louis and the West Coast. The U.S. Census Bureau reports that Phoenix ranks 21st in city population, with 1,846,600 residents, while Denver ranks 22nd with 1,827,100.

1987

April 12: Texaco files for bankruptcy even though it shows assets of $34.9 billion.

October 1: An earthquake in Los Angeles registers 6.1 on the Richter scale; six are killed and 100 are injured.

December 18: Texaco agrees to pay Pennzoil $4 billion, ending their four-year legal battle.

Also in 1987:

Utah is the only state in the Union without an X-rated adult movie theater.

1988

Fires destroy half a million acres of Yellowstone National Park.

1989

February 27: The Intel Corporation of California introduces a million-transistor microchip.

March 24: The tanker *Exxon Valdez* runs aground in Alaska's Prince William Sound, spilling 11 million gallons of crude oil.

October 19: An earthquake registering 7.1 on the Richter scale rocks San Francisco and Oakland; 40 people die in their cars when the upper deck of an Oakland highway collapses.

Also in 1989:

The U.S. Court of Claims grants the Sioux a $40 million award based on the Treaty of 1868.

1990

March 30: Idaho's Governor Cecil Andrus vetoes a bill that would have banned most abortions.

December 3: A major earthquake that was predicted for New Madrid, Missouri, fails to occur.

Also in 1990:

Larry McMurtry writes *Buffalo Girls*.

1991

March 3: An amateur video camera operator records the beating of the black Los Angeles motorist Rodney King, 25, by police officers.

Also in 1991:

California records a fifth consecutive year of drought.

University of Oklahoma Law School professor Anita Hill accuses U.S. Supreme Court nominee Clarence Thomas of sexual harassment.

The author A. B. Guthrie dies at age 90.

Kevin Costner's film *Dances with Wolves* becomes the second western to win the Academy Award for Best Picture.

1992

January 14: Male and female condors are released into the wild in California. (The last surviving condors had been captured in 1987 and bred in captivity.)

March 1: Washington senator Brock Adams announces that he is dropping his reelection campaign shortly after a Seattle newspaper reports that eight women claim he sexually mistreated them.

April 29: Riots rock Los Angeles in the wake of the acquittal of the policemen charged with beating the motorist Rodney King; 52 deaths and $1 billion in damage result from the riots.

June: Two major earthquakes rock southern California.

November 3: The Democrat Bill Clinton, governor of Arkansas, is elected the 42nd president of the United States.

1993

April 9: Major league baseball comes to Denver, as the Colorado Rockies defeat the Montreal Expos 11–4 in the Rockies' first home game.

April 19: As many as 89 members of the Branch Davidian Cult, including leader David Koresh, perish in a fire at their compound in Waco, Texas, after a 52- day stand-off with authorities that claimed the lives of four federal agents during the initial confrontation.

May 31: Archaeologists announce the findings of a recent excavation of the site of the Wagon Box Fight (August 2, 1867) near Fort Phil Kearny in Wyoming.

June 5: The singer Conway Twitty, 59, dies.

Also in 1993:

Clint Eastwood's *Unforgiven* becomes the third western to win the Academy Award for Best Picture.

BIBLIOGRAPHY

BOOKS

Adams, Ramon F. *A Fitting Death for Billy the Kid.* Norman: University of Oklahoma Press, 1960.

Ambrose, Stephen E. *Crazy Horse and Custer.* New York: Doubleday, 1975.

Baker, Pearl. *The Wild Bunch at Robbers Roost.* New York: Abelard-Schuman, 1965.

Bancroft, Caroline. *Six Racy Madams.* Boulder, Colo.: Johnson Publishing, 1965.

———. *Tabor's Matchless Mine.* Boulder, Colo.: Johnson Publishing, 1960.

Barry, Louise. *The Beginning of the West: Annals of the Kansas Gateway to the American West, 1540–1854.* Topeka: Kansas State Historical Society, 1972.

Bartlett, Richard A. *Great Surveys of the American West.* Norman: University of Oklahoma Press, 1962, 1980.

Beal, Merrill D. *"I Will Fight No More Forever": Chief Joseph and the Nez Percé War.* Seattle: University of Washington Press, 1963.

Beck, Warren A., and Haase, Ynez D. *Historical Atlas of the American West.* Norman: University of Oklahoma Press, 1989.

Berg, Francis M. *North Dakota: Land of Changing Seasons.* Hettinger, N.D.: Flying Diamond Books, 1977.

Blevins, Winfred. *Dictionary of the American West.* New York: Facts on File, 1993.

———. *Give Your Heart to the Hawks: A Tribute to the Mountain Man.* Los Angeles: Nash Publishing, 1973.

Bowman, John S., Gen. Editor. *The World Almanac of the American West.* New York: Pharos Books, 1986.

Breihan, Carl W. *Great Gunfighters of the West.* New York: New American Library, 1977.

———. *Great Lawmen of the West.* New York: Bonanza Books, 1963.

Brown, Dee. *Bury My Heart at Wounded Knee.* New York: Holt, Rinehart, 1971.

Butler, Ron. *The Best of the Old West.* Austin: Texas Monthly Press, 1983.

Chrisman, Harry E. *1001 Most-Asked Questions About the American West.* Chicago: Swallow Press, 1982.

Chronicle of America. Mount Kisco, N.Y.: Chronicle Publications, 1989.

Clements, John. *Chronology of the United States.* New York: McGraw Hill, 1975.

Cody, William F. *An Autobiography of Buffalo Bill (Colonel W. F. Cody).* New York: 1920.

Colorado Historical Association. *The Historical Encyclopedia of Colorado.* Denver: Colorado Historical Association, 1958.

Connell, Evan S. *Son of the Morning Star.* Berkeley, Calif.: North Point Press, 1984.

Cromie, Alice. *Tour Guide to the Old West.* New York: Times Books, 1977.

Croy, Homer. *Jesse James Was My Neighbor.* New York: Duell, Sloan and Pearce, 1949.

Cunningham, Eugene. *Triggernometry: A Gallery of Gunfighters.* New York: Press of the Pioneers, 1934.

Davis, E. O. *The First Five Years of the Railroad Era in Colorado.* Sage Books, 1948.

Debo, Angie. *Oklahoma Foot-Loose and Fancy-Free.* Norman: University of Oklahoma Press, 1949, 1987.

Dennis, Henry C. *The American Indian, 1492–1970.* Dobbs Ferry, N.Y.: Oceana Publications, 1971.

Dippie, Brian W. *Remington & Russell.* Austin: University of Texas Press, 1982.

Dorsett, Lyle W. *The Queen City: A History of Denver.* Boulder, Colo.: Pruett Publishing Company, 1977.

Drago, Harry Sinclair. *Great American Cattle Trails.* New York: Dodd, Mead, 1965.

Eagle/Walking Turtle. *Indian America: A Traveler's Companion.* Santa Fe, N. Mex.: John Muir Publications, 1989.

Ehrlich, Eugene, and Carruth, Gorton. *The Oxford Illustrated Literary Guide to the United States.* New York: Oxford University Press, 1982.

Ewers, John C. *Artists of the Old West.* New York: Doubleday, 1965, 1973.

Ferrell, Robert H., and Natkiel, Richard. *Atlas of American History.* New York: Facts On File, 1987.

Fireman, Bert M. *Arizona Historic Land.* New York, Alfred A. Knopf, 1982.

Flanagan, Mike. *Out West.* New York: Harry N. Abrams, 1987.

Fowler, Gene. *Timber Line.* Sausalito, Calif.: Comstock Editions, 1933, 1960, 1977.

Fulton, Maurice Garland. *History of the Lincoln County War.* Tucson: University of Arizona Press, 1969.

Garrett, Pat F. *The Authentic Life of Billy the Kid.* Norman: University of Oklahoma Press, 1949.

Gille, Frank H. Editor. *Encyclopedia of California.* New York: Somerset, 1984.

———. *Encyclopedia of Texas.* New York: Somerset, 1985.

Gurian, Jay. *Western American Writing, Tradition and Promise.* DeLand, Fla.: Everett/Edwards, 1975.

Haley, James L. *Apaches: A History and Culture Portrait.* New York: Doubleday, 1981.

Hansen, Gladys. *San Francisco Almanac.* San Rafael, Calif.: Presidio Press, 1980.

Hardin, John Wesley. *The Life of John Wesley Hardin.* Seguin, Tex.: Smith and Moore, 1896.

Hart, Herbert M. *Old Forts of the Far West.* New York: Bonanza Books, 1965.

———. *Tour Guide to Old Western Forts.* Boulder, Colo.: Pruett Publishing Company, 1980.

Holliday, J. S. *The World Rushed In: The California Gold Rush Experience.* New York: Simon & Schuster, 1981.

Horan, James D. *Desperate Men.* New York: Bonanza Books, 1949.

———. *Pictorial History of the Wild West.* New York: Crown Publishers, 1954

Hunt, N. Jane. Editor. *Brevet's Nebraska Historical Markers & Sites.* Sioux Falls, S.D.: Brevet Press, 1974.

Jackson, Donald. *Voyages of the Steamboat Yellowstone.* New York: Ticknor & Fields, 1985.

Jessen, Kenneth. *Eccentric Colorado.* Boulder, Colo.: Pruett Publishing Company, 1985.

Katz, William L. *The Black West.* Garden City, N.Y.: Anchor Press/Doubleday, 1973.

Kimball, Stanley Buchholz. *Historic Sites and Markers Along the Mormon and Other Great Western Trails.* Urbana and Chicago: University of Illinois Press, 1988.

Kushner, Ervan F. *Alferd G. Packer, Cannibal! Victim?* Frederick, Colo.: Platte 'N Press, 1980.

Lamar, Howard R. Editor. *The Reader's Encyclopedia of the American West.* New York: Thomas Y. Crowell, 1977.

Lazarus, Edward. *Black Hills, White Justice: The Sioux Nation v. the United States, 1775 to the Present.* New York, Harper Collins, 1991.

Linscome, Sanford A. "A History of Musical Development in Denver, Colorado, 1858–1908." Ph.D. diss., University of Texas, 1970.

Lohaus, Sara, and White, Jan. Editors. *Colorado Christmas.* St. Cloud, Minn.: Partridge Press, 1990.

Lord, Walter. *A Time to Stand: A Chronicle of the Valiant Battle at the Alamo.* New York: Harper and Row, 1961.

McLoughlin, Denis. *Wild and Woolly: An Encyclopedia of the Old West.* Garden City, N.Y.: Doubleday, 1975.

McTighe, James. *Roadside History of Colorado, Revised Edition.* Boulder, Colo.: Johnson Books, 1989.

Marks, Paula Mitchell, *And Die in the West: The Story of the O.K. Corral Gunfight.* New York: William Morrow, 1989.

Marshall, Don. *Oregon Shipwrecks.* Portland, Oreg.: Binford & Mort, 1984.

Martin, Douglas D. *Tombstone's Epitaph.* Albuquerque: University of New Mexico Press, 1951.

Miller, David E. Editor. *The Golden Spike.* Salt Lake City: University of Utah Press, 1973.

Miller, Nyle H., and Snell, Joseph W. *Great Gunfighters of the Kansas Cowtowns, 1867–1886.* Lincoln: University of Nebraska Press, 1963.

———. *Why the West Was Wild.* Topeka: Kansas State Historical Society, 1963.

Morris, John W., Goins, Charles R., and McReynolds, Edwin C. *Historical Atlas of Oklahoma.* Norman: University of Oklahoma Press, 1976.

Morris, Richard B. *Encyclopedia of American History.* New York: Harper and Brothers, 1953.

Neihardt, John G. *Black Elk Speaks.* Lincoln: University of Nebraska Press, 1961.

O'Connor, Richard. *Bat Masterson.* New York: Doubleday, 1957.

O'Neal, Bill. *Encyclopedia of Western Gun-Fighters.* Norman: University of Oklahoma Press, 1979.

Owen, Roger C., Deetz, James J. F., and Fisher, Anthony D. *The North American Indians: A Sourcebook.* New York: Macmillan, 1967.

Patterson, Richard. *Historical Atlas of the Outlaw West.* Boulder, Colo.: Johnson Books, 1985.

Paul, Roman. *The Far West and the Great Plains in Transition, 1859–1890.* New York: Harper and Row, 1988.

Paulson, T. Emogene, and Moses, Lloyd R. *Who's Who Among the Sioux.* Vermillion: University of South Dakota State Publishing Company, 1988.

Ridge, Martin, and Billington, Ray A. Editors. *America's Frontier Story.* New York: Holt, Rinehart and Winston, 1969.

Rosa, Joseph G. *They Called Him Wild Bill: The Life and Adventures of James Butler Hickok.* Norman: University of Oklahoma Press, 1964.

Russell, Don. *The Lives and Legends of Buffalo Bill.* Norman: University of Oklahoma Press, 1960.

Ruth, Kent. *Landmarks of the West.* Lincoln: University of Nebraska Press, 1963, 1986.

Schmitt, Martin F. Editor. *General George Crook: His Autobiography.* Norman: University of Oklahoma Press, 1946, 1960.

Shwayder, Carol R. *Weld County Old & New.* Greeley, Colo.: Unicorn Ventures, 1983.

Siringo, Charles. *A Texas Cowboy.* Lincoln: University of Nebraska Press, 1950.

Smiley, Jerome C. *History of Denver.* Denver: Times-Sun, 1901.

Socolofsky, Homer E., and Self, Huber. *Historical Atlas of Kansas.* Norman: University of Oklahoma Press, 1972.

Sprague, Marshall. *A Gallery of Dudes.* Lincoln: University of Nebraska Press, 1966.

———. *Newport of the Rockies.* Athens: Ohio University Press/Swallow Books, 1961, 1987.

Texas State Historical Association. Editor-in-Chief, Walter Prescott Webb. *The Handbook of Texas.* Chicago and Crawfordsville, Ill.: The Lakeside Press, R. R. Donnelley & Sons, 1952.

Thompson, David. *Nevada: A History of Changes.* Reno, Nev.: Grace Danberg Foundation, 1986.

Thornton, Russell. *American Indian Holocaust and Survival: A Population History Since 1492.* Norman: University of Oklahoma Press, 1987.

Tuska, Jon. *Billy the Kid: A Handbook.* Lincoln: University of Nebraska Press, 1986.

U.S. Adjutant General's Office. *Chronological List of Actions, &c., With Indians From January 15, 1837, to January 1891.* Fort Collins, Colo.: The Old Army Press, 1979.

U.S. Department of Commerce, Bureau of the Census. *We, the First Americans.* Washington D.C.: Government Printing Office, 1988.

Waldman, Carl. *Atlas of the North American Indian.* New York: Facts on File, 1985.

———. *Who Was Who in Native American History.* New York: Facts on File, 1990.

Walker, Henry P. *The Wagonmasters.* Norman: University of Oklahoma Press, 1966.

Waters, Frank. *The Earp Brothers of Tombstone.* London: Neville Spearman, 1962.

Webb, Walter Prescott, *The Great Frontier.* Lincoln: University of Nebraska Press, 1951, 1952, 1964, 1980, 1986.

———. *The Great Plains.* New York: Ginn & Company, 1931.

Wellman, Paul I. *A Dynasty of Western Outlaws.* New York: Doubleday, 1961.

———. *The Indian Wars of the West.* New York: Doubleday, 1956.

Western Literature Association. *A Literary History of the American West.* Fort Worth: Texas Christian University Press, 1987.

Western Writers of America. *Water Trails West.* New York: Doubleday, 1978.

Wilder, Daniel Webster. *The Annals of Kansas.* Topeka, Kans.: T. D. Thatcher, 1886.

Wilson, D. Ray. *Iowa Historical Guide.* Carpentersville, Ill.: Crossroads Communications, 1986.

Windrow, Martin, and Mason, Francis K. *A Concise Dictionary of Military Biography.* New York: John Wiley & Sons, 1975, 1991.

Wolle, Muriel Sibell. *Stampede to Timberline: The Ghost Towns and Mining Camps of Colorado.* Chicago: Swallow Press, 1949, 1974.

Writers Program of the Work Projects Administration. Revised by Joseph Miller. *Arizona, The Grand Canyon State: A State Guide.* New York: Hastings House, 1940, 1966.

———. *New Mexico: A Guide to the Colorful State.* New York: Hastings House, 1940, 1962.

Writers Program of the Work Projects Administration. *Texas: A Guide to the Lone Star State.* New York: Hastings House, 1940, 1969.

———. *The WPA Guide to 1930s Colorado.* Lawrence: University Press of Kansas, 1987.

———. *The WPA Guide to 1930s Oklahoma.* Lawrence: University Press of Kansas, 1986.

Younger, Coleman. *The Story of Cole Younger, by Himself.* Chicago: Henneberry Company, 1903.

NEWSPAPERS

Congregation Emanuel Bulletin (Denver, Colorado)
Also, 19th and 20th century editions of:
Abilene Chronicle, Alta California, Arizona Sentinel, Chicago Tribune, Dallas Herald, Denver Times, Fort Worth Democrat, Leavenworth Daily Times, London Times, Morning Call, New Orleans Times Picayune, New York Times, Rocky Mountain News, San Diego Union, San Francisco Chronicle, San Francisco Herald Examiner, Denver Post, Tombstone Epitaph and *Tombstone Nugget.*

NAME INDEX

This index is arranged alphabetically letter-by-letter. The entries are arranged both alphabetically and chronologically. The **boldface** page numbers indicate boxed features. The *italic* page numbers indicate illustrations and captions.

Frémont, John Charles 25
  birth 16
  as surveyor/explorer: railroad survey
    work 23; explores Minnesota 24; ex-
    peditions West 25-26, 41, 43-45, 55,
    78, 80
  writings 28, 44
  military career: court-martial 33-34; in
    Civil War 133-135, 140
  political career: as California governor
    27-28; presidential race 96, 99, 159; as
    Arizona governor 310, 313, 342, 350
  financial ruin 209
  death 421
French, James 312, 315
French, Nellie 312
Frenzeny, Paul 247
Frewen, Moreton 362
Frey, John 121
Fritz, Caroline 323
Fritz, Charles 313
Frizzell, Lodisa 69-70
Frohock, W. T. 193
Fromme, Lynette Alice "Squeaky" 457
Fuller, Francis 224, 241, 262, 303
Fuller, John 47
Fulton, Kate 298-299
Fulton, Thomas 49

G
Gabelich, Gary 456
Gabriele, Pete 403
Gadsden, James 75, 78
Gage, Henry Tifft 78
Gale, C. 195
Gallagher, Barney 287
Gallagher, H. D. 422
Gallagher, Jack 153
Gallegos, Lucas 322
Gall (Sioux leader) 198, 340
Galvez, Bernando de 12
Gamble, James 135
Gantz, Louis 436
Ganzio, Herman 284
Garces, Father (Spanish explorer) 10, 12
Garcia, Sostero 322
Gardenshire, Emilne 210
Gardiner, Ella 397
Gardiner, J. B. W. 354
Gardner, Thomas 313
Garfield, James A. 343, 345, 357
Garland, Hamlin 17, 346, 445
Garner, Franklin 147
Garra, Antonia 67
Garrad, Hector Lewis 59
Garrett, Elizabeth 182
Garrett, Pat 56
  birth 56
  mother dies 182
  goes west 205, 321
  marriage 331
  as New Mexico lawman: Lincoln County
    sheriff 335, 337, 340, 346, 363; "Billy
    the Kid" pursuit/murder 118, 338,
    344-345, 347, 348, 357
  writings 358
  death 439
Garvey, Thomas 240
Gates, Eleanor 270
Gates, John W. "Bet-a-Million" 242
Gauss, Godfrey 345
Gay, Ebenezer 117
Gazzous, Louis 175
Geary, John W. 49, 98, 101
Gebhardt, William 432
Geddes, Andrew 271
Gentilz, Theodore 44
Gentles, William 299
George, Henry 321
George II, King (England) 9
George White Hair (Osage leader) 51, 67
Germaine, Catherine and Sophie 264
Germaine, John 261
Germaine, Julia and Adelaide 261
Geronimo (Apache leader) 381, 387, 387-
388
  birth 20
  as Apache chief: peace talks 146, 369;
    in custody 322; returns from Mexico

373; leads raids 381, 385, 387; surren-
  ders 386-387, 391; "treasure mine"
  tale 430
  death 439
Gerry, Elbridge 158
Gerry, Melville 390
Gerstäcker, Friedrich 44
Getty, J. Paul 458
Gibbon, John 275, 277, 279, 281, 298
Gibson, Jane 248
Gibson, Paris 405
Gibson, Sam 189
Gibson, T. W. 212
Gihon, Thomas 74
Gilbert, Edward 71
Gillaspy, G. 192
Gillett, James Buchanan 99
Gillett, James Norris 125
Gilmore, Gary 458
Gilpin, William 39, 45, 130-131, 139, 196
Gipson, Fred 439, 453
Glidden, George 288
Glidden, Joseph F. 247, 247, 248, 261
Glover, T. B. 331
Goddard, Cy 246
Goes Ahead (Crow scout) 281
Goff, Orlando 312
Goldrick, O. J. 156
Goldwater, Barry M. 455
Gonzales, Madeiro 18
Good, Andrew 70
Goodale, G. A. 187
Goodale, Tim 54
Goodell, George 362
Goodnight, Charles 23, 126, 190, 221,
  289, 289, 294, 447
Goodwin, John 152, 155
Goodwin, M. F. 320
Goodwin, William and Mary 236-237
Goodyear, Andrew 70
Goodyear, Miles 45
Gordon, D. S. 192, 218
Gordon, Mike 324
Gore, George 82, 92
Gosper, Governor 324
Goss, Nathaniel S. 387
Graham, G. W. 199
Graham, John Gilbert (airplane bomber)
  453
Graham, John (performer) 124, 360
Graham, Martha 447
Granger, Robert S. 167
Grant, George 251
Grant, James Benton 33, 364
Grant, Jedediah 60
Grant, Joe 331
Grant, Johnny 176
Grant, Morgan 137
Grant, Richard 99
Grant, Sam 88
Grant, Ulysses S.
  Civil War 134, 165
  presidency: appointments 206, 209,
    224, 235, 242, 252, 261; elections 198,
    203, 206, 239; Indian affairs 219, 221,
    226, 260, 282; legislation: national
    parks 234; gold standard 242; Wal-
    lowa Valley Reservation 244; Colorado
    Enabling Act 249, 264, 285; Pyramid
    Lake Reservation 262; buffalo preserva-
    tion bill veto 272; travels 270, 243,
    335, 371
Grattan, John 84
Graves, Bingham 237
Graves, "Whiskey" Bill 154
Gray, Mary A. 198
Gray, Robert 12-13
Gray, William 42
Gray Beard (Cheyenne leader) 261
Greathouse, Jim 344
Greeley, Horace 115
  birth 16
  as newspaperman: "Go West, young
    man" slogan 66, 101, 304; on gold dig-
    ging 113; western travels/writings
    115-117, 116, 127, 222
  as politician: Confederate peace confer-
    ence 157; presidential campaign 238

  death 239
Greeley, Mrs. Horace 239
Green, John 206, 210, 244
Green, Ned 434
Greenwood, Alfred B. 117
Greer, Frank Hilton 410
Greer, Nat 361
Gregg, Josiah 26
Gregory, Jackson 357
Gregory, John 115
Grey, Zane 224, 439, 441, 450
Griego, Pancho 270-271
Grierson, B. H. 335
Griffin, Fred 443
Griffin, John C. 40
Grimes, A. W. 311
Grimes, James W. 104
Griswold, Anna 143
Grofé, Ferde 447
Grosch, Hosea B. 167
Grover, Sharp 200
Gunnison, John W. 77-79
Gurley, John 146
Guthrie, A. B. 434, 451, 460
Guthrie, Woody 441, 450, 455
Gutierrez, Apolinaria 56, 331
Gutierrez, Juanita 56
Gylam, Jack 248

H
Hackett, James 21
Haggard, John E. 418
Hagglund, Joel see Hill, Joe
Hahn, Georg Michael 154
Haight, Henry Huntley 193, 214, 313
Hairy Moccasin (Crow scout) 281
Haish, Jacob 247
Hall, Jacob 109-110
Hall, W. P. 236
Halleck, Henry 136
Hallidie, Andrew S. 73, 245
Halsey, Jacob 62
Halton, G. O. 91
Hamilton, Hugh 34
Hamilton, Lewis M. 187, 202
Hamilton, Samuel 121
Hamilton, Tom 121
Hamilton, William 34
Hammerstein, Oscar 450
Hanaway, Frank 437
Hancock, William 292
Hancock, Winfield Scott 185
Hand, Dora 292
Hanks, Camilla 434
Hanrahan, Jim 257
Hardeman, Dick 322
Hardesty, Mrs. Samuel 205
Hard Fish (Sac leader) 64
Hardin, John Wesley 75-76, 215
  birth 76
  21st birthday 256
  as outlaw: shootings/stabbings 162, 214,
    227-229, 244, 256; Webb murder 256,
    298, 432
  marriages 76, 432
  killed 433
Harding, Stephen S. 143
Harding, Warren G. 445
Hardwick, Felix 371
Hargrove, Bob 327
Harlan, Clarence "Cal" 237
Harlan, Kenneth 383
Harman, Fred 435, 449
Harman, Moses 395, 402
Harman, S. W. 270
Harmon, W. R. 218
Harnett, William Michael 420
Harney, William S. 91, 96, 102-103, 169,
  190, 191
Harrell, Ben 248, 250
Harriman, Edward H. 34, 440
Harriman, J. Edward 433
Harrington, E. J. 187
Harrington, H. M. 280
Harris, Jack 362
Harris, Tom 155
Harris, Will 369
Harrison, Benjamin 410, 411, 416, 418-
  419, 421, 431

Harrison, William (judge) 390
Harrison, William Henry (U.S. president)
  14, 16, 25
Hart, Pearl 434
Hart, William S. 223, 282, 451
Harte, Bret
  birth 23
  childhood 73
  influences: Mark Twain 156; Ina Cool-
    brith 254
  jobs: in San Francisco 85; as newspaper-
    man 105, 127; in U.S. Mint 152
  marriage 143
  writings: Outcasts of Poker Flat 58; Out-
    croppings: Being Selections of California
    Verse 170; Lost Galleon and Other
    Tales 193; "Luck of Roaring Camp"
    199; Luck of Roaring Camp and Other
    Sketches 211; Plain Language from
    Truthful James 224
  death 435
Harte, Elizabeth Ostrander 73
Hartman, L. C. 369
Harvey, Fred 276
Harvey, Jack 203
Harvey, Thomas H. 39, 47
Hasbrouck, H. C. 243
Haskell, Daniel H. 50
Haslam, Bob 123, 130
Hasson, Patrick 191-192
Hatch, Bob 357
Hatch, Edward 320, 332
Hawthorne, Nathaniel 156
Hayden, Charles 223, 362
Hayden, Ferdinand V. 92, 211, 228, 238
Hayes, George "Gabby" 381
Hayes, Ira 451
Hayes, Rutherford B. 44, 289, 301, 313,
  315, 332, 335
Haymond, Henry 175
Hays, Alexander 177
Hays, Charles 98
Hays, John C. 123
Head, Harry "the Kid" 343, 343, 346
Headley, A. L. 237
Hearst, Patricia 457-458
Hearst, William Randolph 147, 395
Heath, John 373
Heavy Runner (Blackfoot Piegan leader)
  217
Heber, Brigham 46
Heceta, Bruno 10
Hedges, Willys 402
He Dog (Sioux leader) 275
Heffridge, Bill 300
Heintzelman, Samuel P. 58, 68, 71, 94, 118
Heinze, Fritz 214
Helm, Jack 76, 244
Hemenway, Mary 391
Hemingway, Ernest 454
Henderson, James 78
Henderson, John B. 191
Henely, Austin 265
Henley, Joseph 405
Henry, O. (William Sydney Porter) 142,
  373, 397, 439-440
Henry, Robert 322
Hentig, E. C. 348
Herne, Jim 377
Herrera, Fernando 311
Herron, Francis J. 143
Hertzog, Peter 426
Hetherington, Joseph 97
Heywood, Joseph 286
Hickey, James 350
Hickey, Michael 265, 343
Hickman, Bill 230
Hickok, James Butler (``Wild Bill") 230
  birth 24
  marriage 70, 222, 274
  as army scout 130, 138, 205
  as Kansas lawman: in Monticello Town-
    ship 107; gunfights 132, 167, 167,
    221; Ellsworth County sheriff election
    192; prisoner relocation supervised
    195; Jack Harvey dies 203; in Ellis
    County 209, 211-213; in Abilene 219,
    226-227, 230-231

PLACE INDEX

This index is arranged alphabetically letter-by-letter. Cities are followed by a comma and the state or territory. Geographic features are qualified by a descriptive inside a parentheses. The **boldface** page numbers indicate boxed features. The *italic* page numbers indicate illustrations and captions.

SUBJECT INDEX

This index is arranged alphabetically letter-by-letter. The **boldface** page numbers indicate boxed features. The *italic* page numbers indicate illustrations and captions.

SUBJECT INDEX